# Michael Jackson FAQ

## All That's Left to Know About the King of Pop

Kit O'Toole

Backbeat
Books

An Imprint of Hal Leonard Corporation

Published in 2015 by Backbeat Books
An Imprint of Hal Leonard Corporation
7777 West Bluemound Road
Milwaukee, WI 53213

Trade Book Division Editorial Offices
33 Plymouth St., Montclair, NJ 07042


Printed in the United States of America


Library of Congress Cataloging-in-Publication Data

O'Toole, Kit.
    Michael Jackson FAQ : all that's left to know about the King of Pop / Kit O'Toole.
        pages cm
    Includes bibliographical references and index.
    ISBN 978-1-4803-7106-4
1. Jackson, Michael, 1958–2009—Miscellanea. 2. Jackson 5 (Musical group)—Miscellanea. 3. Rock musicians—United States—Miscellanea. I. Title. II. Title: Michael Jackson frequently asked questions.
    ML420.J175O86 2015
    782.42166092–dc23
    [B]
                                                                    2015030420


www.backbeatbooks.com

For my parents, who never told me to "turn that music down"

# Contents

# Foreword
# by Steve Lukather

When Michael first called, I kept hanging up. I thought it was a joke. He did this to me about three or four times. Then I finally got a call from Quincy Jones's office saying, "That was really Michael, and you should call him back."

Michael was my age, and we kind of connected on that level. He was a total pro. I enjoyed working with him. Quincy brought me in on *Thriller* because I had worked on *The Dude*, and then Steve Porcaro had worked on *Off the Wall*. Quincy was using members of Toto a whole bunch on all of his projects. We did Herbie Hancock, we did James Ingram, we did Patti Austin—right in a row. For like three years, I was on every record that Quincy did.

So, Michael is following *Off the Wall* and, as a young session player, getting a call to do *Thriller*, I figured this was going to be the biggest album of the year. We had no idea it was going to be the biggest album in history. It's a great honor to be part of something that big.

But, you know, people are just now—thirty-some-odd years later—starting to ask about Toto's involvement in this. We were always overlooked. But we had a lot to do with that record; there are songs that are just us and Michael. "Human Nature," that's us with Michael. "Beat It" is Michael, Jeff Porcaro, and me, and Eddie Van Halen did the solo. That's it. I think there's a synthesizer in the front that Steve programmed, and Greg Phillinganes played it—but Greg's part of our family, too. The Paul McCartney duet had most of us on it. But when *Thriller* exploded, they just never mentioned our name. It wasn't just like we played on a tune; some of this stuff, we really put a lot of sweat into.

Take "Beat It"—there was a finished version of it, and Eddie Van Halen did a solo on it. But Eddie accidentally cut the two-inch tape, and it wouldn't sync up again. So Jeff Porcaro and I were given the task of going into the studio with Humberto Gatica and Frankenstein-ing this thing back together, just listening to Michael hitting two and four with drum sticks on a drum case, the lead vocal and Eddie's solo. Only Jeff Porcaro could have made that swing, which he did—and then I overdubbed all of the riff parts, and I played bass on it. I got together with Michael and Quincy in the studio and we worked out some changes in the riff. The final version of "Beat It" was me on all guitars and bass, except for the solo—which is obviously Eddie Van Halen—with Jeff Porcaro on drums, Michael on vocals, and then a little overdub here and there, which I think was either Steve or Greg Phillinganes. It was good fun.

Michael was very physical. When something was in the pocket, his body language would change. He wasn't any kind of great musician. A lot of Michael's demos were made with only vocals. He'd sing all of the parts; he knew what he wanted, but he was really open to other ideas. Though Michael was pretty specific in the studio, if I came onto something that was really good, you could visibly see the body language change. For instance, "Human Nature" is a Toto song with Michael singing. I came up with the guitar part, because Steve Porcaro never had one on the original demo. David Paich and Steve used that demo to create the piece which we then all overdubbed on. And Quincy goes, "You gotta give me some funk, man. You gotta make this funky for me," so I came up with that guitar part. And Steve Porcaro hated it! We joke about it to this day. If you take that part off, all of a sudden, it sounds like a completely different song.

Then, with the McCartney duet, we just were so excited to play on a duet with Michael Jackson and Paul McCartney. Quincy sent over the demo of the song for us to listen to, before we did the track, and we all met over at Jeff's house. We were cracking up; it's such a silly song. "The doggone girl is mine"? We were on the floor. It ultimately was a really cool experience, though, just being able to hang with a Beatle. Then Jeff and I ended up going off with McCartney to work with him in England after that.

We continued working with Michael through the years, too. Steve was on *Bad*. We were on the *HIStory* record. He liked our band; he liked our music, and that meant a lot.

I ended up playing on a lot of big hits, but *Thriller* ended up being the biggest. Who knew?

Steve Lukather,
May 2015

*Musician, guitarist, vocalist, composer, producer, and arranger Steve Lukather says his musical life began when he was given a copy of* Meet the Beatles *at the age of seven. In high school, he met the Porcaro brothers, and the seeds of a multi-platinum band—Toto—were born. By the time Lukather (along with Toto bandmates David Paich and Jeff and Steve Porcaro) took part in the sessions for Michael Jackson's 1982 blockbuster* Thriller, *the guitarist was in the midst of playing countless sessions as a first-call collaborator. That already included key moments across an amazing range of styles, from Boz Scaggs to Earth, Wind and Fire, from Elton John to KISS, among many others. Michael would sell millions of copies of an album that featured Lukather on most of its songs. He later appeared on the Jacksons' album* Victory (1984) *and Michael's later albums* HIStory: Past, Present, and Future, Book 1 (1995), *and* Blood on the Dance Floor (1997), *giving Lukather a unique perspective on Michael Jackson's enduring musical legacy. For news on his latest projects, visit his website,* www.stevelukather.com.

# Introduction

# The Man in the Mirror

*When you say Michael Jackson, people always think of an entertainer. They don't think of the fact that I write songs. I'm not trying to brag, but I write them, and I direct a lot of [the videos]. I don't think [younger artists] are aware of those things, which I think would be inspiring for them.*

—"Michael Jackson: The Star Studded TV Special, the New Album (At Last), the Famous Friends, the 'Wacko Jacko' Image—Does It Add Up to Comeback?" *TV Guide*, November 10, 2001

FADE IN.

INT. DEN IN A SUBURBAN HOME—NIGHT, MONDAY, MAY 16, 1983

An eleven-year-old girl sits on her parents' couch, watching TV after begging them to let her stay up just a little bit longer on a school night. A lover of anything to do with music, she is viewing *Motown 25: Yesterday, Today, Forever* on NBC. Still learning about artists like the Temptations, the Four Tops, and Marvin Gaye, she watches with curiosity. Suddenly, six men in glittering costumes run onto the stage, and she recognizes one performer: Michael Jackson, whose song "Billie Jean" has been airing constantly on the radio. Announced as the reunion of a group called the "Jackson 5," they perform a medley of their greatest hits. The young girl has vaguely heard of a few songs—"I'll Be There" and "The Love You Save" among them. Bowing to enthusiastic applause, the other men leave the stage, leaving Michael standing alone.

His sequined jacket catching the light, he paces the stage, stating that while he loves singing the "old songs," he especially likes "the new songs." A fedora appears out of nowhere; he dons it, assumes his trademark angular pose, and the opening drums to "Billie Jean" kick in. He sings, spins, and freezes on his toes, the theater audience rising to its feet as the entertainer dazzles with his footwork. Then he debuts a new step, instantly making history: Michael effortlessly glides backward, seemingly defying gravity just for a moment. Along with millions of TV viewers, the little girl's jaw drops.

FADE OUT.

EXT. SCHOOL PLAYGROUND—DAY, MAY 17, 1983

Schoolchildren gather during recess, standing on the blacktop. While others play basketball or head for the swings, the little girl stands in a large group of fellow students. They talk about what they had seen the night before, and marvel at Michael's dance moves. How did he *do* that? Debating the mechanics of that backward glide, they attempt it themselves, dragging their sneakers across the pavement in a jerky fashion. For that one moment, the schoolchildren unite in their fascination for music, dance, and a "new" artist named Michael Jackson.

FADE OUT.

For Generation X, Michael Jackson's appearance on *Motown 25: Yesterday, Today, Forever* equaled the Beatles' 1964 debut on *Ed Sullivan*. That one performance not only attracted forty-seven million viewers but also officially launched Michael into the superstar stratosphere. While fans of all ages fondly remember the event, for Michael it was the culmination of a complete artistic reinvention. He had officially graduated from his role as a former child star and lead singer of the Jacksons to become a distinctive singer, songwriter, and dancer in his own right.

When he donned his fedora that night on the Pasadena Civic Auditorium stage, he combined Broadway poses, James Brown steps, 1980s glamour, and everything he had learned from idols and mentors such as Diana Ross, Stevie Wonder, Sammy Davis, Jr., and Jackie Wilson to create a new kind of entertainment. This hybrid consisted of old Hollywood and Broadway along with modern visuals (namely MTV and music video), topped off with elements of R&B, pop, and rock.

After that night, *Thriller*-mania was born. Michael would set new standards for music video, bringing feature-film plots and cinematography to a medium generally known for having artists stand in front of a white background lip-synching their latest hits. Through his concert tours and occasional television appearances, he would merge film and live performance by incorporating movie clips and recreating elements of his music videos for the stage. His dancing also challenged artists to fully entertain audiences, not simply stand in one place and sing their songs. Michael treated audiences to a full-scale production, overwhelming the senses with his multimedia approach to music.

While it is difficult to believe today, Michael was once in danger of becoming a nostalgia act. After the Jackson 5 left Motown, they were forced to rebuild their careers at another label and under a new moniker. In doing so, they hosted a short-lived variety show series and played numerous dates in Las Vegas, treating audiences to medleys of past hits. However, Michael was not satisfied in simply reveling in past successes. He changed his sound, altered his singing style to become more percussive, incorporated the newest dance steps, composed distinctive and at times highly personal lyrics, and constantly experimented with the sonic elements of his songs. In doing so, he reemerged as one of music's most unique artists. In the 1980s, he personified "cool" with his fashion sense and spectacular videos. In his 1941 novel *The Last Tycoon*, F. Scott Fitzgerald writes, "There are no second acts in American lives." Remarkably, Michael experienced *three* acts throughout his four-decade career: the Jackson 5, the Jacksons, and his solo years.

Michael viewed art as transcending conventional boundaries and definitions, and wished to create music and entertainment appealing to broad populations. While he was proud of his soul roots, he bristled at being identified simply as an

"R&B artist" or a "disco singer." He defied traditional categorization, from his early days with the Jackson 5 through his final album, 2001's *Invincible*. During the early years of MTV, the channel typically aired few African American artists' videos—but once Michael's massive popularity could not be denied, the network relented.

To date, no other album has amassed the crossover appeal that *Thriller* enjoyed; for an all-too-brief moment, fans of all different music genres owned that album. Browse through the music collection of a punk, country, metal, or rap fan between 1983 and 1985, and chances are high that a copy of *Thriller* rested comfortably among seemingly disparate albums. No other disc has approached such levels of success.

Michael impacted music, video, dance, and pop culture, and his influence lingers today in artists such as Justin Timberlake, Beyoncé, and Bruno Mars. Yet few books have examined his art, instead focusing on the sensational. Joseph Vogel stands as a notable exception, publishing thorough academic analyses of Michael's solo years in texts such as *Man in the Music* and *Earth Song: Inside Michael Jackson's Magnum Opus*. Virtually no books explore his entire career, from the Jackson 5 through the Jacksons and the solo years. Did he compose his own music? Did he play any instruments? Who were his greatest influences? How did he develop as a singer? *Michael Jackson FAQ* tackles these questions, providing an in-depth look at lesser-known aspects of his art.

Unlike a traditional biography, *Michael Jackson FAQ* takes a different approach to narrating his life story. Instead of reporting facts and figures or engaging in endless speculation about his private life, this book focuses on his remarkable artistic development. In doing so, *Michael Jackson FAQ* has four main goals:

- To closely examine and analyze his music, dance, and other aspects of his art
- To explore how Michael impacted music, dance, and pop culture
- To chart how he progressed as a singer and entertainer
- To spark conversation and debate among fans.

One of the best parts of being a fan is debating with like-minded people about certain recordings. Which version of a song is better, the studio recording or live rendition? What was his best performance? What songs from the Jackson 5 years are the most underrated or overrated? It is my hope that *Michael Jackson FAQ* will inspire such discussions, and will ultimately shed light on a unique performer and his timeless music.

When you attend a wedding reception, odds are huge that "Billie Jean" will entice people onto the dance floor. Flip on your car radio, and chances are staples like "Rock with You" and "The Way You Make Me Feel" will be played as you run your errands. Visit YouTube and view the vast number of videos featuring flash mobs reenacting the "Thriller" zombie dance. Why does Michael's art continue to pervade our culture? *Michael Jackson FAQ* explores this fascinating question, and ultimately celebrates his artistic legacy.

# Acknowledgments

I n writing *Michael Jackson FAQ*, I was fortunate to have an incredible support system to guide me through the process. I thank Bernadette Malavarca at Backbeat Books for her unending patience and useful advice in editing this book. My friend and fellow Beatles scholar Robert Rodriguez first approached me to write *Michael Jackson FAQ*, and I thank him for his faith in me and his unending encouragement.

Steve Lukather's special insight into Michael Jackson's creative process provides deeper understanding of the singer's work. I thank him for writing the foreword, for his enduring work with Toto and numerous artists, and for his superior musicianship.

I am lucky to write for several online music sites, and my editors were incredibly supportive and helpful throughout this project. Nick Deriso and Victor Aaron at *Something Else Reviews*, your encouragement (and great jokes) keep me grounded during the writing process. I also thank Josh Hathaway at *Blinded by Sound* for allowing me to indulge in my love of R&B on your website. Finally, Gordon Miller at *Cinema Sentries*, I have enjoyed writing for you and thank you for all of your support and patience. In addition, I'd like to acknowledge the site *Blogcritics* for first giving me the opportunity to start music blogging, specifically Eric Olsen, Barbara Barnett, Jon Sobel, Constance Phillips, Glen Boyd, and Donald Gibson. Finally, I'd like to extend my thanks to Nort Johnson, who gave me my first break writing for the newspaper *Showcase Chicago* while I was still in college.

In addition to my love of soul and R&B, I am a longtime writer and researcher on the Beatles' music and legacy. As such, I count myself as fortunate to belong to a remarkable community of fellow enthusiasts, and their friendship and advice proved invaluable in writing this book. Jude Southerland Kessler has taught me a great deal about writing and marketing, and has promoted *Michael Jackson FAQ* on her podcast, the *John Lennon Hour*. I thank her for being a mentor and a good friend. Bill King, editor of *Beatlefan* magazine, allowed me time off to work on the book, and has been a friend and ideal editor for twenty years. I'm indeed fortunate to belong to the *Beatlefan* family, and I thank him for hiring me back when I starting graduate school. Glenn Neuwirth helped me find rare Michael Jackson footage, and I treasure our friendship and mutual love of music. Finally, I thank Wally Podrazik for his advice and pointing me toward incredibly helpful sources.

Many of the images on these pages were taken by Chris Savaiano of Savco Corporation—I thank him for taking on this immense project and taking such beautiful images of my memorabilia collection. I also extend my gratitude to Bill Frantz of Bill Frantz Photography, who spent an afternoon taking publicity photos of me in Lake Geneva, Wisconsin.

Finally, I'd like to thank the special Michael Jackson fans and writers who have made it their mission to keep his music and art alive, preserving his legacy for generations to come. Joseph Vogel, Chris Cadman, Craig Halstead, Nelson George, and Adrian Grant deserve special recognition for the books and articles they have published on the King of Pop. Instead of focusing on sensationalism, they have provided insightful and invaluable information on his influence and placed his music in proper context.

Ultimate thanks goes to Michael Jackson himself. He provided the soundtrack to countless lives, forever changed music and pop culture, and broke through racial barriers. I hope this book serves as a proper tribute to his artistic contributions, and I thank him for sharing his gifts with us and expanding our definitions of music and artistry.

# I'm Going to Teach You How to Sing It Out

## The Jackson 5's Musical Influences

When the Jackson 5 burst onto the music scene with their first hit, 1970's "I Want You Back," the group instantly set a new standard for "boy bands" with their intricately choreographed routines, hip stage clothes, and catchy, high-quality tracks. New Edition, New Kids on the Block, the Backstreet Boys, *NSYNC, Take That, and One Direction all owe a debt to them.

Like those groups, the Jackson 5 once counted several artists as inspirations for their singing and stage shows. The following list highlights the most significant bands that directly or indirectly played important roles in the Jackson boys' sound.

### Frankie Lymon and the Teenagers

Long before the Jackson 5, Frankie Lymon charmed teenagers with his sweet vocals and memorable pop tunes. In the early days of rock and roll, Lymon became the first African American teen idol. At just thirteen, the singer recorded the single "Why Do Fools Fall in Love?," a classic that over twenty-five years later was covered by Jackson 5 mentor and Motown labelmate Diana Ross. That hit, along with several others, catapulted him to teen-idol status: the first African American to do so.

Born in 1942, Lymon grew up in New York City, specifically the rough tenements of Washington Heights. As a preteen, Lymon began singing on street corners with local singers Herman Santiago, Jimmy Merchant, Joe Negroni, and Sherman Garnes. Initially calling themselves the Premiers, the doo-wop group were soon spotted by talent scout Richard Barren, who secured the struggling singers an audition with Gee Records in 1955.

Their story began with the audition not only because the label instantly signed them but because the song earned them the contract. Inspired by love letters local fans had written to the group, Merchant lifted one particular sentence—"why do birds sing so gay?"—and based the rest of the lyrics on it. After hearing "Why Do Birds Sing So Gay?," Gee Records head George Goldner signed the Premiers. Soon renamed Frankie Lymon and the Teenagers, the band rearranged the track, now retitled "Why Do Fools Fall in Love?" Released in February 1956, the single soared to #1 on the R&B charts and #6 on the *Billboard* Hot 100, becoming a rare crossover hit. Having just started junior high, Lymon found himself pulled out of school to

One of Michael Jackson's greatest singing and dancing influences, James Brown wowed audiences with his dynamic performing style and heavily rhythmic songs. On the 1967 album *James Brown Sings Raw Soul*, the "Hardest Working Man in Show Business" sang tracks such as "Let Yourself Go" and "Money Won't Change You."    *Author's collection*

immediately begin the rigor of touring. Appearances in movies and on *The Ed Sullivan Show* as well as a spot on DJ Alan Freed's package shows quickly followed.

For a year, Lymon and the Teenagers scored an impressive string of hits, including "I Want You to Be My Girl," "Who Can Explain?," "The ABCs of Love," "I Promise to Remember," "Out in the Cold Again," "I'm Not a Juvenile Delinquent," and "Baby Baby." During the group's 1957 tour of the UK (where their popularity almost exceeded their success in their home country), Lymon recorded the solo single "Goody Goody," leading to his departure from the Teenagers. Unfortunately, Lymon experienced little success on his own, appearing on the charts only once more, with his 1960 cover of "Little Bitty Pretty One." His career took a nosedive after puberty affected his voice, and he died of a drug overdose at age twenty-five in 1968.

While Lymon experienced a tragically short career, his influence still lingers, decades later. His pure voice perfectly suited his songs' sprightly beats and innocent proclamations of love. That charisma, along with the Teenagers' flawless harmonies, undeniably influenced the Jackson 5's style. In his 1988 autobiography, *Moonwalk*, Michael Jackson does not specifically mention Lymon as an influence, but acknowledges that, early in his career, fans compared him to the young singer. Look no further than hits like "ABC" or "The Love You Save" for examples of how Lymon's precise yet lively style influenced Michael's youthful delivery. The connection continued with the Jackson 5's cover of "Little Bitty Pretty One," influenced by Lymon's cover, on the 1972 album *Lookin' Through the Windows*.

## The Ford Falcons (a.k.a. the Falcons)

Michael's father Joseph Jackson started a blues band with his brother Luther in the mid-1950s. Little Michael would often watch the band's rehearsals in the family's living room in Gary, Indiana. No Falcons recordings exist, but in *Moonwalk* Michael recalls the band's covers of early rock and blues classics by Chuck Berry, Little Richard, and Otis Redding. The Falcons played in small clubs around Indiana and Chicago; according to *Moonwalk*, Joseph left the band shortly after discovering his sons' talent. Joseph's website, however, claims that the band split two years later after failing to secure a recording deal.

After leaving the band, the guitarist returned to his full-time job at US Steel, but would still practice his instrument at home. Michael may have been too young to witness the group's shows, but wrote that he was "raised on R&B," thanks to his father's fledgling band. Clearly, Joseph had learned about stage presence, securing gigs, and the challenge of getting noticed in the music business. He would soon pass on those lessons—as well as a healthy respect for early rhythm and blues and rock and roll—to his sons.

## Sly and the Family Stone

While this may be a less obvious connection, the Jackson brothers maintained that the innovative group Sly and the Family Stone played a large role in the Jackson 5's early success. According to music historian Stephen McMillian's 2012 blog post for the Jacksons' official website, Motown house band the Corporation would study Stone's melodies and arrangements and then adapt them for the Jackson 5's early singles. However, Michael's affection for the groundbreaking multiracial band dates to 1968, when he first heard their music. In *Moonwalk*, he says the group completely altered their sound. When Sly and the Family Stone dominated the rock and soul radio stations, he recalls, they greatly influenced the Jackson 5, and that Michael and his brothers owed Sly Stone a great deal.

Sly and the Family Stone may not have sounded exactly like the Jackson 5, but their crossover appeal influenced the Motown act. Rock and soul audiences flocked to their upbeat, positive tracks that defied easy musical categorization. "Dance to the Music," "Everyday People," "Sing a Simple Song," "Hot Fun in the Summertime," and "I Want to Take You Higher" exemplified their sound during 1967–70, although the bass-popping 1969 song "Thank You (Falettinme Be Mice Elf Agin)" provided an early clue as to their later grittier direction. Sly and the Family Stone subsequently became famous for their vibrant stage shows, their flamboyant costumes and dance moves exciting audiences. The Jackson 5's music indeed spanned genres, and the Jackson brothers' concerts incited crowd frenzy with their intricate choreography, flashy ensembles, and constant interaction with fans.

Interestingly, the Jackson 5 would cover "Stand!," a Sly Stone track that hinted at edgier, more overly political albums such as 1971's *There's a Riot Goin' On*. While the Jackson 5 may not have tackled controversial material, they brought their youthful exuberance and enthusiasm to Stone's tale of standing up for one's beliefs. Amusingly, as Michael notes in *Moonwalk*, his brothers would point at their young lead singer and laugh while singing the "Stand!" lyric "There's a midget standing tall."

The young group included "I Want to Take You Higher" as well as "Stand!" in live shows, as evidenced by their inclusion in their Indiana homecoming concert on May 29, 1971 (parts of which, including these performances, were filmed for the 1971 ABC TV special *Goin' Back to Indiana*). The 2010 live compilation *Jackson 5 Live at the Forum* also features their enthusiastic interpretation of "Thank You (Falettinme Be Mice Elf Agin)."

## Etta James

Among the artists the Falcons most likely covered was Etta James, a blues singer who successfully merged blues, rock, and jazz for broad audience appeal. Born in Los Angeles in 1938, James grew up singing in the church. Her passion for R&B and early rock and roll led to her initial breakthrough: the raunchy "Roll with Me Henry," a song James and two other San Francisco singers penned in response to Hank Ballard's "Work with Me Annie." Bandleader Johnny Otis heard the trio and instantly signed them to Modern Records. In 1955, Otis re-recorded the track with the trio—now named the Peaches—and retitled it "The Wallflower," perhaps to avoid having it banned for its suggestive content. The racy single topped the R&B charts for four weeks, but three years later James departed Modern Records and the Peaches for a solo career. By 1958, she had officially begun her journey toward becoming a legendary singer.

Switching to the Chicago label Chess, James released the album *At Last!* in 1961. The album contains what would become her signature song, a heartfelt ballad that James approached with her no-holds-barred singing style. The song spanned several musical genres, which proved crucial to its cracking the *Billboard* Top 100. Tellingly, the disc also includes covers of jazz standards such as "Stormy Weather" and "A Sunday Kind of Love," while James reveals her deep blues roots with her reading of Willie Dixon's "I Just Want to Make Love to You." She earned the respect of rock artists such as the Rolling Stones, who invited her to open for them on select dates during their 1978 tour.

Despite battling drug addiction for much of her life, James continued releasing albums until a year before her death in 2012. While she experienced most success with R&B audiences, her albums and singles registered on the blues, jazz, and Hot 100 charts as well.

In an interview with J. Randy Taraborrelli for his biography *Michael Jackson: The Magic, the Madness, the Whole Story, 1958–2009*, James recalled meeting little Michael when she and the Jackson 5 played Harlem's Apollo Theater in May 1968. As she sang "Tell Mama," she noticed a young boy intently watching her from the stage wings. Annoyed, James walked over to him while the audience applauded, ordering him to stop staring at her. At first, a scared Michael ran away, but he reappeared backstage ten minutes later.

After the show, James said she heard a timid knock on her door: it was Michael, coming to apologize for bothering her. She recited the conversation to Taraborrelli. "I'm sorry, ma'am, but I was just watchin' you 'cause you're so good. You're just *so good.* How do you do that? I never seen people clap like that," James said Michael told her.

Charmed, James invited the young performer into her dressing room. While she could not remember what she told him, she said she was impressed by his intense desire to learn. "I remember thinking as he was leaving, 'Now there's a boy who wants to learn from the best, so one day he's gonna *be* the best,'" James told Taraborrelli.

The connection to the Jackson 5 may not be obvious, but James's desire to transcend easy categories certainly appealed to African American artists wanting their music to be heard on a wider scale. Once virtually excluded from pop-oriented radio stations, 1950s musicians such as James, Little Richard, and Chuck Berry knocked down barriers with their unique blends of jazz, pop, gospel, rock, and blues. Motown took lessons from these pioneers, and these lessons propelled early acts such as the Supremes, the Four Tops, the Temptations, and Mary Wells to stardom.

By 1970, Motown had perfected the art of attracting multicultural audiences to their artists. The Jackson 5 benefitted from their predecessors, their music purchased equally by white and black teens. Even more tellingly, listen to Michael's soaring vocals on "Who's Loving You"—his heart-on-sleeve singing style owes a great debt to James.

## Joe Tex

Along with James Brown, Joe Tex brought funk and a grittier, more guttural type of soul to listeners. Born in Rogers, Texas, in 1933, Tex honed his skills in gospel and R&B, which culminated in him winning a talent contest in 1954. Relocating to New York, he pursued a music career by recording a series of little-noticed singles for King Records from 1955 to 1957. He subsequently bounced around other labels, but during this time he opened for Brown, Little Richard, and Jackie Wilson, perfecting his stage moves and inventing flashy dance routines and exciting microphone tricks.

After penning a track for rival Brown, Tex was noticed by Nashville music publisher Buddy Killen. Killen took Tex to the soon-to-be-famous Muscle Shoals recording studio in Sheffield, Alabama, where they wrote and recorded the 1965 ballad "Hold What You've Got." The track peaked at #2 on the R&B charts and cracked the Top 5 on the Hot 100, rendering it the first Southern soul record to cross over to the pop charts. After his big break, Tex released a string of R&B hits, including "I Want to (Do Everything for You)" and "A Sweet Woman Like You."

Like other artists who influenced the Jackson 5, Tex managed to span genres and served as a pioneer in rap. His huge 1972 record "I Gotcha" channeled Brown yet sounded even rougher, while he dipped his toe into disco with his last hit, the hilarious (if politically incorrect) 1977 dance classic "Ain't Gonna Bump No More (with No Big Fat Woman)." Joseph Jackson presumably listened to Tex's early records, and this influence is particularly evident in the Jackson 5's earliest appearances. In *Moonwalk*, Michael Jackson recalls performing another Tex song, 1967's "Skinny Legs and All," during the fledgling band's early shows in dingy strip clubs and bars. Since the original featured mostly spoken lyrics, Michael would deliver the lines while wandering through the audience, crawling under tables to peer up women's skirts. Patrons would throw money at the young singer, amused by his antics.

Michael clearly took lessons from Tex's onstage banter when performing "Who's Loving You," amusingly and convincingly delivering lines like "I may be young, but I know it's all about" in his opening monologue. During the Jackson 5's 1969 television debut on the *Miss Black America Pageant*, the young lead singer's sometimes intentionally comedic but always energetic moves (pelvic thrusts, strutting across the stage) and his exhortations for the audience to sing along echoed Tex's crowd-pleasing routines. His stutters and grunts certainly recalled Brown, but Tex was also a pioneer of the vocal technique.

Incidentally, Tex's hit record from 1966, the self-penned "The Love You Save (May Be Your Own)," is unrelated to the similarly titled Jackson 5 classic.

## Stevie Wonder

Like Michael, Stevie Wonder joined Motown as a child prodigy. The label struggled to market "Little Stevie Wonder," having him record jazz standards as well as Ray Charles covers. One of Wonder's early tracks, the largely instrumental "Fingertips," served as his breakthrough. The live version, recorded at Chicago's Regal Theater in June 1962, captured the audience's joyous reaction and inspired Motown to release the song as a two-part single a year later. At age thirteen, Wonder found himself topping the R&B and Hot 100 charts (making "Fingertips" only the second Motown single to do so) and becoming the youngest artist to achieve a #1 hit. "Fingertips" ranks as an important single for another reason: the drummer on the track is a then-unknown Marvin Gaye.

Wonder demonstrated how to age gracefully and creatively in the music business. As his voice changed, he recorded more adult pop fare such as "I Was Made to Love Her" and "Signed, Sealed, Delivered, I'm Yours." At this point, the Jackson 5 joined Motown, enabling them to witness Wonder's remarkable transformation from child star to creative genius. Hints of his landmark 1970s work permeate 1971's *Where I'm Coming From*, with "If You Really Love Me" standing out as a multifaceted single with its tempo changes and jazz-influenced chord changes. Its most ambitious and sadly beautiful track, "Never Dreamed You'd Leave in Summer," illustrated how Wonder was increasingly tackling complex, adult themes and moving away from traditional R&B. The song would gain even deeper—and tragic—meaning when Wonder performed it during Michael's 2009 memorial service.

Indeed, the Jackson 5 had the fortune of observing Wonder recording what would become a stunning series of masterpieces: *Music of My Mind* and *Talking Book* (1972), *Innervisions* (1973), and *Fulfillingness' First Finale* (1974). The Jacksons finally collaborated with their labelmate in 1974, when they sang backup on the

#1 single from *Fulfilling-ness'*, "You Haven't Done Nothin'." The overtly political song proved a departure for the Jackson 5, who may have recorded subtly subversive tracks such as "Stand!" but never direct commentaries on current issues. "Jackson 5, sing along with me!" Wonder sings, as the Jackson brothers chant "doo-doo-wop!" in the background.

Motown labelmate Stevie Wonder hugely influenced Michael's career, and the Jackson 5 covered many of his songs on their early albums. Over the years, Wonder and Michael guest-starred on each other's albums, including Wonder's 1987 LP *Characters*.

*Author's collection*

This was not the first time the two acts had recorded together in the studio. A year before, Wonder was supposed to produce the Jackson 5's next album, but the collaboration never surfaced. Listeners received a taste of this would-be project with a survivor from these sessions: "Buttercup," the Jackson brothers' delightful cover of the Wonder-penned track. The song would become a 1982 hit for Carl Anderson, but the Jackson 5's Wonder-produced version remained unreleased until the 2009 compilation *I Want You Back! Unreleased Masters*.

In *Moonwalk*, Michael notes how much he learned from Wonder and Marvin Gaye. Both had taken full charge of their careers, writing and producing their own material as well as publishing their songs. After working with Wonder, Michael and his brothers approached Motown about emulating their elders' independence; Berry Gordy's denial ultimately contributed to the departure of the Jackson 5 (minus Jermaine) from the label.

Artistically, Wonder impacted the Jackson 5 as well as Michael. He served as the best example of transcending musical boundaries to reach massive audiences. Was his sound rock, pop, soul, funk, country, jazz? With each album, Wonder challenged these simple labels by combining elements of each. While the Jackson 5's albums may not have been experimental, they contained top-quality pop that appealed to international fans. Even more tellingly, he inspired Michael and his brothers to compose their own songs, leading to the group gaining full control when they moved to Epic Records.

Not surprisingly, the Jackson 5 recorded several Wonder covers during their Motown tenure: "My Cherie Amour" (*Diana Ross Presents the Jackson 5*, 1969), "I Was Made to Love Her" (recorded in 1969 during the *ABC* sessions and released on the 1979 compilation *Boogie*), and "Don't Know Why I Love You" and "Never Had a Dream Come True" (*ABC*, 1970). They frequently included Wonder tunes in their concert set lists, such as "Superstition" (*The Jackson 5 in Japan*) and "Don't Know Why I Love You" (*Live at the Forum*).

## Marvin Gaye

Like Wonder, Gaye grew artistically at an astounding rate. A pioneer of modern soul music, he proved that soul could be an agent for change as well as an invitation to dance. Signed to Motown in 1961, Gaye gained attention two years later for his danceable early hits "Can I Get a Witness," "Pride and Joy," and "Hitch Hike." His desire to expand his repertoire led to a series of successful duets with Wells, Kim Weston, and, most famously, Tammi Terrell. After Terrell died in 1970 from a brain tumor and his marriage to Anna Gordy (Berry Gordy's sister) collapsed, Gaye went into seclusion. He emerged a year later with a radically different sound and purpose. *What's Going On*, his landmark album, tackled politics and the environment like no previous Motown release.

Despite Motown head Berry Gordy's dire predictions, *What's Going On* became a massive critical and commercial success, leading to Gaye assuming full artistic control of his career. Like Wonder, Gaye followed his own muse, straying into jazz territory with 1972's *Trouble Man* soundtrack, and then candidly exploring sexuality with 1974's *Let's Get It On*. Despite battling intense personal problems, including drug abuse and failed relationships, Gaye continued recording until his untimely death. His smooth yet passionate voice set a new standard for soul vocalists—one that Michael emulated.

During the Jackson 5's Motown tenure, they observed Gaye's transition from pop star to innovator, and noted how Motown ultimately awarded him creative freedom. They learned from both his creativity and his intense stage shows. While not a dancer, Gaye managed to engage audiences with his Frank Sinatra–like command over the crowd. In *Moonwalk*, Michael writes that he attempted to emulate Gaye during the Jackson 5's 1972 tour. "Got to be There" had recently hit the charts, and Michael told the band's road manager that he wanted to run backstage, grab the hat he wore on the recently released *Got to Be There* album cover, and put it on just before launching into the title track. He noticed that Gaye donned a hat just before singing "Let's Get It On," and that the audience would get excited, knowing he was about to sing the sexy song. Unfortunately, the road manager vetoed the idea.

The Jackson 5 covered many Gaye tunes, including "Ain't Nothing Like the Real Thing" (*Lookin' Through the Windows*, 1972, and the 2010 compilation *Live at the Forum*), "Ain't That Peculiar" (recorded during the 1973 tour and released on the compilation *The Jackson 5 in Japan*); and "Pride and Joy" (recorded during the *G.I.T.: Get It Together* sessions and released on the 1976 collection *Joyful Jukebox Music*).

## The Temptations

Future Motown labelmates the Temptations figured early in the Jackson brothers' careers. When Michael was just eight years old, he and his brothers entered a talent contest at Gary's Roosevelt High School. In *Moonwalk*, Michael recalls how Jermaine's bass, Tito's guitar, the group's harmonies, and their dance moves won them the grand prize. Tellingly, their winning entry was "My Girl," the Temptations' massive 1965 hit. The Temptations' influence on the Jackson 5 did not end there, however. Their memorable songs, unparalleled choreography, costumes, and vocal blends have impacted generations of artists. Receiving international acclaim, the Temptations' unique songs reached broad audiences and shattered previous genre boundaries.

The Detroit-based Temptations weathered numerous personnel changes in the years following their formation in 1961. One of the most significant additions was David Ruffin, the remarkable tenor who joined Otis Williams, Eddie Kendricks, Paul Williams, and Melvin Franklin in 1964. Collaborating with singer/songwriter/ producer Smokey Robinson, the Temptations released the new lineup's debut single, "The Way You Do the Things You Do," an across-the-board hit that kicked off a series of thirty-seven career Top 10 hits. While members subsequently came and went, the quintet continually evolved by recording bluesier tracks like "Papa Was a Rollin' Stone," political tracts like "Ball of Confusion," and even psychedelic experiments such as the aptly titled "Psychedelic Shack."

From their Gary beginnings onward, the Jackson 5 clearly learned from the Motown group. Their tight harmonies and elaborate choreography excited audiences in ways that recalled the Temptations, and this continued into the Jacksons' 1984 *Victory* Tour. While the Jackson 5 sported different threads than the Temptations' trademark suits, their funky yet flashy costumes echoed their mentors' attention to detail. They also understood how the Temptations wrote and recorded material addressing universal themes of love and family; while the Jackson 5 did not write their own songs at Motown, they would continue this trend when they took charge of their material as the Jacksons.

In the ultimate tribute to their idols, the Jackson 5 recorded Temptations covers such as "(I Know) I'm Losin' You," from 1969's *Diana Ross Presents the Jackson 5*, and "Hum Along and Dance," from 1973's *G.I.T.: Get It Together*. The Jackson brothers would also include Temptations tracks in their live shows, as evidenced by "Papa Was a Rollin' Stone" from *Jackson 5 in Japan* (originally released in Japan only in 1973, before being issued in the UK in 1986 and receiving limited US distribution in 2004).

## Jerry Butler

The timeless soul crooner brought Chicago soul to the mainstream through his tenure with the Impressions and as a solo artist. Born in Missouri but raised in Chicago, Butler sang in the church choir with Curtis Mayfield, and the two would form the legendary group the Impressions (then billed as "Jerry Butler and the Impressions") in 1957. They recorded the Butler-penned ballad "For Your Precious

Love" in 1958, immediately achieving huge success on the R&B and pop charts. Soon Butler left the Impressions to embark on a solo career, which hit a high point when he signed with Vee-Jay Records in 1960. "He Will Break Your Heart" topped the R&B charts and cracked the *Billboard* Top 10, kicking off a series of hit singles such as "A Lonely Soldier," a cover of "Moon River," and "Find Another Girl."

Changing gears in 1967, Butler switched labels and collaborated with Philly-soul producing/songwriting duo Kenny Gamble and Leon Huff, resulting in his classic album *Ice Man Cometh* (a play on his nickname "Ice Man") and more #1 singles like "Hey, Western Union Man" and "Only the Strong Survive." Throughout the 1970s, he continued recording music that ranged from soul to jazz to blues, although his first love was clearly R&B. However, his powerful voice transcended easy categorization, as he could resemble Frank Sinatra in his phrasing. As the Jacksons watched Butler perform, they took note of his sincere delivery and impeccable timing—traits that would be applied in Jackson 5 classics like "I'll Be There" or their interpretations of standards and soul staples like Stevie Wonder's "Don't Know Why I Love You" (1970).

As struggling singers, the Jackson 5 initially encountered Butler while working the same Chicago and Indiana circuit as other emerging R&B vocalists. Butler would play an indirect but important role in the boys' lives. As Michael writes in *Moonwalk*, the group's first single, "I Want You Back," was co-written by Corporation member Freddie Perren, a onetime pianist for Butler. The Jackson 5 once opened for Butler at a Chicago nightclub, surprising Perren with their polished performance.

Flash forward to 1969, when Motown signed the group; Perren had just composed a song entitled "I Want to Be Free" with Gladys Knight in mind, although he assumed Gordy would probably give the track to the Supremes. When Gordy mentioned to Butler that he had just signed a kids' group from Indiana, Perren realized that he was most likely referring to those Jackson boys. Before long, the renamed "I Want You Back" was a Jackson 5 tune.

Interestingly, after their initial success the Jackson 5 would once again cross paths with Butler. During the group's first national tour in 1970, they headlined a package show on June 20. While the original lineup was to include the Ike & Tina Turner Revue and Rare Earth, the former had to cancel at the last minute. Soul singer Butler stepped in, and in a fascinating role reversal, this time he was their opening act.

## Little Anthony and the Imperials

As 1950s doo-wop was transitioning into soul, one group significantly bridged the gap between the two forms: Little Anthony and the Imperials. Born in 1940 in Brooklyn's Fort Greene projects, Jerome Anthony Gourdine began singing in local groups as a teenager. After graduating high school he joined the Chesters, a four-member harmony group, and to sound grander they changed their name to the Imperials (with DJ Alan Freed soon dubbing their new lead singer "Little Anthony"). After being signed to the End label in 1958, the quintet scored an immediate hit: "Tears on My Pillow," a now-essential early soul single that peaked at #2 on the R&B charts and fared well in the pop realm. Little Anthony's sincere, angelic voice, backed by the group's flawless vocal blend, made them one of the most popular doo-wop groups of the era. Two years passed before they regained their initial success with "Shimmy, Shimmy, Ko-Ko-Bop," a danceable tune that allowed Little Anthony to demonstrate that he could navigate up-tempo tracks as well as ballads.

After a brief break from the Imperials, Little Anthony returned in 1964, as the group commenced a more sophisticated era. While their doo-wop harmonies remained intact, they incorporated jazz chord changes, more complicated vocal arrangements, and Little Anthony's more mature, emotional delivery. Beginning with the 1964 single "I'm on the Outside Looking in," they released a succession of top-quality soon-to-be standards like "Going Out of My Head" (1964) and "Hurt So Bad" (1965, later covered by Linda Ronstadt). They became the first group to played New York's Copacabana, and they continued charting R&B hits into the 1970s. Inducted into the Rock and Roll Hall of Fame in 2009, the group was honored for breaking down barriers for later African American artists.

Little Anthony's multi-range voice particularly excelled in falsetto—a trait that marked the Jackson 5's music as well as Michael's solo material. Note how Jermaine, Tito, Jackie, Marlon, and later Randy Jackson provided smooth harmonies to cushion Michael's voice, a method perfected by Little Anthony and the Imperials over a decade earlier. "The Love You Save," "I'll Be There," and "Daddy's Home" all bear traces of Little Anthony's unique sound.

The Jackson 5 and Little Anthony and the Imperials also share one other thing in common: Bobby Taylor, the man who discovered and mentored the Jackson brothers at Motown. Before forming his own group, Bobby Taylor and the Vancouvers, Taylor sang with various groups after moving to New York City in the mid-1950s. Among the artists he sang with were future members of the Imperials.

## Other Influences

From their early years playing local bars to the Apollo to the Motown revue shows, the Jackson 5 had a unique opportunity to learn from legends of soul and R&B. Many of these artists heavily influenced Michael as a solo performer, and some of these artists will be further discussed later in the book. They include the following:

- Smokey Robinson and the Miracles
- James Brown
- Jackie Wilson
- Sam and Dave
- The O'Jays
- The Isley Brothers
- Diana Ross
- The Four Tops

# Back to Where I Started From

## The Steeltown Recordings

A s the Jackson 5 began honing their skills in local talent shows, bars, nightclubs (such as the Gary mainstay Mr. Lucky's), and talent contests, the next step was to secure a recording contract. Joseph Jackson used his Gary connections to gain the attention of local songwriter and impresario Gordon Keith, a former steel-mill worker who co-owned the local record label Steeltown. Time has clouded certain details of the sessions, but this lesser-known backstory disproves Berry Gordy's story of how Diana Ross "discovered" the Jackson 5, supposedly resulting in their signing with Motown. Today, the Steeltown recordings sound unpolished, but the raw talent—specifically eight-year-old Michael Jackson's precocious vocals—remains intact. No matter the sound quality or the dubious song selections, the Steeltown sessions provides an important glimpse into the Jackson 5's earliest years.

### When Steeltown Met the Jackson 5

Attempting to capitalize on the growing music scene in Gary, Keith founded the small label in 1966 with four partners: Ben Brown, Ludie Washington, Maurice Rodgers, and Willie Spencer. By 1967, the new Steeltown Records had released many singles but had not yet produced a hit. How the Jackson boys arrived at the label remains murky, as several versions of the story exist.

The *Chicago Reader* published an in-depth investigation into the Steeltown story in its issue dated September 10, 2009, with reporter Jake Austen interviewing Keith and several local songwriters. Keith stated that he first became aware of the Jackson 5 after seeing numerous posters advertising their upcoming appearances. Deciding to investigate the act, he contacted the Jacksons' music teacher, Shirley Cartman, through another Steeltown group. Joseph Jackson subsequently invited Keith to their Gary home to hear his boys in person. They quickly won over the label head with their professionalism, and Keith immediately offered to take over their management contract. There was one problem: the Jacksons already had managers—well, sort of.

According to Austen, the Jacksons won a talent contest held at Chicago's Regal Theater in late 1965 or early 1966. Among the attendees were Pervis Spann and

E. Rodney Jones, two disc jockeys from the popular African American radio station WVON. The two were so impressed with the group's performance that they offered to manage the Jackson 5. In later years, Spann would claim to be the first person to discover the act, and while this story is disputed, the Jackson brothers did appear at Spann's nightclub Burning Spear.

While Steeltown was based in Gary, the Jackson 5 recordings actually took place in Chicago. Keith decided he wanted the best showcase for the band, so in November 1967 he asked Joseph to drive his sons to a studio in Chicago's West Englewood neighborhood on West 69th street. At the time, the studio was run by Sunny Sawyer, a local entrepreneur who owned a small record-pressing plant called Apex. In 1965, Sawyer partnered with recording engineer Vaughn Morrison to open Morrison Sound Studio (among musicians and label executives, it was more commonly known as "Sunny Sawyer's studio").

The Jackson 5, along with drummer Johnny Jackson (no relation, but a family friend who would later be falsely introduced as a Jackson cousin) and father Joseph, entered the 1,200-square-foot recording room, filled with high-end microphones and a four-track tape recorder on which only three tracks worked. Rounding out the musicians were Richard Brown on rhythm guitar, Freddie Young on lead guitar, Ray Grimes on bass, Lamont King on bongos, and an unknown conga player. Gary vocalist Delroy Bridgeman, Keith, and Steeltown partner Washington provided additional backup vocals on certain tracks.

During the first session, the Jackson 5 completed four songs: "Big Boy," "You've Changed," "We Don't Have to Be Over 21," and "Some Girls Want Me for Their Lover." Because the four-track recorder did not fully function, the group had to stop and start to allow the engineer to mix down and free up space on the now three-track tape. In Austen's article, Bridgeman recalled seeing the weary Jackson 5 still recording at ten or eleven at night. Once the session was finally over, studio singers Solomon Ard and George Rias returned to the studio the next day to touch up the vocals. Keith then brought the tapes back to a Gary recording studio run by Bud Pressner, a fifty-year music-industry veteran who played saxophone and worked as an engineer on countless local recordings. The Jacksons sat in on the postproduction, although likely did not participate. Keith subsequently sent them to a Chicago-area pressing plant, and the 45-rpm singles were ready for release on January 31, 1968. While the Jackson 5 sold copies at their shows, Steeltown started courting local radio stations to air "Big Boy."

The single sold moderately well locally, attracting the attention of Atlantic Records. Striking a distribution deal with Steeltown, the label reprinted "Big Boy" with the B-side "You've Changed" on the Atlantic imprint Atco. Empowered by the backing of a major label, Steeltown began shopping the record to Chicago stores and radio, most notably the powerhouse Top 40 station WLS. While modest, the single's sales delighted both the Jackson family and the fledgling label.

Taraborrelli's book *Michael Jackson: The Magic, the Madness, the Whole Story* tells a slightly different story. According to the author, the Jackson 5 were referred to Keith after winning the Beckman Junior High talent show in Gary. Taraborrelli mentions them arriving at the "Steeltown studio" rather than Sawyer's Chicago studio. They recorded seven tracks, the author states, returning every Saturday for the next few weeks to complete the songs. Brown recalled that the group posed for publicity photographs in March 1968; not happy with how the photographer positioned them, Brown recalled, Michael rearranged his brothers, kneeled down on one knee, and instructed the photographer to take the picture.

While the "Big Boy" single may have helped, it was ultimately the Jackson 5's return appearance at the Regal Theater that won them the Motown audition. The Jackson 5 opened for Motown act Bobby Taylor and the Vancouvers; blown away by their stage presence, Taylor arranged for the band to shoot an audition tape in Detroit. While Gladys Knight had already alerted Berry Gordy to the group, it wasn't until he saw the now-famous film (featuring Michael's flawless rendition of James Brown's "I've Got the Feelin') that he elected to sign the group. Legal wrangling with Atlantic and Steeltown prevented Motown from releasing the Jackson 5's debut album until almost a year later.

Not surprisingly, Keith tried to capitalize on the Jackson 5's fame by releasing the single "We Don't Have to Be Over 21" in 1970. As Austen notes, Keith hired Gary musician Wilton Crump to add string arrangements; this, he believed, would make the recording closely resemble contemporary Jackson 5 recordings. For the B-side, he included rehearsal footage of Joseph Jackson and his sons jamming in the studio, appropriately titling the track "Jam Session." Later that year, Keith licensed the final Jackson 5 track in his possession: "Some Girls Want Me for Their Lover," which was issued on the New York label Dynamo Records. Instead of having a throwaway on the B-side, Dynamo included "We Don't Have to Be Over 21" once more.

After the Jackson 5 released their debut Motown LP in 1969, Steeltown executive Gordon Keith capitalized on their newfound success by releasing leftovers from the group's 1968 "Big Boy" recording sessions. Steeltown released this single, "We Don't Have to Be Over 21," in 1970.    *Author's collection*

Michael Jackson historians have even questioned the singer's own account of the Steeltown sessions. In *Moonwalk*, Michael recalls that father Joseph brought home crudely recorded songs written by "Mr. Keith," clearly referring to the Steeltown executive. Joseph informed his sons that they had a week to rehearse the tracks for a future recording session. After intense rehearsals, they arrived at "Mr. Keith's studio," which again contradicts the notion that they traveled to Chicago. Michael recalls it being their first time in a recording studio, although that may not have been true (see below). They worked on Mr. Keith's songs for the next few weeks—one Saturday, Joseph Jackson brought his guitar to jam with the boys. This marked the only incident of the Jackson patriarch recording with his sons.

## The Plot Thickens: The One-derful Records Connection

Most historians agree that the Jackson 5 recorded the aforementioned four songs. However, subsequent compilations purporting to contain additional Steeltown tracks have since flooded the market, and the validity of most of the songs and demos are questionable. A sampling of albums claiming to contain the "lost" Jackson 5 tunes includes *Pre-History: The Lost Steeltown Recordings* (1996); *Jackson 5* (2000); *Jackson 5 and Johnny—Beginning Years 1967–1968* (1989); and *Original Steeltown Recordings* (2009). Music experts and Michael Jackson/Jackson 5 collectors have been fooled by several "outtakes" that were recorded by the multitudinous acts that appeared after the Jackson brothers' success.

According to Austen, one piece of early Jackson 5 footage does exist: a home-recorded tape of the Jacksons jamming on cover songs with their father. The circa-1967 session occurred in one of three places: Keith's basement, the Jacksons' Gary home, or the home of music teacher Cartman. Who currently owns this tape is unknown.

Yet another complication occurred in 2009, when Chicago guitarist Larry Blasingaine was interviewed on the radio show "Sitting in the Park" on WHPK-FM Chicago. Blasingaine claimed that in July 1967, the then-fifteen-year-old session musician entered the Chicago label One-derful's building, only to find his friends the Jackson 5 recording there. Blasingaine instantly recognized the group since his band, the Four Dukes (later known as Larry and the Hippies) played the same local circuit as the Jackson 5. Eddie Silvers, who had written "Big Boy" for the band, supposedly called in Blasingaine to help Jermaine Jackson with the bass part of the track. Next, Silvers asked the guitarist to sit in the session; he recorded a guitar part, then left.

When Austen confronted Keith and Spann about this version, they disputed Blasingaine's recollections. Keith said that Spann and Jones had the Jackson 5 rehearse at One-derful studios and even hired One-derful guitarist Jimmy Jones to tutor the group; Spann challenged this story. However, Keith also insisted that when he hired the group, he had to negotiate with not only Spann and Jones but also the Leaner Brothers.

George Leaner founded One-derful Records in 1962 with his brother Ernie. As one of Chicago's few black-owned labels, One-derful may have briefly had a contract with the Jackson 5. Austen investigated the story, interviewing Billy McGregor, a singer and songwriter who claimed to have seen Joseph bring Michael alone for an audition in 1966. McGregor insisted that Michael sang "Tobacco Road" for George, who liked what he heard but was hesitant about hiring a minor. Former One-derful employee Otis Hayes added that in 1967, WMPP DJ Louis Jefferson brought the Jackson 5 to the studio to audition for Hays, Jones, and George Leaner. This session won over Leaner, who expressed his desire to sign them to a recording contract.

The Jackson boys, accompanied by their parents, would supposedly drive in from Gary to the One-derful offices three or four days a week. Hayes said that he, Silvers, and Jimmy Jones would work with the group, coaching them on their vocals and jamming on songs. After five months, Leaner was impressed with their progress, but ultimately chose not to sign them due to the cost and issues concerning child labor laws.

The One-derful story remained a mystery until 2010, when Austen published a follow-up piece entitled "Now Playing: The Jackson Find" in the *Chicago Reader*. An extremely fragile tape was discovered in the One-derful archives, and after careful digital restoration, it revealed the lost "Big Boy" session featuring Blasingaine's guitar as well as a Hammond B-3 organ part absent from the Steeltown version. For unknown reasons, the Leaner brothers had decided to shelve the material, selling their Jackson 5 contract to Steeltown.

As this new theory suggests, the group may have recorded this early version of "Big Boy," perhaps as a "dress rehearsal" of the final version. Silvers may have intended this as a demo to shop to other artists and labels. Austen dismisses the notion that Steeltown released the One-derful version of "Big Boy," as Steeltown definitely had the group re-record the track at Sawyer's studios. (The identity of the organ player remains unclear, but was possibly Silvers or studio drummer Jimmy Jones.) Silvers could have given Steeltown the demo, however, with the label then basing its arrangement on the first rendition.

After careful restoration, One-derful finally released the 1967 "Big Boy" in 2014, but only as a limited edition 45-rpm single. The first 500 subscribers to *The One-derful! Collection*, a 147-track, seven-CD (or twelve-LP) set issued via Secret Stash Recordings, received a 45 of this lost Jackson 5 recording.

Whether it's the One-derful or Steeltown sessions, these early recordings paint the clearest picture of the pre-Motown, raw Jackson 5 sound.

## The Verified Steeltown Singles

The following list includes the Steeltown singles that have been verified as authentic Jackson 5 recordings.

### "Big Boy"

This first single was composed by saxophonist Eddie Silvers, who played with a group called the Soul Merchants. He also worked as a music director for One-derful Records; as previously mentioned, this meant the Jackson 5 recorded an earlier version of the tune before heading to Steeltown Records. In *Moonwalk*, Michael fondly remembers the track's "killer bass line" and its innocent tale of a boy wanting to fall in love. He admits that since he was only nine at the time of the recording, he did not fully understand the meaning of the song: "I just sang what they gave me."

Music critic Nelson George points out in *Thriller: The Musical Life of Michael Jackson* that the lyrics were meant to appeal to a specific African American entertainment trope: the young boy mimicking the mannerisms of a man. Michael was imitating Gaye or Ronald Isley in his smooth delivery, George notes; and such swagger coming from a child was a staple of amateur night shows. Here he is trying to downplay his youth; wisely, Motown stressed just the opposite when the group eventually joined the label.

Anchored largely by the bass line and rhythm guitar, Michael sings lead while his brothers (possibly aided by overdubbed studio singers) execute doo-wop-influenced backup vocals. While not a perfect performance, his lead definitely hints at the dynamic singer he would soon become. At nine, he could ad-lib like a pro (just listen to the fadeout for evidence) and confidently croon that he is a "big boy now" that wants someone to love. As the lyrics explain, he is through with childhood toys; instead, he wants to take the object of his affection to the movies. At times, Michael struggles with maintaining the pitch, particularly in the first and second verses, but his voice emerges strong and steady during the crucial choruses.

## "We Don't Have to Be Over 21"

As Austen describes, this up-tempo pop number was written by Sherman Nesbary, a Chicago composer who recorded singles under stage names such as Verble Domino and Little Sherman and the Mod Swingers. The tight bass lines and strong drums, along with the sprightly melody, are clearly derivative of Motown. Like "Big Boy," it borrows from the "young boy imitating grown man" theme.

Michael does not mention this track in *Moonwalk*, and it does not exude the same confidence of "Big Boy." The Jacksons' harmonies are not strong (particularly when they try to sing in falsetto), but Michael tries to channel his idol James Brown by crying "looky here!" at one point. The fast rhythm tries to encourage dancing, but the song still sounds forced, with Michael unable to cut loose and improvise.

## "You've Changed"

The B-side to the "Big Boy" single, this song has a solid Gary connection: songwriter Jerry Reese. Again, the bass part imitates James Jamerson, the ace player who belonged to Motown's house band, the Funk Brothers. It revisits the same theme as "Big Boy" and "You Don't Have to Be Over 21," with Michael reminiscing about when he met his girlfriend as a child who "never ever ever wore curls." The lyrics never rise to the level of Motown's best singles, with lines like "Instead of wearing a ponytail / You wear a little red wig" not exactly rivaling Smokey Robinson.

However, one can hear the Jackson 5 learning how to control their vocals, to work together to inspire energy and excitement among listeners. Jermaine, Jackie, Tito, and Marlon's voices rise to the foreground, illustrating how they had refined their vocal blend. The call-and-response section during the bridge foreshadows fun pop tracks like "ABC."

Steeltown may have overemphasized the "kid becoming a man" trope, but Motown was not above drawing from the same well. In "The Love You Save," the lyrics talk about the couple "playing tag in grade school," clearly taking advantage of Michael's youth.

## "Some Girls Want Me for Their Lover" (also known as "Michael the Lover")

An amusing track featuring Michael boasting about how the girls cannot resist him, "Some Girls Want Me for Their Lover" was composed by Keith under the pseudonym "William Adams." The 1970 version released on the Dynamo label over-dubbed strings in an ill-advised attempt to imitate the Jackson 5's Motown sound. The strings almost overwhelm the band's vocals and the funky bass line. The majority of the lyrics consist of Michael repeating the title phrase, although toward the end he assumes the role of a girl cooing, "Michael, I love you." Steeltown may have seen the potential for the pint-sized singer to become a teen idol, so Keith composed lyrics that would make girls swoon. As usual, Michael inserts James Brown–style phrases like "looky here!"

As with the other Steeltown Recordings, the track reveals the Jackson brothers to be still in the imitative stage. Only Motown would allow them to develop their uniqueness and distinguish themselves from other soul groups.

## "Jam Session"

This generic, poorly recorded jam was most likely intended as just a rehearsal. However, it remains the only recording where Joseph plays lead guitar with his sons. Michael pounds on the bongos, demonstrating an early flair for percussion. An instrumental, the track presents a vivid picture of how the Jackson 5 sounded in early rehearsals, with Joseph Jackson teaching them about classic R&B. The percussive talent Michael shows in the jam reveals how developed his skills were at such a young age. In later years he became a "percussive singer," mimicking drums and cymbals through beat boxing. It is obvious in this otherwise nondescript recording that he had a natural affinity for rhythm.

## Questionable Tracks

The following songs have been included on Steeltown compilations, but today their authenticity is in serious doubt. Confusion occurred when Steeltown issued the single "Let Me Carry Your Schoolbooks" b/w "I Never Had a Girl" by a group called the Ripples & Waves Plus Michael in 1971. Rumors circulated that the mysteriously named act was actually the Jackson 5, despite Steeltown's denial. The song was subsequently included on several compilations purporting to derive from the Jackson 5's Steeltown sessions. The mystery was finally solved in 2003, when Keith filed a lawsuit against the Brunswick label. In the mid-1990s, the company released *Pre-History: the Lost Steeltown Recordings*, clearly meant to piggyback off Michael's *HIStory* collection. Keith discovered that the two Ripples & Waves Plus Michael tracks were on the album, and subsequently sued Brunswick. At last, a few songs previously thought to be Jackson 5 relics were discredited; the real artists were a Gary band managed by Keith.

Most likely the tracks listed below were also recorded by soundalike acts that appeared in the Jackson 5's wake, and should be approached with caution. Only the five previously mentioned songs have been identified as genuine.

- "Baby You Don't Have to Go"
- "Stormy Monday"
- "Boys and Girls We're the J5"
- "My Girl"
- "Soul Jerk"
- "Under the Boardwalk"
- "I Found a Love"
- "Saturday Night at the Movies"
- "Tracks of My Tears"
- "A Change Is Gonna Come"
- "Lonely Heart"

## From Steeltown to Motown

Despite its best efforts, Steeltown simply could not provide the distribution and promotion the Jackson 5 required for mass exposure. In addition, Keith and the label executives seemed at a loss as to crafting the group's image. Should they be marketed as innocent kids, precocious youth, or on the same level as adults? These early recordings demonstrate that, while the Jackson brothers possessed raw talent, they needed a mentor to help refine it, shape it, and develop their unique sound. As George states, the Steeltown recordings lacked a "point of view"—a distinctive hook that would distinguish the Jackson 5 from the many anonymous soul singers struggling for attention. In other words, they needed to transition from imitators to innovators, and the Motown label possessed the tools and experience to help the Jacksons accomplish such a lofty goal.

# 3

# If It's in the Stars, They're Surely on My Side

## How the Jackson 5 Were Really Discovered

he story became legend: Motown superstar Diana Ross discovered the young boys from Indiana and brought them to the attention of Berry Gordy. The Jackson 5's debut LP, *Diana Ross Presents the Jackson 5*, includes liner notes supposedly written by the singer. She discovered the group in Gary, Indiana, Ross explains, as she showers them with praise for being "honest. Straight out. No tricks. No gimmicks." To further emphasize the Ross/Jackson 5 connection, she introduced the group on national television during a 1969 episode of ABC-TV's *The Hollywood Palace*. If Motown's biggest female star was giving this unknown "kiddie group" her imprimatur, they *must* be good.

There was only one problem: the story was a complete fabrication. As Gordy admits in his autobiography, *To Be Loved*, the "Ross discovered the Jackson 5" tale figured into his "strategic plan" to introduce the group to the world. The true story involves hard work, some luck, and multiple figures that played crucial roles in the Jackson 5's journey from Gary to Los Angeles.

### The Gary/Chicago Years

As Jake Austen notes in his September 10, 2009, *Chicago Reader* article "The Jackson Find," several Gary residents have claimed that they discovered the Jackson 5. There are elements of truth in each story, although Michael does not identify the players in *Moonwalk*. Several names do surface, however, some of whom have already been discussed in chapter 2.

### Pervis Spann and E. Rodney Jones

These two disc jockeys worked at Chicago's premiere African American station WVON and often attended local talent contests. In the 1960s, WVON became the most successful station in the black community; according to David Whitels's

2001 *Chicago Reader* article "Not So Smooth Operator," WVON claimed 44 to 48 percent of daytime African American listenership by 1964. In a *Billboard* dated March 28, 1964, the magazine cited the station's rapid growth, noting that WVON "unbelievably" was ranked second in the ratings, topped by Chicago powerhouse WLS. Owned by label chief Leonard Chess, WVON boasted a lineup of popular DJs dubbed the "Good Guys," whose roster included Pervis Spann and E. Rodney Jones.

Not content with being simply on-air personalities, the Good Guys transitioned into promotion and club ownership. Spann developed a relationship with Chicago's famed Regal Theater, booking talent for the establishment. Along with fellow DJ Jones, the duo founded the Burning Spear, a club that featured local and nationally known artists. Spann and Jones also hosted talent shows, which allowed them to dabble in artist representation. In 2001, Spann told Whitels that he booked the Jackson 5 at the Burning Spear; after viewing their show, he approached them with a proposition: he and Jones would serve as their managers. "All that crap about Diana Ross discovered 'em? She didn't have nothing to do with it!" he proclaimed.

However, the 2009 *Chicago Reader* article "The Jackson Find" states that Spann and Jones attended a talent show at the Regal Theater, where they witnessed the Jackson 5 win a contest in late 1965 or early 1966. Impressed, the duo immediately offered to manage the group. The contract—often just a handshake, Spann told Whitels—would be short-lived after Steeltown records expressed interest in the group. No matter the confused details, Spann and Jones most likely played early roles in garnering the Jackson 5 exposure in the black community.

## Genevieve Gray and Yjean Chambers

The two Roosevelt High teachers in Gary, Indiana, encouraged the Jackson brothers to enroll in local talent contests, starting in 1965. Frustratingly little information exists on these two figures, and Michael only discusses his teachers generally in *Moonwalk*. However, Chambers briefly mentioned the group in a 1999 *Education Week* article entitled "A Blueprint for Change." Then seventy-seven years old, she explained how school auditoriums served as a "speaking and listening chamber and laboratory," and recalled guiding the Jackson 5 toward talent shows. Chambers subsequently left Roosevelt in 1972 to teach speech and theater at Purdue University in Hammond, Indiana. After returning to her hometown, she served on the Gary school board.

## Shirley Cartman

Teachers frequently play crucial roles in people's lives, and Shirley Cartman's part in the formation of the Jackson 5 is no exception. Originally Tito Jackson's music teacher, Cartman encouraged the Jackson brothers to develop their talent and enter local talent shows, and she used her connections to earn the boys auditions.

In 1966, Cartman worked at Beckman Junior High School in Gary, teaching eighth grade orchestra. That year her class included Tito, whom she soon learned was part of a family band called the Jackson 5. Tito was interested in auditioning for the school's annual talent-show fundraiser, and he knew that Cartman ran the event. Thus, in 1967, Tito approached her about having him and his brothers try out for the show.

According to Chris Cadman and Craig Halstead's account in *Michael Jackson: The Early Years*, there was a big problem: the show occurred during regular school hours, which would prevent Michael, Marlon, and Jermaine (all students at Garnett Elementary School) as well as Jackie (who attended Roosevelt High) from participating. Cartman persuaded Joseph and Katherine Jackson to allow their sons to miss school; next, she visited their home for the big audition. Impressed, she immediately accepted them, and they went on to win the talent show.

As the Jackson 5 continued winning local talent shows, Joseph grew concerned that the band would never earn paying gigs. Once again Cartman took charge; according to Cadman and Halstead, the teacher suggested hiring a drummer, Johnny Jackson; arranged for promotional photos; and even penned some original songs for the group to sing. No actual footage of these recording sessions has ever surfaced, however. Perhaps her biggest contribution was an introduction: she recommended the group to Gordon Keith, owner of Steeltown Records.

## Gordon Keith

The Steeltown Records cofounder later maintained that he had known of the Jackson 5 before Cartman contacted him; however, she persuaded him to sit in on one of their sessions. Impressed, he signed the Jackson 5 to his small Gary label and sent them to Chicago for recording sessions.

As detailed in the previous chapter, Gordon Keith oversaw the Jackson 5's first officially released recordings and penned two of their songs, "Big Boy" and "You've Changed." After the Jackson 5 signed with Motown, they re-recorded the latter song for their debut album, *Diana Ross Presents the Jackson 5*.

While the singles sold only modestly well in the Gary and Chicago markets, they did receive some airplay. This exposure proved crucial for the group, landing them more gigs and earning them some professional recording experience. Keith worked with the Jackson 5 for a very limited time, but he played a valuable role in the group's journey to Motown.

## Art Roberts

The WLS-AM DJ gave the Jackson 5 early exposure on his local dance show *Swinging Majority* in early 1968. One of the city's most popular DJs, Roberts served double duty hosting the *American Bandstand*–inspired program, which aired live on Chicago's WCIU-TV, Channel 26, Saturdays at 4:00 to 5:00 p.m. Featuring local entertainers of the day, the weekly program featured teenagers dancing to its house band, the Destinations.

Former band-member Reed Kailing recalled how artists fought to appear on the show for exposure and to receive WLS airplay. In a 2009 interview with Sam Tweedle's blog Confessions of a Pop Culture Addict, he mentioned that if bands playing shows in Chicago refused to perform on the show, Roberts would pass on their records. "That's where I met Michael Jackson and the Jackson 5," he said. "They were just little kids. I mean everybody did Art's show."

The Jackson 5 first earned attention thanks to their first Steeltown single, "Big Boy." Jake Austen credited Steeltown president Ben Brown with bringing the record and band to Robert's attention. Interestingly, the show featured the co-headliner Ides of March, the Berwyn, Illinois, group best known for their hit "Vehicle." Little information exists about the exact date of the episode, and no footage can be found. However, Roberts can be credited with providing the Jackson 5 with crucial early television exposure.

## Gladys Knight

Wending their way through the talent show circuit in 1967, the Jackson 5 found themselves playing amateur nights at Chicago's Regal Theater. At the time, Knight and the Pips were rising stars, playing the same circuit. The Jackson 5 won the Regal Theater contest for three straight weeks, eventually earning them a spot opening for Gladys Knight and the Pips. That night, Michael writes in *Moonwalk*, Knight and her group debuted their new single, "I Heard It Through the Grapevine."

Impressed by the group's talent, Knight mentioned them to Motown's Gordy. She even recruited a few Motown executives to see them perform, hoping they would send good reports to Gordy. Not interested in a "kiddie act," Gordy still passed on the group, but he would change his mind a year later.

After the Jackson 5 joined the Motown label, they would occasionally cross paths with Knight and the Pips. Their paths would cross a few years later; the Jackson 5's first hit, "I Want You Back," was originally called "I Want to Be Free" and intended for Knight.

## Bobby Taylor

Perhaps the most important player in the Jackson 5's early career, Bobby Taylor served as both artist and talent scout for Motown. In June 1968, Taylor and his group the Vancouvers (including guitarist Tommy Chong, who would go on to greater fame as one half of the comedy duo Cheech & Chong) played Chicago; according to Austen, the group was touring behind their biggest single, "Does Your Mama Know About Me."

Taylor and his band were playing Chicago clubs and theaters, and one night they witnessed an opening act: the Jackson 5. As Taylor told author Nelson George in *Thriller: The Musical Life of Michael Jackson*, once he saw Michael Jackson and his brothers perform James Brown's "I Got the Feelin'" and "Cold Sweat," he knew he had to work with these talented kids. This performance occurred at the Regal Theater; amazed by their raw talent, Taylor arranged for them to travel to Detroit to film an audition tape.

Staying with Taylor, the Jacksons refined their act for their big test. As George notes, Taylor drilled them in harmonics and enunciation. "The leap from raw live performance to studio professionalism can be a big one, and Taylor, as much as anyone, provided Michael and his brothers with that initial education," Nelson

Bobby Taylor doubled as the leader of the group Bobby Taylor and the Vancouvers and as a talent scout, songwriter, and producer for Motown. He arranged for the Jackson 5 to audition for Berry Gordy, and produced the Jacksons' first album.

*Author's collection*

states. The black-and-white footage features Michael turning in an astounding rendition of Brown's "I Got the Feelin'," complete with sliding footwork. Interestingly, Taylor viewed Michael as primarily a soul singer in the tradition of Ray Charles, not a pop star.

Once Gordy viewed the audition, he signed the group away from Steeltown and assigned Taylor as their producer. For weeks, the Jackson 5 recorded material at Motown's Detroit studios, all under Taylor's watchful eye. Backed by the Motown house band the Funk Brothers, Taylor and the Jacksons recorded over two dozen classic soul covers, some of which appeared on the debut LP *Diana Ross Presents the Jackson 5*. These sessions included The Temptations' "(I Know) I'm Losing You" and "Born to Love You"; Marvin Gaye's "Chained"; Stevie Wonder's "My Cherie Amour"; and the Four Tops' "Standing in the Shadows of Love." Other covers included Sly and the Family Stone's "Stand!," the Delfonics' "Can You Remember," and even Keith's Steeltown composition "You've Changed."

The most famous song resulting from the Taylor sessions remains the Jackson 5's memorable interpretation of The Miracles "Who's Lovin' You." Michael's precocious lead vocal virtually redefined the song, and it remains the most popular version of the Smokey Robinson–penned classic.

When Gordy heard the tapes, he grew disenchanted; while Taylor envisioned the Jackson 5 as an old-school soul act, Gordy wanted them to achieve crossover success. Thus the two parted ways, with Gordy forming the Corporation songwriting and production team (see chapter 4) to complete the album in Los Angeles. Taylor did not receive a production credit on *Diana Ross Presents the Jackson 5*, even though his work comprises much of the LP.

While Taylor worked with the Jackson 5 for only a short time, he served as a major force in their early careers. He more than anyone else truly discovered the group, brought them to Motown, and honed their singing skills until they sounded completely professional. Without Taylor, the Jackson 5 may never have earned a Motown audition.

## George Leaner

The Leaner brothers cofounded One-derful Records, one of Chicago's few black-owned labels, in 1962. The label's first release, McKinley Mitchell's "The Town I Live in," performed well on the R&B charts. After that initial success, George Leaner (with assistance from brother Ernie, who owned distribution company United Distributors) created an in-house production team as well as recruiting local songwriters and musicians. Larry Blasingaine's band Larry and the Hippies frequently served as the backing band. As the label grew, so did its roster, which included Otis Clay ("That's How It Is") and the Five Du-Tones ("Shake a Tail Feather").

As detailed in chapter 2, Michael auditioned twice for George Leaner—once alone, the other time with the Jackson 5. Deciding to work with the band, George had the group recording at One-derful's Chicago studios in 1967. After months of rehearsing the young talents, George ultimately decided not to sign the group due to their ages. When the label folded in 1968, the Jackson 5 connection was all but forgotten.

Thanks to Jake Austen's 2009 *Chicago Reader* article "The Jackson Find," One-derful Records' crucial link to the Jackson 5 was finally revealed. Buried in the vaults was a dusty tape containing the group's original recording of "Big Boy," laid down months before they moved to Steeltown Records. This important find illustrates how Michael's vocal talent developed, with the song featuring a very young performer still finding his way as a singer. Therefore, George Leaner can be credited with providing the Jackson 5 with their earliest professional recording session, even though it remained buried for over four decades.

## Motown Years

After years of toiling in obscurity in Gary, the Jackson 5 finally received their big break through Taylor's Motown connections. When the group relocated to Los Angeles, a team from the label applied its marketing and musical expertise to help the Jackson 5 become Motown's most popular early 1970s act.

## Weldon McDougal III

While he served as a promotions man for Motown's East Coast office, Weldon McDougal III met the Jackson 5 before they were hired at the label. In a 2010 interview with the J5 Collector website, he remembered meeting the group at the High Chaparall nightclub in Chicago. Still on the talent-show circuit in 1969, they had won yet another contest that night; after the performance, McDougal was introduced to Jackson patriarch Joseph Jackson. Joseph informed the promotions man of the boys' desire to audition for Motown; McDougal replied that he could not personally book them but advised them to contact Taylor. The following day, McDougal met Taylor and mentioned the talented group of kids he had seen the night before.

Once the Jackson 5 joined Motown, McDougal's mission was to promote their debut single, "I Want You Back." He suggested that the Jackson 5 embark on a five-city tour behind the record; the label balked at the potential expense. Thus McDougal, Berry Gordy, and the other Motown executives devised the "Diana Ross protégés" plan, hoping that Motown's number-one star could open doors for the group. McDougal distributed postcards advertising this connection, but few radio stations initially played the single. Once the Jackson 5 appeared on *The Ed Sullivan Show* on December 14, 1969, however, stations began contacting the promotions man for copies. "I Want You Back," he stated, broke down barriers in that pop stations as well as R&B powerhouses wanted to air the song.

## Berry Gordy

Gordy, of course, became the major architect of the Jackson 5's careers. In *Moonwalk*, Michael recalls the Motown CEO telling them that he would make them the best-selling act in the world, promising their next three songs would reach #1. According to McDougal, Gordy and the in-house songwriting and producing team the Corporation composed songs they dubbed "bubblegum soul."

While Gordy had heard of the Jackson 5 through Knight, he remained reluctant to hire a "kids act" until Suzanne de Passe and Taylor convinced him of their talent. The Taylor-coached audition tape ultimately won Gordy over: as he remembers in his autobiography, *To Be Loved*, the group performed "Ain't Too Proud to Beg," "I Wish It Would Rain," "Tobacco Road," and "I Got the Feelin'." Interestingly, he claims to have been present at the taping, although Michael and most other sources recalled it differently. In any case, Gordy would later write of how he instantly recognized Michael's star quality: "This little kid had an incredible knowingness about him that really made me take notice. He sang his songs with such feeling, inspiration and pain—like he had experienced everything he was singing about."

After extensive negotiations (including fending off people who claimed to be the Jackson 5's managers), Gordy finally moved the Jacksons to California in March 1969. Until they got settled, the boys stayed with Gordy and Ross, rehearsing and learning the business. Meanwhile, Gordy devised his marketing strategy and brainstormed potential hit singles. As he mentions in *To Be Loved*, the Motown head wanted to pattern the Jackson 5 after Frankie Lymon and the Teenagers, even down to having their debut single, "I Want You Back," resemble "Why Do Fools Fall in Love?" To do this, Gordy formed an in-house production team called the Corporation (further discussed in chapter 4). The group started with a bang, composing the Jackson 5's instant classic "I Want You Back."

In addition to guiding the group's music, Gordy devised a backstory. He designated Ross to "present them," inventing the story that she had discovered the band in Gary. In addition, he billed Michael as eight instead of ten years old, a tactic designed to increase the "cute" factor.

As Gordy details, he quickly rolled out his plan: first, he introduced the group to the Motown Corporation on August 11, 1969. Next, the Jackson 5 opened for

Ross and the Supremes at the Forum in Los Angeles. Building on the increasing buzz, Gordy released the "I Want You Back" single on October 7; over a week later, the Jackson 5 appeared on the television show *The Hollywood Palace* (featuring Ross as guest host). By January 31, 1970—just a few months after the Jacksons relocated to Los Angeles—the Jackson 5 had their first #1 record.

From crafting their image to writing their material, Gordy stands as one of the master architects of the Jackson 5's career.

## Suzanne de Passe

Gordy's creative assistant, de Passe served as the Jacksons' manager and teacher. She constructed their public image, essentially serving as their stylist. In *Moonwalk*, Michael stresses that she played a major role in the Jackson 5's early development. Calling her one of their managers, he writes that she "trained us religiously" and served as both mentor and friend. According to Taraborrelli, de Passe accompanied Ralph Seltzer, head of Motown's creative department and legal division, to the Jackson 5's initial Detroit audition. Bringing the footage to Gordy, she helped persuade the Motown head to sign the group.

When the Jackson boys arrived in Los Angeles, de Passe was put in charge of creating their image. She and her team of stylists crafted everything from the boys' hairstyles to their clothes, dressing them in bright colors and funky styles appropriate for the era. Who could forget the fringed fest and magenta cowboy hat little Michael wore during the group's debut *Ed Sullivan Show* appearance? De Passe purchased the attire, along with the other group members' costumes, off the rack in New York's Greenwich Village.

De Passe served as assistant choreographer, chaperone, stylist, and mother figure for the Jackson 5. Due to her close relationship with the group, she was primarily responsible for persuading Michael to reunite with his brothers for the 1983 *Motown 25* TV special.

## Diana Ross

While Ross did not discover the Jackson 5, she played a significant role in their (as well as Michael's) early career. When the Jackson brothers first relocated to Los Angeles, they stayed alternately with Gordy and Ross while the Jackson parents sold the Gary home and purchased a suitable L.A. house. Ross instantly became a mentor to Michael; in *Moonwalk*, he identifies her as his mother, lover, and sister in one person.

When Gordy asked her to present the new group as her discovery, it came at a crossroads in Ross's life. On the verge of leaving the Supremes, she was about to embark on a solo career. Associating herself with an untested act may have been risky, but she trusted Gordy's judgment and had seen them perform. In the months before the Jackson 5 made their public debut, the boys lived with her sporadically. Gordy believed Ross could teach young Michael about being a Motown star and educate him in dealing with media. In *Moonwalk*, Michael fondly recalls going to museums with Ross, adding that she became a surrogate mother to him. She taught him professional discipline, as she maintained a demanding schedule filled with recording and personal appearances.

According to Taraborrelli, Ross influenced Michael in other ways. He noticed her tendency to sing "ooh's" at various points in a song, almost as exclamations.

He would incorporate this tic in his music with his brothers as well as the solo material. In addition, he took note of her commanding presence, both on and off the stage. Finally, her devotion to her image—that of a glamorous, elegant diva—clearly made an impact on Michael, as he and his brothers gradually adapted to their partially invented backstory, their clothes and attitudes adding to the "clean cut, all-American" image Gordy wanted them to project. Ross may have never visited Gary when the Jackson 5 began performing, but her influence loomed large over the group and Michael as a solo artist.

Released in 1969, *Diana Ross Presents the Jackson 5* perpetuated the myth that the Motown diva "discovered" the Indiana youngsters. An accompanying essay supposedly written by Ross emphasizes the group's genuine talent and honesty.

*Author's collection*

## It Takes a Village

Who discovered the Jackson 5? While the Ross story proved effective for publicity and for properly introducing the group to the public, the true answer is more complicated. Rather than one person, a series of teachers and musicians, disc jockeys and entrepreneurs, and record company executives all played important roles in the Jackson 5's road to fame. It takes a village to create a star, and thus several parties share the credit for teaching the Jacksons professionalism. They taught the Jacksons valuable lessons that they would carry with them throughout their careers, and Michael would further incorporate what he learned into his extraordinarily successful solo years.

# 4

# Show Me a Reason and I'll Soon Show You a Rhyme

## Jackson 5 Songwriters and Musicians

In their early years, the Jackson 5 provided their own backing music. Jermaine Jackson played bass; Tito Jackson provided guitar; Jackie, Marlon, and Michael Jackson contributed vocals. According to J. Randy Taraborrelli, numerous neighborhood boys served stints in the band playing various instruments, most notably drummer Johnny Porter Jackson and keyboardist Ronny Rancifer. Johnny and Ronny traveled to California with the family, even living at the Jacksons' Encino estate. The two remained with the Jackson 5 until the group departed Motown.

However, other musicians and songwriters played integral parts in the Jackson 5's phenomenal success. After Berry Gordy fired Bobby Taylor as the group's producer (see chapter 3), the Motown CEO assembled a team of songwriters and producers whose sole aim was to create hits for the teen group. Dubbed the Corporation, the four-person crew wrote and guided the Jackson 5's output until 1972. Hal Davis then took over the group until they left the record label.

In addition to these songwriters, supplemental musicians performed on the Jackson 5's recordings, often drawing from the West Coast's top studio band/collective, the Wrecking Crew. This group of mostly unknown players contributed some of the best-known guitar licks, drum sections, and other crucial instrumental elements on the Jackson 5's albums. Each of these groups played a major part in the group's development; indeed, the Jacksons would never have achieved success without their contributions.

### Songwriters

In the 1960s, Motown's top songwriters were the legendary Detroit trio of Brian Holland, Lamont Dozier, and Eddie Holland. They virtually invented the Motown sound, writing an astounding number of hits such as "Stop! In the Name of Love" and "You Can't Hurry Love" (the Supremes); "Heat Wave" and "Jimmy Mack" (Martha and the Vandellas); "Reach Out I'll Be There" and "Baby I Need Your Loving" (the Four Tops); and "Can I Get a Witness" and "How Sweet It Is to

Be Loved by You" (Marvin Gaye). By 1968, the Holland-Dozier-Holland name had become so renowned that they demanded a larger share of royalties. Gordy refused, and the trio left Motown to start their own label.

In response to Holland-Dozier-Holland's departure, Gordy established a new team of songwriters, all of whom brought youth and energy to the Jackson 5's unique sound.

## The Corporation

Frustrated with songwriters and producers achieving star status, Gordy decided to create an in-house songwriting and producing team that would be largely anonymous to the record-buying public. Individual names were never included in liner notes; instead, production credits on any Motown release simply read "The Corporation."

The group's members included Alphonso Mizell, Freddie Perren, and Deke Richards—all proven songwriters—and Gordy. According to Taraborrelli, Richards devised the name to stress the democratic nature of the songwriting team. Gordy clearly agreed with this idea; as he writes in his autobiography, his "creative commando team" was to be "anonymous, unified team where nobody's personal names or egos could get in the way"—a thinly veiled reference to the Holland-Dozier-Holland triumvirate. Unlike his involvement with prior Motown groups, Gordy would assume a very active role in launching the Jackson 5 as well as writing and producing their early hits.

The Corporation, the quartet of Motown songwriters and producers, created many of the Jackson 5's greatest hits. They also helmed some of the group's early albums, including 1970's *ABC*.    *Author's collection*

The group's roots trace back to Washington, D.C., where pianist Perren and bassist Mizell met as schoolmates. Relocating to California, they met guitarist Richards, a seasoned songwriter who had been part of a previous Motown in-house team, the Clan (responsible for the Supremes' groundbreaking hit "Love Child"). The three collaborated on a song entitled "I Wanna Be Free," originally intended for Gladys Knight and the Pips. When they brought the track to Gordy, he suggested rewriting it as a bubblegum pop hit for a teenage act. In fact, he had a specific teen group in mind: the Jackson 5.

After the trio revised the track as "I Want You Back," the Corporation entered the studio to record the song with the group. According to Ed Hogan's All Music entry on the Corporation, the session featured Perren and Mizell on piano; Wilton Felder (later known as a member of jazz fusion group The Crusaders) on bass; David T. Walker and Louis Shelton on guitars; Don Peake on additional bass; and Gene Pello on drums. The Corporation composition landed the Jackson 5 their first #1 hit by January 1970.

After that initial success, the Corporation continued producing hits for the Jacksons. "ABC" and "The Love You Save" effectively harnessed the boys' youthful energy, seamlessly blending R&B, pop, and rock to create songs with mass appeal. The following year, 1971, brought the next Corporation-driven hit, "Mama's Pearl," a slightly grittier-sounding song emphasizing the band's funky roots. They extended their production skills to the Jermaine Jackson solo single "Daddy's Home," another Top 10 R&B and pop hit.

While they did not pen the tracks, the Corporation's production work on the *Jackson 5 Christmas Album* deserves attention. The drums burst through on cuts such as "Santa Claus Is Coming to Town," and Michael Jackson's voice adds charm and vitality to old favorites such as "I Saw Mommy Kissing Santa Claus" (see chapter 10 for a full discussion of this album).

*Skywriter,* the Jackson 5's 1973 album, would mark the Corporation's last significant collaboration with the band. "Hallelujah Day," a Top 10 R&B hit, served as the group's final hit written and produced by the Corporation; by the following year, Hal Davis had assumed control of subsequent Jackson 5 productions, marking an important transition from bubblegum to a more mature, dance-oriented sound.

Nevertheless, the Corporation played a tremendous role in the Jackson 5's earliest (and biggest) successes as they possessed a talent for mixing elements of varying musical genres to create songs appealing to diverse audiences. As Paul Friedlander explains in his 2006 book *Rock and Roll: A Social History*, Motown would "tastefully blend musical ingredients into a coherent, pleasing, and commercially successful sound"—a rare talent that paid dividends. In this vein, the Corporation alone is responsible for crafting some of the best and most sophisticated pop material in the history of popular music.

### Essential Corporation Compositions and Productions

- "I Want You Back" (*Diana Ross Presents the Jackson 5*, 1969)
- "Nobody" (*Diana Ross Presents the Jackson 5*, 1969)
- "Santa Claus Is Coming to Town" (*Jackson 5 Christmas Album*, 1970)
- "I Saw Mommy Kissing Santa Claus" (*Jackson 5 Christmas Album*, 1970)

- "ABC" (*ABC*, 1970)
- "The Love You Save" (*ABC*, 1970)
- "Goin' Back to Indiana" (*Third Album*, 1970)
- "Mama's Pearl" (*Third Album*, 1970)
- "Maybe Tomorrow" (*Maybe Tomorrow*, 1971)
- "Never Can Say Goodbye" (*Maybe Tomorrow*, 1971)
- "Hallelujah Day" (*Skywriter*, 1973)

## Hal Davis

The producer and songwriter Hal Davis headed Motown's Los Angeles offices and was involved with the Jackson 5 from *Third Album* onward. When the Corporation split in 1973, Hal Davis assumed full producer status and steered the Jackson 5's career in a contemporary R&B direction. That year's "Dancing Machine" encapsulates this change, previewing the disco sound that would dominate the Jacksons years at Epic.

Known as "Mr. Motown" in the Los Angeles offices, Davis made inroads as a producer in the early 1960s. His most significant discovery, singer Brenda Holloway, provided a turning point in his career. Before meeting the vocalist, Davis had recorded a few songs of his own, including 1960's "Read the Book of Love" and the 1961 single "My Only Flower" b/w "You're the Girl," all for small labels. However, his work with Motown artists cemented his status as an in-demand producer, overseeing albums by Stevie Wonder, Marvin Gaye, and crooner Tony Martin. His big break came when he produced Holloway's 1964 single "Every Little Bit Hurts." Holloway recalled how he worked for the County of Los Angeles during the day and produced records at night. She embarked on a romance with Davis, but it proved short-lived.

Quickly gaining a reputation for being a relentless worker and an efficient talent scout, Davis relocated to Los Angeles to head then new Motown West offices. In addition to his work with the Jackson 5, he produced the phenomenally successful 1973 album *Diana & Marvin*, a collection of duets by Motown's two top stars.

Davis first entered the Jackson 5's orbit in 1970, when Gordy and the Corporation were trying to compose additional hits in the style of "I Want You Back" and "ABC." Meanwhile, Davis had teamed up with Motown singer and songwriter Willie Hutch as well as bassist Bob West to compose "I'll Be There." According to Gordy, Davis woke up the Motown head at five o'clock in the morning to inform him they had just written a sure-thing hit for the Jackson 5. After listening to their demo, Gordy decided that he liked the concept but suggested they revise the lyrics to better reflect the group's clean-cut teenage image. With that change and Michael Jackson's soulful vocal performance, "I'll Be There" quickly became the group's fourth #1 single. Having proven himself to Gordy, Davis then joined the Jackson 5 creative team.

Davis's debut as Jackson 5 architect was 1973's *G.I.T.: Get It Together*, which produced two hit singles: "Get It Together" and "Dancing Machine," both kicking off the new Jackson 5 era. Co-written by Davis, "Get It Together" features the earworm-worthy chorus, "Get it together or leave it alone / If you don't want my lovin' I'll be gone." "Dancing Machine" reflects the early disco years, coming just a short time before dance music would dominate the charts. Combined with a robotic sound and fun word play ("Automatic, systematic / Full of color, self-contained / Tuned and channeled to your vibes"), the single showcases Michael Jackson's emerging sexuality and maturity. He spits out aggressive, sensual lines, talking about the "sexy lady," a "dynamite attraction" who will "really blow your mind." Taraborrelli argues that "Dancing Machine" foreshadows the techno-pop sound that would explode during the 1980s. Indeed, Donna Summer's "I Feel Love" may have taken a few cues from this landmark record.

Davis proved to be what the Jacksons would later remember as "a stern taskmaster and a teacher," according to George's *Thriller: The*

"Hallelujah Day," from the 1973 album *Skywriter*, was the final hit written and produced for the Jackson 5 by the Corporation.                 *Author's collection*

*Musical Life of Michael Jackson*. Nevertheless, his work with the Jackson 5 produced some of their most memorable singles. "I'll Be There" stands as one of Michael Jackson's finest performances, his lilting vocals wrenching every ounce of emotion from the heartbreaking words. In *Moonwalk*, Michael credits Davis and assistant/ vocal coach Suzee Ikeda with guiding him through his vocal performance. He had grown rapidly as an interpreter, and Davis was partially responsible for this crucial transformation.

### Essential Compositions and Productions
- "I'll Be There" (*Third Album*, 1970)
- "Get It Together" (*G.I.T.: Get It Together*, 1973)
- "Dancing Machine" (*G.I.T.: Get It Together*, 1973)
- "It's Too Late to Change the Time" (*G.I.T: Get It Together*, 1973)
- "I Am Love (Parts 1 & 2)" (*Dancing Machine*, 1974)
- "Whatever You Got, I Want" (*Dancing Machine*, 1974)
- "The Life of the Party" (*Dancing Machine*, 1974)
- "Forever Came Today" (*Moving Violation*, 1975)
- "All I Do Is Think of You" (*Moving Violation*, 1975)

## Jobete Publishing

When Gordy was working as an independent songwriter, he became frustrated with a standard practice in 1958: publishers often refused to pay him royalties from his compositions. Thus he took another step to ensure that he and fellow songwriters would receive their fair share of royalties from their original songs. He established Jobete Publishing (deriving the name from the first two letters in his three children's names) and signed Smokey Robinson as its first client. At that point, Robinson suggested that he also form his own record company, resulting in the debut of Tamla Records in 1959.

Gordy recruited numerous songwriters to work for Jobete; while there were later disputes over salaries and royalties, the budding composers managed to see their work be interpreted by some of Motown's biggest stars. As Friedlander writes, Motown songwriters excelled at composing lyrics with universal meaning—a conscious move to appeal to mass audiences. The following section lists significant composers and behind-the-scenes players on various Jackson 5 albums. This discussion includes only songwriters who composed tracks specifically for the Jackson 5, not those who wrote songs the Jackson 5 subsequently covered.

## Willie Hutch

After receiving his big break writing and co-producing the Fifth Dimension's 1967 album *Up Up and Away*, Hutch became known as a go-to lyricist. When Davis was composing "I'll Be There," he contacted Hutch to assist him with lyrics. After the song became one of Motown's best-selling singles, he signed with the label to write and produce for artists such as Smokey Robinson, Marvin Gaye, Diana Ross, Junior Walker, and the Four Tops. In addition, he continued working with Michael and the Jackson 5 while releasing solo albums and scoring films such as *The Mack* and *Foxy Brown*.

### Key Compositions
* "I'll Be There" (*Third Album*, 1970)
* "How Funky Is Your Chicken" (*Third Album*, 1970)
* "Just Because I Love You" (*Joyful Jukebox Music*, 1976)
* "Love Call" (*Jackson 5: I Want You Back! Unreleased Masters*, 2009)

## Suzee Ikeda

Originally signed as a singer for Motown, Suzee Ikeda became better known for her behind the scenes work for other artists. In *Moonwalk*, Michael fondly recalls working with her on his vocals for "I'll be There"; he calls her "my other half" and states that Ikeda stood next to Michael, coaching him on his vocal delivery. She did not write songs specifically for the Jackson 5, but she was credited as "production assistant" on several albums.

## Leon Ware

The Detroit-born singer and songwriter recorded several solo albums before joining Motown in 1960. He briefly left the label to write for artists including Ike and

Tina Turner, but returned in 1972. Co-writing hits such as Michael's "I Wanna Be Where You Are," he went on to write hits for the Four Tops and Minnie Riperton. His most notable work occurred with Marvin Gaye, with whom he co-wrote every track on the singer's classic album *I Want You*.

**Key Compositions**
- "Don't Say Goodbye Again" (*G.I.T.: Get It Together*, 1973)
- "It's Too Late to Change the Time" (*G.I.T.: Get It Together*, 1973)
- "If I Don't Love You This Way" (*Dancing Machine*, 1974)

## Pam Sawyer

One of Motown's chief songwriters, Pam Sawyer hailed from England. After marrying an American musician, she relocated to the United States and settled in New York. When their marriage disintegrated, Sawyer remained in American to pursue a songwriting career. She paired with singer/songwriter Lori Burton, with whom she penned a UK hit for Lulu, "Try to Understand." This achievement earned them an audition with Motown, specifically the Holland-Dozier-Holland team. Once the duo signed to Jobete, they sent their compositions to Detroit; after Burton left the label, Sawyer partnered with several other writers. She was also a member of the Clan, a pre-Corporation team that composed the Supremes single "Love Child."

**Key Compositions**
- "2-4-6-8" (*ABC*, 1970)
- "Christmas Won't Be the Same This Year" (*Jackson 5 Christmas Album*, 1970)
- "The Wall" (*Maybe Tomorrow*, 1971)
- "Touch" (*Skywriter*, 1973)
- "Don't Say Goodbye Again" (*G.I.T.: Get It Together*, 1973)
- "It's Too Late to Change the Time" (*G.I.T.: Get It Together*, 1973)
- "If I Don't Love You This Way" (*Dancing Machine*, 1974)
- "Window Shopping" (*Joyful Jukebox Music*, 1976)
- "I Ain't Gonna Eat My Heart Out Anymore" (*Boogie*, 1979)

## Jerry Marcellino

The Motown songwriter and producer worked with the Jackson 5, particularly after Hal Davis took over as the Jackson 5's chief collaborator.

**Key Compositions**
- "Skywriter" (*Skywriter*, 1973)
- "World of Sunshine" (*Skywriter*, 1973)
- "Get It Together" (*G.I.T.: Get It Together*, 1973)
- "I Am Love (Parts 1 & 2)" (*Dancing Machine*, 1974)
- "Whatever You Got, I Want" (*Dancing Machine*, 1974)
- "What You Don't Know" (*Dancing Machine*, 1974)
- "It All Begins and Ends with Love" (*Dancing Machine*, 1974)
- "Breezy" (*Moving Violation*, 1975)

- "Call of the Wild" (*Moving Violation*, 1975)
- "Time Explosion" (*Moving Violation*, 1975)
- "Penny Arcade" (*Boogie*, 1979)
- "Love Comes in Many Different Flavors" (*Jackson 5: I Want You Back! Unreleased Masters*, 2009)

## Mel Larson

An in-house songwriter, Larson wrote numerous tracks for the Jackson 5 as well as Michael's first solo albums. He frequently collaborated with Marcellino.

### Key Compositions

- "World of Sunshine" (*Skywriter*, 1973)
- "Get It Together" (*G.I.T.: Get It Together*, 1973)
- "I Am Love (Parts 1 & 2)" (*Dancing Machine*, 1974)
- "Whatever You Got, I Want" (*Dancing Machine*, 1974)
- "What You Don't Know" (*Dancing Machine*, 1974)
- "It All Begins and Ends with Love" (*Dancing Machine*, 1974)
- "Breezy" (*Moving Violation*, 1975)
- "Call of the Wild" (*Moving Violation*, 1975)
- "Time Explosion" (*Moving Violation*, 1975)
- "The Eternal Light" (*Joyful Jukebox Music*, 1976)
- "Through Thick and Thin" (*Joyful Jukebox Music*, 1976)
- "One Day I'll Marry You" (*Joyful Jukebox Music*, 1976)
- "Penny Arcade" (*Boogie*, 1979)
- "Love Comes in Many Different Flavors" (*Jackson 5: I Want You Back! Unreleased Masters*, 2009)

## Christine Yarian

Married to Corporation member Perren, Christine Yarian wrote with the Motown production team until the group disbanded in 1973. In addition to writing for the Jackson 5, she co-wrote tracks for Michael's Motown solo albums.

### Key Compositions

- "Hallelujah Day" (*Skywriter*, 1973)
- "Love Don't Want to Leave" (originally appeared on *Jackie Jackson*, 1973; later included on Jackson 5 compilations such as *Soulsation!*)
- "You're My Best Friend, My Love" (*Joyful Jukebox Music*, 1976)
- "Make Tonight All Mine" (*Joyful Jukebox Music*, 1976)

## Donald Fletcher

A frequent collaborator of Davis, Fletcher wrote much of the Jackson 5's later, more dance-oriented material.

**Key Compositions**

- "Dancing Machine" (*G.I.T.: Get It Together*, 1973)
- "Get It Together" (*G.I.T.: Get It Together*, 1973)
- "Body Language (Do the Love Dance)" (*Moving Violation*, 1975)

## Unlikely Songwriters

Along with Jobete's stable of songwriters, some unexpected composers contributed notable songs in the Jackson 5 catalogue. Most of these artists were in the early stages of their careers, and eventually embarked on other musical genres (funk, disco) or different occupations (actor, minister).

## Clifton Davis

Mention this name, and images of 1970s and 1980s television are conjured. His one-year tenure on the 1974 sitcom *That's My Mama* first brought him attention, but his most successful role was as Reverend Rueben Gregory on the Sherman Hemsley vehicle *Amen* (1986–1991). Since then he has appeared in countless television shows, from *Party of Five* to *Living Single*. His talents extend to film, his most notable turn as Mayor Tyrone Smalls in the 1999 Oliver Stone film *Any Given Sunday*. During the 1980s, he added "minister" to his list of achievements, becoming an ordained minister in the Seventh Day Adventist Church. Today he appears onstage, most recently in Disney's Broadway production of *Aladdin*. Before his acting career took flight, however, Clifton's gifts as a singer and songwriter attracted the attention of Gordy and Motown.

In the 1971, the struggling actor and budding composer amassed a songwriting portfolio that he shopped to various publishers. When Clifton approached Jobete, his material included a particular standout: "Never Can Say Goodbye." According to Graham Betts's *Motown Encyclopedia*, Hal Davis and Jerry Marcellino happened to be in an adjoining office when the track's melody drafted through the thin walls. Intrigued, Davis entered the neighboring room and expressed his desire for the Jackson 5 to record the tune. That night, the producer met with arranger Gene Page to lay down the backing tracks; two days later, the Jackson brothers recorded their vocals. At first Motown's departmental heads believed the song was too mature for the teen group, but after Gordy heard the track, he declared it a smash.

Buoyed by the hit single, Clifton returned to Motown with another offering: "Lookin' Through the Windows," a song that would become the title track to the Jackson 5's fifth album. The single did not match the sales of "Never Can Say Goodbye," but it did crack the R&B singles Top 5 and reached #16 on the *Billboard* Hot 100. However, "Lookin' Through the Windows" experienced greater success in the UK, peaking in the Top 10. His association continued with "Uppermost," the *Skywriter* track featuring chord changes slightly reminiscent of "Never Can Say Goodbye."

After his collaboration with the Jackson 5, Clifton continued recording his own songs, venturing into gospel as well as pop and R&B. Today he may be best known for his acting, but "Never Can Say Goodbye" assures his place in music history.

## George Clinton

Known as a pioneer in funk and a major influence on hip hop, George Clinton melded funk with 1960s psychedelia to create the groups Parliament and Funkadelic. Songs such as "Give up the Funk (Tear the Roof Off the Sucker)," "Flashlight," "Free Your Mind and Your Ass Will Follow," and "Chocolate City" remain 1970s funk classics, and countless hip-hop artists have sampled their beats, guitar riffs, and bass lines. Clinton's solo hit "Atomic Dog" has also stood the test of time, with rappers like Snoop Dogg sampling its title phrase. So thinking of the multicolored-haired Clinton penning songs for the Jackson 5 may seem like a stretch, but the group recorded a few of his tracks.

For 1970's *ABC*, the Jackson 5 tackled Clinton's composition "I Bet You," a gritty funk jam that prefigures his acid-soaked Parliament/Funkadelic sound. The fuzzy guitar soars throughout as the Jackson 5's echoing background vocals, creating a surprisingly psychedelic atmosphere for what Gordy deemed a "soul bubblegum" group. While not written specifically for the group—Funkadelic recorded it that same year—the song demonstrates Clinton's ongoing association with the record label.

One of his most surprising compositions may be "Little Christmas Tree," the 1973 Michael holiday track later tacked on to reissues of the *Jackson 5 Christmas Album*. The wistful ballad seems atypical of Clinton's harder-driving, spacey work, but it demonstrates how his early tenure with Motown made him an adaptable songwriter.

## Gloria Jones

The singer/songwriter cemented her place in R&B history with the 1965 burner "Tainted Love," a song that returned to the charts in 1982 thanks to Soft Cell's synthesizer-led cover. Jones's thumping original, featuring blaring horns and her gospel-soaked vocals, differs greatly from the robotic 1980s version, but the latter stands as the bigger hit. Similar in sound, her other best-known single, "Heartbeat," tore up dance floors.

Joining Motown as a songwriter, Jones initially wrote under a pseudonym, "LaVerne Ware," to separate her still-active singing career from her behind-the-scenes position. After her Motown tenure, Jones achieved fame for another reason: her romance with T. Rex singer Marc Bolan. She joined the group as a backup singer in 1973; her subsequent relationship with Bolan produced a son. They often collaborated professionally, writing and producing songs together, but their partnership ended tragically on September 16, 1977. After dining at nearby restaurant, Jones was driving the couple back to their house when she hit a tree, instantly killing Bolan. After she recovered from the accident, she resumed her singing and songwriting career; most recently, she has served as music supervisor for several films.

Frequently collaborating with Sawyer, Jones penned numerous tracks for the Jackson 5. Her major credits include "2-4-6-8" from *ABC*; "Christmas Won't Be the Same This Year" from the *Jackson 5 Christmas Album*; "Teenage Symphony," not released until the 2009 Michael compilation *Hello World: The Motown Solo Collection*;

"It's Too Late to Change the Time" from *G.I.T.: Get It Together*, and "One Day I'll Marry You," not released until the 1979 collection *Boogie*.

## Other Composers

Countless songwriters wrote Jackson 5 album tracks, but unfortunately little is known about these gifted composers. The following is a list of honorable mentions.

- Lester Lee Carr: "How Funky Is Your Chicken" (*Third Album*, 1970)
- Joyce Chambers: "Don't Want to See Tomorrow" (*Lookin' Through the Windows*, 1972)
- Stephen Bowden: "Don't Want to See Tomorrow" (*Lookin' Through the Windows*, 1972)
- Terri McFadden: "Don't Want to See Tomorrow" (*Lookin' Through the Windows*, 1972)
- Ron Rancifer: "I Am Love (Parts 1 & 2)" (*Dancing Machine*, 1974)
- Beatrice Verdi: "Reach In" (*Third Album*, 1970)
- Don Fenceton: "I Am Love (Parts 1 & 2)" (*Dancing Machine*, 1974)
- Gene Marcellino: "Whatever You Got, I Want" (*Dancing Machine*, 1974)
- Ruth Talmage: "She's a Rhythm Child" (*Dancing Machine*, 1974)
- George Gordy: "The Young Folks" (*ABC*, 1970)
- Allan Story: "The Young Folks" (*ABC*, 1970)
- Clarence Drayton: "We're Going to Change Our Style" (*Joyful Jukebox Music*, 1976)
- Nita Garfield: "We're Here to Entertain You" (*Joyful Jukebox Music*, 1976)
- Liz Shaw: "Moving Violation" (*Moving Violation*, 1975)
- Harold Beatty: "Moving Violation" (*Moving Violation*, 1975)
- Brian Holland: "All I Do Is Think of You" (*Moving Violation*, 1975)
- Michael L. Smith: "All I Do Is Think of You" (*Moving Violation*, 1975)
- Judy Cheeks: "We're Gonna Change Our Style" (*Joyful Jukebox Music*, 1976)

## Musicians

Equally important as the songwriters were the musicians who played on the Jackson 5's recordings. They assumed crucial roles in crafting the patented Motown Sound, one which derives from the sound quality of the transistor radio. According to Friedlander, Gordy recognized that teenagers often listened to music through car and transistor radios, both of which produced subpar sound quality. Thus the label altered its mixes to make the best of these lackluster devices, which led to the Motown Sound's three essential ingredients: vocals, drums, and tight bass lines. As Friedlander describes it, "The vocals showcased the attractive singing voices, harmonies, and lyrics; the drums kept time and provided a forceful backbeat; and the bouncy bass impelled the listener to physical excitement (like dancing)." The other instruments remained in the background, providing what Friedlander calls a "cumulative musical effect."

A common misconception is that Motown's legendary house band the Funk Brothers played on Jackson 5 recordings. By the time the group joined the label, however, Motown had shifted much of its operations to Los Angeles, creating Motown West. While some Funk Brothers members moved to the West Coast, others remained in Detroit, thus effectively ending the studio band. Unfortunately, credits were not a priority on liner notes, and thus many incredible musicians remained largely unknown for their crucial roles in Motown hits. Some artists who played in the band later became famous in their own right, and they got their start through playing with the Jackson 5 and other Motown acts. The following section profiles some of those who contributed important ingredients to the label's most beloved songs.

## The Jazz Crusaders

Later known as a trailblazing jazz and R&B group, laying down the foundations for the acid jazz movement, the Jazz Crusaders' members often guested on Motown West recordings. Originally formed in 1950s Houston, Texas, as the Swingsters, the group's core members included Joe Sample (keyboards), Wilton Felder (bass and saxophone), Wayne Henderson (trombone), Hubert Laws (flute), and Nesbert "Stix" Hopper (drums). After relocating to California, they rechristened themselves the Jazz Crusaders and secured a contract with the Pacific Jazz label. By this time Laws had elected to leave, heading to New York. Now a quartet, the Jazz Crusaders recorded several albums for Pacific Jazz while maintaining separate careers as session players. Sample and Felder contributed to several Jackson 5 singles, laying down grooves that would drive the songs' energy. Examples include Sample's keyboards on "Dancing Machine" and "I'll Be There" as well as Felder's crucial bass lines on "I Want You Back" and "The Love You Save."

## Session Musicians

None of the Jackson 5's greatest songs would have become a reality without the talents of top session musicians. In California, Motown had a wealth of gifted artists to choose from, some from the famed session group the Wrecking Crew. Motown drew from a variety of other sources, including many jazz musicians who would moonlight as session players. In addition, Corporation members often played instruments in addition to their songwriting and producing duties. The following section lists significant musicians who appeared on several Jackson 5 recordings as well as on other Motown albums. Frustratingly little information exists on who appeared on specific Jackson 5 records; perhaps someday Motown will open its vaults for music researchers and fans to learn the full stories behind the Jackson 5's most significant recordings.

### Keyboards
- Mike Rubini
- Clarence McDonald
- Don Randi
- Larry Knechtel

## Guitar

- Arthur Wright: "I'll Be There"
- David T. Walker: "I'll Be There," "I Want You Back"
- Thomas Tedesco
- Louie Shelton: "I'll Be There," "I Want You Back"
- Weldon Parks (who also co-wrote "Dancing Machine")
- Don Peake: "I Want You Back"
- Wah Wah Watson (who later played on Michael Jackson's *Off the Wall* album)

## Bass

- Ron Brown
- William Salter: "Dancing Machine"
- Bob West: "I'll Be There"

## Drums

- Ed Greene
- Gene Pello: "I'll Be There," "I Want You Back"
- Paul Humphrey
- James Gadson: "Dancing Machine"

## Percussion

- Gary Coleman
- Bobbye Porter
- King Arisen
- Sandra Crouch (twin sister of gospel legend Andraé Crouch)
- Jerry Steinholtz
- Jackie Johnson: tambourine, "I'll Be There"

## Arrangers

- Gene Page: "Never Can Say Goodbye" "Sugar Daddy," "Corner of the Sky," "I Saw Mommy Kissing Santa Claus"
- Mel Larson: "Skywriter," "I Am Love (Parts 1 & 2)"
- Jerry Marcellino: "Skywriter," "I Am Love (Parts 1 & 2)"
- James Carmichael: "Santa Claus Is Coming to Town," "Never Can Say Goodbye," "Little Bitty Pretty One," "Corner of the Sky," "Doctor My Eyes," "Whatever You Got I Want," "What You Don't Know," "I Am Love (Parts 1 & 2)," "The Christmas Song"
- Arthur Wright: "Dancing Machine," "Get It Together," "The Life of the Party," "Body Language (Do the Love Dance)"
- John Bahler: "Little Bitty Pretty One," "Lookin' Through the Windows," "Doctor My Eyes," "I Am Love," "Body Language (Do the Love Dance)"
- Michael L. Smith: "Forever Came Today"

# 5

# Ain't No Words to This Song, You Just Hum and Dance Along

## Notable TV and Concert Appearances

I n *The Motown Album*, author Ben Fong-Torres explains why the Jackson 5 were tailor-made for television. During a politically turbulent era filled with challenging psychedelic soul and acid rock, he writes, "Motown could offer a wholesome family group dressed in 'fros and mod duds and singing nonthreatening pop music." Indeed, the Jackson 5's clean-cut image and songs about first love appealed to 1970s teenagers while not offending their parents. However, their TV appearances and concerts revealed that they were more than just a family-friendly, sanitized act. Their showmanship and ability to perform songs ranging from standards to hits from various genres demonstrated their versatility and staying power.

### TV Appearances

From their debut 1969 TV appearance to their Las Vegas variety shows, the Jackson 5 transitioned from soul bubblegum group to mature entertainers.

#### August 22, 1969: *Miss Black America Pageant*

For their national TV debut, the Jackson 5 performed a spirited version of "It's Your Thing." Not yet attired in their hip clothes, the identically clothed group dances while a young Michael Jackson assumes the lead vocal. The way he handles the microphone and works the stunned crowd foreshadowed the superstar he would eventually become.

#### October 14, 1969: *The Hollywood Palace Special* (ABC)

Guest hosted by Diana Ross, this variety show introduced the larger pubic to the new singing sensation. Ross announces the group as her personal discovery, and show-business legend Sammy Davis Jr. even performs James Brown's "There Was a Time" with Michael. Dressed in similar clothes to their *Miss Black America Pageant* appearance, the slightly nervous group perform covers of Sly and the Family Stone's "Sing a Simple Song" and the Delfonics' "Can You Remember." After

The Jackson 5's first TV special featured an array of 1970s comedians, singers, and athletes, including Rosey Grier, Bill Russell, Tom Smothers, Bill Cosby, Bobby Darin, and Diana Ross (in a brief cameo appearance). This "playbill" appeared on the back cover of the *Goin' Back to Indiana* soundtrack album.                                            *Author's collection*

Michael shyly states that "it's on sale everywhere," they launch into "I Want You Back," this time lip-synching to the record while executing their signature choreography.

## December 4, 1969: *The Ed Sullivan Show* (CBS)

In the most crucial appearance of their early career, the Jackson 5 landed on *The Ed Sullivan Show*. Looking very different in their funky, hip attire (Michael wearing his now famous purple fedora and vest), the polished group kick off their set with Sly and the Family Stone's "Stand!" before launching into Michael's legendary interpretation of Smokey Robinson's "Who's Loving You." At just eleven years old, the singer had already made the song his own. They close their set with "I Want You Back," using the same choreography as on the *Hollywood Palace* appearance. Sullivan then joins them onstage and points out Ross in the audience, repeating the oft-told story of her discovering the group.

## January 31, 1970: *The Andy Williams Show* (NBC)

The Jackson 5 started the New Year by continuing the variety show rounds, this time making a stop at the *Andy Williams Show*. By this time, "I Want You Back" had reached #1, and thus Williams's announcement of the group elicits screams from the audience. Once again sporting bright colors, the group sings a live rendition of the song. Tellingly, the camera focused mostly on young Michael.

## February 21, 1970: *American Bandstand* (ABC)

Dick Clark notes how the Jackson 5's new single has sold over two million copies, prompting enthusiastic applause. Singing live, they perform "I Want You Back," and are then interviewed by Clark. Clark mainly talks to Michael, who at one point takes the microphone from the host to introduce the band's organist and drummer. Charmed, Clark inquires as to how long Michael has been singing (three years), how hold he is (nine, as per Motown's instructions), and what his favorite groups are (the Beatles, Three Dog Night, and Blood Sweat & Tears).

Next they debut "ABC," which they lip-sync, before closing with a funked-out cover of "Zip-a-Dee-Doo-Dah" followed by a short version of "There Was a Time." Interestingly, Clark reintroduces the group by comparing Michael to Frankie Lymon—something that Gordy most likely encouraged. The entire group executes impressive choreography, with Michael showing off his flawless James Brown moves.

## May 5, 1970: *The Ed Sullivan Show* (CBS)

Making a triumphant return to *The Ed Sullivan Show*, the Jackson 5 repeat "I Want You Back" but add their current smash single "ABC," which they originally debuted on *American Bandstand*. They conclude the appearance with their newest song, "The Love You Save," which features some fresh choreography and allows Michael to display his latest spins and slides. Due to Jermaine Jackson's extended singing part, he receives more attention than before in this follow-up *Sullivan* appearance.

## September 17, 1970: *The Jim Nabors Show*

The Jackson 5's variety show circuit continued with a stint on *The Jim Nabors Show*. Clearly the producers considered Michael the star, as the rest of the Jacksons stand behind him on a platform while he dances in the foreground. In the next segment, they debut "I'll Be There," with Michael mostly shot alone and close up. Apparently cutting the song for length, they trim a lyric from Jermaine's solo. Nabors later joins the Jackson 5 for a rather unusual duet on the folk song "Shortnin' Bread." Interestingly, the Jackson 5 also participate in a skit featuring Nabors playing a Gomer Pyle–like busboy, with a focus on Michael. Another noteworthy number is their a-cappella rendition of the Beatles' "Let It Be," a song they would perform on *The Tonight Show* years later.

## March 29, 1971: *AM America* (NBC Los Angeles)

A local version of *The Today Show*, this program had host Stephanie Edwards briefly interview the group, again focusing mainly on Michael Jackson (who now claims to be eleven years old). They perform their newest single, "Never Can Say Goodbye."

## April 18, 1971: *Diana!* (ABC)

Diana Ross's first solo TV special, *Diana!* showcases the singer at the onset of her new solo career. As well as including guests Danny Thomas and Bill Cosby, the show also features her "discovery," the Jackson 5. Dressed in even funkier 1970s costumes, they perform "Mama's Pearl," "Walk On," "The Love You Save," and "I'll Be There." Ross joins them for a cover of "Feelin' Alright," with Michael and the host playfully shoving each other aside as they bust out their dance moves.

The show's most famous segment, however, is Michael channeling Frank Sinatra on "It Was a Very Good Year." Leaning against a lamppost, wearing a tuxedo and a fedora, with a trench coat slung over one shoulder, he croons lyrics altered to fit his age. The stage transforms into a restaurant scene, leading into a skit where he and Ross play a couple breaking up, allowing Michael to demonstrate his budding acting skills and his desire to become a well-rounded entertainer.

The Jackson 5 appeared on mentor Diana Ross's first solo special, *Diana!*, which ABC broadcast on April 18, 1971. The show's best-known segment features Michael Jackson channeling Frank Sinatra while crooning "It Was a Very Good Year."

*Author's collection*

## September 16, 1971: *Goin' Back to Indiana* (ABC)

At last the Jackson 5 earned their own TV special, featuring skits interspersed with concert footage filmed during their homecoming appearance in Gary, Indiana. Included are live renditions of "Stand!," "Feelin' Alright," "I Want to Take You Higher," "Walk On," "The Love You Save," and "Goin' Back to Indiana." Some of the music performances were filmed in a studio, including short versions of "I Want You Back" and "Maybe Tomorrow."

The special also featured skits starring Bill Cosby, Tommy Smothers, Bobby Darin (then a Motown labelmate of the Jackson 5), Diana Ross, Rosey Grier, Ben Davidson, and basketball stars Bill Russell, Elgin Baylor, and Elvin Hayes. The subsequent soundtrack album sold over 2.6 million copies, while an extra track from the special, an ebullient version of "Mama's Pearl," surfaced on the 2010 collection *Live at the Forum*.

## November 4, 1971: *The Flip Wilson Show* (NBC)

It was a coup for the Jackson 5 to appear on comic Flip Wilson's weekly show, as it was one of the top-rated variety shows of the day. The appearance begins with Wilson bantering with the group, demanding to be part of the Jackson 5. Grabbing Michael by the collar and amusingly calling him "shorty," he eventually persuades the group to "audition" him. After Wilson leaves the stage, the Jacksons perform a live rendition of "Never Can Say Goodbye" featuring some particularly intricate choreography and a new ending. Michael looks noticeably taller in this appearance, during which he and his bandmates also treat the studio audience to a greatest-hits medley of "I Want You Back," "ABC," and "The Love You Save."

## March 3, 1972: *Hellzapoppin'* (ABC)

This variety show featured some particularly strong and energetic Jackson 5 performances of "Sugar Daddy," "Got to Be There," and "Brand New Thing." The *Hellzapoppin'* appearance is noteworthy for two reasons: the debut of Michael's solo single, and younger brother Randy Jackson's first television appearance with the Jackson 5. He dances a bit, then plays percussion with the group. Their combined performance foreshadowed Randy eventually joining the group once they left Motown.

## June 5, 1972: *The Dating Game* (ABC)

In a rather unusual television appearance, Michael served as a contestant on *The Dating Game*. He awkwardly interviews three girls approximately his age and then chooses a winner. Unlike on previous TV appearances, he does not perform any songs.

## July 1, 1972: *American Bandstand* (ABC)

While this was not Michael's first visit to *American Bandstand*, it did mark his debut as a solo artist. Dressed in a flowered vest and bellbottoms, he lip-synchs to "I Wanna Be Where You Are" and "Rockin' Robin." While he could not perform complicated dance routines because of the small set, he manages to work in some James Brown footwork. He also performs the ballad "Ben" before the Jackson brothers finally join him for a rendition of "Lookin' Through the Windows."

## September 15, 1972: *The Sonny & Cher Comedy Hour* (CBS)

Michael continued embarking on his solo career, but he still performed with his brothers, including on the enormously popular *Sonny & Cher Comedy Hour*, on which they sang "Lookin' Through the Windows." As on *American Bandstand*, Michael then mimes to "Ben" alone, and also briefly banters with the show's hosts.

## October 21, 1972: *Soul Train* (syndicated)

When the group finally landed on *Soul Train*, they treated the studio dancers to a mini concert. Interestingly, the set backdrop simply reads "Jermaine"—an attempt to promote Jermaine's burgeoning solo career. They sing "I Want You Back," "Lookin' Through the Windows," and "Corner of the Sky." Jermaine also performs his hit singles "That's How Love Goes" and "Daddy's Home," with the Jacksons providing backing vocals.

## October 26, 1972: *The Flip Wilson Show* (NBC)

The Jackson 5 returned to Wilson's show, with Michael and the group participating in skits with the host. In addition the group performed a slowed-down cover of "Ain't Nothing Like the Real Thing." Jermaine continues promoting his new solo work with "That's How Love Goes" (introduced by Randy).

## November 5, 1972: *The Jackson 5 Show* (CBS)

In the group's second TV special, a noticeably taller Michael leads his brothers in a live, in-studio performance of "I Want You Back," which includes some new lyrics that allow the members to introduce themselves. Michael also lip-synchs to "Ben," while the group reconvenes to sing "Daydreamer" (complete with the group superimposed in cartoons and appearing in skits). The show concludes with a live medley of "ABC," "I'll Be There," and "The Love You Save." Randy once again appears, playing percussion on "The Love You Save." They appropriately close with "Never Can Say Goodbye." Guests include *Laugh-In* comics Jo Anne Worley and Johnny Brown.

## November 9, 1972: *Top of the Pops* (BBC 1, UK)

The group finally crossed the pond to appear on the first of two UK shows, starting with high-energy performances of "Lookin' Through the Windows" and "Rockin' Robin" on *Top of the Pops*. Both were performed live, with Tito adding a guitar solo to the latter track.

## November 10, 1972: *Royal Variety Show* (ITV, UK)

Participating in the annual *Royal Variety Show*, the Jackson 5 performed "I Want You Back," "ABC," and "Rockin' Robin." A highlight is an a cappella rendition of "Thank You," which transitions into "The Love You Save." Michael increasing command of the stage is obvious as he works both sides of the stage and shows off increasingly intricate footwork. Randy plays bongos, but is not introduced.

## March 27, 1973: *The Academy Awards* (NBC)

Michael's recording of "Ben" was nominated for Best Song, thus he performed the track during the 1973 telecast. Charlton Heston introduced him, with the young singer lip-synching (with apparently few nerves) to the original recording.

## September 26, 1973: *Bob Hope Special* (NBC)

As they moved into the Hal Davis era, the Jackson 5 debuted their more dance-oriented sound on this *Bob Hope Special* appearance. Randy provides backing percussion on "Get It Together," while the teenaged Michael demonstrates his mastery of the "robot" dance move during "Dancing Machine," although the camera curiously cuts away during his signature step. (In his autobiography, Michael claims he debuted the robot move during his November 1973 *Soul Train* appearance, but he actually premiered the step here, on Hope's show.)

## November 3, 1973: *Soul Train* (syndicated)

The Jackson 5 returned to *Soul Train* as teenagers, with Michael making a huge impression on the in-studio dancers with his "robot" routine during "Dancing Machine." As he struts up and down the small platform, the crowd can be heard cheering. Other songs include "Don't Say Goodbye Again," and "Get It Together." Michael then takes a solo turn by miming to "With a Child's Heart," while Jermaine sings lead on "You're in Good Hands." In an amusing segment, the dancers ask the group questions, including whether the Jackson 5 had ever met the Osmonds, and whether they would ever record together, because they were "so similar."

## January 10, 1974: *One More Time* (ABC)

In their third television special, the Jackson 5 perform a mixture of new tunes and classic hits. Sporting a slightly deeper voice, Michael leads the group in a medley of past hits: "I Want You Back," "ABC," "I'll Be There," "Ben," "Daddy's Home," "Never Can Say Goodbye," and "The Love You Save." Special guests include the Mills Brothers, a classic jazz and pop vocal group who engage in a duet with the Jackson 5 on "Up a Lazy River" and "Opus One." The result is an interesting "old and new" contrast, and an acknowledgment of the young group's musical roots.

## January 30, 1974: *The Sonny & Cher Comedy Hour* (NBC)

The group returned to *The Sonny & Cher Comedy Hour* to perform "Dancing Machine," this time prominently featuring Randy on bongos. They sing to the original recording, with Michael adding some vocal variations.

## February 19, 1974: *American Music Awards* (ABC)

Clark's music awards ceremony debuted in 1974, and two teen idols cohosted the show: Michael Jackson and Donny Osmond. On Osmond's YouTube channel, he offers the following caption alongside the vintage video clip: "The inaugural American Music Awards. Terrible lines that were written for Michael and me. We did our best to deliver them." In an odd twist, 1970s child actors Rodney Allen Rippy and Ricky Segall are brought on as "mini" versions of the two teen stars.

## March 2, 1974: *16th Annual Grammy Awards* (CBS)

The Jackson 5 presented the award for Best Rhythm and Blues Group in a surprising way: in addition to announcing the nominees, they sing snippets of each song. In an interesting coincidence, the winner was Gladys Knight and the Pips, a group partially responsible for discovering the Jackson 5.

## March 11, 1974: *Free to Be . . . You and Me* (ABC)

Marlo Thomas's children's show introduced themes atypical of earlier children's shows, namely psychological issues and feminism. Packed with stars, this 1974 program impacted a generation of kids. Michael appeared on the show with Roberta Flack, the two duetting on "When We Grow Up." Here Michael demonstrates early acting talent, showing glimpses of the humor and dancing that would resurface during *The Wiz*.

## March 16, 1974: *The Carol Burnett Show* (CBS)

Here the Jackson 5 participate in skits and perform their latest hits. In one famous bit, Burnett plays a prim and proper music teacher who leads her class through "This Old Man," with each Jackson 5 member singing a verse. The band then perform "ABC," "teaching" Burnett the lyrics. Randy continues in his increasing role, with Burnett introducing him as the "newest member of the group." Next, the group sings a medley of the Mills Brothers, Andrews Sisters, the Coasters, and the Supremes (featuring Michael's amusing imitation of Diana Ross's signature poses). Another segment features the group singing "Life of the Party." They conclude with a live rendition of "Dancing Machine."

Janet Jackson made her television debut on this show, duetting with Randy on "The Beat Goes On." Overall, the Jacksons seemed to be auditioning for their own variety show, demonstrating their versatility.

## April 1974: *The Mike Douglas Show* (syndicated)

Talk show host Mike Douglas welcomed the Jackson 5 to his program by curiously describing them as "fast, and good, and just too much." They perform "It's Too Late to Change the Time" and "Dancing Machine." Along with guest Dom Deluise, Douglas interviews the group, asking Randy why the group has not been called the "Jackson Six" since he joined. Randy responds that they should just rename themselves the "Jackson 5½." He then explains that he learned how to play the bongos by hitting oatmeal boxes, to which Deluise jokes that the Jackson brothers told him to "beat it."

## April 4, 1974: *The Tonight Show* (NBC)

Guest host Bill Cosby introduces the group, who perform live renditions of "Dancing Machine," "Never Can Say Goodbye," and a cover of "Let It Be." Cosby then interviews them, mainly focusing on Randy (with other guest Jack Klugman sitting on the very end of the couch). Next they treat the audience to a medley of

"Let It Be" and "Never Can Say Goodbye," the former sung a cappella. In addition, they sing a new medley featuring two popular songs of the day, "Killing Me Softly" and "By the Time I Get to Phoenix," and, strangely, "Danny Boy."

## April 9, 1974: *The Merv Griffin Show* (NBC)

The group continued to tread the talk show circuit with a visit to Merv Griffin's popular 1970s program, performing versions of "It's Too Late to Change the Time" and "Dancing Machine."

## April 10, 1974: *Sandy in Disneyland* (CBS)

Actress, singer, and dancer Sandy Duncan hosts this special, taped at Disneyland. Typical of a 1970s variety show, the program boasts a curious variety of guests, including Ernest Borgnine, Ted Knight, Loggins & Messina, Marty Ingels, and Ruth Buzzi. Dressed in pirate and sailor attire, the Jackson 5 sing a medley of "I Want You Back" and "ABC."

## September 1974: *Jerry Lewis MDA Telethon*

Lewis's annual telethon this year featured the Jackson 5, who perform a live rendition of "Dancing Machine."

## September 22, 1974: *The Sonny Comedy Revue* (ABC)

On the premiere episode of his short-lived variety show, Sonny Bono welcomes the Jackson 5, who play "Life of the Party."

## October 19, 1974: *Soul Train* (syndicated)

Michael appears alone to lip-synch to "If I Don't Love You This Way" and "What You Don't Know."

## November 19, 1974: *The Tonight Show* (NBC)

The Jackson 5 return to promote *Dancing Machine*, and this time Johnny Carson is back as host. The group perform "It's Too Late to Change the Time" and then speak briefly with Carson. There is an atypically long pause as they set up for their next number, "Dancing Machine."

## January 25, 1975: *The Carol Burnett Show* (CBS)

After engaging in brief repartee with the host, the group launch into "Forever Came Today." Later in the show, they perform "Body Language," with Vicki Lawrence dancing alongside them.

## February 18, 1975: *American Music Awards* (ABC)

Michael and Janet appear briefly to present the "Favorite Soul Group" award to Gladys Knight and the Pips.

## March 16, 1975: *Cher* (CBS)

Now hosting her own show, Cher performs a long medley with the Jackson 5, dancing along with Michael as they sing "I Want You Back," "I'll Be There," "Never Can Say Goodbye," "The Love You Save," and "Dancing Machine." They also appear together in a gospel song parody and perform "I Am Love," which is introduced by Cher and Janet.

## June 16, 1975: *Dinah!* (ABC)

Dinah Shore welcomes the Jackson 5 to her talk show, on which they sing "Moving Violation" and "Forever Came Today." She then sings a medley of "You Are My Sunshine" and "You Are the Sunshine of My Life" with Michael, and briefly interviews him separately from the group. He also performs "One Day in Your Life" and a particularly jubilant version of "We're Almost There." While Shore and Michael's voices do not blend well, they seem to charm each other during their short conversation.

## June 28, 1975: *American Bandstand* (ABC)

The group's final appearance on *American Bandstand* as the Jackson 5 was a mixture of group and solo performance. As usual, the Jackson 5 lip-synch to "Dancing Machine" and "Moving Violation," with Randy backing them on bongos. Next, Michael takes his solo turn with his rendition of "Just a Little Bit of You." Dick Clark conducts brief interviews after each song.

## January 24, 1976: *Soul Train* (syndicated)

For their final *Soul Train* appearance as the Jackson 5, the band perform several group and solo cuts. In an interview with host Don Cornelius, Michael talks about his future plans, which include acting and "recording other artists." He then croons "One Day in Your Life" and "We've Got Forever" before displaying impressive spins while singing "Just a Little Bit of You." As a group, the Jackson brothers lip-synch to "Forever Came Today" and "All I Do Is Think of You." As an interesting addition, Cornelius plays a clip of their first *Ed Sullivan* appearance. Noticeably absent is Jermaine, who had left the group to remain at Motown.

## June 21, 1976: *The Tonight Show* (NBC)

In their final days as the Jackson 5, the group returned to *The Tonight Show*, featuring guest host Freddie Prinze. During the interview they promote their upcoming TV variety series, introduce the Jackson sisters (who are sitting in the audience), and cheerfully banter with comic Prinze. Before the interview, the brothers sing a medley of "Without a Song," "You've Got a Friend," "Behind Closed Doors," "You've Made Me So Very Happy," "You Are the Sunshine of My Life," and "You and Me Against the World," while Michael takes a solo turn on the song "Happy."

## Addendum: The *Jackson 5ive* Cartoon Series

While the band did not personally appear in the Saturday morning cartoon series, their images (characters loosely based on their personalities, voiced by actors) and original music permeated the show. In *Moonwalk*, Michael Jackson recalls how the series inspired his love for the movies and animation in general. He wrote that he loved being a cartoon, that he and his brothers loved watching themselves on television.

Wanting to capitalize on the Jackson 5's massive popularity, Motown enlisted Rankin/Bass Productions, founded by Arthur Rankin Jr. and Jules Bass. Now best known for stop-motion holiday specials such as *Rudolph the Red-Nosed Reindeer* and *Santa Claus Is Coming to Town*, the company also produced traditional animation. *The Jackson 5ive* aired on ABC for two seasons from September 11, 1971, to October 14, 1972. The series returned in syndication in 1984–85, at the height of the *Thriller* era.

## Concerts

Despite their young ages, the Jackson 5 maintained a punishing tour schedule from 1970 until early 1976. They played to national and international audiences, featured interesting opening acts (most notably an emerging band called the Commodores), and drew record crowds at some dates. Memorable gigs include their stint in Las Vegas and their 1974 tour of Africa, an event Michael would note as a significant moment in his life and career. Their set lists evolved over time, eventually encompassing more than just their greatest hits. As with their television appearances, they demonstrated their adaptability, performing everything from current hits to 1930s standards.

### 1970: *Jackson 5 First National Tour*

The group's 1970 tour included a date at the Forum in Los Angeles that represented the pinnacle of Jackson 5 mania, as detailed below.

- May 2: Spectrum, Philadelphia
- June 19: Cow Palace, San Francisco: With opening acts Tina Turner and Rare Earth.
- June 20: Forum, Los Angeles: This date represented the pinnacle of Jackson 5 mania. Playing to a record crowd of over 18,000 people, the group treated the audience to a mix of current hits and classic covers. Unfortunately, the group experienced technical problems at the start of the show, which took some time to be resolved. The band started with their traditional concert opener, Sly and the Family Stone's "Stand!," but then Jermaine's amp stopped working. As the anxious crowd waiting, the crew scrambled to fix the sound. While the concert finally resumed, Jermaine's bass remained buried in the mix. The 2010 collection *Live at the Forum* omits the troubled performance of "Stand!" but does include Michael's frustrated cry of "What's wrong with his amp?" at the end of "I Want You Back."

*Goin' Back to Indiana*, the Jackson 5's first TV special, aired on ABC on September 16, 1971. Its soundtrack cracked the *Billboard* Top 20 and peaked at #5 on the R&B Albums chart. *Author's collection*

Despite the technical issues, the Jackson 5 turned in an energetic performance, with the screaming audience seemingly urging on Michael. Highlights include a funky rendition of Traffic's "Feelin' Alright" and Michael's fiery lead vocal on "I Don't Know Why I Love You." His note-perfect performance of "Who's Loving You" reveals Michael's ability as a vocalist at just eleven years old, as he rivals seasoned singers with his phrasing and emotion. Proving the group needed little enhancement in the studio, they deliver faithful renditions of "ABC" and "I Want You Back."

Already a master of stage patter, Michael cheerfully leads the audience in mass sing-alongs and even teases their backing band, accusing them of thinking they are cooler than the Jackson 5. Announcing the Jackson 5 will do "their own thing," they launch into a shuffling cover of "It's Your Thing," with Michael channeling James Brown with interjections such as "hit me, man!"

At one point a breathless Michael acknowledges the presence in the audience of Ross, "the lady who made us all good." They even work her name into their ending medley, segueing from "Thank You (Falettinme Be Mice Elf Agin)" to their traditional closer, "We Want to Thank You." Michael can be heard softly giggling as they sing their thanks to Motown's best-selling female singer.

- October 9: Boston Gardens, Boston
- October 10: Cincinnati Gardens, Cincinnati
- October 11: Mid-South Coliseum, Memphis

- October 16: Madison Square Garden, New York
- October 17: Olympia Stadium, Detroit
- October 18: International Amphitheatre, Chicago
- November 28: Rochester, War Memorial Auditorium, Rochester
- December 27: Charlotte Coliseum, Charlotte
- December 28: Greensboro Coliseum Complex, Greensboro: On this date, the group played to a record crowd of 12,275.
- December 29: Nashville Municipal Auditorium, Nashville
- December 30: Jacksonville Veterans Memorial Coliseum, Jacksonville

**Set List**

The Jackson 5 performed the following songs on their 1970 tour:

- "Stand!"
- "I Want You Back"
- "ABC"
- "Feelin' Alright" (cover of the Three Dog Night version)
- "Who's Lovin' You"
- "I'll Be There"
- "Mama's Pearl"
- "Zip-a-Dee-Doo-Dah"
- "Yesterday"
- "Can You Remember?"
- "There Was a Time"
- "It's Your Thing"
- "I Found That Girl"
- "Thank You (Falettinme Be Mice Elf Agin)"
- "Walk On" (an instrumental rendition of Isaac Hayes's "Walk On By")
- "The Love You Save"

## 1971: *The Jackson 5 Second National Tour*

On the Jackson 5's second tour, they featured a permanent opening act: the Commodores, Motown labelmates and newcomers to the music scene.

- January 2: Miami Beach Auditorium, Miami Beach
- January 3: Mobile Civic Center, Mobile
- January 29: University of Dayton Arena, Dayton
- January 30: Veterans Memorial Auditorium, Columbus
- January 31: West Side Leadership Academy, Gary
- March 27: Hirsch Memorial Coliseum, Shreveport
- March 28: Municipal Auditorium, New Orleans
- April 1: Mid-South Coliseum, Memphis
- April 2: Curtis Hixon Hall, Tampa
- April 4: Mississippi Coliseum, Jackson
- May 28: Spectrum, Philadelphia
- May 29: Indiana State Fairgrounds Coliseum, Indianapolis
- May 30: Myriad Convention Center, Oklahoma City
- July 16: Madison Square Garden, New York: The *New Musical Express* reviewed this concert in its issue dated August 14, 1971, titled "In New York It's Jackson Power," focusing on how policemen formed a line in front of the stage during the entire performance. Screaming fans enjoyed the show, with the article noting that the Jackson brothers "certainly earn their money, powering into

every number enough energy to get a space craft off a launching pad!" The unknown writer singled out Jermaine's rendition of "Bridge over Troubled Water" but proclaimed Michael's status as the "real powerhouse of the act" that "takes lead vocals and leaves onlookers breathless."

- July 17: Charleston Civic Center, Charleston
- July 18: Hampton Coliseum, Hampton
- July 20: Charlotte Coliseum, Charlotte
- July 21: Toledo Sports Arena, Toledo
- July 23: International Amphitheater, Chicago
- July 24: Cincinnati Gardens, Cincinnati
- July 25: Detroit Olympia, Detroit
- July 27: Flint Fairgrounds Coliseum, Flint
- July 28: Allen County War Memorial Coliseum, Fort Wayne
- July 30: Pittsburgh Civic Arena, Pittsburgh
- July 31: Baltimore Civic Center, Baltimore
- August 1: Dorton Arena, Raleigh
- August 2: Macon Coliseum, Macon
- August 7: Carolina Coliseum, Columbia
- August 10: Curtis Hixon Hall, Tampa
- August 11: Boutwell Memorial Auditorium Birmingham
- August 13: Kansas City, Municipal Auditorium, Kansas City
- August 14: Kiel Auditorium, St. Louis
- August 15: Mid-South Coliseum, Memphis
- August 17: Montgomery, Garrett Coliseum, Montgomery
- August 18: Assembly Center, Tulsa
- August 20: Denver Coliseum, Denver
- August 22: Hollywood Bowl, Los Angeles
- August 28: Ohio State Fair, Columbus
- August 29: Iowa State Fair, Des Moines
- August 31: Canadian National Exhibition, Toronto
- September 9: Michigan State Fair, Detroit
- September 12: Honolulu International Center Arena, Honolulu
- October 15: International Amphitheatre, Chicago
- December 27: Houston Coliseum, Houston
- December 28: Memorial Auditorium, Dallas
- December 29: Hampton Coliseum, Norfolk
- December 30: Richmond Coliseum, Richmond

## 1972: The Jackson 5 US Tour and European Tour

For the first time, the group toured internationally.

- January 1: Municipal Auditorium, Nashville
- January 2: Greenville Memorial Auditorium, Greenville
- January 18: City Auditorium, Atlanta: Headlining the first annual Martin Luther King Birthday Commemoration concert

- February 12: Kiel Auditorium, St. Louis
- March 26: Hirsch Memorial Coliseum, Shreveport
- March 27: Municipal Auditorium, New Orleans
- March 29: Curtis Hixon Hall, Tampa
- March 31: State Fair Coliseum, Jackson
- April 1: Mid-South Coliseum, Memphis
- June 30: Madison Square Garden, New York
- July 1: Civic Center, Baltimore
- July 2: Coliseum, Norfolk
- July 7: Richmond Coliseum, Richmond
- July 8: Charlotte Coliseum, Charlotte
- July 9: Coliseum, Greensboro
- July 14: Cincinnati Gardens, Cincinnati
- July 15: Civic Center Arena, Pittsburgh
- July 16: Public Auditorium, Cleveland
- July 18: International Amphitheatre, Chicago
- July 21: Civic Center, Tulsa
- July 22: Memorial Auditorium, Dallas
- July 23: Houston Coliseum, Houston
- July 24: Municipal Auditorium, New Orleans
- July 29: International Amphitheatre, Chicago
- July 30: International Amphitheatre, Chicago
- August 4: Carolina Coliseum Arena, Columbia
- August 5: Municipal Auditorium, Atlanta
- August 6: Municipal Auditorium, Nashville
- August 11: Civic Center, Savannah
- August 12: Constitution Hall, Washington
- August 13: Civic Center, Charleston
- August 17: Kentucky State Fair, Louisville
- August 18: Municipal Auditorium, Kansas City
- August 19: Kiel Auditorium, St. Louis
- August 20: Indiana State Fair, Indianapolis
- August 22: Missouri State Fair, Sedalia
- August 25: Cow Palace, San Francisco
- August 26: Forum, Los Angeles: Just two days before Michael's fourteenth birthday, the Jackson 5 returned to the Forum for a very different performance than their 1970 visit. Now comparative veterans with several hits under their belts, they tore through a medley of their biggest singles. Another significant addition was Michael's solo set, demonstrating how Motown intended to transform him into a teen idol in his own right. Signs of Michael's changing voice abounded, such as his slightly deeper vocals on "Sugar Daddy."
- August 27: Sports Arena, San Diego
- August 29: Honolulu International Center Arena, Honolulu
- September 27–October 1: Save the Children Concert, International Amphitheatre, Chicago: a benefit concert held in conjunction with the Reverend Jesse Jackson's Operation PUSH Black Expo.

- October 5: International Amphitheatre, Chicago
- November 2: Concertgebouw, Amsterdam, Netherlands
- November 4: Circus Krone, Munich, Germany
- November 5: Stadhalle Offenbach, Frankfurt, Germany
- November 6: Olympia, Paris, France
- November 9: Odeon, Birmingham, England
- November 10: Bellevue, Manchester, England
- November 11: Empire, Liverpool, England: According to Adrian Grant, this show broke previous Liverpool attendance records, including Beatles concerts.
- November 12: Empire Pool (now Wembley Arena), London, England: Noted British music journalist David Nathan covered this date for *Blues & Soul*'s December 1972 issue, expressing amazement at how a "black act" could create Beatlemania-type hysteria among multiracial teenagers. After a number of opening acts, including Junior Walker and his All-Stars, the Jackson 5 took the stage to deafening screams. Nathan praised Jermaine's vocals on "I Think I've Found That Girl" and Randy's conga-playing ability. His assessment of Michael's talents today seem relatively modest: "He certainly has a fine professional stance," he stated, and pondered how the Jackson 5 would develop over time. Amusingly, Nathan concluded by stating that while the group may have talent, "I wouldn't myself rush out and see their act again—if only because of the danger to life, limb, and eardrums!"

## Jackson 5 World Tour, 1973–75

The group's first world tour took place over a three-year period, during which they played over 160 shows.

# 1973

The Jackson 5's 1973 live shows took in dates in Japan and Australasia, as well as several tours of the US.

- March 2: Coliseum, Oklahoma City
- March 3: Coliseum, Monroe
- March 4: Houston Astrodome, Houston
- April 27: Tokyo Imperial Theatre, Tokyo, Japan
- April 28: Yubin Chokin Hall, Hiroshima, Japan
- April 20: Koseinankin Hall, Osaka, Japan
- May 1: Festival Hall, Osaka, Japan
- May 2: Budokan, Tokyo, Japan
- May 5: Coliseum Complex, Portland
- May 6: Seattle Center Coliseum, Seattle
- May 18: Spectrum, Philadelphia
- May 19: Dayton Hara Arena, Dayton
- May 20: St. John Arena, Columbus
- June 23: Brisbane Festival Hall, Brisbane, Australia
- June 26: Festival Hall, Melbourne, Australia

- June 29: Beatie Park, Perth, Australia
- July 1: Apollo Stadium, Adelaide, Australia
- July 2: Hordern Pavilion, Sydney, Australia
- July 4: Town Hall, Christchurch, New Zealand
- July 5: Athletic Park, Wellington, New Zealand
- July 13: Boston Gardens, Boston
- July 14: Veterans Memorial Coliseum, New Haven
- July 15: Civic Center, Providence
- July 17: Hiram Bithrom Stadium, San Juan
- July 20: Civic Arena, Pittsburgh
- July 21: Pocono State Fair, Long Pond
- July 22: Madison Square Garden, New York
- July 24–25: International Amphitheatre, Chicago
- July 28: Olympia Stadium, Detroit
- July 29: Saratoga Perfect Arts, Saratoga
- August 3: Richmond Coliseum, Richmond
- August 4: Hampton Roads Coliseum, Hampton
- August 5: Civic Center, Baltimore
- August 7: Greensboro Coliseum, Greensboro
- August 8: Municipal Auditorium, Nashville
- August 10: Carolina Coliseum, Columbia
- August 11: The Omni, Atlanta
- August 12: Convention Center, Miami
- August 17: Mid-South Coliseum, Memphis
- August 18: Kiel Auditorium, St. Louis
- August 19: State Fair, Indianapolis
- August 21: Municipal Auditorium, New Orleans
- August 22: Memorial Auditorium, Dallas
- August 24: Cow Palace, San Francisco
- August 25: Convention Center, Fresno
- August 26: Forum, Los Angeles
- August 28: Suffolk Downs, Boston
- August 29: Man & His World Exhibition, Montreal
- August 31: State Fair, Columbus
- September 2: Honolulu International Center Arena, Honolulu

## 1974

At the beginning of the year, the Jackson 5 performed a series of concerts in Dakar, Senegal. They were the brainchild of Johnny Secka, a Senegalese entrepreneur who had relocated to the United States. Wanting to attract American soul acts to play in Senegal, he approached Joe Jackson with the idea during the 1973 Academy Awards ceremony, according to the J5 Collector Blog. After Michael Jackson performed "Ben," Secka met the Jackson patriarch and expressed his interest in bringing the group to Africa.

A deal was struck, and the Jackson brothers were greeted in high style when they landed in Dakar. A troupe of African dancers in traditional garb welcomed the group, and Michael Jackson recalled the experience as a highlight of his early career. He said it made him proud of his African heritage, and that the African people had given Michael and his brothers qualities that made them stronger; for that, he said, he was forever grateful.

Secka also commissioned a documentary. Titled *The Jackson 5 in Africa*, the hour-long film narrates the group's visit and provides a history of Dakar and West Africa. Premiering at the United Nations in November 1974, it played in select markets. While not a huge success, the movie offers a peek at the Jackson 5's stage show as they perform "Hum Along and Dance," "Feelin' Alright," and "You Need Love Like I Do (Don't You)."

- February 1–3: Senegal Demba Diop Stadium, Dakar (three shows)
- February 22: Houston Astrodome, Houston

## Las Vegas Concerts

Toward the end of the Jackson 5's Motown tenure, Joseph Jackson booked the group to play a series of dates at the MGM Grand Hotel in Las Vegas. Wanting to build a family entertainment dynasty modeled after the Osmonds, he decided to increase the act from five to nine. Randy had already joined the group as a percussionist, and the father added Janet (who had previously appeared on variety shows with her brothers), La Toya, and Rebbie.

As Michael recalls in *Moonwalk*, the family figured their eclectic mix of old hits and covers would appeal to Vegas tourists. He explained that the shows involved skits, and new songs kept tourist crowds engaged. Audiences delighted in the music and skits, including Janet's now famous Mae West impersonation. Having nine children participate in the show was, as he later recalled, Joe Jackson's dream come true.

In *Moonwalk*, Michael looks back with fondness on the Las Vegas shows. Rather than simply playing the hits, he states, they could demonstrate their range. At this point, his voice was changing, so they would include ballads to break in his new vocal style. This freedom ultimately ended their Motown tenure—after enjoying complete creative control over their stage shows, they found it difficult to return to Motown's Los Angeles studios and record what Gordy, his producers, and his songwriters dictated.

- April 9–24 (fifteen shows)
- August 21–September 3 (fourteen shows)
- November 20–December 3 (fifteen shows)

### Set List

The following list represents a typical Las Vegas set by the Jackson 5:

- "Skywriter"
- "Killing Me Softly"
- "Ben"
- "Papa Was a Rollin' Stone"

- "Danny Boy"
- "By The Time I Get to Phoenix"
- "Bei Min Bist Da Schön" (Andrews Sisters salute)
- "The Love You Save"
- "I'll Be There"
- "ABC"
- "I Want You Back"
- "Love Is Strange" (duet with Janet and Randy Jackson)
- "When I'm Calling You"
- "I Got You Babe" (Janet and Randy Jackson)
- "The Beat Goes On"
- "Dancing Machine"

## Other 1974 Dates

Alongside their Vegas engagements, the Jackson 5 played the following shows in the US and abroad in 1974.

- April 26–28: Sahara Tahoe Hotel, Lake Tahoe (three shows)
- May 13: RFK Stadium, Washington, D.C.
- June 22: Forum, Los Angeles
- June 24–30: Mill Run Theater, Chicago (seven shows)
- July 8–14: Circle Star Theater, San Carlos (seven shows)
- July 16: New Jersey State Fair, Trenton
- July 21: Coliseum, Richmond
- July 26: Memorial Auditorium, Buffalo
- July 27: Madison Square Garden, New York
- July 29–August 4: Front Row Theater, Cleveland (seven shows)
- August 6: Von Braun Civic Center, Huntsville
- August 7: Auditorium, New Orleans
- August 10: Kiel Auditorium, St. Louis
- August 11: Municipal Auditorium, Kansas City
- August 16: Civic Center, St. Paul
- August 17: World Expo, Spokane
- September 5–October 1: South American Tour (Panama, Venezuela, Brazil)
- October 4–6: Sahara Tahoe Hotel, Lake Tahoe (three shows)
- October 7–November 1: Far East Tour (Japan, Hong Kong, Australia, New Zealand, Philippines)
- November 3: Coliseum, Oakland

## 1975

The Jackson 5 played the following US and international dates in 1975; exact details for the shows in the West Indies and Mexico are not available.

- January: the West Indies
- February 7: Radio City Music Hall, New York
- March 8: National Stadium, Kingston, Jamaica: Opening for Bob Marley and the Wailers.
- June 11: Chicago Stadium, Chicago
- July 6: NYCB Theatre, Westbury Music Fair, Westbury

- September 1: Memorial Stadium, Mount Vernon
- December: Mexico

## 1976: *The Final Jackson 5 Tour*

The group undertook their final tour as the Jackson 5 this year, by which time they had departed Motown and would shortly thereafter change their moniker to the Jacksons. Jermaine would also depart the group to remain with Motown. All concerts during their finale occurred in the Philippines.

- February 13–15: Folk Art Theater, Manila, Philippines
- February 17–19: Amanita Coliseum

# 6

# Whenever You Need Me, I'll Be There

## The Unique Singing Chemistry of Michael and Jermaine Jackson

While Michael Jackson sang lead on most Jackson 5 singles, Jermaine Jackson often provided crucial harmonies and solos along with his brother. On tracks such as "ABC" and "I Want You Back," a particular highlight was Michael and Jermaine trading lines toward the end of the songs. Interestingly, the Corporation suggested this part for practical reasons as well as aesthetic ones. In *Moonwalk*, Michael recalls the move as a salute to early Jackson 5 influence Sly and the Family Stone. On tracks such as "Dance to the Music," "Family Affair," and "Everyday People," several different voices would appear on the track. Emulating the technique of having different band members take a turn in the solo spotlight, the Jackson 5 added Jermaine's section on "The Love You Save."

In addition, the Corporation did so with the Jacksons' stage show in mind. Since their concerts included complicated dance routines, Michael writes, they could not always sing complicated lines alone. Calling the verses "tongue-twisting," he says the Corporation split up the lines between Michael and Jermaine so they could share the burden. Interestingly, he adds that the Corporation also penned songs that would encourage fan participation, so that teens could easily trade lines while singing and dancing at parties.

However, Michael and Jermaine's call-and-response routine elicited more than screams, sing-alongs, and dancing. Their voices complemented each other, even though they opposed each other in some ways. Jermaine's voice was deeper, more mature, and more restrained. He represented the older, smoother figure, his vocals evoking images of the sensitive, worldly boyfriend in older teenage girls' imaginations. By contrast, Michael epitomized youth and unbridled energy; while his higher range underscored his young age, his phrasing and emotional delivery rivaled any seasoned pro. Together, their voices exemplified the Jackson 5's boundless enthusiasm and illustrated a constant theme of their songs: the excitement of first love.

Songwriters and producers clearly enjoyed the interplay between the two brothers, and would write parts specifically for such interaction. What follows is a selection of such songs, along with discussions of how Michael and Jermaine's vocal blend was a vital contributor to the Jackson 5 sound.

## "I Want You Back" (1969)

While Jackie Jackson also has a brief solo on the Jackson 5's first hit, it is Michael and Jermaine's back-and-forth section that stands out. As the track marches toward its conclusion, Michael's voice increases in urgency. Jermaine croons lines begging for the girlfriend to give him another chance, leading to Jermaine and Michael's cries of "baby!" Their singing styles contrast, with Michael's uninhibited, almost shouting delivery mixing well with Jermaine's passionate yet more retrained vocals. Jackie's falsetto nicely asks the unnamed girl to forget about the past, but Jermaine's cry of "let me live again!" negates the politeness and adds a note of desperation. One more interaction occurs with Jackie, Jermaine, and Michael, with Jermaine's voice gradually meeting Michael's enthusiasm when he cries out "give me back what I lost!" As the song fades out, an emotional Michael punctuates Jermaine Jackson's cries of "baby!" with James Brown–like "oh's!" Their interaction intensifies the desperation of young love, leading to the song's explosive climax. It represents a release of emotion, moving from sadness to desperation, and would mark the first in a series of tracks spotlighting the Jackson brothers' chemistry.

## "ABC" (1970)

This 1970 single could almost be considered a Michael and Jermaine duet, as the two exchange numerous parts. Jackie makes a brief cameo, but once again the duo of Jermaine and Michael creates the biggest impression. As on "I Want You Back," their vocal interaction increases the energy in terms of tempo and feeling. Using the school metaphor, the lyrics reflect the Jackson 5's youth, yet the urgency in Michael and Jermaine's voices suggest something deeper.

The song begins with Michael addressing his crush, saying that she entered school to learn. Jermaine chimes in with "Like *I* before *E* except after *C*" before Michael makes clear that he has something even more valuable to teach: love. While his delivery exudes innocence, Jermaine's sounds more commanding when he instructs the girl to sit down and repeat the lesson.

After the chorus, Jermaine's slightly raspy voice instructs the girl that "I'm gonna teach you how to sing it out," followed by Michael's enthusiastic reply: "Come on let me show you what it's all about!" This exchange contains just a hint of sensuality, particularly in Jermaine's voice. It remains in the age-appropriate category, yet it appealed to their young fans' growing curiosity about adult love.

As "ABC" continues, the brothers trade verses indicating that lessons in love were just as important as "reading, writing, and arithmetic." When Jermaine urges, "Listen to me baby, that's all you got to do," Michael responds with the chorus. Again, the contrasting voices indicate the innocent and mature sides of love, with Jermaine's grittier voice contrasting with Michael's higher, purer one. As the song fades out, however, Michael's voice rises in volume and intensity, symbolizing the unabashed excitement of young love.

The 1970 single "The Love You Save" contains one of Michael and Jermaine Jackson's most energetic back-and-forth exchanges.    *Author's collection*

## "The Love You Save" (1970)

Featuring a slightly faster tempo than "ABC," "The Love You Save" admonishes a young woman for ruining her reputation. Michael and Jermaine take turns lecturing the girl, with Michael professing his love as Jermaine warns her about succumbing to other boys' charms. "They'll label you a flirt!" Michael cries out, as Jermaine chimes in with a more dire prediction: "They'll turn your name to dirt."

After the bridge, the duo engages in one of the best back-and-forth exchanges in the Jackson 5 catalogue. Jermaine reiterates the chorus as Michael warns, "Someday you may be all alone." As they alternate between shouting "stop it!" and "save it!" Jermaine repeats that, if she doesn't, she'll be "headed for the danger zone." The back-and-forth continues as the song fades out, the singers repeating key phrases from the song to persuade the unnamed girl. The Corporation obviously wrote the lyrics with live performance in mind, correctly predicting that the brothers' duet would enhance "ABC's" already abundant energy. Their contrasting voices accomplish exactly that.

## "I'll Be There" (1970)

The track that solidified the Jackson 5's genuine talent and Michael's singing prowess, "I'll Be There" also ranks as one of pop's best ballads. While Jermaine and Michael Jackson do not sing a duet, as in "ABC," their brief interaction greatly amplifies the track's emotional impact. During the bridge, Jermaine solos, proclaiming his undying love for his intended: that he will "build my world of dreams around you" and will be her strength and will never let go. When Michael responds with "Let me fill your heart with joy and laughter," it compliments Jermaine's plea for a mature, committed relationship.

Interestingly, the lines contrast in subject matter as well as tone. Jermaine's verses seemed grounded in reality, acknowledging life's hardships, while Michael's sound more wistful and idealistic. Also serving a supportive function, Jermaine interjects phrases like "so glad" and "yeah baby," as if to encourage his brother to pour his heart into his performance. The result is a truly moving vocal from both brothers, each underlining the romanticism expressed in the lyrics.

Thirteen years after the song's initial release, the brothers demonstrated their enduring musical chemistry during their *Motown 25* performance. As the Jackson 5 (here 6, including Randy) rendered a tightly choreographed medley of their greatest hits, the most genuine moment occurred during "I'll Be There."

When Jermaine begins singing his part, a beaming Michael strolls over to his brother, threw his arm around him, and held up his microphone for Jermaine. Instead of crooning into his own mic, Jermaine shares one with Michael, as they did during their younger days. They smile at one another, clearly remembering the original recording and their frequent vocal collaborations. Along with Michael's "Billie Jean" solo turn, the touching moment became the other highlight of the telecast.

As recorded on Motown 1171
by the JACKSON 5

**I'LL BE THERE**

Bob West, Hal Davis, Willie Hutch, Berry Gordy, Jr.

95¢

son 5 jack

the
JACKSON 5

While 1970's "I'll Be There" may be best known for Michael's soaring lead vocal, Jermaine's contribution to the song's bridge also proved crucial to its power.

*Author's collection*

## "Mama's Pearl" (1970)

One of the Jackson 5's funkiest tracks, this song features a heavier, bass-driven rhythm than the group's other hits. It contrasts with "The Love You Save" in that this time the narrator essentially seduces the girl, urging her to "give my love a whirl." She apparently teases the boy, drawing the line at anything beyond kisses, due to her mother's wishes. Thus "Mama's Pearl" should surrender to the narrator's love, with the chorus calling her a "goody girl" who needs to "let down those curls."

After Michael's upbeat delivery, the entire group joins in the argument, pleading with her to not be afraid. Jermaine chimes in that "we've got the first step made." Jackie adds that the decision is ultimately hers, but Jermaine's strong, gritty voice commands her to "let yourself go." Michael takes the lead again, repeating the "let yourself go" lyric, but with his childish voice. Thus Jermaine's singing represents slightly less innocent wooing, while Michael's contrasting style emphasizes cuteness—and, for parents, safety.

The duet continues when Jermaine recites the "we've got the first step made" line alone, adding, "I've got what you need." Again, Michael's higher range and youth remove the sexual connotations from the phrase, bringing the song back to innocence and first love. As the song fades out, Jermaine and Michael call back and forth, echoing the "let's fall in love" lyrics. As with previous singles, "Mama's Pearl" utilizes their opposing voices to express different sides of teen romance and, at the same time, increase the song's overall energy.

"Mama's Pearl" was not originally envisioned as a duet. The demo, available on the compilation *Come and Get It: The Rare Pearls*, features just Michael on lead vocal. At that point the chorus repeated the line "guess who's making whoopee to your girlfriend" and contained very different lyrics. Fortunately, the song was drastically rewritten, with the multilayered vocal arrangements adding dimension to the funky track.

## "2-4-6-8" (1970)

This hand-clapping slice of bubblegum soul, co-written by Gloria Jones ("Tainted Love"), plays with a schoolyard rhyme, transforming it into a love song. "Two-four-six-eight, who do you appreciate?" the Jackson brothers chant, with Michael Jackson replying confidently, "I'm the one who wants to be your baby!" The wah-wah-pedaled guitar wails as Michael belts out amusing lines such as "I may be a little fella but my heart is big as Texas!"

In this track, Jermaine assumes the familiar role of big brother, defending Michael in his quest to win a girl's love. He may be small, Jermaine admits, but "he wanna be your fella," yet "you pay him no mind." Their singing relationship extends beyond sound in "2-4-6-8"—here they are dramatizing the sibling relationship, with the older brother assisting his younger, less experienced sibling in winning a young lady's love.

## "Sugar Daddy" (1971)

Two years into the Jackson 5's popularity, Motown realized that the group contained two potential breakout solo stars: Jermaine and Michael. The two would soon record their own singles and albums, but "Sugar Daddy" represents the label's most overt attempt to transform the brothers into solo artists. While still credited to the Jackson 5, the song features Michael and Jermaine sharing lead vocals and tells the story of a young man who buys his girlfriend expensive gifts. Friends tell him that the girl steps out with other guys and only wants him for his money, but her love thrills him too much. The tempo, melody, and bass line resemble "I Want You Back," but the lyrics sound more cynical.

Michael sings the first verses, lamenting how he thought he was the young woman's only boyfriend, before Jermaine contributes an angry response. He has seen her walking with other guys, and she is "step, step, steppin' on my toes," he chants, in perfect syncopation. Michael sounds less bitter, more shocked at how everyone thinks he is her "standby Santa Claus."

Both singers harmonize on the next few lines, the mood becoming more contemplative. Her kisses keep him coming back for more, and the chorus stresses the narrator's resignation at ending up as a sugar daddy. They alternate lines about how they will give her all their money, following her anywhere she likes. In an interesting twist, Jermaine executes his back-and-forth routine with the entire Jackson 5; they spell out the words "sugar daddy" as he cheers them on with phrases like "what it is" and "listen to me," perhaps mimicking a preacher and choir.

Another aspect of "Sugar Daddy" reveals the Michael and Jermaine dynamic: theme. Tellingly, Michael sings the section evoking candy images to describe his dysfunctional romance (including the humorous line "Mary Jane said I'm just your lollipop, sucker"). Earlier, Jermaine had revealed that he has a "sweet tooth" for the young woman's love, but he avoids further candy metaphors. By strictly focusing on heady romance and

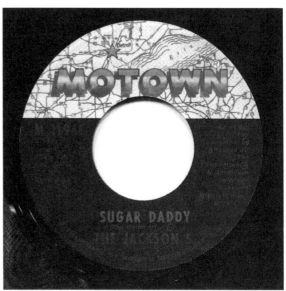

Michael and Jermaine Jackson further displayed their singing chemistry with the funky 1971 track "Sugar Daddy."
*Author's collection*

struggles with her infidelity, Jermaine establishes his maturity—and, compared with young Michael, his experience in love. These older/younger and mature/innocent oppositions are rooted in Michael and Jermaine's singing relationship, and they add a deeper meaning to what could be trivial bubblegum material.

## "Ain't Nothing Like the Real Thing" (1972)

Having Jermaine and Michael share lead vocal duties on this *Lookin' Through the Windows* track was an interesting strategy. After all, the 1968 original cast Marvin Gaye and Tammi Terrell as lovers singing of their romance. Here the Jackson brothers trade off vocals, again juxtaposing Michael's innocence with Jermaine's deeper, more experienced voice. This has the effect of showing different reactions to new love, perhaps representing the first blush of love (Michael) and the subsequent committed, mature relationship (Jermaine). While the Jackson 5 version mostly stays true to the original in terms of arrangement, it lends the Gaye/Terrell duet another perspective.

## "Dancing Machine" (1973)

Michael's maturing voice takes center stage on both the *G.I.T.* and *Dancing Machine* versions of this song. However, Jermaine provides some solo vocals on the line "She's moving, she's grooving, dancin' till the music stops now." Unlike earlier Jackson 5 tracks, "Dancing Machine" has Michael and Jermaine on an equal footing vocally. Now a teenager, Michael can sing lines about the female "dancing machine's" sexiness and how she's "super bad." Only the older Jermaine could convincingly deliver such lyrics when the group began; now his input does not pack quite the same punch. Yet the contrast in the higher and lower voices adds sonic depth to the track, providing some varying goals other than Michael's higher range.

## "Lucky Day" (1974)

An outtake from the *Dancing Machine* sessions (later released on the compilation *I Want You Back! Unreleased Masters*), this lost gem features a duet between the two singers. Like the single "Dancing Machine," this song showcases Michael's changing voice, thereby exposing the altered dynamics between the brothers. Against a thumping beat, a still-youthful Michael earnestly croons about the lucky day that he met his girlfriend. His voice soars as he sings that he has never felt love like this before, and his enthusiastic delivery lets the listener vicariously experience the first blush of new love.

Jermaine enters the picture in the next verse, his deeper voice and subtle but confident performance again suggesting a worldliness that Michael does not yet possess. He sings of how his dreams have come true; how she has become a permanent part of him. In the final line, "How can I forget this lucky day," he navigates an intriguing chord change that marks a departure from the traditional pop song. The brothers then alternate during the chorus, the beat suggesting old school Motown yet the wah-wah guitar places the track firmly in the mid-1970s. While not one of the Jackson 5's most memorable songs, "Lucky Day" further highlights how Michael and Jermaine's singing had changed over time.

## "Moving Violation" (1975)

The title track to the Jackson 5's last Motown album, this disco-influenced track displays Michael and Jermaine's contrasting styles. While Michael's voice had slightly deepened and possessed more sophistication, Jermaine's deeper voice provides contrast. The two exchange lines during the first chorus repetition and first verse. "You drove me out of my mind," Michael croons. "You've been careless with my love!" Jermaine exclaims. As the entire group chants "pushing me back, pushing me back," the song deepens in emotional intensity.

While the song works well on the dance floor, it also represents the waning days of Michael and Jermaine's singing relationship. The electric guitar slices through the song, adding a hint of rock bite to the angry track.

## "Body Language (Do the Love Dance)" (1975)

Motown clearly intended *Moving Violation* to capitalize on the emerging disco scene, picking up where *G.I.T.* and *Dancing Machine* left off. This highly danceable track exemplifies this method, with Michael and Jermaine trading lines about shaking it "to the east" and "to the west." The synthesizers and "ow's" suggest onetime opening act the Commodores, the funk beat slightly echoing Lionel Richie's band's 1974 hit "Machine Gun."

The Jackson 5 performed this song on an episode of *The Carol Burnett Show*, with cast member Vicki Lawrence showing off her dance moves with the Jackson brothers. The beat and Michael and Jermaine's vocals call out to not only the woman in the song but to listeners, commanding them to get on the floor and surrender to "the love dance."

## "Window Shopping" (1976)

By 1976, the Jackson 5 had departed Motown and renamed themselves "the Jacksons." Sitting on a pile of unreleased Jackson 5 material, their former label began releasing compilations of outtakes from previous recording sessions. The first of these collections, *Joyful Jukebox Music*, contains material yielded from the *Skywriter* and *G.I.T.* sessions. A previously unreleased outtake, "Window Shopping" allowed Michael and Jermaine to share lead vocals over a Supremes-esque beat and melody (think "You Keep Me Hangin' On") while the other Jacksons contribute "whoo-whoo" backing vocals straight out of a Gladys Knight and the Pips record.

The lyrics address the narrator's reluctance to commit, though his new relationship has clearly made him reconsider. At the song's beginning, Michael sings of the love interest controlling him, but Jermaine's part clarifies this seemingly negative statement. "I thought I had my game up tight," he sings, meaning that he tried to appear nonchalant but the woman had deeply affected him. After the chorus, Jermaine returns to decry his former ways, now "I'm trying to tie a knot onto you."

While he mainly sings during the chorus, Michael's higher range communicates the narrator's heretofore hidden romantic, monogamous side. "You're priceless merchandise / Precious merchandise," he proclaims. Unlike Jermaine's lines, Michael's verses utilize the buying and selling metaphor alluded to in the track's title. "Window Shopping" remains a curious mixture of romance and commerce, which partially explains why it never appeared on any previous Jackson 5 release. Still, it stands as a variant on Michael and Jermaine's typical method of letting Michael sing the majority of the lyrics while Jermaine contributes single lines or occasional harmonies.

## "Through Thick and Thin" (1976)

Originally recorded during the *Moving Violation* sessions, this outtake finally surfaced on the *Joyful Jukebox Music* compilation. A tender love song written by Mel Larson and Jerry Marcellino, it allows Jermaine and Michael to share lead vocals. A swell of strings sets the romantic mood, with the entire group harmonizing on the title. Jermaine pleads for his girlfriend's forgiveness, admitting he had neglected her. Michael's tenor chimes in, swearing, "I'm going to prove my love for you."

The backing harmonies and Jermaine's declaration of love recall classic 1970s groups like the Stylistics or Harold Melvin and the Blue Notes. The arrangement also foreshadows the Jackson 5's collaboration with Kenny Gamble and Leon Huff, its strings and lush vocals echoing tenets of the Philadelphia Sound.

## "Just Because I Love You" (1979)

The now rare compilation *Boogie*, released in the wake of the Jacksons' successful career resurgence, contains a hodgepodge of remixes, alternate takes, and outtakes dating from the group's Motown tenure. It includes this Willie Hutch–penned ballad, recorded during 1971's *Maybe Tomorrow* sessions, a notable entry in that it features mostly Jermaine on lead vocals. In this case, Jermaine describes his new love affair as Michael comments on his behavior.

Over a string- and flute-enriched arrangement, Jermaine cements his teen-idol status. He softly croons about how he stares at his new love and says ridiculous things because of his feelings. In turn, Michael amusingly clarifies his brother's altered state: "He's slowly going out of his head," he sings, with a lilting voice. Strangely, Michael repeats the title phrase, changing the point of view, yet Jermaine's ending ad-libs defiantly declare his intention to marry the unnamed girl. Once again the brothers exchange voices, but here Michael plays the younger brother role, clearly puzzled by his big brother's behavior. Jermaine's smooth vocals not only establish his "dreamy" status among female fans, they underscore his older age and, presumably, more extensive experience in love.

## "Torture" (1984)

Since Jermaine departed the group as the Jackson 5 left Motown, he did not resume his duets with his younger brother until 1984's *Victory*. Michael sang on few *Victory* tracks, but he did appear on the single, "Torture." The rock-inflected track lets the brothers trade vocals, with Jermaine performing the opening lines. Now on equal footing, the two narrate a dark story of a mysterious woman who apparently entraps the narrator. While she seems to be submissive—"Loneliness or hearts on fire / I am here to serve all masters," Michael sings, from the woman's perspective—she alone provides the pain and/or pleasure.

The brothers alternate verses in the bridge, harmonizing on the lines concerning whether the woman is torturing the main character. The entire group chimes in for the final chorus, determining that the woman's form of torture is denying the narrator her love. This became the closing track in the duo's singing relationship, not counting their duet on "Tell Me I'm Not Dreamin' (Too Good to Be True)," recorded for Jermaine's self-titled 1984 solo album. Unfortunately, it failed to reflect the charisma and unique partnership that drives so many vintage Jackson 5 tracks. By 1984, Michael had become a star in his own right, and he had largely outgrown the Jacksons act. Here, they sound as if they recorded their vocals separately, as there's little interaction between the two singers.

While their collaboration lasted only about six years, the Jackson brothers' singing dynamic stands out as a key ingredient in the Jackson 5's catalogue. Their contrasting voices and chemistry made Michael and Jermaine duets often-unappreciated treasures in the group's biggest hits.

# 7

# Let the Music Take Your Mind, Now

## Some of the Jackson 5's Most Unusual Cover Songs

A s discussed in chapter 4, the Jackson 5 owed much of their success to the talented team of Motown songwriters. The label also selected material the Jackson 5 could cover; not surprisingly, other Motown songs were popular choices. In other cases, Gordy and his staff would monitor the *Billboard* Hot 100, identifying current hit singles the Jackson 5 could record. This technique led to the group covering unlikely tunes ranging from 1940s standards to country songs.

### "I Was Made to Love Her" (recorded 1969; released on *Boogie*, 1979)

At first glance, having the Jackson 5 cover Stevie Wonder's classic "I Was Made to Love Her" seems like a no-brainer. After all, their Motown labelmate scored a Top 5 *Billboard* Hot 100 hit and topped the R&B Singles charts with this up-tempo number. However, the Jackson 5's radical makeover of Wonder's track radically changed the tempo, rendering it in a slow blues groove that at times completely obscures the original.

Recorded during the *ABC* sessions, this version of "I Was Made to Love Her" shows off Michael's precocious vocals, demonstrating how his roots remained firmly in rhythm and blues. His cries of "I love my baby! Oh!" and convincing readings of lines such as "All through thick and thin / Our love just won't end" demonstrate his singing prowess at just eleven years old. Why the Corporation decided to reconfigure Wonder's pop-soul track into a slow blues jam remains a mystery—one that may also explain why the track never surfaced until the 1979 compilation *Boogie*.

### "Mama Told Me Not to Come" (recorded 1970; released on *Come and Get It: The Rare Pearls*, 2012)

Who thought a twelve-year-old singing about a drug-filled orgy would be a great idea? Motown executives may have wanted to capitalize on a current hit record, as with the Jackson 5's cover of Jackson Browne's "Doctor My Eyes." Composed by Randy Newman, "Mama Told Me Not to Come" first appeared on Eric Burdon's 1966 solo album, then on Newman's 1970 disc *12 Songs*. Three Dog Night's 1970 version, however, became the big hit, topping the *Billboard* Hot 100. Noticing the song's success, the Corporation probably thought the Jackson 5 could sell even more copies of their own version. Wisely, their cover was shelved until the 2012 compilation *Come and Get It: The Rare Pearls*.

Recorded in summer 1970, "Mama Told Me Not to Come" here receives a soul makeover, with Michael adopting a comical, gravelly voice to sing the words about an out-of-control party. When the brothers harmonize on the chorus, Jermaine repeats the title phrase. Unlike the paranoid tenor of the Three Dog Night rendition, this version emphasizes humor and a cartoon-like atmosphere. At one point Michael converses with his "mama," who sounds like one of the Chipmunks. Weirdly, one of the Jacksons then cries out, "Anything but the whip!"

To make sure listeners understand that they are still children, the Jacksons talk over the instrumentation, offering statements like "I gotta go, man, it's past my bedtime!" and "C'mon, man, I don't wanna miss *The Flintstones*!" Despite these child-centric lines, the clumsy remake still retains the original's lines about whiskey, scary "cigarettes," a passed-out woman, and "things I ain't never seen before." Despite their attempts at humor, the Jackson 5's version of "Mama Told Me Not to Come" stands as one of their most age-inappropriate covers.

## "Man's Temptation" (recorded 1970; released on *I Want You Back! Unreleased Masters*, 2009)

A leftover from the *ABC* recording sessions, this Curtis Mayfield–penned song features the Jackson 5's stellar harmonies and a soulful Michael lead. However, Mayfield's world-weary ballad blends soul, gospel, and blues into a concoction best suited for a seasoned singer. Gene Chandler (best known for "Duke of Earl") first recorded it in 1962, followed by Mayfield's group the Impressions in 1966 and Isaac Hayes in 1971. While the Jackson 5 capture the song's doo-wop harmonies, they cannot effectively communicate the inner torment the narrator experiences.

Mayfield's lyrics tell the story of a man's struggle to be faithful to his woman. Michael's voice radiates power beyond his tender age, but his lack of experience means he cannot convincingly deliver lines such as "She's trying to ruin my happy home with a man's temptation." He sings of conflict, of how he must choose between two women. While the older Jacksons trade other verses, Michael assumes the emotionally climactic words, directly addressing the beautiful temptation as "little miss" and admitting that a pretty woman "makes me want to shout," repeating the title phrase as the song fades.

When the Corporation selected "Man's Temptation" for the group, they may have simply followed the "young boy pretending to be a man" trope (see chapter 2). The Jackson 5 first encountered this phenomenon while recording for Onederful and Steeltown, with tracks like "Big Boy" reflecting this cultural artifact. For some audiences, hearing Michael's still-childlike voice speak for an angst-ridden man may have seemed cute, but Mayfield's emotionally wrenching words demand sincerity, and a preteen simply cannot emulate world-weariness.

At Michael's memorial service, Smokey Robinson expressed amazement at how the young singer could effectively convey passion and heartbreak in "Who's Loving You." While Michael convincingly communicated complex emotions in that case, he could not match the anguish required in "Man's Temptation" that only an older, more experienced artist like Chandler, Hayes, Marvin Gaye, or Otis Redding could approach.

## "Shortnin' Bread" (*The Jim Nabors Hour*, 1970)

Throughout the 1970s, the Jackson 5 (later the Jacksons) appeared on innumerable variety shows. Often, the programs called upon them to act in silly skits or engage in unlikely duets with the hosts. However, one can only wonder why Jim Nabors and his staff thought this song would be an appropriate duet between the host and his sole guests, the Jackson 5. While the lyrics derive from James Whitcomb Riley's 1900 song "A Short'nin' Bread Song—Pieced Out," the song is frequently identified with plantation life. The PBS documentary *Slavery and the Making of America* identifies "Shortnin' Bread" as a recreational song—one that slaves and their families would sing, listen, and dance, their voices, hand-clapping, and foot-stomping their chief instruments.

Considering the song's history, "Shortnin' Bread" is indeed an odd choice for a Jackson 5/Nabors number. During the show, the Jackson brothers sat on risers; Nabors joined the boys, and all of them sing the song with gusto. As J5 Collector points out, Motown must have been aware of the track selection, as a line from the Jackson 5's "Love Comes in Different Flavors" was inserted into the number ("Thank your folks for the recipe," revised as "Thank your mom for the recipe").

Despite the song's appearance on TV, "Love Comes in Different Flavors" remained unreleased until the 2010 collection *I Want You Back! Unreleased Masters*. While this version is a "hipper" arrangement, filled with heavier percussion and the patented Jackson 5 harmonies, it stands out as one of the stranger and most borderline offensive covers in their history.

## "Bridge over Troubled Water" (*Third Album*, 1970)

When one thinks of Simon & Garfunkel, the term "teen idols" most likely does not leap to mind. The folk-rock duo wrote and recorded some of the most powerful anthems of the 1960s and early 1970s, commenting on the era's rapid changes ("Mrs. Robinson"), fear of alienation and losing one's way ("Sounds of Silence"), and finding strength and peace in a time of strife ("Bridge over Troubled Water").

In 1969, Paul Simon penned the track as his version of gospel, being particularly inspired by Reverend Claude Jeter and the Swan Silvertones. The group's best-known song, a recording of "Oh, Mary Don't You Weep for Me," features Jeter

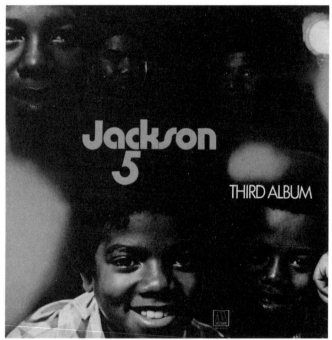

Simon and Garfunkel's popularity in the late 1960s and early 1970s explains Motown's decision to have the Jackson 5 record "Bridge over Troubled Water." Featuring Jermaine on lead vocals, it appeared on 1971's *Third Album*.                    *Author's collection*

shouting the line, "I'll be your bridge over deep water if you trust in my name." Expanding on that idea, Simon wrote this song, its lyrics meant to serve as the "bridge" over the "troubled water" of the 1960s. Combining folk-rock with spirituality, the song features Art Garfunkel on lead vocals, his delicate but emotional voice rising to a crescendo at the chorus. The profoundly moving title track propelled Simon & Garfunkel's to the top of the charts, making it the most successful single of their careers.

As Gordy and the Corporation were heading the Jackson 5's follow-up album to the smash *ABC* disc, they clearly saw an opportunity for the group to prove they were more than just a bubblegum pop act. "Bridge over Troubled Water" featured dense lyrics and a lovely melody; in addition, it blurred musical categories, rendering it a hit with multigenerational audiences. Thus the Jackson 5 found themselves recording their interpretation for *Third Album*, with Jermaine Jackson assuming most of the lead vocals. While it seems out of place for the boy band to croon the "silver girl" section (its meaning a mystery to this day), the track's uplifting mood works with the Jackson 5's positive image. The idea of friends supporting each other in difficult times resonates with audiences, and covering such material would lend the Jackson 5 credibility as artists wanting to move beyond the pop realm.

## "Doctor My Eyes" (Lookin' Through the Windows, 1972)

The Jackson 5's 1972 release *Lookin' Through the Windows* found the group searching for an identity; the Jackson brothers were maturing, with Michael Jackson gradually transforming from cute-as-a-button wunderkind to a teenager. Perhaps this change in direction explains this unusual choice of cover: Jackson Browne's "Doctor My Eyes," the narrative of a world-weary man trying to maintain some sense of optimism. Browne had worked on the track since 1971, with its original lyrics expressing an even more pessimistic view. When he finally recorded it for his self-titled debut album, it had a fast beat and David Crosby's clear harmonies.

Browne's music was a product of the 1970s, when the country was experiencing the fallout from the 1960s' turbulence. The Vietnam War raged on, Watergate would soon bring down the presidency, and the counterculture's mantra of "make love, not war"

The Jackson 5's 1972 version of Jackson Browne's "Doctor My Eyes" remains one of the group's most unusual covers.                    *Author's collection*

had started fading. These former hippies graduated from college and were finding their way as adults, struggling to stay true to their youthful ideals. Browne songs such as "Running on Empty" and "The Pretender" perfectly capture this inner conflict. "Doctor My Eyes" is no exception, as its narrator expresses concern that he has seen so much that he may become immune; in other words, he may "hear their cries," but he remains numb, having seen "the evil and the good without hiding."

Given these mature themes, quite why the Jackson 5 covered the track remains unclear. However, "Doctor My Eyes" was a huge 1972 hit, peaking at #8 on the *Billboard* Hot 100. Berry Gordy and Motown production team the Corporation likely noticed the tune's popularity, figuring it would give the Jackson 5 crossover appeal. As with other Motown acts, the Jackson 5 transcended genres and defied labels, and thus covering a rock track would emphasize how the group reached general audiences. In addition, they would soon outgrow their "kiddie band" status, and they needed to prove that they could handle more than bubblegum pop.

Still, "Doctor My Eyes" seems a mismatch for the youthful Jackson 5. As usual, Michael sings the track with gusto, his brothers providing tightly blended backing harmonies. His childlike voice remains at odds with the weariness of the song's narrator, however. The Jackson 5 makeover performed well in the UK, with the single peaking at #9 in 1973. Yet while they may have achieved some measure of success with "Doctor My Eyes" internationally, it remains one of the strangest covers in the Jackson 5 repertoire. Perhaps their teenage fans simply responded to the bouncy beat, overlooking the lyrics' pessimism.

## "Touch" (*Skywriter*, 1973)

One of the most controversial songs in the Jackson 5 catalogue, "Touch" raises questions of age-appropriateness in music. While it was not surprising that the group would cover a Supremes track—after all, they were label-mates—"Touch" moves far beyond the innocence of "Baby Love" or "Stop in the Name of Love," instead venturing into more sensual territory. Originally featured on the 1971 Supremes album of the same name, it marked the group's first release after Diana Ross departed the trio. Now featuring Mary Wilson, Jean Terrell, and Cindy Birdsong, the Supremes failed to crack the Top 40 with their "Touch" single.

*Skywriter* (1972) contains one of the Jackson 5's most controversial covers: "Touch," a highly sensual Supremes track many fans and critics felt to be age-inappropriate for the group.    *Author's collection*

According to Graham Betts's *Motown Encyclopedia*, "Touch" revealed escalating tensions between Motown and the Jackson 5. During the *Skywriter* sessions, Michael and Jermaine expressed great discomfort with the song, a seductive ballad on which the brothers take turns describing how they would please a woman in bed. Age-inappropriate and inconsistent with their squeaky-clean image, "Touch" drew criticism from the band, who wanted to gain more control over their own material. The label refused, instead dictating what they would record rather than encouraging the Jackson 5 to compose tracks of their own.

Jermaine and Michael's tepid enthusiasm permeates the song. Hearing a very young Michael sing about satisfying a woman is more alarming than hearing it from Jermaine's smoother, deeper voice, making for a discomfiting listen.

## "Reflections" (*G.I.T.: Get It Together*, 1973)

Not surprisingly, the Jackson 5 often covered other Motown artists. However, their version of the Supremes' 1967 hit stands as a curious entry in the Jackson 5 catalogue. While they were generally not known for straying into psychedelia, this cut features spacey sound effects and odd backing harmonies before switching abruptly to a classic soul arrangement.

Released during the height of psychedelia and a tense political climate, the original "Reflections" marked a shift in Motown's sound, foreshadowing cuts such as the Temptations' "Psychedelic Shack." The song's prominent use of the synthesizer was novel, although it would quickly become a major staple in pop music of the 1970s. Although it did not encompass the typical Motown sound, the track soared to #2

For the 1973 LP *G.I.T.: Get It Together*, the Jackson 5 covered the Supremes' "Reflections." An unusual amalgamation of psychedelia and soul, the group attempted to reproduce the 1960s vibe while adding their thoroughly modern harmonies.     *Author's collection*

on the *Billboard* Hot 100 and #4 on the R&B Singles chart.

Continuing the tradition of having the Jackson 5 cover proven hits, Hal Davis selected this Supremes classic for the 1973 album *G.I.T.: Get It Together*. The Jackson 5 version begins with bongos and a synthesizer, clearly attempting to replicate the original's otherworldly atmosphere. However, the effect is largely ruined with the Jacksons' chanting of "reflect, reflect" and what sounds like bubbles popping. Michael and Jermaine sing lead capably but cannot match the wistfulness of Diana Ross's original vocal. The horns, strings, and bass root the song firmly in soul, yet the bubbly sounds occasionally appear, stressing the song's psychedelic origins.

Overall, the sonic atmosphere, undermined by the Jacksons' constant "reflect" refrain, does not enhance the nuanced meaning of lyrics such as "through the mirror of my mind . . . trapped in a world that's a distorted reality." Quite simply, the youthful voices along with the frenzied arrangement—is it trying to be soul or pop tinged with '60s rock?—add up to one of the group's stranger covers.

## Medley: "Killing Me Softly with His Song / By the Time I Get to Phoenix / Danny Boy" (Las Vegas, 1974)

The Jackson 5 performed this odd medley on their 1974 tour, during including their Las Vegas stints and various TV appearances. Michael sings lead on "Killing Me Softly," while Jermaine Jackson takes over vocals on "By the Time I Get to Phoenix." Marlon and Jackie Jackson harmonize on "Danny Boy," with the entire group weaving all three songs together toward the conclusion. The first two tracks were major 1960s and 1970s hits, while the beloved Irish ballad "Danny Boy" has been recorded by countless artists.

Written about singer/songwriter Don McLean, "Killing Me Softly with His Song" was first recorded in 1971 by its composer, Lori Lieberman, but Roberta Flack's tender 1973 version was the monster hit. Similarly, Jimmy Webb's original 1965 recording of "By the Time I Get to Phoenix" did not have the impact of Glen Campbell's 1967 version. Two years later, soul legend Isaac Hayes recorded an almost twenty-minute version of the lead character's doomed romance.

These tracks, along with "Danny Boy," seem like strange choices for the Jackson 5. Indeed, they seem very mature for a still relatively young group. However, the Jacksons were in a very different place by 1974: Michael's voice was changing as he entered his teenage years, and the act had outgrown its initial bubblegum sound. In addition, the brothers and father Joseph Jackson bristled under Motown's control, wanting more control over their material. Thus they decided to prove that they were more than just "ABC" or "I Want You Back"; instead, they demonstrated their well-rounded musical background and ability to sing a variety of classic and contemporary tunes. In turn, their audience would expand, rendering them the perfect Las Vegas entertainers.

"Killing Me Softly" and "By the Time I Get to Phoenix" were huge hits, with the former encompassing the early 1970s singer/songwriter movement. "By the Time I Get to Phoenix" had already received country and soul makeovers, thus allowing them to explore both genres. While "Danny Boy" is an odd addition, it did showcase the Jacksons' tight harmonies and musical diversity. The Jackson 5 never recorded the medley for an album, but they performed it several times in concert, and on TV variety shows such as NBC's *The Tonight Show*.

## Medley: "Opus One / Bei Mir Bist Du Schön / Yakety Yak / Stop! In the Name of Love / Dancing Machine" (*The Carol Burnett Show*, 1975)

For this 1975 TV appearance, the Jackson 5 (now including Randy Jackson) performed a medley that paid tribute to vocal groups. The Coasters' "Yakety Yak" may not be a stretch, and "Stop! In the Name of Love" was not the first time the group covered the Supremes. The tracks that stand out are the Mills Brothers' "Opus One" and the Andrews Sisters' "Bei Mir Bist Du Schön," two standards that remain strange choices for the Jackson 5.

The Jackson 5 members introduced each song in a connecting segment. Michael misidentified "Opus One" as dating from the 1930s—in fact, it was written by Syd Oliver and Sid Garris in 1943. Big band greats Tommy Dorsey, Ted Heath, and Gene Krupa each had hits with their versions, with the Mills Brothers releasing their cover in 1954. One of the longest-running vocal groups in music history, the Mills Brothers applied their perfectly blended voices to pop and jazz, influencing artists from Dean Martin to the Bee Gees. Perhaps their tight harmonies appealed to the Jackson 5, although it may have surprised audiences to hear the pop and soul group dabble in jazz.

Like the Mills Brothers, the Andrews Sisters established themselves as masters of harmony. Specializing in swing and boogie-woogie, the trio—LaVerne, Maxine, and Patty Andrews—rose to fame in the late 1930s through records and radio performances. Their first big hit, a cover of the Yiddish tune "Bei Mir Bist Du Schön," features English lyrics transcribed by lyricist Sammy Cahn. Roughly translated as "To Me You Are Beautiful," the lovely song effectively showcased the sisters' peerless vocal blend. They would eventually become icons of World War II, entertaining the troops and recording popular wartime hits such as "Boogie Woogie Bugle Boy." Other than music, the Andrews Sisters and the Jackson 5 seem to have very little in common, and "Bei Mir Bist Du Schön" is not a typical choice for teen bands. (Interestingly, "Bei Mir Bist Du Schön" would later reappear on the Jacksons' TV variety show, this time performed by Rebbie, La Toya, and Janet.)

As they made clear throughout their medley, however, the Jackson 5 saw themselves as continuing the tradition of harmony groups. While their connection to the Coasters and the Supremes is obvious, their debts to the Mills Brothers and the Andrews Sisters are more subtle. Both acts exemplified tight vocal blends, and the Andrews Sisters integrated showmanship into their performances. For proof of the sisters' charisma and dancing prowess, view their electric rendition of "Boogie Woogie Bugle Boy" from the 1941 Abbott and Costello film *Buck Privates*.

The Jackson 5's 1975 *Carol Burnett* appearance and their Las Vegas shows allowed the group to demonstrate their vocal and stylistic range as they transitioned from teen bubblegum act to well-rounded entertainers. By choosing material dating from the 1940s to the 1970s, the brothers appealed to a multigenerational audience, acknowledged their predecessors, and demonstrated their maturity as entertainers.

Not all of these songs proved effective or appropriate for the Jackson 5. However, they showed the group's ability to adapt to different genres—a skill that would serve Michael well in his acting career, his stage shows, and his solo material.

# 8

# Find Out What You're Missin'

## Buried Gems and Underrated Album Tracks

**E**veryone knows the Jackson 5's biggest hits. Dig deeper into their studio albums and select compilations, however, and one will find tracks that Motown never released as singles, or that simply did not experience great chart success. These songs may never receive radio airplay, but they deserve attention for their underrated vocals, instrumentation, and lyrics. The following list presents buried treasures located on studio albums and on compilations Motown released after the group left the label. For more recent compilations, outtakes, and live versions, see chapter 9.

### "Nobody" (*Diana Ross Presents the Jackson 5*)

Anyone who wondered if the Jackson 5 were the "real deal" need only listen to this deep funk track. Written by the Corporation, this workout allows Michael and Jermaine Jackson to interact, trading lines and urging each other to great vocal heights. Here Michael demonstrates just how much he had learned from his mentors, his vocals borrowing elements from Jackie Wilson and James Brown as he belts out lines like, "I get steaming hot / Every time you light my fire." These seem like unlikely lyrics for an eleven-year-old to deliver, yet Michael does so with aplomb. A relentless groove provided by popping bass and hard-driving drums round out this unfairly overlooked track.

### "Who's Loving You" (*Diana Ross Presents the Jackson 5*)

Yes, this Smokey Robinson and the Miracles cover gradually gained legendary status. Aspiring young singers have performed the track on talent shows such as *Showtime at the Apollo* and *The X Factor* in attempting to prove their vocal chops. Yet no one has come close to Michael Jackson's lead vocal on this slow burner, not even Robinson. At Michael's memorial service, Robinson recalled when Berry Gordy first told him that the Jackson 5 would record his song for their debut album. He expressed disbelief that an eleven-year-old boy could convincingly sing a song about passion and heartbreak; once he heard Michael's astounding performance, he was quickly converted.

"Who's Loving You" became a staple of Jackson 5's concerts, and the live renditions almost equal the studio version. Yet hearing the group's rendition on their debut disc—reliving the moment when Michael hits that difficult yet break taking note as the music drops out—still thrills.

## "I'll Bet You" (ABC)

One of the Jackson 5's more unusual covers, this 1969 Funkadelic track was penned by group leader George Clinton. First appearing on the group's self-titled debut LP, "I'll Bet You" seems a strange choice for a soul/bubblegum act. The original uses sounds effects such as a spaceship landing, echoing voices, and distorted guitar to create a psychedelic atmosphere. Why the Corporation deemed the over six-minute acid funk jam appropriate for the Jackson 5 remains a mystery, although the drum and bass resemble the early Motown Funk Brothers sound.

Not surprisingly, the Jackson 5's rendition is smoother and shorter. The entire group shares vocals, although Michael primarily sings lead. Geoff Brown sneers at their cover in the 2009 edition of his book *Michael Jackson: A Life in Music*, calling it "an attempt to recreate a Norman Whitfield–styled psychedelic funk production for the Temptations as a wild Funkadelic extemporisation," apparently drawing comparisons with the Temptations' hits "Psychedelic Shack" and "Ball of Confusion." Brown concludes that the Jacksons did not possess Funkadelic's vocal abilities; in fact, the Jackson 5 displays an impressive talent for conquering a difficult track. Clinton composed complicated tracks with challenging chord changes, which Funkadelic and its offshoot Parliament performed admirably. While the Jacksons cannot match an adult group's singing range, they can convincingly perform the unusual melody and bluesy vocals the song requires. "I'll Bet You" challenges the listener to reconsider the Jackson 5 outside the boundaries of the teen-pop genre.

## "Can I See You in the Morning" (*Third Album*)

Written by Deke Richards, this *Third Album* track combines rock, psychedelia, and R&B to create a sophisticated track for a teen-pop group. The lyrics may be a bit too sophisticated—indeed, age-inappropriate—but Michael's supple voice handles unusual chord changes with apparent ease. The percussion snakes though as the lead singer coos lines such as "Like I seen you late at night . . . Come and make me feel alright . . . Come and take me, do with me just what you please." The Jacksons provide beautiful harmonies, adding to the sensuality of the track. Despite the questionable lyrics, the track remains a remnant of 1960s psychedelia and acid-tinged rock, allowing the Jackson 5 to demonstrate their stylistic range and singing skills.

## "Goin' Back to Indiana" (*Third Album*)

"I just want to do my thing!" Michael cries out in this impeccably produced song. And the group do their thing well on this catchy, upbeat track. The retro rock-and-roll feel receives a soulful makeover with piercing horns, but the sizzling guitar solos return "Goin' Back to Indiana" to its rock and blues roots. The ending cheers about Indiana add a youthful flair to the track, conjuring images of high-school pep rallies. The group's 1971 TV special derived its name from this bouncy ode to their hometown—a song that could double as the perfect concert opener.

## "How Funky Is Your Chicken" (*Third Album*)

Songwriters Willie and Richard Hutch struck gold with this dance-floor burner, giving many of the Jackson brothers vocal solos in which they are essentially bragging about their ability to do the "chicken" and enticing listeners to show off their best moves. Most likely written with teen parties in mind, the song's funky beat and popping bass lines render the beat impossible to resist. "How Funky Is Your Chicken" may not contain world-changing lyrics, but this tale of a dance battle remains relentlessly catchy.

## "Petals" (*Maybe Tomorrow*)

Written by the Corporation, this danceable number features a spirited Michael and some impressive backing harmonies from his brothers. Recorded in August 1970, "Petals" tells the story of a fickle love interest. The catchy chorus lingers long after the track ends: "Throwing petals, petals, tossing petals on the ground / Yesterday she picked me up just to throw me down!" Michael cries. When the rest of the group members execute a series of cascading vocals, each

*Maybe Tomorrow*, the Jackson 5's first studio album since 1970's *Third Album*, contains not only the hit "Never Can Say Goodbye" but two other stellar Michael lead vocal performances: "Petals" and "It's Great to Be Here." *Author's collection*

overlapping the other, it demonstrates how the Jacksons had become masters of harmony.

## "It's Great to Be Here" (*Maybe Tomorrow*)

With some assistance from Jermaine, Michael proclaims that "it's great to be here in your arms" in this up-tempo love song. The Corporation-penned track borrows the buzzing guitar sound from "ABC" to complement the steady rhythm. As the song continues, Michael's voice transitions from a muted tone to screaming, joyous exaltations toward the end. This lesser-known track demonstrates his increasing mastery over his voice with its well-crafted phrasing and delivery.

## "My Little Baby" (*Maybe Tomorrow*)

This *Maybe Tomorrow* tune may not contain the Corporation's most thought-provoking lyrics ("you keep me warm as toast"), but when Michael cries, "I'm sticking with you girl," his voice gradually rising on the final word, he oozes sincerity. The funky, upbeat track charms with its declarations of true love, for which Michael receives some vocal assistance from Jermaine. Its call-and-response chorus will linger long after "My Little Baby" fades out. Bass-pumping pop/soul never sounded so joyous.

## "If I Have to Move a Mountain" (*Lookin' Through the Windows*)

This Corporation-penned ballad features a first-rate Michael vocal, ranging from soft and sweet to the soaring, powerful chorus. By 1972 he had developed rapidly as a vocalist and interpreter, and this lesser known track is a prime example. "So if I have to move a mountain / Simply to prove that you're my love," he cries, his nuanced vocals wrenching every ounce of emotion from the words.

The B-side to the "Little Bitty Pretty One" single, "If I Have to Move a Mountain" received little attention. In *Michael Jackson: A Life in Music*, author Brown dubs the song as an average ballad. Yet the track foreshadows Michael's power as a solo artist—compare "If I Have to Move a Mountain" with a single from the same year, "Ben." The similarities in vocal technique are striking: the way Michael holds the notes, enunciates, and modulates volume and voice intensity cannot be overlooked. Indeed, the singer would record "Ben" at the same time as the *Lookin' Through the Windows* sessions.

## "I Can Only Give You Love" (*Lookin' Through the Windows*)

Songwriters Richard and Willie Hutch strike again with this up-tempo pop song, slightly reminiscent of "ABC" or "The Love You Save." The throbbing bass and driving beat power the track, anchored by Michael and Jermaine Jackson's lead vocals. Smartly tapping into teenage insecurity, the composers tell the story of the narrator's quest to win a girl's heart. Alternating lines, the Jackson brothers observe that Jimmy, Billy, and Bobby may have status (baseball star, football captain, and son of wealthy parents, respectively), but this suitor can give the young woman his love. "I've made no claim to fame, you won't know my name," they croon. But "if it's love that you need," the narrator can provide that.

Why did Motown not release "I Can Only Give You Love" as a single? The lyrics perfectly suited the Jackson 5's teen idol image, portraying them as caring, devoted boyfriends. Their teenage female fans would have swooned at Michael and Jermaine's pleas to accept their love. In addition, the strong beat is tailor-made for dancing, and would have generated energy from concert audiences. Perhaps the beat and bass too closely resembled earlier Jackson 5 hits, thus mislabeling it a "knockoff" of their patented bubblegum pop sound.

## "Boogie Man" (*Skywriter*)

"The boogie man's gonna get ya!" the Jackson 5 cry out in this *Skywriter* track, a perfect addition to any Halloween playlist, perhaps as a complement to later spooky Michael Jackson numbers like "Thriller," "Is It Scary," "Ghosts," and "Blood on the Dance Floor." Once again, songwriter Richards attempts to entice teen fans onto the dance floor, but he also incorporates humor into the track. Hearing Tito Jackson and other group members attempt an evil laugh is amusing, making "Boogie Man" a humorously spooky addition to the Jackson 5 catalogue.

## "I Can't Quit Your Love" (*Skywriter*)

A Four Tops cover, "I Can't Quit Your Love" features horns that burst through a classic Motown marching beat. The Jackson brothers execute classic backing harmonies reminiscent of the Four Tops and the Temptations. However, Michael's impressive vocal performance steals the show, sounding less childish and more typically teenaged. Listen for his James Brown–esque "ow's" and note how he can now effectively sing lines such as "You snap your fingers and I feel on fire / Like silly spinning wheels of desire" at fifteen years old. When he reaches a scream on the last word of the lyric, "You know I can't quit your love ooh yeah!" his R&B origins shine through.

## "Uppermost" (*Skywriter*)

One of *Skywriter*'s best tracks, this Clifton Davis–penned track incorporates jazz-influenced chord changes with a slight Latin beat. Strings and electric guitar wind around Michael's supple voice, underscoring the singer's emerging maturity. No typical eleven-year-old could handle the tempo changes and wide-ranging medley, thus a teenaged Michael could accomplish those tasks with greater ease. While not as memorable as Davis's hit composition "Never Can Say Goodbye," the light and airy track provides the perfect background for a breezy summer day. Brown terms "Uppermost" a "sneakily attractive track," perhaps referring to its laid-back atmosphere.

## "Ooh, I'd Love to Be with You" (*Skywriter*)

Similar to "Uppermost," the song "Ooh, I'd Love to Be with You" reflects the growing soft-rock movement of the early 1970s. This Fonce and Larry Mizell composition is based on a Latin-tinged rhythm, with Michael and Jermaine sharing lead vocals. One can almost feel the summer heat as Michael croons the opening words, "Old man sun / He don't have to come / I'll keep you warm with your smile." Brown also notes the arrangement's similarity to Timmy Thomas' slinky 1972 single "Why Can't We Live Together," which is most evident in the percussion.

"If I Have to Move a Mountain," from the 1971 LP *Lookin' Through the Windows*, showcases Michael's rapid development as an interpretative vocalist.    *Author's collection*

## "You Made Me What I Am" (*Skywriter*)

A rare foray into gospel, "You Made Me What I Am" serves as a song of gratitude to the Lord. Michael's spirited lead vocal, along with the Jacksons' backing harmonies, reenacting the scene of a preacher standing in front of his choir, addressing the congregation. A Corporation track, it utilizes horns, flute, and a straight-ahead beat (accented by tambourine) to place the listener in church. "Fame and fortune / Can't change my name / That's not the life I want to lead, no, no," Michael exclaims, his brothers chanting "Testify, testify!" at one point. Both catchy and inspirational, "You Made Me What I Am" stands as an unusual entry in the Jackson 5 catalogue.

## "Get It Together" (*G.I.T.: Get It Together*)

Now directed by Hal Davis, the Jackson 5 formally kick-started their second phase with this funky, disco-inflected track. Exceptionally produced with crystal-clear sound, the horns, keyboards, strings, guitar riffs, and underlying bass introduce the album's dance vibe. In addition to being a fun, highly danceable song, "Get It Together" provides the first hint of Michael's emergence as an adult pop artist. His mannerisms on this and other *G.I.T.* tracks would resurface on future Jacksons albums as well as his *Off the Wall* and *Thriller*.

## "Don't Say Goodbye Again" (*G.I.T.: Get It Together*)

This mid-tempo love song, co-written by Pam Sawyer and Leon Ware, may not have the best lyrics ("I can see through you just like cellophane"), but the pleasant track allows Michael to further display his maturing vocals. If he pitched his voice a bit lower, it could have easily ended up on *Off the Wall* as much as a Jackson 5 album. Its lush, string-filled sound also predicts the Jacksons' eventual venture into Philadelphia soul territory with Kenny Gamble and Leon Huff.

## "Mama I Gotta Brand New Thing (Don't Say No)" (*G.I.T.: Get It Together*)

An unusual combination of funk, rock, and disco, the Norman Whitfield–penned track attempts to combine the Jackson 5's classic sound with mid-1970s trends. The popping bass accompanies a particularly aggressive Michael, who spits out lyrics concerning a "country boy" who has left home to find success. But will he turn his back on his morals? The narrator addresses his mother throughout the track, the buzzing guitar reflecting his frustration with his mother's words of warning. "Mama said, 'My son, my son you're only sixteen / I know being a star is your dream' / But I think it's time you stop all this foolin'," Michael yells, representing the mother's growing frustration and the main character's anger about her attitude. Pounding piano is introduced into the mix as the tempo increases, leading to a frenzied conclusion.

Brown claims that Whitfield and Davis tried to shoehorn the Jackson 5 into a Temptations-esque arrangement. While the tone and vocal harmonies undoubtedly reflect the Temptations' classic style, the Jackson 5 still manages to make the song their own. Unlike other *G.I.T.* tracks, "Mama I Gotta Brand New Thing" features virtually all the Jacksons' voices, making the track a full group production.

## "It's Too Late to Change the Time" (*G.I.T.: Get It Together*)

The Sawyer and Ware composition puts Michael's singing abilities to the test with rapidly changing tempos, challenging melodies, and unusual chord changes. He certainly proves himself by varying his volume and pitch; in addition, vocal tics that would become major components in his solo work first surface here. Note how he sings the line "It's too late-uh, too late to change the time"—that "uh" an inflection he would return to multiple times. The "ooh's" he adds at various points also show up in later tracks like "Don't Stop 'Til You Get Enough."

## "You Need Love Like I Do (Don't You?)" (*G.I.T.: Get It Together*)

Previewing the sexier voice and image that would guide his late-1970s and 1980s material, Michael unleashes his sensual vocals on this Gladys Knight and the Pips cover. As Jermaine sings lines, Michael adds "oh yeah," and "ain't it true," communicating just how much he yearns for the woman's love. Note how the ending trumpet notes and percussion meld right into the *G.I.T.* mix of "Dancing Machine," where Michael would fully unleash his seductive vocals to tell the story of the song's "sexy lady" as well as coaxing listeners onto the dance floor.

## "I Am Love" *(Dancing Machine)*

A large departure from the traditional Jackson 5 sound, this slow number functions as both a ballad and protest song. While the song appears in its entirety on *Dancing Machine*, only part of "I Am Love" was released to radio. The single was split into two halves due to its length, with "Part 1" on the A-side and "Part 2" on the B-side. Mostly sung by Jermaine, it incorporates gritty guitar with mellow keyboards. "Part 1" sounds like a slow blues jam with a slightly spacey sound; "Part 2" transforms into an extended rock and blues jam reminiscent of a Parliament record, with some early Doobie Brothers sprinkled throughout.

While some lyrics plead for the unnamed woman to come back, others suggest that the narrator may be discussing more than romantic love. As he declares in the title, he represents love and wants to be "your friend and your lover / Your sister and your brother." Ambitious and experimental, "I Am Love" intrigues with its mysterious lyrics and melting pot of music genres.

## "(You Were Made) Especially for Me" *(Moving Violation)*

Another precursor to the Jacksons' tenure with Gamble and Huff, this horn and string-filled up-tempo number screams Philly soul. Now sounding like the adult Michael, his voice smoothly glides over the catchy melody, repeating the title phrase with enthusiasm. In retrospect, this track should have been released as a *Moving Violation* single, as it would have scored well on R&B radio stations.

## "Breezy" *(Moving Violation)*

This jazzy mid-tempo song features Michael and Jermaine on co-lead vocals, the lovely chord changes reflecting the title. Harmonies, a scratchy guitar riff, and keyboards round out the instrumental section, further emphasizing the fusion elements of the track. Clearly, songwriters Mel Larson and Jerry Marcellino wanted to expand the Jackson 5 into an adult contemporary market, and "Breezy" is a step in that artistic direction.

## "Make Tonight All Mine" *(Joyful Jukebox Music)*

When Motown released its first "unreleased tracks" compilation after the Jackson 5 departed the label, the label unearthed material initially left on the cutting room floor. While some *Joyful Jukebox Music* tracks illustrate why certain songs did not make the final album cut, with others it remains a puzzle as to why they were hitherto unreleased. A perfect example is "Make Tonight All Mine," a finger-snapping pop number dating from the *G.I.T.* sessions. Featuring an energetic Michael lead vocal and irresistible beat, it is one of the "should have been" hits of the Jackson 5 catalogue. Most likely Davis deemed it unsuitable for the overarching dance vibe of *G.I.T.*, although it could have fit in with the diverse *Dancing Machine*. Indeed, "Make Tonight All Mine" effectively updates the classic Jackson 5 bubblegum soul sound, rendering it the adult version of "I Want You Back," "ABC," or "The Love You Save."

## "One Day I'll Marry You" (*Boogie*)

Dating from the *Third Album* sessions, this charming love song stayed locked in the Motown vaults until the second compilation, *Boogie*. The Sawyer/Ware composition followed the "young boy mimicking a grown man" trope the Jackson 5 had visited before in early songs like "Big Boy." While his brief monologues sound a bit corny, Michael's singing conveys the starry-eyed love expressed in the lyrics. "If you think I'm gonna give you up / Throw away that sweet word 'love' . . . One day I'll marry you," he proclaims, effortlessly hitting high notes to convey his emotion. While still very young, he possessed a phrasing ability that rivaled singers twice his age. The long-lost track stresses innocence and the first blush of love, and Michael conveys both themes just through his powerful voice.

## "If I Can't Nobody Can" (*Come and Get It: The Rare Pearls*)

Recorded circa November 1972, this track, penned by Freddie Perren and Christine Yarian, did not reappear until 2012's *Come and Get It: The Rare Pearls*. Why this track never appeared on an original Jackson 5 album is a mystery, as "If I Can't Nobody Can" is a funk workout that would have signaled a departure from the group's bubblegum sound. Perhaps this radical change is why the song initially being left on the cutting room floor. Luckily, *Come and Get It* revealed this hidden

The gatefold from the *Maybe Tomorrow* album shows the Jackson 5 in their funkiest 1970s outfits, including fringed vests and multicolored shirts.                    *Author's collection*

gem, a bass-popping track featuring a maturing Michael vocal. Predating the disco era, the song would have found a place on dance floors had it been released just a few years later.

## "Love Trip" (*Come and Get It: The Rare Pearls*)

From the Jackson 5 to the solo years, Michael demonstrated his prowess as a balladeer. This unusual love song, composed by Jack Perricone, features the singer's sweet, pure voice, containing just a hint of sensuality. Recorded in February and March 1973, "Love Trip" includes elements of 1960s psychedelia in the chorus. "At the magic in your fingers making music flow," Michael croons. "Her tender touch taking you each place you want to go / Each fingertip taking you on a love trip," the Jacksons respond, as the echoing flute and electric sitar (the same instrument used at the beginning of the Stylistics' "You Make Me Feel Brand New") add a mystical element to the song. A woman's voice softly repeats the phrase "love trip" to enhance the almost hallucinogenic quality of the narrator's love for his girlfriend.

"Love Trip" represents a curious cross between 1960s rock and 1970s soul, contrasting smooth soul with acid-rock elements. The Jackson 5 would further experiment with this hybrid sound on their 1975 song "I Am Love," off *Dancing Machine.* Even more significant is Michael's growing confidence in his voice, which he uses to seduce as well as entertain. "I'll Be There" marked the beginning of these experiments, and "Love Trip" illustrates how far he had developed this talent in just a couple of years.

While these tracks may not have been released as singles—in some cases, they stayed unreleased until almost forty years after they were recorded—they provide glimpses into the Jackson 5's artistic development. In addition, they allow listeners to experience how Michael gained confidence as a singer and performer.

# 9

# Give Me Some Joyful Jukebox Music

## Odds and Ends

During the Jackson 5's seven-year tenure with Motown, the group spent an extraordinary amount of time in the recording studio. In addition to their eleven studio albums and the live collection *Goin' Back to Indiana*, the Jackson brothers recorded numerous demos, outtakes, and extra material. According to Taraborrelli, the Jackson 5 recorded 465 songs for Motown during 1969–75; only 174 were released during their tenure at the label. Some of these outtakes later resurfaced on compilations such as *Joyful Jukebox Music, Boogie, Soulsation!, I Want You Back! Unreleased Masters*, and *Come and Get It: The Rare Pearls*. However, Motown still owns archival audio recordings that may someday see official release. The following is a list of such rarities; while some tracks have since been compiled in collections, others maintain their bootleg status. Tracks that have since appeared on later compilations are noted; otherwise the songs remain unreleased.

### 1969

The Jackson 5's first recordings for Motown relied heavily on cover versions of the label's other artists. Originals by the Corporation and other in-house songwriters are also present in the following list.

#### "Oh, I've Been Bless'd"

Recorded during the *Diana Ross Presents the Jackson 5* sessions, this song remained unreleased until the 1979 compilation *Boogie*.

#### "After You Leave Girl"

Bobby Taylor wrote this track for the Jackson 5, meant for inclusion on *Diana Ross Presents the Jackson 5*. The song was eventually released on *Come and Get It: The Rare Pearls*.

#### "Listen I'll Tell You How"

Recorded during the May 1969 *Diana Ross Presents the Jackson 5* sessions, the Taylor-penned song later appeared on *I Want You Back! Unreleased Masters*.

## "1-2-3"

The original title for "ABC," this early demo version features slightly different lyrics, such as "1-2-3, easy as A-B-C."

## "7 Rooms of Gloom"

One of several Four Tops songs the Jackson 5 covered, this track never saw official release.

## "I'm Your Sunny One (He's My Sunny Boy)"

Recorded circa 1969 or 1970, most likely for *Diana Ross Presents the Jackson 5*, the song later surfaced on *Come and Get It: The Rare Pearls*.

## "Since I Lost My Baby"

Recorded in August 1969, the Temptations track later appeared on *Come and Get It: The Rare Pearls*.

## "Ain't No Mountain High Enough"

According to Chris Cadman and Craig Halstead's discography *For the Record*, the Jackson 5 laid down two versions of this hit single. The first closely followed Ross's version, complete with spoken introduction and slower tempo. In addition, they recorded a rendition matching Marvin Gaye and Tammi Terrell's up-tempo reading; both remain unreleased.

## "If I Can't (Nobody Can)"

This Freddie Perren and Christine Yarian composition remains unreleased.

## "Lavender Blue"

The Jackson 5's cover of this Burl Ives composition, which first appeared in the Walt Disney film *So Dear to My Heart* (1948), remains unreleased.

After the Jackson 5 left Motown, the label released *Joyful Jukebox Music*, the first of several compilations containing previous unreleased outtakes.                *Author's collection*

## "To Sir with Love"

The 1967 film of the same name was helmed by Lulu's definitive version; the Jackson 5 recorded their own take, but it remains unreleased.

## "It's Your Thing"

While this was finally issued on the "Rare and Unreleased" disc in 1995's *Soulsation!* compilation, the Jackson 5 had not only completed a studio recording but had performed live several times. One of their most notable versions was during the 1969 *Miss Black America Pageant,* their first national TV appearance. The previously unreleased rendition, an Isley Brothers cover, dates from the *Diana Ross Presents the Jackson 5* sessions.

## "Reach Out I'll Be There"

A Four Tops cover, this track has a rather unusual history. According to Cadman and Halstead, the Jackson 5 originally recorded it for inclusion on their debut album. Early copies of *Diana Ross Presents the Jackson 5* (US edition) lists "Reach Out I'll Be There" as the final track on side B, but did not actually appear on the album. Subsequent copies corrected the error, but the song saw new life when it was included on the *Soulsation!* collection.

## "For the Rest of My Life"

According to Cadman and Halstead, this circa-1970 track was a duet between the Jackson 5 and Diana Ross. Long rumored to exist, "For the Rest of My Life" has not been officially recognized by Motown and has not surfaced.

## "Baby It's Love"

Also allegedly recorded in 1970, the second apparent Ross/Jackson 5 collaboration has not been confirmed by Motown.

## "A Fool for You"

Eventually surfacing on the 1995 compilation *Soulsation!*, this Ray Charles cover was originally recorded on February 12, 1970, under the direction of the Jackson 5's first producer, Bobby Taylor.

## Other Rare Recordings

- "After the Storm (the Sun Will Shine)"
- "Where Did Our Love Go" (Supremes cover)
- "(Loneliness Has Made Me Realize) It's You That I Need" (Temptations cover)
- "Love Feels Like Fire" (Four Tops cover)
- "Since You've Been Gone" (Four Tops cover)

- "Loving You Is Sweeter Than Ever" (Four Tops cover)
- "How Sweet It Is (to Be Loved by You)" (Marvin Gaye cover)
- "What Becomes of the Brokenhearted" (Jimmy Ruffin cover)
- "Ooh Baby, Baby" (Smokey Robinson and the Miracles cover)
- "Kentucky Road"
- "What Does It Take (to Win Your Love)" (Jr. Walker and the All Stars cover)
- "A Place in the Sun" (Stevie Wonder cover)
- "Fingertips" (Stevie Wonder cover)
- "For Once in My Life" (cover of Stevie Wonder version)
- "Heaven Help Us All" (Stevie Wonder cover)
- "If You Really Love Me" (Stevie Wonder cover)
- "Signed, Sealed, Delivered" (Stevie Wonder cover)
- "Yester-Me, Yester-You, Yesterday" (Stevie Wonder cover)
- "Baby I Need Your Lovin'" (Four Tops cover)
- "(Neither One of Us ) Wants to Be the First to Say Goodbye" (Gladys Knight and the Pips cover)
- "Back in My Arms Again" (Supremes cover)
- "Come and Get It"
- "She Say 'Want'" (a.k.a. "She Say 'What'")
- "That's How Love Is"

# 1970

While the Jackson 5 still covered songs by other Motown artists, they were increasingly recording original compositions by the Corporation and other in-house songwriters.

## "Ask the Lonely"

Motown scrapped this Four Tops cover, recorded in 1970, until a 1983 compilation entitled *Motown Superstars Sing Motown Superstars*. This remixed version was eventually replaced by the original recording on 1995's *Soulsation!* collection. According to Cadman and Halstead, a demo exists but has never surfaced.

## "Iddinit"

Recorded during the 1970 *ABC* sessions, this Deke Richards/Freddie Perren/Alphonso Mizell composition was never heard until the 2009 *I Want You Back! Unreleased Masters* compilation. The complete version was featured as a bonus track on *Come and Get It: The Rare Pearls*.

## "We Can Have Fun"

Recorded over two days in 1970—January 8 and February 11—the track remained unreleased until the *Soulsation!* compilation.

## "Guess Who's Making Whoopee with Your Girlfriend"

One of the most fascinating outtakes in Jackson 5 history, this racily titled track is the Corporation's first draft of "Mama's Pearl." The Jackson 5 recorded the song in the summer and fall of 1970, but Gordy deemed the song age-inappropriate. The demo leaked onto the Internet many years later, before seeing official release as part of 2012's *Come and Get It: The Rare Pearls*.

## "You Ain't Giving Me What I Want (So I'm Taking It All Back)"

Recorded on January 8, 1970, the song remained in the Motown vaults until the *Soulsation!* collection. The original working title was "Your A, B, C, and D's"; perhaps Motown executives deemed it too similar (in title, at least) to "ABC."

## "Everybody Is a Star"

One of many Sly Stone covers, the Jackson 5 remake was recorded during the 1970 *Third Album* sessions. A demo version may exist, but a more polished version is included on the *Soulsation!* boxed set.

## "I Hear a Symphony"

Dating from the *ABC* recording sessions, the track has since been released on several compilations. It made its debut on the 1986 Michael Jackson collection *Looking Back to Yesterday* (part of Motown's *Never-Before-Released* series); a version featuring an alternate vocal appeared on *Soulsation!* Finally, it appeared yet again on the 2009 release *Hello World: The Motown Solo Collection*. A demo version may exist, but has not surfaced.

## "Jamie"

Recorded during the *Third Album* sessions, this Eddie Holland cover eventually appeared on the *Soulsation!* boxed set. The composer's original version is included on his 1962 album *Jamie*.

## "Just a Little Misunderstanding"

A cover of the Contours' 1962 album track, the Jackson 5 recorded it for their *Third Album*. While it did not make the cut, it later appeared on *Soulsation!* A demo version may exist, but it has not surfaced in any form.

## Medley: "I Want You Back / ABC / The Love You Save"

*I Want You Back! Unreleased Masters* included this never-before-released alternate version of the medley the Jackson 5 performed on a 1971 episode of *The Flip Wilson Show*.

## "Movin'"

Recorded in 1970, this song remained unreleased until *Come and Get It: The Rare Pearls*.

## "Money Honey"

Intended for inclusion on *ABC*, this Jackson 5 cover of Clyde McPhatter and the Drifters boasts an interesting backstory. Cadman and Halsted note that Gordy fired original Jackson 5 producer Bobby Taylor during the recording. Hal Davis completed the work on "Money Honey," which ultimately failed to make the *ABC* lineup. It was eventually released on the *Soulsation!* collection.

## "Come and Get It (Love's on the Fire)"

Another Corporation compassion, this 1970 track became the inspiration for the collection title *Come and Get It: The Rare Pearls*.

## "I Got a Sure Thing"

Recorded in January 1970, this William Bell and Booker T. Jones song was shelved until 2012's *Come and Get It: The Rare Pearls*.

## "Love Comes in Different Flavors"

Dating from the 1970 *ABC* sessions, this Mel Larson, Jerry Marcellino, and Deke Richards track resurfaced on *I Want You Back! Unreleased Masters*.

## *Jackson 5 Christmas Album* Outtakes (1970)

In addition to their album recording sessions, the Jackson 5 also worked on their first and only holiday release. A surprisingly large number of tracks failed to make the final album lineup.

## "I Want You to Come Home for Christmas"

This *Jackson 5 Christmas Album* track failed to make the final lineup and remains unreleased.

## "Children's Christmas Song"

Another *Jackson 5 Christmas Album* outtake, the song was originally recorded by the Supremes in 1965.

## "It's Christmas Time"

Dating from the 1970 *Christmas Album* sessions, this remains unreleased.

## "That's What Christmas Means to Me"

Originally a hit for Stevie Wonder, the song failed to make the final *Christmas Album* track list and remains unissued.

## "Purple Snowflakes"

Their take on Marvin Gaye's Christmas song was shelved and did not appear on the *Christmas Album.*

## "Twinkle, Twinkle Little Me"

A 1965 Christmas hit for the Supremes, "Twinkle, Twinkle Little Me" was meant for the *Jackson 5 Christmas Album* but was ultimately shelved.

## Other Christmas Album Outtakes

- "Christmas Everyday"
- "Silver Bells"
- "White Christmas"
- "Silent Night"
- "My Favorite Things"
- "Joy to the World"
- "God Rest Ye Merry Gentlemen"

# 1971

Many of the Jackson 5's outtakes from 1971 did not officially resurface until over forty years later.

## "If You Want Heaven"

Recorded in February 1971, this song was shelved until *Come and Get It: The Rare Pearls.*

## "You Can't Hurry Love" (Supremes cover)

The circa-1971 Supremes cover appeared on 2012's *Come and Get It: The Rare Pearls.*

## "Love Call"

The Jackson 5 recorded the Willie Hutch composition on October 12, 1971; a test pressing exists, as pictured in Cadman and Halstead's *For the Record,* but "Love Call" has never been released.

## "Coming Home"

Recorded during the 1971 *Lookin' Through the Windows* sessions, a version was included on the *Soulsation!* boxed set. A demo exists, but it has not appeared in bootleg form.

## "You Better Watch Out"

The Jackson 5 recorded a version in October 1971, but it was not released until 2012's *Come and Get It: The Rare Pearls.*

## "Someone's Standing in My Love Light"

Recorded in January 1971, the song finally appeared on *Come and Get It: The Rare Pearls.*

# 1972

As the Jackson 5 transformed into more seasoned performers, Motown seemed conflicted as to whether the group should continue recording teen pop material or songs with mature themes. Judging from the outtakes listed below, Gordy had them stick to familiar material and cover versions.

## "Would Ya? Would Ya?" (a.k.a. "Wouldja" and "Would Ya Would Ya Baby")

This song, composed by Freddie Perren and Christine Yarian, was recorded in December 1972, finally seeing release on 2012's *Come and Get It: The Rare Pearls.*

## "Love Scenes"

Recorded in August 1972 for *Skywriter*, this track finally appeared on *Soulsation!*

## "Up on the Roof"

This iconic Gerry Goffin and Carole King composition first became a hit for the Drifters in 1963; James Taylor later covered it for his 1979 album *Flag*. The Jackson 5 laid down their version in March 1972, but it was not officially issued until 2012's *Come and Get It: The Rare Pearls.*

## "Be My Girl" (often misidentified as "Paper Doll")

The Jackson Five performed this track during their 1972 tour, apparently intending for it to be a single. Jermaine Jackson sang lead on the song, but it was never released.

Motown released certain songs as B-sides that never appeared on any albums. One example is "I'm So Happy," the flip side to the "Sugar Daddy" single.

*Author's collection*

## "Going My Way"

Co-written by Don Daniels, Richard Hutch, and Theresa McFaddin, this song dates from February/March 1972. It was eventually issued on *Come and Get It: The Rare Pearls.*

## "Keep off the Grass"

Recorded in 1972, the song was eventually issued on *Come and Get It: The Rare Pearls.*

## "Papa Was a Rollin' Stone"

Throughout their careers, the Jackson 5 performed this Temptations hit several times in concert. A version appears on the album *Live in Japan*, originally released in Japan only but finally reissued in the US in 2004. The song made another appearance on the Jacksons' 1976 variety show, then during a Mexico tour stop in 1976. No studio recordings have surfaced, but a 1972 version is said to exist.

## "Makin' Life a Little Easier for You"

Recorded in March 1972, this Corporation-penned track stayed unreleased until *Come and Get It: The Rare Pearls.*

## "Ooh, I'd Love to Be with You"

This 1972 composition by Richards, Perren, and Mizell has a convoluted history, according to Cadman and Halstead. Jackie Jackson recorded the track for his 1973 solo album, while yet another version was originally listed as a track on the *Soulsation!* compilation. However, the track that actually appeared on the boxed set was "Ooh, I'd Love to Be with You," taken from the *Skywriter* sessions. To add to the confusion, the authors note, the 1995 *Soulsation!* press release initially identified the track as "Are You the One." Whether a true Jackson 5 version exists is unclear.

# 1973

The following list contains outtakes from 1973.

## "Let's Go Back to Day One"

Oddly, the liner notes to *Come and Get It* list this track as having been recorded in April 1972 and June 1973. Why the Jackson 5 waited a full year before attempting the Patrice Holloway and Gloria Jones track remains a mystery.

## "Love Trip"

This Doug McClure and Jack Perricone song was recorded in February and March 1973 but was not released until *Come and Get It: The Rare Pearls.*

## "I'll Try You'll Try (Maybe We'll All Get By)"

An outtake from the *Skywriter* sessions, this song, composed by Wade Brown and David Jones Jr., was issued on *I Want You Back! Unreleased Masters*.

## "Label Me Love"

Recorded in May 1973, the Jackson 5's rendition of this song was included on 2012's *Come and Get It: The Rare Pearls*.

## "Didn't I (Blow Your Mind This Time)"

This rare track—a cover of a classic Delfonics hit—appeared on Jackie Jackson's 1973 solo album, and featured the rest of the Jackson 5 on backing vocals.

## "Jumbo Sam"

Written by Mel Larson, Don Fenceton, and Jerry Marcellino, this track was recorded during the 1973 *Skywriter* sessions. It remained shelved until the 2012 collection *Come and Get It: The Rare Pearls*.

## "Can't Get Ready for Losing You"

Dating from the 1973 *Skywriter* sessions, this track eventually appeared on the *Solution!* boxed set. Its composer, Willie Hutch, ended up recording "Can't Get Ready for Losing You" for his 1973 solo release *Fully Exposed*.

## "Let's Have a Party"

Intended for 1973's *Skywriter*, this song remained unreleased until the 1995 *Soulsation!* boxed set.

## "I Can't Get Enough of You"

Recorded in December 1973, the Jackson 5 did not release their version of this Eddie Horan composition until *Come and Get It: The Rare Pearls*.

# 1974

Signs of the Jackson 5's artistic maturity are evident in these outtakes, some of which resulted from a brief collaboration with labelmate Stevie Wonder.

## "A Pretty Face Is"

According to Cadman and Halstead, Stevie Wonder confirmed the existence of this outtake in a 1988 Japan interview. He wrote the track for the Jackson 5 in 1974, although he later said he intended the song as a duet with him and Michael Jackson. The two recorded a version for Wonder's 1988 album *Characters*, but it remains unreleased.

The Jackson 5 and Stevie Wonder almost recorded an album together, but ultimately the project fell through. The group did sing backup on Wonder's "You Haven't Done Nothin'," from his 1974 album *Fulfillingness' First Finale.*    *Author's collection*

## "Cupid"

Recorded circa January 1974, this song, written by Clay Drayton and Tamy Smith, finally surfaced on *Come and Get It: The Rare Pearls.*

## "Buttercup"

Another standout Jackson 5 "lost song," this Stevie Wonder composition was written and recorded around the time of the 1974 *Dancing Machine* sessions. Wonder and the Jackson 5 were considering collaborating on an album; unfortunately, the project never happened. This slice of R&B and pop features classic Wonder chord changes, a sweet Michael Jackson lead vocal, and ebullient backing vocals courtesy of the Jackson brothers. "Buttercup" paints the most vivid picture of what the aborted Wonder/Jackson 5 collaboration may have sounded like. Years later, singer Carl Anderson covered the song for his 1982 album *Absence Without Love*; luckily, listeners finally heard the Jackson 5 version via the 2009 collection *I Want You Back! Unreleased Masters.* Only one Jackson 5/Wonder collaboration was officially issued: "You Haven't Done Nothin'," included on Wonder's 1974 LP *Fulfillingness' First Finale.* Toward the end of the track, Wonder cries out, "Jackson 5, sing along with me," as the Jackson execute precise doo-doo-wop harmonies.

## "Lucky Day"

Recorded in January/February 1974 during the *Dancing Machine* sessions, this Don Daniels– and Terri McFadden–penned song was officially released on *I Want You Back! Unreleased Masters.*

## Uncertain Dates

The following tracks were not specifically labeled with a year, thus the dates given are rough estimates.

### "Twenty-Five Miles"

One of the best "lost" Jackson 5 tracks, this Edwin Starr cover features an incredibly soulful Michael Jackson lead vocal. The exact date of recording remains unclear—circa 1969 is the best guess—but a remixed version appears on the 1987 compilation *The Original Soul of Michael Jackson*. The original mix finally appeared on 2009's *Hello World*; although Michael Jackson solely sings lead, the other Jackson brothers sang backup but were uncredited.

### "Give Me Half a Chance"

The Jackson 5 recorded the song around 1970–73, but it was not released until the compilation *Looking Back to Yesterday*.

### "That's What Love Is Made Of"

The Jackson 5 recorded the song in 1970–73, but it was not released until the compilation *Looking Back to Yesterday*.

### "Since I Lost My Baby"

A cover of the Temptations' hit from 1965.

### "If the Shoe Don't Fit"

This Corporation production was recorded circa 1970–71 but did not see release until 2012's *Come and Get It: The Rare Pearls*.

### "Our Love"

This Deke Richards–penned track was recorded circa 1972–73, eventually appearing on *Come and Get It: The Rare Pearls*.

## Play That Record Again for Me

In a relatively short time span, the Jackson 5 recorded a vast amount of material; much of it still remains in the Motown vaults. More compilations of rare Jackson 5 tracks may reveal these lost treasures in the coming years.

# 10

# It's That Time of Year When Good Friends Are Near

## How the *Jackson 5 Christmas Album* Became a Modern Classic

R iding high on the phenomenal success of their first three albums—*Diana Ross Presents the Jackson 5*, *ABC*, and *Third Album*—the Jackson 5 released their first and only holiday album on October 15, 1970. The *Jackson 5 Christmas Album* appeared under numerous Christmas trees that year, hitting #1 on the *Billboard* 200 and becoming the best-selling holiday collection of the year. It went on to top the *Billboard* Christmas Albums chart for three years, and has sold over 3.5 million copies worldwide.

Since then, the *Jackson 5 Christmas Album* has been remastered and rereleased, most recently as 2009's *Jackson 5 Ultimate Christmas Collection* (featuring bonus tracks and remixes). Tracks such as "I Saw Mommy Kissing Santa Claus" and "Santa Claus Is Coming to Town" endure as staples on all-Christmas radio stations. Motown may have intended the collection to simply capitalize on the Jackson 5's newfound success, but the album has stood the test of time.

In the December 1987 issue of *Ebony*, Mike Worthington, a manager at Sam Goody's Third Avenue store, was asked about the album's lasting appeal. "The *Jackson 5 Christmas Album* has become a standard," he replied. In 2004, the *New Rolling Stone Album Guide* deemed the album a "small gem." Critic Ron Wynn writes in the *All Music Guide to Soul* that it is "one of the greatest holiday albums ever" and that "their versions of these dusty hymns and carols could even charm Scrooge."

*Billboard* magazine recognized the album's sales potential in its issue dated December 5, 1970. In the album reviews, the magazine notes that the "boys come on strong" with their renditions of classic Christmas carols, citing newer songs such as "Someday at Christmas" (not actually new, since Stevie Wonder had recorded it years before) and "Give Love on Christmas Day" as "potent numbers." Music journalist Nelson George fondly remembers the album in his memoir *City Kid: A Writer's Memoir of Ghetto Life and Post-Soul Success*, calling it one of his favorite childhood memories. "Bonded by the Jacksons singing 'Little Drummer Boy' and 'I Saw Mommy Kissing Santa Claus,' we danced around our living room with giddy energy," he writes.

Despite critical acclaim and massive popularity, little is known about the making of the *Jackson 5 Christmas Album*. In recent years, Michael Jackson authors have glossed over the collection entirely, with the *Motown Encyclopedia*'s Graham Betts dismissing it as "obligatory," despite calling "Santa Claus Is Coming to Town" a standout track. Geoff Brown goes a step further in his 2010 book *Michael Jackson: A Life in Music*, dubbing the album a "seasonal cash-in" and intimating that it pales in comparison to Phil Spector's *A Christmas Gift for You*. However, *Rolling Stone* recognized the album's lasting appeal in an article dated December 30, 1976, "Chestnuts Roasting on an Electric Guitar," calling it "mellow" and "ingratiating" and noting that it strikes an effective balance between whimsical material and sentimental favorites.

As with other Jackson 5 albums, the Corporation and new producer Hal Davis assembled to select the tracks and compose originals. Once Deke Richards (guitar), Freddie Perren (keyboards), Fonce Mizell (keyboards), and Berry Gordy had determined the track listing, the Jackson 5 commenced the recording sessions in July 1970.

## "Have Yourself a Merry Little Christmas"

This classic begins with a straightforward arrangement, with Jermaine Jackson assuming lead vocals. With lush strings adding a sentimental touch to the proceedings, the Jackson 5's street-corner harmonies lend a touch of soul to the Ralph Blane/Hugh Martin–penned original. As the song ends, the tempo suddenly increases as the Jackson 5 launch into a spirited rendition of "We Wish You a Merry Christmas," substituting some of the original lyrics with amusing lines such as "The Jackson 5 wish everybody . . . a groovy new year." Michael punctuates the words with "na-na's," letting Jermaine take the spotlight.

## "Santa Claus Is Coming to Town" (Produced by Hal Davis)

One of the best-known tracks from the *Christmas Album*, this youthful and energetic version of the J. Fred Coots and Haven Gillespie original remains a mainstay on all-Christmas radio stations. Michael's childlike voice suits the subject matter perfectly, his cries of "whoa, yeah" and "one more time, now!" evoking James Brown. Motown released the song as a single in November 1970, with "Christmas Won't Be the Same This Year" gracing the B-side. While now a beloved favorite, the track was only a minor hit, reaching #43 on the UK charts.

## "The Christmas Song"

Made famous by Nat King Cole, this Mel Tormé–composed standard receives a soulful makeover here. Jermaine once again assumes lead vocals, with the Jacksons providing lush backing harmonies. As the song fades, they weave lines from "Jingle Bells" into the lyrics, the chord changes adding a layer of romanticism and images of cozying up to a warm fire.

## "Up on the House Top"

One of the album's highlights, this spirited number features what *Rolling Stone*'s David McGee called a "feisty rendition" with "prominent, energetic bass playing." Indeed, the bass pulses with energy, along with driving drums and horns. Michael plays with the original lyrics, working in all the brothers' names and mentioning their love of basketball, dancing, girls, and other fun pursuits. As the Jackson 5 chant "pitter-patter," Michael recites the reindeer's names, enticing listeners to dance to a drastically remade carol. Why Motown did not release "Up on the House Top" as a single is a mystery.

## "Frosty the Snowman" (Produced by Hal Davis)

From the moment little Michael croons "uh huh, Frosty," one realizes that the Jackson 5's version will differ from the Steve Nelson and Jack Rollins original. The bass, drums, and guitar riff are pure Jackson 5, and the entire group sings the lyrics (with Tito receiving a rare solo). They do not alter the lyrics, but the thumping beat and wah-wah guitar lend the favorite a modern, soulful spin.

## "The Little Drummer Boy" (Produced by Hal Davis)

This beloved classic receives a straightforward treatment, with Michael singing lead. Tito's deep voice can be heard emphasizing the drumbeat throughout. Strings enhance the song's dramatic weight, and Michael's pure vocals fit the track's serious topic perfectly. In his 1971 *Rolling Stone* article, "The Jackson 5: The Men Don't Know but the Little Girls Understand," Ben Fong-Torres declares this rendition the most soulful version ever recorded.

## "Rudolph the Red-Nosed Reindeer" (Produced by Hal Davis)

Johnny Marks's charming Christmas standard needs little more enhancement, so the Jackson 5 adhere closely to the original, with the exception of percussion emulating the reindeer's hooves on the rooftop. Jermaine sings lead, with the Jackson brothers singing backing harmonies.

## "Christmas Won't Be the Same This Year" (Produced by Hal Davis)

One of a handful of originals penned for the group, "Christmas Won't Be the Same This Year" delivers the patented Jackson 5 sound. The bass, guitar, and drums provide an irresistible rhythm tailor-made for dancing. Jermaine's lead vocal suits Pam Sawyer and Laverne Ware's words perfectly, cementing his teen idol status. Unlike other *Christmas Album* tracks, "Christmas Won't Be the Same This Year" begins with brief dialogue between the Jacksons. After establishing that Jermaine is pining over a breakup, the group launches into this catchy song, the B-side to the "Santa Claus Is Coming to Town" single.

## "Give Love on Christmas Day"

Written by the Corporation, this second original lets Michael showcase his impressing phrasing ability. Stressing the importance of love over material things, Michael croons lyrics such as "no greater gift is there than love" with sincerity. Very much in the vein of another melancholy Motown Christmas carol, "Someday at Christmas," the song lends a reflective tone to an otherwise jolly collection. The bridge is particularly effective, with a slightly speeded-up tempo and complicated chord changes that Michael navigates with ease.

## "Someday at Christmas" (Produced by Hal Davis)

Originally recorded by Stevie Wonder in 1967, this somewhat political Christmas tune sounds like a precursor to such politically aware carols as John Lennon's "Happy Xmas (War Is Over)." Wonder's performance stressed the song's serious antiwar message, whereas the Jackson 5's rendition speeds up the tempo and amps

up the bass with complicated runs. Michael's passionate lead vocal (augmented by Jermaine's solo) renders it catchy, though the message does become somewhat obscured with this soul-pop treatment.

Fong-Torres's 1971 *Rolling Stone* cover story on the Jackson 5 proclaims the track a stellar illustration of Michael's wise-beyond-his-years vocal style. When he sings the antiwar lyrics, Fong-Torres wrote, the singer's "high, earnest voice" communicates the song's serious message with sincerity. Older singers like Stevie Wonder may have effectively delivered the

*The Jackson 5 Christmas Album* (1970) capitalized on the group's enormous popularity as well as the season, resulting in solid sales. Today, many of its tracks remain staples on Christmas radio playlists.

*Author's collection*

song's plea for peace, but young Michael manages to transcend his tender age with his emotional reading. "He's not even a grownup yet, and yet he knows," Fong-Torres concluded.

## "I Saw Mommy Kissing Santa Claus" (Produced by Hal Davis)

The other best-known track from the album, "I Saw Mommy Kissing Santa Claus" benefits from Michael's charming singing. While the kissing sound effects and the brief dialogue among the brothers may sound corny, the xylophone parts underscore the song's childish perspective. The brothers' backing vocals of "kissing, kissing" draw chuckles, and the sections where only percussion, the xylophone, and keyboards kick in enhance the track's whimsy.

## 2003 Remaster

The 2003 remaster contains the original album as well as an intriguing outtake.

### "Little Christmas Tree"

Michael recorded this solo song in September and November 1972, and it is notable for two reasons. First, it represents a time when Michael's voice was changing, as was his childish image. Listen closely to his voice and one can detect how his higher vocals were gradually succumbing to adolescence. Second, "Little Christmas Tree" boasts an unusual songwriter: George Clinton, who penned the track with Artie Wayne. The track originally appeared on the 1973 collection *A Motown Christmas*, a successful release that topped the *Billboard* 200.

## 2009 Ultimate Christmas Collection Bonus Tracks

The 2009 version contains bonus material including promotional singles, remixes, and a rare Michael solo holiday recording.

### "Season's Greetings from Michael Jackson"

This spoken greeting was originally issued on a 1973 promotional single.

### "Little Christmas Tree"

As on the 2003 remastered addition, the *Ultimate Christmas Collection* includes the 1973 Michael solo holiday track.

### "Season's Greetings from Tito Jackson"

This spoken greeting was originally issued on a 1973 promotional single.

## "Up on the Housetop" (DJ Spinna Re-Edit)

The original *Jackson 5 Christmas Album* song here receives a remix form DJ Spinna that differs little from the original.

## "Season's Greetings from Jackie Jackson"

This spoken greeting was originally issued on a 1973 promotional single.

## "Rudolph the Red-Nosed Reindeer" (Stripped Mix)

As with the bare-bones versions on the 2009 collection *Michael Jackson: The Stripped Mixes*, this remixed version places Michael and the other Jacksons' vocals in the forefront.

## "Season's Greetings from Jermaine Jackson"

This spoken greeting was originally issued on a 1973 promotional single.

## "Someday at Christmas" (Stripped Mix)

As with "Rudolph the Red-Nosed Reindeer" above, this version of "Someday at Christmas" strips away extra effects to allow the Jackson brothers' vocals to shine.

## "Give Love on Christmas Day" (group a-cappella version)

This lovely track alone is worth the price of the *Ultimate Christmas Collection*. Anyone wondering if the Jackson 5 could really harmonize need only listen to this a-cappella version of the *Jackson 5 Christmas Album* track. Michael's lead singing particularly impresses, his bare voice displaying impressive technical ability for a preteen. His impeccable timing and pitch rival that of any seasoned entertainer.

## "J5 Christmas Medley"

This spliced-together medley functioned as a promotional tool for the original Christmas album, presenting highlights from the collection.

# Counting Off the Days Till Santa Claus Comes

In releasing the *Jackson 5 Christmas Album*, Motown may have been capitalizing on the group's meteoric rise to fame. Pop stars commonly record holiday records, as they are guaranteed bestsellers and tailor-made for gift giving. As Geoff Brown states, music labels frequently view Christmas albums as "cash-ins." *Jackson 5 Christmas Album* surpasses these low expectations through its high-quality production and the Jackson 5's relentless energy. Michael's charming lead vocals combined with Motown's patented beats makes for a timeless record families play at annual family gatherings.

# People Making Lists

## The Essential Jackson 5 Playlist

Duuring their relatively short tenure with Motown, the Jackson 5 recorded an impressive amount of top-shelf pop and soul. What cannot be overlooked, as previously mentioned, is their interesting array of covers. While Jackson 5 collections exist, do they accurately present a picture of the group's multi-genre roots? Which songs best encapsulate his singing and performing style? Are there particular tracks that encompass the various genres comprising his sound? It is a challenge, and one that remains largely subjective. In compiling the hypothetical collection below, the following several factors were considered:

- song popularity
- vocal performance
- timeless quality
- distinctive instrumentation
- lyrical quality.

In creating a playlist, only officially released tracks were considered. Remixes, extended versions, and unofficially released material require separate lists. This proposed collection provides an overview of the Jackson 5's short but influential career.

### Diana Ross Presents the Jackson 5 (1969)

- "I Want You Back"
- "Who's Lovin' You"
- "Stand!"

### ABC (1970)

- "The Love You Save"
- "2-4-6-8"
- "Never Had a Dream Come True"
- "One More Chance"
- "ABC"

### Third Album (1970)

- "I'll Be There"
- "How Funky Is Your Chicken"
- "Goin' Back to Indiana"
- "Mama's Pearl"

## The Jackson 5 Christmas Album (1970)

- "Santa Claus Is Comin' to Town"
- "I Saw Mommy Kissing Santa Claus"
- "Give Love on Christmas Day"
- "Up on the House Top"

## Maybe Tomorrow (1971)

- "Never Can Say Goodbye"
- "Petals"
- "It's Great to Be Here"

Most groups would not release a greatest-hits collection after just a few years in the business. Yet the Jackson 5 had racked up enough hits by December 1971 to merit such a release, which also included the previously unreleased track "Mama's Pearl."     *Author's collection*

## Goin' Back to Indiana (Live, 1971)

- "I Want to Take You Higher"
- "Feelin' Alright"

- "Walk On / The Love You Save"

## Lookin' Through the Windows (1972)

- "Lookin' Through the Windows"
- "I Can Only Give You Love"

- "If I Have to Move a Mountain"

## Skywriter (1973)

- "The Boogie Man"
- "Uppermost"

- "Ooh, I'd Love to Be with You"

## G.I.T.: Get It Together (1973)

- "Get It Together"
- "Don't Say Goodbye Again"
- "You Need Love Like I Do Don't You"

- "Mama I Gotta Brand New Thing (Don't Say No)"
- "Dancing Machine"

Illustrating the Jackson 5's teen-idol status, their early albums frequently included inner-sleeve advertisements such as this one from *Skywriter*. Teenagers sent their money to receive pictures, magazines, and other souvenirs featuring their favorite group members.

*Author's collection*

### The Jackson 5 in Japan (1973)

- "Lookin' Through the Windows"
- "Got to Be There"

- "Superstition"

### Dancing Machine (1974)

- "Dancing Machine"
- "I Am Love"

- "If I Don't Love You This Way"

### Moving Violation (1975)

- "Moving Violation"
- "Body Language (Do the Love Dance)"

- "(You Were Made) Especially for Me"
- "Breezy"

### Joyful Jukebox Music (1976)

- "Love Is the Thing You Need"

- "Through Thick and Thin"

### Boogie (1979)

- "One Day I'll Marry You"
- "Just Because I Love You"

### Soulsation! (1995)

- "Can't Get Ready for Losing You"
- "You Ain't Giving Me What I Want (So I'm Taking It All Back)"

### I Want You Back! Unreleased Masters (2009)

- "Buttercup"
- "Lucky Day"
- "Love Comes in Different Flavors"

### Live at the Forum (2010)

- "There Was a Time" (1970 concert)
- "Who's Loving You" (1970 concert)
- "Never Can Say Goodbye" (1972 concert)
- "I Wanna Be Where You Are" (actually from the Save the Children concert, but included on this compilation)

### Come and Get It: The Rare Pearls (2012)

- "Feelin' Alright" (studio version)
- "Jumbo Sam"
- "Keep an Eye"
- "Movin'"
- "You Better Watch Out"
- "Keep off the Grass"
- "If I Can't Nobody Can"
- "Love Trip"

While one playlist cannot fully capture the Jackson 5's sound and influence, this selection of up-tempo numbers, ballads, covers, and live renditions presents an overview of their career. Listening to these hits and album tracks may inspire future generations to dig deeper into the group's catalogue. In addition, Michael Jackson fans can trace his development as an interpretative vocalist through the mix, as he introduces techniques he would hone to perfection in his solo work.

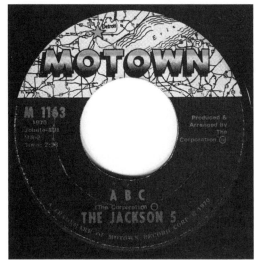

"ABC" not only topped the charts in 1970, it has endured through hip-hop artists frequently sampling its melody, its beat, and Michael's outstanding lead vocal.    *Author's collection*

# 12

# Make Me a Believer in Rock 'n' Roll Fever and Bring Back the Memories

## What the Jackson 5 Contributed to Modern Music and Pop Culture

When the Jackson 5 released the single "ABC" in 1970, it not only became a huge hit but also signaled a change in pop music. *Billboard*'s April 25 Hot 100 chart revealed a surprising phenomenon: the Jackson 5 had knocked the Beatles from the #1 position, with "ABC" supplanting "Let It Be" as the week's best-selling single. The young band repeated this feat just a few months later, when "The Love You Save" topped "The Long and Winding Road" as the nation's top song on July 27, 1970.

This chart action reflects a changing of the guard, when the biggest band of the 1960s dissolved their partnership, giving way to a new generation of artists. In this case, newcomers the Jackson 5 injected youth and a new R&B sound to mainstream music, paving the way for future boy bands, child singers, and quality pop music. They raised the bar for bubblegum pop, proving that its songs need not be instantly disposable. In addition, they melded soul with teen pop—a mixture that had not been seen since Frankie Lymon and the Teenagers. Finally, the Jackson 5 released early dance records that predicted one of the biggest genres to emerge from that decade: disco. Rather than an instantly forgettable teenage boy band, the Jackson 5 served as a catalyst that propelled soul and R&B onto the pop charts.

### African American Impact

While hard to believe now, the Jackson 5's success with both African American and white audiences was deemed surprising in the early 1970s. In a November 27, 1970, *Life* article entitled "A Black Teen Breakthrough," Albert Goldman expressed apparent disbelief that the Jackson 5 could create hysteria evoking Beatlemania. Alan Smith published a similar article in the May 29, 1971, issue of the *New Musical*

*Express*, curiously titled, "Jackson 5: Jacksons Give Teenyblacks Hope." The author drew frequent comparisons with 1960s made-for-TV-act-turned-real-band the Monkees, writing that in America, the Jackson 5 bridged "that big gap between black awareness and the whole Monkees thing."

The Jackson 5 impacted African American audiences deeply, although 1970s writers apparently struggled with describing the effect. In his essay commemorating the Jackson 5's 1997 induction into the Rock and Roll Hall of Fame, Ben Fong-Torres states that the group's fashions and cute choreography suggested "black bubblegum. Pseudo-psychedelic fashions to the hokey hilt." Indeed, Smith's piece confirmed this initial assessment: "You've heard of teenybop? The Jackson Five are Teeny-black, Afro hairstyles and smiling faces, and many a dream of escape from the ghetto will have been nurtured on their real-life discovery and swift trip to national fame."

Black teen audiences did identify with the Jackson 5, but in a more profound way than Smith suggests. Benefitting from retrospection, dancer Stephen McMillian fondly recalled in a *Soul Train* blog entry how he and other 1970s teens imitated the group's hairstyles and fashion choices. "It was the first time that they had a young group in the music industry whom they could look up to, admire and emulate," McMillian writes, in his 2013 essay "Classic *Soul Train* Album Spotlight: The Jackson 5's *ABC*."

Music critic and historian Nelson George writes of his pride in the group in *Thriller: The Musical Life of Michael Jackson*. He recalls seeing them at Madison Square Garden in New York and being mesmerized by their fashions and hair. "Their Afros, perfect ovals of jet-black hair, look like halos," he states. "Though the crowd is very integrated, there's a palpable sense of pride emanating from the many black families in attendance." For the audience, the Jackson 5's natural hair and clothes promoted their background. "The Jackson kids were unusually well dressed. Their immaculately maintained Afros signaled black pride," George writes, adding that their stage costumes mixed psychedelic elements with streetwise touches like applejack caps.

In the 1972 *New Musical Express* article "The Jackson Five: Five Pranksters Puppets," Roger St. Pierre discussed the band's multiracial appeal with Tito Jackson. While Tito Jackson stated that in the northern United States they played to primarily African American audiences, their appeal in the South was split evenly among black and white listeners.

Not since Lymon and the Teenagers had the music world seen African American teen idols, and the Jackson 5 encountered some barriers. Peers such as the Osmonds received regular coverage in teen magazines, while the Jackson 5 would appear far less often in major publications such as *16* and *Fave*. As Taraborrelli writes, "Because of their color, the Jackson 5 could never be perceived as teen idols in those magazines, despite all of their success and good looks." It took the African American teen magazine *Right On!* to garner the Jackson 5 the press coverage they desired, with the publication featuring the group on its premiere 1971 issue. It continued promoting the group until their 1975 departure from Motown.

While *Right On!* may have inspired teenage girls to swoon over their favorite stars, the publication symbolized how African Americans played a large part in pop culture. As George explains in *Thriller*, rather than promoting black nationalism, it presented the black teen as a desirable consumer market. Remarkably, this was a relatively new idea in the early 1970s. "It was the *Tiger Beat* of the bushy Afro, bell-bottomed, body poppin', *Soul Train*–watching generation," George states. "It was written for kids who'd experienced the civil rights struggle through television and newspaper headlines. We were gonna have more fun than our parents, and the J5, in multicolored gear, was a symbol of a more carefree vision of black life."

In addition, the Jackson 5 were the first group since the Beatles to be immortalized in cartoon form. While the Beatles' cartoon series featured the Fab Four in zany adventures, accompanied by their biggest hits, the Jackson 5 cartoon held a greater significance. As George states, "When I think of this series, the word 'normal' comes to mind. Having black kids (alongside Bill Cosby's Fat Albert) on television on Saturday mornings helped to make black people less exotic to white peers." Like the Beatles or cartoon bands like Josie and the Pussycats and the Archies, the Jackson 5 could engage in hilarious adventures. "The cartoons weren't profound, but they had an impact," George concludes.

Through their music and image, the Jackson 5 achieved more than simply entertaining their enthusiastic fans. They provided African American teens with a sense of pride, as they could relate to five young men who looked like them and dressed like them. In their television specials, the Jackson brothers professed their love of basketball and used current slang, emphasizing that they were regular kids despite their fame. In Fong-Torres's essay to commemorate the Jackson 5's induction into the Rock and Roll Hall of Fame, he quotes a fan letter written to the now defunct *Soul* magazine during the height of the group's popularity. "I want to say how proud all us kids are to have a group like the J5 today," the fan, C. E. from New York, wrote. "It wasn't too long ago when kids got on the stage and were laughed at. The J5 can communicate with young and old, black and white."

## Youthful Takeover of Music

When the Jackson 5 knocked the Beatles out of the #1 position on the *Billboard* Hot 100, it signaled the group's ascension into "music hero" status. It also ignited the beginning of a new force in R&B and pop: youth. While teenagers certainly bought records by the Beatles, the Rolling Stones, the Supremes, and other popular acts, most of these idols were not teens themselves. At eleven years old, Michael Jackson introduced the concept of the child star not only to Motown but to the music world in general. In turn, teens gained renewed power as a commercial market.

In his *Life* article, Albert Goldman noted that the Jackson 5 symbolized what he called a "take-over everywhere in the teen music business by the teens themselves." Citing other family groups such as the Osmonds, the Cowsills, and the Partridge Family (the latter a made-for-TV act who were not related and did not play their own instruments), Goldman argued that these acts as well as the Jackson 5 "point to a novel configuration in pop culture centering on images of childhood and the family instead of adolescence and rebellion."

In addition, Goldman discussed the then-new target market: the preteen (or "sub-teen," as he called it in 1970). Pointing out that they bought Monkees records, *16* Magazine, and other bubblegum pop records, he concluded that preteens "are fast becoming the hottest creative and consuming public for pop culture."

The Jackson 5 indeed set records for scoring hits at such young ages. As of 2014, Michael Jackson ranks as the youngest artist to top the *Billboard* Hot 100, as he was just eleven years old when "I Want You Back" reached #1 in January 1970.

More importantly, the Jackson 5 injected a needed dose of youth to Motown and pop music in general. In his Rock and Roll Hall of Fame essay, Ben Fong-Torres assesses their impact. At a time when Motown was suffering an identity crisis, its competitors usurping its claim to representing the "Sound of Young America," the Jackson 5 spearheaded the label's commercial and creative resurgence. "At a time of acid rock and psychedelic soul, of war protests and black power, Motown could offer a wholesome family group in 'fros and mod duds, dancing, playing and singing non-threatening pop music," he writes.

Interestingly, Roger St. Pierre would note in the 1972 *New Musical Express* article "The Jackson Five: Five Pranksters Puppets" that while the Jackson 5 most appealed to teens in the UK, their US impact seemed broader. In the US, they hit all age groups. He cited Tito Jackson's explanation of "I'll Be There" as expanding beyond bubblegum.

Today, teens and tweens remain crucial markets in pop culture. The Jackson 5's record and concert sales illustrated adolescents' desire to see and hear artists they can also consider peers. Long after the Jackson 5 departed Motown, their impact lingers through youthful artists such as Debbie Gibson, Tiffany, Britney Spears, Christina Aguilera, Justin Bieber, and Usher.

## General Pop Music Impact

As the Jackson 5 aged, their music grew in sophistication and content. At the same time, dance music began emerging from New York's black and gay clubs, although disco had not yet reached the mainstream. The Jackson 5 embraced this new genre, recording some of the art form's earliest hits. Beginning with the 1973 album *G.I.T.: Get It Together*, Michael Jackson and his brothers experimented with disco through songs such as "Get It Together," "Dancing Machine," and "Body Language (Do the Love Dance)," adding their polished sheen to the emerging music movement. Music critic Tony Sclafani explained their contribution in a June 26, 2009, MSNBC.com article entitled "Jackson Changed Course of Music, Society": "They brought R&B to white preteens, helping to create the eventual audience that would be receptive to disco."

Another genre has embraced the Jackson 5: hip hop. Since the 1980s, artists have sampled sections of the group's biggest hits, with these hooks providing the basis for classic rap and hip-hop tracks. The following list represents just a few of them:

- "Candy Girl"—New Edition (1983, samples "ABC")
- "Overweighter"—Heavy D. and the Boyz (1987, samples "ABC")

- "Chillin' with Santa"—Derek B. (1987, samples Jackson 5's version of "Up on the House Top")
- "Ev'rybody Loves a Star"—Doug E. Fresh (1988, samples "One More Chance")
- "Dancin' Machine"—MC Hammer (1990, samples "Dancing Machine")
- "O.P.P."—Naughty by Nature (1991, samples "ABC")
- "Jump"—Kriss Kross (1992, samples "I Want You Back")
- "Baby Come Back"—K-Ci & JoJo (1997, samples "Whatever You Got, I Want")
- "Izzo (H.O.V.A.)"—Jay Z (2001, samples "I Want You Back")
- "Something Big"—Mary Mary (2011, samples "Mama's Pearl")

All of these tracks relied on the Jackson 5's knack for memorable grooves and youthful vigor to power their songs. In addition, the nostalgia factor drew first generation fans to hip hop, lending credence to the relatively new genre. By incorporating classic Jackson 5 hooks, these artists brought the Motown group to new generations, ensuring the Jackson brothers' longevity.

## Impact on Current Artists

The Jackson 5's pioneering experiments combining pop with disco reverberate in artists ranging from the Bee Gees to Justin Timberlake and Usher. Sclafani points out that Prince's first hit, "I Wanna Be Your Lover," borrows from Michael Jackson's singing style as well as the group's beat.

Today's pop music scene has seen an explosion in electronic dance music (EDM) and electro-pop, a trend that the Jackson 5 foresaw in the early 1970s. As J. Randy Taraborrelli posits in *Michael Jackson: The Magic, the Madness, the Whole Story*, singles like "Dancing Machine" were years ahead of their time, "and on to the electric sound of the eighties—the style of 'Dancing Machine' is similar to a sound that, a dozen years later, would be known as 'techno-pop.'"

While the Jackson 5 contributed to disco and techno-pop's foundations, they also inspired generations of young artists—many family groups—to record pop that appeals to teens while incorporating irresistible dance beats or memorable lyrics. These groups span from the 1970s to today; they range in ages and sound but all owe a great debt to the Jackson 5.

## The Sylvers

Viewed as the South's answer to the Jackson 5, the Sylvers featured nine of ten siblings from a large family. Hailing from Memphis, the group found early success with 1972's Leon Sylvers–penned single "Fool's Paradise," a grittier record than their later pop-oriented material. Energetic choreography accompanied the 1976 crowd-pleaser "High School Dance" and the charmingly innocent "Hot Line."

Drawing further parallels to the Jackson 5, the group tried spinning off one member into a solo career. Young Foster Sylvers, who possessed vocals eerily similar to those of a young Michael Jackson, scored a 1973 R&B hit with "Misdemeanor," a track All Music's Jason Ankeny dubbed "one of the most underrated funk jams ever." In an odd coincidence, Foster Sylvers recorded "Misdemeanor" at eleven years old—the same age Michael first achieved fame with the Jackson 5.

Interestingly, they shared even more in common with the Jackson brothers: songwriter/ producer Freddie Perren. Perren co-wrote and produced the Sylvers' biggest hit, 1975's "Boogie Fever." Leon Sylvers experienced the greatest career success, becoming a top songwriter and producer for such acts as New Kids on the Block, Howard Hewett, Shalamar, the Whispers, and Smokey Robinson.

## DeBarge

Among the legends present at the *Motown 25* celebration in 1983 were young newcomers DeBarge. The quintet's presence was no accident—indeed, Motown heavily promoted them as the new Jackson 5, a group of fresh-faced siblings who recorded mostly smooth R&B. Composed of four brothers (El, Mark, James, and Randy) and one sister (Bunny), DeBarge released hit singles from 1981 until about 1985, but drug problems and family squabbles ultimately resulted in the group's 1989 breakup.

Their first few years showed much promise, with El DeBarge's sweet and smooth vocals evoking Michael's style. While the siblings did not execute difficult choreography, their mix of ballads and up-tempo numbers landed on the

A member of the family group the Sylvers, Foster Sylvers was being groomed to be the next Michael Jackson. His 1973 solo hit "Misdemeanor," penned by older brother Leon, is an underrated soul workout. *Author's collection*

Motown had high hopes for its 1980s family act DeBarge, with publications such as *Rolling Stone* hailing them as the new Jackson 5. Their 1982 album *All This Love* produced several hits, including the title track and the ballad "I Like It." *Author's collection*

R&B and pop charts. While their 1981 debut failed to produce hits, their second effort, *All This Love*, soared up the charts courtesy of the singles "I Like It," "Time Will Reveal," and the title track. Their brand of R&B mixed with adult-contemporary sounds culminated in their 1983 release *In a Special Way*, which featured yet another hit, "Love Me in a Special Way." Motown continually groomed the group to become the next Jackson 5, leading to their appearance on *Motown 25* and the inclusion of their song "Rhythm of the Night" in the 1985 Motown film *The Last Dragon*.

Buoyed by the massive success of "Rhythm of the Night," DeBarge racked up two more hits, "You Wear It Well" and "Who's Holding Donna Now?," before El DeBarge departed the group to start a solo career, his best-known song being "Who's Johnny?" from the *Short Circuit* soundtrack. Chico DeBarge also tried his luck, scoring the moderate 1986 hit "Talk to Me." While DeBarge did not achieve the longevity and lingering influence of the Jackson 5, their sound smoothed and updated the Jackson brothers' brand of pop for the 1980s.

## New Edition

The 1980s' answer to the Jackson 5, the original quintet (Ricky Bell, Michael Bivins, Bobby Brown, Ronnie DeVoe, and Ralph Tresvant) scored hits combining R&B and hip hop, predating the "new jack swing" sound that would explode later in the 1980s and early 1990s. When Brown departed the group in 1989 to embark on a solo career, Johnny Gill joined the group as they were moving away from their previous bubblegum sound. All members eventually experienced success as solo

artists (Brown, Gill, Tresvant) and in a spinoff group (Bel Biv DeVoe), but they would occasionally reunite and perform as they did as Boston teenagers.

Unsurprisingly, they were discovered when they performed "The Love You Save" in a 1980 talent contest. Boston entrepreneur Maurice Starr signed them to his Streetwise label and co-wrote their first single, "Candy Girl," a track that mimicked the rhythm and chord changes of "ABC." After the song topped the R&B charts, they released an album of the same name. "Popcorn Love" and "Is This the End?" followed, drawing the attention of MCA. After legal wrangling, New Edition fired Starr and

New Edition were the 1980s incarnation of the Jackson 5; their 1984 self-titled album provided their breakthrough, spawning the hits "Cool It Now" and "Mr. Telephone Man."
*Author's collection*

signed with the larger label; Starr would go on to repeat his "boy band" success with New Kids on the Block.

The move greatly benefitted New Edition, however, as they experienced their greatest success yet with their 1984 self-titled album. "Cool It Now" effectively updated the Motown sound for the '80s generation, while "Mr. Telephone Man" continued the retro vibe. When Gill joined the group, they scored another smash with "Can You Stand the Rain." The group then went on hiatus to pursue solo projects; the six reunited in 1996 for the *Home Again* album, which spawned the #1 R&B single "Hit Me Off." While they have since broken up and reunited, their place in R&B history is assured. Their difficult choreography, youthful-voiced lead singer, and initial pop sound evoked memories of the Jackson 5.

## Hanson

While they did not experience a lengthy career, this trio from Tulsa, Oklahoma, are remembered for the relentlessly catchy 1997 hit "MMMBop." The Hanson brothers co-wrote their music, played their own instruments—a rare quality for a "boy band"—and their harmonies suggested talent surpassing their tender ages. The members were Isaac, aged sixteen (guitar); Taylor, thirteen (lead singer and keyboardist); and Zac, eleven (drums). From 1992 to 1995, they shopped their material to several labels, finally earning a contract with Mercury Records on the strength of an early version of "MMMBop." The label paired the trio with a few producers, including the red-hot Dust Brothers, who had recently helmed Beck's *Odelay*. The result was a mix of pop with hip-hop beats and scratches, and the revamped "MMMBop" topped the *Billboard* Hot 100. They next released the follow-up single "Where's the Love," but it failed to achieve the same commercial success.

While Hanson never replicated their 1997 hit album *Middle of Nowhere*, they continue recording for independent labels. Their significance primarily rests with their role in ushering a new wave of teen pop, powered by acts such as the Backstreet Boys, Christina Aguilera, Britney Spears, and *NSYNC. Taylor's vocals echo Michael Jackson's on Hanson's early recordings, and tracks like "MMMBop" echo the Jackson 5's exuberance and boundless youthful energy.

## *NSYNC

Continuing the 1990s teen pop boom was *NSYNC, a boy-band quintet that emerged from Orlando, Florida, in 1996. J. C. Chasez and Justin Timberlake met as performers on the new *Mickey Mouse Club* TV show; after both returned to Nashville, they embarked unsuccessfully on solo careers. Relocating to Orlando, they formed *NSYNC by adding Chris Kirkpatrick, Joey Fatone, and Lance Bass. Recording their debut album in 1998, the group became an instant hit in Europe. Once the singles "I Want You Back" and "Tearing Up My Heart" ranked high on European charts, the group decided to test their luck in their home country. An American tour of roller rinks followed, as did a Christmas album. They were poised for even bigger success, except for one obstacle: their manager.

By 1999, *NSYNC was represented by Lou Pearlman, an impresario who had previously launched the Backstreet Boys to stardom. Wanting to sever their contract and sign with the Jive label, the group engaged in prolonged legal proceedings with Pearlman that delayed their follow-up album, *No Strings Attached*, for several months (in an echo of New Edition's problems firing Starr, Pearlman's mentor). Once these contract issues were resolved in 2000, *No Strings Attached* exploded through hits such as "Bye Bye Bye," "It's Gonna Be Me," and "This I Promise You." *Celebrity* followed in 2001: a more mature effort that displayed Timberlake's emergence as a lead singer and songwriter. *NSYNC split soon afterward as Timberlake's solo career took off, although Chasez did release his own solo album, *Schizophrenic*.

*NSYNC's sound did not precisely mimic the Jackson 5's, but their close harmonies, elaborate choreography, hip stage costumes, and teen heartthrob image owe a great debt to the Motown band. Those two worlds came together in 2001 when Michael joined *NSYNC onstage at the MTV Music Video Awards for a rendition of the band's then-current hit "Pop."

## Honorable Mentions

Countless other boy bands can thank the Jackson 5 for paving the way for their tight choreography and genre-spanning sound, proving that bubblegum pop need not be inherently disposable. The following list includes some honorable mentions:

- Five Star (1980s)
- New Kids on the Block (1980s)
- The Jets (1980s)
- Backstreet Boys (1990s–2000s)
- Take That (1990s)

- Boyz II Men (1990s)
- Boyzone (1990s–2010s)
- Westlife (1990s–2010s)
- One Direction (2010s)

## Never Can Say Goodbye: The End of an Era

Due to creative control disputes, the Jackson 5 departed Motown in 1975, renaming themselves the Jacksons. Jermaine Jackson stayed behind, but the quintet (now officially including Randy Jackson) moved on to CBS Records, entering a new phase in their professional development. While their sound matured as they gradually assumed complete control over songwriting and production, their tight harmonies and compelling stage shows remained. Those two elements were what propelled the Jackson 5 to fame, and their influence on music and pop culture continues, forty years later.

# 13

# The Good Times We Shared Together

## The Jacksons Meet Gamble and Huff

**B**y the mid-1970s, the Jackson brothers found themselves at a crossroads. Exasperated by Motown's refusal to grant them more creative control, coupled with declining album sales, the group lobbied to depart the label. Two obstacles hindered the move, however: Berry Gordy claimed that he owned the name "Jackson 5," and Jermaine Jackson had recently married Gordy's daughter Hazel, placing him in the middle of two families. After prolonged legal proceedings, five of the six Jacksons severed ties with the label, but Gordy forced them to change their group moniker to simply "The Jacksons." Jermaine elected to remain with Motown, with Gordy promising him a higher-profile solo career.

Finally free, the Jacksons signed with CBS Records subsidiary Epic, effectively starting their next career phase. Now older, the group needed to craft their sound to fit current tastes and move away from the bubblegum image. CBS recruited Kenny Gamble and Leon Huff, the songwriters and procedures who had developed Philadelphia soul through their label Philadelphia International (another CBS subsidiary), to helm the Jacksons' debut album. The duo had a solid track record, composing and producing hits for Melvin and the Blue Notes, the O'Jays, and Billy Paul, thus it seemed a no-brainer for the team to pen hits showcasing the Jacksons' tight harmonies and soulful sound.

Released in 1976, *The Jacksons* spawned the hit "Enjoy Yourself," but the album performed modestly. Critics seemed underwhelmed with the effort, with *Rolling Stone* critic Ken Tucker dismissing the album in his 1977 review for its "drab disco numbers," "shabby ballads," and "perfunctory" instrumentation. Today's music critics continue to pan *The Jacksons*, with All Music's Jason Elias singling out its "derivative tracks" and "by-the-numbers Philly tracks that could have been easily done by Lou Rawls." Only Michael Jackson's skilled lead vocals, Tucker and Elias agreed, saved the album from oblivion. In *Thriller: The Musical Life of Michael Jackson*, even Nelson George sums up the group's two-album stint under Gamble and Huff as average.

Almost forty years later, does *The Jacksons* deserve the same judgment, or has time proved beneficial to the album? An examination of the album's inception and recording reveals an alternative interpretation—in essence, *The Jacksons* represents the group's immersion into disco, early experiments with songwriting, and their emergence as adult entertainers. The roots of their 1978 comeback with *Destiny* lay here, along with early signs of Michael as a contemporary R&B solo artist.

## "Show You the Way to Go": The Jacksons Move to Epic

Still acting as his sons' manager, Joseph Jackson eyed CBS Records when he and the boys grew dissatisfied with Motown in 1975. Along with a solid contract, CBS offered Gamble and Huff, proven hit makers who deftly melded the popular disco sound with old school soul, with lush string arrangements providing the perfect cushion for lead singers' voices. The O'Jays' "Back Stabbers," Melvin and the Blue Notes' "The Love I Lost" (often cited as one of the first disco records), the Three Degrees' "When Will I See You Again," and People's Choice's "Do It Any Way You Wanna" became hits in the clubs and on the charts. At the same time, Gamble and Huff proved they could write more than danceable records, as they worked social commentary into singles such as the O'Jays' "For the Love of Money" as well as Harold Melvin and the Blue Notes' "Wake Up Everybody" and "Bad Luck."

As Taraborrelli writes in *Michael Jackson: The Magic, the Madness, the Whole Story*, Joseph admired CBS's commitment to black music but felt that Philadelphia International was too small a label for his sons. Joseph and the Jacksons completed negotiations with CBS and Epic by June 1975, but the band could not enter the recording studio for the next eight months. The Jackson 5's Motown contract did not expire until March 1976; since the Jacksons left Motown before their contract ended, they agreed not to release any new albums during that time period. To fill the time, Joseph struck a deal with the CBS network to air a Jacksons variety series (see chapter 16); in between filming episodes, the Jacksons recorded their debut album for their new label.

Wanting the Jacksons' first effort to be strong, CBS/Epic recruited Gamble and Huff to helm the project. In turn, the duo tapped their in-house Philadelphia International producers Dexter Wansel, Gene McFadden, and John Whitehead to assemble a solid song lineup. In a few years, McFadden and Whitehead would evolve into disco artists on their own with the anthem "Ain't No Stopping Us Now." For the first time, the Jacksons would be allowed to write some of their own material, with two original compositions making the final cut: "Blues Away," Michael's debut as a songwriter, and the group effort "Style of Life." Philadelphia International's house band MFSB ("Love Is the Message," "T.S.O.P.") rounded out the album personnel, completing a promising lineup that would help the Jacksons transition into modern, adult performers.

While the Jacksons worked on their variety series, Gamble and Huff crafted demos and planned for the group to meet them in Philadelphia for the recording sessions. The duo informed Joseph that they would not interfere with the Jacksons' patented harmonies but would pen songs that would play to their strengths.

In a February 1977 interview with David Nathan for *Blues & Soul*, four of the five Jacksons (curiously, the article does not specify which ones) stated that while they initially wanted to work with Earth, Wind & Fire founder Maurice White, they found willing collaborators in Gamble and Huff. "When we first went down to Philly, they allowed us to listen to the material they'd prepared for us and we selected what we liked!" the unnamed Jackson brothers said. "They gave us complete freedom. And we went for songs with nice melodies, with messages, songs that had some kind of meaning."

## *The Jacksons* **Recording Sessions**

In *Moonwalk*, Michael recalls learning how to write and develop a song by watching Gamble and Huff in the studio. He watched the songwriters present the tracks to the group, with Huff playing piano as Gamble sang the tunes. These demos taught Michael what he dubbed the "anatomy of a song," particularly Gamble's gift for melody. "I'd sit there like a hawk, observing every decisions, listening to every note," he writes.

*The Jacksons* is more than just their first collaboration with Gamble and Huff: it also contains the Jacksons' first original compositions, "Blues Away" and "Style of Life." Finally granted control over some of their material, Michael and his brothers were eager to flex their new writing muscles. During breaks from shooting the Jacksons' variety series, the brothers would record demos of their new tracks at home. As Michael describes in *Moonwalk*, he and his brothers felt great pride in the two songs, but they waited to bring them to Gamble and Huff until they were perfected.

Recording sessions took place during the summer and fall of 1976; in order to capture the Philly sound, the Jacksons traveled to Gamble and Huff's Sigma Sound Studios in Philadelphia. Clearly, the Jacksons relished altering their sound and image to fit current tastes. As Geoff Brown writes in *Michael Jackson: A Life in Music*, "In its balance between dance floor, love interest and concern for the moral and physical future of mankind and the planet . . . [it] set the pattern for the first phase of the rest of their lives." Already hallmarks of Gamble and Huff productions, those themes would reappear on future Jacksons albums such as *Destiny* and *Triumph*.

As Brown notes, Michael's voice had clearly matured in depth and scope, and Gamble and Huff's arrangements fully exploit his new vocal talents. He also mentions that Michael was given more freedom to interpret the lyrics as he wished; indeed, *The Jacksons* foreshadows the Michael Jackson of *Off the Wall* in terms of singing embellishments and improvisations.

The Jacksons' self-titled 1976 album marked their debut with new label CBS/Epic Records. *Author's collection*

## "Enjoy Yourself" (Kenny Gamble, Leon Huff; recorded June 1976)

A favorite of Michael's, this highly danceable track stands as the group's first hit under the "Jacksons" moniker. He would cite its infectious beat, catchy guitar riff, and horns as the song's strongest ingredients. Indeed, "Enjoy Yourself" capitalized on the growing disco craze while retaining old school soul roots through street-corner harmonies. Rarely had Michael sounded like he was having as much fun as when he chants "just get on down!" as the song fades out. "Enjoy Yourself" became the brothers' first hit as the Jacksons and highlighted Michael's emerging role as full front man for the group.

As a side note, "Enjoy Yourself" became the Jacksons' first single to be certified gold by the Recording Industry Association of America (RIAA). Motown never participated in the RIAA because they did not allow the organization to audit their books, according to Lisa Campbell's *Michael: The Complete Story of the King of Pop.*

## "Think Happy" (Kenny Gamble, Leon Huff; recorded October 1976)

A rumbling beat followed by a keyboard riff leads to a tight string section accenting the rapid tempo before a rock element is introduced through electric guitar. The Jacksons execute cascading harmonies on the chorus, with Michael using vocalizations that would make frequent appearances on future records (raspiness, grunts, and stutters).

## "Good Times" (Kenny Gamble, Leon Huff; recorded October 1976)

One of the album's highlights, the beautiful love song features an emotional performance by Michael. Chronicling the end of a love affair, the track focuses on happy memories rather than the bitterness of the breakup. "I treasure my experience with you," Michael sings, painting pictures of a young love. "Good Times" stresses how the main character learned about love and a long-lasting relationship from his brief romance. Short horn blasts punctuate phrases such as "learning how to give, learning how to live, learning how to love," again underscoring the knowledge gained from a relationship's beginning and end. The ballad fits with the album's themes of optimism, but in a mature, nuanced fashion.

## "Keep on Dancing" (Dexter Wansel) (recorded October 1976)

Anyone looking for evidence of how much Michael had developed as a vocalist need look no further than this dance floor–worthy track. His raspiness toward the end of the track adds energy and a slight edge to an otherwise upbeat "get on the floor" kind of song. Geoff Brown pans this track, stating that the tempo resembles "an insistent thud" instead of a fast pace, the tempo suddenly accelerating halfway into the track. While it does not rank among the strongest Jacksons tunes, it contains what would become a common Michael refrain: "get on up!" This phrase may also pay tribute to Michael's music and dance idol James Brown.

The group filmed a music video for the song, performed it on the 1977 season of *The Jacksons,* and included it in the *Destiny* tour BBC broadcast.

## "Blues Away" (Michael Jackson; recorded October 1976)

Michael's excitement over his debut solo composition is palpable in his autobiography, *Moonwalk*. While he never performed it in concert during the solo years, he still praises it as a "light song about overcoming a deep depression," citing Jackie Wilson's "Lonely Teardrops" as an influence. Singing in a lower register, almost whispering, and using vocalizations such as accentuating the "t" in the word "but" ("but-uh"), Michael sings of positivity in the face of possible rejection. He hopes his love interest will agree to be with him, but even if she turns him down, he croons, "I've got the power" and "you can't take my blues away / No matter what you say." Is music itself the cure for his blues?

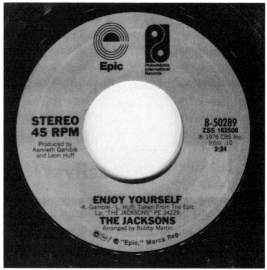

"Enjoy Yourself," the Kenny Gamble/Leon Huff–penned single from *The Jacksons*, marked two important firsts for the group: Randy Jackson's debut as an official member and their first hit as the Jacksons.

*Author's collection*

The lighthearted vocal blend his brothers provide at the end, gently scatting over the string-filled arrangement, suggests the answer.

To underscore Michael being the song's primary composer, he performed the song alone during a 1977 episode of the *Jacksons* variety show.

## "Show You the Way to Go" (Kenny Gamble, Leon Huff; recorded October 1976)

Featuring strings and smooth harmonies, "Show You the Way to Go" best reflects the Philly Soul sound. Michael singled out the track as his favorite from the album, even stating it was one of the best tracks the Jacksons ever recorded. "I loved the hi-hat and strings fluttering alongside us like birds' wings," he writes in *Moonwalk*. Here the narrator informs the listener that he may not hold all the answers, but he knows one thing: "We can come together / And think like one," he sings. Just follow him, Michael croons, and trust that he holds the key to peace. While this sounds messianic, in context he serves as a dynamic leader, emboldening listeners with his unending faith that humanity can "get the job done."

While this track failed to sell well in the US, it performed better than "Enjoy Yourself" in the UK. On June 25, 1977, "Show You the Way to Go" knocked Kenny Rogers's "Lucille" out of the top spot on the charts. According to Cadman and Halstead's *Michael Jackson: The Early Years*, the Jacksons could not perform their hit single on *Top of the Pops*, so the show aired a live rendition from the 1977 Jacksons' TV variety show instead. The track lingered on into the *Destiny* years, making an

"Show You the Way to Go," the second single from *The Jacksons*, was Michael Jackson's favorite from the album.     *Author's collection*

appearance during a concert broadcast by the BBC during that tour.

## "Living Together" (Dexter Wansel; recorded October 1976)

Extending the message behind "Show You the Way to Go," "Living Together" further expresses hope and optimism for humanity. Interestingly, Michael writes in *Moonwalk* that the lyrics indirectly address the turmoil the Jacksons had experienced leaving Motown. Only by uniting as a family and working together could they survive and rebuild their careers. In addition to strong Jacksons harmonies, the track also features intricate, pulsating percussion that propels the song and reflects its lyrics. Have a good time, because life is short: "Have yourself a good, good time / But don't you know it's getting late?" they sing. Only by "living together," as the title states, can the world dwell in "sweet, sweet peace," as Michael pleads in the track.

"Living Together" made an appearance on the Jacksons' 1977 TV series.

## "Strength of One Man" (Gene McFadden, John Whitehead, Victor Carstarphen; recorded October 1976)

The song's chord changes and popping bass lines, particularly toward the end, are among the most noteworthy elements of the track. Michael executes vocal tics that would resurface in later tracks, such as the way he repeats key lines such as "tell me." At one point his finger snapping can be heard—a technique he would use in later recordings such as "Billie Jean."

## "Dreamer" (Kenny Gamble, Leon Huff; recorded October 1976)

Like other Jacksons tracks, "Dreamer" radiates an idealistic view of the world. However, the ballad communicates naïveté in romance. Over fluttering strings and tinkling vibes, Michael admits that he will always be a dreamer; while he was dreaming of peace in previous tracks, here he refers to unrequited love. "A romantic fool, that's what I am," he sings, with a sigh. As his brothers harmonize on key lines such as "dreaming my life away," Michael sings in a lower register of how his vision of love is just that: a transient vision. "Dreamer" is a particularly melancholy love song, a story of a man who finds love only in his nightly dreams and fantasies.

"Dreamer" was released as a single in the UK as the follow-up to "Show You the Way to Go." The Jacksons performed the track on *Top of the Pops*, and the song peaked at #22 on the British charts. In *Moonwalk*, Michael cites the track as one of his personal favorites. Expressing the belief that Gamble and Huff wrote the track to address his personality, he writes that he had always been a dreamer, that he would use his imagination to set goals and conquer any roadblocks.

## "Style of Life" (Tito Jackson, Michael Jackson; recorded October 1976)

Predominantly written by Tito, "Style of Life" emulates earlier Jackson 5 dance cuts like "Dancing Machine." The main difference, according to Michael, was that "we kept it a little leaner and meaner than Motown would have cut it." Brown's *Michael Jackson: A Life in Music* criticizes the track for having too many producers and voices, or "group democracy gone berserk." Clearly, Tito and Michael wanted to compose a danceable track in the vein of "Enjoy Yourself" or "Living Together," and it does not quite achieve that goal. However, it contains some intriguing Michael lead vocals—he plays with his vocal range, using a lower register in the lyrics while occasionally soaring into falsetto. The Jacksons performed the track during the 1977 season of their TV variety show.

## *The Jacksons*: An Important Milestone

While The Jacksons produced the hit single "Enjoy Yourself," the album did not result in a triumphant career comeback. It peaked at #6 on *Billboard*'s R&B chart and #36 on the pop chart, and stalled at #54 in the UK. The record was certified gold, but it sold disappointingly fewer copies than the band had during their Jackson 5 heyday.

Their next Gamble and Huff–produced effort, 1977's *Goin' Places*, fared worse, with only the third single, "Different Kind of Lady," gaining any notice. Jackson writes in *Moonwalk* that while he appreciated the duo's Philly soul style, he believed it ultimately overshadowed the Jacksons' own voices. Disillusioned, he would find new creative inspiration by accepting a part in the movie version of *The Wiz* (see chapter 32). Meeting Quincy Jones on the set and taking greater creative control over subsequent Jacksons albums would result in a commercial and critical resurgence for the group.

In *Thriller*, Nelson George sums up the Jacksons' two albums under Gamble and Huff as "so-so" but points out that "studying under the masters of the message song" allowed Michael and his brothers to eventually gain complete control over the composition and production of their albums. While *The Jacksons* may not have gained massive commercial and critical acclaim, it represents an important stage in Michael Jackson's professional development. It was here that he debuted vocal tics that would become trademarks less than a decade later, namely hiccups, raspiness, repeating key phrases, James Brown–esque grunts, and alternating between his normal voice and falsetto. Gamble and Huff's songs and arrangements allowed Michael to stretch his vocal style and experiment with his rapidly maturing voice.

The image on the back cover of *The Jacksons* album, as well as its vibrant front photograph, displayed the maturing look of the former boy band.                                                    *Author's collection*

He sounds aggressive, assuming his place as the group's leader. *The Jacksons* showcases the Michael Jackson that Generation X and younger age groups most recognize—the confident voice and persona that dominate *Off the Wall*, *Thriller*, *Bad*, and his 1990s work.

Before Michael transformed into a superstar, he had to move away from the Motown bubblegum sound and prove his ability to interpret songs as an adult. *The Jacksons* stands as an important step in this process, with the Philadelphia-soul sound providing a lush, more mature sonic landscape for Michael and his brothers to embark on their career's next phase. In addition, Michael's role as composer officially begins with the album, and he would further establish his worth as a hit-maker just a couple of years later with *Destiny*.

# 14

# Blame It on the Boogie

## How the Jacksons Collided with Disco and Reignited Their Careers

A fter their second album under Kenny Gamble and Leon Huff, 1977's *Goin' Places*, the Jacksons found themselves at a crossroads. The album had failed to gain much traction on the charts, and the Philadelphia-soul makeover did not revitalize the group's careers. Had they made a mistake leaving Motown? Were they suffering from the loss of Jermaine Jackson, who had elected to stay with Berry Gordy's label? Would their future entail playing Las Vegas, performing Jackson 5 hits to please a nostalgic crowd?

A year later, two factors significantly impacted the Jacksons, leading to their chart resurgence. First, they assumed complete artistic control of their material, beginning with their 1978 album *Destiny*. Acting as producers and chief songwriters, the group immersed themselves in current pop and R&B trends, incorporating their classic harmonies to create a modernized Jackson sound. More importantly, however, their career resurrection occurred at the same time that disco dominated the charts and popular culture. In danger of becoming a nostalgia act playing Las Vegas variety shows, the Jacksons grabbed onto the trend, wrote sophisticated yet fun dance tunes, and made a triumphant return to the charts.

This chapter tells two stories: the rise of disco, and the Jacksons' entrance into that world.

### You Should Be Dancing: The Rise of Disco

While the term "disco" may conjure images of multicolored floors, white polyester suits, platform shoes, and mirror balls, the genre is a culmination of several social movements, political events, and shifts in culture and morality. Thanks to 1960s activism and pop culture, relaxed attitudes toward drug use and sexuality also contributed to this new music. These factors created the perfect storm for disco to emerge, providing a way for people to celebrate their newfound freedom.

The often-turbulent 1960s drove a stake into the conservative attitudes dominating previous decades, forever changing the status of previously disenfranchised groups. Led by figures such as Martin Luther King Jr., and Malcolm X, the civil rights movement began the long fight toward equality and the ending of segregation in schools and other public spaces. A police raid on New York gay club the Stonewall Inn incited rioting on June 28, 1969, an event that sparked the gay liberation movement. Feminism also gained momentum, with the publication of Betty Friedan's *The Feminine Mystique* inspiring protests against workplace discrimination and reproductive rights.

Along with these social movements, a change in social mores took place. The introduction of the pill in 1960 granted women more power in their sexuality, as taking it provided convenience and control over one's body. In addition, the stigma surrounding recreational drugs lessened; rather than being seen as deadly, they were now considered tools for enlightenment. Teenagers and college students indulged in both drugs and sex during the 1969 Woodstock Festival, with both activities infused with political meaning as much as simply partying at a rock concert. Youth were consciously separating from their parents' generation, exercising their sexual and moral freedoms while rejecting their government's command to fight in Vietnam.

This revolutionary spirit dimmed in the early 1970s with the Watergate scandal. For two years, Americans lived through the nightmare of investigations, court battles, and hearings, culminating in President Richard Nixon's resignation in 1974. People were left disillusioned, feeling betrayed by their leaders and frustrated that 1960s activism had failed to radically change politics. Looking for escapism, Americans would soon find it in a hedonistic kind of music.

In the midst of this social hurricane, disco music began emerging in predominantly gay clubs around 1970. These establishments were largely underground; one such example was New York's the Loft, a series of private parties DJ David Mancuso would host in his home. Using a self-built sound system, Mancuso spun everything from classic soul to jazz and classical. Attracting dancers and aspiring DJs, these parties spawned the careers of soon-to-be-legendary club figures such as Larry Levan, Frankie Knuckles, David Morales, and Nicky Siano. In these early days, DJs would fuse songs that contained similar beats, inventing mixes where one song blended seamlessly into the next. They would create their own extended play songs, using multiple turntables to lengthen a track for maximum dance-ability. Before these records, James Brown's heavily rhythmic tracks and extended instrumental sections laid the groundwork for extended play disco songs.

Meanwhile, this new four-on-the-floor, beat-driven music slowly found its way to the mainstream. Few agree on the first disco record, but early examples frequently cited include Jerry Butler's "Only the Strong Survive" (1969), Eddie Kendricks's "Girl You Need a Change of Mind" (1972), Manu Dibango's "Soul Makossa" (1972), and Harold Melvin and the Blue Notes' "The Love I Lost" (1973). By 1975, disco was making a greater dent on the charts with anthems such as "Love Is the Message" by MFSB, "The Hustle" by Van McCoy, and the Bee Gees' first foray into the form, 1975's "Jive Talkin'." Discotheques opened throughout the US and around the world, with straight and gay fans enjoying dance music featuring a foolproof beat designed to make everyone move.

In the late 1970s, disco had taken over the charts and dominated pop culture. Famous gay clubs such as New York's Paradise Garage and Chicago's the

Warehouse flourished, while the era's most notorious nightclub, Studio 54, attracted attendees from the famous and the everyday (or at least those who would pass inspection outside the selective club, with the bouncer moving aside the velvet rope to allow entrance). Along with music by Donna Summer, Chic, the Village People, and countless other acts, these clubs offered hedonism. Dancers would indulge in their sexual and drug-infused fantasies, both inside and outside the club. Popular songs of the era such as the Andrea True Connection's "More More More," Rod Stewart's "Do Ya Think I'm Sexy?," and Summer's "Hot Stuff" embodied this promiscuity and freedom. At Studio 54, a prop would descend over the flashing dance floor every night: a huge "man in the moon" with a coke spoon dangling under his nose. Little else better illustrates the relaxed, casual attitude toward drug use during this time.

While the disco era culminated in the 1977 classic *Saturday Night Fever*, the genre began its decline only two years later. During "Disco Demolition Night," Chicago DJ Steve Dahl blew up over 10,000 disco records between double-header White Sox games on July 12, 1979. The "disco sucks" trend was born, due in part to overexposure. The music saturated commercials; Studio 54–brand jeans went on sale; one-hit-wonder disco records came and went; and Arthur Murray studios in every suburb offered disco dancing classes to seniors. Overnight disco became uncool, with all-disco radio stations rapidly switching formats. Disco hung on until about 1980, although the music never died; it simply went back underground in the clubs, transforming into house music.

Evolving out of the civil rights, gay, and feminist movements, disco provided a way for these previously disenfranchised groups to express themselves through dance, dress, and community. For mainstream audiences, the music served as an ode to letting go. For a night they could forget the trauma of Watergate and feelings of post-1960s disillusionment. Chic's 1979 hit "Good Times" best summarizes the era; over a catchy, bass-driven rhythm, the female singers coo at listeners to "leave your cares behind," "put an end to this stress and strife," and instead celebrate hedonistic desires such as "clams on the half shell, and roller skates." Despite political turmoil, inflation, and other woes, they insist, "These are the good times / Our new state of mind."

Despite these goodtime lyrics, the underlying message of disco remained political. As Alice Echols writes in *Hot Stuff: Disco and the Remaking of American Culture*, people drunkenly performing the "Y.M.C.A." dance at wedding receptions overlook the music's revolutionary roots. "The hotness of seventies' disco doesn't just refer to its raunchiness or its rhythmic drive; it also signifies its politically incendiary quality," Echols states. "Thirty-five years ago disco was the opportunity for people—African Americans, women, and gays in particular—to reimagine themselves and in the process to remake America."

## Turn the Beat Around: The Jacksons Meet Disco

The Jacksons may have revitalized their careers with the disco-friendly albums *Destiny* and *Triumph*, but their first brush with the genres dates back to their

Jackson 5 days. Their 1973 album *G.I.T.: Get It Together* (their first under producer Hal Davis) seized on the trend early with hits such as the title track and "Dancing Machine." As Michael writes in *Moonwalk*, disco served as the group's break from their bubblegum image. Some critics may dislike disco, Michael says, but it became the Jacksons' ticket into the adult world. The music figured into their 1974 live sets when they performed the aforementioned songs as part of their Las Vegas cabaret act.

When their Motown contract expired, the group elected to sign to Epic Records, although Jermaine, who had married Berry's daughter Hazel, stayed with Motown as a solo artist. But before the group moved on, they released one final LP, *Moving Violation*, in 1975, which contained the type of music that would usher in the disco era. Their version of "Forever Came Today," an extended take on the Supremes hit, packed dance floors when it was released in 1976 and became a #1 disco hit.

After the Jacksons joined CBS Records, they had to wait until their Motown contract expired before recording any new material. To fill this gap, the family filmed *The Jacksons*, a variety show that aired on CBS during the 1976 summer season. High ratings led to the network ordering more episodes for the 1976–77 TV season. Not surprisingly, disco figured prominently in the series, with the siblings performing hits such as "Enjoy Yourself," "Show You the Way to Go," "Style of Life," "Living Together," "Dancing Machine," and "Body Language," among other danceable hits.

After the Jacksons collaborated with Kenny Gamble and Leon Huff on the Philadelphia soul–inspired *The Jacksons* and *Goin' Places* (discussed in chapter 13), the Jackson brothers gained complete artistic control by forming their own production company, Peacock Production, and taking full charge over their 1978 album, *Destiny*. Except for "Blame It on the Boogie," the Jacksons wrote all the tracks, with a definite ear toward the popular disco trend. This move toward sophisticated dance music paid dividends for the group, as *Destiny* sold four million copies worldwide, peaked at #11 on the *Billboard* 200, and scored the Top 10 hit "Shake Your Body (Down to the Ground)" and "Blame It on the Boogie," a #3 R&B smash. Their follow-up, 1980's *Triumph*, performed even better, reaching #10 on the *Billboard* 200 and earning club play with the singles "Walk Right Now" and "Lovely One."

What follows is an overview of their best disco-infused tracks from *Destiny* and *Triumph*.

## Destiny

*Destiny* represents the Jacksons' full immersion in disco and demonstrates their rapidly growing songwriting skills.

### "Blame It on the Boogie"

If any song captures the disco era, it's "Blame on the Boogie," a tale of hitting the clubs with a girlfriend. "Sunshine / Moonlight / Good times / Boogie!" the Jacksons chant, as Michael enthusiastically sings how the music and dance has

The Jacksons' 1978 album *Destiny* served as a creative and commercial rebirth for the group. They composed most of the tracks and produced the entire project themselves, with the resulting album immersing the Jacksons in the burgeoning world of 1970s disco.
*Author's collection*

freed him. "I've changed my life completely, I've seen the light, believe me!" he cries, reflecting many disco-dancers' transformative experiences. Clearly the narrator is an expert, claiming to have spent the night in "Frisco at every kind of disco." In *Moonwalk*, Michael discusses how much he enjoyed performing the track, calling it an "a fun, up-tempo song that allowed the band to work as a unit, and that he loved…" "slurring the chorus" by singing the words in one breath.

The only *Destiny* track not written by the Jacksons, "Blame It on the Boogie" was composed by Michael (Mick) George Jackson, an English musician who, with brothers Peter and David, formed the band "Jacko" and released songs in their adopted home, Germany. According to Mick's website, he became part of the 1977 Munich disco scene and released his first single "You Turn Me On" that year. Around this time he wrote "Blame It on the Boogie" with brother Peter and drummer Elmar Krohn; the song won Mick an album deal with Atlantic.

Meanwhile, the budding singer's publisher offered the track to the Jacksons (in *Moonwalk*, Michael recalls producer Bobby Columby bringing the song to their attention); they recorded the song and released it as the first single off *Destiny*. Mick's original version was released before the Jacksons' in the US, but both versions came out within days of each other in the UK. According to Mick

STEREO
45 RPM
Produced by
The Jacksons
Engineered by
Don Murray

Epic

8-50595
ZSS 164453
℗ 1978 CBS Inc.
3:32

BLAME IT ON THE BOOGIE
-M. Jackson - D. Jackson - E. Krohn-
THE JACKSONS
Executive Producers: Bobby Colomby
and Mike Atkinson

The first single released from *Destiny*, "Blame It on the Boogie" became a Top 20 hit everywhere but the US, where it peaked at a disappointing #54 on the *Billboard* Hot 100.                    *Author's collection*

Jackson's official website, the British press dubbed this the "Battle of the Boogie," with radio stations and music publications taking sides as to which rendition was superior. Michael commented on this battle in an October 7, 1978 interview with *Record Mirror*, expressing disappointment in the confusion. "I've heard the other version and it's okay, but it just hasn't got the groove like ours has," he said. "He only put out his version when he'd heard ours which wasn't a very nice thing to do because the record company had promised us that wouldn't happen."

In any case, "Blame It on the Boogie" perfectly captured the dance craze and spirit of the times, and propelled the Jacksons back onto the charts.

### "Shake Your Body (Down to the Ground)"

Co-written with brother Randy, "Shake Your Body (Down to the Ground)" proved a perfect fit for discotheques. Light, optimistic, and celebratory, the song synthesizes the disco experience: finding love and escapism through dance. The object of the narrator's affection tries to resist him, but he still wants to "get closer to your soul." How will he accomplish such a task? Dancing, shouting, and shaking that body to the music. As the 2004 *Rolling Stone Album Guide* states, Michael's furious performance and the relentless beat "made dancing seem like very serious business indeed."

The song's smoothed-over funk arrangement, along with an irresistible bass line (courtesy of keyboardist Greg Phillinganes), enhances the track's dance-ability. As Taraborrelli explains, "Shake Your Body" "personified the contemporary disco trend with its crackling lead vocal by Michael, whip-snapping chorus from the brothers and insistent, persistent backbeat. It is still regarded by many music critics as the perfect dance record." If anyone were to put together a time capsule of the disco era, "Shake Your Body" as well as "Blame It on the Boogie" would be perfect candidates.

### "Things I Do for You"

Ten years after *Destiny*'s release, Michael compared this track thematically to *Off the Wall*'s "Working Day and Night." Indeed, the lyrics detail working hard but receiving nothing in return. While "Working" involved the narrator lamenting his troubled relationship, "Things I Do for You" extends beyond an unequal romance. Michael's strident vocal reveals his trepidation toward being used. "Always wanting something for nothing," he rhythmically chants, "especially what they don't deserve." He complains of being in a "bad situation" involving people "taking me to the extreme." These negative images would return on *Triumph* and Michael's post–*Off the Wall* work, namely mistrust and wariness toward others.

Despite these dark themes, the horns and scratchy guitar riff keep "Things I Do for You" appropriate for nightclubbing. Dancers probably did not listen past Michael gulps, whoops, and cries of "taking over!" to understand the pain underneath. Themes aside, as *Rolling Stone* noted in a 1979 review of the Jacksons' Nassau Coliseum concert, "The Jacksons' Family Entertainment," songs such as these proved that "the best dance music being turned out these days isn't just *boom-boom-boom* but a sophisticated fusion of pop, swing and R&B, with a strong Latin flavor."

## Triumph

The Jacksons' 1980 follow-up, coming hot on the heels of *Off the Wall*, demonstrated the group's mastery of the disco genre. Along with the brothers, the album boasted an all-star roster of musicians, many of whom had worked on *Off the Wall* and would go on to play on Michael's other solo albums. Bassist Nathan Watts, keyboardist Greg Phillinganes (also co-producer of the album), guitarist Michael Sembello, percussionist Paulinho da Costa, and horn player/arranger Jerry Hey represent just a selection of the names involved in the project.

*Triumph* would solidify the Jacksons' comeback, cracking the *Billboard* Top 10 Albums and becoming their best-selling album since 1972's *Lookin' Through the Windows*.

Critics heaped praise on *Triumph*, ranking it slightly above *Destiny* in quality. *Blues & Soul*'s John Abbey said it "really is a triumph" and predicted that it would become "a major, major hit for the talented brothers — and deservedly so because this album is the perfect continuation to *Destiny*." *Triumph* represents not only the Jacksons' last (and greatest) group effort but also their final foray into disco. Still reeling from the "disco sucks" backlash, the genre was in its final stages in 1980, and the Jacksons successfully demonstrated how the music could be elevated from its "Shake Your Booty" stereotypes.

### "Can You Feel It"

One of the Jacksons' best tunes, "Can You Feel It" is a modern R&B masterpiece of orchestration, choir-led backing vocals, horns, and uplifting vocals from Michael and Randy Jackson. The lyrics describe part of the disco dream: "All the colors of the world should be / Lovin' each other wholeheartedly," Michael cries. "We're all the same." Part of the Studio 54 ideal was that for one night, everyday people could party and revel in the music right alongside the rich and famous. As long as someone can tear up the dance floor or display a distinctive look, he or she can supposedly achieve the same social status as club regulars like Andy Warhol, Diana Ross, Liza Minnelli, or Halston—albeit in a transitory manner.

Interestingly, Michael did not consider "Can You Feel It" to be dance music. In *Moonwalk*, he even describes it as the "closest thing to a rock feel that the Jacksons had ever done." He also considered the track a nod to Gamble and Huff in terms

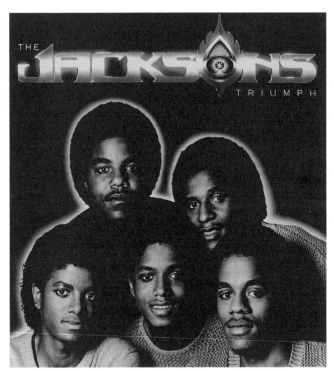

Released shortly after Michael's huge solo success, *Triumph* encapsulated the last days of disco, fusing dance with rock elements on cuts such as "This Place Hotel." *Author's collection*

of lyrical meaning, echoing classic Philly soul tracks like the O'Jays' "Love Train" or the *Jacksons* song "Living Together." The inspiring lyrics, accompanied by adult and children's choirs, turn "Can You Feel It" into a powerful anthem. "Can You Feel It" remains relevant because it departs from the typical Jacksons sound, its dramatic, sweeping feel proving an unusual, disco-tinged track providing the perfect start to a solid album.

### "Lovely One"

In *Moonwalk*, Michael describes this dance track as an extension of "Shake Your Body (Down to the Ground)," but in a smoother style. The track performed well in dance clubs, ranking at #1 on the Dance Singles/Club Play charts along with "Can You Feel It" and "Walk Right Now." Written by Michael and Randy, "Lovely One" describes an attempted seduction, the protagonist wooing a woman he has noticed walking down the street. Think of the song as a funky precursor to "The Way You Make Me Feel," with the narrator begging her to give him a chance.

"Lovely One" features a slamming beat and a particularly enjoyable Michael vocal. He hiccups, gasps, and displays his knack for percussive vocalizing. "G'on with your bad self!" he yells, slightly mimicking James Brown. His scatting toward the end is an explosion of pure joy, his enthusiasm easily reaching the listener. The blaring, staccato horns allow for maximum dance-ability, even if the lyrics do not typify a freedom-celebrating disco tune.

### "Your Ways"

The most underrated track in the Jacksons' catalogue, "Your Ways" sounds like a vintage Earth, Wind & Fire number with some jazz thrown in. Michael acknowledges this experimental vibe in *Moonwalk*, explaining that he tried using a "newer, more ethereal voice" for his lead vocal. Paulinho da Costa displays the same intricate percussive skills he utilized on "Working Day and Night," the finger-snapping rhythm and sharp horn blasts luring people to the dance floor. A Jackie

Jackson composition, the tune discusses a woman whose mysterious behavior both frustrates and bewitches the narrator.

Eerie, synthesizer-driven chords lend a spooky tone to the song, although a jazz-inflected keyboard solo and popping bass contribute a good time vibe appropriate for the disco. Here Michael showcases his evolution as a singer, pitching his voice higher and sustaining select notes to convey frustration as he cries, "I don't understand your ways!"

### "Everybody"

A continuation of *Off the Wall*'s "Get on the Floor," even reprising the line "I love the way you shake your thing," this ode to surrendering to dance accurately summarizes the disco era. Lush strings, horns, and flutes accompany the tune, adding levels of urban sophistication. Michael described "Everybody" as "playful," comparing its sound to "going up the glass elevator to the top floor while looking down, rising effortlessly." While that description may be hard to quantify, its straightforward, gentle, "Rock with You"–like beat made for easy dancing, and its lyrics celebrate the disco life.

In a clear voice, Michael announces that he has "had my days of standing on shaky ground" and longs for a "life so fancy-free." Escapism through music and the dance floor provides release, and like the narrator in "Blame It on the Boogie," his life is forever altered. He leaves his worries behind because he has "tasted the good life and it's fine / No more pain and strife." He admires a woman grooving on the dance floor, so romance (long term or temporary) is a possibility. "We're here to live so free," he cries, the phrase serving as a mantra for the 1970s disco era.

### "Walk Right Now"

A tune that sailed to the top of the Dance Music/Club Play charts, "Walk Right Now" was actually one of Michael's least favorite tracks off *Triumph*. In *Moonwalk*, he complains that the arrangement overwhelmed the Jacksons, comparing the busyness to Gamble and Huff's Philly soul arrangements on *The Jacksons* and *Goin' Places*. Yet the driving, heavy beat, popping bass, and resounding guitar riff make the feet move, and the chorus soars to a climax thanks to cascading strings and the Jacksons' close harmonies. Michael's trademark "hee-hee's" underscore the rhythm as the horns push the tempo. The instrumental break definitely recalls Gamble and Huff with its melancholy chord changes and orchestral arrangements, but the handicapping beat and Michael's energetic lead vocal clearly proved irresistible to DJs.

### "Wondering Who"

Written by Jackie and Randy Jackson, "Wondering Who" features a rare Jackie lead vocal. The robotic feel recalls "Dancing Machine" but updates it with a smoother sound typical of early 1980s R&B. Vocoder-heavy backing vocals slightly echo techno-driven tunes like Summer's "I Feel Love," but the chord changes and arrangement suggest a slight jazz influence. In fact, "Wondering Who" would not sound out of place on Quincy Jones's 1981 album *The Dude*. "Welcome to the night," Jackie croons, the rapid tempo encouraging the narrator to forget his tortured romance and surrender to the rhythm. "Stop holding on, start being strong," the brothers answer, resembling a Greek chorus. Typical of a disco love song, the tune's objective is to escape daily misery through the dance.

In an interview with the *New Musical Express*'s Danny Baker dated April 4, 1981, Marlon and Tito Jackson described the role disco played in the Jacksons' lives: "Disco music was one of the greatest things that happened in the world. Never before did we see blacks and whites under the same roof dancing to the same songs. It stopped people giving attention to the colour of a performer's skin." Culturally, disco offered a voice for previously disenfranchised groups and celebrated the loosening of sexual morays.

Disco tune lyrics celebrated hedonism as an escape from disillusionment and the apparent stalling of the 1960s political revolution. This phenomenon was nothing new, as a sampling of songs popular during the Depression illustrates: "Happy Days Are Here Again," "Get Happy," and "We're in the Money (The Gold Diggers Song)" are just a few examples. The mid-to-late-1970s disco boom proved a lifesaver for the Jacksons' careers, returning them to the charts and kick-starting Michael's solo career. Rather than remaining a nostalgia act, the Jacksons became relevant again, all thanks to people just wanting to dance their troubles away.

# 15

# The Spark That Lit the Fire Inside of Me

## Michael Jackson as Budding Songwriter

When the Jackson 5 (minus Jermaine Jackson) left Motown, they looked forward to more control over their material. Their move to CBS Records, they hoped, would allow them to include their own compositions on their albums. As diligent Motown students, the Jackson siblings witnessed some of the best soul songwriters and artists at work. They learned what qualities comprised a hit, how to write memorable lyrics and melodies, and how to compose songs that best showcased specific vocal ranges. No one absorbed these lessons more than Michael Jackson, a singer who longed to become a songwriter.

Michael finally earned the opportunity to stretch his composing muscles when he and his brothers recorded 1976's *The Jacksons* under Kenny Gamble and Leon Huff. With each subsequent album, Michael assumed more writing duties, working up to writing virtually all the songs on his solo album *Bad* (1987). Before he could write "Billie Jean" or "Smooth Criminal," however, he had to develop his skills as part of the Jacksons.

### State of Independence: The Struggle to Become a Songwriter

As he revealed in a deposition concerning the song "Dangerous" dated February 17, 1994, Michael first experimented with songwriting at age seven, finally publishing his debut composition at fifteen. Throughout his career he wrote an astonishing number of songs, only a fraction of which made the final album lineups. For example, he explained that while nine of his songs appeared on *Bad*, he had written sixty or seventy others for the project that remained in his archives. By 1994, he estimated that he had composed two hundred songs, only fifty or sixty them released to the public. During this testimony, he described writing seventy songs for the *Dangerous* project, but only a dozen made the final cut. These numbers are impressive for any artist, but they particularly amaze since he could not read music. Watching and learning from professionals proved his best education, as numerous influences encompassed his work.

On March 27, 2005, on his radio show *Keep Hope Alive*, the Reverend Jesse Jackson asked his longtime friend about how he developed his songwriting craft. Michael's time at Motown, specifically under the tutelage of composing team

Holland-Dozier-Holland, had clearly played a significant part in his growth. He also mentioned the Beatles and singled out Broadway composers Richard Rogers, Oscar Hammerstein, Leonard Lowe, Harold Arlen, and Johnny Mercer for their melodies. In addition, he cited other unlikely sources such as Irish pub songs and praised African music for its strong rhythms.

In other interviews, Michael revealed another early inspiration: classical music. During his last major interview, Michael told *Ebony* in 2007 that Tchaikovsky's *Nutcracker Suite* influenced him as a child in terms of composition. Often, albums would contain a few strong, potential hit singles; the other tracks were filler or "album songs." As he listened to the work, he began asking questions: "'Why can't every one be like a hit song? Why can't every song be so great that people would want to buy it if you could release it as a single?' So I always tried to strive for that."

As Michael quietly honed his writing skills, his desire to record more of his own material had reached boiling point by 1975. As previously mentioned, Motown's policy was to have in-house writers compose tracks for the artists to record. While Stevie Wonder and Marvin Gaye had successfully battled for complete artistic autonomy, the Jackson 5 had not fared so well. As Taraborrelli explains in *Michael Jackson: The Magic, The Madness, the Whole Story*, Joseph Jackson wanted Michael and his other sons to assume greater songwriting responsibilities for another reason: money.

Joseph discovered that if his sons owned the publishing rights to their songs, they would receive greater royalties: in addition to earning an artist's royalty, they would also receive a songwriter's royalty on every record sold. Taraborrelli breaks it down in numbers: by the mid-'70s, the rate was an additional two cents per copy sold, split equally with the song's publisher. "Therefore, the B-side of a million-selling song, the side that rarely if ever gets radio airplay, could be worth up to $20,000. At least, Joseph reasoned, the boys should be able to write their own B-sides."

Motown's own composers were signed with the label's publishing company Jobete, and thus would split the proceeds with the Jackson 5. So, for every two cents the group made on the sale of the record, 50 percent of it went to the publisher. Joseph approached Gordy with the idea of the Jacksons forming their own music publishing company; the Motown head resisted, also demonstrating a lack of confidence in the brothers' writing abilities.

Meanwhile, in 1974 Michael and the Jackson 5 worked with Stevie Wonder, recording a few of his compositions for a proposed joint album. While they laid down a few tracks (including "Buttercup," which would later surface on the 2010 compilation *I Want You Back! Unreleased Masters*), the project ultimately stalled. Yet the Jackson 5 witnessed Wonder writing and recording his own material, maintaining complete artistic control as he issued one stellar album after another. They guested on the *Fulfillingness' First Finale* track "You Haven't Done Nothin'," again witnessing their mentor working in the studio.

Eventually they returned to work on their own album, 1974's *Dancing Machine*. After his experience with Wonder, Michael was increasingly frustrated with being prohibited from submitting his own compositions or owning publishing rights. As Taraborrelli writes, Michael complained about this to Gordy, arguing that "he had some strong songs he could have added to the package. If he could have had just one song on the album, Michael said, it would have shown that Gordy had confidence in him as a songwriter."

## One More Chance: The Early Years

Michael's first major composition debuted on *The Jacksons*: "Blues Away," a breezy, lighthearted track that would serve as a template for the upbeat, escapist themes that dominate *Off the Wall*. While Michael rarely performed the song live, he held great affection for his first songwriting effort. The lyrics dealt with overcoming depression, of using laughter to ward off sadness. Starting off on a strong note, "Blues Away" appeared as the B-side to the "Show You the Way to Go" single.

Throughout his career, Michael enjoyed collaborating with other songwriters, artists, and producers on his work. He demonstrated this streak on his other *Jacksons* contribution, "Style of Life," co-written with brother Tito. This funky, disco-friendly track was featured as the flip side of the "Enjoy Yourself" 45.

Their 1977 follow-up, *Goin' Places*, again featured the writing and producing work of Gamble and Huff. Rather than the Philly soul-drenched sound of their previous album, their follow-up leaned heavily toward the disco trend. As on *The Jacksons*, Michael and his brothers contributed two original songs: "Different Kind of Lady" and "Do What You Wanna."

Credited to "The Jacksons," "Different Kind of Lady" was released as the third single off *Goin' Places*—a step up from writing B-sides. In *Moonwalk*, Michael describes the song as standing out "like a ball of fire" from other tracks, with the scratchy guitar riff and Philly horns adding a funkier sound. Here Michael demonstrates a more aggressive sound than the smooth overtones of songs such as "Show You the Way to Go," with staccato and raspiness creeping into his voice. His cries of "ha!" would become trademarks in his later work.

Also credited to "The Jacksons" in the album liner notes, "Do What You Wanna" appeared as the B-side to the "Goin' Places" single. Resembling a 1960s-era Motown single with its cheerful, up-tempo beat, "Do What You Wanna" departs from the album's dominant disco sound.

## Burn This Disco Out: The Evolution of Dance and Writing Hits

After amicably parting with Gamble and Huff, the Jacksons finally exercised complete creative control. As detailed in chapter 14, disco proved to be the Jacksons' creative and commercial savior, with the group recording their two most successful albums, *Destiny* and *Triumph*, at the height of the era. Michael found writing in the genre a natural fit, given his dancing skills and heavily rhythmic singing style. "As it turned out, writing disco songs was a natural for me because I was used to having dance breaks incorporated into all the major songs I was asked to sing," he writes in *Moonwalk*.

Unlike previous releases, *Destiny* boasted virtually all Jacksons compositions, the lone exception being "Blame It on the Boogie." Michael was specifically credited as a songwriter on three tracks: "Shake Your Body (Down to the Ground)," "All Night Dancin'," and "That's What You Get (for Being Polite)," all co-written with Randy. "Shake Your Body" proved to be Michael's biggest breakthrough as a composer, as it became the biggest hit off *Destiny*.

The original demo for "Shake Your Body" reveals the inner workings of the song, with Randy playing keyboards and Michael belting out the lyrics in virtually the same fashion as in the final version. As Taraborrelli writes, the track perfectly capitalized on the disco trend with its "crackling lead vocal by Michael, whip-snapping chorus from the brothers and insistent, persistent backbeat. It is still regarded by many music critics as the perfect dance record and one of the Jacksons' strongest efforts." The sales reflected this assessment, as the single peaked at #7 on the pop charts and sold two million copies worldwide.

"All Night Dancin'" may contain a slapping bass typical of a disco tune, but the rapid tempo does not typify the easy, four-on-the-floor beat made for dancing. With Michael enthusiastically encouraging listeners to dance all night, the chord changes, lengthy instrumental sections, and the brothers' cries of "dancin!" suggest a number from a Broadway show more than a song played in a nightclub. Michael's whoops and yells of "that's the way I like it!" suggest his enjoyment while recording the track. Rock guitar solos inject grittiness into the track, a trait Michael would continue in his solo career.

One of Michael's most intriguing early compositions, "That's What You Get (for Being Polite)" describes an insecure man looking for love to rescue him from his misery. His later recollections of the song, however, suggest the song signified more than just a typical love ballad. He explained in *Moonwalk* that he wanted to stress that despite his fame, he faced the same insecurities that all teenagers do. In particular, Michael feared that life was passing him by while he tried to establish his career.

Containing an arrangement and chord changes reminiscent of a Philadelphia International production, "That's What You Get" includes lyrics that reveal more about Michael's state of mind than anything else he had written up to that point. "Jack still cries day and night / Jack's not happy with his life," he almost whispers. "Jack still sits all alone / He lives the world that is his own." These words not only describe someone wanting love in his life, but someone who is a prisoner of his fame. As he mentioned in several interviews, Michael felt isolated from normal life as a result of his career, and his cries of "give him love" in this

"Blues Away," from *The Jacksons*, represents Michael Jackson's first officially released original composition.
*Author's collection*

track echo his sentiments about desiring friendship. "That's What You Get" may sound smooth and sophisticated on the surface, but underneath lies a darker connotation.

Fresh off the critical and commercial success of *Destiny* and *Off the Wall,* Michael brimmed with confidence as an artist and songwriter. Adrian Grant, author of *Michael Jackson: A Visual Documentary 1958–2009,* cites an interview from June 24, 1979, in which Michael exuded excitement and a fervent desire to top *Destiny.* "*Triumph* will be much better, much more creative than *Destiny,*" he said. "We've learned a lot since we made that. We didn't have a chance to be as creative on it as we would have liked. We were rushed. We were pressured. It was the first album we wrote—and we had to prove to the Epic people we could write. Now the pressure is off. We don't have to prove anything any more."

If Jacksons fans thought *Destiny* was a major leap from their Jackson 5 days, they were in for a bigger surprise with *Triumph.* Disco was in its final days, and the Jacksons' 1980 album (along with *Off the Wall*) helped elevate the genre to a more sophisticated level. It mixed in gospel, rock, and hints of jazz to demonstrate that the music need not be a just a straightforward 4/4 beat with variations of "boogie down" lyrics; instead, it could communicate complex emotions beyond escapism.

Now a fully fledged songwriter, Michael composed every track on Triumph except "Wondering Who," a Jackie and Randy Jackson effort. Only one track was written by Michael alone: "This Place Hotel," a gothic tale of doom that foreshadows future works like "Thriller" and "Blood on the Dance Floor" in its dark themes. It remains one of Michael's finest and most fascinating compositions, stimulating the feet and mind. Since many of *Triumph*'s tracks have already been discussed in chapter 14, this chapter will focus on two songs: "This Place Hotel" and "Give It Up."

Originally titled "Heartbreak Hotel," "This Place Hotel" was one of Michael's favorite songs, according to *Moonwalk.* Calling it his most ambitious composition, he says it addresses revenge and its aftermath. In addition, he states that he wanted audiences to interact with the song in four ways: listening, dancing, singing along, and experiencing fright. Sister La Toya Jackson provided the opening scream, immediately setting the scary tone; female backup singers contributed eerie vocals to accompany the track. In order to return listeners to a safe place, he tacked on a slow piano-and-cello coda to leave them with a more positive feeling.

While chiefly credited to Tito Jackson, The Jacksons' "Style of Life" (the B-side to the "Enjoy Yourself" single) was co-written by Michael.    *Author's collection*

"Hope is dead," he quietly sings, pitching his voice lower. He has arrived at this place, "Heartbreak Hotel," because his girlfriend accused him of cheating. The hotel seems to be run by "wicked women," possibly other women he has hurt in the past. Michael paints himself as a falsely accused victim entrapped in this place of despair. "Someone's evil to hurt my soul," he cries, with his spurned girlfriend promising that she will destroy love as he knows it. "Someone's stabbin' my heart!" he wails. A guitar foreshadowing Eddie Van Halen's solo on "Beat It" or Slash's various appearances on future Michael cuts pierces through the gloom, the notes slashing through the strings as Michael sings high pitched "oohs!" as if in pain. "This Place Hotel" (listed as such on the album cover to avoid any confusion with Elvis Presley's "Heartbreak Hotel") illustrates how rapidly Michael had evolved as a songwriter, moving beyond commanding listeners to "shake your body down to the ground" and instead conveying dark themes in a complex, cinematic way.

Co-written with Randy, "Give It Up" faintly echoes Gamble and Huff's signature sound but allows the other brothers to sing as well, particularly Marlon. Singing in falsetto, Michael emulates the airy vibe of the song, accentuated by floating strings. Unlike "This Place Hotel," "Give It Up" paints a picture of idealized love, asking the love interest to surrender to his affections. At first the narrator seems unsure that he and his girlfriend are truly experiencing love, but concludes that they must surrender to this new emotion. "And one day we'll see the moon / Take my hand and we'll fly away," Michael sings seductively, with the chorus urging the woman to believe in this fantasy. "You've got to believe in something," Marlon croons. Despite this dreamy scene, the song's coda resembles a march, an unusual touch for a ballad.

## State of Shock: The 1980s and Worldwide Fame

When the Jacksons reunited for their final group effort, *Victory*, Michael had established himself as a superstar and song craftsman. For reasons detailed in chapter 20, his involvement with *Victory* remained minimal. Yet he collaborated on three tracks: "Be Not Always," "State of Shock," and "The Hurt."

Co-written with Marlon, "Be Not Always" is a simple ballad, with Michael singing over acoustic guitar and strings. A predecessor to some of Michael's "message songs," the song calls for people to feel compassion and strive for peace. With his voice occasionally breaking, he mourns war and death, pointing the finger at listeners that "we turn our backs on life" and should "bow our heads in shame" over current events. While not as powerful as "We Are the World," "Be Not Always" offers a glimpse at Michael's emerging activism.

In contrast to the serious tone of "Be Not Always," "State of Shock" is a fun, rock-saturated duet with the Rolling Stones' Mick Jagger. Co-written with guitarist Randy Hansen, "State of Shock" was originally intended as a duet with Queen's Freddie Mercury. An admirer of Queen's music, Michael worked on several songs with Mercury between 1981 and 1983; for unknown reasons, these tracks were shelved. Jagger ended up on the final version, with the track becoming *Victory*'s biggest hit. A tougher version of "The Girl Is Mine," "State of Shock" features the two singers battling over the same girl. Sexy and at times amusing ("I need mouth-to-mouth resuscitation," Jagger purrs at one point), the song continues Michael's ongoing fascination with incorporating harder rock into his pop and R&B-inflected material.

Finally, Michael collaborated with Randy as well as Toto members David Paich and Steve Porcaro on "The Hurt," a rare example of Michael not singing lead on his own composition. The synthesizer-dominated track details a doomed love affair, with the narrator clearly tormented over feeling used. "Can't get away, babe / Can't let you go," he croons, communicating his confusion. The woman has cheated on him and made him cry, yet he cannot live without her. These are very familiar themes, but "The Hurt" contains a distinctly 1980s polished sheen.

## I've Done My Time and I Have Paid the Price: Becoming a Proven Songwriter

From his Jackson 5 days on, Michael strived to improve his songwriting skills. Although he could not read or write music, he could play some keyboards, guitars, and percussion. While he received schooling during his Motown tenure, he was never formally trained in the art of composition. Yet he possessed a rare talent for conceptualizing music entirely in his head. During his 1994 "Dangerous" deposition, he said that "the lyrics, the strings, the chords, everything comes at the moment like a gift that is put right into your hand. And that's how I hear it." In a *New Musical Express* blog post titled "The Incredible Way Michael Jackson Wrote Music," dated April 2, 2014, Lucy Jones compared him to Wolfgang Amadeus Mozart. "Just as Mozart could hear whole symphonies in his head, Jackson fully realized his songs before they were put down on paper."

During interviews conducted between the 1980s and 2009, Michael often described songwriting as being as natural as breathing. When Regina Jones asked about his process during a March 2002 *Vibe* interview, he explained that "I don't sit at the piano and think, I'm going to write the greatest song of all time. It doesn't happen. It has to be given to you." His technique may not be quite that simple, however, as he told *Ebony* in 2007 that he would first write a rough draft to formulate the chorus and melody, and then, once he honed those elements to his satisfaction, transcribe the words and music to tape.

Michael may have portrayed his songwriting technique as straightforward, but those who worked on his albums have provided additional insight. Engineer Rob Hoffman, who worked on the *HIStory* project, recalled that Michael would bring a new song into the studio and sing every single instrument part to the musicians, instructing them how he wanted them to play. "He would sing us an entire string arrangement, every part. Steve Porcaro [Toto] once told me he witnessed MJ doing that with the string section in the room. Had it all in his head, harmony and everything," Hoffman said. "Not just little eight bar loop ideas. He would actually sing the entire arrangement into a micro-cassette recorder complete with stops and fills."

*Off the Wall* and subsequent solo albums showcase Michael as a fully developed composer, but he developed his skills as a member of the Jacksons. From "Blues Away" to "State of Shock," his advancement in lyrical themes and instrumental complexity can be traced. Disco proved to be a freeing creative force for the singer, as "Shake Your Body" demonstrated Michael had the chops to compose crossover hits. After *Triumph*, Michael would move on from pure disco to write tracks that transcended "get on the floor" themes and rather explored psychological issues as well as traditional romantic subjects.

In *Moonwalk*, Michael candidly reveals his struggle to become an accepted songwriter. "People used to underestimate my ability as a songwriter . . . when I started coming up with songs, they'd look at me like: 'Who really wrote that?' I don't know what they must have thought—that I had someone back in the garage who was writing them for me? But time cleared up those misconceptions." Indeed, time, experience, and hard work all contributed to Michael's emergence as a respected composer, and his increasing role in Jacksons albums served as the beginning of his artistic transformation.

# 16

# Can You, Can You Feel It, Feel It in the Air

## The Jacksons' Notable TV Appearances, Music Videos, and Concerts

When the Jacksons began their new career with CBS Records, they embarked on a new musical phase as well as adopting a new name. Now having to rebuild their audience and retool their sound, they utilized television to promote their records and played numerous concerts to launch their updated, disco-based tunes. This chapter details the Jacksons' notable television guest spots and concert tours; in addition, it covers their short-lived CBS variety series.

### Television Appearances

After changing labels and names, the Jacksons began reintroducing themselves to the public. They appeared on various variety shows as well as talk shows, showcasing their new look and sound.

### February 8, 1977: *Mike in Hollywood '77* (syndicated)

On this special edition of *The Mike Douglas Show*, the Jacksons lip-synch to "Enjoy Yourself," "Dreamer," and "Show You the Way to Go." In between the performances, Douglas interviews the brothers about their offstage life. The host also praises Michael's moves, stating that he can spin like a top.

### May 19, 1977: *Top of the Pops* (BBC1, UK)

Singing live to a prerecorded track, the Jacksons perform "Show You the Way to Go." A footnote: Michael's jacket, with epaulets, is reminiscent of the military jackets he would popularize in the 1980s.

### May 21, 1977: *Musikladen* (Radio Bremen, Germany)

Singing live, the Jacksons make their debut appearance on the popular German music show (its title roughly translating to "music shop"), performing "Enjoy Yourself" and "Keep on Dancing."

## May 30, 1977: *Numero 1* (TF1, France)

A French TV special hosted by Joe Dassin, this show featured the Jacksons lip-synching to "Keep on Dancing."

## May 3, 1978: *Rock 'n' Roll Sports Classic* (ABC)

Rock's answer to the *Battle of the Network Stars* specials, this odd show pitted the day's hottest musicians against each other in various competitions. The Jacksons participate in various events, including basketball, swimming, the 100-yard dash (Jackie Jackson beat Michael in the competition), and the team long jump. Michael is briefly interviewed, and the show airs a short clip of them performing "Enjoy Yourself."

## January 25, 1979: *Musikladen* (Radio Bremen, Germany)

Returning to Germany, the Jacksons treat the in-studio audience to a lip-synched rendition of "Blame It on the Boogie."

## February 2, 1979: *Midnight Special* (NBC)

Hosted by the legendary DJ Wolfman Jack, this late-night weekly show became a must-stop for any popular act. The Jacksons were no exception. They perform "Shake Your Body (Down to the Ground)," pulling audience members onstage (including a dancer dressed in a policeman's uniform) to groove with them toward the end of the number, while their rendition of "Destiny" features a special guest: Jermaine Jackson. The Jacksons bring the audience to its feet with the disco track "Things I Do for You" before finally reprising "Shake Your Body (Down to the Ground)," this time with the dancers remaining onstage with the group for the entire song; even Wolfman Jack joins the party.

## February 3, 1979: *Soul Train* (syndicated)

This special episode saluted the Jacksons' ten years in the music business. Featuring group and solo Michael performances, the show opens with a vintage clip of the Jackson 5 performing "I Want You Back" on the show on October 7, 1972. The Jacksons lip-synch the tracks "Things I Do for You" and "Shake Your Body (Down to the Ground)," the latter performance notable for Michael pulling dancers onto the stage toward the end of the song.

After an airing of the new video for "Blame It on the Boogie," Michael receives a solo spot, singing the *Destiny* track "Push Me Away." Host Don Cornelius interviews Michael about his time filming *The Wiz* and living in New York, with the singer amusingly describing his favorite haunt, Studio 54, as "neat."

During the taping, Michael shot an additional interview with Cornelius, for broadcast at a later date, in which he further described his time filming *The Wiz*. When Cornelius asked Michael if he would still come back to *Soul Train* even after becoming a movie star, the singer laughed and declared "definitely!" Interestingly, though, this appearance would be the final time Michael visited the *Soul Train* set.

## February 10, 1979: *American Bandstand* (ABC)

Performing to a screaming, dancing teenage audience, the Jacksons show off their tight choreography and Michael's undeniable front-man charisma. As on *Soul Train*, Michael pulls dancers onstage with the band during "Shake Your Body (Down to the Ground)," with the group repeating the *Midnight Special* routine of a policeman appearing onstage. Host Dick Clark seems surprised by the addition, adding that he thought they were all being arrested for real! Clark clearly felt affection for the group, having known them since the beginning of their careers.

After a brief interview, Michael once again performs "Push Me Away" alone, before being joined by his brothers for "Things I Do for You." His moves during the latter number foreshadow the steps (spins, sideways kicks, pointed toes) that would become signature during his 1980s videos and concerts. It's an electrifying and unjustly overlooked TV appearance that functions as a sneak preview of Michael Jackson the Superstar.

## March 1979: *Top of the Pops* (BBC1, UK)

The Jacksons returned to the British show to sing "Destiny." Perhaps to energize the rather subdued audience, Michael leaps to his feet at the end of the track to perform impressive spins and sideways kicks.

## April 9, 1979: *ABBA Special: Disco in the Snow Part 1* (BBC1)

In one of the Jacksons' more unusual appearances, the brothers traveled to Switzerland to film lip-synched versions of "Shake Your Body (Down to the Ground)" and "Blame it on the Boogie." They dance and play guitars in the snow, a snowman gazing on the scene as children on skis stand in a half-circle around them. This ABBA special aired in the UK only.

## January 1980: *20/20: Interview with Sylvia Chase* (ABC)

ABC's news magazine *20/20* profiles Michael and his brothers, focusing on the Jacksons' concerts as well as the success of *Off the Wall*. Along with live footage, Michael discusses his newfound solo fame with correspondent Sylvia Chase.

# Music Videos

MTV may have been five years away, but the Jacksons seized upon the music-video trend early. Unlike during their Jackson 5 days, the siblings would no longer have to guest star on every variety show to promote their latest singles—they could make a video instead.

## "Enjoy Yourself" (1977)

The Jacksons' first video, this shows them lip-synching to the song while performing high-energy choreography. Performing in front of several cut-up mirrors, the brothers sport the height of disco fashion: white sequined suits and silver platform shoes. In the 2009 *Washington Post* retrospective "Sara Kaufman Analyzes the Magic Behind Michael Jackson's Dancing," Kaufman discussed how Michael showed off moves that would become his trademarks, including smooth but rapid spins and what ballet dancer Mikhail Baryshnikov termed "his simple, bouncy walk across the stage, that was what was most beautiful and arresting, swinging his hips, kicking his heel forward. That's to me what he is: that superior confidence in his body as a dancer."

## "Blame It on the Boogie" (1978)

Directed by Peter Conn, this simple clip shows Michael and his brothers lip-synching to their latest hit against a black background. Along with the Jacksons, the other "star" of the video is its then-cutting edge special effects. As Michael and his brothers dance, they appeared to leave "trails" behind them courtesy of the Quantel DFS 3000 digital framestore, also known as the Scanimate analog computer system. The effects were created by special-effects firm Image West, Ltd., a company that was responsible for animation in the first *Star Wars* film.

## "Can You Feel It" (1981)

The first single off *Triumph* was accompanied by an expensive, effects-laden video conceived, written, and produced by Michael. Directed by Bruce Gowers and Robert Abel, the story involves the larger-than-life Jacksons towering over an imaginary city, sprinkling glitter and holding rainbows over an ecstatic crowd of adults and children. While the special effects underwhelm today, "Can You Feel It" offers a glimpse into what would become a Michael Jackson mainstay: the extravagant, epic music video.

## "Torture" (1984)

Tensions among the brothers led to Michael and Jermaine walking off the "Torture" set. Stand-ins completed Michael's dance sequences, with a wax figure of the singer used for close-ups. The Jeff Stein–directed video remains significant for its choice of choreographer: a then-unknown Paula Abdul.

## "Body" (1984)

Another single off *Victory*, and again neither Jermaine nor Michael appear in the video. It presents the story of an audition for Jacksons backup dancers, with several close-ups of the sexy female dancers' busts and legs. The video ends with Jackie, Randy, Marlon, and Tito performing a dance routine, supposedly "onstage" with the lovely ladies.

## "2300 Jackson Street" (1989)

The Jacksons briefly reunited for the *2300 Jackson Street* album, the title track being the only one to include Michael. Shot in March 1989, the Greg Gold–directed video features all of the Jacksons except La Toya and Marlon, much of it filmed during a staged family reunion. Much of the singing in the video is courtesy of Jermaine, Tito, Randy, and Jackie Jackson, with Michael, Janet, and Rebbie each taking brief solos.

## The Jacksons (CBS TV Series)

When the Jacksons departed Motown for CBS Records, they could not record another album until their previous label contract expired. Needing some media exposure, father Joseph Jackson seized upon a unique offer: CBS wanted a summer series to compete with the popular variety show *The Osmonds*, hosted by a family often branded as the Jacksons' chief rivals. Joseph urged his children (except Jermaine) to participate, figuring it would not only produce needed revenue for the family but also boost sales of the Jacksons' future albums.

Michael would later admit in interviews and his autobiography that he despised having to dress in silly costumes and perform what he thought were corny skits for the shows. He feared overexposure and losing credibility with audiences. In addition, the grueling shooting schedule allowed little time for intricate choreography or intensive rehearsals. "On the show our sets were sloppy, the lighting was often poor, and our choreography was rushed," he later complained.

Despite his misgivings, the four-week run earned solid ratings; consequently, CBS renewed the show for the latter half of the 1976–77 season (much to Michael's dismay). The show failed to catch on, however, ending its run after eight weeks.

The first show starring an African American family, *The Jacksons* was a mixture of comedy and music featuring guest stars. While Michael may not have enjoyed the experience, he demonstrated an even more impressive dancing ability, channeling Fred Astaire and Gene Kelly in numbers like "Get Happy" and a dance-off with the Nicholas Brothers.

### Episodes

The two brief seasons of *The Jacksons* featured the following guests:

**Season I**
- June 16, 1976: Sonny Bono
- June 23, 1976: Mackenzie Phillips
- June 30, 1976: Ed McMahon
- July 7, 1976: Joey Bishop

**Season 2**
- January 19, 1977: Redd Foxx
- January 26, 1977: Carroll O'Connor
- February 2, 1977: Dom DeLuise, George Miller, Muhammad Ali
- February 16, 1977: Georgia Engel, David Letterman
- February 23, 1977: John Byner, the Nicholas Brothers
- March 2, 1977: Lynda Carter
- March 9, 1977: Tim Conway, David Letterman

## TV Special Appearances

The Jacksons came back together for a pair of special TV performances.

### May 16, 1983: *Motown 25* (NBC)

The Jacksons reunited—this time with Jermaine—for the *Motown 25* special, taped on March 25 at the Civic Auditorium in Pasadena, California. Performing a medley of their greatest hits, they charmed the crowd with their classic choreography and still-sparkling chemistry. A complete discussion of this event is located in chapter 28.

### September 7 and 10, 2001: *Michael Jackson 30th Anniversary Special* (CBS)

Taped over two nights at New York's Madison Square Garden, this CBS special features a Jacksons reunion. Performing together for the first time since the *Victory* tour, the brothers treated the audience to renditions of "Can You Feel It," "I Want You Back," "Shake Your Body (Down to the Ground)," "ABC," "The Love You Save," and "I'll Be There." During the September 7 taping, *NSYNC joined the group onstage for "Dancing Machine."

## Concerts

From 1977 to 1981, the Jacksons mounted national and world tours to promote their first four albums. (The 1984 *Victory* tour is fully discussed in chapter 20.) While the group played an impressive number of dates, one common theme emerged: Michael was becoming a star, increasingly dominating the concerts with his extraordinary—and still evolving—dancing and singing skills. By the *Triumph* tour, almost half the set list was devoted to *Off the Wall*, firmly establishing Michael's arrival as a solo artist.

### The Jacksons Tour (May 1977)

This two-and-a-half-week European tour included a May 19 Royal Command Performance at King's Hall, Glasgow, Scotland, in celebration of the Queen's Silver Jubilee. In *Moonwalk*, Michael singles out meeting the Queen as a highlight of his career and discusses how his family's travels through Europe provided an invaluable education. The Jacksons' jaunt also included dates in Amsterdam, Bremen, and Paris.

### Goin' Places Tour (January 22–May 13, 1978)

The Jacksons began a world tour that included Europe and the US. Little information exists on the exact number of shows, although they played a date on February 19, 1978, at City Hall in Newcastle, England. Chris Cadman and Craig Halstead list three dates in Trinidad: February 24 and 25 in Port of Spain, and February 26 in San Fernando.

Another rare artifact exists from this tour: a picture disc of the *Goin' Places* album that was to be sold at their concert at Los Angeles' Dodger Stadium on

May 13, 1978. The *New Musical Express* ran a review of a performance in Fort Worth, Texas, though writer Cliff White seemed unimpressed by the show's slickness and "clockwork predictability." He complained of a lack of spontaneity, and even criticized Michael for not attempting the splits in the manner of his idol, James Brown.

A typical set list, according to Cadman and Halstead, was as follows:

- "Think Happy"
- "Get It Together"
- "Forever Came Today"
- "I Am Love"
- "Keep on Dancing"
- "Ben"
- "Show You the Way to Go"
- "Goin' Places"
- "Never Can Say Goodbye"
- "Got to Be There"

- "Sugar Daddy"
- "I Wanna Be Where You Are"
- "I'll Be There"
- "I Want You Back"
- "ABC"
- "The Love You Save"
- "Find Me a Girl"
- "Dancing Machine"
- "Enjoy Yourself"

## Destiny Tour (January 22, 1979–September 26, 1980)

Now in full control of their careers, the Jacksons undertook a world tour to promote *Destiny*. Opening in Bremen, Germany, the itinerary included Britain, Holland, France, and Kenya, with concerts in Madrid, Amsterdam, Geneva, London, Brighton, Preston, Sheffield, Glasgow, Manchester, Birmingham, Halifax, Leicester, Cardiff, Bournemouth, Paris, and Nairobi.

### International Dates

The international leg of the *Destiny* tour took in the following shows:

The Jacksons' 1979 World Tour supporting *Destiny* covered three continents and nine countries.

*Author's collection*

- January 22, 24, 26: Wilhelm Kaisen Platz, Bremen, Germany
- January 27: Festhalle, Frankfurt, Germany
- January 28–30: Madrid, Spain
- February 1–2: Amsterdam, Netherlands
- February 6–9: Rainbow Theatre, London, England
- February 10: Top Rank, Brighton, England

- February 11: Preston, Lancashire, England
- February 12: Wakefield, West Yorkshire, England
- February 13: Sheffield, South Yorkshire, England
- February 14–15: Geneva, Switzerland
- February 16: Apollo, Glasgow, Scotland
- February 17–18: Manchester, England
- February 19: Halifax, England
- February 20: Leicester, England
- February 21: Cardiff, Wales
- February 23–24: Rainbow Theatre, London, England: According to Cadman and Halstead, one of these dates was filmed for a BBC TV special. In 1982, the Jacksons sued to prevent the syndication of the special; they sought $600,000 in damages and ordered that all bootlegged copies be destroyed.
- February 25: Poole, England
- February 26: Concertgebouw, Amsterdam, Netherlands
- February 29: Avignon, France
- March 2: Le Palace, Paris, France
- March 6–10: Johannesburg, South Africa
- March 12–15: Stade De L'Amite, Dakar, Senegal
- March 19–21: Johannesburg, South Africa

## First US Leg

The Jacksons' spring tour of the US included the following performances:

- April 14–15: Cleveland, Ohio
- April 19 and 22: Valley Forge Music Fair, Valley Forge, Pennsylvania
- April 25–27, 29: Chicago, Illinois
- May 3: Bayfront Center, St. Petersburg, Florida
- May 4: Fort Pierce, Florida
- May 6: Jacksonville Memorial Coliseum, Jacksonville, Florida
- May 10 and 12: The Summit, Houston, Texas
- May 13: Baton Rouge, Louisiana
- May 16: Birmingham-Jefferson Civic Center Coliseum, Birmingham, Alabama
- May 18: The Omni, Atlanta, Georgia
- May 20: Mid-South Coliseum, Memphis, Tennessee
- May 24: Pine Bluff Convention Center, Pine Bluff, Arkansas
- May 26: Municipal Auditorium, Kansas City, Missouri
- May 27: Fairgrounds Arena, Oklahoma City, Oklahoma
- May 30: Hirsch Memorial Coliseum, Shreveport, Louisiana
- June 1: The Scope, Norfolk, Virginia
- June 3: Carolina Coliseum, Columbia, South Carolina
- June 8: Charlotte Coliseum, Charlotte, North Carolina
- June 9: Capital Centre, Landover, Maryland
- June 10: Greensboro, North Carolina

## Second US Leg

The *Destiny* tour resumed in the fall.

- September 26: RFK Stadium, Washington, D.C.
- October 2–3: Municipal Auditorium, New Orleans, Louisiana
- October 4: Hirsch Memorial Coliseum, Shreveport, Louisiana
- October 5: Municipal Auditorium, Mobile, Alabama
- October 6: Von Braun Civic Center, Huntsville, Alabama
- October 7: Louisville Gardens, Louisville, Kentucky
- October 12: Spectrum, Philadelphia, Pennsylvania
- October 13: War Memorial, Rochester, New York
- October 14: Civic Arena, Pittsburgh, Pennsylvania
- October 18: Saginaw Civic Center, Saginaw, Michigan
- October 19: Market Square Arena, Indianapolis, Indiana
- October 20: Kiel Auditorium, St. Louis, Missouri
- October 21: University of Dayton Arena, Dayton, Ohio
- October 25: Fairground Coliseum, Columbus, Ohio
- October 26: War Memorial Auditorium, Syracuse, New York
- October 27: Buffalo Memorial Auditorium, Buffalo, New York
- October 28: Civic Center, Springfield, Massachusetts
- November 1: Wings Stadium, Kalamazoo, Michigan
- November 2: Chicago Stadium, Chicago, Illinois
- November 3: Convention Centre, Cleveland, Ohio
- November 4–5: Cobo Hall, Detroit, Michigan
- November 6: Civic Center, Baltimore, Maryland
- November 8: Nassau Coliseum, Hampstead, New York: *Rolling Stone* ran a positive review of this performance in its issue of January 24, 1980, particularly focusing on Michael as a confident presence onstage. Writer Stephen Holden singled out "I'll Be There," "Rock with You," Don't Stop 'Til You Get Enough," and "Shake Your Body (Down to the Ground)" as highlights. Holden described Michael's dancing as "the hundred-yard dash done as a boogie by a teenage Fred Astaire" and analyzed his vocal qualities. "The combination of his breathlessly enthusiastic adolescent's voice perched midway between alto and tenor and his puckish physical zeal makes him seem as mythically ageless as Peter Pan."
- November 9: Richmond Coliseum, Richmond, Virginia
- November 10: Hampton Coliseum, Hampton, Virginia
- November 11: Cumberland County Auditorium, Fayetteville, North Carolina
- November 14: Tarrant County Convention Center, Fort Worth, Texas
- November 15: Riverside Centroplex, Baton Rouge, Louisiana
- November 16: Jackson Coliseum, Jackson, Mississippi
- November 17: Civic Center, Lake Charles, Louisiana
- November 18: Hofheinz Pavilion, Houston, Texas
- November 20: Municipal Auditorium, Columbus, Georgia
- November 21: Greenville Auditorium, Greenville, South Carolina
- November 22: Civic Center, Savannah, Georgia

- November 23: Macon Coliseum, Macon, Georgia
- November 24: Nashville Municipal Auditorium, Nashville, Tennessee
- November 25: The Omni, Atlanta, Georgia
- November 29: University Arena, Albuquerque, New Mexico
- November 30: McNichols Sports Arena, Denver, Colorado
- December 2: Neal Blaisdell Center, Honolulu, Hawaii
- December 6: Memorial Coliseum, Portland, Oregon
- December 8: Seattle Center Coliseum, Seattle, Washington
- December 9: Pacific National Exhibition AR., Vancouver, British Columbia, Canada
- December 13: Swing Auditorium, San Bernardino, California
- December 14: Arizona Veterans Memorial Coliseum, Phoenix, Arizona
- December 15: San Diego Sports Arena, San Diego, California
- December 16: Oakland Coliseum, Oakland, California
- December 18: The Forum, Inglewood, California

## Third US Leg

After an eight-month gap, the Jacksons played a final run of *Destiny* shows in the fall of 1980.

- September 5: Neal Blaisdell Center, Honolulu, Hawaii
- September 17–19, 25–26: The Forum, Inglewood, California

### Set List

The following list represents a typical set on the *Destiny* tour.

- "Dancing Machine"
- "Things I Do for You"
- "Ben"
- "Keep on Dancing"
- Medley: "I Want You Back / ABC / The Love You Save"
- "I'll Be There"
- "Enjoy Yourself"
- "Destiny"
- "Show You the Way to Go"
- "All Night Dancin'"
- Encore: "Blame It on the Boogie"

## *Triumph* Tour (July 8–September 26, 1981)

The Jacksons toured behind their critically and commercially successful album, with their pyrotechnic-filled shows ultimately chronicled on the 1981 album *The Jacksons Live!* When *Rolling Stone* published a special issue on June 4, 1987, featuring "Live! 20 Concerts That Changed Rock & Roll," it ranked the *Triumph* tour among its choices. "With spectacular lighting, sensational pyrotechnics and flashy ensemble footwork, the Jacksons danced and dazzled their way through a tight hour and twenty minutes' worth of snappy boogie numbers and cool ballads," David Fricke wrote.

In *Moonwalk*, Michael explains that he and his brothers worked hard to create a perfect tour. They hired magician Doug Henning to design special effects such as having Michael disappear in a burst of smoke at the end of "Don't Stop 'Til

You Get Enough." Tying in what Michael dubs the tour's "*Close Encounters*" theme with the Jacksons' new production company Peacock, he explains that his concept "was trying to make the statement that there was life and meaning beyond space and time and the peacock had burst forth ever brighter and ever prouder." Competing with other showmen such as the Commodores and Earth, Wind & Fire, the Jacksons believed they needed to prove they were still a formidable band after over ten years in the business.

Despite the group effort, the dynamics had definitely changed. As Nelson George states in *Thriller: The Musical Life of Michael Jackson*, "Although the tour is named after the Jacksons' latest album, in truth it should have been called the '*Off the Wall* tour featuring some cuts from *Triumph*.'"

The fourth and final single from 1980's *Triumph*, "Walk Right Now" reached #7 on the UK pop charts but performed modestly in the US.    *Author's collection*

## US Leg

The *Triumph* tour became the Jacksons' most successful ever, with the band playing to over 600,000 fans and grossing $5.5 million. While at the time Michael claimed it would be his last tour with the group, just a few years later he would agree to one more: the ill-fated *Victory* tour.

- July 9: Mid-South Coliseum, Memphis, Tennessee
- July 13: Buffalo, New York
- July 10: The Myriad, Oklahoma City, Oklahoma
- July 11: Reunion Arena, Dallas, Texas
- July 12: Albuquerque, New Mexico
- July 15: HemisFair Arena, San Antonio, Texas
- July 17: Riverside Centroplex, Baton Rouge, Louisiana
- July 18: Municipal Auditorium, Mobile, Alabama
- July 19: Civic Center, Lakeland, Florida
- July 22: The Omni, Atlanta, Georgia
- July 24: Greensboro Coliseum, Greensboro, North Carolina
- July 25: Charlotte Coliseum, Charlotte, North Carolina
- July 26: Hampton Coliseum, Hampton, Virginia
- July 28: Lakeland Civic Center, Lakeland, Florida

- July 31–August 1: Washington, D.C.
- August 2: Buffalo Memorial Auditorium, Buffalo, New York: *Billboard* ran a positive review of this concert in its September 5, 1981, edition (the magazine lists it as occurring on August 23, but Cadman and Halstead cite it as August 2). Reviewer Hanford Searl dubbed Michael a "whirling dervish of high kicks, twirls and dance steps," praising his "intense vocals" and citing the brothers for adding "harmonic depth to Michael's soaring falsettos and frequent blues ramblings."
- August 4: Richmond Coliseum, Richmond, Virginia
- August 5: Maple Leaf Gardens, Toronto, Canada
- August 7: Nassau Veterans Memorial Coliseum, Uniondale, New York
- August 8: Riverfront Coliseum, Cincinnati, Ohio
- August 10: Veterans Memorial Auditorium, Columbus, Ohio
- August 12: The Omni, Atlanta, Georgia
- August 13: Civic Arena, Pittsburgh, Pennsylvania
- August 15: The Spectrum, Philadelphia, Pennsylvania
- August 16: Providence Civic Center, Providence, Rhode Island
- August 18–19: Madison Square Garden, New York City, New York: Nelson George describes the New York stop as a game changer for the Jacksons and a preview of Michael's future multimedia career.

The Jacksons' only official live album, *The Jacksons Live!*, was released in November 1981. Peaking at #30 on the *Billboard* 200 and #10 on the R&B charts, the double LP chronicles the group's *Triumph* tour.

*Author's collection*

Opening the show with the "Can You Feel It" video, he maintains, forecast Michael's ongoing fascinating with mixing film and live performance. The singer would continue to use this technique throughout his life, including filming a new sequence to "Smooth Criminal" that was to be used in the 2009 *This Is It* concerts.

- August 22: Chicago Stadium, Chicago, Illinois
- August 23: Hara Arena, Trotwood, Ohio
- August 26: Mecca Arena, Milwaukee, Wisconsin
- August 28: Market Square Arena, Indianapolis, Indiana
- August 29: Joe Louis Arena, Detroit, Michigan
- September 2: Checkerdome, St. Louis, Missouri
- September 3: McNichols Arena, Denver, Colorado
- September 5: Chicago Stadium, Chicago, Illinois
- September 7: Convention Center, Las Vegas, Nevada
- September 8: Kemper Arena, Kansas City, Missouri
- September 10: Denver, Colorado
- September 16: San Diego Sports Arena, San Diego, California
- September 17: Cow Palace, Daly City, California
- September 18–19, 25–26: The Forum, Inglewood, California (all four shows sold out)

# 17

# Shake Your Body Down to the Ground

## Odds and Ends

U nlike the Jackson 5 years, not as many outtakes, unreleased material, and rarities exist from the Jacksons era. The following is a brief description of Jacksons tracks that did not appear on official albums. Tracks that have since appeared in later compilations are noted; otherwise the songs remain unreleased.

### "People Got to Be Free" (1976)

Prior to their move to CBS/Epic Records, the Jacksons recorded a series of home demos with Motown mentor Bobby Taylor. One of these demos is a cover of the Rascals' 1969 classic, although the Jacksons' version was never released.

### "Piece of the Pie" (1976)

Another Bobby Taylor collaboration, this song remains unreleased.

### "We're All Alone" (1976)

While the Jacksons version never went past the demo stage, Boz Scaggs recorded this song for his smash album *Silk Degrees*. The most famous and successful version remains Rita Coolidge's 1977 cover, a Top 10 hit in the US and UK.

### "Rock in a Hard Place" (1976)

Another Bobby Taylor collaboration, this remains unreleased.

### "Different Kind of Lady" (*Goin' Places* picture disc version, 1977)

One of the rarest Michael Jackson and Jacksons collectibles, the *Goin' Places* picture disc was a limited-edition item created to be sold at their concert at Dodger Stadium, Los Angeles, on May 13, 1978. Although it contains the same tracks as the standard version of *Goin' Places*, the track "Different Kind of Lady" had undergone a slight change on the picture disc, with the opening horns eliminated.

## "Shake Your Body (Down to the Ground)" (demo, 1978)

Michael's first self-penned hit, he co-wrote this *Destiny* track with Randy. While Randy wrote the original music and lyrics, Michael refined the sound. The two recorded a demo in 1978, originally titled "Shake a Body." In the studio, the Jacksons stuck very closely to the demo's structure. The early demo eventually surfaced on the 2004 boxed set *Michael Jackson: The Ultimate Collection.*

## "Shake Your Body (Down to the Ground)" (12-inch disco mix, 1978)

Featuring an enhanced rhythm track and a slightly more robotic sound, the 12-inch single (with a disco remix of "Blame It on the Boogie") was tailor-made for discos worldwide, reaching #20 on the Dance Music/Club Play Singles.

## "Blame It on the Boogie" (extended disco remix, 1978)

This seven-minute mix features slightly different vocals, and was

The Jacksons' second album with Gamble and Huff, 1977's *Goin' Places*, failed to replicate the success of the previous year's *The Jacksons*. The third single released from the album, "Different Kind of Lady," was a Jacksons composition. *Author's collection*

"Find Me a Girl," the B-side to the "Different Kind of Lady" single, was the fifth and final single from *Goin' Places*. The Gamble and Huff–penned track peaked at #38 on the R&B charts. *Author's collection*

released along with "Shake Your Body (Down to the Ground)" to dance chart success.

## "That Girl" (1978)

Written between 1978 and 1980, "That Girl" was a group effort, with Michael, Jackie, Marlon, Randy, and Tito all contributing to it. Cadman and Halstead state that the song was recorded, but it failed to make *Destiny* or *Triumph*.

## "You Told Me Your Lovin'" (1979)

Michael wrote this track in 1979, but it is unknown whether it was intended for *Off the Wall* or *Triumph*. Randy revised the lyrics and music; both the original and Randy's rendition exist, but have never been released.

## "Slipped Away" (1980)

Co-written with Marlon, this song was intended for *Triumph*, but it failed to make the final lineup. It remains unreleased.

## "Walk Right Now" (1981)

This *Triumph* cut was released in several forms, including a limited-edition picture disc (UK only) and an extended disco mix.

## "Doing Dirty" (1982)

Michael collaborated on this track with Marlon Jackson, and it was eventually considered for the *Victory* album. It has never been issued in any form.

## "State of Shock" (1983)

While the *Victory* version features a duet between Michael and Mick Jagger, the track originated as a collaboration with Queen lead singer Freddie Mercury. In 1983, Michael invited the rock singer to his family's Encino estate to record three demos: "State of Shock," "Victory," and "There Must Be More to Life Than This." For unknown reasons, they never completed the tracks. The Michael/Mercury "State of Shock" has never been officially released but is available on bootlegs.

## "There Must Be More to Life Than This" (1983)

Another demo Michael recorded with Mercury, this song's roots trace back to Queen's 1982 album *Hot Space*. According to Cadman and Halstead, Mercury originally wanted the song for that album, then for Queen's next album, *The Works*. With Mercury on piano, the duo finally recorded the demo in 1983, this time for inclusion on *Victory*. They recorded for five or six hours, with Michael improvising lyrics. Ultimately they abandoned the song, but Mercury revived and reworked it for his 1985 solo album *Mr. Bad Guy*.

To date, the Michael/Mercury version has never been officially released. Bootleg versions leaked online in 2002, one being a brief snippet of Mercury discussing the song while Michael sang it solo. Years later, another version surfaced, thought to be a fan-made mash-up of Mercury's 1985 version with Michael's 1983 demo.

## "Victory" (1983)

The final Michael/Mercury collaboration, the demo of this track included another ingredient: Mercury's personal assistant, Peter Freestone. According to Cadman and Halstead, the singers lacked a drum machine; thus Freestone provided unusual percussion by slamming a bedroom door in time with the rhythm. While the track did not appear on the Jacksons' album, it did supply the project title. "Victory" remains unreleased.

## "Bad Company" (1983)

Tito Jackson composed this track for *Victory*, but it remains unreleased. Cadman and Halstead describe it as an up-tempo song with a Tito guitar solo.

## "Buffalo Bill" (1983)

This Michael composition was first considered for *Victory*, then for *Bad*. Inspired by the story of James "Wild Bill" Hickok, the song was recorded but never released. Cadman and Halstead cite engineer Bruce Swedien as stating that it contained a symphonic opening, prominent backing vocals by the Jacksons, and a memorable melody. It remains unreleased in any form.

## "Torture" (12-inch version, 1983)

The extended 12-inch dance mix features enhanced percussion and lengthened instrumental sections.

## "Nona" (1983)

Jackie Jackson composed this track as an ode to actress Sophia Loren. "Nona" failed to make the *Victory* lineup and has never been issued.

## "Power" (1983)

Recorded by the Jacksons, this Jackie-penned song was eventually shelved. According to Cadman and Halstead, Jackie described "Power" as containing a positive message about people coming together. While the Jacksons version has not been heard, the song was finally recorded by Tramaine Hawkins for her 1987 album *Freedom*.

## "Still in Love with You"

Randy wrote and sang lead on "Still in Love with You," a track intended for *Victory*. The song remains unreleased.

## "Time Out for the Burglar" (1987)

Jackie and Randy Jackson collaborated with six other writers on this Jacksons track, which was ultimately reworked to tie in with the Whoopi Goldberg movie *Burglar*. Jackie, Randy, Jermaine, and Tito perform on the final recording; Michael and Marlon (who had departed the group to pursue a solo career) declined to participate. It reached #88 on the US R&B charts but failed to crack the *Billboard* Hot 100 or impact the UK charts.

## Unknown Title (Japan Tsunami relief, 2005)

During a February 2005 interview on the Fox News show *At Large with Geraldo Rivera*, Michael discussed a track he and Randy wrote to raise money for the victims of the recent tsunami in Japan. A brief clip was shown of the two working in the studio, listening to playback. The song was shelved, however, due to Michael's ensuing legal problems.

# 18

# Music Is a Teacher

## Michael Jackson's Transformation from Child to Adult Vocalist

U nlike many artists, Michael Jackson sang professionally from ages eight to forty-nine. As such, listeners have had the unique opportunity to experience how his voice and singing style gradually changed. From *Diana Ross Presents the Jackson 5* to *Off the Wall*, Michael rapidly matured in vocal technique, developing what would become his signature style. Fans who came of age during the 1980s are well aware of his staccato vocals as well as his use of "hee-hee's," hiccups, "dah's" (to accent the percussion), and "shamon's," but may be surprised at his earlier singing, where these traits are largely absent. The Jacksons represent a crucial stage in his career, where he transitioned into a distinctive vocalist with an aggressive, confident style.

Prior to the Jacksons era, the Motown years featured a very young Michael, a singer showing extraordinary promise and technique beyond his years. He was still a child, however, and his vocals on such as classics as "ABC" and "I Want You Back" stress his youth. Nowhere is this clearer than in "ABC's" second verse, with the playground singsong section of "Teacher's gonna show you / How to get an 'A.'" In *Thriller: The Musical Life of Michael Jackson*, Nelson George frequently describes Michael's Jackson 5 voice as "angelic" and "the voice of a choirboy," heavily reliant on his upper register.

In the journal article "'You Can't Win, Child, but You Can't Get Out of the Game': Michael Jackson's Transition from Child Star to Superstar," Jacqueline Warwick analyzes "Who's Loving You" to illustrate Michael's childhood technique. The song's dramatic, full-voiced beginning, Warwick posits, showcases how "Michael Jackson's prepubescent voice was striking for its clarity, strength, and agility, as evidenced in the acrobatic melisma." Within this section he moves through an entire octave, although Warwick notes his full-voiced enthusiasm is typical of many child singers.

Michael's voice began changing in 1973, as evidenced by the slightly lower pitch used on cuts such as "Dancing Machine." Yet in concerts, he was still expected to perform earlier hits like the aforementioned "I'll Be There" and "Ben," and footage from the era demonstrates his increasing difficulty matching his original performances. Just a year before, Michael confronted Berry Gordy about wanting more control over his vocal choices. Gordy agreed, allowing the singer some latitude during the "Lookin' Through the Windows" song recording sessions.

As he explains in *Moonwalk*, he began adding his own vocal flair, ad libbing and experimenting with different effects. He continued experimenting, adding the "dahs" that became a Michael Jackson trademark on the *G.I.T.: Get It Together* track "It's Too Late to Change the Time."

Once he reached puberty, Michael's singing changed not only to accommodate his deeper range but to convey his maturity as a man and artist. While other authors cite *Off the Wall* and his partnership with vocal coach Seth Riggs (discussed in chapter 37) as the turning point in his technique, few focus on his time in the Jacksons as a vocal crossroads. Before his massive late-1970s success, Michael had been refining his singing methods, with his training coming to fruition on 1980's *Triumph*. Certain tracks from *The Jacksons* to *Triumph* perfectly illustrate Michael's road from child star to adult interpretive vocalist.

## The Jacksons (1976)

As Geoff Brown writes in *Michael Jackson: A Life in Music*, the Gamble and Huff arrangements work partially well thanks to Michael's growing vocal maturity. Brown cites how his voice had "taken on richer colours," and as such the producers allowed him more freedom to ad-lib and interpret lyrics as he saw fit.

### "Think Happy"

One of the Jacksons' lesser-known tracks, "Think Happy" demonstrates how far Michael had traveled as a vocalist. Geoff Brown describes how Michael executes "the little decorations of gasps and squeals on the end of words" present on previous Motown cuts like the aforementioned "It's Too Late to Change the Time." From the song's onset, a new, more confident Michael is immediately established. "There ain't no reason, hah! / For you to be sad," he exclaims. As the track concludes, he executes a series of "ha's," "oh's," and "na's" that resemble scatting, a technique that blends perfectly with the speeded-up tempo and pounding piano.

### "Strength of One Man"

While the other brothers sing solos on this track, Michael's performance dominates. "Tell me!" he chants, snapping his fingers in time to the beat (another trait that would reappear on future recordings). He hits his stride in the closing moments; as his brothers harmonize on the phrase "strong enough because the road is tough," Michael improvises, grunting, uttering James Brown–like "well's" and letting raspiness creep into his pure voice while reiterating the phrase "strong enough." The young Michael of "The Love You Save" would not have had the sophistication and experience to have pulled off such vocal tricks.

### "Blues Away"

Michael's first published composition has been discussed already in chapter 15, but it also belongs on this list for his vocal performance. Note how his singing style fluctuates throughout "Blues Away," as if he is testing the subtle shades of his voice. In the first stanza he adopts a whispering tone, matching the daydreaming quality of the lyrics. "I'd like to be yours, tomorrow," he sings shyly, clearly hoping that his intended will accept his offer. But in the second verse, he increases the volume to sing with full voice: "Hey baby, what's your thinkin'?" he demands, anxious for her answer. Although he insists in the chorus that his spirit will not be dampened no matter what she decides, his singing style suggests apprehension. He would fully develop these skills on later tracks like "Human Nature," "Lady in My Life," and "Stranger in Moscow."

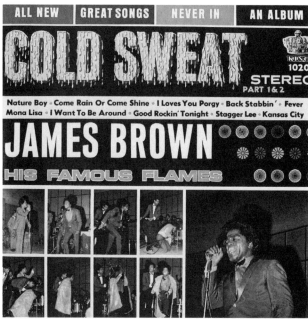

James Brown influenced Michael Jackson not only in dance but also in vocal style. Michael's grunts and heavily rhythmic style echo Brown's earlier work on classics such as "Cold Sweat," the title track from his 1968 album.        *Author's collection*

## Goin' Places (1977)

In just a year, Michael had gained even more confidence as a vocalist, freeing himself from lingering inhibitions remaining from the Motown days. Here, he allows sensuality to enter his voice, exuding sexual desire. For the first time, he utilizes his voice as a tool of seduction, a technique that would become essential on his solo albums.

### "Music's Takin' Over"

"Get down!" Michael commands listeners, and his rhythmic vocal urges that everyone obey. Rasps, grunts, repeating key phrases, alternating between "well's" and "um's," and drawing out notes all make appearances on this track. Think of this performance as a preview for "Working Day and Night." He has clearly learned how to use his voice as a percussive instrument.

### "Different Kind of Lady"

Geoff Brown dubs this *Goin' Places* track "a dry run for 'Shake Your Body (Down to the Ground),'" and the disco beat, scratchy guitar riff, and bass line do sound like a rough draft of that future hit. Michael's growling on "she's so fine, she's all mine" is a significant departure from his Jackson 5 work, introducing the overt sexuality he would constantly revisit in future tracks like "Dirty Diana" and "Give In to Me." The James Brown influence continues, the "ha's!" and "well's" punctuating the song's frenetic beat.

## "Find Me a Girl"

Unlike his Motown recordings (both with the Jackson 5 and solo), Michael's performance on this ballad contains a hint of sensuality. While the brothers execute classic 1970s soul harmonies, he adds roughness to their smooth sounds. "I'm gonna be good to her," he sings, emphasizing the "oo" sound in "good" and exhaling after the word "her." There's a barely constrained desire in these lines, and his singing underscores this emotion. "I'm gonna make good, good lovin'," he later snarls, pitching his voice lower. His "mmm's" suggest more than just an accent; the way he draws out the consonants conveys desire. He would utilize this technique in other sensual ballads such as "Lady in My Life" and even up-tempo songs such as "Rock with You."

## Destiny (1978)

Having amicably split from Gamble and Huff, the Jacksons decided to produce their next album themselves to achieve total artistic control. On *Destiny*, Michael would develop the vocal tics that would be his trademark from 1979 to 2001; think of the tracks discussed below as warm-ups for *Off the Wall*.

### "Blame It on the Boogie"

As discussed in chapter 14, "Blame It on the Boogie" signified the Jacksons' full immersion in disco. Here Michael takes full charge, demonstrating his mastery of the dance track that would fully bloom on *Off the Wall*. As on previous cuts, he growls certain lines ("Don't blame it on the good times") but also injects energy by pitching his voice even higher on ending ad-libs such as "Blame it on yourself, ain't nobody's fault." In *Moonwalk*, Michael reveals that he experimented with controlling his breath on certain lines: "I had fun slurring the chorus: 'Blame It on the Boogie' could be sung in one breath without putting my lips together," he explains.

### "Shake Your Body (Down to the Ground)"

One of Michael's best early compositions, "Shake Your Body" not only merges funk and disco, it allows the singer to turn in one of his most inspired vocals. He alternates between his usual tenor and falsetto, drawing out certain consonants ("playing hard to get-tah"), and punctuating the beat with sharp, high-pitched "oohs." Another favorite phrase, "taking over," was also born in this track. Other artists would utilize this phrase to signify the dance taking over one's spirit, most recently Justin Timberlake in his 2013 hit "Take Back the Night."

# Triumph (1980)

After *Off the Wall*, Michael reunited with his brothers for their last truly collaborative album. Now Michael has emerged as a singer and songwriter, his vocals further honed by new vocal coach Seth Riggs and producer Quincy Jones (both discussed in chapter 37).

## "This Place Hotel (a.k.a. Heartbreak Hotel)"

In *Thriller: The Musical Life of Michael Jackson,* Nelson George describes this Michael-penned track as containing "almost the entire vocabulary of Michael's mature vocal mannerisms. . . . Just as the song's paranoid subject matter and production point toward Michael's future, so does Michael's vocal approach, which makes this performance a preview of greatest hits to come." Indeed, everything is here: the hiccups, the "hee-hee's," and the judicious use of his raspy tone. He also digs into the lower ranges of his voice for the first and second verses, adding to the song's eerie content and vibe.

## "Lovely One"

Michel turned in a particularly joyful performance on this dance track, singing mainly in his upper register. He even gulps in time to the beat in the final moments of the track, contributing his own percussion.

"Lovely One" introduces yet another classic Michael phrase: "g'on," as in the line "g'on with your bad self." He would revisit that technique on "The Way You Make Me Feel," when he could cry out "g'on girl!" Stevie Wonder told *Rolling Stone* in 2014 that Michael later said that he had borrowed "g'on" from a line in Wonder's 1984 song "Go Home." Its presence in "Lovely One," however, proves the phrase predates Wonder's hit.

## "Your Ways"

One of the Jacksons' more unusual tracks, "Your Ways" approaches jazz as much as R&B and funk. Geoff Brown explains how Michael sings in falsetto for much of the track, calling his style "wispy" and "ghostly." In *Moonwalk,* Michael states that he tried out a "newer, more ethereal" style on this song, with the spooky keyboard riffs lending an otherworldly element to the entire track.

## "Everybody"

Listen closely for Michael's occasional finger snaps as he sings much of the dance track in falsetto. His vast vocal range is displayed here, showing he could stretch his vocals to accommodate any style. Falsetto perfectly compliments dreamy lyrics such as "'Cause we're here to live so free," emphasizing the song's theme of escaping everyday life through dance.

## Bonus Track: "You Can't Win (Parts 1 and 2)" (*The Wiz*, 1979)

Technically, "You Can't Win" was Michael's first solo single on Epic Records. In *The Wiz*, Michael performs the song in character as the Scarecrow, lamenting how the crows keep taunting him and how and life keeps throwing obstacles in his path. Looking downcast, he sings the Charlie Smalls–penned song as the crows dance around him, delivering the chorus in a derisive manner. In this original version, Michael emphasizes the character's pain, drawing out the ending line "you can't get out of the game" using the lower ranges of his voice.

Longtime mentor Diana Ross's breathy, emotional style influenced Michael as a singer. Ross continued scoring hits into the 1980s with albums such as 1984's *Swept Away*.

*Author's collection*

Shortly after the film and soundtrack were released, Michael and Quincy Jones returned to the studio to re-record the song with a disco beat, then released it as a single (labeled "Parts 1 and 2") in 1979. The drums and bass thump through the speakers as the horns pierce through the funk. On this version, Michael sounds joyful, the backup singers sometimes functioning as a gospel choir. Part 1 consists of the original lyrics, while Part 2 is a funk workout with the keyboards providing a danceable beat. Michael lets go, testing the upper ranges of his voice, becoming one with the percussion with his scatting and whooping. He even laughs at various points, his happiness radiating from the speakers. In short, he perfects the vocal tics that would pervade *Triumph* and all his future recordings.

The re-recorded version was released as a single in 1979 (with Part 2 later recycled as the B-side to "The Girl Is Mine" but retitled "Can't Get Outta the Rain"), peaking at #81 on the *Billboard* Hot 100 and #42 on the R&B Singles chart. "You Can't Win" garnered renewed interest when it was included on the 2004 *Ultimate Collection* boxed set, with Renée Graham of the *Boston Globe* raving about this buried gem: "It's a revelation. Halfway through the main song, Jackson lets out a whoop, and the tune evolves from a pop-soul confection into a true R&B delight, spiced with barking horns and hand-claps as funky and loose as anything Jackson has ever done."

Throughout his life, Michael constantly experimented with his voice, adopting a tougher, raspier style from 1987's "Bad" onward.

*Author's collection*

Leading Michael Jackson scholar Joseph Vogel has written extensively on Michael's solo career and analyzes his vocal style in *Man in the Music.* Vogel posits that the singer's style transcends language, with his grunts, whoops, stuttering, scatting, interjections, and slurring of words all methods of communicating emotion. "The idea is to make the audience 'feel' the song as a sense impression," he concludes, "rather than focusing entirely on the words."

Jackson borrowed elements of this technique from jazz singers such as Ella Fitzgerald, but he also integrated James Brown's exclamations and grunts, Diana Ross' sighs and "whoo's" between verses, and Otis Redding's raspiness and occasional "yeah's" as if to accentuate a lyric's meaning. As Michael aged, he studied these greats and incorporated bits of their style into his technique.

It is important to note that Michael was not simply mimicking these artists; rather, he combined what he picked up from them with lessons learned at Motown, plus a dash of the interpretive skills he was developing even as a child. As he transitioned from the Jackson 5 to the Jacksons, he realized he had to change his singing, not only to suit his maturing voice but to fit current trends. *Off the Wall* was the vocal turning point for Michael, as Quincy Jones wanted him to move beyond bubblegum pop into more sophisticated material.

"We tried all kinds of tricks that I'd learned over the years to help him with his artistic growth, like dropping keys just a minor third to give him flexibility and a more mature range in the upper and lower registers, and more than a few tempo changes," Jones told the *Los Angeles Times* in 2009. He recommended voice coach Seth Riggs to help Michael expand his range; as Jones recalled, Riggs "gave him vigorous warm-up exercises to expand his top and bottom range by at least a fourth, which I desperately needed to get the vocal drama going."

After *Off the Wall*, Riggs became Michael's vocal consultant, coaching him through recording albums and even touring with him. Riggs told Taraborrelli that the singer possessed a three-and-a-half-octave range, moving from basso low E up to G and A-flat above high C. Michael was a natural tenor, but he was capable of reaching a baritone note.

While his changing voice can be assessed in highly technical terms, one thing is certain: he became a percussive singer, a vocalist whose style depended on rhythm and dance. As *Telegraph* critic Neil McCormick wrote in 2009, "Jackson was a dancer at heart, and his vocal prowess expressed itself playfully within and around the rhythm." Michael showed a unique talent for rhythm from his Jackson 5 days, but his years with the Jacksons enabled him to mold this gift into a distinctive style that would become his musical calling card, and in turn influence generations of singers.

# 19

# Show You the Way to Go

## The Essential Jacksons Playlist

O nce the Jackson 5 departed Motown, they lost their name and a member, Jermaine Jackson, who decided to remain with the label. After signing with Epic Records and adding younger brother Randy, they dubbed themselves "The Jacksons" and recorded seven albums. As previously mentioned, the Jacksons owed a great debt to disco, their careers revived by such dance-friendly hits as "Blame It on the Boogie" and "Shake Your Body (Down to the Ground)." These songs also boasted a mature sound that greatly diverged from their initial bubblegum roots. In addition, Michael as well as other group members took full control over their material, composing their own songs and producing the albums.

This *Billboard* ad from November 18, 1978, celebrated all the gold and platinum albums and singles the Jacksons had scored since their Jackson 5 days.

*Author's collection*

Compiling an ultimate Jacksons playlist needs to reflect these musical changes. In assembling the hypothetical collection below, the following several factors were considered:

- song popularity
- vocal performance
- timeless quality
- distinctive instrumentation
- lyrical quality
- significant elements that appear in future songs.

In creating this playlist, only officially released tracks were considered. Remixes and extended versions require separate lists. Because this book examines Michael Jackson's work, Jacksons tunes not including him are excluded.

## The Jacksons (1976)

- "Enjoy Yourself"
- "Living Together"
- "Show You the Way to Go"
- "Good Times"
- "Dreamer"
- "Blues Away"

## Goin' Places (1977)

- "Different Kind of Lady"
- "Jump for Joy"
- "Even Though You're Gone"
- "Goin' Places"
- "Find Me a Girl"

## Destiny (1978)

- "Blame It on the Boogie"
- "Shake Your Body (Down to the Ground)"
- "Destiny"
- "Things I Do for You"
- "That's What You Get (for Being Polite)"

Another early Jacksons composition, "Do What You Wanna" dated from 1977's *Goin' Places*. It served as the B-side to the Jacksons' 1978 single "Blame It on the Boogie"—an odd choice given that the group had recently severed ties with previous producers Kenny Gamble and Leon Huff.

*Author's collection*

## Triumph (1980)

- "Can You Feel It"
- "Lovely One"

- "This Place Hotel (Heartbreak Hotel)"
- "Everybody"

- "Time Waits for No One"
- "Walk Right Now"

## The Jacksons Live! (1981)

- "Can You Feel It"
- Medley: " I Want You Back / ABC / The Love You Save"

- "This Place Hotel (Heartbreak Hotel)"
- "I'll Be There"

## Victory (1984)

- "Torture"

- "State of Shock"

## 2300 Jackson Street (1989)

- "2300 Jackson Street"

# 20

# Living and Hoping, but I'm Coping

## The Troubled 1984 *Victory* Album and Tour

I t was supposed to be a reunion album and tour celebrating the Jacksons' considerable accomplishments in music. After Michael's historic *Motown 25* performance, Joseph and Katherine Jackson decided that the family could benefit from their son's massive success. They persuaded him to take part in a multimillion-dollar deal involving Pepsi commercials, an album, and a Pepsi-sponsored tour. This time the reunion would include Jermaine Jackson, who had recently departed Motown for Arista Records.

By the end of 1984, all projects were doomed by health issues, infighting, mismanagement, controversy, and negative reviews, culminating in Michael's onstage breakup with the group. This chapter explores this tumultuous year with a look back at the album and tour.

### One More Chance: *Motown 25* and the Birth of *Victory*

After completing his "Billie Jean" performance at the Pasadena Civic Center Auditorium, Michael basked in the applause. His brothers and father greeted him backstage, showering him with compliments on his astounding solo spot. They immediately began to discuss the possibility of a reunion tour, but Michael showed little enthusiasm for the idea. After his mother spoke with Michael, he reluctantly agreed to the album and tour.

### Just Can't Stop This Feeling: The *Victory* Album

Unlike previous Jacksons albums, *Victory* did not represent a true group effort. The brothers rarely worked or recorded together, as solo compositions comprised the track list. Members of Toto such as Steve Lukather, David Paich, Steve Porcaro, and Jeff Porcaro played on the album, as did Michael and Quincy Jones mainstays Paulinho da Costa and Jerry Hey. Michael was minimally involved, contributing only two songs: "State of Shock" (discussed elsewhere in this book) and the slow track "Be Not Always." Otherwise, he shared lead vocals with Jermaine on "Torture," the first single, and co-wrote "The Hurt" with brother Randy, Steve Porcaro, and Paich. In addition to "State of Shock," "Be Not Always," and "Torture," Michael contributed ending ad-libs to "Wait." Recording sessions reportedly took place from November 11, 1983 to May 7, 1984, although engineer Bruce Swedien remembered working on "State of Shock" in June 1984.

Swedien fondly recalls recording "State of Shock" and "Be Not Always" in his book *In the Studio with Michael Jackson*, describing the first song as having "a fantastically strong, rock and roll edge" and being "quite different from the more pop-oriented songs that Michael [later] did with Paul McCartney." The other, "Be Not Always," was a personal favorite of the engineer, who dubs it "a beautiful ballad with a bit of a message for Michael's fans. I love this song."

While trouble was brewing behind the scenes, the Jacksons presented a united front to the press. In an interview with *Jet* entitled "The Jackson Family Talk about Michael" and dated March 26, 1984, the brothers discussed their excitement over the upcoming LP. Marlon Jackson mentioned that he and Michael had collaborated on "Be Not Always" and described it as "a song about children." Tito, Randy, and Jackie Jackson reported that twenty songs had already been written, and that they were rushing to complete the album before the tour began.

Two months later, Michael told *Jet* that Marlon took on a particularly prominent role on the album. "I think out of everybody in the family, Marlon tries harder than anybody . . . . When Jermaine left the group, Marlon had the courage to step into his spot on stage, sing the songs and fill in the gap with harmony," he said, in the article "Michael and the Jacksons Get Ready for Tour." "He's writing songs that are so good. I'm real proud, really . . . On the next album [*Victory*], listen to his lead vocals." After the tour ended, Tito mentioned he had received positive feedback on his *Victory* composition "We Can Change the World," leading him to contemplate a solo career. He discussed these possibilities in a *People* magazine article dated December 30, 1984, "Tito and Randy: Facing Life After the Victory Tour."

In the May 21 *Jet* article, the family reported that Michael was involved with the set design for the upcoming tour as the other brothers completed work on the album. These seemingly frantic preparations may have ultimately harmed *Victory*, as Jermaine would admit years later.

Fans expecting *Thriller*-like tracks were most likely disappointed with *Victory*, as most of the songs are synthesizer-driven R&B. While not as strong or focused as *Triumph*, it does contain a few highlights. "State of Shock," a duet with Mick Jagger, continues Michael's experiments with fusing rock and R&B. The guitar riff stands out, accenting Michael and Jagger's furious performances. Jagger uttered some amusing lines, as if recognizing the song's exaggerated sexuality ("I need mouth-to-mouth resuscitation," Jagger purrs).

Fans from the Jackson 5 days most likely loved Michael and Jermaine singing together on "Torture," another rock-tinged track that features unusually controversial lyrics for the group. The protagonist tells of a doomed love affair, the "torture" referring to the relationship's end. Amazingly, the song found itself in the crosshairs of the Parents Music Resource Center, a Washington, D.C.–based

# PEPSI PRESENTS THE CONCERT TOUR AMERICA IS THIRSTING FOR.

## THE JACKSONS, REUNITED.

Michael, Tito, Jackie, Jermaine, Randy and Marlon are together again. And for the first time in over eight years, all the Jackson brothers are planning a major concert tour across the country.

Pepsi-Cola is proud to sponsor and partici-

pate in the event that will surely be the most exciting and talked about musical tour of 1984. We wish to congratulate and thank Don King and Joe Jackson, exclusive tour promoters, for their help in making this relationship possible. It's nice to be part of the family.

PEPSI

Riding the wave of *Thriller*-mania, Michael Jackson joined his brothers (including Jermaine) for their first tour in three years.                     *Author's collection*

organization formed by Tipper Gore (wife of future US vice president Al Gore). Fearing a rise in violent and sexually explicit lyrics, the group urged the music industry to place warnings on albums concerning content, similar to a movie rating system. They interpreted the lyrics—which include lines such as "Tell me what's your pain or pleasure" and "I am here to serve all masters"—as sadomasochistic.

On September 19, 1985, during a hearing on record labeling before the Committee on Commerce, Science, and Transportation, pastor Jeff Ling of Virginia's Clear River Community Church testified, "Even the Jacksons' mainstream pop music today, their song, 'Torture'" was released as a video, and was shown on national TV. That video included pictures of women dressed in leather bondage, masks, with whips in their hands, in chains, and wrapped up in handcuffs." Despite these remarks, the "Torture" video aired on MTV and other video networks, and *Victory* did not carry a warning label.

Other highlights include the Randy-penned "One More Chance," a ballad that could have been released as a single. Randy's lilting voice repeats "Say you love me" toward the song's end conveys ongoing convincingly. Years later, Janet Jackson covered the tune as the B-side for her 1991 single "If." "The Hurt" contains a solid falsetto lead from Randy and a melancholy, synthesizer-driven melody. Finally, one of the more danceable tracks, "Wait," should have been released as a single rather than "Body," as it features a throbbing beat, the Jacksons' backing harmonies, and heavily rhythmic ad-libbing from Michael as the song concludes.

Infighting adversely affected the publicity for the album. Michael and Jermaine refused to appear in videos for the singles "Torture" and "Body"; in the former clip, Michael is represented by a wax dummy. On the twelfth anniversary of the *Victory* tour, *Entertainment Weekly* published a retrospective on the event. As Kate Meyers reported, no video was filmed for "State of Shock," while the singers reportedly refused to perform any *Victory* tracks during the Jacksons' tour.

Expectations for the LP were huge, mainly due to Michael's massive popularity. Ultimately, *Victory* sold over seven million copies worldwide, opening at #4 on the

*Billboard* 200. It topped the US R&B/Hip-Hop Albums chart, selling 185,000 copies in its first week. A few months later, the album reached double-platinum status for sales of over two million copies. Not surprisingly, the duet between Michael and Mick Jagger performed best, reaching #3 on the *Billboard* Hot 100 and Dance Music/Club Play Singles charts. The second single, "Torture," peaked at #17 on the Hot 100 and #12 on the Hot R&B/Hip-Hop Singles & Tracks chart. Least successful was the final single, "Body," which barely cracked the Top 50 pop charts and the Top 40 R&B singles.

While these statistics would be satisfactory for almost any artist, they did not match the enormous hype surrounding *Victory*'s release. As *New York Times* critic Robert Palmer noted, one issue was sheer competition: upon the Jacksons' album release, Bruce Springsteen's *Born in the USA* ruled the charts. In addition, Prince's *Purple Rain* soundtrack was riding high, spurred by the success of its lead single, "When Doves Cry." Palmer's article, dated July 7, 1984, included an interview with Vince Alletti, chief buyer at the Manhattan Tower Records, who reported that in his store, *Purple Rain* was outselling *Victory* two-to-one.

Sales aside, another issue complicating *Victory* was its tepid reviews. Palmer deemed it "a slickly produced, catchy and danceable collection of pop and dance tunes by brothers who have been developing individual singing and writing styles and don't seem to have as much in common musically as they once did when they aren't sweetly harmonizing vocally." He lamented Michael's lack of involvement, stating that the album needed one producer to ensure consistency, and predicting Jermaine's later complaint: "The pressure to get the album recorded and out in time for the tour may have prevented some of the participants from having second thoughts about improving particular songs, instrumental parts, or sound mixes."

The *New Musical Express* panned *Victory*, with Barney Hoskyns declaring that "what's sad is the sound itself: the lack of everything which made *Triumph* so various and so vigorous. Sound here is hard slabs. Nothing curves or curls. Every beat is mechanical and identical." Ultimately he dismissed the album as "slow digital death." When All Music's William Ruhlmann looked back on the LP years later, he stated that, "In retrospect, *Victory* is a competent album of slick contemporary R&B, occasionally goosed toward greatness by the appearance of one of pop music's most identifiable voices."

The *Chicago Tribune*'s review from July 5, 1984, focused on *Victory*'s inconsistencies, although deemed it "a slick, state-of-the-art merger of catchy pop and mainstream funk, heavy on synthesizers and up-tempo, danceable tunes." Critic Lynn Van Matre called "Be Not Always" "one of the few songs that carries any sense of heartfelt sincerity" but praised "Wait" as "appealing" and Randy's lead vocal on "One More Chance" as proving that "Michael isn't the only family member to manage a floating falsetto with ease."

Years later, Jermaine Jackson expressed his own dissatisfaction with *Victory*, as Cadman and Halstead state in *Michael Jackson: The Early Years*. "As far as I'm concerned the 'State of Shock' single was a mistake. The whole fiasco occurred because it was decided that we had to have product to sell while we were on the road. As a result, a substandard Jacksons album was released, which damaged our reputation."

## All for One and One for All Is What We All Should Be: The *Victory* Tour

The long and complicated saga of the *Victory* Tour brought a disappointing end to the Jacksons' stage career. Disorganization and financial mismanagement, compounded by offstage squabbles, doomed plans for a European tour and any further group projects. Audiences still flocked to see the shows, mainly due to "*Thriller*-mania"—after all, this would be the only opportunity to see Michael perform live. Ultimately, the 55-date, 23-city tour sold 2.3 million tickets, earning the Jacksons about $5 million each. According to Cadman and Halstead, Michael donated his proceeds to three charities: the United Negro College Fund, the Ronald McDonald Camp for Good Times (a charity for terminally ill children and their families), and the T. J. Martell Foundation for Leukemia and Cancer Research.

As Taraborrelli and other authors have chronicled, it was family matriarch Katherine who finally convinced Michael to participate in the *Victory* Tour. Troubles began when Joseph and Katherine hired boxing promoter Don King to organize the tour; Michael did not trust King, and their mutual dislike permeated the launch press conference at New York's Tavern on the Green on November 30, 1983. As *Rolling Stone* reported in the article "Trouble in Paradise?" from its issue dated March 15, 1984, "The gathering turned into a marathon mouth-fest for the bombastic King, who declaimed to the crowd in fine P. T. Barnum style before yielding the floor to a fifteen-minute documentary—about Don King. The reporters were amused; the Jacksons, sitting sullenly behind their sunglasses, did not appear to be." (Six years later, King and Michael apparently buried the hatchet, as the promoter made a cameo appearance in the singer's 1989 "Liberian Girl" video.)

In addition to friction between King and Michael, health issues almost derailed the tour. Earlier in the year, the Jacksons filmed a Pepsi commercial to tie in with the tour. Shot at the Shrine Auditorium in Los Angeles, the advertisement showed the Jacksons performing "live in concert," with Michael dancing down a flight of stairs, explosions going off on either side of the staircase, before joining his brothers at the front of the stage. During the January 27 shoot, an infamous accident occurred: the pyrotechnics malfunctioned, with sparks landing in Michael's hair. Filming abruptly stopped, and Michael was rushed to the hospital with third-degree burns to his scalp. He recovered just before the tour began.

While *Victory* was supposed to feature all six brothers, Jackie was forced to miss most of the tour due to knee surgery. He traveled with the family but could not perform until the December 9 Los Angeles date—the final show of the tour. However, he did appear onstage briefly during their September Quebec shows, joining the Jacksons for a rendition of "Shake Your Body (Down to the Ground)."

Health issues turned out to be the least of the tour's difficulties. When the tickets went on sale, the Jacksons were accused of inflating prices and gouging fans' pockets. First, tickets cost $30 apiece—at the time, big acts like Springsteen and the Rolling Stones charged $16. Michael had reportedly thought $20 was a fair price but was outvoted by his brothers. In addition, an unusual buying procedure was announced: tickets could only be purchased in sets of four by mail order, with no guarantee that the show would not already be sold out by the time the order was

Released on July 2, 1984, *Victory* cracked the Top 5 of the *Billboard* R&B
and pop album charts.                                    *Author's collection*

received. These entries would then be selected at random by a computer; fans
whose names were not drawn would get refunds, but these took four to six weeks
to process. Adding in the $2 service charge for mail orders, the average fan would
spend $122—with the distinct possibility of not receiving any tickets.

Fans and the media panned the decision—and since Michael was the most
famous member of the Jacksons, he was often blamed personally for the unusual
policy. The turning point came when the *Dallas Morning News* published a letter
written by eleven-year-old fan Ladonna Jones in July 1984. Wanting to see her idol,
she had earned money by doing chores for neighbors and babysitting. When she
discovered that would have to buy four tickets, she realized she could not afford
the concert. She penned an open letter to Michael, which ran in the newspaper.
"Dear Michael," she wrote. "I've always believed you to be a person of feeling up
until now. I'm so disappointed in you. How could you of all people be so selfish?
Is your appearance here in Texas Stadium only for the rich?"

When Michael learned about the letter, he made a decision. Holding a press
conference before the Jacksons' Kansas City concert on July 5, he announced that
he and the concert promoter were ending the current ticket policy, canceling the
mail-order system and no longer requiring a four-ticket purchase. He added that
he was donating his share of the *Victory* Tour proceeds to charity. As for Ladonna,
she received four tickets to the concert, a limousine ride, clothing to wear, to the
show, and a meeting backstage with Michael—an event she described in the 2009
*Dallas Morning News* article "Woman Recalls 1984 Meeting with Michael Jackson."

The ticket debacle, along with Michael's obvious disagreements with King and rumors of family infighting, made daily headlines. As *Rolling Stone* reported, plans for the *Victory* Tour had originally included a concert film and a live satellite broadcast of one of the shows; for unknown reasons, neither happened.

In *Moonwalk*, Michael admits that he did not want to do the tour, but decided that he would devote 100 percent of his energy to draw audiences. He designed an 8-story stage incorporating 64,000 pounds of sound and lighting equipment, all of which took 240 people 5 days to assemble for each gig, as *Entertainment Weekly*'s Meyers later wrote.

While Michael enjoyed performing with his brothers again, he was unhappy with their performances. He lamented not having enough time to perfect dance routines and the lighting and said he had a difficult time settling for what he viewed as imperfect performances.

Michael goes on to claim that he and his siblings knew this would be their final tour; he even mentions that "The Final Curtain" was the original name for the project. However, Taraborrelli reports that Michael shocked his brothers when he made his surprise announcement during their Los Angeles show on December 9, 1984: "This is our last and final show. It's been a long twenty years, and we love you all."

## 1984 Tour Dates

The Jacksons toured the USA and Canada over the course of five months, playing to over two million fans.

- July 6–8: Arrowhead Stadium, Kansas City, Missouri: The Jacksons kicked off the tour with three sold-out shows, playing to 135,000 fans, breaking the previous record of nearly 58,000 in 1977. Critic Nelson George attended the July 6 show, and mentions in *Thriller* that the tempo on numbers such as "Off the Wall" and "Human Nature" was too fast. Overall, he states, "the truth, of course, was that this was a Michael Jackson solo tour, nothing more or less."
- July 13–15: Texas Stadium, Dallas, Texas: According to Adrian Grant, the July 13 show drew several celebrities, including Dave Lee Roth, Emmanuel Lewis, and Prince. The July 14 gig proved very special; since guitarist Eddie Van Halen was in town with Van Halen, he joined Michael onstage to reproduce his famous guitar solo on "Beat It."
- July 21–23: Gator Bowl Stadium, Jacksonville, Florida: The Jacksons performed three sellout shows, playing to 135,000 fans. That number broke previous Gator Bowl records set by the Rolling Stones, the Beatles, and the Who. In *Times-Union*'s review dated July 22, 1984, Kevin Bezner summarized the special effects–heavy show as "part Walt Disney World and part Music Television," positing that the Jacksons were the first group to fully integrate music video effects into the concert arena. While Bezner marveled at the stage design—he stated that the Jacksons were the first to use robotics at a concert—he concluded that "Michael Jackson . . . out-dazzles the electronics."
- July 29–31: Giants Stadium, East Rutherford, New Jersey: In *Thriller: The Musical Life of Michael Jackson*, George recalls this as a "remarkable show," with Michael

seeming more engaged with the band and audience. "With a sneering intense scowl on his face, Michael shook his pelvis, moonwalked, and sang with heart and a whole lot of deep-fried soul," he writes. The *New York Times*' Jon Pareles thought the special effects put too great a distance between audience and performer. "But the most spectacular special effect was the most basic one—Michael Jackson's fancy footwork and high, heartfelt singing."

- The *New Musical Express*'s Barney Hoskyns, on the other hand, seemed over-whelmed by the effects and extravagance of the show. "'Heartbreak Hotel' was an electric shock of colour and jerking movement," he wrote, "'Human Nature' was layered silk, waves of love, and Michael was in total command."
- August 4–5: Madison Square Garden, New York: In contrast to the Giants Stadium shows, George recalls, the Madison Square Garden shows exuded less energy. "This performance felt like a group of men punching a clock. Michael, in particular, seemed tired and remote," he writes.
- August 7–9: Nevland Stadium, Knoxville, Tennessee
- August 17–19: Pontiac Silverdome, Detroit Michigan: According to Grant, the Detroit shows found Michael in a particularly good mood due to the Motown connection. At one point he shouted "We love you Motown!" to the audience, then ended the show by tossing his black sequined jacket to a lucky fan.
- August 25–26: Rich Stadium, Buffalo, New York
- September 1–2, 28–29: JFK Stadium, Philadelphia, Pennsylvania: These shows attracted some of the largest audiences of the tour, with the Jacksons playing to 60,000 fans each night. Celebrities such as Springsteen and Sly Stone were in attendance.
- September 7–8: Mile High Stadium, Denver, Colorado
- September 17–18: Montreal Olympic Stadium, Montreal, Quebec, Canada: Grant notes that these dates marked the first time the Jacksons acknowledged the *Victory* album in concert, with the newly completed "Torture" music video played on the screen above the stage. Overall, the brothers would play for more 116,540 concertgoers at these two sell-out gigs.
- September 21–22: RFK Stadium, Washington, D.C.
- October 5–7: Canadian National Exhibition Stadium, Toronto, Ontario, Canada
- October 12–14: Comiskey Park, Chicago, Illinois: The *Chicago Tribune*'s October 13 report captured the excitement of the first night of their Chicago stop. "It was Michael Jackson. Live. On stage. In concert. He didn't even have to sing. When he moved his hips, the fans screamed. When he threw his sunglasses into the crowd, they went wild. And when he danced, Comiskey Park erupted," Mark Zambrano raved. *Tribune* music critic Lynn Van Matre disliked the special effects, calling them "spectacle simply for spectacle's sake," but concluded, "For pop/funk far performed and staged with flair the brothers are hard to beat."
- October 19–20: Municipal Stadium, Cleveland, Ohio
- November 2–3: Orange Bowl, Miami, Florida
- November 9–10: Astrodome, Houston, Texas
- November 16–19: BC Place Stadium, Vancouver, Canada: The Jacksons played three nights to over 107,000 fans, and the *Georgia Straight*'s review of the first

show suggested the special effects were the highlight. Writer Steve Newton particularly liked "Michael's vanishing trick, in which he was corralled into a silver box by two huge, black automated spiders and then lifted into the air and blown up–only to reappear on a platform stage left." However, he criticized the sound system, saying, "With ten musicians playing and the five Jacksons singing, the result was one shrill barrage of sound."

- November 30, December 1–2, December 7–9: Dodger Stadium, Los Angeles, California

## Typical Set List

The Jacksons played the following songs during their 1984 tour:

- "Sword in the Stone" Introduction
- "Wanna Be Startin' Somethin'"
- "Things I Do for You"
- "Off the Wall"
- Medley: " Ben / Human Nature"
- "This Place Hotel"
- "She's Out of My Life"
- Medley: " Let's Get Serious / Dynamite / Tell Me I'm Not Dreamin' (Too Good to Be True)"
- Jackson 5 medley: "I Want You Back / The Love You Save / I'll Be There"
- "Rock with You"
- "Lovely One"
- "Working Day and Night"
- *Encore 1*
- "Beat It"
- "Billie Jean"
- *Encore 2*
- "Shake Your Body (Down to the Ground)"

## Time Has Made Promises: *Victory's* Legacy

The *Victory* Tour grossed approximately $75–90 million, setting a record for the largest grossing tour of all time at that point. While it was marred by negative press, disagreements, burgeoning costs, and initial ticket mismanagement, it stands as a document of the *Thriller* era. For the first time, audiences could see and hear Michael perform "Billie Jean" and "Beat It" live. In addition, he could partially recreate those singles' videos onstage through costume and dance.

As previously mentioned, the *Victory* Tour marks the first major tour of the music video age, a time when video and live performance were being fully integrated. Today, videos are often essential components to a concert, setting a mood or dazzling audiences with special effects. Large-scale tours are the norm. However, the *Victory* Tour captured Michael Jackson at the height of his fame, demonstrating that he had fully surpassed the "little Michael" era to become a star in his own right. In *Moonwalk*, Michael wrote that during the Victory days, he felt on top of the world.

# 21

# Come Together and Think Like One

F ew would argue the Jackson 5's place in music history—their 1997 induction into the Rock and Roll Hall of Fame solidifies their legendary status. However, the Jacksons years have traditionally received less attention, even thought their sales and music proved just as solid as during their Motown era. Along with launching Michael's solo career, the group contributed to R&B and pop in several ways. They introduced movie production values into music videos; upped the ante in concert staging; and created a genre-spanning music that defied the easy categorization of "R&B" music.

## Music Videos as Art

Michael is rightly considered a pioneer in music video, transforming it from artist lip-synching in front of a white screen to the creation of a mini movie. Masterpieces such as "Beat It" and "Thriller" are most often cited as the best examples. However, the Jacksons created another short epic over a year before "Billie Jean": "Can You Feel It," the lead single from *Triumph*. At a time when only a fraction of artists released "music clips," as they were first called, the Jacksons starred in a special effects–filled film written and produced by Michael.

Costing a then-astronomical $140,000, "Can You Feel It" features animation courtesy of Robert Abel, a pioneer of the "photo-fusion" technique. It combines still photography with video and computer graphics, creating a psychedelic effect with Day-Glo colors. Abel & Associates would go on to design the graphics for 1982's *Tron*. Directed by Abel, the ten-minute mini-movie casts the Jacksons as demigods bringing color, love, and happiness to the world. "Word Jazz" poet Ken Nordine provides the beginning narration.

The music video broke several rules for the time, including its over-eight-minute length and the way the sound effects occasionally obscure the music. Even more shockingly, the Jacksons never sing or lip-synch the lyrics during the entire video. Michael would expand these concepts in his own videos, experimenting with animation and creating short movies such as "Thriller," "Bad," "Black or White," and "Remember the Time."

Since "Can You Feel It" premiered in 1981, countless artists have taken cues from its unprecedented production values, with musicians as varied as Madonna, Guns N' Roses, Lady Gaga, and, yes, Janet Jackson later releasing lengthy, high-budget, arty videos bearing production values worthy of a feature film.

## New Standard in Concert Staging

When the Jacksons mounted their 1981 tour supporting *Triumph*, the group wanted to reestablish their reputation as one of music's best live acts. Hiring magician Doug Henning, they decided to emulate the science-fiction film *Close Encounters of the Third Kind* in staging and special effects. State-of-the-art lighting, pyrotechnics accompanied the intricate choreography and sparkling costumes. Michael consciously began each performance with "Can You Feel It"; in *Moonwalk*, he explained that he viewed the song as an attempt to emulate the orchestration and power of *Also Sprach Zarathustra*, the Richard Strauss work that later gained fame as the opening theme to *2001: A Space Odyssey*.

Music critic Nelson George told *Rolling Stone* in 1987 that the 1981 tour was a "primo black arena rock show. In his own book *Thriller: The Musical Life of Michael Jackson*, George recalls seeing the group during their 1981 Madison Square Garden stop. "It was the first concert I attended where the songs were performed in the shadow of music videos," he writes, referring to the Jacksons' performances of "Can You Feel It," "Don't Stop 'Til You Get Enough," and "Rock with You." All three had videos, and the stage show referred to those clips through costumes that mirrored those he wore in the original films. The entire show began with a projection of the "Can You Feel It" clip, a harbinger of how Michael would combine film and live performance at his own concerts.

Today, effects-filled extravaganzas, along with Broadway-worthy costumes and choreography, are commonplace in rock concerts. Elaborate sets, complete with projections and special effects, evolved into a prerequisite for a pop act. Attend any Katy Perry, Lady Gaga, Pink, Usher, Beyoncé, Madonna, or Justin Timberlake show and witness the Jacksons' lasting legacy.

## Genre-Spanning Music

Traditionally, radio stations aired music slotted into specific categories: R&B aired on contemporary stations, rock on all-rock stations, and pop on Top 40 channels. *Destiny* and *Triumph* transcend these labels, bridging elements of dance, pop, soul, and rock into a polished mixture. As *Record Mirror*'s Mark Cooper wrote in 1981, "The Jacksons are the mightiest boogie force in American music, busy at their best constructing a new musical language—percussive R&B funk—that reminds me somehow of rockabilly, maybe because both are about being possessed. Possessed by the twin demons of sex and dance. A boogie that's all twitch and turn and sexy shake, punctuated by yelps, growls, shrieks and the punchiest brass this side of *Raging Bull*."

The *New Musical Express*'s Danny Baker struggled to describe the band's sound in his interview dated April 4, 1981, calling them "the world's premier soul dance band. From chic (small c) disco across to electronic funk. When the Jacksons turn to funk they use no guitars. They have made the use of percussion into an unmatchable style. . . . It's what goes on in those pauses that makes it funk, not because there are a thousand drums keeping the rhythm alive."

The Jacksons did not invent genre-spanning soul, as the tide was already turning toward a new sound. In *Thriller*, George points out that both the Jacksons' albums and Michael's solo material lack the grittier sounds that dominated early-1960s and 1970s soul. Their tracks did not bear marks of what George calls a "traditional soul structure," probably because the sound had become passé.

It was no accident that when the Jacksons founded their production company in the late 1970s, they named it Peacock Music. As Michael told *Blues & Soul* in August 1979, the bird is "a symbol of what we are trying to say through our music and it is summed up by the fact that the peacock is the only bird that integrates all of the colours into one." The siblings' musical message, he explained, in the article "Michael Jackson: Michael's Peacock Music," was that love unites all races.

In an infamous 1980 interview with John Pidgeon (during which Michael commanded that Pidgeon relay his questions through baby sister Janet), the singer expressed disgust over music stereotypes. "I hate labels, because it should be just music. Call it disco, call it anything, it's music to me, it's beautiful to the ear, and that's what counts," he said. "When you go to our concerts, you see

every race out there, and they're all waving hands and they're holding hands and they're smiling. You see the kids out there dancing, as well as the grown-ups and the grandparents, all colors, that's what's great."

Out of the Jacksons' releases from 1976 to 1984, *Triumph* stands as their most critical and commercially successful. Eleven years after its original release, *Spin* magazine ranked *Triumph* at #5 on its list of the "Ten Most Underrated Albums of All Time." Writer Simon Reynolds justified his choice by naming it "a better Michael Jackson album than either *Off*

Another indication of the Jacksons' newfound creative control could be found on 1978's *Destiny*. The back cover featured a lavish image of a peacock, symbolizing the brothers' newly formed production company, Peacock Productions. *Author's collection*

"Goin' Places," the title track from the Jacksons' 1977 album, served as the group's final collaboration with Gamble and Huff.                    *Author's collection*

*the Wall* or *Thriller.*" Is it a dance, rock, R&B, or pop record, or a combination of the four? While "Heartbreak Hotel" suggests rock, "Walk Right Now" and "Lovely One" entice listeners to the dance floor. Switching gears, "Your Ways" resembles jazz-fusion more than a traditional R&B song. *Destiny* began the genre-spanning method, with the brothers contributing danceable R&B and pop, leaning heavily toward disco. *Triumph*, however, best encapsulates the Jacksons' vision of crossover music uniting seemingly disparate audiences.

While the Jacksons may not have directly influenced hip hop, they did set a precedent for combining various types of music for mass appeal. In the early 1980s, rap and hip hop were relegated to house and block parties, and rarely heard on the radio. Then came the "big boom" of the genre: 1986's "Walk This Way," the groundbreaking collaboration between Run DMC and Aerosmith. For the first time, two distinctly different genres joined forces to illustrate their commonalities. Since that massive hit, rap and hip-hop artists have combined elements of rock, pop, soul, dance, and even country to create chart-topping hybrids.

Unlike in the early 1980s, today's rap and hip-hop acts defy easy categorization. Nelly is a prime example of this phenomenon, his singing style and willingness to collaborate with seemingly incompatible musicians like Tim McGraw challenging conventional "rap" stereotypes. A glance at today's *Billboard* Top 100 demonstrates how rappers have scored with pop audiences; in the early 1980s, artists such as Big Sean, Lil Wayne, Flo Rida, and Kanye West would not be seen alongside teen pop. Rap and hip hop now stand as staples on radio and the charts, enjoyed by fans from widely varying backgrounds and musical tastes.

## Bringing the Harmony: The Jacksons' Lasting Impact

A dazzling video, extravagant stage shows, and genre-spanning music comprise the Jacksons' legacy. Technology and evolving trends (namely the rise of disco) enabled them to achieve goals that would have been impossible during the Jackson 5 years. Unfortunately, their final album and tour as a complete group would not run smoothly, as detailed in chapter 20. But while the Jacksons may be best known as the final launching pad for Michael as a solo artist, their influence lingers in artists from the 1980s, 1990s, 2000s, and beyond.

# 22

# Grab a Song and Come Along

## The Lost Solo Albums

**E**ngineer Bruce Swedien wrote about his experiences working with Quincy Jones and Michael Jackson in his 2009 book *In the Studio with Michael Jackson*. At one point he describes his first meeting with songwriter/producer Rod Temperton, who would become a prominent figure in Michael's career. "Rod had flown all night on the red-eye from New York to begin work on Michael Jackson's first solo album," Swedien recalls, referring to *Off the Wall*.

This sentence reflects a common misperception, namely that Michael never recorded a solo album until his 1979 masterpiece. In fact, he had released four solo albums while at Motown. While they met with varying degrees of success, they represent his formative years as a singer trying to establish an artistic identity separate from his brothers.

This chapter looks back at his four Motown releases: *Got to Be There* (1972), *Ben* (1972), *Music and Me* (1973), and *Forever, Michael* (1975). In addition, it explores the collection *Farewell My Summer Love 1984*, a compilation Motown released at the height of *Thriller*-mania.

### You Can Sing Your Melody

In the wake of the Jackson 5's success, Motown head Berry Gordy saw another golden opportunity for Motown. The cute, young, and talented Michael had captured the hearts of teenage girls and impressed older fans with his precocious stage presence. Why not "spin off" Michael from the Jackson 5, establishing him as a solo act and potential teen idol? Gordy approached Michael with the idea in 1971; when the singer began recording his debut solo LP, *Got to Be There*, he became the first Motown act to start a solo career while still a member of another group.

As usual, Michael would not choose his own material; as with the Jackson 5, the Corporation and other Motown producers would write songs and find appropriate cover tunes. In a 1972 interview with *Disc & Music Echo*'s Phil Symes, Michael defended his lack of creative control. Admitting that he had little say over the song selection, he insisted, "If I feel I'd like to comment on a song I do and the producers take notice of what I say." He also stressed that he had no plans to leave his family group.

## Got to Be There (1972)

To prime the public for this album, Motown released the title track as a single in 1971 (the B-side being "Maria [You Were the Only One]"). It became an instant

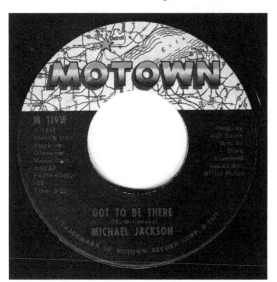

hit, reaching #4 on both the *Billboard* R&B chart and the Hot 100. Michael's cover of Bobby Day's 1958 bubblegum smash "Rockin' Robin" fared even better; pared with the B-side "Love Is Here and Now You're Gone," the track soared to #2 on the R&B and pop charts. The final US single, "I Wanna Be Where You Are" (paired with "We've Got a Good Thing Going") reached #2 on the R&B charts but peaked at #16 on the Hot 100. In the UK, Motown released one more single: Michael's cover of the Bill Withers classic "Ain't No Sunshine," which peaked at #8.

Upon the album's release, *Billboard* predicted, in its issue dated February 12, 1972, that it would be a "blockbuster." While it did not attain that status, *Got to Be There*'s performance pleased Motown, as it reached #3 on the R&B chart and

Michael Jackson's debut solo LP, 1972's *Got to Be There*, spawned the hit title track. Released in late 1971, the single provided a preview of Michael's rapidly developing skills as a first-class interpretive vocalist.

*Author's collection*

#14 on the *Billboard* 200. It sold 900,000 copies in the US alone and was certified gold by the Recording Industry Association of America (RIAA). In addition to the Corporation, *Got to Be There* also features Hal Davis and Willie Hutch as producers.

## Album Highlights

In addition to the title track, *Got to Be There* contains several hidden gems as well as familiar hits.

### "Ain't No Sunshine" (Bill Withers)

Listening to Michael's soulful rendition of Bill Withers's classic blues-tinged ballad, it is difficult to fathom that Michael was only thirteen when he recorded it. His wise-beyond-his-years voice and delivery effectively convey the anguish and pain that permit every word.

### "I Wanna Be Where You Are" (Arthur "T-Boy" Ross and Leon Ware)

One of the singer's finest early solo singles, "I Wanna Be Where You Are" surpasses the typical bubblegum pop song with its use of harpsichord, strings, and flute. In addition, Michael displays the full range of his voice and his impressive ability to navigate difficult chord changes. Finally, "I Wanna Be Where You Are" boasts an interesting co-writer: Arthur "T-Boy" Ross, younger brother of Diana Ross.

### "In Our Small Way" (Beatrice Verdi and Christine Yarian)

While not a huge hit, "In Our Small Way" retains significance as Michael's first "message" song, an omen of the message songs he would later record as part of the Jacksons and, even more significantly, on *Bad*, *Dangerous*, *HIStory*, and *Invincible* (see chapter 30 for more on this). According to Geoff Brown's *Michael Jackson: A Life in Music*, the song's lyrics reflect the political unrest lingering from the 1960s. "Ecology was then a new, hip concern while brotherly love had become a flawed concept thanks to the Vietnam War and the failure of peaceful protest and demonstration to deliver much in the way of equal opportunity, unless it was to die for your country." Lyrics concerning changing the world in the smallest of ways became popular around this time, particularly in Marvin Gaye and Stevie Wonder's songs, as well as various Philadelphia soul singles.

### "Got to Be There" (Elliot Willensky)

An absolutely beautiful love song, the album's title track showcases Michael's impressive range and emotive style. He can softly croon "when she says hello to the world" yet cry out "I need her sharing the world beside me" with gusto. While the single proved Michael's hit-making potential, not all critics were convinced of his longevity. "With 'Got to Be There' riding high in the *NME* chart, the argument still rages—is Michael Jackson an example of schmaltzy show business gimmickry at its worst, or is he really a stupendous if precocious new talent?" pondered Roger St. Pierre in his critical piece "Michael Jackson: Schmaltz or Genius?"

Decades later, it is little wonder that *Rolling Stone* ranked "Got to Be There" at #30 on its "50 Best Michael Jackson Songs" list, calling it "surprisingly sultry." "Few pop stars of the time—let alone ones that were still thirteen years old—ventured into sweetly suggestive lyrics like 'Got to be there in the morning / And welcome her into my world.' Was he referring to the classroom or the bedroom? Either way, he was convincing."

### "Rockin' Robin" (Leon Rene)

Michael's cover of the 1958 Bobby Day hit proved to be the album's biggest success, with the singer's cheerful and youthful voice exuding charm. The song may not be as sophisticated as "I Wanna Be Where You Are," but the arrangement perfectly suits the light-as-air pop sound, complete with tweeting bird (courtesy of a flute).

## Ben (1972)

Thanks to a horror film starring a killer rat, Michael scored his first #1 solo hit and biggest-selling album to date. Michael recorded the title track to the movie *Ben*, a sequel to the 1971 horror flick *Willard*. It became a #1 hit, earning him a Golden Globe for Best Song and an Academy Award nomination for Best Original Song. Eager to capitalize on this massive success, Motown titled Michael's sophomore solo effort *Ben*. To ensure the buying public understood that the album contained

After Michael's rendition of the theme song from the horror flick *Ben* became a huge hit, Motown scrambled to assemble an entire album to capitalize on the tune's popularity. The original cover for *Ben* features images of the killer rats from the film, superimposed over a photograph of a pensive young Michael.    *Author's collection*

Perhaps due to the menacing image of Ben and his rat army, Motown soon reissued the album minus the vermin, this time with only Michael on the cover.    *Author's collection*

the hit song, a photo of rats was initially superimposed on the bottom half of the LP's cover. Fearing that the rats might scare children, however, Motown soon replaced this cover with one featuring a close-up of a pensive Michael. Today, the "rat" cover is a collector's item.

While the Corporation remained involved, *Ben* featured additional producers, including Hal Davis, Byhal Davis, Mel Larson, Jerry Marcellino, and Bobby Taylor (for more information on these figures, see chapter 4).

The "Ben" single proved to be Michael's biggest Motown solo hit, topping the *Billboard* Hot 100, peaking at #5 on the R&B chart, and reaching #3 on the Adult Contemporary chart. Propelled by the hit, the album reached #5 on the *Billboard* 200 and #4 on the *Billboard* R&B chart. Ultimately, the album sold approximately five million copies worldwide.

*Rolling Stone*'s 1972 review of *Ben* was quite positive, with Vince Alletti stating that it was "on the whole a much stronger album than the first." In addition to the title track, he singled out "What Goes Around Comes Around" as a highlight. "[It is] full of hurt bitterness for the girl he is finally strong enough to renounce — but very danceable. That Michael can carry this combination off so smoothly and passionately (the contradictions!) is a sign of ever-increasing maturity."

## Album Highlights

The album may be best known for its title track, but it also includes two of Michael's best cover songs.

### "Ben" (Walter Scharf and Don Black)

Anyone doubting the fourteen-year-old's talent had definitive proof in this sweetly poignant song about friendship. Hearing Michel's earnest delivery, his voice rich with innocence and slight anger on lines such as "They don't see you as I do / I wish they would try to," it is evident that he had continued honing his singing technique and could already hold his own as an interpretive vocalist.

Not surprisingly, *Rolling Stone* ranked "Ben" at #28 on its list of Michael's fifty best songs, calling it "one of the most bizarre Number One hits of the Seventies" due to its subject matter but admitting that few understood the track's original "pro-vermin subtext." The magazine quoted songwriter Black as stating that Michael liked the idea: "He's quite an animal-lover—very sensitive. He enjoys anything that crawls or flies." In *Moonwalk*, Michael cites the song as one of his favorites, and states that he loved watching the film just to see his name appear in the end credits.

### "People Make the World Go 'Round" (Thom Bell, Linda Creed)

Another message song, this Stylistics hit receives a funky yet sincere treatment on *Ben*. Hearing Michael sing lyrics concerning the world's problems, covering poverty, politics, and pollution may seem strange coming from a teenager, but he belts out the words with conviction. Ultimately, he croons, it is up to everyone to solve these seemingly insurmountable obstacles: a topic he would return to frequently throughout his career.

### "Shoo-Be-Doo-Be-Doo-Da-Day" (Sylvia Moy, Henry Cosby, Stevie Wonder)

Stevie Wonder served as an early mentor for Michael, and the young singer repays the favor with this fun cover of a Wonder classic. Michael adds his own flair, uttering James Brown–esque "ow's" and scatting—both trademarks of his later vocal style.

## Music & Me (1973)

As he entered his teenage years, Michael's looks began to change, as did his voice. Clearly he was outgrowing his "cute little Michael" phase, and Motown was at a loss as to how to market him. Thus began a two-album slide for the singer, the first being 1973's *Music & Me*. As with the Jackson 5's work of the time, Hal Davis produced the album.

Because he was touring with the Jackson 5, Michael could do little to promote *Music & Me*. As such, the album's sales suffered, as did its singles. The first release, "With a Child's Heart," features the B-side "Morning Glow"; the song peaked at #50 on the *Billboard* Hot 100, faring better on the R&B charts by reaching #14. "Morning Glow" was released as a single in the UK only. Strangely, the title track (with the B-side "Johnny Raven") charted only in Holland and Turkey. Overall,

*Music & Me* only made it to #50 on the *Billboard* 200, although it reached #24 on the R&B charts. It ultimately sold over two million copies worldwide.

Critically, *Music & Me* received mixed reviews. In his October 1973 "Consumer Guide" column for the *Village Voice*, Robert Christgau awarded the album a "B-minus," arguing, "I listened hard and decided that he's not yet a very good singer. Genuinely sexy and genuinely clean, when Motown provides the material. But if he's a real interpreter, I'm too old to understand where the interpretations are coming from."

## Album Highlights

*Music & Me* may not have experienced commercial success, but select tracks demonstrate Michael's growing skills as an interpretive singer.

### "With a Child's Heart" (Sylvia Moy, Henry Cosby, Vicki Basemore)

Stevie Wonder first recorded this touching ballad about never losing one's sense of childhood innocence and optimism. Interestingly, the music (featuring a jazzy instrumental section) contrasts with this idealistic portrait of youth, sounding melancholy. When Michael recorded his version for *Music & Me*, he gave a wistful sound to lyrics such as "With a child's heart / Nothing can ever get you down." These words would take on new meaning as Michael transitioned into adulthood, eventually chronicling his lost youth in songs such as "Childhood."

### "Up Again" (Freddie Perren, Christine Yarian)

In the hands of a lesser singer, this fluffy pop song might have sounded ridiculous, with lyrics referring to Humpty Dumpty and clichés such as "into each life some rain must fall." Yet Michael's pure voice radiates the idealism that comes with young love. "I'm up again I never let you down / Nothing's ever gonna stop me now!" he cries, testifying to the power of his girlfriend's devotion. The arrangement maintains a circus-like atmosphere, perhaps underscoring the narrator's innocence. Geoff Brown describes the track as containing optimistic lyrics accompanied by a "perky melody with hooks picked out by calliope."

### "Euphoria" (Leon Ware, Jacqueline Hilliard)

One of Michael's more unusual songs, "Euphoria" was an early anti-drug song that nevertheless uses psychedelic, swirling keyboard effects and wah-wah guitar. As he repeatedly spells out the word, he stresses that a state of euphoria can be achieved "knowing no ills, needing no pills" and by "Living the way that you choose / Healthy and clean." Clearly, the track was aimed at Michael's teen audience, presenting him as a positive role model for youth, yet still hip.

### "Music and Me" (Jerry Marcellino, Mel Larson, Don Fenceton, Mike Cannon)

"We've been together for such a long time," Michael croons, summarizing his already long relationship and passion toward music. Similar to "Up Again," "Music and Me" could have been dismissed as sappy and syrupy, yet Michael sings it with conviction. When he almost whispers "There have been others / But never two lovers like . . . music and me," there is little doubt that this rang true for Michael, even as a young teenager.

## Forever, Michael (1975)

Hoping to improve upon his last album's disappointing performance, Motown released Michael's final solo LP for the label, *Forever, Michael*, in 1975. By this time, Michael's voice and appearance had changed considerably, and his young adulthood once again stymied Motown record executives. As on *Music & Me*, Michael lobbied for more creative control, offering to submit his own compositions. Gordy refused, further persuading Michael that he and his brothers needed to leave the label. Unlike the previous outing, *Forever, Michael* boasts several producers, including Edward Holland Jr., Brian Holland, Hal Davis, Freddie Perren, and Sam Brown III.

The LP spawned two singles, both meeting with modest success. "We're Almost There," the first release, reached #7 on the *Billboard* R&B chart but stalled at #54 on the Hot 100. The follow-up, "Just a Little Bit of You" (paired with "Dear Michael") fared much better, peaking at #4 on the R&B chart and #23 on the Hot 100. While *Forever, Michael* performed solidly with R&B audiences, reaching #10 on the charts, it only charted at a disappointing 101 on the *Billboard* 200. To date, it has sold one million copies worldwide.

Despite its lackluster sales, some critics appreciated *Forever, Michael*. Christgau's 1975 review in the *Village Voice* awarded the album an "A-minus," with the critic stating, "At sixteen, however, Michael's voice combines autonomy and helpless innocence in effective proportions." Geoff Brown labels the album as underrated, featuring more mature arrangements suitable for a young man rather than a little kid.

### Album Highlights

Motown may have struggled with Michael's teenage image on *Forever, Michael*, but the album still contains some underrated dance tracks as well as ballads.

#### "We're Almost There" (Edward Holland Jr., Brian Holland)

Michael's voice had changed substantially in tone and technique by 1975, and "We're Almost There" immediately demonstrates that fact. The first track on the album, it establishes that a new Michael Jackson has emerged—one who is confident and mature. Brown described his new voice as having "a quiver of emotion in it, a slightly rasping edge," comparing its sound to Gladys Knight or Candi Staton.

#### "One Day in Your Life" (Sam Brown III, Renée Armand)

While over-arranged, "One Day in Your Life" provides an effective showcase for Michael's rapidly developing skills as an interpreter. His voice emits longing, regret, and a touch of hope as he chronicles a recent breakup. He warns his ex-girlfriend that she will regret losing their young love, that one day she will realize what they shared. "You'll remember me somehow / Though you don't need me now," he croons, adding that he will wait for her. This delivery, radiating tenderness and emotion, would come in handy when he recorded later ballads such as "She's Out of My Life."

### "Just a Little Bit of You" (Edward Holland Jr., Brian Holland)

This up-tempo number recalls old-school Motown but incorporates a slight disco beat. Written by two members of the Holland-Dozier-Holland triumvirate, the lyrics expand upon the adage "an apple a day keeps the doctor away," this time positing that a woman's love fends off any emotional or physical ailments. Using a more aggressive voice, Michael alternates between sweetly crooning and belting out lines such as "So don't send no doctor to my door / 'Cause Doctor John been here before." While he had not adopted his staccato vocal technique yet, he previews his ability to combine pop, dance, and funk in this fun single.

### "You Are There" (Sam Brown III, Randy Meitzenheimer, Christine Yarian)

Brown calls this track's arrangement "Chi-Lites meets the Stylistics," which is an apt description. The song makes use of the electric sitar, a popular instrument in early-1970s soul, most notably on the Stylistics' "You Make Me Feel Brand New." "You Are There" also panders to Michael's teenage girl audience, with lines such as "Like a rainbow after rain / Like the night follows day / You're the answer to the prayers I say" sung with a sigh. The lyrics may be corny, but Michael's lilting voice sounds genuine, which surely make the girls swoon.

## Bonus LP: *Farewell My Summer Love 1984*

Calling *Farewell My Summer Love 1984* a Michael Jackson solo album is admittedly a stretch; after all, Motown simply compiled leftover tracks from 1973 recording sessions, labeled the project a "lost Michael Jackson album" that had been "newly discovered," overdubbed additional instrumentation, then released it at the height of *Thriller*. Michael later expressed anger at his former label trying to cash in on his fame, telling author J. Randy Taraborrelli, "It's not fair. I had no control over that music. I don't even like some of those songs."

The album was initially released with "1984" as part of the title, but the numbers were dropped from subsequent pressings. A poster accompanied the LP, mainly promoting the album itself. The first single, the title track, performed well in the US and UK due to Michael's massive popularity. It reached #38 on the *Billboard* Hot 100 and #7 on the UK charts. However, the next release, "Touch the One You Love," failed to chart, and the final single, "Girl You're So Together," was issued in the UK only, just cracking the Top 40 there. *Farewell My Summer Love* stalled at #46 on the *Billboard* 200, but reached #9 on the UK albums chart. Overall, it has sold over three million copies worldwide—a far cry from *Thriller*'s numbers.

In addition, Motown received much criticism for a seemingly tacky cash grab. "To put it mildly, the title of Michael's album (Motown) is a blatant, opportunistic cheat. None of these songs was recorded more recently than ten years ago when Michael was fifteen. . . . It's too bad that his old label found it necessary to foist this deception on his fans," *People* said, in its review dated June 25, 1984. When *Rolling*

*Stone* discussed the album thirty years later in its "50 Best Michael Jackson Songs" list, it too acknowledged the curious timing of its release. "In 1984, a recording of Michael Jackson reading the tax code would probably have charted. Keenly aware of this, Motown released an album of unused MJ material."

## Album Highlights

*Farewell My Summer Love 1984* is less of a solo album and more of a rarities compilation. Yet it features enjoyable cover versions and some interesting new compositions courtesy of Motown's songwriters.

### "You've Really Got a Hold on Me" (Smokey Robinson, Ronald White, Robert Rogers)

"You've Really Got a Hold on Me" enabled Michael to pay tribute to personal hero Smokey Robinson. After all, Michael earned early acclaim with his astounding cover of "Who's Loving You," both on record and in concert. While the modern instrumental overdubs and added backing vocals are unnecessary, Michael's soulful performance remains intact.

Clearly cashing in on Michael's enormous popularity, Motown included an insert within each copy of *Farewell My Summer Love.* This booklet advertised the Jackson 5 catalogue, a new greatest hits compilation, picture discs, and posters—all accompanied by a "glove" mimicking his signature prop.

*Author's collection*

### "Melodie" (Mel Larson, Jerry Marcellino, Deke Richards)

This cheerful slice of up-tempo bubblegum pop would have probably played well in concerts, or could have been transformed into a Jackson 5 track. Its driving rhythm and Michael's peppy vocals tell the story of a girl who reminds him of his love for music. "Melodie, you're my symphony," he cries out. His optimism knows no bounds; "Beautiful morning, oh happy day," he sings, because every word his beloved utters is "music to my ears." The song exudes youthful optimism and the blush of first love through Michael's charming performance.

### "Touch the One You Love" (Artie Wayne, George S. Clinton)

As previously mentioned, George Clinton penned several tracks for Motown. One such composition, "Touch the One You Love," remained unreleased until this collection. Its finger-snapping rhythm and catchy chorus ("You got to touch the one you love / If you want the one you love to touch you") encourages listeners to sway and sing along. It would have been suitable for a Jackson 5 track, particularly

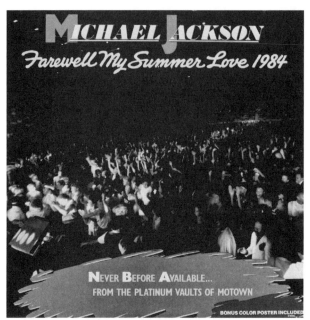

As *Thriller* was breaking sales records, Motown compiled outtakes from Michael's solo albums for the label. The resulting collection, *Farewell My Summer Love 1984*, performed modestly on the charts despite being dubbed a "lost album." Pictured is the original release; the "1984" was removed from future pressings.                    *Author's collection*

for his harmonic backing vocals, but Michael's lead vocal channels Diana Ross in its ability to engage the audience. Think of this track as Michael's version of "Reach Out and Touch Somebody's Hand."

### "Farewell My Summer Love" (Keni St. Lewis)

A throwback to classic Motown, "Farewell My Summer Love" sounds as if it could have been recorded by the Four Tops. Just listen for the beginning "ooh's" straight from "Baby I Need Your Lovin'." The album's biggest hit single tells the story of bidding a summer love goodbye, with both having to return to school. Teenagers can relate to the story—or dream of having such a romance—and Michael's tenor maintains an air of innocence. "When you return to your hometown / And you discuss your trip / Will I be the guy that you put down?" he asks, expressing his insecurity and doubt that their relationship will survive long distance.

Despite its minor success, *Rolling Stone* ranked "Farewell My Summer Love" at #41 on its list of the fifty best Michael Jackson songs. Calling it "innocent," the magazine praised Michael's singing: "Fittingly for a song about adolescent sadness, Michael's performance is a snapshot of his voice just as it was changing; there are even some hints of his mature power."

## Lost in the Past Somewhere

When the Jackson brothers departed Motown for CBS Records, they began a new phase in their careers. Michael did not resume his solo career until 1979 (although he technically released his first single in 1978 as part of the soundtrack to *The Wiz*), with *Off the Wall* quickly overshadowing the four solo LPs he recorded at Motown. *Got to Be There, Ben, Music & Me,* and *Forever, Michael* may not have been massive hits, but their contents provide hints as to what Michael would eventually become. On these LPs, he was developing the interpretive skills and mannerisms that would distinguish him from his peers, leading to his impressive 1980s reinvention.

# 23

# You Are Not Alone

## Michael Jackson as Backup Singer

While Michael Jackson rarely made guest appearances on other people's records, he occasionally made exceptions for friends, family, and colleagues. By singing backup on various tracks, he demonstrated his range, singing on everything from rock to reggae. This chapter highlights some of these cameo appearances and attempts to answer a longtime mystery: did Michael really sing with the Doobie Brothers?

### "Who's Right, Who's Wrong"—Kenny Loggins (1979)

A cut off Loggins's soft-rock album *After the Fire*, "Who's Right, Who's Wrong" is a slice of mid-tempo blue-eyed soul. Co-written by Richard Page (Mr. Mister), the song features Michael's backing vocals and unmistakable ad-libs. In an interview with Ultimate Classic Rock dated October 29, 2014, Loggins revealed that he met Michael at a benefit and asked if he would like to sing on his next record. Having just finished *Off the Wall*, Michael agreed. "Had I really thought it through, I should have probably recorded something up-tempo with him. I kick myself and think that was a waste of his talent. Great tune and everything, but just not the right tune for Michael Jackson to be singing on," Loggins said.

Nevertheless, Loggins stressed how he enjoyed working with Michael, encouraging him to put more of his own style into the track. "He was a total sweetheart and was willing to go in any direction. I remember at one point I said, 'Put more of your 'thing' on it, it feels a little too stiff.' And he said, 'You mean you want it stinky?' 'Yeah! I want it stinky.' So he put more juice on it."

### "Save Me"—Dave Mason (1980)

The former Traffic member and Michael Jackson seems like an unusual combination, but their mixture of rock and soul works well on this up-tempo rocker. Mason, who wrote the rock classic "Feelin' Alright" and later scored a soft rock hit with "We Just Disagree," was recording his album *Old Crest on a New Wave* in a neighboring studio as Michael made *Off the Wall*.

"I needed someone to sing a high harmony on 'Save Me,' so when Michael was on a break I asked him if he would sing on the track," Mason told the *Journal News*'s Kevin Phelan. "To which he responded, 'When I was twelve years old, I was doing a TV special with Diana Ross. At the end of the show Diana and I sang 'Feelin' Alright,' so yes, I'd love to sing on your song.' He came to the studio and sang the heck out of it."

"Save Me" was released as a single, but peaked at #71 on the *Billboard* Hot 100 and #72 on the R&B Singles chart.

## "I'm in Love Again"—Minnie Riperton (1980)

While Michael's voice is more prominent here than is typical for a "backup vocalist," the focus is more on Riperton. After her untimely death, her husband Richard Rudolph and Quincy Jones sorted through unfinished music to find vocals suitable for release. These vocals were isolated from these recordings, and then new music and additional singers were added to complete the tracks. Jones brought in contemporary artists who had previously worked with Riperton or whose styles closely matched her unique vocal approach. In addition to Peabo Bryson, Stevie Wonder, George Benson, and Patrice Rushen, Michael lent his vocals to the album, including "I'm in Love Again," the second track on *Love Lives Forever*.

Soul songstress Minnie Riperton released several successful albums during her all-too-short career between 1970 and 1979 (including 1975's *Adventures in Paradise*, pictured here). A year after her 1979 death, vocals from her 1978 demos were overdubbed onto new arrangements. Popular singers from 1980 added lead and backing vocals. The resulting posthumous collection *Love Lives Forever* features the jazzy ballad "I'm in Love Again," a virtual duet with Michael.                                                    *Author's collection*

The album has a jazz slant, which proved a challenge for Michael. The ballad features strings along with Hubert Laws's fluttering flute solo, Riperton's lighter-than-air voice effortlessly navigating the melody. Michael mainly provides accents, as if filling in gaps from the original recording. Still, his tenor melds with Riperton's high-pitched range quite well; it would have been fascinating to hear the duo collaborate on more material.

## "All I Do"—Stevie Wonder (1980)

After recording the soundtrack to the documentary *Journey Through the Secret Life of Plants*, Wonder returned to his R&B roots with 1980's *Hotter Than July*. Among its numerous standout tracks is "All I Do," a song he wrote over a decade earlier for Tammi Terrell. With the song updated to subtly reflect the then-dominant disco sound, Wonder recruited longtime friend Michael to sing backup. The younger singer was in good company, as he joined a group consisting of the O'Jays' Eddie Levert and Walter Williams along with Betty Wright. Unlike the other tracks mentioned in this chapter, Michael's voice is barely audible, but he is listed in the liner notes.

While "All I Do" has since become a beloved radio and concert staple, it was never released as an A-side. Instead, it saw release as the B-side of "That Girl," the first single off Wonder's greatest hits collection *Stevie Wonder's Original Musiquarium I*.

Michael often collaborated with his mentor, Stevie Wonder, from the Jackson 5 years onward. On Wonder's 1980 disc *Hotter Than July*, Michael backed up his friend on the second track, "All I Do." *Author's collection*

## "Goin' Back to Alabama"—Kenny Rogers

Before artists such as Garth Brooks, Shania Twain, and Faith Hill scored pop hits, Kenny Rogers crossed over into pop territory by expanding his sound beyond country. In 1980, Lionel Richie penned the ballad "Lady" for Rogers, and it was included as a previously unreleased track on his *Greatest Hits* collection. The song became a Top 10 smash, leading Rogers and Richie to collaborate on more material, including several tracks on the country star's 1981 album *Share Your Love*.

Richie told *Jet* in 1985 that he called his friend Michael to ask if he would sing backup on "Goin' Home to Alabama," a track Richie had written for Rogers. According to Cadman and Halstead's *Michael Jackson: For the Record*, Michael was already a fan of Rogers, so he needed little convincing. After the session, Richie joked, "We decided that if we never had another hit record, we could always make $100,000 a year singing background parts."

With a melody reminiscent of the Commodores' "Sail On," "Goin' Home to Alabama" lets Rogers sing of starting over again in his hometown. "He can pick himself up, dust himself off, and start all over again," Rogers sings, with Richie and Michael crooning behind him. Unlike on cuts like "Save Me" or "Who's Right, Who's Wrong," Michael vocalizes his sections in a straightforward manner, restraining his R&B mannerisms in favor of the track's pop/country flavor. As Stephen Holden wrote in his 1981 *New York Times* review of the album, "'Goin' Back to Alabama,' in which Michael Jackson sings back-up, is a rousing gospel-styled anthem of self-affirmation."

## "The Dude"—Quincy Jones (1981)

The least surprising entry in this chapter, "The Dude" is the title track from Jones's 1981 album. One of his finest collections, *The Dude* produced the hits "Just Once"

and "One Hundred Ways," both featuring James Ingram. Unlike those smooth ballads, the title song reflects early hip hop with its lead rapping. Co-written by Jones, Patti Austin, and frequent Jones collaborator Rod Temperton, the song is centered on a self-assured, streetwise character who has "a PhD in how to make ends meet." Michael and fellow backup vocalists Austin, Syreeta Wright, Jim Gilstrap, and Lalomie Washburn serve as a Greek chorus, chanting lyrics such as "See him steppin' down the street / No forgettin', he's the Dude."

*The Dude* serves as a sonic companion to *Off the Wall*, particularly since it includes many of the same musicians. In addition, it fuses soul, pop, R&B, dance, jazz, and world music in a very similar manner to Jones and Michael's masterpiece.

Repaying his friend Quincy Jones for his production work on *Off the Wall*, Michael joined the backup singers on "The Dude," the title track from Jones's 1981 album.
*Author's collection*

## "Just Friends"—Carole Bayer Sager (1981)

Michael first worked with the songwriter when he recorded her composition "It's the Falling in Love" for *Off the Wall*. Returning the favor, he sang backing vocals on "Just Friends" for her solo album *Sometimes at Night*. Sager co-wrote this sad ballad about the end of a romance with then-husband Burt Bacharach; Michael co-produced the song with Bacharach. The two singers express regret that they cannot go back to just being friends; one line, however, suggests that their affair may not be over: "I don't ever wanna feel so much again . . . Unless it's you . . . again." Occasionally Michael speaks rather than sings his verses, at one point sighing, "I wish you'd understand." Other than "She's Out of My Life," "Just Friends" may be the most mature love song Michael ever recorded.

Michael and Sager continued their friendship for decades, writing material together. One song they co-wrote, "You Are My Life," appeared on his final album, *Invincible*.

## "Don't Let a Woman (Make a Fool Out of You)"—Joe King Carrasco (1982)

How did Michael end up singing with the self-proclaimed "King of Tex-Mex Rock and Roll"? In one of his most unusual collaborations, Michael sang backup on Joe King Carrasco's "Don't Let a Woman (Make a Fool Out of You)," a track that bears more than a passing resemblance to Bob Marley's "No Woman, No Cry." The Texas-born guitarist, singer, and songwriter and his band the Crowns first became known for their 1979 anthem "Party Weekend." One of the first American bands to be signed to England's Stiff Records (best known for artists like Elvis Costello), they created what Carrasco's website describes as "a stylistic borderland of pop rock and Latin rhythms . . . [his] cross-cultural stew blends cumbias, vamp, salsa, surf, reggae, blues, and Latin-tinged polkas."

According to Carrasco's former manager Joe Nick Patoski, the unlikely collaboration occurred in fall 1981, as the guitarist and the Crowns were recording their album *Synapse Gap*. While the group recorded at Studio 55 in Los Angeles, the Jacksons were in an adjoining studio mixing their *Jacksons Live* album. Carrasco's entourage and the Jacksons became friendly, often hanging out in the building's rec room and sharing meals. One day, Carrasco mused how it would be fun to have Michael sing harmonies on "Don't Let a Woman (Make a Fool Out of You)"; he approached the singer, and Michael agreed.

As Patoski later recalled on his blog, "So there he was, headphones covering his ears, trying to figure out just who was this Joe 'King' character, while he professionally stepped up to a microphone facing Joe, nailing the high harmonies and making Joe sound good. Someone by the mixing board wisecracked that Joe's vocals should be mixed out of the recording so we could release a dub version of Michael Jackson singing the song."

In a 2013 interview with the *Dallas Observer*, Carrasco remembered the event differently. He said that he often saw Michael sitting alone in a studio office and ended up chatting with him about Marley and African music. "One day, I told him that I didn't have anyone in my band who could sing high," he told Darryl Smyers. "He said he would like to sing on my album. . . . Michael was a real nice guy, and we became good friends. His voice was amazing. He could do these amazing five-part harmonies. I have a tape somewhere of him singing those five-part harmonies."

## "State of Independence"—Donna Summer (1982)

Best known for the hit "Love Is in Control (Finger on the Trigger)," the 1982 album *Donna Summer* was produced by Jones and featured much of the cast from *Off the Wall* and *The Dude*. "State of Independence" is derived from a seemingly mismatched duo: Vangelis ("Chariots of Fire") and Jon Anderson, lead singer of the progressive rock group Yes. The two first recorded the song for their 1981 album *The Friends of Mr. Cairo*, but "State of Independence" failed to chart. Summer's cover performed much better, peaking at #41 on the *Billboard* Hot 100 and #31 on the R&B chart.

A curious mixture of new wave, pop, and R&B, "State of Independence" boasted an impressive roster of backup singers: Michael, Brenda Russell, James Ingram, Dionne Warwick, Kenny Loggins, Lionel Richie, and Stevie Wonder.

## "Somebody's Watching Me"—Rockwell (1983)

At the height of *Thriller*-mania, a mysterious single emerged. "Somebody's Watching Me," a song by an unknown artist named Rockwell, featured what sounded like a British singer lamenting his lack of privacy. Then came the chorus: "I always feel like somebody's watching me," it wailed, and here the singer sounded familiar. Indeed, it was Michael singing those choruses, leading fans to wonder why such a big star would appear on a seemingly anonymous artist's record. The answer: "Rockwell" was in reality Kennedy William Gordy, son of Motown founder Berry Gordy.

Legend has it that Rockwell submitted audition tapes under this assumed name to avoid any nepotism issues; not realizing his true identity, his father signed him to Motown. According to Cadman and Halstead's *Michael Jackson: For the Record*, Michael agreed to sing on "Somebody's Watching Me" when Rockwell first played him the demo. With Jermaine singing background, Michael performed the hook, recording his vocals in just over an hour.

Accompanied by a strange, horror-themed video (in which Michael did not appear), the single was released in January 1984. While Rockwell's half-rapped vocals comprised much of "Somebody's Watching Me," it was Michael's prominent backing vocals that propelled the track up the charts. It reached #2 on the *Billboard* Hot 100 and #6 on the UK charts, ultimately earning Rockwell his first and only gold single. Once his true identity as Berry Gordy's son was revealed, he continued his music career; after failing to repeat the success of "Somebody's Watching Me," he left the music industry in the late 1980s.

## "Papa Was a Rollin' Stone" / "So Shy"—Bill Wolfer (1983)

Bill Wolfer had already established a reputation as a top session musician, playing keyboards on "Billie Jean" and previously performing on Stevie Wonder's *Hotter Than July*, when he was signed to the Solar Records label in 1982. The following year he released *Wolf*, a fusion album clearly influenced by Quincy Jones's *The Dude*. Due to his connections, Wolfe recruited an impressive lineup of guest artists for his first album, including Michael and Wonder.

Michael sings on two cuts: a cover of the Temptations' "Papa Was a Rolling Stone" and "So Shy." Sounding like a cross between Devo's robotic new-wave sounds and Herbie Hancock's "Rockit," "Papa Was a Rolling Stone" is sung almost entirely through a synthesizer. The Maxine sisters (Oren, Julia, and Maxine) and Michael sing the chorus. In addition, the up-tempo "So Shy" sounds like a *Hotter Than July* outtake with a Wonder-esque lead vocal and a synthesizer-driven beat. Again, Michael's vocals are not prominent, but he is among the chorus of voices singing "na-na's" at various points. *Wolf* ended up as a modest hit, peaking at #50 on the R&B chart.

## "Don't Stand Another Chance"—Janet Jackson (1984)

In the early 1980s, Janet struggled to establish her musical identity. Her second album, 1984's *Dream Street*, melded pop and R&B in the hopes of scoring some hits on both charts. The lead single, "Don't Stand Another Chance," saw Marlon and Michael lending their support; Marlon co-wrote and produced the song, while Michael contributed ad-libs. The funky keyboards and strong, danceable beat propelled the song to #9 on the R&B/Hip-Hop Singles and Tracks chart and #23 on the Dance Music/Club Play Singles chart (the latter due to its superior 12-inch mix). Listen for the reference to "Shake Your Body (Down to the Ground)" in the extended version.

Despite Janet's performance of "Don't Stand Another Chance" on *American Bandstand* and her new role on the TV series *Fame*, *Dream Street* failed to achieve great success, peaking at #147 on the *Billboard* 200. Two years later, she would team with Jimmy Jam and Terry Lewis to create *Control*, and the rest is history.

## "To Satisfy You"—Bryan Loren (1992)

Singer, songwriter, and producer Loren's professional relationship with Michael dates back to *Dangerous*; the two collaborated on several tracks for the project but none made the final album. During that time, the duo also co-wrote "Do the Bartman," a song Michael composed in honor of his favorite TV show (see chapter 33 for further explanation). Eventually, a Loren/Michael composition did appear on an album: "Superfly Sister" finally emerged on 1997's *Blood on the Dance Floor*.

During the *Dangerous* sessions, they wrote the light ballad "To Satisfy You"; when Michael elected to pass on the song, Loren asked if he could record it. Not only did Michael agree, he volunteered to sing backup. A rare cut, "To Satisfy You" was included on Loren's 1992 album *Music from the New World*, which was released in Japan only.

## "Whatzupwitu" / "Yeah"—Eddie Murphy (1993)

While younger fans may know him better as Donkey from *Shrek* or from comedy classics like *Beverly Hills Cop* and *Coming to America*, few may remember Murphy's flirtation with becoming a recording artist. After receiving some acclaim for his singing on *Saturday Night Live*, he pursued a solo career that initially had positive results. His 1985 debut album, produced by Rick James, spawned the hit "Party All the Time"; his 1989 follow-up failed to repeat that success. Deciding to try again in 1993, he recruited his friend Michael to appear on two tracks from the album *Love's Alright*: "Whatzupwitu" and "Yeah."

"Whatzupwitu" features Michael singing the chorus using a funky nasal voice—All Music's Steven McDonald later noted that Michael "steals 'Whatzupwitu' outright." The accompanying video, also starring Michael and Murphy, shows the two men clowning with each other while appearing to float in a blue sky. Children skip around them as animated flowers and peace signs float by. Presumably Michael appeared on the song and in the clip to thank Murphy for his work on Michael's "Remember the Time" video.

Another *Love's Alright* track, "Yeah," features an all-star chorus harmonizing on the word "yeah"; the single benefitted Murphy's Yeah Foundation charity. Michael served as a part of a truly impressive group, including Babyface, Jon Bon Jovi, Garth Brooks, En Vogue, Johnny Gill, Amy Grant, Aaron Hall, MC Hammer, Heavy D., Howard Hewett, Julio Iglesias, Janet Jackson, Elton John, Patti LaBelle, Paul McCartney, Teddy Pendergrass, Richie Sambora, Luther Vandross, Audrey Wheeler, Barry White, and Stevie Wonder.

## "Why" / "I Need You"—3T (1995)

Michael's appearance on this boy band's singles is logical: after all, 3T's members were his nephews. Tito's three sons Toriano Adaryll Jackson II (also known as Taj), Taryll Adren Jackson, and Tito Joe Jackson (also known as T. J.) released their debut album, *Brotherhood*, in 1995. Michael and Kenneth Komisar co-produced the disc; while it did not fare well in the US, it performed impressively abroad, reaching #11 on the UK album chart as well as #2 in France.

The Babyface-written single "Why" prominently features Michael on the chorus, his vocals blending perfectly with those of his nephews. The black-and-white video is most charming when it shows Michael kidding around with the boys, occasionally pretending to upstage them or trying to make them laugh as they sing their solos. The second single off *Brotherhood*, "Why" reached #2 on the UK charts.

"I Need You" combines a traditional love song with a gospel feel, similar to Michael's own "You Are Not Alone." Toward the track's end, Michael contributes a brief ad-lib in a raspier voice than is heard on "Why." This time the video only featured 3T; their famous uncle did not appear. Again, "I Need You" performed best in the UK, peaking at #3.

## The Great Mystery: Did Michael Collaborate with the Doobie Brothers?

In 2003, director Bryan Michael Stoller was shooting his film called *Miss Cast Away and the Island Girls*; a longtime friend of Michael's, he asked the singer to make a cameo appearance in the movie. Stoller shot the scene at Neverland, and in the midst of the filming, Michael received a call from Elizabeth Taylor. As the two chatted, Stoller kept the video camera rolling for extra "behind the scenes" footage. During the conversation, Michael told Taylor that he sang backup on the Doobie Brothers' 1978 tracks "Minute by Minute," "What a Fool Believes," and "Here to Love You." Singing the backing vocals to the first two songs during the call, he demonstrated that he was familiar with those parts. After Michael's death in 2009, *Entertainment Tonight* aired this video excerpt; subsequently, every book and Michael Jackson website has reported this as fact.

However, when you listen to those three *Minute by Minute* tracks, Michael's voice is not audible. Additionally, he is not listed on the album credits (although he acknowledges this in the video). Did he really sing on these songs? The Doobie Brothers camp has been strangely silent on this topic. On Michael McDonald's official website, his forum administrator responded to the topic on August 21, 2009: "There is absolutely no truth to this on confirmation from Michael. McD sang all the parts on 'What a Fool . . .' and he did not sing on 'Minute by Minute' either. MJ was having a fantasy moment it seems."

Original Doobie Brothers member Patrick Simmons cast further doubt on the story in a 2014 interview with Ultimate Classic Rock. "No, it's not. He was kidding around while someone had a video camera going. I don't know if he ever told her [Elizabeth Taylor] the truth," Simmons insisted. He confirmed that Michael frequently visited the band during their *Minute by Minute* rehearsals. "He was a good guy—he was always hanging around a lot, and he did come into the studio for our rehearsals once in awhile," Simmons said. "I wish we had called him in for that, and I know he would have done it in a second, but I don't think it ever entered our heads to invite him. I don't know why—I guess because we were a band and we wanted to do everything ourselves." Simmons added a bit of intrigue, however, when he mentioned that Michael "did come and sing backgrounds with us on several occasions at shows."

Another layer to the mystery lies in a *Rock & Soul* magazine cover story from March 1980, reporting on "Michael Jackson's L.A. Jam." The Doobie Brothers celebrated their tenth anniversary by hosting a party at the Friar's Club in Beverly Hills, and the Jacksons attended the bash. Rufus Thomas, Eddie Floyd, and Sam & Dave all performed, but the highlight of the evening occurred when Michael, Kenny Loggins, and Pablo Cruise, among many others, turned in a "rip-roaring forty-minute rendition" of "Shake Your Body (Down to the Ground)." Clearly the Doobie Brothers and Michael traveled in the same circles, as Michael had previously recorded with Loggins, who often collaborated with McDonald. Did Michael really sing backup for the Doobie Brothers? Based on Simmons's comments as well as those from McDonald's site administrator, it looks unlikely.

# 24

# To Escape the World I've Got to Enjoy That Simple Dance

## Michael Jackson's Greatest Dance Teachers

Michael Jackson's legendary *Motown 25* performance cemented his reputation as not only a first-rate singer but a trendsetting dancer. View any *Soul Train* or *American Bandstand* episodes from March 1983 onward and you'll see dancers executing his signature moves. The sideways kick, standing on tiptoes, pelvic thrusts—all of these steps remain iconic. As discussed in chapter 28, Michael may have perfected the moonwalk, but he did not invent it. Indeed, Michael's dance teachers hailed from everywhere from Broadway to the Apollo, from movies to television. The following list profiles the most important figures and explores how their moves impacted one of entertainment's greatest dancers.

### Bob Fosse

Michael cited Bob Fosse as an inspiration. In the 2012 documentary *Bad 25*, Karen Langford, longtime legal advisor and archive manager for the Michael Jackson estate, displays a memo written during the making of the "Smooth Criminal" video. In longhand, Michael wrote, "For Criminal Dance look at all the great dances on tape. 'Study the greats and become greater.' Get all Bob Fosse Movie dances, study these inside out, know every cut, move, music, etc." He cited specifically *All That Jazz*, the Fosse-directed film loosely based on the choreographer's life story, as a film to examine.

Judging from this note as well as several of Michael's videos, Fosse's moves loom large in Michael's repertoire. Fosse's angular style, replete with sexual overtones and playfulness, became a mainstay of Michael's performances. Both dancers shared a common dance idol: Fred Astaire, whose elegance and dramatic flair inspired Fosse to create a technique that can be seen on Broadway as well as in music videos such as Beyoncé's "Single Ladies (Put a Ring on It)."

Born in Chicago in 1927, Fosse enrolled in ballet and tap as a child. By his teenage years he led a double life: high-school student by day, professional dancer by night. He frequently performed at strip and burlesque clubs in between acts; the sexually free atmosphere would permeate his work for his entire career. After serving in the navy, Fosse relocated to New York to break into theater. While he won roles in Broadway shows and later films, he failed to make an impression as a performer. When Broadway's George Abbott and Jerome Robbins saw Fosse's brief dance in the 1953 film version of *Kiss Me, Kate* they immediately hired him as choreographer for their new show *The Pajama Game*. The success of that 1954 show and Fosse's innovative routines officially launched a career that would soon earn him a Tony, an Emmy, and an Oscar.

From the *Pajama Game* to *Pippin*, *Sweet Charity* to *Chicago*, *Damn Yankees* to *Dancin'*, Fosse established himself as a pioneering choreographer. His moves were about angles, having dancers pose dramatically, elbows and knees bending in sharp directions. Sensuality played an important role, with pelvic thrusts and rolling hips subtly recalling Fosse's early years performing in burlesque clubs. Accented by props such as derby hats and white gloves, he encouraged dancers to utilize their entire bodies, incorporating elements of mime and comedy.

Michael Jackson often incorporated Bob Fosse's classic moves—pelvic thrusts, angular poses, exaggerated hand gestures, and overt sensuality—into music videos such as "Beat It" and "Smooth Criminal" as well as live performances of cuts such as "Dangerous." Fosse's semi-autobiographical 1979 film *All That Jazz* contains musical sequences that encapsulate the choreographer's signature style.    *Author's collection*

While no definitive proof exists that Michael Jackson patterned his moves after Fosse—he never publicly mentioned seeing the dancer's films or shows—the resemblance is undeniable. One example occurs in the 1974 film *The Little Prince*, directed by frequent Gene Kelly collaborator Stanley Donen. This musical retelling of Count Antoine de Saint-Exupéry's children's book features a sequence choreographed and performed by Fosse entitled "Snake in the Grass." Portraying the reptilian character, Fosse slithers through the desert, his slinky moves incorporating spinning, posing with a fedora, rapid footwork, and even a pre-moonwalk type of step. Clad in mostly black, cigarette dangling from his mouth, Fosse manages to conjure images of a smoothly gliding snake while maintaining his trademark moves of angles and pantomime.

Fosse's film and theater work peaked during the 1970s, and therefore it is quite possible that Michael may have seen *The Little Prince, Cabaret, All That Jazz*, or even his close friend Liza Minnelli's 1972 TV special *Liza with a Z*. In any case, Michael utilized props (including the fedora and single glove) to accentuate his movements, and would pause at sharp angles. Sensuality also played a huge role in his steps, as he undulated his body, incorporating pelvic thrusts and positioning his hands over his groin to stress sexuality. Unlike Astaire and Kelly's more restrained style, Fosse and Jackson welcomed risqué elements, thus further engaging audiences. Indeed, combining Fosse's Broadway style with hip-hop choreography became established Michael Jackson trademarks.

## Essential Performances

Fosse's influence on Michael is most evident in the following videos:

- *Motown 25* performance of "Billie Jean" (1983)
- "We Are Here to Change the World" from *Captain EO* (1986)
- "Bad" (1987)
- "The Way You Make Me Feel" (1987)
- "Smooth Criminal" (1988)
- "Jam" (1992)
- *MTV Music Video Awards* performance of "Dangerous" (1995)
- "Scream" (1995)
- "You Rock My World" (2001)
- *Michael Jackson 30th Anniversary* performance of "The Way You Make Me Feel" (2001)
- *American Bandstand* performance of "Dangerous" (2002)

## James Brown

Perhaps the single greatest influence on Michael's career, the Godfather of Soul impacted the King of Pop's dance moves as well as his singing style. James Brown's brand of showmanship remains unparalleled, and his explosive style and gravity-defying footwork are still imitated. Watching from the wings at the Apollo, Michael carefully observed the master and adapted his style to fit his performances. When Bobby Taylor filmed the Jackson 5 for their Motown audition, their rendition of "I Got the Feeling"—complete with little Michael's perfect Brown imitation—played a crucial role in winning over Berry Gordy.

In *Moonwalk*, Michael fondly recalls studying how Brown commanded the stage: He learned every step, spin, and turn and noted how Brown would give one hundred percent to every performance.

The future soul legend came from extreme poverty; born in 1933, he spent the first four years of his life living in a one-room shack in Barnwell, South Carolina. After his parents split, he was sent to live with a brothel-owning aunt in Augusta, Georgia. Dropping out of school at twelve, he worked a series of odd jobs while singing in the church choir. He eventually landed in jail, serving a three-year sentence for auto theft, and met singer and pianist Bobby Byrd while incarcerated. After prison the two reconnected, with Byrd inviting Brown to join his vocal group, the Gospel Starlighters, in 1955. Quickly Brown established himself as a formidable front man, renaming the act the Famous Flames and earning the attention of King Records. Their demo of "Please, Please, Please" scored them their first hit in 1956.

After the Famous Flames failed to duplicate their initial success, Brown left the group and relocated to New York two years later. This move proved beneficial, as Brown recorded with new musicians and cut a series of hit singles such as "Try Me," "Night Train," and "Prisoner of Love." Relentlessly touring the country, Brown constantly honed his live act, learning every current dance step and adding his own flair. Spinning and falling to the floor, sliding across the stage, throwing and catching the microphone while executing a spin, having a bandmate throw a cape over him (only to toss it off dramatically moments later): Brown pioneered these moves, which never failed to excite audiences. His signature steps, which remain mainstays in entertainment, include the camel walk, the mashed potato, and the fast split. The most significant move, the boogaloo, formed the backbone of popping and locking and served as an important part of Michael's routine.

As previously mentioned, Michael meticulously studied Brown's exciting footwork and adapted it as his own. While he displayed these moves in numerous music videos, he particularly utilized them during his concerts. Audiences screamed as his feet flew across the stage, executing spins and tossing the microphone stand in a similar manner to his idol. At the height of *Thriller*, Michael made a cameo appearance during Brown's concert at Los Angeles's Beverly Theater on August 20, 1983, singing a few lines and dancing alongside the Godfather of Soul. Twenty years later, he presented Brown with a Lifetime Achievement Award at the BET Awards, draping a golden cape on his mentor before busting out his own Brown-influenced moves. As Michael professed numerous times throughout his life, he owed the Hardest Working Man in Show Business a great debt.

## Essential Performances

Michael paid tribute to his idol in innumerable performances, but the following videos best exemplify Brown's enormous influence on his student's moves:

- Motown audition tape performance of "I've Got the Feeling"
- Solo tours behind *Bad*, *Dangerous*, and *HIStory*
- "Jam" (1992)
- "Scream" (1995)
- "2 Bad" (*Ghosts*, 1997)
- "Ghosts" (Ghosts, 1997)

## Fred Astaire

The highly skilled Astaire deftly blended ballroom, ballet, and tap, formal and casual, on the stage and on film. Born in 1899, the Nebraska native began dancing as a child, eventually developing a vaudeville act with older sister, Adele. Like Michael,

Fred Astaire appeared on big stages while still in his teens; he reached Broadway at eighteen years old, soon starring with Adele in the stage production of George and Ira Gershwin's *Funny Face*. After Adele retired in 1932, Fred relocated to Hollywood to break into film. Initially paired with Joan Crawford for the 1933 film *Dancing Lady*, he broke through when he teamed up with his longest-serving leading lady, Ginger Rogers. From 1933 until 1939, the two brought elegant dancing to the masses, performing seemingly effortless routines often clad in formalwear.

While his dancing with Rogers exemplified elegance and precision, Astaire's solo numbers showed early signs of experimentations. In *Top Hat*'s "Top Hat, White Tie, and Tails" (1935), he transforms his cane into a weapon, pretending to "shoot down" his backing dancers with a gun.

After he and Rogers split, Astaire never paired with one consistent partner again. Yet he choreographed innovative solo routines that fully exploited new developments in cinematography or used props in creative ways. Examples abound, including dancing with multiple images of himself in the "Puttin' on the Ritz" number from *Blue Skies* (1946). Two years later, he incorporated percussion by kicking drums with his feet in the ebullient "Drum Crazy" segment from *Easter Parade*. His experimental streak exploded in *Royal Wedding* (1951), where he makes a hat rack come alive during "Sunday Jumps" and appears to dance on the ceiling during the famous "You're All the World to Me" sequence.

Fred Astaire's elegant moves and formal style, personified in films such as 1936's *Swing Time*, played a key role in Michael Jackson videos such as "Smooth Criminal" and "Billie Jean."    *Author's collection*

A particularly influential routine occurs in *The Band Wagon* (1953), namely one that incorporates precise choreography and distinctive costuming. In "Girl Hunt Ballet," Astaire plays a sharp-suited gangster fighting off tough guys while wooing women. His ability to dance while fending off his enemies, showing impressive athleticism, illustrates Astaire's well-rounded style.

Throughout his life, Michael made no secret of his admiration for this song-and-dance man. He dedicated his biography *Moonwalk* to Astaire, calling him a "*real* showman" and recounting how the dancer called him the morning after the *Motown 25* performance. Calling Michael a "hell of a mover," Astaire added that Michael was an "angry dancer," just like him. Michael later dubbed the comment the greatest compliment he had ever received. He even visited the dance great and his longtime choreographer, Hermes Pan, and showed them how to do the moonwalk.

Comparing Astaire's films with Michael's videos reveals just how much Michael Jackson learned from the master. Building from Astaire's affinity for incorporating props, Michael made them crucial parts of his routines. The fedora is the greatest example, as he used it to extend the length of his arms or create a character. His smoothness and elegance strongly recall Astaire's elegant style, yet he blends other influences to thoroughly modernize the formal style.

## Essential Performances

The influence of Astaire's elegant moves is shown in several of Michael's videos, including the following:

- "Billie Jean" (1983)
- *Motown 25* performance of "Billie Jean" (1983)
- "Smooth Criminal" (1988)
- *MTV Music Video Awards* performance of "Dangerous" (1995)
- "Scream" (1995)
- "Blood on the Dance Floor" (1997)
- "You Rock My World" (2001)
- *American Bandstand* performance of "Dangerous" (2002)

## Gene Kelly

This Broadway-turned-movie star created numerous iconic moments, from glee-fully splashing in puddles in *Singin' in the Rain* to the still-astounding sixteen-minute ballet sequence in *An American in Paris*. Seamlessly transitioning from ballet to jazz to tap, Gene Kelly brought a multicultural approach to dance. As opposed to Astaire, he often performed in casual clothing, incorporated acrobatics, and brought a distinctively masculine quality to his movements.

Born in Pittsburgh, Pennsylvania, in 1912, Kelly took dance lessons while playing sports in school. These two qualities merged when he taught dance classes to help pay for college; after graduation, he started auditioning for Broadway. His breakthrough occurred in 1940, when he won the title role in the musical *Pal Joey*. Drawing the attention of MGM head Louis B. Mayer, his performance earned him a contract with the movie studio. His film debut started his new career in a big way: costarring with Judy Garland in *For Me and My Gal* (1942), directed by the legendary Busby Berkeley.

Like Kelly, Michael exploited cinematography to showcase his moves. In 1945's *Anchors Aweigh*, Kelly danced with cartoon mouse Jerry—the first time live action and animation had merged. For *On the Town* (1949), he insisted that select song and dance sequences be filmed on New York streets rather than on studio lots. Visually, the ballet-filled conclusion of *An American in Paris* stands as his ultimate achievement; the vivid colors and recreations of famous paintings play vital roles

Gene Kelly's innovative choreography introduced casual dress, acrobatics, and masculinity into dance in films such as the 1952 classic *Singin' in the Rain*.
*Author's collection*

in his dances with costar Leslie Caron. His most ambitious work, *Invitation to the Dance* (1956), contains no dialogue; instead, it relies on dance and mime to narrate three stories. In its final segment, "Sinbad the Sailor," Kelly expands upon the live action and animation he first explored in *Anchors Aweigh*, dancing with Hanna-Barbera characters such as Tom and Jerry.

Finally, Kelly brought a playful quality to high art. He would perform ballet with cartoon characters, recreate vaudeville numbers, inject comedy into otherwise skillful dancing (most notably his "Moses Supposes" routine with Donald O'Connor in *Singin' in the Rain*), or flirt with women through his moves. His signature routine from *Singin' in the Rain* possesses a childlike quality with his splashing in puddles or climbing lampposts. This was not the first time he had showed youthful, playful exuberance in his art—he even danced on roller stakes in 1944's *Cover Girl*.

Michael clearly took notes from Kelly's films, as he borrowed these ingredients and transformed them into his own style. In his videos, Michael brought dance to the streets, a trait Kelly incorporated in his films. "Bad" shows Michael and his tough colleagues busting moves in a dingy subway station. He would also dress in informal attire, such as the T-shirt he wears in "In the Closet" and the jeans in both versions of "They Don't Care about Us." As he jumps and dances on the basketball court with Michael Jordan in "Jam," he executes his routines in an extremely casual atmosphere.

While not as athletic as Kelly, Michael constantly tested the limits of his body, whether standing on his toes for an extended time or spinning until he hit the floor. He too experimented with animation in his clips, namely by costarring with a Claymation-made donkey in *Moonwalk*'s "Speed Demon" piece.

While "Speed Demon" displayed technical prowess, it also proved Michael Jackson could incorporate humor into his art. He first displayed this talent in *The Wiz* but would occasionally return to this persona in his videos. He and his duet partner, Paul McCartney, perform a vaudeville-like routine in "Say Say Say," perhaps referring to Kelly's similar scenes in *For Me and My Gal* and *Singin' in the Rain*.

As is well known, Michael often flirted with women onscreen through dance. He teases co-star Ola Ray in the "Thriller" clip, dancing circles around her and pretending to scare her. "The Way You Make Me Feel" stands as the ultimate example, with Michael seducing a woman in both sexual and playful ways. Note how he briefly imitates the way she walks, or when he dives head first into a car to follow her. He also displays these traits in "Smooth Criminal" and "You Rock My World," albeit with less comedic flair.

In addition, Michael borrowed another Kelly trait: dancing in white socks and loafers. These two elements drew attention to his feet and ultimately became one of his trademarks. Watch Kelly in *An American in Paris*, *Singin' in the Rain*, or *Summer Stock* (1950) and notice how his cuffed pants, white socks, and loafers enhance his footwork. Michael added sequins to his socks to draw further attention, and continued this pattern until his last public performances in 2001 and 2002.

## Essential Performances

Kelly's humor, athleticism, and casual style are present in some of Michael's most iconic videos:

- "Don't Stop 'Til You Get Enough" (1979)
- "Say Say Say" (1983)
- "Thriller" (1983)
- "The Way You Make Me Feel" (1988)
- *Moonwalker* version of "Speed Demon" (1988)
- "Jam" (1992)
- "You Rock My World" (2001)
- Madison Square Garden performance of "The Way You Make Me Feel" with Britney Spears (2001)

## Marcel Marceau

While not strictly a dancer, Marcel Marceau pioneered miming techniques that Michael transformed into dance. In a 2007 interview with *Jet*, Michael described how the entertainer would "defy the laws of gravity" in his live performances. After viewing them, the singer explained, he would try and incorporate the steps into his dance routines.

Born in Strasbourg, France, in 1923, Marceau saw his first Charlie Chaplin film at five years old. After viewing the Little Tramp's brand of pantomime, Marceau became obsessed with learning the art. After World War II ended, he studied at the Charles Dullin School of Dramatic Art in Paris. Rapidly establishing himself as a gifted mime, he developed his signature character: Bip the Clown, who sported white makeup, wore a striped shirt, and donned a battered silk opera hat. From 1947 onward, he created skits featuring the character in comical situations (similar to Chaplin's Little Tramp). He also invented routines and movements still widely known, such as "Walking Against the Wind" and "The Cage."

Widely known worldwide, Marceau finally conquered America when he toured there in 1955. Through live appearances and television specials, he exposed worldwide audiences to pantomime, establishing organizations to promote miming in the United States.

A longtime fan, Michael briefly shared a stage with his idol in 1995. At a December 4 press conference to promote his upcoming HBO special *One Night Only*, he brought on a surprise guest: Marceau, who was also to perform during the concert at New York's Beacon Theater. The two clowned for the cameras, with Marceau mimicking Michael's poses as the singer imitated the mime's patented routine: being trapped inside an invisible box. The two exchanged smiles and seemed to enjoy appearing together; unfortunately, Michael collapsed from exhaustion two days later, forcing the cancelation of the event.

While the moonwalk did echo Marceau's "Walking Against the Wind" skit, the singer did not learn the move from the entertainer. He did, however, subtly incorporate the routine into his videos and concerts. Witness "Jam," where he performs the move several times. Another technique Michael learned from Marceau is how to inhabit a character through dance and body movement—a lesson he took to heart as he played the Scarecrow in *The Wiz*. He returned to this method while imitating zombies in "Thriller," virtually walking on air in "Scream," and conjuring spirits in *Ghosts*.

## Essential Performances

Michael incorporated Marceau's miming technique into several dance steps, most evident in the following videos:

- *The Wiz* (1977)
- "Thriller" (1983)
- "Jam" (1992)
- "Scream" (1995)
- "2 Bad" from *Ghosts* (1997)

## The *Soul Train* Effect: Jeffrey Daniel, the Electric Boogaloos, and the Original Lockers

*Soul Train* set trends in dance during the 1970s. Featuring a mix of amateur and professional artists, the program showcased the newest steps and catapulted relatively unknown dancers such as Jody Watley and Rosie Perez to international fame. Host Don Cornelius instituted the immensely popular "*Soul Train* line," where individuals could show off their hottest moves while sashaying down a gauntlet of dancers. Occasionally, *Soul Train* highlighted dance groups who would demonstrate the latest trends, locking and breakdancing serving as two major examples. Among the show's fans (and occasional guests) was Michael, who regularly viewed *Soul Train* to keep track of emerging dance moves. From the Jackson 5 years through his early solo career, the singer studied the steps of several prominent dance groups, ultimately calling upon select artists to teach them their moves.

## The Lockers (1973–76)

Boasting future stars of music and television, the Lockers brought street dance to the mainstream. The original lineup featured seven performers: founder Don "Campbellock" Campbell, Toni Basil, Dave Gregory Pope (a.k.a. Greg Campbellock Jr.), Fred "Mr. Penguin" Berry (better known as *What's Happening*'s Rerun), Leo "Fluky Luke" Williamson, Bill "Slim the Robot" Williams, and Adolfo "Shabba Doo" Quinones. Campbell first created the art form in the early 1970s, when he debuted his particular style in Los Angeles clubs. His jerky moves involved briefly "freezing" an arm or leg extension and incorporating possibly exaggerated facial expressions in time to the rhythm. Some of the movements bordered on comedy, such as randomly pointing at people or distributing high fives. At times robotic, the steps required some athleticism and flexibility.

After winning innumerable dance contests and gaining notice for his unique style, Campbell and his new dance partner, Damita Jo Freeman, learned of a new show entitled *Soul Train*. Having relocated from Chicago to Los Angeles, the producers were looking for fresh local talent. According to a 2013 Soultrain.com interview with Campbell, the duo enrolled in the show's weekly dance contests; working their way through several semi-finals, they finally won and earned a spot on the program.

After leaving *Soul Train* in 1973, Campbell formed his own dance troupe called the Lockers (originally called the Campbellockers) featuring local talent culled from the clubs. Campbell mentioned that his goal was to make the Lockers multidimensional, including various races, ethnicities, and dance styles. Their flamboyant costumes and energetic style led them to appear on numerous variety shows such as *Saturday Night Live*, *The Tonight Show*, and *The Carol Burnett Show*, but Campbell's greatest memory came when his troupe made two triumphant returns to *Soul Train*, on January 25, 1975, and September 18, 1976. Soon after the second performance, Berry and Basil left to pursue solo careers; while other dancers joined the Lockers, the original lineup is considered the most groundbreaking.

## Electric Boogaloos

This Los Angeles–based troupe popularized popping as an outgrowth of locking. Robotic yet fluid, the dance involves loose-jointed movements and rapid "popping" moves using elements of miming. Boogaloo Sam, a dancer from Fresno, California, first created the art after watching the Lockers perform on *Soul Train*, developing the steps with younger brother Poppin' Pete. By 1977, Sam had formed the Electric Boogaloo Lockers, later dropping the "Lockers" term to avoid confusion with the other dance form. The closely synchronized steps, given titles such as "crazy legs" and "twist-o-flex," were closely associated with late-1970s funk and gradually evolved into hip hop and breakdancing.

The Electric Boogaloos received mass exposure on April 19, 1980, when they demonstrated their moves on *Soul Train*. Unlike the Lockers, the Electric Boogaloos featured sleeker yet glitzier costumes that accented their rapid movements. Less comical than locking, the style involves precision and moves such as an earlier form of the moonwalk. While athletic, it does not include the high kicks and jumps that locking emphasized.

## Jeffrey Daniel (dancer, songwriter, singer, and choreographer)

The late-1970s and early-1980s group Shalamar enjoyed an impressive run of dance and funk hits such as "Make That Move," "A Night to Remember," and "Dancing in the Sheets." Before that, however, two members served lengthy stints on *Soul Train*, namely Watley and Jeffrey Daniel. Daniel would play a major role in Michael's evolution as a dancer, teaching him the moonwalk and other moves that would become famous during the *Motown 25* performance.

Daniel began his career as a teenage dancer on *Soul Train*, inspired by Campbell's locking form. He became a student of the West Coast Street Dance movement, a conglomeration of jazz, popping, locking, robotics, house and hip hop. Forming his own group Eclipse, Daniel debuted his moves along with members Casper Canidate and Cooley Jaxson in a 1979 *Soul Train* episode. Performing a routine to Michael's "Working Day and Night," the three executed the moonwalk and demonstrated their own spin on popping and locking, namely smoother movements that were less jerky and exaggerated. Seeing this performance, the singer contacted Daniel and his partners to teach him their dance style, particularly a step Daniel called the "backslide"; Michael later renamed it the moonwalk.

After his Shalamar tenure, Daniel frequently collaborated with Michael, serving as a consulting choreographer on the "Bad" and "Smooth Criminal" videos as well as the *Ghosts* film. He advised Michael on his tours as well, and several videos demonstrate just how much Daniel and the West Coast Street Dance movement impacted the entertainer.

## Essential Videos

Always attentive to dance trends, Michael fashioned his steps after moves executed by *Soul Train* dancers and other dance groups. This modern style dominates the following key videos:

- "Beat It" (1983)
- *Motown 25* performance of "Billie Jean" (1983)
- "Thriller" (1984)
- "Bad" (1987)
- "Smooth Criminal" (1988)
- "Jam" (1992)
- "Scream" (1995)
- "Ghosts" (1996)

## Honorable Mentions

In addition to these great entertainers, Michael studied other artists who were pure showmen, often watching them from the wings when he was a child. The following list consists of such honorable mentions:

- Jackie Wilson
- Sam and Dave
- Charlie Chaplin
- Sammy Davis Jr.

# 25

# Let the Madness in the Music Get to You

## *Off the Wall* vs. *Thriller*: The Face-Off

One question has inspired much ink and heated discussions: which is the superior Michael Jackson album, *Off the Wall* or *Thriller*? The two discs hold much in common: not only were they huge chart successes, they also represent major turning points in Jackson's career. Both signaled significant artistic growth, and their artistic influences linger on today's charts. However, their sound, songwriting, and overall attitude differ, even though both were helmed by frequent Jackson collaborator and producer Quincy Jones.

Is one album truly superior to the other? A track-by-track analysis, along with an examination of the creation process, may provide some answers. Such a comparison may not definitively answer these questions, but it inspires a starting point for discussion. Therefore, let's begin the ultimate face-off: *Off the Wall* vs. *Thriller*. The battle will be decided on individual songs, production quality, and cultural impact. Sales figures will not ultimately determine the victor, as commercial success does not always equal artistic vision.

### Contestant One: *Off the Wall*

While filming *The Wiz* from October 3 to December 30, 1977, Michael learned a great deal about acting and filmmaking. This early exposure to moviemaking transformed into a lifelong love he would frequently explore through his music videos and longer films *Moonwalker* and *Ghosts*. After Michael's death, his children stated that he had planned to focus solely on filmmaking after the *This Is It* tour. Another fateful moment occurred on the *Wiz* set on the day that music supervisor Jones encountered Michael filming a scene. As the scarecrow, the singer mispronounced the name "Socrates"; Jones quietly pulled him aside and corrected him. They became fast friends, and after filming ended Michael asked Jones if he could recommend a producer for an upcoming solo album. Jones suggested that he produce Michael's future project.

He later said that his desire was to present Michael as a mature, sophisticated talent, incorporating intricate arrangements that showcase Michael's full vocal range.

Michael and Jones amassed an impressive amount of material—Jackson wrote or co-wrote three tracks, while Jones recruited emerging talent Rod Temperton (then best known for his band Heatwave) to contribute three more songs. Paul McCartney and Stevie Wonder penned two memorable tunes, while close Jones associate Tom Bahler donated the timeless ballad "She's Out of My Life." To ensure the best sound, Jones tapped the best studio talent available to provide backing, such as guitarist Larry Carlton, keyboardist George Duke, trumpet player/arranger Jerry Hey, keyboardist David Foster (who would go on to a hugely successful songwriting and producing career), Steve Porcaro (who found even greater fame as part of the band Toto), master percussionist Paulinho da Costa, and vocalist Patti Austin. From December 1978–June 1979, Jones and Jackson recorded *Off the Wall* at several Los Angeles studios, including Allen Zentz Recording, Westlake Audio, and Cherokee Studios.

## "Don't Stop 'Til You Get Enough"

A prime example of Michael's prowess as a percussive singer, this track sounds the alarm, namely the arrival of a mature, artistically evolved, and confident singer. For the first time, listeners hear Michael sing in previously unheard lower ranges. The days of "Dear Michael" are gone, evidenced by Michael pitching his voice lower as he recites the opening lines. "Because the force, it's got a lot of power," he murmurs, shortly before exclaiming "ooh" as if releasing such power and energy. While danceable, the song also boasts intricate and unusual percussion courtesy of da Costa and other backing musicians. Horns punctuate the beat, with Michael's refrain of "Keep on with the force don't stop" further accentuating the rhythm.

Michael composed the track with help from brother Randy Jackson, who plays percussion on the demo. In *Moonwalk*, Michael reveals that he inserted the spoken introduction over just the bass line in order to build tension, which soon explodes in a rush of strings and percussion. Jones composed the percussion-heavy fadeout, with guitars resembling kalimbas (African thumb pianos).

"Don't Stop 'Til You Get Enough" announces Michael's arrival as a major talent in his own right and proves that dance music can feature an interesting arrangement as well as an infectious beat. Although Randy and Jones assisted with arrangements, "Don't Stop" represents Michael's first solo writing credit. It started his songwriting career with a bang, earning him a #1 hit and a Grammy.

## "Rock with You"

Considered one of Michael's trademark songs, the track was actually written by Temperton. As he mentions during an interview included on the 2001 release *Off the Wall: Special Edition*, Temperton wrote differently in order to accommodate Michael's unique vocal style. Along with the strong drumbeat and sensual keyboards, Michael's vocal performance marks an artistic turning point. Michael discusses this change of voice in *Moonwalk*, stating that he knew "Rock with You" required a more natural sound rather that singing the entire track in a high pitch.

Unlike Michael's other songs, "Rock with You" boasts a distinctively sensual singing style. When he instructs his prospective partner to "let that rhythm get into you" and not to fight the lure of the beat, Michael lures his partner not only to the floor but also into romance. Temperton's lyrics emphasize that love lingers long after the song ends, therefore the dance means much more than just a spin on the floor. By singing in a lower register and an occasionally breathless style, Michael convincingly assumes the role of leading man, sealing his status as a disco-era sex symbol.

"Rock with You" quickly became a critical and commercial favorite, earning praise for Jones's arrangement as well as Michael's singing technique. In "'And When the Groove Is Dead and Gone': The End of Jacksonism," Mark Fisher pronounces it "a love song to dance itself," seeing "the whole universe in a disco mirror ball" and "simultaneously bringing a tear to the eye and a shuffle to your feet."

## "Working Day and Night"

Another Michael composition, this song again makes use of Jackson's talents as a percussive singer. He later identified the track as a showcase for master percussionist da Costa, with his background vocals trying to keep up with da Costa's "grab bag of toys," as he calls them in *Moonwalk*.

Upon closer listening, one can hear his scatting and panting interwoven into the rhythm (a technique he would revisit many times during the remainder of his solo career). As on "Don't Stop," brother Randy Jackson assisted with much of the percussion on the original demo and played on the final studio version. Blaring horns and a scratchy guitar riff lend a funky vibe to the song, thus distinguishing it from other, smoother *Off the Wall* cuts.

Despite working hard every day, the narrator complains, he receives no affection from his lover; in fact, he suspects his girlfriend is cheating on him. In *Moonwalk*, Michael compares this track thematically to the *Destiny* song "The Things I Do for You." His ad-libbing and scatting before the song fades out illustrate Michael's innate rhythmic ability, while his "ooh's" and other exclamations evoke pure joy. Not surprisingly, Michael included this song in several live set lists, including during the *Bad* and *Dangerous* world tours.

## "Get on the Floor"

Michael co-wrote this track with Brothers Johnson member Louis Johnson, and it remains one of the lesser-known *Off the Wall* tunes. It may not be as artistically significant as other songs, but it stands as an artifact of the late disco era. The popping bass and cries to "shake that thing" may typify 1970s dance music, but the bridge departs from the formula. "Get up won't you g'on down," he chants, as the bass and drums back him. Michael's lead vocal and multilayered backing vocals sing in unison, ending with Michael's laughter as he begins the final delivery of the chorus.

That infectious laughter reveals Michael's affection for "Get on the Floor," a feeling he discusses in *Moonwalk*. He cites bassist Johnson as providing "a smooth-enough bottom" for his voice to glide over the words, allowing him to increase his volume with each chorus.

After meeting Quincy Jones on the set of *The Wiz*, Michael asked the veteran producer and arranger to oversee his next solo project. The result, *Off the Wall*, has been inducted into the Grammy Hall of Fame and is consistently included on "greatest albums of all time" lists.                    *Author's collection*

## "Off the Wall"

The second side kicks off with the title track, an eccentric yet accessible song Temperton wrote specifically for Michael's voice. In *Off the Wall: Special Edition*, he states that he liked writing heavily rhythmic melodies for Michael's precise vocal chops. "The melodies he would sing on up-tempo songs was [sic] very rhythmically driven. And so I tried to write melodies that were short notes, a lot of short notes to give him staccato rhythmic things he could do." Temperton also noticed that Michael preferred tracks with layered harmonies, so he would include both short notes and intricate harmonies in his compositions.

The start of the song sounds like the beginning of a horror movie, the quivering synthesizer lines accentuated by Michael's hysterical laughter. But as the beat enters the fray, Jackson clarifies that he means living "off the wall" in a positive sense. He entices the listener to enjoy life, shed inhibitions, and "let the madness in the music get to you." Like "Rock with You" and "Don't Stop," it allows Michael the freedom of exploring rhythm through his voice, utilizing his full range, and being cushioned by Jones's lush arrangement.

## "Girlfriend"

Paul McCartney originally wrote this track for Michael, but he decided to record it himself for his 1978 Wings album *London Town*. Michael still expressed interest in recording the song, however, which led to its being dramatically revised for *Off the Wall*. Comparing the two versions reveals how Michael and Jones altered the beat, heavily emphasizing the subtle rhythm-and-blues aspects of McCartney's composition and completely eliminating the original bridge. Because McCartney and Michael approached "Girlfriend" in radically different ways, it's fruitless to deem one better than the other. Instead, Michael's version remains a charming amalgamation of McCartney's melodic style with Jackson's dance-oriented background.

## "She's Out of My Life"

One of Michael's most enduring ballads, the track was written by composer Tom Bahler. As Jones explains in the 2001 *Off the Wall: Special Edition*, he already had Bahler's demo version and was waiting for the right singer to record it. After recording a demo with Michael backed by acoustic guitar, Jones led the studio sessions. At the end of the emotional song, Jackson breaks down, with a sob clearly heard as he sings the final word: "life." According to Jones, Michael cried at the end of every take (estimated between eight and eleven), so the producer decided to leave in the obvious sobbing. "I said, 'Hey—that's supposed to be there, leave it on there,'" Quincy adds. "She's Out of My Life" proved so popular with fans that Michael included it in various world tours: the Jacksons' *Triumph* and *Victory* tours, the *Bad* and *Dangerous* world tours, and the 1996 Royal Brunei concert. Backed by a very simple, keyboard-dominated arrangement, it showcases Michael's talent as an interpretive vocalist.

## "I Can't Help It"

Co-written by Stevie Wonder and composer Susaye Greene, this song shows off Wonder's gift for melody with just a hint of jazz. Michael's voice shines on this track, as he seemingly effortlessly croons the notes over the airy arrangement. Keyboardist Greg Phillinganes plays subtle fills as da Costa and drummer John Robinson add understated percussion. Demonstrating his sophisticated singing skills, Michael scats and utilizes his broad vocal range. As he writes in *Moonwalk*, Michael enjoyed the track for its complicated melody, which made the song more enjoyable for him to sing.

The song also allowed Jones to apply his jazz background to R&B—a feat that Epic Records feared he could not pull off. Like *Thriller*, *Off the Wall* appeals to various music genres in order to garner a wider audience, and "I Can't Help It" is a prime example of this technique.

## "It's the Falling in Love"

While Michael's version may be the most famous, the song's composer, Carole Bayer Sager, first recorded it for her 1978 album *Too*. Co-written by David Foster, the original version strongly resembles the *Off the Wall* rendition, although Sager did not perform it as a duet (Michael McDonald did provide backing vocals). Jones protégé Patti Austin lends her talents to the cut, with her voice closely blending with Michael's throughout the track. Popping bass, blaring horns, and Robinson's tight drumming inject even more energy into the song, making it a perfect fit for the dance floor.

Michael recorded too few duets with female partners, so "It's the Falling in Love" stands as a rare treat for listeners. Their chemistry is evident toward the end of the track, when the two singers ad-lib and exclaim "yeah yeah yeah!" in apparent joy. Austin and Michael sound as if they are thoroughly enjoying performing together, and that infectious spirit radiates through the song. Along with "I Can't Help It," "It's the Falling in Love" represents, as John Swenson writes in the *Rolling Stone Illustrated History of Rock & Roll*, "a master vocalist at the height of his interpretive power."

## "Burn This Disco Out"

*Off the Wall* closes with this dance track, a signal to the rapidly approaching end of the disco era. Temperton wrote the tune specifically for Michael's heavily rhythmic singing style, as he did "Off the Wall."

The song lets Michael cut loose in front of Jones's top session players. Jones wisely arranges the horns so they punctuate the strong beat, while Johnson's popping bass typifies dance music from the period. The lyrics may not address anything other than getting down, but when Michael chants "Gonna dance, gonna shout / Gonna burn this disco out," he commands dancers to the floor. It serves as an appropriate end to *Off the Wall* in several ways: it summarizes the upbeat tone of the album; it captures Michael's strengths as a percussive singer; and it unintentionally signals the end of the 1970s disco craze.

## Contestant Two: *Thriller*

While *Off the Wall* marked Michael's remarkable maturity as an artist, it also represented personal disappointment for the singer. After winning only a single Grammy Award in 1980—Best Male R&B Vocal Performance for "Don't Stop 'Til You Get Enough"—Michael vowed that his next solo effort would exceed all expectations and shatter sales records. Reteaming with Jones, he amassed thirty songs, nine of which would appear on *Thriller*. Recording sessions took place from April 14 to November 8, 1982, at Westlake Recording Studios, with much of the *Off the Wall* personnel returning for the follow-up. Notable additions were further members of Toto such as David Paich (keyboards) and Jeff Porcaro (drummer and brother of keyboardist Steve Porcaro). Another significant difference was the presence of major artists McCartney and guitarist Eddie Van Halen, along with the actor Vincent Price.

*Thriller* became an instant success due to the quality of the material, Jones's elegant yet more aggressive production, and Michael's supple vocals. Jones and Michael intentionally wrote and selected songs that would appeal to a crossover audience: "Beat It" for the rock fans, "The Girl Is Mine" for an older audience, and "P.Y.T. (Pretty Young Thing)" for funk aficionados, for example. For a rare moment in history, *everyone* owned this album, regardless of age, race, or musical tastes.

## "Wanna Be Startin' Somethin'"

A Michael composition, this song introduces a more refined artist, one that incorporates international flavors into his music. Vocally Michael approaches the track differently than on *Off the Wall*, utilizing short notes and interweaving his scatting with the percussion. Listening closely to the song through headphones reveals his voice stuttering "da da da da da" along with da Costa's drum-machine patterns and other percussion work. The lyrics are less about seduction and more about protection, paranoia, and alienation. As Hey's horns provide short bursts of power, Michael bemoans the fact that unnamed forces continually harass his loved one. "Talkin', squealin', lyin'," he cries, later asserting that these naysayers reduce people to "vegetables" or defenseless souls.

Despite these dark themes, "Wanna Be Startin' Somethin'" maintains its upbeat feel via the infectious rhythm and the famous "ma ma se, ma ma sa" chant. Unfortunately this section attracted some controversy, as Cameroonian saxophonist Manu Dibango claimed Michael lifted the chant directly from his 1972 hit "Soul Makossa." Dibango filed suit shortly after *Thriller*'s release, with the case eventually settled out of court.

Despite the issue of authorship, the track remains a signature tune from the album and a fan favorite. Michael included the song in set lists for tours ranging from the Jacksons' 1984 *Victory* through his solo 1997 *HIStory* tour. Look no further for an illustration of Jackson's skills as a percussive singer than this cut.

## "Baby Be Mine"

Another Temperton composition, "Baby Be Mine" dates from 1981, with the first demo recorded in 1982. Boasting synthesizers arranged by Temperton, the steady beat is provided by N'Dugu Chancler, the same drummer featured on "Billie Jean." The mid-tempo, disco-inflected track most recalls *Off the Wall* in its blaring horns and hints of jazz. Note the catchy yet complicated vocal exchange toward the conclusion, where Michael sings the lead vocal ("So baby, be mine girl / And girl I'll give you all I got to give") over the backing vocalists' part ("Girl, be mine, show me how it should be / Hold me tight every night, it's all right"). The effect is rhythmic, with two seemingly disparate parts blending seamlessly. Considered by some critics a "filler" track and never released as a single, "Baby Be Mine" elevates contemporary R&B to a sophisticated, mature level.

Incidentally, the backing vocals consists of Michael's voice overdubbed several times. Engineer Bruce Swedien marveled at his ability to perfectly replicate each part in both pitch and timbre. "Michael is such an expert at doubling his backgrounds and other vocal parts that he even doubles his vibrato rate perfectly. . . . His pitch is flawless!" Swedien states, in his book *In the Studio with Michael Jackson*.

## "The Girl Is Mine" (with Paul McCartney)

In *Moonwalk*, Michael writes that he wanted to repay a favor—namely Paul McCartney penning "Girlfriend" for *Off the Wall*. In *Thriller: The Musical Life of Michael Jackson*, Nelson George compares "The Girl Is Mine" to McCartney's "Silly Love Songs," describing the latter as a "whimsical 1976 statement of artistic purpose about the value of feel-good, sing-along songwriting." "The Girl Is Mine" furthers this goal, George argues, due to its playful lyrics and whimsical vocals. When Michael and McCartney banter toward the end of the track, one can hear

# Michael Jackson/Paul McCartney "The Girl Is Mine"

Michael's duet with Paul McCartney, "The Girl Is Mine," was the first single released from the *Thriller* album. Linda McCartney took the photograph displayed on the 45's picture sleeve.
*Author's collection*

the smiles on their faces, as if they are not taking the imagined "fight" very seriously.

Michael composed the basic track early in the *Thriller* sessions, recording several solo demos (one later surfacing on the *25th Anniversary Edition*). According to *Thriller 25: The Book*, the recording took place on April 14, 1982, at the Westlake Recording Studios in West Hollywood. Released six months later as a single, it provided the public with a preview of *Thriller* (which would hit record stores two months later) and a rare union of superstars spanning two generations.

*Thriller 25: The Book* also points out that "The Girl Is Mine" stands as the first time "a pop song appeared as a sung dialogue and a 5-minute musical." Upon its release, the single topped the Adult Contemporary and R&B Singles charts and peaked at #2 on the *Billboard* Hot 100. While not considered *Thriller*'s critical high point, the track is a light-hearted slice of 1980s pop and a passing of the torch from a 1960s icon to a burgeoning 1980s star.

## "Thriller" (featuring Vincent Price)

One of Michael's most iconic songs, "Thriller" derives from a Temperton demo entitled "Starlight." The songwriter brought the demo, complete with synthesizer programming, to Michael's Encino home. As Temperton told the *Guardian*'s Peter Lyle in 2007, Jones challenged him to rewrite the song; after all, the composer had managed to deliver a tune that doubled as the title for Michael's last album, *Off the Wall.* "I went back to the hotel, wrote two or three hundred titles, and came up with the title 'Midnight Man.' The next morning, I woke up, and I just said this word. . . . Something in my head just said, this ["Thriller"] is the title. You could visualise it on the top of the *Billboard* charts."

During the recording session, Jones and Michael constantly tinkered with the track. Wanting an impressive-sounding opening chord sequence, Jones drew inspiration from a notable source: Prince's "1999." Brian Banks, who played synthesizer on the album, recalled the incident in the *Telegraph* article "Michael Jackson's

*Thriller,* Michael's *Off the Wall* follow-up, remains the best-selling album of all time. In 2003, *Rolling Stone* ranked the album at #20 in its "500 Greatest Albums of All Time" list.                    *Author's collection*

Monster Smash" dated November 25, 2007. "You know the opening sound on that? Duh-da da, Dur-duh duh? Well that was the sound—that big, bitey chord sound at the opening of '1999'—he wanted that, but bigger, for 'Thriller,'" Banks said.

As they listened to the playback, Jones and Michael brainstormed changing chords and adding sound effects such as wolves howling to transform the track into something darker. The final element added was Vincent Price's spoken section; amazingly, Temperton wrote the rap on his way to the studio the day it was recorded. Jones had called the songwriter the night before, explaining that he had decided to abandon their original plan of having Price improvise his spoken part. Agreeing to write a script for the actor, Temperton wrote three verses the next morning while waiting for a car to bring him to the studio (only two were used in the final track).

What resulted was a playful yet convincingly menacing song integrating gothic and horror elements with 1980s R&B. Its funky bass line, memorable melody, swirling and menacing keyboards, and Michael's emotive, actor-worthy vocal performance (listen to his reading of lyrics such as "Night creatures call and the dead start to walk in their masquerade") add up to not only a standout *Thriller* cut, but one of the most memorable singles of the 1980s.

## "Beat It" (featuring Eddie Van Halen)

Michael and Jones conceived of *Thriller* as possessing mass appeal, of continuing music appealing to every audience—pop, R&B, adult contemporary, and rock. As Jones told the *Guardian* in 2007, he envisioned a "black version" of the Knack's 1979 hit "My Sharona." Michael informed the producer that he had written a song fitting that description: "Beat It," a track addressing nonviolence. As he writes in *Moonwalk*, Michael composed the lyrics with school kids in mind, urging them to stay out of trouble and avoid violence whenever possible. Members of the group Toto recorded the backing track—according to guitarist and bassist Steve Lukather, Jones did not like their original rendition, deeming it too heavy for Michael. After recording the track, Jones decided on a lead guitarist: Eddie Van Halen, the legendary leader of Van Halen. As the guitarist told the *Guardian*, "Everybody [from his band, Van Halen] was out of town and I figured, 'Who's gonna know if I play on this kid's record?'"

"Beat It" allowed Michael to stretch his vocal chops, adding a toughness he would further explore on his subsequent album *Bad*. Rarely had an R&B artist flirted so openly with rock elements; indeed, "Beat It" transcends genres, uniting seemingly dissimilar audiences. As he explains in *Moonwalk*, Michael wanted to write a song that was "totally different from the rock music I was hearing on Top 40 radio at the time," and he succeeded with this unique hybrid.

## "Billie Jean"

The tale of a stalker who claims that Michael fathered her baby, "Billie Jean" remains one of the most hypnotic, distinctive R&B/pop songs ever recorded. In *Moonwalk*, he clarifies that no one "Billie Jean" existed—instead, the lyrics described a composite of groupies that he and Jackson 5 encountered over their careers. Interestingly, Jones and Michael clashed over the tune for two reasons: the title and the opening beats. Michael revealed in his autobiography that Jones suggested changing the title to "Not My Lover" to avoid listeners confusing the title character with tennis legend Billie Jean King.

Secondly, Jones objected to the almost thirty-second-long introduction—a highly unusual feature of a pop song. As the producer told the *Telegraph*'s Lyle in 2007, "He had an intro you could shave on it was so long. I said, 'It's too long, we gotta get to the melody quicker.' He said, But that's the jelly! That's what makes me wanna dance.' Now, when Michael Jackson tells you that's what makes him want to dance, the rest of us had to shut up."

"Billie Jean" symbolizes a major thematic difference between *Thriller* and *Off the Wall*. While Michael's first collaboration with Jones celebrated dance and love (albeit heartbreak and frustration as well as idealized romance), *Thriller* takes on a paranoid tone. Like "Wanna be Startin' Somethin'," "Billie Jean" concerns predators wanting to disrupt the narrator's very being. The former addresses unnamed forces reducing the protagonist to a "vegetable," crying out that "my baby's dying!" as if his relationship is also in peril. In this case, the narrator is threatened by a groupie who apparently seduces him and then, through her "schemes and plans," as Michael snarls, attempts to entrap him with claims of paternity. The disco days of rocking with you are over, and have been replaced by a menacing, sinister overtone. Despite these dark themes, "Billie Jean" soars with its distinctive beat, tense strings, scratchy guitar riff, and Michael's anguished vocals.

## "Human Nature"

One of *Thriller*'s most hypnotic and mysterious tracks, "Human Nature" also contains one of Michael's best vocal performances. Here he demonstrates how he could alter his voice to fit a song's mood. On this mid-tempo track, he applies a seductive tone, whispering in some sections, taking deep, hissing breaths as he moves from one verse to another. During a 2008 *Los Angeles Times* roundtable marking the twenty-fifth anniversary of *Thriller*, critic Serena Kim described the singer as "a sensual vampire flying over the city looking for juicy necks to bite" in this unusual track. While this assessment may not fit every listener's interpretation of the lyrics, Michael's sighs and lighter-than-air vocal fills invoke the song's sensual nature.

Written by Steve Porcaro of Toto and songwriter John Bettis, "Human Nature" was based on a melody Porcaro had written almost as an afterthought. As Jones told the *Telegraph* in 2007, Toto had sent the producer a tape with two songs. At first, Jones remained unimpressed with the tracks, but "at the end, there was all this silence and then . . . 'Why, why, da-dum dah dah da-dum dah dah, why, why . . . .' Just a dummy lyric and a very skeletal thing and I get goose bumps talking about it." Michael agreed, describing the track in *Moonwalk* as "music with wings" containing a beautiful melody reminiscent of Toto's hit "Africa."

After deciding he liked the tune, Jones tapped lyricist John Bettis to pen lyrics to Porcaro's melody; on the final version, Toto cushioned Michael's subtle reading of the words with synthesizer chords that snake in and out of the verses as Steve Lukather's tasteful guitar fills added intimacy. The effect remains as bewitching today as it did in 1982.

## "P.Y.T. (Pretty Young Thing)"

For years, "P.Y.T." flew under the radar, overshadowed by *Thriller*'s massive hit singles. Yet the track has grown in popularity, today receiving even more radio airplay as it did upon its release. Even Fox's musical series *Glee* covered the song in "Silly Love Songs," the twelfth episode of the show's second season.

James Ingram, an R&B singer who had recently scored a hit with the ballad "One Hundred Ways" (a song off Jones's solo album *The Dude*), composed the funky song along with mentor Jones. However, the title "P.Y.T." originates from a demo recorded by Michael and keyboardist Greg Phillinganes; this version eventually surfaced on the 2004 *Ultimate Collection* boxed set. Unimpressed by their version, Jones passed the catchy title on to Ingram, who crafted this slice of early 1980s R&B.

Michael's vocal performance charms as he coos at a lovely woman lines like "where did you come from, baby / And ooh, let me take you there." As Nelson

George writes in *Thriller: The Musical Life of Michael Jackson*, "Michael's man-child quality is what really sells the song. His boyishness takes the edge off the leer implicit in the lyric." Sisters La Toya and Janet sing backup during the bridge; in the liner notes, they are humorously identified as being among the "pretty young things" in the song. The robotic, vocoder-enhanced voice used throughout the track provides the funk, as does the strong, driving beat. A fun track reflecting the upbeat tone of *Off the Wall*, "P.Y.T. (Pretty Young Thing)" entices listeners to get on the dance floor.

## "The Lady in My Life"

Another example of a *Thriller* song gaining more popularity years after its initial release, "The Lady in My Life" reveals an overtly romantic side to the singer. As Michael admits in *Moonwalk*, he found the ballad to be the most difficult *Thriller* tune to record due to its sultry mood and content. After numerous takes, Jones finally presented Michael with a scene to act out: Michael would play someone begging for his lover to be with him. Returning to the studio, Michael ordered the lights off and the curtain closed between the studio and control room to allow for privacy. Feeling less self-conscious, he accomplished the task.

Jones first commissioned the song as a possible track for Frank Sinatra, most likely for the Jones-produced 1984 album *L.A. Is My Lady*. George describes "Lady in My Life" as having Temperton's trademark intricate melodies and chord changes. While Michael's voice more than meets Temperton's challenging notes, it's his closing ad-libs that distinguish "Lady in My Life" from a typical soul ballad. He modulates his voice, reaching impossibly high notes on lines such as "I need you by my side" and letting a desperate raspiness creep into his vocals as he commands his lover "don't you go nowhere." Constantly evolving as an interpretive vocalist, Michael demonstrates just how much he has developed as a singer since his Jackson 5 days on this slow burning track.

## Showin' How Funky and Strong Is Your Fight: The Showdown

In just three years, Michael experienced what most artists can only dream of: recording two back-to-back groundbreaking albums. Now that we have demonstrated just why *Off the Wall* and *Thriller* are worthy musical opponents, other factors can be compared: sales, critical response, and overall musical and cultural impact.

## Round One: Sales and Awards

*Off the Wall* spawned four Top 10 singles—the first US album to do so—with "Don't Stop 'Til You Get Enough" and "Rock with You" hitting #1. In the UK, five hit singles were released (including "Girlfriend"), setting a record in British music history. By December 10, 1979, *Off the Wall* was certified gold and platinum; the LP would ultimately sell over twelve million copies worldwide. In 1980, Michael added several new awards to his shelves—he earned three American Music Awards

(Favorite Soul Single, for "Don't Stop 'Til You Get Enough"; Favorite Soul Album; and Favorite Male Soul Artist).

One particular trophy would provide crucial motivation for *Thriller*, however. At the 1980 Grammy Awards, Michael earned just one award: Best Male R&B Vocal Performance for "Don't Stop 'Til You Get Enough." In *Moonwalk*, Michael discusses his disappointment with this lone nomination, along with being classified in the "R&B" category alone. This snub would change his career, however, as it inspired him to create an album no one could ignore: *Thriller*.

As is well known, *Thriller* broke every conceivable sales record. After its release in December 1982, *Thriller* topped the US *Billboard* 200 chart for an astonishing thirty-seven weeks; while sales figures vary greatly, estimates range from sixty-five to one hundred million copies worldwide. All seven singles released from the album reached the Top Ten singles charts.

Michael dominated the 1984 Grammy ceremony, winning an impressive eight awards including Best Pop Male Performance, Best Rock Male Performance, Record of the Year, and Album of the Year. The album also earned him eight American Music Awards and three MTV Video Music Awards. By February 7, 1984, *Thriller* had received yet another distinction from the *Guinness Book of World Records*, which named it the world's best-selling album. Sales continued decades after its release, with the Recording Industry Association of America (RIAA) certifying the album twenty-nine times platinum in 2009.

On sales figures alone, *Thriller* emerges victorious in this round. Critical reception, however, may tell a different story.

## Round Two: Critical Reception

Upon its release, *Off the Wall* received almost instant critical acclaim. *Rolling Stone* praised the work in its November 1, 1979, issue, with critic Stephen Holden citing Michael's "feathery-timbered tenor" and "ultradramatic phrasing, which takes huge emotional risks and wins every time" and ultimately rating it a "triumph" for both Jones and Michael. In 1982, *Billboard* ran a positive review pointing out his "bell-clear vocal style" and the album's overall "brassy arrangements." In comparing *Off the Wall* to *Thriller*, *New Musical Express* reviewer Gavin Martin called the former a work of "scorching fury," an album that elevated disco to a more sophisticated level: "It put the cap on a genre and broke into a whole new mould, a truly explosive sound: a peak of achievement which others had to aim for." Reminiscing about *Off the Wall* in its review of *Thriller*, *Billboard* declared it "one of the most acclaimed albums in recent years."

Over thirty years later, *Rolling Stone* ranked *Off the Wall* at #68 on its "500 Greatest Albums of All Time" list, stating that the up-tempo tracks "remain more or less perfect examples of why disco didn't suck" and "still get the party started today." All Music's Stephen Thomas Erlewine called it a "visionary album" that found a way to combine disco with rock, pop, soul, and jazz, ranking it above *Thriller* in quality and effect.

While it is hard to believe today, *Thriller* did not inspire the same universal acclaim. In the December 4, 1982, edition of *New Musical Express*, Gavin Martin claimed that in trying to follow up a blockbuster like *Off the Wall*, Michael seemed to run out of fresh material. "The ones put into action here reek of desperation, falling back on old showbiz lags like Vincent Price and Eddie Van Halen to cover the lack of inspiration in the music," he wrote. He dismissed "Beat It" as "a feeble attempt at tough, street wise posin' written specially for the occasion by Michael 'Muscles' Jackson," and labeled many of Michael's self-penned songs "acutely embarrassing." Declaring the singer's second collaboration with Jones a disappointment, he squeezed in a final dig: "It would be awful to think that it took them the best part of that time to make a record as weak as this."

*Billboard* took a more positive view on December 11, 1982, praising its energy as well as its mix of contemporary ballads and dance floor–ready material. Only *Rolling Stone*'s review accurately predicted *Thriller*'s impact, rating the album four stars. Writer Christopher Connelly proclaimed the album a major step forward in Michael's artistic development, explaining that it contained a "deeper, if less visceral, emotional urgency than any of his previous work, and marks another watershed in the creative development of this prodigiously talented performer."

Yet other critics appeared bothered by the album's slick production. While *New York Times* reviewer John Rockwell deemed *Thriller* a superior pop record, he criticized Michael for allowing Jones to "depersonalize his individuality with his superbly crafted yet slightly anonymous production." Rockwell also declared that Michael refused to reveal his innermost emotions, instead hiding "his emotionality behind smoothly indistinctive pop songs and formulaic arrangements, defenses so suavely perfect that they suggest layers of impenetrable, gauzy veils."

Virtually every *Thriller* review compared the album to *Off the Wall*—mostly unfavorably. On December 19, 1982, *Billboard*'s R&B columnist Nelson George mentioned Michael's new release in just one paragraph, which he tacked onto the end of a feature on Prince. While he deemed *Thriller* an "instant classic," he judged it "not as strong" as *Off the Wall*. Despite the comparison, *Rolling Stone* ultimately rated *Thriller* at #20 on its "500 Greatest Albums of All Time" list for its unprecedented crossover appeal. But because *Thriller* initially received some mixed reviews, *Off the Wall*'s almost unanimously positive reception renders it the winner of this round.

## Round Three: Legacy

The last round proves the most difficult: which album made the greatest impact? Both *Off the Wall* and *Thriller* contain sounds that are still heard today, and they shattered records and changed the music industry in different ways. *Off the Wall* emerged during the final days of disco, but instead of merely echoing current trends, the album elevated the genre to a sophisticated level. Rock, soul, pop, funk, and jazz melded seamlessly with dance to create a fresh sound. Unlike the Village People, increasingly anonymous one-hit wonders, and throwaways like Rick Dees's "Disco Duck," tracks like "Don't Stop 'Til You Get Enough" and "Rock with You" represent dance music with a brain, a symphony of strings and intricate percussion that stimulate the intellect as well as the feet.

In addition, *Off the Wall* serves as Michael's debut as a mature, nuanced vocalist. He stretched his voice to new heights and, more notably, low ranges never heard before on a Jackson 5 or Jacksons record. Listen to how his voice dips and soars on "Don't Stop," or flutters and scats through "I Can't Help It." "Rock with You" features some of Michael's most seductive vocals, yet he transitions effortlessly into the speedy, rhythm-propelled track "Working Day and Night." The album contains something for every musical taste, be it adult contemporary ("She's Out of My Life"), breezy pop ("Girlfriend"), or dirty funk ("Get on the Floor").

Since its release in 1979, countless artists have tried duplicating this range and elegance. Avowed fan Justin Timberlake has most patterned his career after his idol on tracks such as the *20/20 Experience (2 of 2)* song "Take Back the Night." In a *Chicago Tribune* review of Timberlake's album dated September 30, 2013, critic Greg Kot labeled the track "classic disco . . . which sounds like it could have been lifted from Michael Jackson's classic 1979 *Off the Wall* album." From Beyoncé's *Dangerously in Love* to Usher's *8701*, modern artists have used *Off the Wall*'s crossover appeal and sophisticated, well-produced sound as a template.

*Thriller* caused ripple effects in the industry that are still felt. Extending *Off the Wall*'s themes, Michael and Jones created songs that would appeal to various musical tastes. In 1983, everyone owned a copy of the LP, from rock fans to soul aficionados. No other work held such mass appeal, and it has yet to be equaled. Cuts like "Beat It" illustrate how seemingly disparate genres could combine to form a new sound; its rock and R&B sound paved the way for future mash-ups like Run DMC and Aerosmith's massive hit "Walk This Way."

By experimenting and testing the limits of traditional pop music, Michael redefined radio-friendly singles. Against Jones's wishes, Michael chose to begin "Billie Jean" with a thirty-second buildup of strings, drums, and bass before his voice enters the picture. In an atmosphere where singles delivered the chorus immediately to hook listeners, songs like "Billie Jean" broke radio rules. In addition, *Thriller* broke barriers: in the early 1980s, radio was strictly segmented; if a song did not fit the rock format, for example, it would not be played on a rock station. Since *Thriller* crossed so many genres, it defied easy categorization, thus its tracks received airplay on rock, soul, Top 40, and adult contemporary stations—a rare feat for any artist.

As is discussed elsewhere in this book, *Thriller* also changed music video with its groundbreaking short films. Even more significantly, Michael became the first black artist to receive major airplay on MTV, at a time when the network played few African American videos due to its "rock" format.

Considering these factors, round three can be declared a tie, as each album impacted the music industry in different yet enormously significant ways. Both contain groundbreaking tracks and present Michael as a mature, accomplished, and original artist. With Jones's production, *Off the Wall* and *Thriller* influenced subsequent generations and still sound as fresh today as they did upon their release.

Who wins this ultimate showdown? Let the debates begin.

# 26

# The Sound of a Crescendo

## How *Bad* Updated Michael Jackson's Signature Sound

ichael Jackson found himself in an unenviable position in 1985: while he was still riding high on the massive success of *Thriller*, as well as the importance of "We Are the World," he felt increased pressure to produce a blockbuster follow-up album. A 1987 *Spin* cover story hysterically described him as "running scared" in achieving such a monumental task. How could he possibly duplicate *Thriller*'s record-breaking sales, groundbreaking singles, and innovative videos? Setting a goal to exceed *Thriller*'s critical and commercial success, Michael dived into the *Bad* sessions with two more objectives: to toughen his image and update his sound. The title track would embody his grittier voice, but the synthesizers used on *Bad* would also define the LP's modern feel and musical impact.

As Geoff Brown notes, the musical landscape had evolved in the few years between *Thriller* and *Bad*. Harder beats had surfaced, hip hop began creeping into mainstream pop, and producers such as Jimmy Jam and Terry Lewis had introduced synthesizers such as the Roland TR-808 into R&B. As a result, Michael incorporated these pounding beats and new technology into *Bad*. (He would not fully embrace hip hop until 1991's *Dangerous*, however, as covered in chapter 29.)

### We'll Work It Out: The *Bad* Sessions

As he embarked on his *Thriller* follow-up, Michael decided that the album should contain sounds not heard on previous recordings. Zach O'Malley Greenburg states in *Michael Jackson, Inc.: The Rise, Fall, and Rebirth of a Billion-Dollar Empire* that Michael asked keyboardist John Barnes to assist him in finding unconventional instrumentation to mix into tracks. "They'd wander around Southern California and record everything from machinery clanking to birds chirping to cars whizzing past, hoping to capture something that could be woven into the fabric of a hit song," O'Malley writes.

Before entering the studio, however, Michael worked extensively at his home studio, dubbed "the Laboratory," with frequent collaborators Matt Forger, Barnes, and Bill Bottrell (who would later be revealed as the mysterious rapper on "Black or White"). The group—who would become known as the "B-Team," as opposed to Jones's "A-Team" of Bruce Swedien, Greg Phillinganes, and Jerry Hey (see chapter 37)—helped Michael realize his goal of sonic innovation.

One tool proved essential in creating such unusual instrumentation: the synthesizer. The Fairlight CMI and the Synclavier PSMT are just two examples of technology that changed 1980s pop and R&B. As Forger told Vogel in his *Atlantic* article "How Michael Jackson Made 'Bad,'" from September 10, 2012, "It really opened up another realm of creativity. The Fairlight had this light pen that could draw a waveform on the screen and allow you to modify the shape of it. The Synclavier was just an extension of that. Very often we would end up combining two synthesizer elements together to create a unique character."

Both synthesizers allow the user to finely adjust the tone and character of each sound. "We were doing a lot of sampling and creating new sound characters and then creating a combination of sample sounds mixed with FM synthesis," Forger added. "Michael was always searching for something new. How much stuff could we invent ourselves or research and find? There was a whole lot of that going on. That was what the Laboratory was about."

In his book *In the Studio with Michael Jackson*, Swedien recalls the first day of the *Bad* sessions as taking place on Monday, January 5, 1987, although other accounts by Vogel and Quincy Troupe claim the sessions began in late 1986. The engineer reunited with Michael and Quincy Jones at Westlake Audio's new Studio D. Much of Jones's "A Team" came back for *Bad*, but Jones also recruited jazz organist Jimmy Smith, singer/songwriter Siedah Garrett (another Jones protégé), and the Andraé Crouch Choir to diversify the material—a tactic that Michael would continue to employ on subsequent albums.

Keyboardist Greg Phillinganes recalled these early sessions in "An Oral History of Michael Jackson's *Bad*," published in *Time* on August 22, 2012. "By the time we were working on *Bad*, Mike's ideas became stronger and clearer. Songs like 'Al Capone,' titles like that, even as working titles, show that Mike had a tremendous cinematic approach to the making of his music."

Michael's growing confidence resulted in clashes with Jones and the Westlake crew, as he would frequently bring virtually completed songs to the studio for Jones to finish. Unlike the recording sessions for *Thriller* and *Off the Wall*, the *Bad* sessions allowed Michael to gain more control over the production. He would disagree with his mentor on track choices and overall sound, although their arguments were often exaggerated by the press. Still, at one point Jones reportedly walked out on the project when he learned that Michael had secretly entered the studio after hours to alter some tracks. Jones did win a significant victory when he persuaded Michael to cut the number of tracks down to eleven; originally Michael had intended *Bad* to be a double album featuring thirty songs.

As he writes in *Moonwalk*, Michael sometimes argued with Jones about technology. Michael wanted the latest drum and synth sounds in order to make Bad sound as futuristic as possible; Jones did not always agree with this method.

Wanting *Bad* to sound as contemporary as possible, Jones and Michael utilized what would become the signature instrument of the 1980s: the synthesizer. Russ Ragsdale, assistant engineer on the album, told Vogel that Michael wanted to create work that barely resembled the *Thriller* material—in other words, he wanted to be a sonic innovator. To achieve this goal, Ragsdale explained, Jones and the "A-Team" filled the studio with synth stacks as well as the largest Synclavier (another pioneering instrument that allowed the musician to become a virtual one-man-band) available at the time.

"It took over 800 multitrack tapes to create *Bad*; each song was a few hundred tracks of audio," Jones said. Swedien would create the hard-hitting drum tracks Michael desired by recording them on 16-track tape, then transferring them to digital in order to retain the booming analog sound. Jones called the resulting effect "big legs and tight skirts." As Nelson George explains in his liner notes for *Michael Jackson: The Ultimate Collection*, many *Bad* tracks feature "a combination of digital drum sounds, fat keyboard created bass lines, and other percussive elements that pulse like heart beats and slam like fists."

In a blog entry for Headphone.Guru posted on March 31, 2015, Christopher Currell, a guitarist, producer, sound designer, and audio engineer, recalled the day Michael called on his Synclavier expertise. In the summer of 1985, Michael contacted the producer and Synclavier programmer, asking for private tutoring on the instrument. Currell subsequently designed a learning program for the King of Pop and met with Michael in his home studio. Their first three-hour session involved Currell teaching Michael how to boot up the Synclavier and call up its sound library; intrigued, Michael asked him to return the next day for more lessons. For the next six months, the musician and programmer would visit Michael daily, organizing his computer storage tapes and helping to create new sounds for the singer's demos.

Enjoying their collaboration, Michael asked Currell to assist with the *Bad* album, operating the Synclavier and working with Jones and Swedien to best incorporate the new technology into the songs. Later, Currell would say that while "live tracks" were recorded, Michael consistently preferred the Synclavier-powered sound, and as such the technology ultimately dominated the album. As the sessions continued at Westlake Audio, some of the musicians who played on *Bad* were not initially happy to see to the Synclavier programmer. When veteran bassist Nathan East met Currell, he said, "So YOU'RE the reason why no one was being called."

Another key player, John Robinson, programmed the drum tracks on an Oberheim drum machine. "Most drum machine parts I had heard sounded very mechanical. Not so with these tracks. They sounded amazing! The feel was great!" Currell recalled.

The Synclavier also allowed Michael's vocals to gain power in emotion as well as volume. After Michael double- and triple-tracked his harmonies, Currell would sample them on the Synclavier and insert them in places where the harmonies appeared. "This procedure also reduced vocal fatigue from just repeating the same things multiple times . . . especially on repetitive out-choruses that went on for five minutes for dance mixes," Currell explained.

Nick van der Wall (a.k.a. "Afrojack"), a DJ who mixed a new version of "Bad" for the *Bad 25* release, told *Time* magazine that "the sonic professionalism on the original *Bad* album was just next level. Nowadays they do it a lot but back then this was the newest of the newest, like crazy stereo effects, on a technical level of engineering and music production." Swedien would later name *Bad* his favorite Michael Jackson album, partly because it contains an impressive variety of sounds.

## It's Just a Feeling: *Bad* Tracks and New Technology

Certain *Bad* tracks exemplify how Michael melded technology and his songwriting prowess to create a modern, tougher sound. Other tracks, such as "Man in the Mirror," "Just Good Friends," and "I Just Can't Stop Loving You," are discussed in chapters examining Michael's social activism and best-known duets.

### "Bad"

Originally titled "Pee," the album's title track was originally intended as a duet between Michael and Prince. When Prince declined, Michael assumed the lead vocal and transformed the song into a manifesto, announcing his intention to stand up to his critics. While the electronic beat largely dominates the song, another essential component is the Hammond B-3 and MIDI organ solos courtesy of jazz organ legend Jimmy Smith. Swedien also credits Michael's mouth percussion, which the engineer amusingly dubs the "How Now Brown Cow," as adding depth to the catchy beat.

Its electronic sound came courtesy of the Roland D-50, an instrument that allowed artists to incorporate loops and samples as well as effects such as reverb. The Synclavier played a crucial role in blending Smith's organ part and Phillinganes's keyboards, and processed nine different bass sounds (including bass courtesy of the synthesizer, organ bass pedal, and electric bass) to create the final mix heard in the iconic track.

In addition to its electronic sound, a significant element of "Bad" remains Michael's first use of the phrase "shamone." According to the Roots' Questlove, the exclamation serves as a tribute to another iconic soul singer. As mentioned in Spike Lee's *Bad 25* documentary, Mavis Staples often chanted the word in classic Staple Singers cuts such as "I'll Take You There." Staples verified this hypothesis on September 3, 2010, in an interview with the *Washington Post*'s Chris Richards. "My mother called me one day. She said, 'Mavis, this little Michael Jackson done stole your word!' I said, 'What?'" Staples recalled. "And he was [on television, singing the song 'Bad.']: 'I'm bad,

*Bad*'s title track introduced Michael's tougher image and sound, its synthesizers placing it firmly in the present.          *Author's collection*

you know it, shamone, shamone.' See, I said 'shamone' in 'I'll Take You There.' It's just a word I made up! Instead of saying 'come on,' I said 'SHA-mone.' You know, trying to be slick. And he picked up on it. And it made me feel so good."

## "The Way You Make Me Feel"

Michael Bearden, musical director and keyboardist for the canceled *This Is It* concerts, revealed in a September 2009 *Keyboard Magazine* interview that the original keys on the song were produced using a Yamaha CS-80. Phillinganes also described his memories of the recording in *Rolling Stone*'s "50 Best Michael Jackson Songs." "That was one of my favorites. I remember how much fun I had laying down those offbeat parts, the bass line, all that stuff, and watching the expression on Michael's face." The magazine ranks the song at #2 on its list.

Michael frequently cited Stevie Wonder as a major inspiration, and "The Way You Make Me Feel" is a classic example of this. In the 2014 *Rolling Stone* feature "Michael Jackson Remembered: The Tributes," Wonder recalled riding on an elevator with Michael, with the two spontaneously singing the track together. At one point Wonder mentioned how much he loved the line "go on, girl," and Michael promptly confessed that he adapted the phrase from Wonder's 1984 song "Go Home."

Swedien is particularly proud of how he blended Michael's vocal mannerisms seamlessly throughout the entire song. He adds that the song's shuffling rhythm makes it a standout. Vogel agrees, further emphasizing how track combines technological and organic elements to create a perfect slice of pop. "The relentless steel-shuffling motion of the beat is juxtaposed with all kinds of natural, improvisational qualities that give the song its charm: the vocal ad libs, the finger snapping, the blues harmonies, the percussive grunts and gasps, the exclamations," he writes, in "How Michael Jackson Made 'Bad.'"

## "Speed Demon"

In *Moonwalk*, Michael calls "Speed Demon" a "machine" song, and as such the techno-sound of this track as well (as the entire *Bad* album) suits the song well. Michael reportedly penned the track as a reaction to getting a speeding ticket on the way to the studio one day, Jones having challenged him to write a song about the maddening experience. According to Currell, the demo version featured a synthesizer playing a sweeping note right before the solo. Instead, the programmer suggested sampling the sound of a racecar shifting gears; after processing the noise through the Synclavier, the effect became a vital part of the final version.

In addition to the unusual percussion and metallic vibe, "Speed Demon's" other star is Michael's vocal performance. As Jay Cocks stated in his *Time* review of *Bad*, published on September 14, 1987, "There is a great singer at work here, doing vocal stunts on tracks like 'Dirty Diana' or 'Speed Demon' that are as nimble and fanciful as any of his dance steps." Indeed, Michael's voice sounds entirely different on "Speed Demon," as he alternately growls and spits out the lyrics, barely containing his anger at being restrained in terms of speed or, one could argue, his creativity. "Pull over boy, and get your ticket right," he snarls, clearly assuming the voice of the policeman. The rest of the lyrics clearly defy the authority figure, as Michael proclaims that he is "stoppin' at nothin'" and "gotta have it my way."

Perhaps most telling is a line toward the song's conclusion, where he declares, "You're preachin' 'bout my life like you're the law." One can assume that the song answers his critics as well as the fictional policeman. As a final wink to his musical past, Michael inserted the line "the life you save could be your own"—a nod to the Jackson 5 hit "The Love You Save."

## "Liberian Girl"

While this mid-tempo love song features layers of synthesizers, it still sounds organic due to Michael's seductive vocals. Currell's Synclavier, along with synthe-sizers programmed by Steve Porcaro and played by Barnes, Michael Boddicker, David Paich, and Larry Williams, place the track firmly in the modern age. Jones expresses his affection for "Liberian Girl" in the liner notes to the 1999 compila-tion *From Q, With Love*, revealing that he felt the song should have been a major hit. Swedien also believed the track was a standout, citing its "big, block background harmonies."

The technology may be impressive, but Michael's sensual vocal performance breathes life into the song. Using a breathy singing style, he tells of his deep love for a beautiful woman, evoking dreamlike images of movies and a vision of "happily ever after." His passion rescues the song from being corny, with his sighs and interjections such as "all right" and "baby" injecting sexuality into the otherwise sweetly romantic lyrics. Sounds of birds tweeting introduce the song, setting the exotic tone. A close listen reveals Michael occasionally snapping along with the percussion.

Toward the end of "Liberian Girl," Michael unleashes the full power of his voice, allowing grittiness to permeate his singing. Here he has clearly surrendered to passion and desire, and Michael acts out this "scene" with his voice alone. This technique exemplifies Forger's description of Michael's composition and singing skills. "He wanted a beginning, a middle and an end, and he wanted it to be a story and it could be translated not only into a song but a terrific—what Michael always called 'film shorts,' as opposed to 'music videos,'" he told *Time* for the magazine's "Oral History of Michael Jackson's *Bad*."

## "Another Part of Me"

This danceable track originally debuted a year before *Bad* in the Disney World feature film *Captain EO* (see chapter 32). It was not originally intended for *Bad*—Michael favored another composition, "Streetwalker." But as Jones revealed on the 2001 *Bad Special Edition*, he spotted Michael's then-manager Frank DiLeo dancing to "Another Part of Me" in the studio one day; deeming this reaction a sign of the song's catchiness, he persuaded Michael to include the track on the album. "Streetwalker" remained unreleased until the 2012 *Bad 25* compilation, and remains one of Michael's "should have been" hits.

Hard-driving programmed drums slam throughout the song, although more traditional instruments provide the essential rhythmic elements. Jerry Hey's trumpet arrangement punctuates the beat, while scratchy guitar riffs courtesy of Paul Jackson Jr. and David Williams further underscore the beat. As the track fades out, listen for some particularly sophisticated yet catchy trumpet lines that lend a jaunty and jazzy air to the song. Michael's spirited singing communicates the song's uplifting message of unity and a belief that "we're bringing brighter days."

## "Dirty Diana"

This hard rocker ranked at #26 on *Rolling Stone*'s "50 Best Michael Jackson Songs" list. Billy Idol's guitarist Steve Stevens provided the crunchy guitar. "[Michael] kept asking me about rock bands: 'Do you know Mötley Crüe?'" Stevens told *Rolling Stone*. However, another crucial element of the song came courtesy of Synclavier expert Denny Jaeger. His vast array of what Vogel calls "new sound characters and soundscapes" impressed Michael, who called upon him to assist with sounds for "Dirty Diana" as well as "Smooth Criminal."

"Dirty Diana" can be seen as a sequel to "Billie Jean" as it details a ruthless groupie. Critics accused the song of being misogynist, but in a 1987 *Ebony/Jet* interview, Michael cited the track as being among his favorites. "It's a life story of a groupie. Hate to say the word 'groupie' but that's what it is. And it's something that I've experienced and a lot of people who grow up on the road, like me," he told

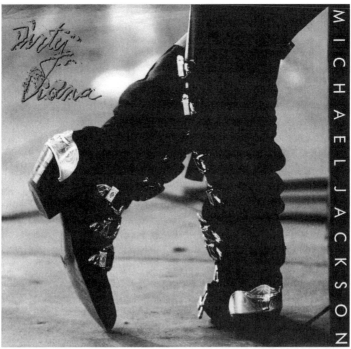

Michael frequently experimented with combining harder rock with R&B, with this fusion most evident in the #1 single "Dirty Diana."

*Author's collection*

interviewer Darryl Dennard. Michael alternately screams and sobs, revealing his moral conflict. Should he remain faithful to his lover, or surrender to Diana's seduction? Stevens's wailing guitar pierces through the cacophony of guitars and slamming drums, further emphasizing the anger and anguish the narrator experiences over this siren.

If anyone doubts Michael's talents as an actor, the section where he screams "come on!" before the music drops out, then sobs "no, no" as the song returns to its original volume, should prove otherwise. Through its hard rock feel and Michael's emotional performance, "Dirty Diana" portrays a common situation that many artists must face while on the road.

## "Smooth Criminal"

This classic track benefitted from another kind of percussion: Michael's heartbeat. Requiring someone with professional equipment capable of recording the human heart, Michael contacted Dr. Eric Chevlen to undertake the task. Using Chevlen's equipment, Currell recorded it directly into the Synclavier, with which he digitally processed the heartbeat, allowing him to alter the speed. Thus the pulsating beat can be heard at the beginning of "Smooth Criminal," slowly speeding up to match the song's tempo.

Michael spent time tinkering with the sound and lyrics, with earlier versions such as "Al Capone" eventually surfacing on releases such as *Bad 25* and *Xscape*. "Al Capone" could have been included on an album in its initial version with its slamming rhythm and Michael's staccato vocals.

Nevertheless, "Smooth Criminal" eventually became one of Michael's signature tracks, thanks to its gangster theme, growling vocals, memorable lyrics (namely "Annie are you OK?"), and groundbreaking music video. An abrupt synthesizer chord first pierces the air, followed by heavy breathing and Michael's heartbeat. The distinctive bass line and the echoing, pounding drums then enter the scene, introducing Michael's almost whispering voice. He narrates the story of Annie, a woman who has been murdered (and possibly raped) by the "smooth criminal." Gruesome images of "bloodstains on the carpet" along with sounds of gunfire add to the foreboding imagery.

Multilayered backing vocals (all performed by Michael) form a Greek chorus, repeatedly asking about Annie's status. Michael responds, crying "I don't know!" and "I don't know why!" As a side note, two friends and colleagues contributed important elements to the song: Swedien portrays the officer who shouts "OK, I want everybody to clear the area right now!" while DiLeo provides the heavy breathing and "creaking" in the track, according to the original liner notes.

## "Leave Me Alone"

*Rolling Stone* ranked "Leave Me Alone" at #38 on its "50 Best Michael Jackson Songs" list. Interestingly, the track was initially available only on the CD release as well as the 2001 cassette edition. Subsequent versions, such as *Bad Special Edition* and *Bad 25*, now also include "Leave Me Alone." Despite its original scarcity, the track made a mark on critics. "This funky shuffle was Jackson's shot back at the tabloids, powered by dueling keyboard lines, not to mention Michael's own emphatic Stevie Wonder–esque synthesizer-vocal solo," *Rolling Stone* writes. Its strident beat echoes "The Way You Make Me Feel," but instead of radiating flirtatious fun, it stresses anger, frustration, and aggression.

Quite simply, "Leave Me Alone" represents one of Michael's finest compositions and most heartfelt vocals. While the lyrics apparently address a doomed love affair, they reflect Michael's frustration with the tabloids. "Just stop doggin' me around," he snarls. In contrast to the passive resistance expressed in "Beat It," he proclaims here that there comes a time when one must fight for one's reputation. When he sings "It's the choice that we make / And this choice you will take," he seems to directly ask fans whether they will choose to believe the tabloid-fueled rumors or respect his privacy.

Interestingly, at the end of this song Michael communicates his confusion and conflicting feelings. Returning to the love story, he yells, "Don't come beggin' me" and "Don't come lovin' me," yet in the next breath proclaims his love for the unnamed woman. As "Leave Me Alone" fades out, he furiously chants, "I don't want it," as if trying to convince himself that this tempestuous relationship must end. He finally releases a high-pitched "ooh!" as if expressing his anguish and indecision.

## Just Stop Doggin' Me Around: Critical Reception

Not all critics praised Michael's use of technology on *Bad*. Brown criticized the tracks for relying heavily on the "dink-donk-dunk of synthesizers" which encouraged Michael to sing in a tougher—and, in Brown's opinion, unconvincing—manner. Richard Cook's *Sounds* review, published on September 12, 1987, also expressed a disliking for the dominance of technology. Cook stated that the only organic bass appears on "I Just Can't Stop Loving You"; otherwise, the synthesizers create the bass lines, which Cook claimed created "a clean pneumatic carpet." In his *Bad* retrospective for SoulTrain.com, pop culture historian and music journalist Jason Elias dubbed the album "a synthetic, 'cold' production that came from the increasing use of digital in the recording chain that proliferated in this era."

Cook's review singled out Jones's production as a problem. "Instruments interlock as exactly as they have to in all modern dance music, yet Jones permits none of the sparseness which makes Cameo intriguing, little of the supple bandspread which Luther Vandross creates," he wrote, accusing Jones of stuffing songs with "a wealth of detail which finally weighs heavy on the listener."

David Stubbs published an even harsher review in the December 2001 issue of *Uncut*. Commenting on the release of the album (along with *Off the Wall* and *Thriller*), he stated that "*Bad* (1987) ain't bad, but with its aggressive, box-girder rhythms, it indicates the 'hardening' of Michael Jackson—an abandonment of his previous, liquid grace in favour of a puerile and dubious obsession with machismo on the title track, 'Speed Demon,' and the petulant 'Leave Me Alone' as he retreats, under siege from worshippers and detractors alike, into a private compound of his own mawkish and perverse fantasies."

While Richard Cromelin's *Los Angeles Times* review, dated August 31, 1987, ultimately praised the album, he also criticized the production. "If the aims are modest, there's nothing low-key about the way producer Quincy Jones assembles a track, and his sound is typically forceful, vivid, rich, and deep. It also tends to be a little mechanical—especially the way he splices in Jackson's tightly woven multi-tracked backing vocals."

The music journalism archive Rock's Backpages held a discussion with its editors to reassess *Bad* on the eve of the *Bad 25* release, with writer Kate Allen reporting that "the general consensus was that it was an overproduced album by an artist creatively frozen by a debilitating obsession with topping his already superlative achievements. And that's pretty much the conclusion music history has resigned *Bad* to as well."

Conversely, *Rock & Roll Disc* writer Tom Graves specifically praised *Bad*'s pristine sound quality. "On television and radio, the limited sound reproduction does enormous injury to a song such as 'Bad' which is dependent upon the listener hearing dozens of tiny details. One must give Jackson and Quincy Jones credit for the meticulous, laborious production," he wrote. *Time*'s review concurred with Graves, calling the album "a state-of-the-art dance record" and praising Michael's vocal abilities. Robert Christgau awarded *Bad* a "B+" in his September 1987 *Consumer Guide* review, arguing that "anybody who charges studio hackery is too narrow-minded to be able to hear pros out-doing themselves. Studio mastery is more like it, the strongest and most consistent black pop album in years."

While it did not sell as many copies as *Thriller*, *Bad* remains a towering achievement for any other artist. It became the first album in music history to spawn five consecutive #1 singles, and nine of its tracks reached the US Top 10. *Bad* sold over forty-five million albums, and several of its videos broke new ground in choreography ("Bad," "Smooth Criminal"), animation ("Leave Me Alone"), and cinematography ("Bad," "Smooth Criminal," "The Way You Make Me Feel"). It also marks the beginning of a tradition Michael could continue for the rest of his career: including socially conscious songs on every album (see chapter 30).

Regardless of the initially mixed reviews, *Bad* now stands as Michael's statement of independence and the start of his transition into hip hop and new jack swing. Having written nine of the eleven tracks on the album himself, he demonstrated how much he had grown as a songwriter since his first attempts during the Jacksons years. No longer the student, Michael had transitioned into a full creative partner to his mentor, Jones.

Forger told *Time* that *Bad* functions as the artist's statement of independence. "For me, it really was that point in time when Michael took the reins of his solo career and you could understand Michael's personality musically. It's not that you couldn't before that, it's just that in his solo career now he had taken all the encouragement that Quincy [Jones] had given him, and it was just that extension."

## All Is Going My Way: *Bad* as Personal and Artistic Statement

When Michael first worked with the Philly soul songwriting and producing team Kenny Gamble and Leon Huff, he said they taught him the "anatomy of a song": how to dissect a composition into its individual parts. He learned how those elements then combined to create a powerful and memorable track. *Bad* represents Michael's mastery of his mentors' technique, as he experimented with unusual instrumentation to create thundering percussion as well as other offbeat sounds. While he remained fascinated with technology and wanted the album to stand firmly in the "now," Michael never lost sight of his songwriting skills, his peerless vocal abilities, and his knack for creating pop that lingers in the brain long after the song ends.

A final significant aspect of *Bad* is its foreshadowing of Michael's future immersion in hip hop. As John Murph would note in his 2012 reassessment of *Bad* for the *Atlantic*, dated September 19, 2012, "The album makes for a fascinating transitional record to Jackson's 1991 album, *Dangerous*, particularly in its sonic design. The hot-ice beats on songs like 'Bad,' 'Speed Demon,' and 'Smooth Criminal' hinted at Jackson's exploration into new jack swing and hip-hop." Chapter 29 delves into his official hip-hop debut, *Dangerous*, and looks at how *Bad* and later releases further demonstrate Michael's full acceptance and appropriation of the genre.

# 27

# Just Good Friends

## The Duets

M ichael Jackson was a true collaborator. Judging from his appearances on others' albums as well as tracks from his own LPs, he clearly enjoyed singing with his peers, molding his voice to blend with others' styles. This chapter surveys some of his most significant duets from his solo years, focusing on tracks ranging from 1979 to the 2010 posthumous collection *Michael* (the Justin Timberlake remix of "Love Never Felt So Good" is excluded, since it is a "virtual" duet). Artists who performed rap breaks on Michael's tracks are not included here as they are discussed in chapter 29.

### "Ease on Down the Road" with Diana Ross (*The Wiz*, 1978)

The Broadway and film versions of *The Wiz*'s showstopper number "Ease on Down the Road" feature Michael and Ross performing in character as the Scarecrow and Dorothy. It was released as a single in 1978, peaking at #17 on the R&B singles chart, #41 on the Hot 100, and #45 in the UK. The single came in various forms, including the original album version, the single edit, and the 12-inch extended mix (tailor-made for discos).

In his autobiography, *Q*, Quincy Jones admits that he reluctantly produced the *Wiz* soundtrack as a favor to his friend, the director Sidney Lumet. Impressed by Michael's work ethic, Jones said working with the singer was the only positive experience during the project. According to the producer, the two bonded one day during the 1977 shoot. While filming a scene, Michael repeatedly mispronounced the name "Socrates," yet no one had corrected him. Jones took Michael aside and gently informed him about the mistake; Michael was so grateful for Jones's advice that the producer felt a connection with the young talent. "Right then and there I committed: 'I'd like to take a shot at producing your new record.'" The rest, as they say, is history.

While *The Wiz* may not have been a box-office hit, "Ease on Down the Road" became a classic. Michael and Ross's voices blend well, with both of them energizing each other with their spirited performances. In 1981, the duo performed the track on Ross's TV special *Diana*, and their broad smiles suggested the fun they must have experienced in the 1977 recording studio.

## "It's the Falling in Love" with Patti Austin (*Off the Wall*, 1979)

The lone duet recorded for *Off the Wall*, "It's the Falling in Love" was composed by Carole Bayer Sager and David Foster. Sager's original version first appeared on her 1978 album *Too*, and Jones recruited Foster and Tom Bahler (writer of "She's Out of My Life") to rearrange the track for *Off the Wall*. Next, he tapped Austin, a jazz singer and Jones protégé who would prominently feature on the producer's 1981 album *The Dude*. Add Louis Johnson's popping bass and Wah-Wah Watson's funky guitar riffs, and the result is a sprightly love song with touches of disco and funk. Michael and Austin's voices interweave so closely that they sound identical, melding into one during the chorus. The lyrics portray the complications of young love; while they celebrate the "possibility of more to come," they also address a relationship's paradoxes. While the feeling of falling in love may produce a high, the *being* in love can induce tears as well as laughter.

## "The Girl Is Mine" with Paul McCartney (*Thriller*, 1982)

While "The Girl Is Mine" does not mark Michael's first collaboration with the ex-Beatle (McCartney wrote the *Off the Wall* track "Girlfriend"), it does represent the first time the duo sang together. But the song was more than just a hit single—it transformed into a multigenerational moment, an apparent passing of the torch from a 1960s legend to an emerging 1980 superstar.

In 1981, Michael approached McCartney to collaborate on some tracks and "write some hits," as he states in *Moonwalk*. According to Taraborrelli, the duo penned "The Girl Is Mine" while watching cartoons; Michael soon recorded a demo with just his voice. In 1983, McCartney told *Newsweek* that he initially had misgivings about the song, particularly concerning the word "doggone." "When I checked it out with Michael, he explained that he wasn't going for depth—he was going for rhythm, he was going for feel," McCartney said. "And he was right. It's not the lyrics that are important on this particular song—it's much more the noise, the performance, my voice, his voice."

"The Girl Is Mine" was released just a month before *Thriller* hit the shelves. As Michael explains in *Moonwalk*, he felt that a track with two such strong names must be released first to avoid overexposure. The song performed well, reaching #2 on the *Billboard* Hot 100 and topping the R&B and Adult Contemporary charts. It did experience critical backlash, though, with Gavin Martin dismissing it in his *New Musical Express* review as "very pretty and perfectly innocuous." While *Rolling Stone*'s Christopher Connelly called the song "syrupy," he praised Michael's "raw ability and conviction make material like 'Baby Be Mine' and 'Wanna Be Startin' Somethin'' into first-class cuts and even salvage 'The Girl Is Mine.' Well, almost." Even McCartney admitted to *Newsweek* in 1983 that "the song I've just done with Michael Jackson, you could say that it's shallow."

Reassessing the song in 2008, *Los Angeles Times* critic Ann Powers acknowledged the song's charms yet still decried its "cornball lyrics," adding that it was "borne forward on a beat light as hair mousse." While "The Girl Is Mine" may not be as groundbreaking as "Beat It" or "Billie Jean," it remains significant for its legendary pairing and for its forward-thinking theme: interracial love. *Newsweek* recognized this fact in 1983, asking, "Have American radio stations ever before played a song about two men, one black and the other white, quarreling over the same woman?"

Looking back, it is clear that the song did blaze trails in terms of its lyrical themes. In addition, the playful banter between Michael and McCartney suggests the two were fully aware of the silliness of some the dialogue. "Paul, I think I told you, I'm lover, not a fighter!" Michael utters at one point, barely restraining a giggle.

## "Say Say Say" with Paul McCartney (*Pipes of Peace*, 1983)

Written at the same time as "The Girl Is Mine," "Say Say Say" became one of Michael's biggest hit singles. As of 2010, *Billboard* ranks the song as his best-performing single, having topped the Hot 100 for six weeks beginning in December 1983. According to the Beatles Bible website, the pair first worked on the melody and arrangement, then recorded rough versions in May 1981 at London's AIR Studios, and in March and April 1982 at Los Angeles' Cherokee Studios. During these sessions they also laid down overdubs to "The Girl Is Mine" and "The Man." After "The Girl Is Mine" single was released in late 1982, Michael and McCartney

reunited in England in February 1983 to complete "Say Say Say" and "The Man" at Abbey Road Studios.

Unlike "The Girl Is Mine," these two songs were helmed by George Martin, the legendary Beatles producer who had re-teamed with McCartney for his 1982 album *Tug of War*. Now producing the ex-Beatle's follow-up album, *Pipes of Peace*, Martin oversaw the Jackson and McCartney recording sessions. Cadman and Halstead's *Michael Jackson: For the Record* quotes Martin as expressing his admiration for the younger singer: "He actually does radiate an aura when he comes into the studio, there's

One of Michael's most successful duets, "Say Say Say" is just one of three songs he wrote and recorded with Paul McCartney. While their first collaboration, "The Girl Is Mine," appears on *Thriller*, "Say Say Say" and "The Man" are included on McCartney's 1983 LP *Pipes of Peace*. *Author's collection* no question about it . . . He does know what he wants in music and he has very firm ideas."

While "Say Say Say" radiates a feel-good, up-tempo pop sound, the lyrics tell a different story. The singers lament a woman who has abandoned them, who has rejected their love and left them almost childlike in their grief. "Take, take, take what you need, but don't leave me with no direction," McCartney sings, with Michael adding, "What can I do, girl to get through to you . . . Standing here baptized in all my tears." The anguish in Michael's voice is evident through his increase in volume and intensity, while McCartney provides a calmer perspective, arguing that the woman will one day regret her actions.

"Say Say Say" became a massive hit, in part because of its humorous and well-shot video. Directed by Bob Giraldi, the clip features the con-artist duo of "Mac and Jack," who travel the countryside selling snake oil and performing vaudeville routines. La Toya Jackson, Harry Dean Stanton, and Art Carney all appear in small roles.

## "The Man" with Paul McCartney (*Pipes of Peace*, 1983)

The final Jackson/McCartney collaboration was only an album track; according to Cadman and Halstead, the song was to be released as a single in February 1984, but Michael's record company blocked it, fearing it would compete with the *Thriller* releases. The planned 12-inch version featured an extended remix of "The Man" as well as the album version. While the single was only officially released in Peru, it was also available as a promo 45 only in several other countries.

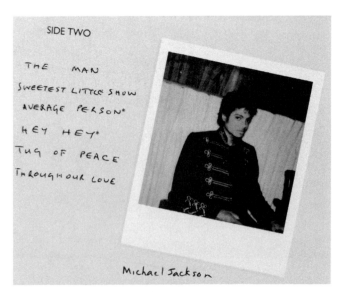

The gatefold from Paul McCartney's *Pipes of Peace* album includes a snapshot of Michael working in the studio during the "Say Say Say" and "The Man" sessions.          *Author's collection*

"The Man" would probably not have been nearly as successful as "Say Say Say," but it has its charms. Michael and McCartney harmonize closely on the breezy melody, their voices soaring on the line, "I'm alive, and I'm here forever." The two alternate verses, singing together on the chorus, telling the story of an inhibited man who eventually releases his childlike joy, experiencing freedom while apparently flaunting societal rules ("He's not like me and you," they clarify).

## "State of Shock" with Mick Jagger (*Victory*, 1984)

In the early 1980s, Michael collaborated on three tracks with Queen lead singer Freddie Mercury: "There Must be More to Life Than This," "Victory," and "State of Shock." Scheduling issues forced the duo to discontinue working on the songs, but Michael resurrected "State of Shock" in 1984 for the Jacksons' upcoming album *Victory*. He called upon the Rolling Stones' Mick Jagger to re-record Mercury's parts, and they met in the studio in June 1984.

As engineer Bruce Swedien recalled in a 2009 *Gainesville Sun* interview, Michael insisted that Jagger warm up his vocal cords before recording. "Mick didn't hesitate," he said. "By then, everyone knew how good Michael was. If Michael Jackson says warm up, you warm up—even if you are Mick Jagger."

While promoting his 1985 solo album *She's the Boss*, Jagger discussed his collaboration with the King of Pop. "How was working with Michael? Quick," he told the *New York Times*' Robert Palmer. "He had the two of us practice scales for two hours and then we recorded the vocals in two takes. When he sent the finished track to me later I was kind of disappointed in the production and the mix. But I think he's a really good singer."

An extension of "Beat It's" rock and soul fusion, "State of Shock" reached #3 on the *Billboard* Hot 100 and #4 on the R&B Singles chart. While Jagger may not have been pleased with the mix, the song exposed him to different audiences, including pop and dance fans. The single performed impressively on the Dance Music/Club Play Singles chart, peaking at #3.

## "Tell Me I'm Not Dreamin' (Too Good to Be True)" with Jermaine Jackson (*Dynamite*, 1984)

During the peak of Thriller-mania, Michael recorded a duet for Jermaine Jackson's new album, *Dynamite*. While the duo performed it during the *Victory* Tour, "Tell Me I'm Not Dreamin'" was never released as a single. According to Lisa Campbell's *Michael: The Complete Story of the King of Pop*, Michael did not want to appear on the song but felt obligated to do so. Therefore he asked CBS Records head Walter Yetnikoff to invent a story that the CBS subsidiary Epic (Michael's label) was blocking Arista (Jermaine's label) from issuing the single. While the song was never released as a single, it received substantial radio airplay, thus boosting sales of Jermaine's LP.

Co-written by Michael Omartian (who also produced the album), Jay Gruska, and Bruce Sudano, "Tell Me I'm Not Dreamin'" features a funky beat with slightly eerie synthesizer chords, all anchored by Jermaine and Michael's intense vocals. In an April 2012 interview with jermainejacksonmusic.com, Gruska described the brothers' working relationship as "professional on every level—superb singing and outstanding musicianship. Much attention to detail and no one grooves harder."

Despite not being a chart-topping single, "Tell Me I'm Not Dreamin' (Too Good to Be True)" earned a 1985 Grammy nomination for Best R&B Performance by a Duo or Group with Vocals, and gives Jackson 5 fans one final taste of their vocal chemistry (as discussed in chapter 6).

## "I Just Can't Stop Loving You" with Siedah Garrett (*Bad*, 1987)

Jones protégé Siedah Garrett never could have guessed that her voice would grace the first single off Michael's highly anticipated album *Bad*. During the making of the album, several other singers were considered for the duet, including Barbra Streisand, Whitney Houston, and Aretha Franklin. Eventually Jones and Michael selected Garrett, then a staff songwriter. By then, "Man in the Mirror," a track co-written by the singer, had already been recorded for the album. As Garrett told *Billboard*'s Gary Graff in 2012, Jones called her back into the studio; thinking he wanted her to help with finishing touches on "Mirror," she was surprised to learn that the producer had another project for her.

As Garrett sat in the studio, Jones and Michael were working on a ballad. Jones suddenly asked Garrett if she liked the song; when she responded positively, he revealed the real reason behind Garrett's visit: she was to sing on "I Just Can't Stop Loving You" with Michael. She fondly recalled the session in the article as well as in the documentary *Bad 25*, noting that Michael jokingly threw popcorn at her while she laid down her vocals. Despite the in-studio hijinks, Michael and Garrett exude romance on the record, with Garrett's sighs and Michael's defiant tone on lines like "My life ain't worth living / If I can't be with you." The album version contains a seductive spoken introduction by Michael, but the single and radio edit excised this section.

The ballad introduced *Bad* with a bang, topping the *Billboard* Hot 100, Adult Contemporary, and Hot R&B/Hip Hop Singles charts. It also hit #1 in the UK and several other countries and quickly became a live favorite. During the *Bad* World Tour, Michael performed the duet with then-backup singer Sheryl Crow; Garrett joined Michael for the *Dangerous* Tour a few years later.

## "Just Good Friends" with Stevie Wonder (*Bad*, 1987)

Another duet from *Bad*, "Just Good Friends" proved the perfect title for these two artists. Michael whoops, "hee-hee's," and beat boxes over the beat as Wonder scats, sounding as if they were having a ball in the studio. They playfully fight over a woman, the synthesizer-provided funk thumping harder than many other *Bad* tracks. Interestingly, despite having two top composers singing on the song, neither one wrote it: Terry Britten and Graham Lyle, a popular '80s hit-making team, provided the lyrics.

Among reviewers, "Just Good Friends" received the lowest marks of any *Bad* track. Davitt Siegerson's *Rolling Stone* review rated it as a song that "starts well but devolves into a chin-bobbing cheerfulness that is unforced but also, sadly, unearned." John McCready's *New Musical Express* review likened the song to *Thriller*'s "The Girl Is Mine," dismissing both as "saccharin diversions." While it may not be *Bad*'s strongest track, it provides insight into Michael and Wonder's longtime personal and professional relationship.

## "Get It" with Stevie Wonder (*Characters*, 1987)

Repaying his mentor for appearing on *Bad*, Michael recorded this danceable R&B tune for Wonder's album *Characters*. Wonder told *Rolling Stone*'s Jeffrey Ressner in 1987 that recording the vocals posed geographical challenges. When Wonder performed a London concert, he picked an audience member to fly a tape of "Get It" back to Los Angeles so Michael could record his section. It ended up being completed in Tokyo, where Michael was kicking off his *Bad* Tour. Jones and Michael entered a studio in between dates to finish his vocals.

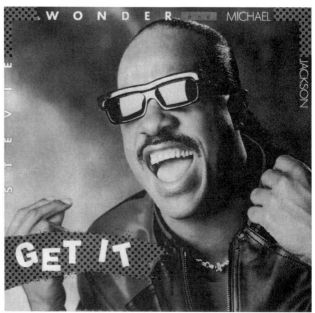

The best part of "Get It" occurs toward the end, when the two singers ad-lib and playfully urge each other to intensify the energy. Handclaps can be detected, although it is unclear who is responsible for the sound (Michael often clapped along with his vocals, as can be heard on many of his tracks). Listening to this joyful

Continuing their frequent collaborations, Michael Jackson joined Stevie Wonder for the playful duet "Get It," which appears on Wonder's 1987 album *Characters*. That same year, Wonder would return the favor by singing on the *Bad* track "Just Good Friends." *Author's collection*

coda, it is difficult to believe that the two were not singing side by side in the studio.

Released as a single in 1988, "Get It" reached #11 on the *Billboard* Adult Contemporary chart and #4 on the Hot R&B/Hip-Hop Songs chart but peaked at #80 on the Hot 100.

## "Scream" with Janet Jackson (*HIStory*, 1995)

One of Michael's most eagerly anticipated duets, "Scream" marked the first time he and his superstar sister shared lead vocals. A track from *HIStory*, "Scream" seethes with rage and indignation (chapter 34 offers a fuller discussion of this and other *HIStory* tracks). The single's release on May 31, 1995, jolted fans expecting a ballad, a fun dance track, or a signature "Heal the World"–style song. Instead, Michael curses (although a percussive sound partially masks the word) and rails against the press and his critics. "The lies are disgusting," he spews, as Janet Jackson snarls, "You're sellin' out souls / But I care about mine." The industrial background, provided by producers and co-writers Jimmy Jam and Terry Lewis, pulsates with barely contained anger.

It may have been an atypical Michael Jackson song, but "Scream" performed extremely well on the charts. It reached #5 on the Hot 100, topped the Hot Dance Club Play chart, and peaked at #2 on the R&B Singles chart. The $7 million Mark Romanek–directed video boasted state-of-the-art special effects and a dance sequence with the siblings. Showing Michael and Janet roaming in a spaceship, sporting space-age/punk clothes and makeup, it projected a new, defiant image for both singers.

## "Hold My Hand" with Akon (*Michael*, 2010)

The first posthumous single, "Hold My Hand" dates to 2008, when songwriter Claude Kelly presented R&B singer Akon with the song. He thought Akon would pass it on to Whitney Houston, but the singer informed Kelly that he wanted to record it himself. A few months later, Kelly told *Billboard*'s Mariel Concepcion, "Akon plays the song for me and all of a sudden I hear Michael Jackson's voice. I was literally shaking by the time the song was over." "Hold My Hand" was intended for Akon's next album as well as a rumored Michael album, but leaked onto the Internet. Feeling "devastated," Akon never released the song.

Akon first met Michael during the *Thriller 25* recording sessions, when the two collaborated on a remake of "Wanna Be Startin' Somethin.'" "The connection was just instant. It felt like we'd known each other for years. I knew everything about Mike, and it was really surprising that he knew everything about me," Akon said in the 2009 *Billboard* article "Akon on Michael Jackson: 'He Was Completely Happy.'" By the time of 2010's *Michael*, the singer believed "Hold My Hand" should finally be heard. Akon issued a statement printed in outlets such as the *Los Angeles Times* blog Pop & Hiss. "Its time has definitely come; now in its final state, it has become an incredible, beautiful, anthemic song. I'm so proud to have had the chance to work with Michael, one of my all time idols," he said.

The reggae-tinged song is a mid-tempo ballad, with Akon sounding eerily like Michael at various points. Released with an accompanying video featuring Akon and archival Michael footage, it performed modestly on the charts, just cracking the *Billboard* Top 40 and R&B Singles charts.

## "All in Your Name" with Barry Gibb (recorded in 2002, released as a digital single in 2011)

Barry Gibb first reported to *Billboard* in December 2002 that he was collaborating with Michael on new material. Nothing surfaced from these collaborations until 2011, when Gibb decided to release a song the duo had recorded entitled "All in Your Name." According to the May 26, 2011, edition of the *Guardian*, the track was originally written in protest against the war in Iraq. The longtime friends worked on the track in December 2002, and Gibb treasured the experience. "We loved collaborating and he was the easiest person to write with. The more we got to know each other the more those ideas entwined, and it all came to this song," he said.

Although "All in Your Name" was originally supposed to be a protest song, it evolved into another meaning. "[The song] is in fact the message that Michael wanted to send out to all his fans all over the world that he did it all for them and for the pure love of music," Gibb told the *New Musical Express* in 2011.

According to the *Guardian*, the duo recorded the song at Miami's Middle Ear Studio; Michael had written parts of the track and brought to Gibb for further work. For unknown reasons, Gibb shelved "All in Your Name" until 2011, when he remastered and released the track on his own website on June 25—the second anniversary of Michael's death. An accompanying video pieced together Hi8 video footage shot by Gibb's son Ashley of the 2002 recording session.

The sweeping "All in Your Name" primarily features Gibb, but Michael sings the powerful chorus. While Gibb later downplayed the antiwar sentiments, the lyrics clearly refer to the futility of the Iraq war: "There's just one religion, one family of love," Gibb sings. In the dramatic chorus, Michael alternates between tenor and falsetto, increasing the volume as he roars, "That it's all in the game, it's all in your name / Carry me to the gates of paradise, they're the same." While "All in Your Name" would most likely have never become a hit due to its overtly religious themes, it serves as a fascinating document of how Michael's voice had lost none of its power.

# 28

# Dance on the Floor in the Round

## How Michael Jackson's *Motown 25* Performance Changed Music and Pop Culture

**B**aby Boomers witnessed the birth of American Beatlemania while watching *The Ed Sullivan Show* on February 9, 1964. Generation X alumni experienced the closest they ever came to this phenomenon while viewing the *Motown 25* special on May 16, 1983. The next day, children were displaying curious behavior: on school playgrounds everywhere, kids began walking backward, their feet dragging across the pavement. Adults swarmed record stores, snapping up copies of a particular album.

Through one performance, Michael Jackson had transformed into a bona-fide star, turning the moonwalk into a nationally known dance and propelling sales of *Thriller* into the stratosphere. For younger generations, Beatlemania had returned in the form of a single-gloved, fedora-tossing man who excited the theater audience and transfixed television viewers. Jackson's iconic rendition of "Billie Jean" would produce a ripple effect in the television and record industry, and still inspires today's artists to combine their singing talent with dynamic stage presence.

### Origins of the TV Special

The *Motown 25* special went through what the entertainment industry dubs "development hell" until NBC finally took a chance on the program. Motown Productions president Suzanne de Passe had previously approached CBS and ABC with an idea: reunite Motown's biggest stars for one night. She presented a list of the talent that would appear, including what was to be the evening's crowning moment: a long-awaited reunion of Diana Ross and the Supremes. After both networks passed on the idea, de Passe gave it one more try: she met with Peter Calabrese, then NBC's vice president of specials and late-night programming. As he gazed down the list of proposed acts, he saw one name: the Jackson 5. He asked if Michael Jackson had confirmed his participation; de Passe responded that Jackson was still considering the offer. She expressed confidence, however, that Motown CEO Berry Gordy would successfully convince him to take part in the celebration.

Despite Michael's ambivalence, Calabrese decided *Motown 25* would attract a desperately needed younger audience to the network. However, NBC's Head of Entertainment Brandon Tartikoff refused to commit to the show. Meanwhile, Motown remained vague as to Jackson's participation. Finally, Calabrese issued an ultimatum to de Passe: deliver Jackson and have him perform his smash-hit single "Billie Jean," or no deal. According to Calabrese's book *How Michael Jackson and the Moonwalk Saved NBC*, de Passe called two days later and confirmed that the singer agreed to appear. This proved to be the deciding factor, as Tartikoff finally gave the special the green light, still not entirely convinced that it would deliver solid numbers for NBC.

Negotiations resumed to persuade Michael to appear on the TV special. Stung by his negative experience with the CBS variety show *The Jacksons*, he had resolved never to appear on television again. In his biography *You Are Not Alone: Michael Through a Brother's Eyes*, Jermaine Jackson recalled a phone conversation with his brother. "I don't want to do no more TV. I want to be doing music videos and live performances. I don't *want* to do what the Osmonds are doing," Michael told him.

Michael narrates the story slightly differently in his autobiography. Still smarting from his negative experiences of working on the family's summertime variety show, he had rarely performed for television after that. He finally acquiesced to Gordy's pleas after insisting on performing "Billie Jean" in addition to the Jackson 5 medley. According to Jackson, Gordy readily agreed to his demands, even though the song and *Thriller* were on Epic Records, not Motown.

## Rehearsal and Costume Choices

After successful negotiations, Jackson and his brothers (including Jermaine) began rehearsals at the family's Encino compound. According to Michael, he choreographed the group's routine (with input from Jermaine and Marlon) and relentlessly rehearsed them. True to his perfectionist nature, Michael had every session videotaped so they could review the footage, making adjustments where necessary.

Michael and his brothers showed up for rehearsals at the Pasadena Civic Auditorium shortly before the final taping. The group ran through their medley—not at full volume, Michael later noted, as they were saving their energy for the final performance. The crew responded positively to their renditions of their greatest hits, and then Michael walked through "Billie Jean." At this point, as he recalls in *Moonwalk*, Michael had not planned out the entire routine. Nevertheless, he constantly consulted with the *Motown 25* production team, quizzing them over camera angles. "Michael wanted to know what those shots were, how many cameras he had and at what angles. All this before the editing process!" Jermaine Jackson remembers.

The next day, Michael instructed his assistants to find what he called a "spy's hat." He wanted to look slightly dangerous and edgy. Accounts vary as to his jacket—in *Moonwalk*, Michael claims he found the sequined jacket while recording *Thriller*. In later interviews, Katherine Jackson remembered Michael finding the garment in her closet, then borrowing it to wear on the show. Jermaine repeats this assertion in his memoir. Nevertheless, Michael writes that it was "so show-business" that he felt it was the perfect attire for his television appearance.

Another crucial aspect to his performance: that soon-to-be ubiquitous sparkly glove. According to his autobiography, Michael had been wearing one glove as since the late 1970s. "I felt that one glove was cool," he writes. "Wearing two gloves seemed so ordinary, but a single glove was different and was definitely a look." He mentions donning the glove during the *Destiny* and *Triumph* tours with the Jacksons, but no one noticed until that fateful night. Like the jacket, he felt the glove was "so show-business," as were the white socks. Michael admitted wearing them while they were "uncool," to the point where his brothers teased him. Yet the sequined socks drew the eye to his footwork—a trick Gene Kelly used in movies such as *Singin' in the Rain* and *Summer Stock*. In *Moonwalk*, Michael reveals his motto: if a particular fashion is taboo or considered too bizarre, he will wear it.

On the eve of the *Motown 25* taping, Michael retreated to the kitchen of the family's estate, cranked "Billie Jean" at top volume, and commenced choreographing his routine. He explained, "I kind of let the dance create itself. I really let it talk to me; I heard the beat come in, and I took this spy's hat and started to pose and step, letting the 'Billie Jean' create the movements." These movements included the moonwalk, a step he had practiced for months. Although he did not invent the dance (as discussed in chapter 26), he refined it to match his Broadway-influenced style.

## High Tension: Taping the Show

During the *Motown 25* taping on March 25, Michael anxiously waited in the wings for his name to be called. He practiced his routine backstage, then instructed crewmember Nelson Hayes to sneak him the hat in between the Jackson 5 medley and his solo spot. According to Jermaine, Michael Jackson also found time to sneak into Ross's dressing room to snoop through her suitcases.

Meanwhile, tension was building onstage the Civic Auditorium. The night's expected highlight—the reunion of Ross, Mary Wilson, and Cindy Birdsong (original Supreme Florence Ballard had passed away years earlier)—turned out to be the night's biggest disaster. The discord between Ross and Wilson had abated little over time and fully emerged during the taping. While Ross and Birdsong agreed to wear black-and-white gowns, Wilson appeared in a fiery red dress. When Wilson made her entrance, the audience responded, briefly upstaging the Supreme star. Then Ross became frustrated when Wilson and Birdsong walked alongside her on stage rather than staying behind the lead singer.

The final straw came when Wilson took over on lead vocals, apparently covering for Ross's confusion; in response, Ross pushed her former bandmate. Attempting to smooth over this highly uncomfortable scene, other Motown acts quickly took the stage for a group sing-along of "Someday We'll Be Together." Wilson then made the mistake of introducing Gordy—unbeknown to her, de Passe had instructed Ross to do so—prompting Ross to yell at Wilson. Editors carefully excised much of this footage from the show before it aired in May, leading to an abbreviated, fragmented Supremes reunion.

In contrast, the Jackson 5 reunion proceeded smoothly; whatever backstage tensions there may have been vanished during rehearsals and the final performance. To create anticipation, the show introduced the group by showing a compilation of classic Jackson 5 clips. This ingenious move excited the audience to the point that they were already on their feet and screaming when all six brothers leapt onto the stage. While their clashing costumes unintentionally emphasized how the members had long since formed their own identities, they quickly demonstrated that they still had a unique chemistry that thrilled audiences.

As if little time had passed, the six brothers immediately fell into line, executing the choreography almost flawlessly. Bedecked in sequined jacket and sparkling white socks, Michael was the main focus—he spun, strutted, and sang the Jackson 5's major hits: "I Want You Back," "The Love You Save," and "I'll Be There." When the group pulled out their signature move—pointing and moving their heads in perfect synchronization—the audience cheered wildly. Wisely, the group began with the two high-energy tracks, saving the

Boasting an all-star roster, the NBC TV special *Motown 25* intended to celebrate the label's vast history. No one could have predicted that Michael would steal the show with a song released by another label, his solo performance looking forward rather than lingering in the past.                                    *Author's collection*

most moving moment for their signature ballad. When Jermaine's part occurred, Michael walked over to him, grinning, insisting that his brother share a microphone with him. Their smiles and embraces demonstrated that this performance symbolized the family's reunion, no matter how brief. Despite the family squabbles, the Michael/Jermaine singing partnership remained.

## Michael in the Spotlight

When the music ended, the six brothers warmly embraced, all exiting the stage except Michael. Now alone, he thanked the audience and began a brief but significant speech. "I have to say those were the good old days. I love those songs. Those were magic moments with all my brothers, including Jermaine," he said, in a shy manner. Suddenly he stared at the audience, signaling something huge was about to happen. "You know, those were the good songs. I like those songs a lot. But especially, I like . . . the new songs."

Anticipating what was about to happen, the audience rose to its feet, cheering even before the first drumbeat to "Billie Jean" began playing. Since the song was in the middle of its seven-week run at the top of the *Billboard* charts, fans instantly recognized those drums. As Christopher Smith writes in his *Los Angeles Times* article "Michael Jackson's 'Motown 25' performance—In Person," "The place exploded. I'm pretty blasé about crowd response, but this was different. It wasn't a roar; more the sound of simultaneous shrieks from all over the auditorium, like everyone being scared at once. A couple rows in front of me, two women in my sight line were violently hugging, almost tackling each other, while riveted on the stage, as though they were unconsciously trying to hold onto the moment more than each other."

Viewers may not have realized it, but they had just witnessed a transitional moment. Little Michael Jackson, the child star, had faded away, replaced by the mature, independent Michael Jackson—one that would momentarily skyrocket in fame and reputation.

Hayes secretly passed Michael the fedora; Jackson planted it firmly on his head, spun around, and assumed his signature position—an angular, Bob Fosse–esque pose, toes pointed, intensity radiating from his posture. The audience screamed as the unmistakable first beats of "Billie Jean" boomed over the speakers. He chose to lip-sync rather than sing live, but his spellbinding dancing made up for it. Tossing the hat across the stage, he began his now legendary routine. He executed flawless spins, his white socks flashing as he paid homage to James Brown's style of fast footwork. The kicks, the moves that seemed to defy gravity, and even some flashes of humor (such as miming combing back his hair in a '50s-style slicked-backed hairdo) dazzled the crowd. But the best was yet to come.

The instrumental break kicked in, and history was made: Michael glided backward, his feet appearing to hover over the stage floor. Gasps could be heard as he ended the move with a flourish: standing on his toes. As Smith writes, "His lankiness underscored the razor sharp moves he was throwing off, each held for a millisecond, poses struck for the world to drink him in. That first moonwalk triggered a resumption of the shrieks—not surprisingly, later on in the lobby there were people trying and failing to mimic that move." Then the song ended, and Michael froze in place as he absorbed the wild applause and cheering. Bowing and blowing a kiss, he jogged off the stage. Even Gordy was spellbound. "It was the most incredible performance I'd ever seen," he recalls, in his autobiography, *To Be Loved.*

## "Coronation" of a Superstar

Writer Steven Ivory, who attended the night's taping, described what followed the singer's exit as pandemonium. "The show had to be halted so that the entire production and building could regain its composure; so that men in the audience could straighten their ties and women could adjust their wigs," he wrote, for the *Electronic Urban Report.* The aftereffects, he said, were as "if Jackson had dropped a bomb on the place, walked away and left us there to negotiate the soulful fallout." A male voice boomed over the auditorium, pleading with audience members to sit down. "Folks dabbed water from their eyes, hugged one another and high-fived strangers. Performance? We'd just witnessed a coronation."

As Michael later revealed in *Moonwalk*, and his 1993 interview with Oprah Winfrey, at first he criticized his own performance. He had intended to remain on his tiptoes for a longer time—an error that clearly no one else noticed. As he mulled over this "mistake" backstage, a little boy ran up to him and praised his dancing. Then, he told Winfrey, "I knew I did a good job, because I know children don't lie." At the *Motown 25* after party, stars such as the Temptations, the Four Tops, and the Supremes crowded around him, showering him with praise. The next day, his idol Fred Astaire called him, raving over his moves. "You're a helluva mover," he recalls Astaire telling him, in *Moonwalk*. "You put the audience on their asses last night!" Michael later said it was the greatest compliment he ever received and the only one he ever believed.

In his final major interview, Michael reminisced further about that night with *Ebony* magazine in 2007. "One of the things that touched me the most about doing that was, after I did the performance—I'll never forget. There was Marvin Gaye in the wings, and the Temptations and Smokey Robinson and my brothers, they were hugging me and kissing me and holding me," he said. "That was my reward. These were people who, when I was a little boy in Indiana, I used to listen to Marvin Gaye, the Temptations, and to have them bestow that kind of appreciation on me, I was just honored."

## Editing and More Editing

Before the show aired in May, editors worked to salvage the ill-fated Supremes reunion and show other performers in their best light. Calabrese recalled Jackson attending editing and audio mixing sessions of his performance, instructing de Passe and *Motown 25* director Don Mischer on virtually every aspect. While this may seem controlling, Michael explained his reasoning in the 2007 *Ebony* interview:

> I direct and edit everything I do. Every shot you see is my shot. Let me tell you why I have to do it that way. I have five, no, six cameras. When you're performing—and I don't care what kind of performance you are giving—if you don't capture it properly, the people will never see it. It's the most selfish medium in the world. You're filming WHAT you want people to see, WHEN you want them to see it, HOW you want them to see it, what JUXTAPOSITION you want them to see. You're creating the totality of the whole feeling of what's being presented, in your angle and your shots. 'Cause I know what I want to see. I know what I want to go to the audience. I know what I want to come back. I know the emotion I felt when I performed it, and I try to recapture that same emotion when I cut and edit and direct.

Used to Michael's perfectionism, de Passe agreed to most of his edits. Then came the next hurdle: should the performances be shown in their original sequence or reordered for the best impact? Calabrese explains in his book that he insisted on having the Jacksons segment occur in the middle of the two-hour special. "When the other networks are showing commercials and viewers are channel-surfing, Michael will be moonwalking across NBC," he writes.

This move—and Michael's riveting performance—paid off big for the network. An estimated forty-seven million viewers tuned in, topping the week's ratings of all network shows. Just four months after it was broadcast, *Motown 25* received an Emmy for Best Special of the Year, thanks in no small part to Michael's electrifying role in the program. He even earned an individual Emmy notation for his performance, but lost to Leontyne Price for *Live from Lincoln City*.

Nonetheless, *Thriller* sales spiked after the show. Michael's onetime co-manager, Ron Weisner, told *Billboard* in 2009 that manufacturing plants had to slow down pressings of other albums to keep up with the demand for more *Thriller* copies. The rest is history: the album topped the year-end charts in the United States, Europe, Asia, and Canada. While sales figures vary widely, *Thriller* is estimated to have sold between 50 and 110 million copies worldwide and is listed by the *Guinness Book of World Records* as the greatest-selling album of all time, thanks in no small part to that *Motown 25* appearance. Michael's rendition of "Billie Jean" became so iconic that whenever he performed the song in concert, he wore a fedora, a glove, and a sequined jacket, replicating the original dance routine.

## Aftermath and Legacy

Michael Jackson's "Billie Jean" performance may have propelled *Thriller*'s sales and NBC's ratings, but its additional effects have rippled throughout the music industry. As Jaap Kooijman writes in "Michael Jackson: *Motown 25*, Pasadena Civic Auditorium, March 25, 1983," it bridged the gap between live performance and the music video. Some of the moves he executed—standing on his tiptoes, lightning-fast spins, kicking and twisting his leg—derived from the original video clip. To emphasize the live/film connection, Michael elected to lip-sync rather than sing live. While this may previously have been frowned upon, here it was a deliberate choice. He focused on dancing, avoiding appearing out of breath.

Shortly thereafter, other artists partially recreated their videos on the stage—a practice still very much in evidence today. Madonna's "scandalous" performance of "Like a Virgin" at the 1984 MTV Video Music Awards; *NSYNC's live recreation of their "Pop" video for the 2001 MTV Video Music Awards show (appropriately featuring a surprise Jackson cameo); and Ylvis's shot-by-shot replica of the 2013 novelty "What Does the Fox Say?" during a 2013 appearance on *Late Night with Jimmy Fallon* can all trace their roots back to that *Motown 25* performance. In concert as well as in music videos, artists could no longer just remain stationary, strumming their instruments and singing. Instead, elaborate staging and choreography took over, some of it worthy of Broadway productions.

Michael's performance also helped break down MTV's racial barriers. Until Michael's breakthrough, the music channel featured an "all rock" format—in other words, predominantly white artists. When the network initially refused to air the "Billie Jean" video in March 1983, Walter Yetnikoff, the head of CBS Records, threatened to pull his label's artists from the channel unless MTV relented (this story was later disputed by onetime MTV senior executive/VP of programming Les Garland). After the *Motown 25* appearance, the barriers officially fell at the station.

Steven Ivory, who attended the show's taping, stated, "If you were a Jackson fan and Black, you were awash in a wave of cultural pride that transcended mere pop music to fasten itself onto American history outright. To be sure, the five minutes Jackson was onstage alone somehow elevated the whole race." MTV could no longer deny his popularity, finally placing the "Billie Jean" video in heavy rotation, as well as the follow-up, "Beat It." By December 1983, the cable channel turned the premiere of the groundbreaking clip "Thriller" into a major event, sealing Jackson's stature as a global superstar. In turn, R&B artists finally received respect

Out of print for over twenty years, *Motown 25* finally received the deluxe DVD treatment in 2014.

*Author's collection*

from MTV, eventually paving the way for hip hop's growth on the channel.

The *Motown 25* program also shattered barriers in radio. Before *Thriller*, American radio remained fairly segregated—rock, pop, and R&B existed on separate stations and rarely met in the middle. Other genres, such as the emerging house music movement and hip hop, found no home on radio. However, *Thriller* quickly became the album everyone owned, no matter their music taste, age, or background. Michael's "Billie Jean" performance further crossed boundaries, attracting a wide audience previously unheard of in radio. In that moment, rock, soul, and dance merged to create modern entertainment for the masses.

Will such a moment occur again? The prospect is unlikely, as the media and popular culture have changed since 1983. After cable became widespread, television audiences were fragmented. Suddenly choices were not limited to the three big networks, and endless channels appeared, appealing to every imaginable interest. The Internet further sliced up viewership, with music videos now relegated to YouTube, Vevo, and other streaming platforms. Add exclusively online channels, Spotify, endless online sources (Netflix, Amazon, iTunes) and the ability to watch shows on demand through tablets, smartphones, computers, TiVo, DVR, and other technology leads to one inescapable fact: the "water cooler" effect has forever changed. Today, mass audiences rarely view the same shows simultaneously, thus diminishing the shared experience. Moments such as the Beatles' first *Ed Sullivan* appearance and Michael's groundbreaking *Motown 25* appearance simply cannot occur in 2015; sadly, radio and television may be returning to the pre-*Thriller* days of musical segregation.

Originally intended as a commemoration of the label's twenty-fifth birthday, *Motown 25* ultimately went down in history as the night Michael introduced his signature moonwalk, demonstrating that he was a musical force in his own right. The fedora, the spangled white glove, the sparkly socks, and the loafers: all became synonymous with the performer, and his style, voice, and dance moves have been mimicked—but never duplicated—ever since that show.

# 29

# Why You Wanna Trip on Me?

## *Dangerous* Liaisons: How Michael Jackson's 1991 Album Demonstrated His Mastery of Hip Hop

W hile Michael Jackson did not initially embrace hip-hop music, he eventually integrated it into his songs. Through incorporating rap breaks and hip-hop beats, he utilized the genre to change his image and explore new topics. *Dangerous* was the first of his albums to feature the immensely popular sound (particularly in the form of "new jack swing"). Under songwriter/producer Teddy Riley's guidance, Michael combined hip hop with his signature rhythmic style to fully embrace the newer musical form. After *Dangerous*, he would continue to use hip hop on 1995's *HIStory* and 2001's *Invincible*, but his 1991 effort symbolizes his acceptance and growing mastery of the genre.

The journey was a long one, however. Quincy Jones had reportedly urged him to incorporate the rapidly growing musical form on *Bad*, but Michael resisted. While he had brought street-dance moves such as popping and locking to the masses—essential components of early hip hop—he was unsure about experimenting with the music itself. Nevertheless, he watched with interest as hip hop emerged from an underground reaction to slick R&B to a worldwide phenomenon.

### 3 Feet High and Rising: Rap and Hip Hop's Emergence

By the mid-1980s, the music scene was shifting from a smooth, pop-focused sound to one that was considered "real" and "gritty." Rap had first emerged in the early 1970s, when teenagers in New York's South Bronx and Harlem began extracting rhythms and melodies from current records, then adding their own rhymes and poetry over these instrumentals. As the disco movement gained momentum (see chapter 14), teenagers who could not afford admission to the downtown clubs hosted their own house and block parties. Local DJs worked these events, with DJ Kool Herc emerging as a prominent creator of "mutant disco," a mixture of R&B, soul, funk, and obscure disco that rebelled against the slick dance music dominating radio airwaves. As these mixes grew in popularity, other pioneers emerged, such as Grandmaster Flash and Afrika Bambaataa. In addition to DJs, rappers gained fame for their wordplay and ability to "battle" other artists in who could best energize the crowd or deliver the most creative insults.

Rap finally reached the mainstream with the Sugar Hill Gang's 1979 hit "Rapper's Delight," a sometimes-humorous record where the group members rapped over the drum and bass lines to Chic's disco tune "Good Times." Grandmaster Flash and the Furious Five expanded the rap genre in 1982 with "The Message," a graphic tale of poverty and violence in the inner city. For the first time, rap signified more than just having a party; it could function as a protest song, a tool for justice. Even though hip hop was finding bigger audiences, it still did not exude crossover appeal—after all, the music was only played on R&B stations.

It took Run DMC to bring rap to massive audiences. Their 1986 collaboration with Aerosmith, "Walk This Way," combined rock and rap to demonstrate the similarities between the two genres; even more importantly, the record was played on Top 40 as well as urban stations. Once the record broke through, it opened the floodgates for other acts such as LL Cool J, Beastie Boys, and Salt-N-Pepa; by the end of the decade, rap turned more realistic and violent with groups like Public Enemy and NWA. When *Yo! MTV Raps* started airing on the music channel in 1988, it was official: rap and hip hop were powerful forces in modern music.

Michael was clearly aware of these trends, as evidenced by his dance moves. Popping and locking, which evolved into breakdancing, was an essential part of the burgeoning hip-hop culture, and its practitioners showcased these steps on *Soul Train*. As discussed in chapter 24, Michael carefully observed these dancers, eventually paying a few of them to teach him moves like the one that would later be known as the "moonwalk." Even as early as 1974, Michael experimented with popping and locking during performances of "Dancing Machine." For the remainder of his career, he combined the smooth dancing of Fred Astaire with the robotic B-boy moves of the 1970s.

In addition to his dancing, from *Off the Wall* onward Michael established himself as a skilled beatboxer. Since he could not play any one instrument proficiently, he would sing every single instrument into a cassette recorder, including the percussion section. Author Randall Sullivan tells a very different story in *Untouchable: The Strange Life and Tragic Death of Michael Jackson.* According to Sullivan, Michael astounded. . ." Michael astounded people with his drumming, piano playing, and guitar and bass plucking. Paddy Dunning, the proprietor of an estate and recording studio in Ireland, recalled Michael jamming with local musicians during his 2006 stay. Sullivan claims that Michael always traveled with a Casio keyboard and had taught himself how to play.

Whether or not he could compose using instruments, one skill was never in question: his beatboxing ability. According to Truemichaeljackson.com, sound engineer Rob Hoffman says his beatboxing skills were "without parallel, and his time was ridiculous." Listen closely to early tracks such as "Working Day and Night," "Get on the Floor," and "Wanna Be Startin' Somethin'," and one can hear his beatboxing woven into the percussion. For a live demonstration, view the 1993 special *Michael Jackson Talks to Oprah*, where he treats Oprah Winfrey and the audience to a reproduction of the rhythm track from *Dangerous*'s "Who Is It."

Despite the hip-hop inspired moves and beatboxing, however, he refrained from recording any straightforward rap or hip-hop records until he could no longer deny its rapidly growing popularity.

## An Uneasy Alliance: When Michael Met Run DMC

At the height of Run DMC's fame, Michael approached them to collaborate on a tune entitled "Crack Kills." In a *Rolling Stone* cover story dated December 4, 1986, the trio had initially expressed disdain for the entertainer. They claimed Michael was "not us," explaining that they came from the ghetto and that Michael dwelled in "corny and fake" Beverly Hills. Russell Simmons, hip-hop impresario and brother of Run DMC member Joseph "Run" Simmons, stressed his opposition to the duet. "The idea of Michael and Run is kinda soft," he told *Rolling Stone*. "This is something that's certainly not going to make Run DMC bigger or better; it could kill them. It could kill their careers in front of their first audience."

Michael eventually won over Run DMC. Toward the end of the interview, Run described a dinner he and the other group members had shared with the superstar, calling him an "incredible human being" and adding that he asked the rappers about their music. Run added that he had decided to record the song with Michael after all, but "Crack Kills" never surfaced.

Meanwhile, Michael prepared material for his follow-up to *Thriller*, *Bad*, but in a very different climate. By 1986, *Rolling Stone* noted, "Run DMC hats and T-shirts have supplanted Michael Jackson items in American households." Darryl "DMC" McDaniels declared, "The reason why they are listening to us is because we are the Michael Jackson of now. Prince was it when *Purple Rain* came out. But we are what's going on right now. We are the music. We are what's hot."

This attitude dominated rap in the late 1980s and 1990s—as Nelson George points out in *Thriller: The Musical Life of Michael Jackson*, "rappers began attacking R&B acts for being too smoothed out and slick, for not being too black or too strong." Run DMC did not know it at the time, but Michael would soon break out of the "smooth" and "slick" image to create a tougher image with *Bad*.

## Who's Bad? Michael Flirts with Rap Culture

Despite the changes sweeping the charts, Michael elected to stay with his signature sound. However, *Bad*'s title cut approaches rap in its boastful lyrics and harder-driving beat. In a raspier, slight lower voice, Michael throws out taunts like "Just watch your mouth" and "You're not a man," ultimately singing that if the listener cannot respect his words and reputation, "then won't you slap my face." Michael's words echo hip-hop tropes in their bragging about who is better or "badder," listing why he is superior to any other man. Interestingly, Michael originally envisioned the song as a duet with Prince, but the singer declined.

*Bad* failed to duplicate *Thriller*'s success—an impossible feat—but stood as the best-selling album worldwide in 1987 and 1988, and to date has sold almost forty-five million copies. It remains the only US album to generate five #1 singles, an impressive achievement for any artist. However, *Bad* would be Michael's last album to not feature any rappers or hip-hop tunes. His next release, *Dangerous*, would mark a new phase of his artistic development.

## Dangerous (1991)

Upon completing his hugely successful *Bad* World Tour in 1989, Michael turned to his next album. The first sign that he was changing direction occurred when he chose not to recruit longtime collaborator Quincy Jones for the follow-up project. Jones would later claim that he had been urging Michael to embrace hip hop. "'He said, 'Quincy doesn't understand the business any more. He doesn't know that rap is dead.' But it's OK. It wasn't so obvious then," Jones told the *Guardian*'s Johnny Davis in 2010.

While Michael may have initially resisted rap and hip hop, he gradually realized that the related forms were dominating the music charts. Another factor may have been Michael's discomfort with rap's occasionally harsh language and controversial subject matter. In *M Poetica: Michael Jackson's Art of Connection and Defiance*, Willa Stillwater posits that Jackson ultimately became one of hip hop's greatest advocates. "He acted as something of a silent guardian angel, helping hip hop find an audience and quietly answering and deflecting the central criticisms aimed against it: namely, that it was violent and misogynistic," Stillwater says. She adds that he may have chosen not to incorporate rap back in 1987 because it was a musical form that defied the music establishment; at that time, post-*Thriller*, Michael dominated the establishment and mainstream.

For his first full immersion into hip hop, Michael hired Riley, a pioneer of the R&B/hip-hop hybrid new jack swing, to helm what would become *Dangerous*. Riley had helped transform new jack swing into a major force in R&B with his own group, Guy, as well as on Bobby Brown's blockbuster self-titled album. As Susan Fast points out in the 33⅓ volume *Michael Jackson's Dangerous*, Riley and new jack swing allowed the singer to explore "new ways of using his spectacular, agile voice, the dark, industrial grooves, a revived allegiance to the sounds of black music— past (soul and r&b) and present (hip-hop)—his all-grown-up image."

## Recording Sessions

Sessions began at California's Record One but then moved to Larrabee Studios, as Riley later told MusicRadar.com. He employed vintage boards rather than digital equipment to achieve a warmer sound, in keeping with his goal of achieving a simpler sound rather than layering strings over each song. According to Dolan's article in *Rolling Stone*'s 2009 tribute to Michael, the album was actually made over two years in seven different studios. He would shuttle between studios and shooting music videos, with the final cost of *Dangerous* ballooning to approximately $10 million.

For the purposes of this chapter, only *Dangerous* tracks with a distinct hip-hop sound will be examined. Other tracks such as "Heal the World" are discussed in terms of his activism (chapter 30), while songs such as "Will You Be There," "Give In to Me," and "Who Is It" are covered in chapter 37, in the context of Michael's "Studio MVPs."

## "Jam"

"Jam," *Dangerous*'s opening track, sets the stage for Michael's updated sound. Riley reported that the track was Michael's idea; Michael brought it to Riley, who enhanced it out with more instrumentation. "That's the way it worked a lot of the time. He'd come in with an idea and I'd flesh it out in the studio. He bought it to me as a DAT, and he told me there were things he wanted done, and I did them," said Riley.

Riley suggested having Heavy D. appear, as he was Michael's favorite rapper at the time. The lyrics address one of the singer's favorite themes: uniting to solve the world's problems. However, the song also offers a *carpe diem* message with the line "We must live each day like it's the last." Heavy D. demonstrates his superior flow with the rap break, mainly referring to his excitement at "making funky tracks" with his idol the "smooth criminal." Amusingly, in an example of the hip-hop tradition of bragging about one's status, he even mentions other artists he has collaborated with: "Got with Janet, then with Guy, now with Michael."

While the beat and the rap break bear typical hip-hop traits, "Jam" also features Michael's trademark rhythmic singing. As Fast suggests, his style closely mirrors that of his mentor, James Brown. "This song is a full-on tribute to Brown, what with Jackson's clipped and distorted singing style in the chorus, the retro horns," she writes. Michael the actor is also present here, as his voice effortlessly changes from sounding wounded, almost on the verge of tears, to defiant as in the chorus ("It ain't too much for me to jam!").

According to Fast, Michael here employs hip hop as a form of resistance and a call to form a community of

The *Dangerous* track "Jam" features Heavy D. of Heavy D. and the Boyz on the rap break. The rapper also briefly appears in the accompanying video. *Author's collection*

creativity: "Jackson situates himself fully within the world of hip hop as action, as resistance. . . . The lyrics of 'Jam' can, in fact, be viewed as a kind of meta-text on the crucial role of hip hop in contemporary culture: as a creative means through which dissent is expressed and community created."

## "Why You Wanna Trip on Me"

According to Riley, "Why You Wanna Trip on Me" was one of the easier songs to record. It features one organic instrument: Riley's guitar, which blasts through an otherwise typical new jack swing beat. Michael employs a growling voice in the verses, rising to a louder, more emphatic anger in the chorus. The verses feature Michael complaining that while the media focuses on his eccentricities, it is ignoring more pressing problems like poverty, violence, and illiteracy. "Why you wanna trip on me?" he cries, confronting his critics. Over an industrial beat, he again calls for a community to form and solve the world's problems. The hard beat and Riley's piercing guitar grab the listener by the metaphorical lapels, asking them to unite with Michael and make the world a better place instead of becoming bogged down in trivialities.

## "She Drives Me Wild"

"She Drives Me Wild" contains a heavy beat very reminiscent of a rap track, its melody virtually nonexistent during the first verses. Only the chorus introduces the melody, with multitracked backing vocals (all provided by Michael) creating a smooth counterpoint. The lyrics draw on the slang of the day, with Michael growling about how the subject has "got it kickin' in the back." Riley's rap act Wreckx-N-Effect performs the rap break, uttering head-scratching lines like "You got me looking like Buckwheat" and "Oh, shiver me timber."

As Riley explained to MusicRadar, "She Drives Me Wild" mixed in unusual percussion, similar to the techniques used on *Bad*. Car sounds were substituted for drums, courtesy of a sound-effects CD.

## "In the Closet"

Riley reported that this song also originated from an idea Michael brought to him, and that the singer was very specific about the sound he wanted to achieve. "He kind of put his vocals on a Dictaphone when he was in another room. He'd often record the vocals on a Dictaphone and take them into the studio and then see how it would all work out," he said. Notable for containing some of Michael's more sexually explicit lyrics, "In the Closet" retains its hip-hop vibe through its slamming drum tracks.

Keyboardist/arranger (and frequent collaborator) Brad Buxer would later cite this song as one of his favorite tracks from the album. "One day I was in the studio working, and Michael and Teddy came in and put on this track 'In the Closet,' and it was just incredible," he told *Rolling Stone*'s Jon Dolan. "The song was almost atonal. I was like, 'This is the cutting-edge stuff.'"

Critics agreed, citing "In the Closet" as one of the best examples of Michael's fusing of old-school soul with modern beats. In *Rolling Stone*'s *Michael*, Rob Sheffield includes the song among Michael's twenty-five essential moments. "His early-nineties work is the only time MJ really capitulated to music trends, hopping the new jack swing beats of Teddy Riley, yet he sounded right in the pocket. With a mysterious female spoken-word vocal . . . this is a one-of-a-kind item in his songbook."

## "Black or White"

"Black or White" (produced by Bill Bottrell) presents a fascinating juxtaposition of sounds. At first, the acoustic guitar–driven beat and electric guitar lines suggest a pop/rock tune, with the drum pattern subtly suggesting a hip-hop sound. Then the bridge kicks in with a hard rock vibe (appropriate for the defiance of lines like "I ain't scared of no sheets"); directly after that comes the rap section, which is completely dissimilar to the rest of the track. Mysteriously named rapper L.T.B. spits out one of the song's most crucial themes: "I'm not going to spend my life being a color."

Who was the unknown L.T.B., and why would he be prominently featured in a Michael Jackson song? In 2001, the rapper gave up his identity: Bottrell. In an interview with *Vice* dated May 5, 2015, he explained how he and Michael sought to fill a gap in the middle of "Black or White." One morning, while thinking about Michael's lyrics of harmony, Bottrell quickly jotted down a rap part. He recorded a demo, intending for Michael to have LL Cool J or Heavy D. perform the final version. Michael loved Bottrell's performance, though, and insisted that it be used as the song's rap break instead.

"I'm, you know, a songwriter and record producer," Bottrell told *Vice*. "I'm not a rapper, and I did not intend to be a white guy who's rapping on there." Reluctantly acquiescing to Michael's wishes, Bottrell insisted on using the pseudonym L.T.B., which stood for *Leave It to Beaver* ("It's a white suburban kid, I'm making fun of myself," he told *Vice*).

On later reflection, Bottrell added, he thought that the fact that he was a white, inexperienced rapper allowed Michael to underscore the point of the lyrics. "The fact that I'm white and I did that rap kind of speaks to the content of the song. So in his mind, it all came together."

"Black or White" was released to radio stations in two versions: with and without the rap. In 1991, many stations adhered to a strict "no rap" policy, thus necessitating the edit. Perhaps the massive success of the single paved the way for radio to remove the stipulation, finally acknowledging that rap and hip hop had officially entered the mainstream.

## "Remember the Time"

One of the biggest hits off *Dangerous*, "Remember the Time" is a unique hybrid of nostalgia and new jack swing. Michael's warm, playful voice complements the harder beat perfectly, with neither element overshadowing the other. As Susan Fast notes, "It's the first track that doesn't adhere to the 'industrial' sound that so characterizes the album and this makes sense given that it's intended to be

While not containing a rap break, "Remember the Time" represents the typical 1990s "new jack swing" sound that fused hip hop, R&B, and pop.
*Author's collection*

nostalgic for a happier, perhaps more innocent time (not only the lover's past, but a different social past)."

Michael alternates between this creamy singing style (accented by lush background vocals, all performed by Michael) and a more energetic reading toward the song's end, the scatting and crying out suggesting that he has surrendered completely to these sweet memories. This section is even more evident in the accompanying music video, when all music except a finger-snapping sound drops out to fully expose Michael's raw vocals.

Riley reported that he brought the song to Michael, and had intended it to set the tone for the rest of *Dangerous*. According to the songwriter/producer, "Remember the Time" best encapsulates the sound he pioneered with Guy and Bobby Brown. "Sort of like the twisted samples I brought in. There were no samples of other people on that; what I did was make the sounds myself—I was sampling myself. I'd just jam with a riff and think, 'That's a cool bit there . . .' Yeah, it kinda really brought a lot to the production side. It worked." Riley also told MusicRadar he believes the song contains some of Michael's best vocals.

Since its release in 1991, "Remember the Time" has remained one of Michael's most beloved tracks, and as *Vibe* pointed out in 2014, it ignited a new era of R&B. Old school soul set to a modern, harder beat became extremely popular in the early 1990s, with artists such as R. Kelly, Mary J. Blige, and Toni Braxton experiencing great success. Keith Murphy's *Vibe* article from August 29, 2014, posits that the soul, hip hop, and gospel mixture of "Remember the Time" presented a new type of R&B. The track peaked at #3 on the *Billboard* Hot 100, topped the R&B charts, and cracked the Top 10 in more than eleven countries. As Murphy writes, Jackson had taken Riley's new jack swing to new global heights, "making the newest era of rhythm and blues into the go-to pop sound."

## "Dangerous"

The album's title cut allows Michael to rap in his own way. Over a typical new jack swing beat, Michael describes the unnamed subject of the song, a woman who is dangerous. Pitching his voice lower, almost whispering, he mostly speaks the words until the last two lines before the chorus: "The girl was bad / The girl was dangerous." Michael originally recorded the track with co-producer Bottrell; after Riley heard it, he asked if he could rearrange the song to better fit with the rest of the album. Indeed, the demo's bass line echoed "Billie Jean," and the electronic snapping sounds resembled past cuts like "Rock with You." As Riley told MusicRadar, he built upon Michael's hook with an Akai MPC-60 drum machine as well as sounds derived from sample CDs.

Bottrell professed to have no hard feelings about Riley updating the track. "I never felt competition with Teddy, and when MJ suggested Teddy do a version, I had no problem," he later wrote on the GearSlutz forum. "Hey, it's all about the writing. Teddy's version rocks and sounds like the '90s, where mine was stuck in the '80s." As Dolan writes, the result was "a classic-Michael attack on a skeezin' girl, mixing bright strings (a Jackson favorite) with one of the heaviest, starkest beats he'd ever sung over."

## "Can't Let Her Get Away"

An underrated *Dangerous* song, "Can't Let Her Get Away" resulted from a sample CD Riley created; he played various instruments and looped them together to store for future projects. He played that CD for Michael, believing its James Brown-esque rhythms would suit Michael's vocal style.

In *Man in the Music*, Vogel writes that this song is "generally considered one of the least memorable songs on the album," and it was never released as a single. Still, some critics pointed out Michael's energetic performance and relentless beat as standouts. *Village Voice* reviewer Chuck Eddy labeled the track "a nonstop, nonlinear barrage of bopgun pops and bumblebeed beats, vamps and squeaks and gurgles, Cupid's arrows flying through space and what at one point could be a drippy faucet, has as much disco momentum as anything Jackson's waxed since *Off the Wall*." It is a deep cut waiting to be appreciated, an irresistible slice of early-'90s new jack swing made better by Michael's heavy syncopated singing and growling voice, communicating his torment over a tumultuous relationship. If any evidence is needed to demonstrate Michael's mastery and complete acceptance of hip hop, "Can't Let Her Get Away" is it.

## *Dangerous* Outtake: "Serious Effect"

One outtake from these sessions that eventually leaked onto the Internet is "Serious Effect," a collaboration with LL Cool J. The fun, surprisingly sensual, and aggressive track did not make the final cut on *Dangerous*. In a raspy voice, Michael describes the effect of a sensual woman on him, clarifying that "She don't hash / She don't dope" and that he is "so damn glad about it." LL Cool J's rap in the middle underscores Michael's passion: "She's too hot to touch / Too cool for criticism." A funky bass line, slightly off-kilter drum pattern, and synthesizers resembling female backup singers cooing along with the beat result in a tougher, sexier Michael performance. He even briefly raps toward the end, repeating some of the earlier lyrics.

With this track, as well as numerous *Dangerous* cuts, Michael had finally embraced hip hop, although he did not compromise his signature singing style or ability to produce danceable tunes. *Dangerous* became the era's most successful new jack swing album, selling about thirty-five million copies worldwide and spawning eight Top 40 singles. Despite this success, *Dangerous* is often overlooked in favor of *Off the Wall* or *Thriller*. As AllMusic's Stephen Thomas Erlewine writes, "It's the rare multi-platinum, number one album that qualifies as a nearly forgotten, underappreciated record." Today, it seems to be best remembered for being knocked out of the charts by a new and distinctly different act: Nirvana. However, not only did *Dangerous* sell well, it set the stage for Michael to further experiment with hip-hop.

## 2 Bad: Hip Hop on Post-*Dangerous* Releases

*HIStory* and *Invincible* contain a number of tracks featuring rappers and harder beats. As further testament to his embrace of the music genre, several rap and hip-hop artists have paid Michael the ultimate compliment by sampling his music. On 1995's *HIStory*, a newly defiant Michael expressed his anger and lashed back at his critics through harder beats and rage-filled rhymes (some of them performed by Michael). His final album, *Invincible*, includes rap breaks boasting of how he had withstood media scrutiny. However, some tracks just celebrated dance, and guest rappers like Fats underscored that message.

## *HIStory* (1995)

By the time of 1995's *HIStory*, Michael had obviously become accustomed to hip hop. He uses rap to convey anger and his new defiant stance (see chapter 34 for a thorough analysis of the entire album). The Notorious B.I.G. and basketball star/aspiring rapper Shaquille O'Neal make appearances, and Michael spits lines on another track, railing against his critics.

### "This Time Around"

"This Time Around" is notable not only for Michael uttering a profanity for the first time in his music, but for the rap break performed by one of gangsta rap's towering figures. The Notorious B.I.G.—a former drug dealer whose unique flow and vivid storytelling made him a pioneering figure in East Coast rap—seemed to have little in common with the King of Pop. Yet his blunt rap fits in perfectly with the song's seething rage, saying how he has changed his outlook and to choose his friends carefully. "They ain't friends if they robbin' me," he snarls. He describes people tapping his phones; people stalking him, forcing him to carry a gun (another highly unusual ingredient in a Michael Jackson song). However, this unconventional elements transitions into Michael chanting, "He really thought he really had control of me."

### "Money"

No guest rappers grace "Money." Instead, Michael himself raps—surprisingly convincingly. In a low, menacing voice, he rails against "backstabbers" who would betray others for money. "Are you infected with the same disease / Of lust, gluttony and greed?" he asks, confronting listeners with his words. While he sings the chorus in his typical multi-layered vocals, he demonstrates that he has learned new techniques from hip-hop artists. The funky bass line and shuffling beat not only convey his outrage but also encourage listeners to hit the dance floor hard.

### "2 Bad"

Later appearing in the short film *Ghosts*, "2 Bad" confronts people Michael considers to be phony, grittiness entering his voice as he declares, "You are disgustin' me." This time the rap break does not follow the song's overall theme, which is best expressed in the lyric "I'm standin' though you're kickin' me." He would revisit this sentiment on 2001 tracks like "Unbreakable," but here he uses a funky vocal over a thrusting beat. Then-fledgling rapper O'Neal brags about hanging out with Michael, boasting "Nine five Shaq represent with the Thrilla / Grab my crotch, twist my knee, then I'm through." Unlike the tracks discussed above, the rap segment on "2 Bad" appears shoehorned in, perhaps to appeal to more hip-hop aficionados.

### Outtake: "We Be Ballin'" (1998)

Before his final album, *Invincible*, Michael would flirt with hip hop by teaming up with another unlikely collaborator: ex-NWA member Ice Cube. Recorded in 1997, "We Be Ballin'" is a remix of Ice Cube's track "We Be Clubbin," and was intended to be used as part of the NBA's 1998 "I Love This Game" ad campaign. In addition, it was to be released on an NBA compilation album. Shaquille O'Neal contributed an introduction and new verses, then recruited Michael to sing the chorus. Unfortunately, the basketball players subsequently went on strike against the league, forcing the entire project to be abandoned.

## Invincible (2001)

In 2001, Michael found himself at another creative crossroads. He faced a similar situation as in 1991, namely entering a musical landscape that had changed even in the last ten years. Rap and hip hop were the undisputed rulers of the charts, and best-selling pop acts like Usher, while heavily influenced by Michael, had fully embraced the genre.

Deciding to update his sound to compete with acts like Usher as well as *NSYNC and the Backstreet Boys, he hired hot producer Rodney "Darkchild" Jerkins, among other collaborators, to helm his next album. By 2001, Jerkins had produced innumerable hits that combined hip hop's heavy beats with a classic but tougher R&B sound, often including rap breaks. Examples include Joe's 1997 hit "Don't Wanna Be a Player," 1998's "The Boy Is Mine" by Brandy and Monica, Jennifer Lopez's breakthrough 1999 hit "If You Had My Love," 1999's "Say My Name" by Destiny's Child, and 2000's "He Wasn't Man Enough" by Toni Braxton. Now, Jerkins became one of *Invincible*'s key players, producing six tracks.

As detailed in chapter 35, Michael entered the studio wanting a futuristic sound. He collaborated with rappers such as Will Smith and Jay Z, but those cuts did not make the final album. He did work with Jerkins protégé Fats, and a sample from the Notorious B.I.G.'s rap break from Shaquille O'Neal's "You Can't Stop the Reign" was integrated.

Despite working with such artists and material, Michael still expressed some reticence toward hip-hop culture. In a March 2002 *Vibe* interview entitled "MJ: Unbreakable," Michael opined on the culture as well as the music. "I like a lot of it, a *lot* of it," he said. "I don't like the dancing that much. It looks like they're doing aerobics."

### "Unbreakable"

Michael told *Vibe* that although he envisioned a rap break in "Unbreakable," it was Jerkins who proposed the Notorious B.I.G. sample. The bouncing beat and Michael's pointed jabs announce his return. "Why can't you see that you'll never ever hurt me," he cries. The stuttering beat later introduces the rapper, who delivers lines that seem tailor-made for the song's spirit. He brags of his wealth and influence, stating, "My dreams is vivid, work hard to live it." To all his haters, he merely replies, "You're messin' with the devil." As on *HIStory*, Michael uses hip hop to communicate aggression and defiance, challenging his critics to try to wound him.

### "Heartbreaker"

Unlike "Unbreakable," "Heartbreaker" exudes sex and inhibition. As Michael growls and stutters over a slamming beat, Fats provides even more commentary in the rap break. "I thought it was love with this game," he sputters, chanting the lines in warp speed. "One hard player, she's a star player." While "Heartbreaker" works just as well without the rap segment, it does enhance the harder, street-edge quality of the song, backed by its relentless techno beat. As Robert Hilburn wrote in his 2001 *Los Angeles Times* review, "'Heartbreaker' and the title song are also sonic marvels that lead us to think Jackson has thrown away some of the security blankets he's held onto since *Thriller*, and moved into daring new territory. His singing is sassy, defiant, and forceful."

### "Invincible"

Another hard-charging dance track, the album's title song tells of Michael's constant attempts to earn a woman's love. In the hip-hop tradition, Michael compares himself to her current man, bragging, "And he's buying diamonds and pearls, he can't do it like me." When Fats enters via the rap break, he reiterates Michael's message: "He can spit, but his game ain't strong enough." Ultimately, though, Fats seems to give up: "It's like nothing seems to work, she's invincible."

### "You Rock My World" (remix featuring Jay Z)

Jerkins completely reimagined *Invincible*'s lead single, "You Rock My World," with this remix, which features a new rap by Jay Z. While Michael told *Vibe* that he enjoyed working with the rapper, he admitted that adding him to the remix was for commercial as well as artistic reasons. "He's hip, the new thing, and he's with the kids today. They like his work. He has tapped into the nerve of popular culture. It just made good sense."

Featuring a thumping beat, acoustic guitar, and whistling out of a spaghetti western, the remix lets Jay Z deliver playful lines filled with braggadocio: "the Mike Jordan of rap, the Mike Jordan of pop," he announces. Fitting in references to Mike Tyson, Hugh Hefner, Lara Croft, and Steven Spielberg, he sets the scene for Michael's original vocals. Unlike the original version, this recasting of "You Rock My World" focuses less on the classic Michael Jackson sound and more on a tougher hip-hop feel. "Clap, clap, clap, clap!" Jay Z decrees, urging the listener to obey.

In return for Jay Z's appearance on "You Rock My World," Michael recorded backing vocals for the rapper's *Blueprint* track "Girls, Girls, Girls." Due to a dispute with Sony, however, Jay Z was unable to release this track as a single; consequently, Jay Z blocked the release of the "You Rock My World" remix. "Girls, Girls, Girls" finally appeared as a hidden track on the *Blueprint* album, not listed in the liner notes.

## Michael Influences Hip Hop

During the final years of his career, Michael still appeared reluctant to fully accept rap and hip hop. In a 2001 *USA Today* interview, he responded to a question about whether the sexual components of his music and dancing conflicted with his religion. "I never use bad words like some of the rappers," he said. "I love and respect their work, but I think I have too much respect for parents and mothers and elderly people. If I did a song with bad words and saw an older lady in the audience, I'd cringe." Despite this wariness, his decision to incorporate the closely related genres of rap, R&B, and hip hop into his music forever changed his music, vocals, and image. In turn, hip-hop artists and rappers acknowledged his influence on them through their music's ultimate compliment: sampling his songs. The following lists represents just a sampling of these tracks:

- "Candy Girl" by New Edition (1983, samples the Jackson 5's "ABC")
- "O.P.P." by Naughty by Nature (1991, samples the Jackson 5's "ABC")
- "Jump" by Kriss Kross (1992, samples the Jackson 5's "I Want You Back")
- "Right Here (Human Nature Remix)" by SWV (1992, samples "Human Nature")
- "Hey Lover" by LL Cool J featuring Boyz II Men (1995, samples "The Lady in My Life")
- "Izzo (H.O.V.A.)" by Jay Z (2001, samples the Jackson 5's "I Want You Back")

- "All Eyes on Me" by Monica (2002, samples "P.Y.T.")
- "Don't Stop the Music" by Rihanna (2007, samples "Wanna Be Startin' Somethin'")
- "You're My Star" by Tank (2014, samples "This Place Hotel")

## Remember the Time: *Dangerous*'s Impact on Michael Jackson's Music, and Pop Music Worldwide

While Michael may not have fully embraced hip hop and rap until *Dangerous*, he flirted with the genre as early as 1986. By 1991, he felt confident enough to fully immerse himself in the music's stronger beats and industrial sounds. It was not that far from his R&B and dance roots, and thus on tracks such as "Remember the Time" or "Can't Let Her Get Away" he melded a voice influenced by James Brown, Jackie Wilson, and several other classic soul singers with a harder edge. As Vogel notes in "Michael Jackson, *Dangerous*, and the Reinvention of Pop," "Jackson's appropriation of the style is clear. The beats are often more dynamic and crisp, the rhythms more syncopated, the sound more visceral and industrial. Found sounds are used as percussion everywhere: honking horns, sliding chains, swinging gates, breaking glass, crashing metal. Jackson also frequently implements beatboxing, scatting, and finger-snapping."

Along with its ballads and further experiments with rock/pop/R&B hybrids, *Dangerous* marks a turning point in Michael's career, namely his using hip-hop to express anger (as on *HIStory*) and defiance (as on *Invincible*). In turn, he further exposed the genre to the mainstream, and countless artists have paid him back by sampling his music. In an *Ebony/Jet* interview published in November 1992, Michael explained that he intended *Dangerous* to be timeless. "I would like to see children and teenagers and parents and all races all over the world, hundreds and hundreds of years from now, still pulling out songs from that album and dissecting it. I want it to live." Judging by its lasting impact, *Dangerous* not only endures but continues to influence pop music and hip hop alike.

# 30

# We Are Here to Change the World

## Michael Jackson as Musical Activist

When radio stations and news programs paid tribute to Michael Jackson in 2009, one track emerged as his theme song, the one fans tended to play when wanting to reminisce. While "Thriller," "Billie Jean," and "Bad" were frequently aired, it was "Man in the Mirror" that proved most popular. A few days after his death, MTV reported in "Michael Jackson's Posthumous Sales Surge" that "Man in the Mirror" ranked as his most downloaded song. Among many reasons given for this phenomenon is that its uplifting message comforted fans in the wake of Michael's death.

In a web post from June 30, 2009, MTV asked, "Why Is 'Man in the Mirror' Jackson's Top-Selling Song on iTunes?" The post quoted Brian Raftery, author of *Don't Stop Believin': How Karaoke Conquered the World and Changed My Life* as saying that "Man in the Mirror" is "an oversized anthem that makes a vague yet heartfelt pledge for self-improvement. And it's amazingly flexible—it's a song that could be about racism, war, sexuality or even plain old love. Listeners can project whatever they want onto 'Man in the Mirror,' which I think is a big part of its appeal."

As Michael evolved artistically, he expanded his music beyond the realm of dance to social activism, recording songs addressing poverty, the environment, produce, and personal responsibility. *TV Guide* asked Michael during a 2001 interview about his desire to help others through music. "I've done it all my career: 'Heal the World,' 'We Are the World,' 'Will You Be There,' 'Man in the Mirror,' about the planet, earth songs. And nobody was doing it but me, because that's where my heart is. I care."

Beginning with his 1985 composition "We Are the World," Michael used his lyrics and voice to communicate messages advocating social change. However, he had already experimented with such songs on the Jacksons' 1980 *Triumph* album, specifically its lead single, "Can You Feel It." As Geoff Brown writes in *Michael Jackson: A Life in Music*, the track delivers an important announcement: the Jackson brothers have arrived to help bring peace and harmony to the world, but they need everyone's cooperation to accomplish such a task. In other words, humanity must unite to accomplish world peace.

## "We Are the World" (1985)

Released as a single in 1984 to aid famine victims in Ethiopia, Band Aid's "Do They Know It's Christmas" became a massive success. Featuring the UK's biggest artists, the song became the fastest-selling single in the nation's chart history, selling a million copies in its first week and three million by the end of the year. Inspired by the song's success, Band Aid founder Bob Geldof hoped to produce a similar project in America. Meanwhile, singer and activist Harry Belafonte had contacted Ken Kragen, a mega-agent who represented Lionel Richie and Kenny Rogers. He wanted Kragen's help in organizing a benefit concert for Africa; instead, Kragen encouraged him to gather an all-star group of artists to record a single. Originally intended to feature about a dozen artists, USA for Africa rapidly grew to over forty participants, with Kragen having to turn some away.

Kragen tapped client Richie to pen the song. Originally, the singer/songwriter intended on composing the song with Stevie Wonder, but his longtime friend was unavailable. Thus he approached Quincy Jones, the project's producer, to contact Michael to see if he would be interested. Once Michael accepted the invitation, he and Richie immediately began collaborating.

As Richie told *USA Today* in January 2015, the duo listened to anthems from several countries. "We didn't want a normal-sounding song," Richie said. "We wanted bombastic, the biggest thing you got." In *Moonwalk*, Michael states that he would have sister Janet follow him into the bathroom (which had optimum acoustics) and sing notes from the melody. The two songwriters then met several times to refine the melody and write lyrics. Lisa Campbell's *Michael: The Complete Story* reprints Michael's reflections on the composing process. "I love working quickly. I went ahead without even Lionel knowing, I couldn't wait. I went in and came out the same night with the song completed—drums, piano, strings, and words to the chorus. I presented the

"We Are the World," the 1985 single Michael Jackson co-wrote with Lionel Richie, boasted an all-star chorus featuring the era's biggest musical stars. Michael's first overt "message song" raised money for USA for Africa, the Bob Geldof–led organization that raised money to feed Africa's poor. *Author's collection*

demo to Quincy and Lionel, and they were in shock—they didn't expect to see something this quick. They loved it."

An early demo surfaced on the 2004 *Ultimate Collection*, featuring substantially different lyrics than the final version and some African-style backing vocals toward the end. The most striking variation comes during the lines "There's a chance we're taking / We're taking our own lives." When Michael, Richie, Wonder, Jones, and the session musicians met at Kenny Rogers's Lion Share Recording Studio to record the backing track and vocal guides, the songwriters revised the lyrics to read, "There's a choice we're making / We're saving our own lives," to avoid any connotations with suicide.

Michael and Richie revised the lyrics right up until the night before the historic recording session. Jones modeled the backing vocal arrangements after a song he had just finished producing: Donna Summer's "State of Independence" (see chapter 23), which featured several singers that would also appear on "We Are the World." After strenuous preparation, including choreographing each singer's part and contacting each participant (a tape with the guide vocals came with a Jones-penned note requesting that this project had to be kept secret), the final recording session took place on January 28, 1985, the night of the *American Music Awards*. Immediately after the festivities, celebrities were whisked to A&M Recording Studios; when they reached the building entrance, a sign greeted them: "Please check your egos at the door."

As Robert Hilburn wrote in his 1985 *Los Angeles Times* article "Behind the Scenes of a Pop Miracle," the lyrics created an emotional reaction in the singers as well as the record-buying public. He reported that the singers were frequently moved to tears during the all-night recording session. Listeners, in turn, were emotionally affected by the words' simplicity and directness. "Some friends have told me they were so taken by the gentle, uplifting spirit of the song that their eyes filled with tears the first time they heard it," Hilburn wrote.

## "Man in the Mirror" (1987)

Michael's next step in musical activism occurred with this *Bad* track, co-written by Siedah Garrett and Glen Ballard (for more information on these artists, see chapter 37). Amazingly, Garrett had never written a song before this one; mentor Quincy Jones had been quietly urging her to try songwriting, and in 1986 invited her to submit material for Michael's upcoming *Bad* album. Accepting the challenge, Garrett called Ballard for a brainstorming session. As Ballard played keyboards, Garrett searched through her writer's notebook for possible lyrics. A few lines concerning a man looking into a mirror drew Ballard's interest; in just a week, the two completed a demo.

After they presented the demo to Jones, it took only four hours for Jones to fall in love with the tune. He immediately contacted Garrett to praise the track and said Michael would probably request some additions. According to the *Independent*'s Robert Webb, Michael suggested adding a longer middle eight and revising certain

Though not written by Michael, "Man in the Mirror" quickly became "his" song, a gospel-tinged track celebrating his ever-increasing interest in philanthropy and activism. *Author's collection*

lyrics. Jones recruited the Andraé Crouch Choir to underscore the song's gospel influences.

In *Moonwalk*, Michael cites "Man in the Mirror" as one of his favorite songs. He likens its message to John Lennon's lyrics in that the words advocate how one person can make a change. Unlike other protest songs, however, "Man in the Mirror" contains a twist—it stresses that change begins from within; that one must develop compassion before helping others. "Start with yourself. Don't be looking at all the other things. Start with you. That's the truth. That's what Martin Luther King meant and Gandhi too. That's what I believe," Michael writes.

These beliefs shined through when he performed the song at the 1988 Grammy Awards; as he fell to his knees in front of the choir, he exhorted the audience to "stand up" and make a change. His passionate performance earned him a standing ovation.

## "Heal the World" (1991)

Buoyed by the massive success of "Man in the Mirror," Michael fully delved into message songs on 1991's *Dangerous*. "Heal the World" exemplifies his transformation—not only would he use music to bring awareness to issues, he would use direct action to enact change. Shortly after album's release, he announced the formation of his Heal the World Foundation, an organization devoted to improving children's lives around the world. This song served as the foundation's theme song—one that he also performed during his 1993 Super Bowl halftime show.

In an online chat with fans in 2001, Michael listed "Heal the World" as one of his favorite tracks, and it can be seen as a sequel to "Man in the Mirror." In this case, the man has restructured his priorities and is urging listeners to follow his lead. There are ways to alleviate suffering, but only if one cares enough to make the world a better place. He urges people to join him in creating a "world with no fear" and leave a better place for future generations.

Despite his sincere message, some reviewers criticized the track. The *Village Voice*'s Chuck Eddy dismissed it as a "We Are the World" clone, while *Q*'s Mat Snow proclaimed that the song "hits like an insulin overdose." In his *Rolling Stone* review, Alan Light called it a "Hallmark card knockoff" of "We Are the World," while *Billboard*'s Steve Huey labeled it "saccharine." Despite the mixed reviews, "Heal the World" remains one of Michael's most personal songs, one that exemplifies his growing activism and willingness to become involved in causes. As Brown writes in *Michael Jackson: A Life in Music*, the song stands as a plea for unity and harmony in order to preserve the world for future generations.

By 1991, Michael had formed the Heal the World foundation; the track of the same name graced the *Dangerous* album.            *Author's collection*

## "Earth Song" (1995)

"I like songs with emotions and a message, and a sense of immortality," Michael told interviewer Adrian Grant for *Making HIStory*. As discussed in chapter 34, "Earth Song" seethes with anger and despair over damage to the environment. Its booming bass, along with the Andraé Crouch Choir's soaring backing vocals and Michael's emotional performance, force the listener to assume responsibility for damaging the earth and rebuilding it. Michael worked on the song over several years; originally intended for *Dangerous*, it eventually debuted on *HIStory*. His obvious love for the track surfaced during preparations for *This Is It*; he planned on including in in the 2009 concerts, and it would be the final song he rehearsed before his untimely death.

The lyrics constantly address the audience, forcing them to observe "this crying earth, this weeping shore" as well as "all the children dead from war." He suddenly changes to the first person plural, admitting his guilt. "What have we done to the world / Look what we've done," he cries. Unlike "Heal the World," he does not advocate specific action; he also does not demand that listeners look inward, à la "Man in the Mirror." Instead, he turns people's attention to the world, ordering that they acknowledge their role in damaging the earth.

As Brown writes, "The humanitarian and ecological bill so far is enumerated: the destruction of people, flora, fauna, yea the very planet itself." Michael would continue the "holding the mirror to society" theme on *Blood on the Dance Floor*, but in this case revealing humanity's flaws.

## "They Don't Care About Us" (1995)

One of Michael's most misunderstood songs, "They Don't Care About Us" tackles the sensitive issue of racism. Because of its strong language and use of certain ethnic slurs, critics denounced the track before it hit music stores. Horrified, Michael ultimately agreed to re-record the song with new words, to include apologies on future copies of *HIStory*, and censor the offensive language on versions already airing on radio. However, "They Don't Care About Us" actually protested prejudice, assuming the voice of the oppressed and urging revolution. As he later told *Making HIStory*'s Grant, "It's a public awareness song. . . . It's a protest kind of song—it's not a racist song, it's an anti-racist song."

The relentless beat, along with Michael's snarling, half-rapping singing, allows the track to pulsate with rage. The 4/4 rhythm is sparse, yet the throbbing tempo provides a strong background for his messages against prejudice and persecution. Unlike previous tracks, "They Don't Care About Us" contains an "us against them" motif, calling for an end to prejudice, but not in a gentle sense. In other words, the handholding positivity of "We Are the World" or the uplifting "Heal the World" is nowhere to be found here.

The track also resulted in Michael's most overtly political videos: two Spike Lee–directed clips that both emphasize the lyrics' message, but in vastly different ways. The first, commonly called the "prison version," features Michael dressed in prison garb and handcuffs, roaming a jail. He leads inmates in a protest, with the group pounding the tables (causing the camera to shake) as Michael sings and dances around them. Seeing him join in the protests showcases a very different side of Michael—rather than distancing himself from the so-called "thugs," as he does in the "Beat It" video, he identifies himself with the tough prisoners. Violent footage of the Klu Klux Klan, war crimes, and police attacking African Americans is woven throughout; these disturbing images resulted in the video being banned by MTV.

While the second video seemed more uplifting, its setting suggested otherwise. Lee filmed the clip in the poverty-stricken Salvador (Pelourinho) and Rio de Janeiro, Brazil; Michael danced and wandered the slums (sometimes interacting with the police), with residents shadowing him. The cultural group Olodum also played a huge part in the video, as the 200-member collective pound drums that combine African and Brazilian rhythms. Paul Simon had featured such percussion just a few years earlier, on his album *Rhythm of the Saints*. Sporting an Olodum T-shirt, Michael dances and yells as the group plays tribal-sounding rhythms. Two women break through security to hug Michael, one knocking him to the ground; Lee and Michael left these scenes in the video. While not as overtly political as the "prison version," it still communicates messages of defiance and perseverance, even from the oppressed.

## "HIStory"

Upon *HIStory*'s release, critics ripped apart the title track, accusing Michael of hubris. A closer examination of the lyrics, however, reveals that he is not likening himself to historical figures but instead calling upon listeners to emulate the actions of revolutionaries. The song urges people to stand up for their beliefs and never give up.

Brown posits that "HIStory" consists of four parts, each contributing to the track's larger message. Part one weaves newsreels describing significant events in history, accompanied by a sample of Russian composer Modest Mussorgsky's "The Great Gate of Kiev" from *Pictures at an Exhibition*. A marching band segues into a hip-hop beat (an infectious yet plodding rhythm provided by Jimmy Jam and Terry Lewis), which leads into Michael's vocal. His gruff, angry voice introduces part two, where he details how those challenging the status quo will experience obstacles. "He got kicked in the back / He said that he needed that," he half-raps. "He dares to be recognized." In other words, never give up or compromise one's principles.

The third segment moves beyond the individual to general society. He asks how humanity can continue to ignore others' suffering, urging them to take action. The solution is personal responsibility, the obligation to enact change. The final section explicates this answer: "Every day create your history / Every path you take you're leaving your legacy," he sings in the chorus. Live life with purpose and remember every action has a consequence: those are the key messages in "HIStory."

Critics such as the *New York Times*' Jon Pareles claimed "HIStory" was essentially gloomy. In "Michael Jackson Is Angry, Understand?," Pareles claims that Michael "seems more obsessed with dying soldiers and 'victims slaughtered in vain across the land' than with hope." However, Brown counters that the song deserves further consideration, explaining that "this ambitious, complicated concept track deserves more careful unstitching and decoding than it received from critics on its release."

## "Cry"

Michael's second collaboration with R. Kelly differs dramatically from their first hit, "You Are Not Alone." While their first single stands as a classic love song, "Cry" is a plea for unity and cooperation. Released as a single and accompanied by a video—Michael does not appear in the clip due to disputes with Sony—"Cry" received a lukewarm reception from critics. Pareles's *New York Times* review from October 28, 2001, stated the song "applies its grand buildup to one of pop's strangest utopian schemes: asking everyone to cry at the same time, at which point the singer may 'answer all your prayers.'" *Rolling Stone*'s 2001 *Invincible* review opined that the track "more or less succeeds with the kind of life-affirming number Jackson will never (and should never) quite desert."

A sweeping anthem, "Cry" highlights isolation and loneliness, stressing the importance of working together to alleviate suffering. Through the lyrics, he implores the listener to accompany him in this journey. "You can change the world (I can't do it by myself) / You can touch the sky (Gonna take somebody's help)," he and the Andraé Crouch Choir sing in a call-and-response section. As in "Earth Song," the choir acts as the narrator's conscience, urging him forward in his task.

Like his previous message songs, "Cry" forces the audience to view atrocities. "Someone is taking a life," Michael sings. "Where were you when your children cried last night?" The solution is to join him, for everyone to "reach for the truth."

How can this be accomplished? According to the lyrics, "if we all cry at the same time tonight," humanity can experience one another's pain and feel inspired to heal the world's ills. As Vogel points out in *Man in the Music*, some critics viewed these lyrics as "messianic," and lines such as "I will answer all your prayers" certainly bolster that opinion. However, Kelly and Michael's gospel-inflected anthem remains consistent with the King of Pop's other message tracks: it offers self-reflection, unity, compassion, and action.

## "The Lost Children"

The second message song off *Invincible* received the harshest reviews of all. In his *Invincible* review, the *Village Voice*'s Robert Christgau called it "offensive," while *Rolling Stone*'s Hunter dismissed it as "a theater piece in which Jackson insists on singing about imperiled kids." "The Lost Children" does resemble *HIStory*'s "Little Susie" in that it narrates the story of neglected children, but this time Michael expresses slightly more optimism in humanity.

In the first verses, Jackson argues that too many songs merely address romance and daydreaming, but few concern missing children. He asks that people keep these youth in their thoughts, as he does; he sings that his heart weeps as he thinks of these children away from their homes and the love of their parents. A children's choir joins him on the chorus, with additional children's voices heard as the song concludes.

Interestingly, the activism represented here is cerebral and spiritual. The waltz-like track aims for awareness, for listeners to reserve moments out of their days to remember and pray for these lost children (runaways and, presumably, those who have been abducted). Do not forget them, he demands, and hope for their safety and ultimate return. Michael cited "The Lost Children" in his 2001 online chat, explaining that this track, "Speechless," and "Unbreakable" were his favorite songs off *Invincible*.

## "What More Can I Give" (unreleased 9/11 benefit track)

Intended as a sequel to "We Are the World," "What More Can I Give" is instead known for its tangled backstory and ultimate shelving. It began life in 1998, as Michael wrote the track in honor of Nelson Mandela. He had planned on debuting it with an all-star choir during the 1999 Michael & Friends concerts in Seoul and Munich, but for unknown reasons, he did not perform "What More Can I Give" at those shows.

After the catastrophic events of September 11, 2001, Michael retrieved the song from his archives, rewriting it and recruiting a new group of artists. Featuring an A-list roster including Luther Vandross, Celine Dion, Mariah Carey, *NSYNC, Usher, Carlos Santana, and Beyoncé, the charity single was completed on October 19 and then premiered at the "United We Stand: What More Can I Give" concert at Washington DC's RFK Stadium. Footage from the show later aired on ABC that November. At the time, Michael stated that he wanted to raise at least $50 million with the single, with funds to benefit the terrorist attack victims.

In the BBC News article "Jackson Plans Record for Attack Victims," Michael said, "I believe in my heart that the music community will come together as one and rally to the aid of thousands of innocent victims. There is a tremendous need for relief dollars right now and through this effort each one of us can play an immediate role in helping comfort so many people."

Despite the good intentions, troubles plagued the single from day one. When the *United We Stand* performance was aired, Michael was barely shown. This unusual move resulted from an agreement between ABC and CBS; Michael's *30th Anniversary Special* was scheduled to air later in November 2001, so they demanded that Michael not appear on any other show before that airdate. Next, Michael's ongoing disputes with his label Sony resulted in "What More Can I Give" not being released as a single. It was released to radio a year later, and was issued as a digital single in 2003. In addition, its accompanying video finally premiered at the Radio Music Awards.

The lyrics capture Michael's activist streak and demonstrate how he used music for social commentary. As the various artists sing their lines, they ask the audience how much more suffering needs to happen before people take action. What can one give? The answer, the song tells us, is love and prayers. The lyrics ask that humanity pledge to "love and to teach you / To hold and to need you." Compassion and unity, the song argues, can overcome hate and cruelty.

"What More Can I Give" stands as Michael's final message track, and it summarizes his consistent themes: self-reflection, unity, compassion, and action. "How many times can we turn our heads / And pretend we cannot see?" he asks in the song, as he did sixteen years before, in "We Are the World." Throughout his solo career, Michael asked that question in various ways, forcing listeners to hear his narratives and consider what they will do to solve problems and, as he sang, "heal the world."

# 31

# Is It Scary for You?

## Gothic and Horror Elements in Michael Jackson's Films, Songs, and Videos

A s Julian Vigo writes in "Michael Jackson and the Myth of Gender," Michael used horror motifs not only to entertain but also to "bring to the fore issues of social and racial inequality in the United States as seen through cinematic tropes as he borrowed from an expansive tradition of cinematic traditions of song, dance and horror." Just as gothic authors used horror motifs to convey messages concerning social and political uncertainty, so Michael used such themes to explore social ills as well as personal struggles.

### A Brief History of the Gothic

The roots of the gothic novel can be traced back to 1764, when author and English aristocrat Horace Walpole published *The Castle of Otranto: A Gothic Story*, a story that combines trademarks of the genre: a foreign location, a foreboding castle, and a pure maiden fleeing from an evil, lecherous man. It also marks the first time the word "gothic" appeared in the subtitle of a book. Thirty years later, Ann Radcliffe penned the first massively successful gothic novel, *The Mysteries of Udolpho*, and established a common gothic motif: supernatural elements that have logical explanations. Controversy entered the genre with Matthew Lewis's *The Monk*, a salacious novel filled with sexual perversion and gore.

By 1816, one of gothic literature's most enduring characters was introduced to English audiences through *The Vampyre*, John Polidori's story of the outsider who feasts on human blood. That same year, Mary Shelley would publish the tale of the ultimate outsider: *Frankenstein*. The novel not only introduced a creature created from dead bodies but also commented on current events. As Catherine Spooner notes on the BBC's Timeline of Gothic Fiction website, Shelley's tale is considered the first science-fiction novel and can be seen as a warning about the dangers of modern science.

Other significant works include Jane Austen's *Northanger Abbey* (1818), which features a character obsessed with gothic literature. Another major gothic figure, Edgar Allan Poe, published the first of his short stories in 1840, combining gothic themes with psychological terror. Emily Bronte's *Wuthering Heights* (1847) mixed gothic elements with romance, while Robert Louis Stevenson's classic *The Strange Case of Dr. Jekyll & Mr. Hyde* (1886) explored the duality of human nature, contrasting good and evil. Finally, Bram Stoker's *Dracula* (1897) set the standard for the modern vampire, a seductive man who targets, among others, young maidens.

In more recent years, the tradition lives on through authors such as Stephen King (*Salem's Lot*, 1975), Anne Rice (*Interview with the Vampire*, 1976), and Mark Z. Danielewski (*House of Leaves*, 2000). Television programs such as *True Blood* and the *Vampire Diaries*, books such as the *Twilight* series, and films such as *Bram Stoker's Dracula* continue the genre, its popularity unabated.

Placed in a historical context, the gothic novel reflected late Victorian fears. According to Greg Buzwell's article "Dracula: Vampires, Perversity, and Victorian Anxieties," many at that time feared increasing immigration, leading to unfounded concerns over increases in crime and the rise of ghettos. Buzwell also posits that Victorians feared increased promiscuity, which would lead to a sharp rise in sexually transmitted diseases and ultimately moral as well as physical decay. At the same time, women were enjoying unprecedented educational and employment opportunities, allowing them to transcend traditional gender roles. This "New Woman," Buzwell writes, created hostile attitudes and portrayals of such women as "either as a mannish intellectual or, going to the opposite extreme, an over-sexed vamp."

Finally, an explosion in technology (phonographs, Kodak cameras, typewriters, telegrams) as well as scientific advancements in medicine and psychology led to fear of out-of-control modernity. Would machines ultimately overtake humanity? How would life be forever altered? These themes would emerge again in 1920s Jazz Age literature such as F. Scott Fitzgerald's *The Great Gatsby*.

## Major Themes: The Checklist

From their literary beginnings through modern-day adaptations, gothic books and films share several major themes in common. As part of the British Library's *Discovering Literature: Romantics and Victorians*, John Bowen listed seven motifs of the genre. In this chapter, these characteristics will be used as a checklist for determining gothic elements in Michael's music and videos:

- Time and place: contrasts between the modern world and past, and comparisons between wild strange places vs. confinement or imprisonment
- Power: what does it mean to be human? What are our limits? This theme tackles questions of self-control, such as managing internal desires against forces outside oneself. Can all humans resist forces tempting them to do things against their consciences?
- Sexual power: gothic literature often examines extremes such as incest, rape, and violence
- The sublime: in gothic literature, this element concerns the terrifying, awesome, and overwhelming; in other words, not traditional connotations of bliss, such as something that is beautiful or orderly
- Supernatural vs. real: the gothic motif involves two themes that consider this contrast; the first weaves the supernatural into a story, expecting the reader to believe in such magic; the second argues that there is no supernatural world, and that ghosts can be explained in a natural, logical way.

## "This Place Hotel"

Michael's first brush with the gothic occurs on this *Triumph* track, a tale of revenge and love turning sour. In *Moonwalk*, Michael discusses how he intended on taking listeners through a journey, scaring them but ending on a positive note to bring them back to reality. Geoff Brown describes the track as "Hammer horror," referring to the British production company that produced such over-the-top horror films as *The Curse of Frankenstein* and *The Mummy*. In addition, Brown argues that "This Place Hotel" can be seen as a prequel to "Thriller" through its gothic themes. La Toya Jackson's scream introduces the track, along with mournful strings. Background singers wail and vocalize spooky "oohs" during the bridge, an eerie tap-dance sound suggesting ghouls performing a ghostly dance. Besides its sound effects, the lyrics touch upon elements on the gothic checklist.

### Time and Place

Ten years after the dissolution of a romance, the narrator is led back to where he and his lover used to meet for trysts. He vowed he would never return to this place, yet he is drawn to the scene "where my baby broke my heart and left me yearning." His expectations for a nostalgic romp are dashed when he arrives at the hotel, eyes following the couple as they walk to their old room. Immediately he feels imprisoned as one voices cries out "welcome to your doom." As the woman accuses him over a past infidelity, every woman the author knows emerges, surrounding him. "Hope is dead," Michael wails, as the man in the next room informs him he has been a prisoner in this "heartbreak hotel" for fifteen years. Clearly Michael refers to confinement in not only a physical place but also a psychological one. Time does not exist in this place, which isolates sufferers from the everyday world.

### Sexual Power

While not explicit, the song throbs with sexuality, although in a negative sense. The first line, "live in sin," indicates that the sensuality in "This Place Hotel" refers to something destructive. When the narrator reaches the room, he finds his former lover along with "Sefra and Sue, every girl that I knew" waiting for him. They confront him, with the wronged woman crying, "Love is through." What will this group do with the protagonist? The song never answers the question, although these so-called "wicked women" reside in a place "where the vicious dwell," intending to destroy the narrator's soul. Violence of the body and soul are suggested—a common motif in gothic literature.

### Power

How far will humans go to hurt one another? This hotel or wild space represents inhibition, a place where social norms and morays are suspended. What will these women do in a hotel where evil reigns, in search of souls to destroy? Would people condone this behavior in everyday society? "This Place Hotel" questions what forces would drive people to condone and execute revenge, disregarding consequences.

## "Thriller" (song and video)

Michael's first immersion into the gothic, "Thriller" and its video are loving tributes to the horror genre. In his 2010 article "'Did I Scare You?': The Curious Case of Michael Jackson as Gothic Narrative," Dennis Yeo Kah Sin argues that this video revived interest in the gothic and supernatural. In addition to the Rod Temperton–penned lyrics' constant references to scary movies, the song includes vintage sound effects, all capped off by a rap from horror film legend Vincent Price. Engineer Bruce Swedien recalled recording the sound effects in a 2009 interview with *Future Music*, specifically the wolf howl at the beginning. At first Swedien tried recording his Great Dane; after the canine refused, he enlisted Michael to perform the howls himself. The engineer then traveled to Hollywood's Universal Studios, bringing back three doors used to create sound effects to Westlake Studios. He recorded the sounds of the doors creaking, the final touch being Michael contributing the footstep sounds.

For the video, Michael contacted John Landis, director of the comedy/horror film *An American Werewolf in London.* After enlisting top cinematographers, costume designers, master special-effects makeup artist Rick Baker, and A-list choreographer Michael Peters (who had previously worked with Michael on the "Beat It" clip), Landis wrote the script, a story loosely based on the campy classic *I Was a Teenage Werewolf.*

As has been extensively chronicled, "Thriller" set the standard for future music videos. The production cost $900,000 to produce, a record at the time for what was previously considered a throwaway expense. To partially fund the astronomical sum, Landis and Michael issued *The Making of Thriller*, a home-video release that also aired on MTV and Showtime. The preproduction and filming alone shattered expectations, with Landis insisting on almost two weeks of rehearsal for the dancers.

After premiering on MTV, *The Making of Thriller* broke previous sales records, bolstering the still-emerging home-video market. When it was later released on DVD, its sales increased to $9.5 million. The video's influence lingers, with

Michael's first video experiment with horror elements was "Thriller," an ode to monster movies that features still-impressive makeup, innovative choreography, and genuinely scary moments. *Author's collection* artists such as the Backstreet Boys emulating the original. In 2009, the "Thriller" clip became the first music video ever inducted into the Library of Congress's National Film Registry.

Not surprisingly, both the song and video encapsulate several themes of gothic literature.

## Time and Place

*The song*: "Thriller" plays with time and space, tricking the listener into believing the narrator and his girlfriend are being pursued by a monster. The first line specifies that darkness surrounds the couple, with only the moon lighting their way. Suddenly they move from the wilderness to indoors, the sound of the door slamming stressing imprisonment and claustrophobia as they wonder if they'll "ever see the sun."

The scene changes abruptly, with the listener realizing that the couple is actually watching a horror movie on television. Michael playfully sings that if the woman simply cuddles close to him, he will save her "from the terror on the screen." Day and night, inside and outside, wilderness and stability—all are contrasted in the lyrics, the words constantly disorienting the listener.

*The video*: Landis's storyline takes many twists and turns, intentionally confusing the audience to prepare them for the twist ending. With a few exceptions, most of the action takes place outside at night, suggesting that darkness provides little protection and invites mayhem and evil. The movie theater and abandoned house scenes create claustrophobia; in the former, the tightly packed theater increases the female lead's anxiety, forcing her to practically crawl over the other people seated in their row to escape. She soon discovers, however, that leaving the building provides no sanctuary. Crowds appear again in the abandoned house segment, this time zombies cornering the heroine, hampering any escape. The final scene takes place at what is presumably Michael's home—in this case, only one room is shown, mimicking the closed spaces of previous locations.

"Thriller" also plays with time in its three distinct sections. First, Michael and his girlfriend appear in 1950s-style clothes, driving a car from the period. Just as the Michael werewolf character is about to attack the girl, the scene changes to modern day. The couple, now clad in modern clothing, is watching this scene in a movie theater. By switching time periods to something more familiar to modern audiences, Landis provides viewers a false sense of security. Surely Michael and the girlfriend must be safe now? Of course, chaos ensues once they leave the theater, with zombies descending upon them. Michael transforms into one of the walking dead, destroying any sense of safety.

When the zombies chase the terrified girlfriend into an old house and close in on her, the scene changes a final time. Only Michael's hand is seen gently as he gently his love interest awake; at first frightened, she quickly discovers that she had fallen asleep and dreamed the entire episode. Once again, viewers breathe a sigh of relief at this return to normalcy and present day. "C'mon, I'll take you home," Michael says softly, smiling kindly at her. But as they walk away, Michael turns to the camera, revealing his cat's eyes. Has time shifted once again? Is this action occurring in the past or present, in a dream or in the real world? The ending remains ambiguous.

## Sexual Power

*The song*: As with "This Place Hotel," the sexuality present in "Thriller" is not overt. Yet certain lines suggest that the narrator is seducing the woman in the guise of protecting her. "All through the night I'll save you from the terror on the screen," Michael croons, urging her to cuddle closer. His next lines add sly sexuality, as he tells her, "I can thrill you more than any ghost would ever dare try," to hold him tight and share a "killer, thriller." Introducing romance after spending most of the tune painting gruesome pictures of ghouls and monsters takes "Thriller" in different directions, with the juxtaposition of romance and sex with horror a hallmark of gothic literature.

*The video*: A trademark of the gothic motif is the damsel in distress, a woman in constant peril of being violated by savage beings. The "Thriller" clip definitely contains this element. In the first scene, the virginal "good girl" first experiences innocent romance, with her boyfriend giving her his class ring. But this purity is short-lived; when he transforms into the werewolf, he becomes an uninhibited creature intent on conquering the young lady. In the final scene he looms on top of her, leaving his next action to the viewer's imagination.

In the zombie sequence, the woman is in danger once more, this time from the undead. When they chase her into the abandoned house and reach out for her, it is unclear what they will do with her. However, the violence is implied—a gothic motif.

## Power

*The video*: By having Michael transform into other creatures, the short film questions what it means to be human. Do werewolves represent the uncivilized, immoral being that may exist within everyone? The darkness, along with changing into other creatures, encourages Michael and the other characters to abandon society's rules, attacking others without remorse. Classic horror characters such as Frankenstein and the Wolfman exemplify this theme, questioning whether temptation and other outside forces can shatter self-control.

In the last scene, when Michael turns to the camera to reveal his cat's eyes, he incorporates the gothic's fascination with duality in human nature. In *Rock Eras: Interpretations of Music and Society 1954–1984*, Jim Curtis states that in this scene the viewer understands that appearances can be deceiving. The sweet, mild-mannered Michael Jackson may possess a dark, uninhibited side. The eyes expose "a demonic quality which is not illusory but inherent in him. That is to say that by helping us to recognize a demonic quality in him, he is also recognizing that quality in ourselves."

## "Little Susie"

A tale of horror and corrupted innocence, the *HIStory* track "Little Susie" tells the story of a little girl neglected by her parents and society. She tumbles down the stairs to her death, and Michael's lyric paint a vivid picture of her wounds. He forces listeners to confront this tragic scene, questioning how humanity could have allowed such an event to happen. The orchestration, along with Michael's dramatic reading, turns "Little Susie" into a mini-opera, a track not out of place in a stage production such as *Les Misérables*.

### Power

Humanity has failed Little Susie in every way possible. Her father abandoned her, even after her mother and grandfather died. Having most likely suffered physical and emotional abuse (possibly reflecting the "sexual power" motif), Susie tried to survive, yet was ultimately overpowered by an unnamed person. The lyrics clarify that no one cared about her plight, not wanting to become involved. Only the next-door neighbor knows of her pain, yet all he does in the song is tend to her lifeless body, gently closing her eyes. Michael commands listeners as well as the gentleman to treat her with care and respect. Morality dictates that people empathize with another's plight and help alleviate suffering. Yet in this scene the do-nothing neighbors (not to mention her father) cave in to internal desires, putting themselves above others' needs.

When the neighbor closes Susie's eyes, the action symbolizes people avoiding personal responsibility. The eyes represent the conscience, which in this case has been ignored, asking the eternal gothic question: can humans resist forces tempting them to act against their morals? He ultimately implicates bystanders in her death, crying that neglect "can kill like a knife in your soul."

### The Sublime

In the midst of this violent tale, Michael still finds flashes of beauty. He stresses how Susie would "sing in the daytime at noon," and even in death radiates purity and is "so young and so fair." "She lie there so tenderly / Fashioned so slenderly," he gently sings. Yet this is contrasted with her torn dress, the blood in her hair, and her lifeless eyes. By invoking the gothic's unconventional perception of beauty, Michael emphasizes the tragedy of Little Susie's death.

## "Blood on the Dance Floor"

The title track of what Joseph Vogel calls Michael's darkest album, "Blood on the Dance Floor" tells the tale of a woman who appears romantic and sincere, but ultimately physically and emotionally wounds her victims. Long rumored to be about AIDS (which the songwriters denied), the track sets the scene for the entire album, an "exploration of social decay," according to Vogel's *Man in the Music*, that

Critic Joseph Vogel called 1997's *Blood on the Dance Floor*, a collection of songs featuring supranational elements as well as horror tropes, Michael's most gothic album. *Author's collection*

holds a mirror up to its grotesqueness. By forcing people to confront their weaknesses, Vogel writes, Michael hoped society would change. Over a new jack swing–tinged beat, Michael growls the lyrics, gasping between lines, using a similarly aggressive voice to the one he employs on much of *HIStory*.

## Time and Place

As the song title specifies, most of the action occurs on the dance floor. Interestingly, unlike in previous songs such as "Rock with You" or "Off the Wall," the nightclub does not represent liberation. "To escape the world I've got to enjoy that simple dance / And it seemed that everything was on my side," he shouts, indicating that he viewed the dance floor as a positive space. In this case, however, this sanctuary is invaded by the wicked Susie. In this charmed space, her love seemed sincere; now the once exalted floor has become a place of confinement and regret.

## Sexual Power

"Blood on the Dance Floor" pulsates with sexuality. He sings that many may feel that he is in power, seducing her, but she will turn the tables and "put you under."

Being with her is not about love or romance, but taking a chance on a one-night stand. Similar to "Billie Jean," this woman (also named Susie) will harm her lover and make him wish he could "erase the past."

The song's title, along with its images of knives, stabbing, and death, mix sex with violence, a typical gothic theme. In the music video, the Susie character even wears a form-fitting red dress, moving seductively and wielding a knife, just to clarify the lyrics.

## "Ghosts"

A sequel of sorts to "Thriller," "Ghosts" invokes every horror film cliché, painting pictures of ghosts, ghouls, blood, and creaking doors. A blood-curdling scream is heard, along with eerie backing vocals and a metallic beat. However, Michael inserts a plot twist: while monsters and haunted houses may be frightening, the ghost of jealousy is the real force of evil. As with many tracks on *Blood on the Dance Floor*, "Ghosts" challenges listeners to confront their own demons, asking which is scarier—the supernatural, or betrayal and jealousy?

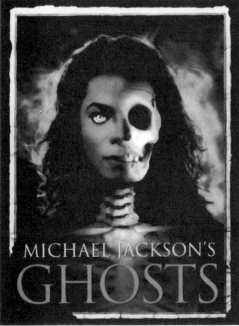

Released in 1996, *Michael Jackson's Ghosts* serves a sequel of sorts to the "Thriller" video, and explores a favorite Michael theme: isolation from society.
*Author's collection*

### Supernatural vs. Real

At first, "Ghosts" resembles a typical horror movie, with Michael searching for explanations for strange sounds and smells. There is an omnipresent spirit in his home—he hears something in the walls, senses a "ghostly smell," and sees a rocking chair moving by itself. However, is this presence truly supernatural? The chorus suggests something even more sinister. "Who gave you the right to hurt my family?" he angrily cries. "You put a knife in my back, shot an arrow in me / Tell me are you the ghost of jealousy?"

These words transform the song into more than just a gothic horror tale: here he suggests that envy and revenge wreak even more havoc, tearing apart families and destroying lives. Clearly the narrator feels he has been stabbed in the back; while scary movies would render this a physical attack, here Michael refers to the action metaphorically. Some force has destroyed his life and disturbed his loved ones, achieving more than any ghost could achieve.

## "Is It Scary"

One of Michael's most autobiographical songs outside of "Childhood," "Is It Scary" remains lyrically fascinating and disturbing. Using gothic motifs, Michael responds to critics who ridicule his eccentricities and render him a "freak." As the song progresses, however, he holds up a mirror and asks an intriguing question: who is the real "freak," him or those who stereotype others? Filled with desperate gasps, sighs, sharp exhales, and beatbox-powered percussion, "Is It Scary" rests on Michael's vocals, his voice emitting pain and anger. "Is it scary for you, baby?" he sneers, before pointing a finger at his accusers: "You know you're scaring me too."

### Power

In gothic fashion, "Is It Scary" explores issues of self-control and civility. While ghosts and ghouls are considered inhuman, and therefore able to commit immoral acts, people are thought to be above such actions because they possess a conscience. But what forces could tempt humans to abandon morals to satisfy inner desires? *Dr. Jekyll & Mr. Hyde* exemplifies this theme, but in "Is It Scary" people do not have to transform into literal monsters. In the lyrics, he accuses people of taunting him, eager to see him become "the stranger" in their lives. But who is strange for wanting to see the grotesque? "The stranger is you," he practically screams. "Like a mirror reveals the truth / See the evil one is you." According to "Is It Scary," people deny their own humanity by enjoying seeing others suffer—a concept known as *Schadenfreude*.

### The Sublime

As Michael transforms into the unusual, he almost sounds seductive. "If you wanna to see eccentrialities [sic] / I'll be grotesque before your eyes," he sighs, using a vocal style similar to the one heard on "Human Nature." "Did you come to me to see your fantasies / Performed before your very eyes?" he softly croons, beckoning the viewer to watch. "Let the performance start!" He makes the grotesque sound seductive and alluring, although he turns the tables by suggesting that people who want to see such sights are the *real* freaks and ghouls. This theme borrows from *Frankenstein*, during which Shelley also poses a question: who is the real monster, the creature or the doctor wanting to create life and defy nature?

### Supernatural vs. Real

Michael may paint himself as a supernatural character, entertaining others with his antics and ability to spin Edgar Allan Poe–style yarns. "Am I the beast you visualized?" he sings, presumably with a wink. What is revealed, however, is that there is no otherworldly presence, no "haunting ghostly treats," "foolish trickery," and "spirits dancing." Instead, the "grotesqueness" on display is lack of compassion and mislabeling others. He accuses critics of ignoring "truth and purity," not empathizing with his loneliness. In other words, all of these supposed "supernatural" events never occur, but are explained in a logical way. This is evocative of such gothic novelists as Ann Radcliffe, who touched upon this dichotomy in works such as *The Mysteries of Udolpho*.

## Ghosts (short film)

As discussed in chapter 32, *Ghosts* is a 1997 film based on a collaboration between Michael and Stephen King. Directed by special-effects/makeup master Stan Winston, the short film stars Michael as a man residing in a castle outside of Normal Valley. The Maestro lives with ghosts and often entertains the town's children with their singing and dancing antics. The town's mayor as well as the youths' parents discover these activities and proceed to storm the castle to drive out the "weird" figure. Spewing insults such as "freaky boy," the mayor orders the Maestro to leave immediately and stop scaring the children. The Maestro challenges the major to a "scare-off": the one most frightened must leave the town.

Through dance and special effects, the Maestro successfully defeats the mayor and wins over the parents with his mischievous sense of humor. By the end, however, it is a young boy who manages to scare the Maestro and adults the most (although the viewer never sees what precisely he does). An ode to classic horror movies like *The Haunting* or *I Was a Teenage Werewolf*, *Ghosts* conveys a message Michael clearly wanted to deliver: those who misjudge others will get their comeuppance. As Yeo Kah Sin states, "it is the freak who becomes real in comparison to the false and grotesque Mayor. The effect of this inversion is that, instead of being saved from the monster, the norm is seen to be that which is monstrous."

### Time and Place

The decor of the castle, along with Michael's poet's shirt, suggests a previous time period; as the mayor, Normal Valley parents, and children enter the building, they have left modern society behind. The crowd (representing the film's viewers) wears everyday clothing, looking out of place in this time warp. Instead of the Maestro being the outsider, the tables are turned: the people are the invaders, the "freaks" in this space. The castle temporarily imprisons the mayor and the town's residents; when the Maestro slams the doors shut, the confinement is complete. In this charmed space, no rules apply—ghosts exist and can walk up the walls, the Maestro can transform into monsters, skeletons, and even a substance that the mayor ingests. In this timeless castle, the Maestro takes charge over the proceedings.

### Power

The segment where the Maestro controls the mayor's body may be the best example of this gothic theme. As the mayor absorbs the Maestro's spirit, he gestures to the crowd as if to reassure them he retains complete control. Yet he starts dancing, thrusting and moonwalking, clearly not under his own power. His facial expressions alternate between anger and abandon as he fights an internal battle for self-control. Ultimately the mayor loses the war, his arms and legs completely manipulated by the mystical Maestro.

As previously discussed, gothic literature and horror films frequently address self-control and how people restrain confront temptation. *Ghosts* tackles the issue quite literally, asking if humans can lose themselves to outside manipulation. In the enchanted castle, the mayor loses his identity to the wilderness filled with spirits. Self-control is rendered useless in this space.

## The Sublime

While not conventionally beautiful, the castle radiates a musty elegance. The ghosts may appear grotesque, wearing tattered clothes and sporting rotted skin, yet their effortless dancing has grace. At times they execute bows, as if acknowledging applause after performing a ballet. The group dance, *Ghosts*'s climax, inspires awe with its terrifying ghouls and gravity-defying moves. Through their synchronized steps, they perform an eccentric ballet that both scares and amazes. Indeed, the segment fits the gothic aesthetic: beauty in disorder and terror.

## Supernatural vs. Real

Are the ghosts real, or are they simply illusions, trickery courtesy of the Maestro? When the mayor accuses the mysterious figure of frightening impressionable children, the Maestro responds with the following argument: "You are right, I do like to scare people, yes. But it is just for fun. Don't you kids enjoy when I do my little . . . you know?" After the mayor runs away, the Maestro asks the crowd, "Did we have a good time here?" These questions suggest that the Maestro is a master magician, conjuring these ghastly images for entertainment. No ghosts remain at the end of the film, as if they never existed.

As the Maestro and the crowd talk, a young boy dons a mask and startles the group. They all chuckle, acknowledging that such creatures do not exist in the natural world. The curtain has been pulled to reveal the wizard; the "behind the scenes" special effects are revealed to separate fantasy from reality. Yet another boy steps forward, grinning evilly, and asks, "Is this scary?" He motions as if he will pull the skin off his face; the camera abruptly cuts away to the outside of the castles, but screams can be heard. Perhaps the ghosts and monsters were not hallucinations or illusions after all; in the castle, the supernatural may reign. Ultimately the viewer must decide what to believe.

## "Threatened"

Michael's final album, *Invincible*, ends with this hard-driving track. Tellingly, *Twilight Zone* creator and narrator Rod Serling's voice permeates "Threatened." The singer portrays himself as a monster haunting a man who is with his former lover. "Every time your lady speaks she speaks of me, threatened," he sneers. Unlike tracks such as "Is It Scary" or "Ghosts," "Threatened" does feature a supernatural creature played by Michael. Perhaps he visualized figures like Dracula, the werewolf, or a zombie, all outsides who invade one's home and spirit in horror films. As Yeo Kah Sin explains, the gothic monster's terror "lies precisely in its indeterminate constitution. The polymorphic shape-shifting potential of the mutant monster resists categorical containment and reinforces the indefinite shapeless mutability of the monstrous." Indeed, the danceable, hip-hop flavored song leaves an uneasy feeling that lingers beyond the dance floor.

## Time and Place

The narrator exists in a timeless expanse, defying death and able to penetrate physical places as well as the psyche. "I'm the living dead, the dark thoughts in your head," Michael growls, cautioning that he can read one's every thought. He identifies himself as the "walking dead" and "your worst nightmare . . . I'm everywhere," stating he might briefly disappear but will always return. Clearly this monster transcends time and place (as Serling's sampled voice clarifies during the song's onset), making him even more frightening. As Yeo Kah Sin states, the gothic monster is located "on a borderline between conceptual oppositions like life and death, man and beast, and natural and supernatural."

## Power

Did Michael and co-writer/producer Rodney Jerkins intend for the lyrics to be vague? They left the words open for interpretation, particularly whether the "monster" in the song is actually a conscience. He can read people's darkest thoughts, constantly haunting them in dreams and daily life. "I'm not a ghost from Hell, but I've got a spell on you," Michael sings, suggesting that this supernatural being may not be as simple as a spooky creature.

The track ends with Serling warning, "What you have just witnessed could be the end of a particularly terrifying nightmare. It isn't. It's the beginning." This presence will never die; it will remain with this unknown person even after death. The human conscience always remains and can haunt one's every decision. Poe uses this motif in the 1843 short story "The Tell-Tale Heart," a tale of a murderer haunted by the beating of the victim's heart. As in traditional gothic literature, the story touches upon the limits of morality and the ability to maintain self-control in the face of temptation. "Threatened" can be seen as an extension of this theme.

Throughout Michael's career, Yeo Kah Sin argues, the singer "established himself from the start as Dorian Gray, Dr. Jekyll and Mr. Hyde, Frankenstein's monster, and Dracula rolled into one." In many of his videos and songs, he used gothic motifs embodied in those characters to explore the boundaries of human nature, his life experience, and the hazy distinctions between fantasy and reality. He may have simply enjoyed disguising himself in theatrical makeup and dissolving completely into other characters, but his frequent use of gothic horror allowed him to explore very personal themes and ultimately force listeners to examine their own contradictions and internal struggles.

# 32

# Left Behind Everything for the Movie Scene

## Michael Jackson as Actor

In the last decade of Michael Jackson's life, he expressed a desire to retire from music and transition into film. During a 2002 interview with *Vibe*'s Regina Jones, he said, "I have deep love for film, and I want to pioneer and innovate the medium of film—to write and direct and produce movies, to bring incredible entertainment." A year earlier, he mentioned a movie he was working on with Liza Minnelli. "I love movies. I'm going to direct more and act more. I feel the most powerful artistic expression in the world is film," he told the November 10–16 issue of *TV Guide*.

*This Is It* presents what would be Michael's final venture into film in one segment: the introduction to his performance of "Smooth Criminal." Michael had filmed a new version of the video, a tribute to 1940s film noir with classic footage seamlessly blended in with new scenes. Dressed in similar attire as in the original "Smooth Criminal" video, Michael watches Rita Hayworth (from *Gilda*) perform. Soon Humphrey Bogart and Edward G. Robinson chase after Michael's gangster character, but he escapes by crashing through a window. The film gives way to the stage, where Michael and his backup dancers launch into the song. As in previous concerts, Michael blended film and live performances in his shows, and had clearly planned on continuing his trademark during the *This Is It* performances.

While Michael could not fully realize his dream of plunging into film full-time, he appeared in several short films as well as a full-length movie. From playing the Scarecrow in 1978's *The Wiz* to his 1996 short film *Ghosts*, he displayed a knack for dissolving into characters and charming audiences with his obvious enthusiasm. This chapter highlights some of his major roles, looking back on his skills as an actor as well as a singer and dancer.

### The Wiz (1978)

By the time Motown bought the rights to this Broadway smash, Michael had already departed the label. However, Berry Gordy knew the film required star power to attract viewers to the box office, and he desperately needed talented singers and dancers to recreate the musical's signature moments such as "Ease on Down the Road" and "Home." Tapping director Sidney Lumet to helm the project, the film immediately encountered controversy when the starring role of Dorothy was awarded not to its originator, Stephanie Mills, but to Diana Ross. According to Nelson George, Ross talked producer Gordy into giving her the part, even though many believed she was too old to play the role. In addition to Ross and Michael, the cast included Richard Pryor, Nipsey Russell, Ted Ross, Mabel King, and Lena Horne (then Lumet's mother-in-law). Quincy Jones served as music supervisor, and the production seemed destined for massive success.

According to Michael, Gordy asked him to audition for the role of the Scarecrow. In *Moonwalk*, he explains that he most connected with the Scarecrow, as he found the Lion too serious and the Tin Man too restrictive for his energetic personality. Once Lumet awarded him the role, Michael and sister La Toya temporarily relocated to New York during the film shoot. Living essentially on his own for the first time, Michael immersed himself in the role and socialized with friends during off hours. He admitted feeling out of his element at first, since the other actors possessed much more experience, but he learned from observing their work ethic.

In addition to memorizing his lines, mastering the choreography, and honing his acting skills, he endured sitting in the makeup chair for four or five hours a day, six days a week. Despite the vast amounts of time he spent in the chair, he enjoyed the experience. "When I was transformed into the Scarecrow," he writes, "it was the most wonderful thing in the world. I got to be somebody else and escape through my character." His idol, Charlie Chaplin, proved a great inspiration to Michael in his dancing and movements; perhaps Michael viewed both the Scarecrow and Chaplin's "Little Tramp" character as underdogs.

Despite Michael's positive experiences, problems plagued the *Wiz* set. According to Quincy Jones's 2002 autobiography *Q*, Lumet ran vastly over budget—the first time the director had ever done so. The music supervisor did not particularly care for the music, only liking "Ease on Down the Road," "Home," and "Brand New Day." Michael stated that his fellow cast members grew impatient with him, mainly over the singer's ability to master the dance steps more easily than the other actors. When *The Wiz* finally hit movie theaters, bad reviews doomed its chances. As Nelson George points out in *Where Did Our Love Go?*, the film needed to

After shooting wrapped, Michael and Quincy Jones re-recorded "You Can't Win" for *The Wiz: Original Motion Picture Soundtrack*. Released as a single in 1979, it became Michael's first solo hit on the Epic label. *Author's collection* gross $60 million to break even, and it earned nowhere near that figure. The soundtrack, however, fared well, with the Ross/Michael duet "Ease on Down the Road" emerging as its biggest hit. A follow-up single, "You Can't Win," also served as Michael's first solo single for Epic.

While *The Wiz* disappointed in terms of revenue and general reviews, Michael earned raves for his performance. Roger Ebert's critique from October 24, 1978, singled out the young actor, stating, "It's good that the Scarecrow is the first traveling companion she meets; Michael Jackson fills the role with humor and warmth." John Skow's *Time* review from October 30, 1978, also praised his performance: "[Dorothy] meets . . . a marvelous scarecrow (Michael Jackson), hung up on his pole and tormented by rascally birds. Jackson sings a piteous lament, to the effect that 'you can't win, you can't break even, and you can't get out of the game.'"

Joel Schumacher, who wrote the screenplay for *The Wiz*, stated in a 2003 A.V. Club interview with Nathan Rabin that he instantly recognized Michael's talent. "He was Michael Jackson the phenomenal talent. He was brilliant and sweet and kind and very well-mannered. I knew that there was no one like him. I knew that he was one of the most talented people of his generation, but I think that had been established ever since he was a little kid. I have no way of knowing whether anybody is going to be anything, but I certainly knew that he was a talent to be reckoned with."

Biographer J. Randy Taraborrelli interviewed Lumet before the film's premiere, and the director gushed over Michael's skills. "Michael Jackson is the most gifted entertainer to come down the pike since James Dean," he said. "He's a brilliant actor and dancer, probably one of the rarest entertainers I have ever worked with."

## Key Scene

While watching Ross and Michael joyously sing and dance together during the "Ease on Down the Road" number is enjoyable, it is Michael's scene introducing the Scarecrow that best showcases his raw talent. As streetwise crows dance around him, taunting his every move, Michael sings "You Can't Win" with sincere pathos. What fascinates is how he communicates the Scarecrow's fear and anguish through body language and facial expressions. He remains strapped to the pole-like structure throughout the number, only able to move his head. While he can barely move his arms and legs, he assumes a bowlegged position as if to emphasize the character's status as a helpless victim.

As the crows execute clumsy but aggressive choreography, Michael rolls his eyes and grimaces, letting his face reflect the Scarecrow's agony (a particularly impressive feat, considering his heavy makeup). When he lowers his voice and lets his body slump as he utters the final line—"you can't get out of the game"—he forces viewers to fully experience his character's pain and hopelessness. This scene perfectly demonstrates Michael's already-impressive acting skills and his understanding of how to use the entire body as well as his voice to emote. This memorable debut role suggested that he could have a future as an actor; sadly, he never made another similar feature film.

# Captain EO (1986)

In 1980, Michael visited the set of *On Golden Pond* to see his friend Jane Fonda. As he grew closer to Jane, her father Henry, and her co-star, Katherine Hepburn, Michael learned more about filmmaking and wanted to delve into acting, according to Grant's *Michael Jackson: A Visual Documentary*. Outside of music videos, his next opportunity came with 1986's *Captain EO*. This would be no standard film, however—instead, it was a special effects-laden project that would double as a short movie and a ride at both Disney World and Disneyland. First announced in July 1985, *Captain EO* boasted an all-star lineup: Michael, Francis Ford Coppola, and George Lucas. Top makeup artist Rick Baker (who had previously worked on the "Thriller" video) and choreographer Jeffrey Hornaday (*Flashdance* and the film version of *A Chorus Line*) rounded out the crew. Strangely, another notable star of *Captain EO*, actress Anjelica Houston, was initially left off Disney's 1985 press releases.

The seventeen-minute project would be ambitious—executive producer Lucas co-wrote the screenplay and designed the *Star Wars*–like characters, while Coppola directed. Since the film doubled as a ride, new theaters had to be built or redesigned to accommodate special effects including tilting floors, laser light shows, and smoke that emitted from the screen. With the project being shot in 3-D, the budget quickly ballooned to $20 million—a record for a short film. Filming took place in the summer of 1985; the *New York Times*' Aljean Harmetz explained that the shooting scheduled prevented Michael from participating in the massive Live Aid event.

Disney clearly held high hopes for *Captain EO*, as it wished to update the parks with new technology and attract customers using big-name talent such as Michael. Hornaday told the *New York Times* critic Janet Maslin in December 1985, "It's real light and very positive. The idea is that music means love. I guess you could say it reflects Michael's point of view.'" The film and ride finally debuted in both parks in September 1986.

The storyline is simple: Michael plays Captain EO, the leader of a "misfit" space crew filled with unusual creatures. They are given a mission: save the world from the Supreme Leader (Houston), an ugly, rage-filled woman who lives on a desolate planet. After arriving, the captain and crew are captured and brought to the leader, who threatens to imprison Captain EO and turn his crew into trashcans. The captain tells her that he will unlock her inner beauty through music. Through his power, he transforms her minions into dancers, who back Michael on two songs: "We Are Here to Change the World" and "Another Part of Me." They sing and dance furiously as the queen's gruesome appearance gradually dissolves to reveal a beautiful woman.

Initial reviews were mixed, mainly due to rumors of out-of-control budgets, last-minute editing, and technical issues with the theaters. In his review for the *Los Angeles Times* dated October 9, 1986, Charles Solomon praised the 3-D effects but concluded that the film was "nothing more than the most elaborate rock video in history: Like a hollow chocolate Easter bunny, it's a glorious surface over a void . . . given that list of credits and the film's lavish budget (rumored to be between $15 million [and] $20 million, although Disney refuses to release any figures), audiences have a right to expect more than empty flash."

A month later, *Los Angeles Times* writer Randy Lewis panned *Captain EO*, awarding it a "turkey" for not living up to the hype. "This pale, Buck Rogers-learns-to-boogie adventure is the best that the combined talents of Michael Jackson, George Lucas, Francis Ford Coppola, the Disney organization and $20 million could buy?"

The *New York Times'* Vincent Canby published a more nuanced assessment of the film, calling it "wild" and "discolike," with a storyline that gets lost in the special effects. He seemed more taken with the 3-D format, stating that "*Captain EO*, beautifully shot and impeccably projected, proves that 3-D can be a trip and not a headache. This is by far the best 3-D I've ever seen." However, Canby describes the main character as "a fairly camp space-savior who transforms the Kingdom of Darkness into the Kingdom of Light through—what else?—the magic of his music."

*Time's* Richard Corliss opined that, while the film may be entertaining, "*Captain EO* is sugar but no spice, coating an audio-animatronic gridwork. What can be exhilarating and depressing about Walt Disney World is true of *Captain EO*: it is a triumph of the artificial, of high-tech wizardry and secondhand emotions."

*Captain EO* ran from 1986–97, appearing at Epcot Center at Disney World, and at Disneyland, Tokyo Disneyland, and Disneyland Paris. In February 2010, *Captain EO* returned to all of the Disney parks as a tribute to Michael, although it closed in Tokyo in 2014.

## Key Scene

As previously mentioned, *Captain EO*'s plot is secondary to the film's special effects. Michael's best scene, the "We Are Here to Change the World" sequence, allows him to dance while fighting off the Supreme Leader's henchmen. Snarling and later grinning, he communicates his determination to conquer the evil queen through his singing and moves. When the leader finally transforms, he emits a beaming smile and kisses her on the hand, displaying childlike glee.

One of the dancers who appears in the scene, nineteen-year-old Marlene Lang Clayman, later told *Entertainment Weekly*'s Lynette Rice about working with Michael on the project. She stated that Hornaday would watch Michael's moves and then choreograph routines based on his natural style. "It was electrifying, the energy you felt off of him. He gave 100 percent, every time. There was no, 'I'm tired, let's just mark it,'" she recalled. When they shot the sequence, Gene Kelly was visiting the set; dancing next to Michael while Kelly looked on was, said Clayman, a once-in-a-lifetime experience.

*Captain EO* would impact Michael's future career in several ways. Several steps from the "We Are Here to Change the World" segment reappeared in the "Bad" video the following year. As Carl Miller points out in "'We Are Here to Change the World': *Captain EO* and the Future of Utopia," Michael wanted to further experiment with 3-D effects for the *This Is It* performances. The film's revival in 2010, Miller argues, stands as "a testament to both the transformative dimensions and the contemporary relevance of Jackson's art."

## Moonwalker (1988)

Michael's next project was more video anthology than conventional feature film. A $27 million venture involving three directors, multiple animators, dancers and choreographers, and numerous special effects, *Moonwalker* was intended as a companion to *Bad*. For complicated reasons, the ninety-minute film was shown in theaters in several countries but released direct to home video in the United States. According to Taraborrelli, Michael's then-agent Frank DiLeo refused to release *Moonwalker* domestically, angering international distributors enough to either cancel future theatrical showings or drastically reduce promotion. Debuting in Japan in October 1988, *Moonwalker* appeared in theaters in Portugal, the Netherlands, Sweden, France, Spain, Finland, South Korea, Australia, the UK, Ireland, and Turkey before finally reaching American shores in January 1989.

*Moonwalker* would set home-video records, becoming the top-selling music videocassette of all time by 1989 (ringing up sales of $12.5 million), breaking Michael's own record for 1984's *The Making of Thriller*. Taking into account other deals as well as sales, *Moonwalker* raked in $30 million, an unheard-of sum for a home-video release.

An ambitious production, *Moonwalker* consists of compilations of vintage performances, music videos, and concert footage. Due to its nonlinear organization, the end credits identify *Moonwalker* as an anthology.

The movie begins with footage of Michael performing "Man in the Mirror" live, interspersed with clips of historical figures such as Martin Luther King, Gandhi, and Mother Theresa. The cut is very similar to the official music video, except with added emphasis on Michael's live rendition. The image of Michael standing alone onstage fades into an autobiographical collage of videos, pictures, animations, and sound clips of past achievements. "Music and Me" plays the background, along with segments of his hits with the Jackson 5 and solo. The medley gives way to what at first seems to be the "Bad" video but is actually footage of some kids comically recreating the dance sequence.

Next comes the "Speed Demon" sequence, a mixture of live action and Claymation courtesy of Will Vinton (best known for the California Raisins ads). The adult Michael runs throughout a movie studio lot pursued by insane fans and assorted crazy characters. To escape the tormentors, he dresses in a rabbit costume (which turns into a Claymation figure); riding a motorcycle, "Spike" eventually fends off the rabid pursuers. When he finally removes the costume, Michael is shocked to learn that it has come to life, resulting in a "dance-off."

After that comes one of *Moonwalker*'s best-known videos, "Leave Me Alone," the creatively animated clip parodying rumors then swirling around the singer. Providing a rare glimpse at the singer's humor, the video features Michael dancing with the Elephant Man's bones and cruising around an amusement park dedicated to Michael's supposed "obsessions" such as Elizabeth Taylor accompanied by Bubbles the chimp.

The film's next segment presents *Moonwalker*'s only storyline: Michael's quest to defeat "Mr. Big" (played by Joe Pesci), an evil character who plans to have every child become addicted to drugs. Three children played by Sean Lennon, Brandon

Quintin Adams (who also appeared in the earlier "Bad" parody), and Kellie Parker are first seen playing in a park with Michael; Michael and Parker subsequently discover a secret tunnel, where they find Mr. Big discussing his plans. The villain sees them and chases them; Parker manages to escape and reunite with the two boys. The three then witness Michael entering an apparently abandoned club, but it instantly transforms into a 1930s speakeasy filled with gangsters. *Moonwalker*'s most famous segment, the "Smooth Criminal" sequence, follows. Suddenly, Parker is kidnapped; when Michael and the boys find Mr. Big's lair, they find the villain hitting the little girl and threatening to inject her with heroin. Eventually, Michael transforms into a robot and then a spaceship, killing Mr. Big and his henchmen while rescuing Parker.

When the kids reunite with Michael, he leads them back to the club, telling them a surprise awaits them. As they enter, the "Come

A feature-length film featuring videos for several *Bad* tracks as well as the bonus cover of the Beatles' "Come Together," *Moonwalker* showcased Michael's acting and dancing skills.        *Author's collection*

Together" sequence begins, with Michael performing his cover in front of an audience. During the closing credits, Ladysmith Black Mambazo perform their composition "The Moon Is Walking," intercut with behind the scenes footage from the "Smooth Criminal" shoot.

A huge hit in Japan, *Moonwalker* finally debuted in the United States in 1989. Reviews from the time were decidedly mixed, with the unconventional format puzzling critics. *Variety* wrote that the film "seems unsure of what it was supposed to be," while because most segments did not explicitly link together, "the whole affair does not make for a structured or professional movie." The reviewer dismisses the "Smooth Criminal" sequence, describing it as "a musical/dramatic piece full of dancing, schmaltzy kids, sci-fi effects and blazing machine guns" and instead cites "Leave Me Alone" as the strongest element of the movie.

The *Washington Post* also seemed unimpressed with "Smooth Criminal," praising the dancing but condemning the sequence's violence and concluding "even the glossy production and glitzy special effects can't mask 'Smooth Criminal's' essential vacuousness." Like the *Variety* critic, writer Richard Harrington singled out "Leave Me Alone" for its innovative animation, humor, and themes. "He's portrayed as a huge, Gulliver-like figure tied down and turned into a virtual amusement park by nasty little creatures; eventually, Jackson rises up and breaks the shackles of perception."

One of *Moonwalker*'s harshest reviews ran in the *Los Angeles Times*, with Dennis Hunt deeming it filled with "juvenile concepts" and calling the "Smooth Criminal" sequence "silly." "Jackson is dead serious about this childish heroic fantasy. You get the feeling that all this adulation has gone to his head-that he's confusing being a pop-music superstar with being a superhero," Hunt opined, adding that he most enjoyed the live performances and Ladysmith Black Mambazo's appearance, and concluding that Michael should have released a concert film rather than an anthology.

The unconventional format, along with the confusion over its theatrical release, may have affected public perception of the project. Movie producer Dennis Jones struggled to explain *Moonwalker*'s concept in the *Los Angeles Times* article "Music Video Makers Bet on 'Moonwalker.'" "Jones had trouble explaining what *Moonwalker* is," Hunt wrote. "He made it sound like a cinematic hodge-podge, bounding from a retrospective of Jackson hits to the movie-like 'Smooth Criminal' segment-presenting Jackson as a crime-fighting hero-to a new version of the 'Bad' video to a Claymation (animated clay figures) sequence." Rumors swirled that while foreign audiences enjoyed the film, American audiences would not pay to see such an unconventional work in the theaters. Jones denied that this was a factor in releasing *Moonwalker* direct to video, however.

Despite the mixed reviews, *Moonwalker* showed off some innovative filmmaking. "Leave Me Alone" features the work of Jim Blashfield, a pioneer in photo-cutout animation. He would take numerous pictures of people or objects in his studio, photocopy the images, and then animate them in post-production. Known for videos such as Talking Heads' "And She Was" and Paul Simon's "Boy in the Bubble," Blashfield was commissioned to helm the "Leave Me Alone" segment. Asked to create a clip poking fun at tabloid-fueled rumors about Michael, he ended up taking photos of Michael over a three-day period, then cutting up those images as well as others, layering them for animation. Overall the process took nine months.

In *Rolling Stone*'s web article "Michael Jackson 20 Greatest Videos: The Stories Behind the Vision," Blashfield reminisced about filming "Leave Me Alone." The singer was very open to the idea of poking fun at his image, Blashfield said, and during the shoot remained "always up and ready to go, good-spirited." Explaining the process, Blashfield said each image was stacked on top of one another on a piece of glass. "There's a splash that shows up throughout the entire video, and that was so time consuming to cut out that we just had one and it was passed around. Whoever was doing the scene and needed the splash would get to use it for a while. There was a guy, he specialized in that splash, and I think he worked on it for weeks."

Elaborate for very different reasons, "Smooth Criminal" was conceived by Michael and director Colin Chilvers as a tribute to film noir and MGM musicals. They patterned the dance sequence after Fred Astaire's moves and image in *The Bandwagon*. In *Rolling Stone*'s "Michael Jackson's 20 Greatest Videos," Chilvers remembered that Astaire choreographer Hermes Pan visited the set the day they filmed the dance. Overall, the filming involved forty-six dancers as well as chore-ographers, hair, and makeup, and every day the director, Michael, and other cast members would view the dailies. "It would be like a party going on in the screening room. Michael would be there as well and they would be hoopin' and hollerin' when they saw themselves and how good it looked—or else, Michael would say, 'We can do better than that,'" Chilvers told *Rolling Stone* in 2014. "Not the usual way to make a Hollywood movie, that's for sure."

The director finally revealed how they accomplished the video's signature move: the lean. Michael and the other dancers' feet were fixed to the floor by fitting their heels into slots; piano wire was used to prevent them from falling over. "If you look in the video, when they come back up from that lean, they kind of shuffle their feet back—they were unlocking themselves from the support they had in the ground," Chilvers said.

As for Michael as an actor, Parker held fond memories of working with the star. She told the Girl in the Video blog that *Moonwalker* took a year to film due to changes in the script. The "Smooth Criminal" sequence alone (originally titled "Chicago Nights," Parker revealed) took a month to complete. "It was the most incredible experience of my life! Without a doubt, it changed the course of my life. Michael and I became great friends," she said. "He was always pushing me to be better and teaching me about the artistic process. To have someone of his creative genius take the time to teach you at the age of ten is like getting the winning lotto ticket."

## Key Scene

While not discussed as much as "Leave Me Alone" or "Smooth Criminal," the "Speed Demon" video stands out for showcasing Michael's wicked sense of humor. Director and Claymation pioneer Will Vinton helmed the sequence, although it was just the latest in their series of collaborations. Vinton first met the star while working on *Captain EO*'s special effects; when Vinton later earned acclaim for his California Raisins ads, Michael called him to ask if he too could get the "raisin treatment." Vinton and Michael worked on the choreography and animation, ensuring that the character would capture the mannerisms of Michael's "Bad"-era persona. "He was just the sweetest person in the world. A really amazing, gentle soul," Vinton told the *Pittsburgh Post-Gazette* in 2009.

When they teamed up again for the "Speed Demon" clip, they combined live and Claymation elements for humorous effect. Before Michael transforms into Spike the rabbit, however, he appears in several scenes where he must interact with animated characters. He accomplishes the task with apparent ease, smiling and joking with what were imaginary elements on the set. In addition, he looks convincingly horrified when tourists, fans, and actors on the studio lot chase after him. While this is done for comedic effect, it also presents a picture of the sense of imprisonment celebrity status can lead to. As he accidentally stumbles onto a movie set where an animated Steven Spielberg is shooting a film, he reacts with both embarrassment and amusement as Spielberg rips into him for interrupting the scene (all while transforming into a lizard).

After he successfully fends off his pursuers, Michael removes the bunny costume, only to see the outfit spring to life. He and Spike then engage in a "dance-off," impressing each other with their smooth and at times gravity-defying moves. When a policeman barges in on the scene, citing Michael for violating a "no-dancing zone," Spike vanishes. The rabbit's face then reemerges in a rock formation. Throughout this sequence, Michael's beaming smile and youthful glee is contagious, encouraging the audience to join in on the fun. He also pokes fun at himself and his overzealous fans, careful not to offend the "normal" fans who respect his privacy. "Smooth Criminal" may have emerged as *Moonwalker*'s most significant and influential segment, but "Speed Demon" charms with its winking humor and Michael's ability to seamlessly interact with animated characters.

## Ghosts (1997)

One of Michael's least well-known projects, *Ghosts* emerged from a story idea by Stephen King. Directed by makeup master Stan Winston, the thirty-five-minute film was screened at the May 1997 Cannes Film Festival and was shown in Finland, Australia, and Denmark. It premiered in the States in October 1996, shown in select theaters as a double feature with King's new horror movie *Thinner*. Strangely, the film has never been available on videocassette or DVD in the United States; in 2002, the film, along with the documentary *The Making of Michael Jackson's Ghosts*, was aired on VH1.

As King recalled in his 2009 *Entertainment Weekly* tribute to Michael, the singer first contacted him in 1993. At the time, the author was involved in the TV mini-series adaptation of his novel *The Stand*. Interested in creating a terrifying music video, Michael asked King to write a screenplay based on an idea he had. He described the story: a man living in a castle is pursued by prim-and-proper towns-people, wanting to drive him away because he is viewed as a bad influence on children.

According to King, they spent three weeks filming *Ghosts* in 1993, then shut down until 1996. At first Mick Garris, who directed *The Stand*, helmed the effort and did preproduction work on it. Harris had previously appeared as a zombie in the "Thriller" video, as he was a friend of director John Landis. In a 2009 interview with *Movieline*, Garris described his experience working with Michael. He revealed that the film began life as a promotional video for *Addams Family Values*; Christina Ricci and Jimmy Workman, who played Wednesday and Pugsley Adams respectively, appeared in the 1993 version. Garris explained that they shot two weeks worth of footage but no musical numbers. Then, when the child abuse allegations surfaced in 1993, the studio no longer wanted Michael to promote the *Addams Family* sequel, thus filming halted.

Michael told a slightly different story in Adrian Grant's *Making HIStory*. He explained that the makers of the *Addams Family* film wanted to use "Is It Scary" as its theme song; Michael ultimately decided not to do it. "So eventually we got out of it," he told Grant. "So I ended up making a short film. I love films, I love movies, and that's why my next mission is to make films. That's what I want the next chapter in my life to be—movies and records."

While Garris did not consider himself among Michael's closest friends, he fondly recalled the brief time he worked on *Ghosts* with the singer, telling Michael Adams, in the article "The Cold Case: Director Mick Garris on Michael Jackson's Forgotten *Ghosts*," of his favorite memories. "We'd finish a take, and if I wanted another, I'd put on Bullwinkle's voice and say, 'This time for sure!'" he said. "The first time, he just laughed and laughed and laughed. Then he'd keep asking, even after the good takes: 'Mick, do Bullwinkle!' That's how I like to remember him."

When filming resumed in 1996, Garris had moved on to the miniseries version of *The Shining*. He recommended Winston, who had worked on special effects during the 1993 shoot, to direct the project. Winston of course already knew Michael, having worked on makeup for *The Wiz*. According to King, his original script was then dramatically altered. "It started out being twelve to fifteen minutes long," Winston told Cadman and Halstead in *For the Record*, "but as we were shooting it grew in power and length."

*Ghosts* was shot over six weeks and cost an estimated $7–9 million, with Jackson funding the project himself. The star faced numerous creative challenges: he would play multiple roles, many of them requiring extensive makeup, and would execute some of the most difficult dance routines of his career. He would sit for three-hour makeup sessions daily, and was in virtually every scene.

*Ghosts* tells the story of the Maestro, a mysterious figure who lives in a haunted castle. The mayor and parents of the neighboring Normal Valley storm the castle, furious that the Maestro and his ghosts have been entertaining their kids with their spooky antics. As the children look on in horror, the mayor demands that the Maestro leave. "You're weird," he snarls, "You're strange. You're scaring these kids." Accusing the mayor of trying to scare *him*, the Maestro challenges the mayor to a kind of "scare off": the first one to make the other scared must leave Normal Valley for good.

Using a dazzling array of special effects and ghoulish makeup, the Maestro proceeds to transform into various grotesque creatures and a skeleton, leading his ghostly dancers in sometimes gravity-defying routines. The Maestro eventually takes over the mayor's body by entering through the hateful character's gaping mouth. He moves the mayor's body, making him moonwalk against his will. As the mayor runs away in terror, the Normal Valley parents are won over by the Maestro, with two boys scaring the Maestro and parents with their own antics.

While King praised *Ghosts* for featuring some of Michael's best dancing, other reviewers seemed confused by the short film. "Though the dialogue is wooden, the conceit hokey, and the acting amateurish, Jackson and the film come alive during lengthy renditions of '2 Bad,' "'Ghosts,' and 'Is It Scary,'" writes the A.V. Club's Nathan Rabin in "Spooktastic Case File #174: Michael Jackson's *Ghosts*." While finding the film entertaining, Margo Jefferson calls it a "tormented film" in *On Michael Jackson*. The *Manila Standard* printed a positive critique in 1997, writing that "it transforms Michael into multiple characters that will surely surprise, thrill and delight his audiences" and adding that the film contains "all the protean morphing and pyrotechnic visual flashes one could want, along with such flashes of wit as having a skeleton do Jackson's celebrated moonwalk."

Michael looked back on the short film in a 2001 audio chat moderated by rock journalist Anthony DeCurtis. "That was one of my most favorite things I've ever done because it's been a dream of mine for a long time to do something like, you know, scary but comical at the same time, and, uh, it's all the elements, just fun," he said. "These ghosts, they weren't really scary, they were fun. They walked up the ceilings. Little kids were laughing at them. They were fun. You know, we don't want to horrify them."

## Key Scene

Without question, Michael's greatest acting in *Ghosts* lies in his portrayal of Normal Valley's mayor. Unrecognizable under his special-effects makeup and costume, Michael portrays an overweight, older character—a bigot who clearly wishes to banish anything he deems different. The singer pitches his voice lower, altering his accent and almost grunting his lines. Even with the makeup, he manages to convey the mayor's disdain and disgust, staring at the Maestro as if he were a sideshow attraction. As the Maestro begins playfully scaring the group, the mayor suddenly looks unsure, his indignation gradually fading. As the ghosts dance on the ceiling and the Maestro transforms into a skeleton, the mayor's mouth drops open, clearly growing terrified.

Michael's most skillful acting occurs when the Maestro's spirit enters the mayor's body, manipulating the man as if he were the Maestro's puppet. In this scene, Michael had to achieve several goals. First, he had to execute his signature moves in a "fat suit," the padding surely severely restricting his movements. Next, he had to stay in character as the hateful mayor, at times standing and waving his hands as if to assure the scared parents and their children that he was still in control of himself and the situation.

Now Michael must dance, but not as Michael Jackson; instead, he must dance as if he is moving against his will. In other words, he would moonwalk or execute a sideways kick, but somewhat stiffly, as if the mayor were fighting his own body. He also had to use his facial expressions to communicate the character's inner struggle to regain mastery of his own body while another force was firmly in command.

That scene demonstrates Michael's growth as an actor as well as a singer and dancer. The role recalls the beginning of his acting career, when he learned about body movement and facial expression to communicate the Scarecrow's misery. Once again, Michael used both techniques to convey the mayor's hateful personality, but *Ghosts* forced him to expand upon those methods. His dancing could also be termed "meta-dancing"—in other words, he had to move as if someone else were attempting to dance like Michael Jackson. He had to imitate himself as if a comedian or other actor with lesser dancing skills would imitate him. Only an experienced and gifted performer could achieve such a difficult goal.

## Honorable Mentions

The following performances are also worth noting:

- "Thriller" (1984)
- "Bad" (1987)
- "The Way You Make Me Feel" (1987)
- "Remember the Time" (1992)
- *Men in Black II* (2002, cameo appearance)

## So Let the Performance Start

While Michael made only a handful of short films and one conventional feature-length movie, he demonstrated natural acting talent developed over a relatively short period of time. He would further hone those skills in his music videos, having to convey a wide range of emotions in five-minute clips. Music and dance may comprise Michael's legacy, but his acting credentials should not be overlooked.

Bob Giraldi, who directed the "Beat It" and "Say Say Say" videos as well as the 1980s Pepsi commercials, says in *Thriller 25: The Book*, "I always thought Michael could give a great film performance—if the role was hand-picked carefully to reflect and respond to his unique artist's personality. I think he got close as the scarecrow in *The Wiz* (1978)—but, along the way, he obviously became larger than the movies, larger than the movies, larger than any role he could play, and larger than life—and now—it may be too late."

# 33

# What Have I Got That I Can Give?

## Songs Michael Jackson Wrote for Other Artists

I n the 1980 *Jet* article "Michael Teams with Sister La Toya Jackson," Michael explained his songwriting process: "Songs come about in the strangest ways. I'll just wake up from sleeping and there is the whole song coming into my head." While he made composition sound simple, it is a difficult skill acquired through extensive experience. As discussed in chapter 15, Michael started honing his craft in the Jacksons days; by the 1980s, he emerged as a proven hit maker through his successes with the Jacksons (*Destiny*, *Triumph*) and solo (*Off the Wall*). Other artists approached him for assistance, knowing his lyrics and voice could guarantee a hit single.

Michael gave songs to others for various reasons. Some were friends; other times he wanted to repay a favor; and sometimes his songs found their way to other musicians through no direct involvement. This overview demonstrates his versatility as a composer, crafting everything from ballads to dance tracks, tackling serious and romantic topics, and even writing for cartoon characters.

### "Night Time Lover"—La Toya Jackson (1980)

Co-written with Michael, "Night Time Lover" appears on La Toya's self-titled debut album. Appearing on the cover of the July 31, 1980, issue of *Jet*, the siblings discussed La Toya's upcoming disco-tinged album. La Toya explained that they had written "Night Time Lover" three years prior for Donna Summer; then called "Fire Is the Feeling," the song never reached the disco diva. When father Joseph Jackson signed La Toya to his new label, La Toya asked Michael if she could record their co-written tune. "He said, 'Fine, but I would have to produce it because I wouldn't want anyone else to do it.'"

The *Jet* article states that the duo wrote several songs together, although only "Night Time Lover" appears on the album. The photos accompanying the story offer a rarely seen sight: Michael at the piano, with the article stating that his fingers glided across the keys throughout their interview. This suggests, contrary to many other sources, that Michael *did* play piano.

Despite Michael's presence and prominent backing vocals, "Night Time Lover" peaked at #59 on *Billboard*'s R&B chart. It would have been interesting to hear Michael record the song, as the falsetto-heavy chorus sounds tailor made for him.

## "This Had to Be"—Brothers Johnson (1980)

Brothers Johnson co-founder Louis Johnson first met Michael while playing bass on 1979's *Off the Wall*; according to Cadman and Halstead, the group's psychedelic soul classic "Strawberry Letter 23" was one of Michael's favorite cuts from 1977. The Quincy Jones protégés were working on their third album, *Light Up the Night*, around the same time that Michael and Jones were writing and recording *Off the Wall*. Thus Michael co-wrote "This Had to Be" with Louis and guitarist George Johnson, also contributing backing vocals. Many of the same musicians from *Off the Wall* also play on *Light Up the Night*, now best known for its biggest hit "Stomp." "This Had to Be" was never released as a single, but its fusion of jazz, funk, and disco is typical of early-'80s R&B.

## "Muscles"—Diana Ross (1982)

This Diana Ross track may be one of Michael's sexiest compositions, but its title derives from a rather unsexy source: his pet boa constrictor. In *Moonwalk*, Michael writes that giving Ross the song was his way of thanking her for her lifelong support. In June 1981, Ross's second album for RCA, *Silk Electric*, was not proceeding well and was badly in need of a hit. Flying home from England, where he had been working with Paul McCartney, Michael suddenly became inspired. "This song popped into my head. I said, 'Hey, that's perfect for Diana,'" Michael told *Interview* magazine in October 1982. "I didn't have a tape recorder or anything, so I had to suffer for like three hours. Soon as I got home, I whipped that baby on tape."

The first of two tracks Michael wrote for mentor Diana Ross, "Muscles" appeared on her 1982 album *Silk Electric*. A Top 10 *Billboard* hit, its title refers to Michael's pet boa constrictor, despite the overtly sexual lyrics.     *Author's collection*

According to Taraborrelli, Michael was initially intimidated by Ross in the studio, but she urged him to give her direction like he might any other artist. Ross coos the lyrics as much as sings them, purring that she wants the subject of the song to have muscles "all over his body." Finger snapping comprises much of the percussion, augmented by a plucked guitar riff.

The collaboration paid off, as Ross scored a #10 hit on the *Billboard* Hot 100. It also reached #4 on the R&B chart and peaked at #15 in the UK. The accompanying video, with Ross surrounded by shirtless, oiled, muscle-bound men, was one of the raciest videos the diva ever filmed.

## "Love Never Felt So Good"—Johnny Mathis (1984, co-written with Paul Anka)

While Michael's demo of this track finally appeared on 2014's *Xscape*, the song dates back to 1983, when he and the legendary songwriter Paul Anka co-wrote a number of tracks together. After plans to record the track fell through, Anka revised it with songwriter Kathleen Wakefield and gave it to Johnny Mathis for the 1984 album *A Special Part of Me*. This version, with its light, jazzy melody, smooth keyboards and an extended sax solo, resembles an Al Jarreau track as much as a typical Mathis tune. Frequent Michael collaborators Jerry Hey (horns) and Nathan East (bass) also played on it.

When Timbaland reworked "Love Never Felt So Good" for *Xscape*, he crafted it to reflect late-1970s/early-1980s disco. The radio version, which includes a virtual duet with Justin Timberlake, uses percussion and beatboxing from "Working Day and Night" and intensifies the beat to lend it a touch of modern dance and hip hop.

## "Behind the Mask"—Greg Phillinganes (1984)

A version of this song with Michael's demo vocals appeared on the 2010 posthumous collection *Michael*, but its origins are more complicated. The tune derives from a 1978 instrumental by the Yellow Magic Orchestra, a Japanese electronic music band considered pioneers in techno, house, and synth-pop. It was originally written for a Seiko Quartz wristwatch commercial, before lyricist and poet Chris Mosdell wrote new lyrics for the song, which group member Ryuichi Sakamoto sang into a vocoder. Liking the result, the band released it on their 1979 album *Solid State Survivor*.

During a trip to Japan that same year, Jones heard the track and instantly liked it. He brought it home to Michael, encouraging him to write new lyrics and record it for *Thriller*. "When Michael Jackson took it, it made it into a love song, kind of, about a woman," Mosdell told the *Boulder Daily Camera* in 2011. "It was a completely different premise to me, but hey, it's Michael Jackson. I let him have that one." Due to copyright issues, however, the song was ultimately left off *Thriller*. Shortly thereafter, keyboardist and longtime Michael collaborator Greg Phillinganes recorded his version of "Behind the Mask" for his 1984 album *Pulse*. Overloaded with 1980s synthesizers and electronic drums, the song reached #77 on the R&B chart but failed to crack the *Billboard* Hot 100 or the UK charts. Eric Clapton would take a stab at "Behind the Mask" on his Phil Collins–produced 1986 album *August*, lending it a bluesier feel with his vocals and guitar soloing.

## "Centipede"—Rebbie Jackson (1984)

Featuring unusual lyrics and a throbbing beat, this slice of 1980s R&B was written by Michael for his big sister Rebbie. He also assumed production duties on "Centipede" and sang backup, with his presence helping to propel the song to #4 on the R&B charts. It also peaked at #24 on the *Billboard* Hot 100 and cracked the Hot Dance Music/Club Play Top 30. Fun fact: Martha Wash—a member of the Weather Girls ("It's Raining Men") and lead singer on dance hits such as C+C Music Factory's "Gonna Make You Sweat (Everybody Dance Now)" and Black Box's "Everybody Everybody"—sang backup on the song.

While Rebbie had previously done session work and cabaret singing, *Centipede* was her first—and most successful—album. The accompanying video features Rebbie springing to life from a painting, lighting shooting from her fingers, and dancing in front of a line of tuxedo-clad men. Tigers and snakes made random appearances as fog machines spew smoke everywhere; in short, it is a classic '80s video.

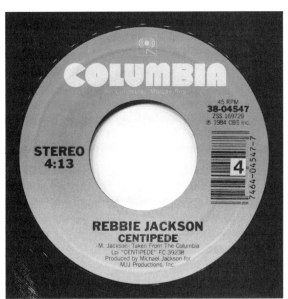

Embarking on a solo career in 1984, Rebbie Jackson turned to her brother for help writing and producing her debut single. Michael Jackson delivered "Centipede," a slinky track that became a Top 5 R&B hit and cracked the *Billboard* Top 30. Michael, La Toya, and the Weather Girls ("It's Raining Men") provide backing vocals.   *Author's collection*

## "Eaten Alive"—Diana Ross (1985)

Michael's second composition for Ross was a collaboration with Barry and Maurice Gibb, who were producing her album *Eaten Alive*. According to Cadman and Halstead, the Gibb brothers first wrote the song in March 1985. Michael heard their demo and offered to revise the words and music in the chorus. Ross recorded the track in mid-1985, with Michael, Barry, and Maurice on backing vocals. Michael attended the recording of the instrumental sections, dancing to the music in the studio to judge its quality. The track was accompanied by an over-the-top music video featuring Ross turning into a panther, complete with fangs and cat's eyes (shades of "Thriller"?).

A hybrid of dance and rock, "Eaten Alive" benefits greatly from Michael and the Gibb Brothers' backing vocals. Michael's voice particularly stands out, his ad-libs toward the end of the track fiercely rhythmic. It would be interesting to hear his 1985 demo, as his own interpretation may have been vastly different from the final version.

*Rolling Stone* did not care for the single, however. In its review dated February 13, 1986, the magazine called Michael's contribution "unhelpful . . . his worst effort since 'Muscles.'" Despite some lukewarm reviews, "Eaten Alive" became a Top 10 R&B hit and was an even bigger success in the clubs, peaking at #3 on the Dance Music/Club Play Singles chart.

## "You're the One"—Jennifer Holliday (1985)

Michael first met Jennifer Holliday while she was starring in Broadway's *Dreamgirls*; in 1985, he co-wrote and produced the ballad "You're the One" for her album *Say You Love Me*. Composed with Alan Kohan, "You're the One" paints a Disney-like picture of finding one's soulmate. "Someday a prince will come your way," she sighs. Until then, she cries to her mother, who advises her that, one day, "You will come to know / The joy and love of one good man."

Their collaboration is mentioned in the *Jet* article "Jackson Pens, Produces New Tune for Holliday" from June 10, 1985. "I think he's just really great, really great," Holliday said. "He's going to be so prominent in the next decade or so because he really knows what he wants to do. The ballad that he wrote for me is not a ballad you write from the tip of your head; it comes from observing and from a gift that is deep within."

She also revealed that guitarist Earl Klugh and other top musicians played on the track, which was recorded in one day. *Jet* reported that it would be released as a single, but ultimately the songs "Hard Time for Lovers" and "No Frills Love" were chosen instead.

## "Alright Now"—Ralph Tresvant (1990)

Perhaps it was fated that Michael and Ralph Tresvant would cross paths. After all, Tresvant was the Michael Jackson–esque lead singer of New Edition, a 1980s update of the Jackson 5. When Tresvant recorded his debut solo album, his producers were Jimmy Jam and Terry Lewis, the duo who would launch Janet Jackson into superstardom and eventually work with Michael on several tracks. The ballad "Alright Now," co-written by Michael and John Barnes in 1989, appears on the CD version of *Ralph Tresvant*.

## "Do the Bartman"—The Simpsons (1990)

At the same time Michael appeared on *The Simpsons*, he informed creator Matt Groening that he wanted to write a #1 song for Bart. He and songwriter Bryan Loren duly wrote "Do the Bartman," a pop-rap single that features Bart rapping about his family, his misadventures, and, of course, his own dance. Nancy Cartwright, the voice of Bart, performed the song; in *For the Record*, Cadman and Halstead quote Loren as saying he and Michael provided the backing vocals. Michael guided Cartwright through her vocals; she presented him with a signed Bart Simpson doll before they began rehearsing. "Michael was absolutely incredible. We had so much fun. It didn't take us very long at all because he knew exactly what he was doing. We started at the top and just ran through it a couple of times, and he couldn't stop laughing," said Cartwright.

While "Do the Bartman" was released as a single in the UK (staying at the top of the charts for three weeks), it received only radio airplay in the US. It did appear on the 1990 album *The Simpsons Sing the Blues*, and a hilarious animated video aired frequently on MTV.

## "I Never Heard"—Safire (1991, co-written with Paul Anka)

"I Never Heard" is a rewrite of "This Is It," one of the Michael and Anka collaborations from the early 1980s. Hailing from Puerto Rico, Latin freestyle singer Safire released two singles before recording her self-titled debut album in 1989. After scoring an adult-contemporary hit with the ballad "Thinking of You," she released her 1991 follow-up album *I Wasn't Born Yesterday*, which features "I Never Heard."

According to *Billboard*, after Michael and Anka recorded demos of their 1983 tracks, Michael took the master tapes. Anka got them back, slightly rewrote the lyrics, and gave the song to Safire in 1991. While the lyrics differ, the vocal and piano lines are virtually identical. Eighteen years later, when the Michael Jackson estate raided the music vaults for previously unreleased material, they found "I Never Heard" (the working title Michael and Anka had given the song) and heard the line "this is it." Realizing that it would tie in with the *This Is It* film, they remastered the track, had the Jackson brothers sing backup vocals, and promoted it as a "new Michael Jackson song."

When Anka learned of this plan, he threatened to sue to the estate for proper credit and share of royalties. He quickly received both and seemed to hold no ill will toward all involved with the project. "They realize it's a mistake, they realize it's my song, they realize it's my production of his vocal in my studio and I am getting 50 percent of the whole project, actually, which is fair," Anka told TMZ, as reported in the *Billboard* article "'New' Michael Jackson Single Written in 1983."

## "Joy"—Blackstreet (1994)

Intended for *Dangerous*, "Joy" featured a melody written by Michael and lyrics by Tammy Lucas. After Michael decided not to record it, he gave it to Blackstreet, the

Co-written with Paul McCartney, "The Man" appears on McCartney's 1983 LP *Pipes of Peace*.
*Author's collection*

side project of *Dangerous* producer Teddy Riley. The track ultimately appeared on the group's self-titled 1994 album, best known for the 1990s jam "No Diggity." This lovely ballad, one of Michael's best compositions that he never recorded, features tight harmonies, an airy melody, and a gentle beat that combines pop and R&B. Blackstreet add a short rap toward the end, lending a touch of hip hop to the track.

Released as a single in 1995, "Joy" peaked at #12 on the *Billboard* R&B/Hip Hop Singles chart, #43 on the Hot 100, and #56 in the UK.

## "Happy Birthday Lisa"—The Simpsons (1991)

One of Michael's more unusual compositions, "Happy Birthday Lisa" is listed under a pseudonym for contractual reasons. A huge fan of *The Simpsons*, Michael voiced a character for the 1991 episode "Stark Raving Dad." After Homer has been committed to a mental institution for being a "free-thinking anarchist," he meets his roommate: Leon Kompowsky, a large white man who claims to be Michael Jackson. In a subplot, Bart promises to get his sister Lisa the best birthday present ever, which turns out to be Michael singing "Happy Birthday Lisa."

While it was later confirmed that he appeared in the episode and wrote the track, Michael was credited on the show as "John Jay Smith," while soundalike Kipp Lennon sang the song. The track later appeared on the 1997 album *Songs in the Key of Springfield*. The episode aired in 1991, but Michael completed his voiceovers a year before.

## "Children's Holiday" / "People of the World"—J-Friends (1998)

In 1995, a devastating earthquake leveled Kobe City, Japan, killing 6,434 people and causing approximately $100 billion in damage. Japanese talent agency Johnny

& Associates gathered three boy bands it represented—KinKi Kids, V6, and Tokio—to form J-Friends, a supergroup that would record songs to raise money for relief efforts. Internationally famous musicians and songwriters were recruited to write and produce songs for the group, including Jon Bon Jovi, Elton John, Maurice White, and Diane Warren.

Michael contributed two songs, the first being "Children's Holiday," which he also produced, and which features a children's choir backing the teenage singers. The lyrics were translated into Japanese, although the "Michael Jackson" touch is unmistakable. Hints of "We Are the World," "Heal the World," and "Will You Be There" resonate in the track. Released as a single in Japan, "Children's Holiday" debuted at #1.

The second song written and produced by Michael, "People of the World," includes lyrics written by Yasushi Okimoto. Sounding quite reminiscent of "We Are the World," it was issued as a single in Japan only.

# 34

# How Does It Feel When You're Alone?

## An Analysis of *HIStory*, Michael Jackson's Angriest Album

**B**y the mid-1990s, Michael Jackson found himself at an artistic and personal crossroads. He had finally emerged from a painful two-year period dealing with allegations of child abuse. While he eventually reached an out-of-court settlement with one of his accusers in January 1994, the ordeal left him scarred. His image took a battering particularly in the United States, with the media chronicling every salacious detail (often based on innuendo and hearsay) of the saga. The ordeal further fueled his addiction to painkillers, resulting in rehab stints and forcing him to cut the *Dangerous* World Tour short.

After emerging from the scandals, Michael appeared determined to rebuild his life and resume his career. In May 1994 he married Lisa Marie Presley, daughter of "the King" Elvis Presley; next he began work on a greatest-hits package entitled *HIStory: Past, Present, and Future, Book 1*. It was originally intending to include only a few new songs, but Michael's creative burst resulted in him recording enough material for a separate album. At last he could address his critics and tell his side of the story. Instead of portraying himself as a victim, he would fight back. Lisa Marie reportedly encouraged him to assume an aggressive stance on the album; indeed, her comments in the June/July 1995 issue of *Vibe* clearly reflected her opinion. "I can't wait for the day when all the snakes who have tried to take him out get to eat their own lunch and crawl back into the holes from which they came," she said, in the article "Action Jackson." "We know who they are and their bluff is about to be called."

Indeed, many of Michael's new *HIStory* songs called people's bluffs, and he radiates anger on virtually every track. For the first time, he uses profanity and projects an even tougher image than on "Bad." Here stood a man who had weathered major storms but now stands defiant and, as he would sing six years later, "unbreakable." Even his voice sounded different, as he spits out lyrics in a raspy, almost whispering style. This new approach sharply divided fans and critics, with many struggling with one question: what happened to the moonwalker who lured listeners to the dance floor with "Rock with You" or the man who playfully flirted with "tenderonis" on "P.Y.T."?

*Rolling Stone*'s review, dated August 10, 1995, was decidedly mixed, praising "Scream," "Tabloid Junkie," "You Are Not Alone," and "Stranger in Moscow," but citing "Come Together," "Earth Song," "Smile," "HIStory," and "Childhood" as examples of Jackson's "rampaging ego . . . desperate for the days when he ruled." Critic James Hunter also noted the rage permeating the collection of new songs in his 1995 review. "He's angry, miserable, tortured, inflammatory, furious," he wrote. "Jackson sketches funky scenarios denouncing greed, blanket unreliability and false accusation."

Jon Pareles appeared indecisive in his June 18 *New York Times* review, "Michael Jackson Is Angry, Understand?" He questioned whether listeners could identify with this anger or view it as a superstar throwing a tantrum, while noting Michael's new sound: "The music has polarized; it's either clipped, choppy and electronic or glossy and sumptuous, only occasionally trying to combine the two. Most of the time, Jackson sounds as if he's singing through clenched teeth, spitting out words in defiance of any and all persecutors."

One of *HIStory*'s harshest reviews came from *Entertainment Weekly*, which awarded the greatest-disc hits an "A" but the new tracks a "C-minus." Lamenting the latter's departure from Michael's earlier, more positive tracks, writer David Browne labeled the entire project "grotesque egomania on display" but did single out "They Don't Care About Us," "Stranger in Moscow," "Money," and "This Time Around" as crisp and confident. Still, he dismissed "Scream" as "flailing" and "You Are Not Alone" as "syrupy."

Twenty years later, and further removed from its original circumstances, *HIStory* has received more positive reassessment from fans and critics. Michael planned on performing "They Don't Care About Us" and "Earth Song" as part of his *This Is It* concerts, while both tracks appear in Cirque du Soleil's tribute shows *The Immortal World Tour* and *ONE*.

In his article "Michael Jackson's Twenty Greatest Hits," Paul Lester stressed that the second disc of *HIStory* contradicted what constitutes a typical Michael Jackson record. "A lot of people couldn't quite get to grips with the notion of Jackson the cosseted multi-millionaire daring to spend one half of an album complaining about his lot," he wrote. "They could accept—relish, even—the idea of the clownishly peculiar Jacko, but they weren't quite ready for Michael's *In Utero*" (a reference to Nirvana's final album). Lester pointed out that "They Don't Care About

Written and produced by R. Kelly, "You Are Not Alone" became Michael's last #1 single. *Author's collection*

Us" foreshadowed *Blood on the Dance Floor* with its "neo-industrial metal-funk" that "suggested Jackson should maybe have collaborated with Trent Reznor."

In *Man in the Music*, Joseph Vogel argues that *HIStory* remains Michael's most underrated album due to its "mixture of sounds, styles, and themes," its fearlessness in tackling political and social issues, and its superior sound quality (thanks in part to the work of engineer Bruce Swedien). It may be one of Michael's least accessible albums, Vogel concludes, but repeated listening can reap great rewards.

*HIStory* is Michael's most personal album, its lyrics allowing a rare glimpse into his inner emotions, fears, and painful memories. With the exception of "You Are Not Alone"—Michael's last #1 single—and his cover of the Beatles' "Come Together" (which dates from the *Bad* sessions and first appeared in the *Moonwalker* film), the album tracks seethe and pulsate with passion. An analysis of select *HIStory* tracks reveals how the disc deserves another listen and a renewed appreciation of its sonic and lyrical experiments.

## "Scream" (with Janet Jackson)

Primarily written by Jimmy Jam and Terry Lewis, "Scream" was not originally intended as a duet. According to Jam, the duo played several tracks for Janet Jackson's consideration; once she heard the "Scream" demo, she said she wanted the track for herself but knew Michael would choose it. Jam thought the siblings would select another track, "Runaway," for the *HIStory* project, but Janet ended up

The greatly anticipated "Scream" excited fans as the first ever Michael and Janet Jackson duet. Its expensive, effects-laden video impressed fans as well as critics.          *Author's collection*

recording it for her *Design of a Decade* greatest-hits collection. "I actually thought ["Runaway"] would've been a great duet for them, but Michael wanted to be real aggressive and real hard. He had things on his mind about how he felt he was being treated in the press," Jam told the *Morton Report*'s Chaz Lipp in 2012.

According to Jam, Michael first recorded his vocals in New York; when Janet saw his aggressive performance, she decided to lay down her section separately at Jam and Lewis's Flyte Tyme Studios in Minneapolis. When Michael later heard her version, he elected to redo his section in Minneapolis. In the end, Jam stated, they used 90 percent of Michael's first performance.

With its heavy industrial sound, complete with breaking glass and snarling backing vocals, "Scream" hardly represents a typical Michael Jackson single. Fans may have instantly recognized his trademark "hoo-hoo's" at the song's onset, but his staccato delivery of rage-filled lyrics took listeners on a very different journey. "Kicking me down / I got to get up," he spits, as Janet adds, "You're selling out souls / But I care about mine." The siblings scream with frustration over lying, sensationalism, injustice, and racial discrimination, but vow they will not give up the fight. As a final shocker, the duo sings "stop fucking with me," marking the first time a profanity has appeared on a Michael Jackson single. In *Man in the Music*, Joseph Vogel quotes assistant engineer Russ Ragsdale as saying that in the recording, Michael could not bring himself to actually utter the word; instead, he made a similar percussive sound. Thus Janet's vocal carries most of the weight on that specific line.

Jam and Lewis would remix "Scream" for *Blood on the Dance Floor*; dubbed "Scream Louder," the song features the bass lick from Sly and the Family Stone's "Thank You (Falettinme Be Mice Elf Agin)."

## "They Don't Care About Us"

A Top 10 hit in several countries, "They Don't Care About Us" fared only modestly well in the US, peaking at #30. This initial reception was partly due to its often-misinterpreted lyrics and controversial content. Before *HIStory* was released, the *New York Times*' Bernard Weintraub ran a scathing article entitled "In New Lyrics, Jackson Uses Slurs," deeming the entire album to be "profane, obscure, angry and filled with rage." He particularly singled out "They Don't Care About Us" for the lyrics "Jew me, sue me, everybody do me / Kick me, kike me, don't you black or white me." These words immediately raised the ire of several Jewish groups, including the Anti-Defamation League, which demanded the lyrics be changed.

In response, Michael immediately apologized, stating that the song was in fact supporting victims of prejudice. "My intention was for this song to say 'no' to racism, anti-Semitism, and stereotyping," he said in a statement to Abraham H. Foxman, national director of the Anti-Defamation League. As stated in Dinitia Smith's *New York Times* article "Jackson Plans New Lyrics for Album," Michael agreed to include an apology on albums that had already been pressed, then re-recorded the lyrics to read "strike me" and "do me" for future pressings. Radio edits obscured the words with a sound effect.

"They Don't Care About Us" was difficult not only thematically but also sonically. Vogel cites engineer Rob Hoffman, who explains that the bridge consisted of over 300 tracks featuring the hard-rock guitar solo, police-scanner recordings, synthesizer effects, and percussion ranging from drums to handclaps. In the GearSlutz forum, he stated that the track was among the most difficult to finish on *HIStory*, as Michael had worked on the song numerous times without matching his high expectations.

Despite the initial controversy, "They Don't Care About Us" stands as a powerful statement against stereotyping and prejudice. When he uses derogatory terms, he illustrates the meaningless labels that are meant to oppress rather than uplift. "Beat me, hate me / You can never break me," he half-raps, speaking for the "invisible" and the ignored; instead of portraying these people as victims, he allows them to fight back, exclaiming, "I'm tired of being the victim of hate." These words not only apply to prejudice in general, but to Michael's situation in 1995. Through his music, he establishes that he no longer views himself as a victim and wishes to defend himself against his critics.

## "Stranger in Moscow"

While less aggressive than other *HIStory* tracks, "Stranger in Moscow" seethes with anger and resentment. At the same time, Michael's vocals are engulfed in extreme sorrow, expressing his feeling of isolation. The singer wrote the lyrics during the *Dangerous* tour, when he was indeed in Moscow. According to Cadman and Halstead's *For the Record*, Michael said "the lyrics are totally autobiographical. . . . That's really how I felt . . . just all alone in my hotel, and it was raining—and I just started writing it." He composed in September 1993, in the early days of the child-molestation allegations. Every word expresses his anguish: "Swift and sudden fall from grace," he croons, almost sounding on the verge of tears. "How does it feel?" The sweeping instrumentation emphasizes his turbulent emotions, while his voice ranges from somber and contemplative to raspy and passionate.

Flashes of anger jolt the listener. "Take my name and just let me be," he sings. He complains of the KGB "doggin' me," a reference to the district attorney who pursued the case against Michael. In this powerful track, Michael portrays himself as a victim and a survivor, asking people to sympathize with his emotional imprisonment.

Many reviewers cited "Stranger in Moscow" as the best *HIStory* song, with the *Los Angeles Times*' Chris Willman calling it "a step removed from the focused paranoia of much of the rest of the album, more akin to the deeper, fuzzier dread of a past perennial like 'Billie Jean.' . . . He sings in the somber, constricted verses, before a sweeping coda kicks up four minutes in and the stalkee suddenly breaks his cool to wail about a desolate, inconsolable loneliness. Here, in this song, is the real genius—and probably real personhood—of Michael Jackson." In Hunter's *Rolling Stone* review, he claimed the song reveals as much angst as any grunge track.

Overall, the sweeping "Stranger in Moscow" deserves more attention, as it stands as one of the best songs Michael wrote and recorded. The pain-filled lyrics, Michael's sincere performance, and the powerful arrangement should stand alongside the singer's greatest songs.

## "This Time Around" (featuring the Notorious B.I.G.)

The rage returns with this hip hop–tinged track, with Michael angrily denouncing his critics and the unnamed—but fairly obvious—people involved in the child-abuse allegations. Like "Scream," "This Time Around" features a Michael never before heard on record—he utters another profanity and sings in a growling tone, professing his resilience and defiance.

Co-written and produced with Dallas Austin, "This Time Around" was initially described in the May 20, 1995, issue of *Billboard* as a "pop/hip-hop track" with a "hand-clapping chorus." Those phrases barely scratch beneath the surface of this scathing track, a declaration that also serves as an indictment against Thomas William Sneddon Jr., then-district attorney of Santa Barbara County, California. Over a slamming, hard beat, Michael shouts that he will defend himself at all costs. Then come the sections aimed squarely at Sneddon: "He really thought he really had / Had a hold on me," he sings. Next he seemingly addresses the family who instigated the 1993 investigation, adding, "They really want to use me / And then falsely accuse me."

To further toughen his image, Michael recruited an unlikely guest to perform the rap break: gangsta rapper the Notorious B.I.G. According to engineer John Van Nest, B.I.G. was starstruck from the moment he entered the studio to record his section. He asked Austin if it was possible to meet Michael; the producer responded that he could do so after he laid down his rap. "During his first take, Dallas and I looked at each other, because it was spot on. Wow. I was impressed, and so was Dallas," Van Nest recalled in the GearSlutz forum. "We listened back, and Dallas was like, 'Wow, I think we got it.' As I recall, we took another take for good measure, but I'm fairly certain that we ended up using the first take."

When Michael finally entered the studio to meet the Notorious B.I.G., Van Nest recalled, the rapper almost dissolved in tears. They played back B.I.G.'s part, which Michael loved. Before they parted, the rapper shyly asked Michael for a photo together, which was quickly taken. "Michael could have this effect on anyone, even the most hardcore rappers!" said Van Nest.

## "Earth Song"

*HIStory* moves from personal trials to world issues, specifically environmental neglect. While it was finally released in 1995, "Earth Song" dates to 1988, when Michael first penned the chorus in a Vienna hotel room. He wanted to write an environmental song from the earth's perspective, and recorded the track's signature cry into a tape recorder. A year later, Michael entered the recording studio with a skeleton of the track but was unsure how to execute the idea. Contacting Bill Bottrell, a producer and engineer he had previously worked with (see chapter 37), he decided to flesh out "Earth Song" for a future album.

The duo honed the lyrics, chorus, and instrumentation to Michael's perfectionist desires. "He wanted it to have the passion and intensity of a gospel song, but the sonic landscape of something like Pink Floyd or Brian Eno, something that borrowed from prog rock, ambient, and world music, but was still classical and accessible. He didn't want it to be too complex or abstract since the song was intended to move masses of people," writes Joseph Vogel, in *Earth Song: Inside Michael Jackson's Magnum Opus*. Eventually, Bruce Swedien and David Foster would become involved, and guitarist/bassist Guy Pratt contributed a key element to the song: its booming bass, courtesy of what Vogel calls a "massive, experimental octave-pedal bass line at Westlake Studio. The deep, soul-vibrating sound heard on the record was achieved by using an octave divider, so that the bass was playing in two octaves at once." The final crucial element, the Andraé Crouch Choir, was added last, with the group standing in a circle as they recorded their response: "What about us?"

By 1991, the then-titled "What About Us" seemed finished and destined for *Dangerous*. But for unknown reasons, Michael decided to leave it off the album. Three years later, he would return to the retitled "Earth Song," recruiting Foster to help him with additional orchestration. In spring 1995, Michael finished the song at Record One in Los Angeles, re-recording parts of his vocals through an entire weekend. When he sang the final ad-libs, the roughness in his voice was partially caused by exhaustion. As Vogel notes, the effect was profound: "It was as if Jackson was channeling from the lungs of the earth—a pained, fierce, prophetic voice, giving utterance to the suffering of the world."

On "Earth Song," the anger is multifaceted. The narrator represents the earth and Michael, alternating between mourning ("Now I don't know where we are / Although I know we've drifted far") and accusatory ("What have we done to the world?"). At the song's climax, the back-and-forth response with the choir, Michael releases his frustration. "What about apathy?" he cries. "Do we give a damn?" A true epic, "Earth Song" contains tension, drama, and a final release of anger toward humanity's carelessness.

## "D.S."

A thinly veiled attack on Sneddon, "D.S." harkens back to Michael's previous dalliances with rock on tracks such as "Beat It," "Dirty Diana," and "Give In to Me." Featuring Slash's rhythm and solo guitar, "D.S." tells the story of "Dom Sheldon"—a "cold man," Michael shouts. The singer holds nothing back, suggesting the character may be a member of the KKK and hold ties with the FBI and CIA. When Michael snarls the opening line, "They wanna get my ass dead or alive," he leaves no doubt that he has returned to his personal travails. One of the song's most controversial elements occurs at the end. "I have not—shall we say—done him the honor of listening to it, but I've been told that it ends with the sound of a gunshot," Sneddon mentioned on his National District Attorneys Association listing.

While the content may be controversial, the song itself emits pure rock and roll, with Slash turning in a fine solo. Had it addressed another topic—or prejudice in general—it could have been a hit for Michael. Alas, its obvious subject prevented it from being released as a single, and listeners may not have appreciated Michael's enraged attack.

## "Money"

One of Michael's most underrated songs, "Money" rails against greed. While the lyrics clearly concern his legal woes, they also address material gluttony. Rapping in a low, almost-whispered voice, Michael sounds virtually unrecognizable until the chorus. He confronts the listener with lines such as "Are you infected with the same disease / Of lust, gluttony and greed?" The bass lines, looped sounds, and shuffling beat pulsate, punctuating Michael's sharpest jab: "You'll do anything for money."

A more familiar Michael Jackson emerges in the chorus, with multilayered backing vocals (all performed by the singer) sweetly harmonizing over depressing words. The unethical person "would lie for you / would die for you / even sell my soul to the devil." While the song's negative tone may have initially repelled fans, its deep funk sounds timeless and deserves another listen. "You're dirty!" he slurs toward the end, suggesting the dirty beat as well as the immoral person he addresses.

## "Childhood (Theme from *Free Willy 2*)"

Anger takes a subtle role in this deeply melancholy track. Here Michael refutes his critics, explaining his seemingly eccentric behavior. In several interviews, he maintained that "Childhood" was his most personal song. As Cadman and Halstead note in *For the Record*, Michael called it "a reflection of my life . . . it's about the pain, some of the joys, some of the dreaming, some of the mental adventures that I took because of the different lifestyle I had, in being a child performer." To underscore the point, Michael included his own drawing in the *HIStory* CD booklet of a young boy clutching a microphone, cowering in fear in a corner.

According to Swedien, Michael sang the song live with the Foster-conducted orchestra. Michael's self-penned words plainly tell his story, and his voice acts out the lyrics' wide range of emotion. His singing takes on a breathy quality when he describes childish fantasies of pirates and kings, but in another line he bluntly asks, "Have you seen my childhood?" While his anger may be muted, he still confronts his critics. "People say I'm not okay," he sighs. "Before you judge me, try hard to love me." In this profoundly sad track, with strings straight out of an old Hollywood movie soundtrack, he argues his case, defending his supposed "strange eccentricities."

## "Tabloid Junkie"

Enraged Michael Jackson returns on this Jam and Lewis–produced track, which is often cited by critics as one of *HIStory*'s standout songs. His raspy delivery is back, his staccato delivery punctuating every word attacking one of his favorite targets: the tabloid press. The lyrics first address the purveyors of scandal sheets, decrying their lies and accusing them of spreading conspiracy theories. "It's slander!" he cries, "You say it's not a sword / But with your pen you torture men."

In the chorus, however, the focus turns on the listener. In this memorable, highly rhythmic section, he warns fans not to believe everything they read. He challenges the audience not to feed the "parasites" by buying the magazines and newspapers. Throughout "Tabloid Junkie," his beatboxing is interwoven with the percussion, placing the rhythm track at the forefront. In his *Rolling Stone* review, "King of Pain: *HIStory: Past, Present and Future, Book 1*," Hunter labeled this song an "adventurous Jam and Lewis thumper . . . the choruses of 'Tabloid Junkie' in

particular sing out with quick-voiced warnings about the failings of media truth."
While Michael may have been lashing out at specific targets, "Tabloid Junkie's"
rebukes of media sensationalism still resonate.

## "2 Bad"

Later appearing in the short film *Ghosts*, "2 Bad" slightly resembles 1987's "Bad" in
its tough attitude. Over a hip-hop beat courtesy of Jam and Lewis, Michael taunts
his tormentors in the chorus: "Too bad about it / Why don't you scream and shout
it," he snarls. Longtime colleague Jerry Hey provides the horns, and basketball
player/aspiring rapper Shaquille O'Neal performs the rap break.

The star, however, is Michael's strident vocals. "You tried to bring me to my
knees," he boasts. "I'm standing though you're kicking me." He accuses his
unnamed enemies of "blood lust" and repeatedly voices his disgust and contempt.
As in "This Time Around," Michael argues that living well is indeed the best
revenge. By surviving, he spits out in "2 Bad," he has already won.

## "HIStory"

The collection's title track seemingly smacks of megalomania, the horn-filled fanfare
and military-influenced beat seemingly echoing the statue on the cover. Yet Jam and
Lewis's lyrics suggest something quite different. Accompanied by a driving beat and

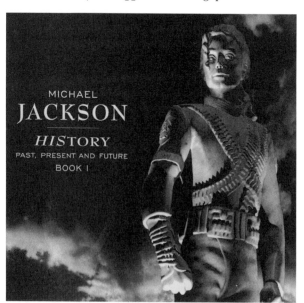

sound samples from famous
speeches, Michael urges listeners to create their own history,
to impact the world in positive
ways. The song begins on an
angry note, with Michael's
raspy voice returning. "He got
kicked in the back . . . He dares
to be recognized," he growls,
describing the abuse revolutionaries often experience. His
voice then becomes smoother,
asking how much suffering
must occur before people
decide to make a change.

The chorus delivers the
song's true message: "Every
day create your history / Every
path you take you're leaving
your legacy." Michael assumes
his angry stance in the next
verse, but here he uses his
anger as a motivator. "Don't

*HIStory* contains not just a greatest-hits collection but also
a disc filled with previously unreleased material, as well as
new recordings. Songs such as "Stranger in Moscow" and
"Childhood" are among the most personal Michael ever
recorded.                            *Author's collection*

let no one get you down / Keep movin' on higher ground," he urges, arguing that nothing should deter one's self-motivation. In 1995, "HIStory" was misinterpreted as an exercise in self-glorification. A close examination of the lyrics, however, reveals its true meaning: stressing each person's responsibility to improve the world. "HIStory" proves the adage of not judging a book—or, in this case, an album—by its cover.

## "Little Susie"

While this track is explored in detail in chapter 31, it is worth including it here for its underlying indignation. Michael mourns the death of innocence as well as the little girl, but also rages against those who turned a blind eye to injustice. He accuses the audience of ignoring her cries for help; she screamed "and nobody's there / She knew no one cared," he sings. The theatrical production mainly invites pity, but it also invokes shame and communicates the narrator's disgust at others' apathy.

## "Smile"

This classic Charlie Chaplin composition clearly does not concern anger. Yet its inclusion here is no accident. The lyrics are about smiling in the face of adversity, even if one must force or feign happiness. Such a positive attitude can turn one's life around—a sentiment Michael had become familiar with by 1995. Rage permeates much of *HIStory*'s new material, but "Smile" suggests some hope. He will smile at his critics, not giving them the satisfaction of destroying him.

Michael sang live over the orchestra, with a piano introduced at the end. The sound resembles the soundtrack to Charlie Chaplin's early films, and Michael seems to enjoy the throwback, snapping his fingers and scatting along. Since Michael was a huge fan of the movie legend, this tribute was intentional. Beyond the homage, however, "Smile" is a final dig at his adversaries, letting them know that nothing they say will bring him down.

## You Can Never Break Me

When Michael Jackson fans first heard *HIStory*, they were undoubtedly startled by its furious tone. The circumstances surrounding its release tainted its initial reception, particularly in the United States. Two decades later, *HIStory* merits a second listen with an open mind. Yes, the collection's new songs throb with undisguised rage. It's the way that Michael channels his ire into an artistic statement and social commentary that fascinates, and the themes of politics, environmental destruction, and human behavior and frailties pack an even greater punch today. As Michael told Adrian Grant in 1998's *Making HIStory*, the album is "about people looking at their lives, and taking any seconds of their well being and making something of yourself—creating a legacy so you can look back and look at what you have done."

# 35

# And with All I've Been Through, I'm Still Around

## Reassessing 2001's *Invincible*

T he year 2001 was to be an exciting one for Michael Jackson: plans included releasing *Invincible*, his first album of entirely new material since 1991's *Dangerous*; filming the long-form video for the first single, "You Rock My World"; and staging two thirtieth-anniversary concerts at Madison Square Garden in New York, which would air as a TV special. He appeared at the 2001 MTV Music Video Awards, showing off his dance moves in a brief appearance with *NSYNC, then granted a rare interview on MTV's *Total Request Live*. Although competing in a field dominated by younger artists such as Britney Spears, the Backstreet Boys, Christina Aguilera, *NSYNC, and Usher, Michael seemed poised for a comeback, ready to regain his crown as the King of Pop.

Unfortunately, several events prevented this desired triumph. Ongoing disputes with his label, Sony, culminated in a lack of promotion for *Invincible*. Filming for the thirtieth-anniversary special concluded September 10, 2001; the next day, the tragic events of 9/11 brought life to a grinding halt. Music and other entertainment sales slumped as the country grappled with the tragedy. *Invincible* was finally released on October 30; it debuted at #1 on the *Billboard* 200, repeating the feat in the UK, Australia, Belgium, Denmark, The Netherlands, Germany, Norway, Sweden, and Switzerland. To date the album has sold thirteen million units worldwide—a solid hit for any performer. By Michael's standards, however, those numbers were disappointing; *Invincible* was his least successful album, selling far fewer copies than recent releases such as *HIStory* and *Dangerous*.

Another factor was the critical response. *Invincible* received mixed reviews, some particularly venomous. In his *MOJO* review, "Michael Jackson: Dead Man, Moonwalking," James McNair stated that the singer "used to be cool, now he just sounds criminal." *Uncut* writer Chris Roberts called the album "awful, and awfully sad," and spent more time discussing Michael's personal life than the music. And in its December 6 review, *Rolling Stone* awarded *Invincible* three stars, with reviewer Hunter praising only "Whatever Happens," a collaboration with Carlos Santana. Otherwise he dubbed ballads such as "Butterflies" "odd" and up-tempo tracks like "Heartbreaker" and "2000 Watts" "generic," with Michael "merely treading water."

*Entertainment Weekly*'s David Browne further panned *Invincible* in its November 9 issue, grading it a C-minus and judging it "curiously lacking in excitement or thrills," with cuts like "Butterflies" and "Break of Dawn" examples of a "squishy bunch" of ballads with "glaringly banal lyrics, pleasantries . . . that could emanate from just about anyone." Browne even managed to work in a reference to Michael's appearance, citing the "frightening new nose he debuts on the cover." *Los Angeles Times* reviewer Robert Hilburn provided a slightly more balanced take, praising "Heartbreaker" for its pounding rhythms and Michael's "sassy, defiant, and forceful" vocals. While he named "2000 Watts" as a dance-club anthem, Hilburn deemed ballads such as "Heaven Can Wait" and "Speechless" unconvincing.

Finally, the *New Musical Express* analyzed the album track-by-track in its issue dated September 12, 2005, concluding that it is a "good R&B record, but certainly not pioneering." Revealing his subjectivity, the reviewer consistently referred to Michael by the British tabloid nickname "Jacko." In a companion review, *NME*'s Mark Beaumont called it a "a relevant and rejuvenated comeback album made overlong and embarrassing by the unavoidable fact that Michael Jackson is a) exceedingly rich and b) a bit of a wanker," focusing mainly on the singer's complicated personal life.

Fourteen years have passed since *Invincible*'s release, allowing listeners some distance from various issues surrounding its 2001 debut. Has the album aged gracefully? While the album may not equal works like *Off the Wall*, *Thriller*, or *Dangerous*, it contains some buried gems that echo moments on those earlier albums. After revisiting the making of *Invincible*, this chapter will analyze some of the disc's best—and least-known—tracks.

## The Making of *Invincible*

*Invincible*'s roots date back to 1997; it was originally scheduled for release on November 9, 1999. Michael granted *TV Guide* a rare interview that year, explaining that he was at work on the new material. "I just try to write wonderful music; and if they love it, they love it. I don't think about any demographic," he told interviewer Lisa Bernhard. "[The record company] tries to get me to think that way, but I just do what I would enjoy hearing." During the discussion, Michael mentioned a track that was intended for the upcoming album: "I Have This Dream," a song co-written with Carole Bayer Sager and David Foster addressing the environment. The composition failed to make the final *Invincible* lineup.

In a 1999 interview with the *Daily Mirror*, Michael appeared optimistic about the upcoming album. Provocatively titled "Michael Jackson: My Pain," the article saw Michael declaring that he was halfway through the project. "It's going to be the best thing I've ever done. I'm putting my heart and soul into it because I'm not sure if I'm gonna do another one after this. . . . This will be my last album, I think," he said. Future plans for the millennium included venturing into film and, remarkably, working on an album with his brothers. Due to endless delays recording *Invincible*, health issues, legal problems, and financial difficulties, however, these plans never came to fruition.

Michael's first full studio album since 1991's *Dangerous*, *Invincible* carried expectations and anticipation. Could he retain his title as King of Pop in the new millennium? Sony, the parent company of the Epic label, initially invested in heavy promotion via TV specials, a video, and advertisements such as this poster.                                   *Author's collection*

Two more years would pass before *Invincible* finally hit music stores. Since 1997, Michael had traveled to recording studios ranging from Montreux, Switzerland, and Norfolk, Virginia, to Los Angeles and Miami. According to Joseph Vogel's *Man in the Music*, Michael worked with a staggering number of artists, writers, and producers at various stages, including Teddy Riley, Dr. Freeze, Babyface, R. Kelly, Will Smith, Puff Daddy, Slash, Boyz II Men, K-Ci & JoJo, Bayer Sager, Foster, Tom Bahler, Lenny Kravitz, Wyclef Jean, Floetry, Brandy, Sisqo, Santana, and Rodney "Darkchild" Jerkins. Jerkins took on the greatest role in *Invincible*, writing and producing much of the album.

While Michael served as executive producer and made the final decisions, working with several writers and producers resulted in a lack of focus. Tracks like "You Rock My World" and "Butterflies" harken back to the classic Michael Jackson sound of *Off the Wall*; other songs like "2000 Watts" and "Heartbreaker" firmly root the sound in modern techno-dance.

In addition, Michael's perfectionist streak and the knowledge that the expectations of his fans, record company, and collaborators were high further delayed the album. In a 2009 interview with *Vibe*'s Linda Hobbs, Jerkins reminisced about this period. He revealed that in addition to Michael's constant travels, he would suddenly suggest throwing out everything they had worked on and starting from scratch. In addition, Jerkins revealed, Michael voiced his concerns on everything from percussion to the overall sound quality. "He looked at everything under a microscope, like, 'The middle frequency is too much'—he was very technical," he recalled.

By the summer of 2001, Michael found himself at a critical juncture: he had worked on *Invincible* for four years, with the cost now at a staggering $30 million. Under pressure from his record company, the singer finally selected sixteen songs out of hundreds for the final lineup (some of the leftover tracks eventually saw release on *The Ultimate Collection* as well as posthumous compilations *Michael* and *Xscape*). Executives at Sony and Epic were reportedly pleased with the final product, and promotion was planned: two Madison Square Garden concerts celebrating Michael's thirty years as a solo artist; a fifteen-minute music video for the first single, "You Rock My World," co-starring Chris Tucker, Michael Madsen, and Marlon Brando; and a media blitz, most notably an appearance on the popular MTV show *Total Request Live*.

In November, a condensed version of the thirtieth anniversary concert aired as a CBS special, earning solid ratings: over twenty-five million viewers tuned in to view contemporary artists such as Destiny's Child, Whitney Houston, and Usher covering Jackson's biggest hits. Michael turned in some fun performances, including a duet with Britney Spears on "The Way You Make Me Feel" and a reunion with his brothers on "Dancin' Machine" as well as other classic Jackson 5 singles. Shortly after the special aired, Sony abruptly ended its reported $25 million promotion campaign, effectively halting any momentum *Invincible* may have gained from the TV program.

## Second Listen: An Alternate Version

Enough time has passed that the original circumstances and complications surrounding the album can be set aside. Critics are correct in that *Invincible* is inconsistent in comparison to stronger efforts such as *Off the Wall* and *Thriller*. It also suffers from "too many cooks" syndrome, as working with only one producer may have guaranteed a clearer vision for the album. Cuts such as "The Lost Children" and "You Are My Life" suffer from saccharine over-arrangements that overwhelm Michael's voice. However, certain dance tracks and ballads contain flashes of classic Michael Jackson, with some anticipating the techno-heavy, dubstep material dominating today's charts.

Numerous critics complained about *Invincible*'s length (almost seventy-eight minutes) and generous song selection (sixteen tracks). What follows is a proposal for an alternate *Invincible*—a shortened lineup that highlights the best material on the album. This hypothetical ten-track, trimmed-down version may encourage a reassessment of the 2001 work and a reconsideration of how his last album fits into his oeuvre.

## "Unbreakable"

Michael reportedly wanted this tough, aggressive track to be the lead single off *Invincible*, but Sony chose "You Rock My World." While the latter contains the classic Michael Jackson sound and features flirtatious lyrics, "Unbreakable" may have better established his intention to regain his title as the King of Pop. Over a hard, slamming Jerkins beat, Michael delivers his version of Elton John's "I'm Still Standing." His snarling, gritty voice convincingly conveys lines such as "And with all that I've been through / I'm still around," summing up the troubles plaguing his life and career in the 1990s. Unlike the wounded figure he portrayed in *HIStory* cuts like "Stranger in Moscow," here he exudes confidence and determined residence. "When you bury me underneath all your pain / I'm steady laughin', while surfacing," he cries, adding a sharp "ha!" after the word "laughin'."

Firmly placing the song in modern hip hop, the song samples the Notorious B.I.G. during the rap break. Taken from the 1996 track "You Can't Stop the Reign" by Shaquille O'Neal, the lines echo the bravado of the rest of the song. When Michael returns, he screams, "You can't touch me, you can't break me" with conviction, crying "g'on" in a similar manner to "The Way You Make Me Feel." The banging bass and rhythmic keyboard riffs enhance "Unbreakable's" danceability, yet the Michael and Jerkins–penned words argue that the singer has not only survived, but is thriving. When asked about the meaning of the song in the 2001 *TV Guide* interview "The Star Studded TV Special, The New Album (at Last), the Famous Friends, the 'Wacko Jacko' Image—Does It Add Up to Comeback?" he responded, "That [I'm] invincible, that I've been through it all. You can't hurt me. Knock me down, I get back up."

## "Heartbreaker"

One of *Invincible*'s most unfairly underrated tracks, "Heartbreaker" is a dancefloor burner and a sonic carnival. Another Jerkins-led production, the electronic beats, beeps, burps, and stutters predict the current popularity of dubstep. To fully appreciate the percussive sounds, listen to the track through headphones or top-of-the-line speakers. Once more Michael stretches his vocal range, singing in a slightly lower key, alternating between shouting and almost whispering. Some lyrics are surprisingly sexual for him, with Michael cooing lines such as "She's got those come-get-me thighs." Yet he simultaneously expresses innocence, claiming he never guessed that she would entrap him with her looks and actions, ultimately breaking his heart. Toward the end, Michael treats the listener to some of his patented beatboxing skills, spitting and sharply exhaling to accent the beat.

Like "Unbreakable," the song features a rap break, this time performed by Jerkins protégé Fats. The producer told MTV's Brian Hiatt in 2000 that Michael specifically asked for an unknown rapper to perform this section. "Michael [said] we need a rapper on a song, and he says he didn't want a known rapper, he wanted an unknown. So I said I got the perfect person." According to Jerkins, Michael appreciated Fats's contribution so much that he asked him to return for the album's title track.

## "Invincible"

On this hip hop–infused dance track, Michael exudes swagger as he pleads for his love interest to notice him. Co-written and produced by Jerkins, its hand-clapping rhythm is accented by the tinny melody, supplied courtesy of keyboards. Michael sputters, shouts, lets an angry raspiness creep into his voice as he sings, "If there's somebody else, he can't love you like me / And he says he'll treat you well, he can't treat you like me." Yet the woman remains unconquerable or "invincible" to his love, seemingly impervious to his wooing.

As Joseph Vogel points out in *The Man in the Music*, "Invincible" presents a confident Michael Jackson, yet "there is also a semi-detached pathos to the song as he longs for a love he seems to know will always elude him." The metallic clangs of the rhythm track and melody echo this detachment, yet the driving beat entices listeners onto the dance floor.

## "Break of Dawn"

One of *Invincible*'s highlights, this ballad features Michael in a seductive mood. Producer Dr. Freeze co-wrote and produced "Break of Dawn," an airy tribute to love in all its romantic and sexual connotations. Featuring birdsongs fluttering in the background and a plodding beat, Michael assumes the persona of "The Lady in My Life" but in a slightly more strident manner. He sings of escapism and travel, both real and in the imagination. As birds subtly chirp in the mix, he encourages his lover to walk outside with him in the park.

The title phrase, "I won't stop 'til the break of dawn," seemingly reeks of dominance, yet he also promises to "soothe" as he holds his lover's hand, keen to enjoy each other's company as well as nature. "It's the day, a brand new day, let's both go outside and play," he croons, keeping the tone light and indeed playful. "Break of Dawn" may contain the "I can love you like no other man can" trope, but the breezy arrangement provides a lush sonic cushion for Michael's voice.

## "Heaven Can Wait"

Lyrically, "Heaven Can Wait" may not be *Invincible*'s strongest track. Critics such as the *Los Angeles Times*' Hilburn cited Michael's "breathless, quivering vocal" on the track, adding that "a tale about turning away an angel who comes to take him to heaven because he wants to stay with his darling, seem aimed at the lower end of *NSYNC's fan base—a difficult stretch for a man of forty-three." Yet the offbeat rhythm pattern, plush background vocals, and Michael's earnest reading of the words still render the track a standout. Mark Anthony Neal agreed with this assessment in his SeeingBlack.com review, calling the song "one of Jackson's best vocal performances since *Thriller*'s 'Lady in My Life.' Jackson is just brilliant, alternately pleading, grunting, demanding and cooing as he brings the song home."

"Heaven Can Wait" dates from 1999, when new-jack-swing pioneer Teddy Riley (who also produced 1991's *Dangerous*) co-wrote the track with Michael. The song was originally intended for Riley's side project Blackstreet; Michael loved it so much that Riley gave it to him instead. In a 2009 interview with Hip-Hop Wired's

Allah Dasun, Riley stated that Michael told him, "I want that song. I need that song in my life." The two wanted the track to be an *Invincible* single, Riley revealed, as it was one of their favorite collaborations. In this unusual ballad, Michael pleads for more time with his lover, wanting to elude death. He even paraphrases a line from the prayer "Now I Lay Me Down to Sleep": "The world could not go on so every night I pray / If the Lord should come for me before I wake." While the lyrical content definitely does not constitute a typical love song, Michael's emotional performance and the off-kilter beat render "Heaven Can Wait" a stellar *Invincible* track.

## "You Rock My World"

The lone hit from *Invincible*, "You Rock My World" bears all the trademarks of a classic Michael Jackson song. Oddly, some critics lambasted the singer for returning to his old sound. In 2001, the *New York Times*' Jon Pareles accused him of recycling "gambits that worked in decades past," like the string arrangements in "You Rock My World," borrowed from "Don't Stop 'Til You Get Enough." Yet co-writer and producer Jerkins would argue that this was precisely the point. In his 2009 *Vibe* interview with Hobbs, Jerkins mentioned that the early material he wrote for *Invincible* was "trying to really go vintage, old-school Mike . . . He kept 'Rock My World.' But he wanted to go more futuristic."

The easygoing beat, reminiscent of "Rock with You," along with multilayered backing vocals (all performed by Michael, typical of his recordings) render "You Rock My World" a throwback to the *Off the Wall* era of sophisticated disco tracks. His flirtatious "come on's" recall "The Way You Make Me Feel," although in this case he definitely wins the girl. "Who'd think that I / Have finally found the perfect love

I searched for all my life," he sings, using a lower register. Even though the woman has changed his life, he sounds content with her rocking his world with her love. One of the sincerest moments on *Invincible* occurs in this song, when he croons, "Girl, I know that this is love / I felt the magic all in the air," a faint jingling sound accenting the feeling. It recalls the earlier, innocent, playful Michael Jackson that had been largely absent on *HIStory* and *Blood on the Dance Floor*, and it's a welcome return.

"You Rock My World" received radio airplay in the US, but the CD single was released only internationally.    *Author's collection*

## "Butterflies"

Written by Marsha Ambrosius, one half of the neo-soul duo Floetry, "Butterflies" is now considered one of Michael's best tracks. As Vogel writes in *Man in the Music*, "It reminds people of what made Jackson's voice such a revelation in the first place, yet benefits from added maturity and sophistication."

The track originally appeared on the group's 2002 debut *Floetic* (best known for its sultry hit "Say Yes") and was brought to Michael's attention by mutual friend and business associate John McClain. After hearing the track, Michael invited Floetry to the studio to work on his vocal arrangements. Floetry member Natalie Stewart recalled the experience in a December 2, 2010, interview with Yazmar, stating that "it was a beautiful experience, and I learned a lot. I took away a lot . . . He had a huge sign on the wall that said 'No B-Sides,' and that read very deeply into my spirit."

Producer Andre Harris oversaw the production, with Ambrosius spending two to three weeks working on vocals with Michael. In a 2014 interview with the Urban Daily, she reported that he was a professional in the studio, frequently asking her advice on his singing. Earlier, Ambrosius had told Yahoo Music's Billy Johnson Jr., "It was incredible, because he continually asked, 'Marsh, what's the next harmony? Girls, does this sound right? What do you think? Is this what you were looking for?' He was so open."

The collaboration worked on several levels. The lovely lyrics capture the first blush of love, and the song challenged Michael to use the full range of his voice. "I caress you, let you taste, it's just so blissful / I would give you anything, just make my dreams come true," he sings, his voice rising a bit higher on every word until climaxing on "make my dreams come true." The lovely melody, accompanied by a gentle but hip hop–grounded beat, contributes to one of Michael's best cuts since his *Off the Wall* days.

## "2000 Watts"

Featuring uncharacteristically deep Michael vocals and a rhythm track reproducing the sound of screeching tires, "2000 Watts" hardly represents the singer's typical material. Co-written by Tyrese and Teddy Riley, the track was originally intended for Tyrese; when Michael heard the demo, he loved it so much that Tyrese agreed to hand it over. An ode to technology and music with a hint of sexuality, "2000 Watts" represents one of Michael's more aggressive dance floor burners: "3-D, high speed, feedback, Dolby / Release two or three, when I reach I can go 'til I hit my peak," he purrs in an uncharacteristically low voice.

The *Invincible* track demonstrates how Michael continually experimented with his voice and explored different musical genres. "2000 Watts" may be rooted firmly in the dance arena, but his virtually unrecognizable vocals and the song's hard, mechanical edge distinguish it from virtually any other Michael Jackson song.

## "Cry"

The second of Michael's three collaborations with R. Kelly (the other two being "You Are Not Alone" and "One More Chance"), "Cry" typifies Michael's love for sweeping message tracks. Andraé Crouch returns to conduct the choir answering Michael's pleas: "You can change the world," the choir harmonizes; "I can't do it by myself!" Michael cries in response. The lyrics call for empathy, that people should weep together to lament wars, violence, and child neglect.

Released as the third single off *Invincible*, it was accompanied by a video, although Michael did not appear in it. Instead, it featured an international, multi-racial, multigenerational line of people holding hands. The CD single was released with two B-sides: the *Bad* outtake "Streetwalker" and "Shout," a hard-driving rock track that just missed the cut for *Invincible*. According to *For the Record*'s Cadman and Halstead, "You Are My Life" replaced "Shout" just before the album's release. In retrospect, "Shout" would have made for an intriguing addition to *Invincible*, as it further exemplifies Michael's obvious affection for electric guitar-driven rockers.

## "Whatever Happens"

The final track on the official *Invincible* release as well as this proposed "pared-down" version, "Whatever Happens" marks yet another sonic departure for the singer. The Latin flavors, lovely acoustic guitar, and piercing solo by legendary musician Carlos Santana all cushion Michael's wide-ranging vocal performance. At times soft and lilting, at other moments raspy and almost screaming, Michael tests the limits of his voice on this cut. Toward the end of the track, one can hear Michael furiously clapping into the mic as he spits out the lyrics, as if completely absorbed in the music.

Of all the *Invincible* tracks, "Whatever Happens" was almost unanimously praised by critics. *Rolling Stone*'s December 6, 2001, review called it "an exceptional song" where Michael sings "in the third person with a jagged intensity." Michael and co-producer Riley created something "handsome and smart," according to reviewer James Hunter, allowing listeners to "concentrate on the track's momentous rhythms, Santana's passionate interjections and [Jeremy] Lubbock's wonderfully arranged symphonic sweeps."

## Another Listen

The beginning of this chapter posed a question: is *Invincible* really a weak album deserving of its negative reviews and disappointing sales? Clearing away the clutter surrounding its 2001 debut allows listeners to experience the album in a new way. Yes, some tracks suffer from too many producers and songwriters; the length deterred some fans; and the album lacks the tight focus of *Off the Wall* and *Thriller*. Yet it does contain some buried gems that deserve to be heard, and its harder dance tracks sound at home with today's techno and dance-driven pop. This chapter's proposed "Alternate Version" of *Invincible* uncovers its underrated songs and invites another perspective on Michael's final album.

# 36

# I Sure Would Like Just to Groove with You

## Notable TV and Concert Appearances

T he 1980s and beyond saw a drastic change in Michael Jackson's concert and television appearances. After his negative experience working on the CBS network's *Jacksons* variety show, he vowed to focus strictly on concerts and music videos. Despite this declaration, he occasionally performed on awards shows, guest starred on TV specials, and filmed concerts for HBO and CBS.

### TV Appearances

The following list highlights some of his most significant television appearances; for the purposes of this book, only shows where he sang at least one song are included (with one notable exception). Some solo performances during the Jackson 5 years are also listed.

### March 27, 1973: *45th Annual Academy Awards* (NBC)

Michael's first solo single, "Ben," was nominated for Best Original song. After Charlton Heston introduced him, Michael performed the track in front of a live audience. Unfortunately, "Ben" lost to "The Morning After" from *The Poseidon Adventure.*

### March 11, 1974: *Free to Be . . .You and Me* (ABC)

Actress Marlo Thomas and the *Ms.* Foundation for Women partnered to produce *Free to Be . . . You and Me,* a children's book, record, and TV special that celebrated gender equality, tolerance, and self-esteem. In the ABC television special, Thomas and other prominent celebrities sing and perform skits teaching life lessons to young viewers. One of the program's most memorable segments is a duet between Roberta Flack and a teenage Michael entitled "When We Grow Up," a song that promotes acceptance each other's differences as well as self-confidence. Flack and Michael romp around a playroom, trying on "grown-up" costumes and wondering what they will look like as adults. Ultimately, they harmonize, "We don't have to change at all."

## March 2, 1981: *Diana* (CBS)

Diana Ross starred in this CBS-TV special, which was later nominated for a Golden Globe for Best TV Special, Variety/Musical. Fresh off his *Off the Wall* and *Triumph* successes, Michael appeared with his onetime mentor to perform two songs. Shot in front of an audience at the KTTV studios in Los Angeles, Michael sings an electric version of "Rock with You," resplendent in his then-customary sparkly tuxedo. Ross joins him for a brief reprise of the song, then the two perform a live rendition of "Ease on Down the Road." With Quincy Jones playing piano behind them, the two reenact their choreography from *The Wiz* (with Michael smirking when Ross apparently comes in too late on a lyric). One of the show's most charming moments occurs when Michael and Ross sit down for a flirtatious chat, each teasing the other about sexiness.

## May 16, 1983: *Motown 25: Yesterday, Today, Forever* (NBC)

This milestone in Michael's career is discussed in detail in chapter 28.

## February 28, 1984: *26th Annual Grammy Awards* (CBS)

Michael did not perform during the ceremony, but his appearance ranks as one of his most important television moments. At the peak of his power, he won a record eight awards during the broadcast. This telecast attracted the largest viewership in Grammy history, with 43.8 viewers tuning in to watch Michael win Record of the Year ("Beat It,"), Album of the Year, Best Recording for Children (*E.T. the Extra-Terrestrial*), Best Pop Performance, Male ("Thriller"), Best R&B Vocal Performance, Male ("Billie Jean"), Best Rhythm & Blues Song ("Billie Jean"), Best Rock Vocal Performance, Male ("Beat It"), and Producer of the Year (shared with Quincy Jones). Bruce Swedien won Best Engineered Recording, Non-Classical, for *Thriller*.

## March 2, 1988: *30th Annual Grammy Awards* (CBS)

In one of his finest solo performances, Michael delivers powerful renditions of "The Way You Make Me Feel" and "Man in the Mirror." The latter song features a live choir and live, improvised vocals by Michael toward the track's end. Unfortunately, *Bad* won in only one of its four nominated categories: Best Engineered Recording, Non-Classical, for Bruce Swedien and Humberto Gatica.

## February 4, 1990: *Sammy Davis Jr. 60th Anniversary Special* (ABC)

Taped at the Shrine Auditorium, Los Angeles, this star-packed tribute to the show business legend celebrated his sixty years in entertainment. However, it also served to fete a clearly frail Davis, who passed away weeks after the show's broadcast. To salute his idol, Michael co-wrote the song "You Were There" the night before the taping, the lyrics addressing how Davis had opened the door for future African American entertainers. Singing it live, Michael gives an emotional delivery to Davis, who sits in the box seats just feet from the stage. At the song's end, he walks over and warmly embraces the clearly moved veteran. Michael never performed the track again.

## June 6, 1991: *MTV 10th Anniversary Special*

It came as no surprise that Michael would participate in this program celebrating the network's tenth anniversary. In front of a live audience, Michael lip-synchs to "Black or White" as his friend Slash performed a new guitar solos. The set slightly resembles the "panther" sequence from the music video, with Michael climbing on top of a graffiti-covered car (and Slash dramatically throwing his guitar through one of the car's windows at the song's conclusion). He closed his mini-concert with a rendition of "Will You Be There," complete with a choir and a Broadway-inspired dance number.

## October 10, 1992: *Live in Bucharest: The Dangerous Tour* (HBO)

Recorded at Michael's October 1 show in Bucharest, this concert was broadcast on HBO nine days later. The first time a full Michael Jackson concert had ever been broadcast, the show garnered the highest ratings in HBO's history and earned Michael a Cable ACE Award. According to a *New York Times* report titled "Michael Jackson, Live, on HBO in October," published on August 13, 1992, it also represented the largest financial deal for a concert performance on television. The article cited undisclosed sources as stating the figure was close to $20 million, with HBO chairman and CEO Michael Fuchs bragging, "With no US tour planned in the near future, this special HBO event could be the only chance that American audiences will have to see Michael Jackson in full concert for years."

## January 19, 1993: *An American Reunion: The 52nd Presidential Inaugural Gala* (CBS)

Top music stars participated in President Bill Clinton's inauguration, including Michael. He performed "Gone Too Soon" in honor of friend Ryan White, who had recently died of complications from AIDS. After offering a rendition of "Heal the World," he ended the evening by joining Fleetwood Mac and other artists onstage for a group sing-along of the band's "Don't Stop" (which had served as the President's campaign theme song).

## January 25, 1993: *American Music Awards* (ABC)

Michael opened the ceremony with "Dangerous," which featured similar choreography to Judy Garland's "Get Happy" segment from the film *Summer Stock*. The performance earned him an ecstatic standing ovation.

## January 31, 1993: Super Bowl XXVII Halftime Show (NBC)

Holding the coveted position of halftime entertainer, Michael turned in a medley of hits at the Rose Bowl Stadium in Pasadena, California, before an audience of 100,000 in the stadium and between 90 and 100 million television viewers.

In his usual dramatic fashion, Michael makes a grand entrance, catapulted onstage as fireworks were set off behind him. Standing perfectly still for a minute and a half as the audience cheered, he finally removes his sunglasses and launches into his set, which includes brief renditions of "Jam," "Billie Jean," Black or White," "We Are the World" (sung by children's choir), and "Heal the World" (with a group of international children standing around him and a choir as he lip-synchs the track).

According to a *New York Times* article from June 29, 2009, "How Jackson Redefined the Super Bowl," Michael's show signified more than just a spectacular set. Traditionally, the NFL had offered halftime shows featuring less-than-youthful talent such as Carol Channing, Pete Fountain, and the Rockettes; the singing and dancing collective Up with People was the closest the Super Bowl came to "young, hip" entertainment. Wanting to attract the desired eighteen-to-thirty-four demographic, the NFL tapped Michael to head the halftime show. Not only did he attract the desired audience, he accomplished another feat: he raised the halftime show ratings higher than the game before it. From then on, the Super Bowl became an event rather than simply a game; today, only major music stars are granted the honor of leading the halftime extravaganza.

Jim Steeg, one the founders of the NFL's special events department, recalled Michael's incredible preparation: "Michael worked harder than anybody [who's done the halftime show], before or since," Steeg told *Sports Illustrated*'s Austin Murphy. He added that he remembered seeing the singer still rehearsing his show the night before the game in a tent outside the stadium.

## March 9, 1993: *Soul Train Music Awards* (WGN America)

In an unusual performance, filmed at the Shrine Auditorium, Los Angeles, Michael lip-synchs "Remember the Time," dressed in costume from the song's video, but in a wheelchair. He later revealed he had injured his ankle while rehearsing, preventing him from dancing. The *Los Angeles Times*' Dennis Hunt wrote in "Jackson Shows Up to Gather Awards, Despite Ankle Injury," that the singer staged a "show-stopping production number" despite the handicap, adding that the *Soul Train Awards* was just one more stop in Michael's continuing "media blitz."

## March 13, 1995: *Soul Train Music Awards* (WGN America)

Returning to the Shrine Auditorium two years later, Michael performs "Dangerous" using the same routine as in previous appearances. He returns later, standing alone, for a rendition of "You Are Not Alone." At first dressed in his "Dangerous" suit and tie, he gradually loosens his tie, unbuttons his shirt, then flirts with audience members who present him flowers. A woman even rushes the stage! For the finale, he calls up adult and child choral groups and improvises live alongside them. While the performance may have been choreographed, he appeared more relaxed, playful, and willing to interact with the audience than in usual TV performances.

## February 25, 1997: *Happy Birthday, Elizabeth: A Celebration of Life* (ABC)

During this special celebrating the actress's sixty-fifth birthday, Michael performs "Elizabeth, I Love You," a song he had recorded in Montreux, Switzerland, in her honor. This appearance would mark the only time he ever performed the track in public.

## September 6, 2001: *MTV Music Video Awards*

While Michael does not sing, he makes a surprise cameo appearance during *NYNC's performance of "Pop." Just as the song has apparently ended, Michael emerges from behind a screen and busts some moves with the group.

## November 13, 2001: *Michael Jackson: 30th Anniversary Special* (CBS)

To mark his thirtieth year in entertainment and promote his upcoming album *Invincible*, Michael held two Madison Square Garden concerts on September 7 and September 10, 2001. Boasting a roster of top artists as well as Michael and his brothers, the two shows were edited into a two-hour November 2001 special. The first hour features tributes from artists such as Whitney Houston, Usher, Mya, and Destiny's Child; the second shows Michael performing his greatest hits, and includes a Jackson 5 reunion. A particular highlight was Michael's rendition of "The Way You Make Me Feel," with Britney Spears acting as the object of his affections. As she giggles, Michael and his dancers reenact the choreography from the original video.

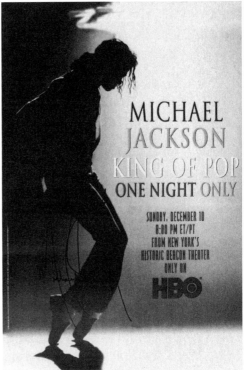

HBO relentlessly promoted *Michael Jackson: One Night Only*, a show scheduled to air on December 10, 1995, following tapings on December 8 and 9 in front of a live audience at New York's Beacon Theatre. Just two days after appearing at a December 4 press conference with Marcel Marceau, however, Michael collapsed during rehearsals, forcing HBO to cancel the show.
*Author's collection*

The special garnered CBS some of its highest ratings of 2001—according to the MTV article "Michael Jackson Special to Re-Air, with Britney This Time," it was the network's biggest Tuesday night program (except sports programming) since 1994, attracting forty-five million viewers.

Michael's set lists included the following songs:

**Friday, September 7**

With the Jacksons:
- "Can You Feel It"
- "HIStory Intro"
- "I Want You Back"
- "Shake Your Body (Down to the Ground)"

- "ABC"
- "The Love You Save"
- "I'll Be There"
- "Dancing Machine" (with *NSYNC)

Solo:
- "The Way You Make Me Feel" (with Britney Spears)
- "Black or White" (with Slash)
- "Beat It" (with Slash)
- "Billie Jean"
- "You Rock My World"

**Monday, September 10**

With the Jacksons:
- "Can You Feel It"
- "HIStory Intro"
- "ABC"
- "The Love You Save"
- "I'll Be There"
- "I Want You Back"

The Jacksons:
- "Dancing Machine"
- "Shake Your Body (Down to the Ground)"

Solo:
- "The Way You Make Me Feel"
- "Black or White" (with Slash)
- "Beat It" (with Slash)
- "Billie Jean"
- "You Rock My World" (with Usher and Chris Tucker)
- "We Are the World" (with all of the above guest artists, plus Kenny Rogers, Yoko Ono, and Quincy Jones)
- "You Rock My World (Reprise)"

## May 3, 2002: *American Bandstand's 50th: A Celebration* (ABC)

Filmed at California's Pasadena Civic Auditorium on April 20, 2002, this concert celebrated the fiftieth anniversary of the longtime teenage dance show. Michael performs "Dangerous" with a group of backup dancers clad in suits, ties, and hats. Suggesting a number out of a Fred Astaire film, he leads the men in precise, tight choreography. According to Chris Cadman's *Michael Jackson: The Maestro*, the singer asked to repeat the performance, as he was unhappy with his first attempt.

## June 24, 2002: *A Night at the Apollo* (C-SPAN)

Taped on April 24, 2002, and later broadcast on the C-SPAN channel, this National Democratic Committee Fundraiser generated $2.5 million for a nationwide voter-registration drive. Introduced by Bill Clinton, Michael lip-synchs to "Dangerous," "Black or White" (with special guest Dave Navarro), and "Heal the World." Diana Ross joins him onstage for the final song. Sadly, this event marked Michael's last public performance.

## Music Videos

Throughout his solo career, Michael's music videos comprised much of his television presence. Aired on MTV, VH1, and international music video channels as well as during shows such as *Soul Train*, *American Bandstand*, NBC's *Friday Night Videos*, and *America's Top 10 with Casey Kasem*, these videos revolutionized the music video as an art form. Many of these clips are discussed in detail in other chapters, but the following list presents a brief videography, including year and director. Only individual videos that were officially released are included; the long-form films *Moonwalker* and *Ghosts* are discussed elsewhere in this book. Posthumous videos are excluded.

- "Don't Stop 'Til You Get Enough" (1979, Nick Saxton)
- "Rock with You" (1980, Bruce Gowers)
- "She's Out of My Life" (1980, Bruce Gowers)
- "Billie Jean" (1983, Steve Barron)
- "Beat It" (1983, Bob Giraldi)
- "Thriller" (1983, John Landis)
- "Say Say Say" (1983, Bob Giraldi)
- "We Are the World" (USA for Africa, 1985, Tom Trbovich)
- "Bad" (1987, Martin Scorsese)
- "The Way You Make Me Feel" (1987, Joe Pytka)
- "Man in the Mirror" (1988, Donald Wilson)
- "Dirty Diana" (1988, Joe Pytka)
- "Smooth Criminal" (1988, Colin Chilvers)
- "Another Part of Me" (1988, Patrick Kelly)
- "Leave Me Alone" (1989, Jim Blashfield)
- "2300 Jackson Street" (with the Jacksons, 1989, Grey Gold)
- "Liberian Girl" (1989, Jim Yukich)
- "Black or White" (1991, John Landis)
- "Remember the Time" (1992, John Singleton)
- "In the Closet" (1992, Herb Ritts)
- "Jam" (1992, David Kellogg)
- "Heal the World" (1992, Joe Pytka)
- "Give in to Me" (1993, Andy Moharan)
- "Who Is It" (1993, David Fincher)
- "Will You Be There" (1993, Vincent Paterson)
- "Whatzupwitu" (with Eddie Murphy, 1993, Wayne Isham)
- "Gone Too Soon" (1993, Bill DiCicco)
- "HIStory Teaser" (1995, Rupert Wainwright)
- "Scream" (with Janet Jackson, 1995, Mark Romanek)
- "Childhood" (1995, Nicholas Brandt)
- "You Are Not Alone" (1995, Wayne Isham)
- "Earth Song" (1995, Nicholas Brandt)
- "Why" (with 3T, 1996, Ralph Ziman)
- "They Don't Care About Us" (Brazil and prison versions, 1996, Spike Lee)
- "Stranger in Moscow" (1996, Nicholas Brandt)
- "Blood on the Dance Floor" (single and Refugee Camp Mix versions, 1997, Michael Jackson and Vincent Paterson)
- "Ghosts" (1997, Stan Winston)
- "You Rock My World" (2001, Paul Hunter)
- "Cry" (2001, Nicholas Brandt)
- "What More Can I Give" (2001, Michael Jackson & Friends)
- "One More Chance" (2003, Nicholas Brandt)

# Concerts

Other than in his music videos, Michael fully established his independence from his family through his concert tours. Starting in 1987, he would assume full control over set design, costumes, choreography, band members, and set lists. The *Bad* World Tour included a few key Jackson 5 songs but mainly focused on his solo material, demonstrating how he had artistically distanced himself from the Jackson 5 or the Jacksons. During his three full tours, Michael broke attendance records and raised the creative bar with each successive show. Unlike other musicians from the era, he fully integrated his most iconic music videos into the show, reenacting the "Thriller" choreography and wearing a similar costume to the multi-buckled jacket and pants he sported in the "Bad" video. From pyrotechnics to innovative dance, Michael established a new standard for rock concerts that today's artists still emulate.

## 1987–89: *Bad* World Tour

Michael's first solo tour, this 123-concert venture was seen by 4.4 million people. By the end of the almost two-year tour he had grossed over $125 million—a record for a single artist.

In the 1990s, the tour became famous for another reason: it introduced the world to Sheryl Crow, the then-unknown backup singer who went on to release the smash 1993 album *Tuesday Night Music Club*. She has since released seven more studio albums, won nine Grammy Awards, and sold over fifty million albums worldwide. In several interviews published after Michael's death, she cited her experience touring with him as one of the happiest times in her professional and personal life. "My most beloved memory, however, was watching him perform 'Human Nature' every night from the side of the stage," Crow told *Time* for its 2009 Michael Jackson tribute. "There was something so genuinely vulnerable in his voice on that song, and watching the freedom with which he danced, doing the moves he invented only made me more keenly aware of the greatness I was blessed to be witnessing."

### First Leg (1987)

The first leg of the tour opened with fourteen sell-out shows in Japan before moving on to Australia.

- September 12–14, 1987: Korakuen Stadium, Tokyo, Japan.
- September 19–21: Hankyu Nishinomiya Stadium, Nishinomiya, Japan
- September 25–27, October 3–4: Yokohama Stadium, Yokohama, Japan
- October 10–12: Osaka Stadium, Osaka, Japan
- November 13: Olympic Park Stadium, Melbourne, Australia
- November 20–21: Parramatta Stadium, Sydney, Australia
- November 27–28: Brisbane Entertainment Centre, Brisbane, Australia: Surprise guest Stevie Wonder joined Michael onstage during the November 28 date to perform "Bad," according to Chris Cadman and Craig Halstead's *Michael Jackson: For the Record*. Other sources reported them duetting on the *Bad* track "Just Good Friends."

## Set List

Michael played the following set during the first leg of the tour:

- "Wanna Be Startin' Somethin'"
- "Things I Do for You"
- "Off the Wall"
- "Human Nature"
- "Heartbreak Hotel"
- "She's Out of My Life"
- "Jackson 5 Medley"
- "Rock with You"
- "Lovely One"
- "Working Day and Night"
- "Beat It"
- "Billie Jean"
- "Shake Your Body (Down to the Ground)"
- "Thriller"
- "I Just Can't Stop Loving You"
- "Bad"

### Second Leg (1988–89)

The second leg of the *Bad* tour began with two months of shows in the US followed by shows in Europe and beyond.

The highly successful *Bad* Tour circumnavigated the globe, with one stop being a three-night stand at Pittsburgh's Civic Arena in 1988.    *Author's collection*

- February 23–24: Kemper Arena, Kansas City, Missouri
- March 3, 5–6: Madison Square Garden, New York, New York
- March 13: St. Louis Arena, St. Louis, Missouri
- March 18–19: Market Square Arena, Indianapolis, Indiana
- March 20: Freedom Hall, Louisville, Kentucky
- March 24–26: McNichols Sports Arena, Denver, Colorado
- March 30–31, April 1: Hartford Civic Arena, Hartford, Connecticut
- April 8–10: The Summit, Houston, Texas
- April 13–15: The Omni, Atlanta, Georgia
- April 19–21: Rosemont Horizon, Rosemont, Illinois
- April 25–27: Reunion Arena, Dallas, Texas
- May 4–6: Met Center, Minneapolis, Minnesota: The *Minneapolis Star Tribune* published an ecstatic review of the May 5 show, singling out Michael's "nasty phrasing" during "Working Day and Night" and his passionate performance of "Man in the Mirror," adding that he seemed to lose himself in the lyrics' emotion. "He's electrifying to watch. He shimmies, shakes, locks and pops, karate kicks, and he does his patented moonwalk," wrote Jon Bream. "He's the baddest dancer among pop music stars, the song-and-dance man of the rock generation."

- May 23–24: Stadio Flaminio, Rome, Italy
- May 29: Stadio Olimpico di Torino, Turin, Italy
- June 2: Prater Stadium, Vienna, Austria
- June 5–7: Feijenoord Stadium, Rotterdam, Netherlands
- June 11–12: Eriksberg Docks Grounds, Gothenburg, Sweden
- June 16: St. Jakob Stadium, Basel, Switzerland
- June 19: Reichstag Grounds, West Berlin, West Germany
- June 27–28: Parc des Princes Stadium, Paris, France
- July 1: Volkspark Stadium, Hamburg, West Germany
- July 3: Mungersdorfer Stadium, Cologne, West Germany
- July 8: Olympic Stadium, Munich, West Germany
- July 10: Hockenheimring, Hockenheim, West Germany
- July 14–16, 22–23: Wembley Stadium, London, England: Michael's Wembley concerts remain among the most significant of his career. He set the world record for playing the most concerts at the venue: seven sold-out dates, entertaining over 504,000 fans. Despite the legendary status of the shows, no official tour footage was released until 2012's *Bad 25* boxed set, which includes the DVD and CD *Live at Wembley July 16, 1988*. The DVD became available for separate purchase soon afterward.
- While audiences clearly packed the stadium to see the superstar, not all critics were impressed. *Sounds* critic Mat Snow appreciated Michael's dancing most: "As it proceeds, you adjust to the idea that Michael at Wembley is better considered a ballet than a concert. His feet upstage everything. From the staccato blur of white socks upwards, you've never seen a dancer so fascinated by the mechanics of his own body." In addition, Snow singled out the "Man in the Mirror" segment as "one of the most strangely moving things I've ever seen. On record a slice of born-again self-improvement, live it embraces the sky in a fervor of gospel choir tinged with the sad afterglow of Prince's 'The Cross.'"
- One of England's most famous rock critics, John Peel, admitted his initial skepticism about the show. "As the costume changes came and went and the stage and lighting effects grew more audacious, he took control with a performance of matchless virtuosity," he wrote, in the *Observer*. "My only wish is that my children could have been there to see this stupendous performance. It is something they would never have forgotten."
- July 26: Cardiff Arms Park, Cardiff, Wales: Playing to over 55,000 fans, the singer drew not only impressive crowds but also months of pre-concert hype. The *Western Mail*'s Mike Smith, in his review dated July 26, 1988, reported that Michael did not disappoint. Critiquing Michael's rendition of "She's Out of My Life," Smith stated, "Jackson doesn't just sing a ballad, he lives it, interrupting the song to wander around the stage, face buried in a hand, wringing out the emotions, and returning to complete it." The venue "erupted" at "Dirty Diana," the latest hit off *Bad*, then enthusiastically reacted to the "moondance," as Smith put it, during "Billie Jean." Overall, he concluded, "What set Jackson apart was that incredible dancing and gesture, perfectly choreographed, that brought theatre and dance to the rock concert."
- July 30–31: Páirc Uí Chaoimh, Cork, Ireland

- August 5: Estadio Municipal de Marbella, Marbella, Spain
- August 7: Vincente Calderon Stadium, Madrid, Spain
- August 9: Nou Camp Stadium, Barcelona, Spain
- August 12: Stade Richter, Montpellier, France
- August 14: Stade Charles Ehrmann, Nice, France
- August 19: La Pontaise, Lausanne, Switzerland
- August 21: Talavera Weisen, Würzburg, West Germany
- August 23: Werchter Festival Grounds, Werchter, Belgium
- August 26–27: Wembley Stadium, London, England
- August 29: Roundhay Park, Leeds, England: Over 90,000 fans serenaded Michael with "Happy Birthday" before he launched into "Another Part of Me." He had just turned thirty years old.

Michael played seven sold-out out shows to a total of 504,000 people at London's Wembley Stadium, breaking previous attendance records set by artists such as Madonna, Bruce Springsteen, and Genesis.

*Author's collection*

- September 2: Niedersachsen Stadium, Hanover, West Germany
- September 4: Park Stadium, Gelsenkirchen, West Germany
- September 6: Linzer Stadium, Linz, Austria
- September 10: The Bowl, Milton Keynes, England: *Melody Maker*'s Carol Clerk ran a review of the show in the magazine's issue dated September 17, 1988, describing it a spectacle of pyrotechnics, spectacular dancing, and elaborate costumes. She added that she enjoyed "the wonderful ham acting of Michael, 'overcome with emotion,' head in hands for long, long seconds, before being able to sing out the last word of 'She's Out of My Life.'"
- September 11: Aintree Racecourse, Liverpool, England: This stop on the *Bad* Tour set another attendance record: 120,000 people.
- September 26–28: Civic Arena, Pittsburgh, Pennsylvania
- October 3–5: Meadowlands Arena, East Rutherford, New Jersey
- October 10–11: Richfield Coliseum, Cleveland, Ohio
- October 13, 17–19: Capital Center, Landover, Maryland: The *Columbia Flier* ran a multi-review, as Prince and Luther Vandross had also recently played concerts at the venue. For Geoffrey Himes, the special effects and choreography lacked spontaneity. "He was so obsessed with keeping perfect control over his public mask that no hint of the private man ever leaked out," he wrote. "His show was a relentless barrage of special effects-exploding flashpots, streaking green

lasers and synchronized Broadway choreography meant to distract one from the show's utter lack of spontaneity or personality."

- October 24–26: The Palace of Auburn Hills, Detroit, Michigan
- November 7–9: Irvine Meadows Amphitheater, Irvine, California
- November 13: Memorial Sports Arena, Los Angeles, California
- December 9–11, 17–19, 24–26: Tokyo Dome, Tokyo, Japan
- January 16–18, 26–27, 1989: Memorial Sports Arena, Los Angeles, California: Michael concluded the very successful *Bad* Tour with a series of five sold-out shows in Los Angeles. After playing to 86,882 fans (including celebrities such as Sylvester Stallone, Yoko Ono with her son Sean Ono Lennon, and Elizabeth Taylor), he donated the proceeds from one of the nights to Childhelp USA, a nonprofit child-abuse-prevention program.

**Set List**

Michael performed the following songs on the second leg of the *Bad* tour:

- "Wanna Be Startin' Somethin'"
- "Heartbreak Hotel"
- "Another Part of Me"
- "I Just Can't Stop Loving You" (duet with backup singer Sheryl Crow)
- "She's Out of My Life"
- "Jackson 5 Medley"
- "Rock with You"
- "Human Nature"
- "Smooth Criminal"
- "Dirty Diana"
- "Thriller"
- "Working Day and Night"
- "Beat It"
- "Billie Jean"
- "Bad"
- "The Way You Make Me Feel"
- "Man in the Mirror"

## 1992–93: Dangerous World Tour

Unlike the *Bad* Tour, the *Dangerous* World Tour reached mostly international audiences. Profits were donated to various charities, notably Michael's newly formed Heal the World Foundation. This time he played sixty-nine concerts, which were seen by approximately 3.5 million people. Upping the ante in special effects, Michael concluded each performance by appearing to put on a jetpack, blasting off, and flying over the crowd's heads and out of the venue. The *Dangerous* Tour was supposed to have a longer duration, but Michael ended it abruptly for health reasons.

### First Leg (1992)

The *Dangerous* tour began with Michael performing to a sell-out crowd of 72,000 in Munich, Germany.

- June 27: Olympiastadion, Munich, Germany
- June 30, July 1: Feijenoord Stadium, Rotterdam, Netherlands
- July 4: Stadio Flaminio, Rome, Italy
- July 6–7: Stadio Brianteo, Monza, Italy
- July 11: Müngersdorfer Stadion, Cologne, Germany
- July 15: Valle Hovin, Oslo, Norway

- July 17–18: Stockholm Olympic Stadium, Stockholm, Sweden
- July 20: Gentofte Stadion, Gentofte, Denmark
- July 22: Werchter Festival Ground, Werchter, Belgium
- July 25: Lansdowne Road, Dublin, Ireland
- July 30–31: Wembley Stadium, London, England
- August 5: Cardiff Arms Park, Cardiff, Wales
- August 8: Weserstadion, Bremen, Germany
- August 10: Volksparkstadion, Hamburg, Germany
- August 13: Weserberglandstadion, Hamelin, Germany
- August 16: Roundhay Park, Leeds, England
- August 18: Glasgow Green, Glasgow, Scotland
- August 20, 22–23: Wembley Stadium, London, England
- August 26: Praterstadion, Vienna, Austria
- August 28: Waldstadion, Frankfurt, Germany
- August 30: Südweststadion, Ludwigshafen, Germany
- September 2: Wild Stadion, Bayreuth, Germany
- September 4: Jahn Stadion, Berlin, Germany
- September 8: Stade Olympique de la Pontaise, Lausanne, Switzerland
- September 13: Hippodrome de Vincennes, Paris, France
- September 16: Stadium Municipal de Toulouse, Toulouse, France
- September 18: Estadi Olímpic Lluís Companys, Barcelona, Spain
- September 21: Estadio Carlos Tartiere, Oviedo, Spain
- September 23: Estadio Vicente Calderón, Madrid, Spain
- September 26: Estádio José Alvalade, Lisbon, Portugal
- October 1: Lia Manoliu Stadium, Bucharest, Romania: Michael's Bucharest stop was filmed and subsequently shown on HBO (as detailed in the television appearances section above). Shown in over sixty countries, it was eventually released on DVD in 2004 as part of the *Ultimate Collection* boxed set; the following year it was reissued as *Live in Bucharest: The Dangerous Tour*, and included footage from his London and Madrid stops.
- December 12, 14, 17, 19, 22, 24, 30, 31: Tokyo Dome, Tokyo, Japan: Longtime friend Slash joined Michael onstage during the December 30 and 31 shows to play guitar on "Black or White."

**Set List**

The set list for these shows comprised the following songs:

- "Jam"
- "Wanna Be Startin' Somethin'"
- "Human Nature"
- "Smooth Criminal"
- "I Just Can't Stop Loving You"
- "She's Out of My Life"
- "Jackson 5 Medley"
- "Thriller"
- "Billie Jean"
- "Black or White" video interlude
- "Working Day and Night"
- "Beat It"
- "Someone Put Your Hand Out" (instrumental)
- "Will You Be There"
- "The Way You Make Me Feel" (performed from Munich to Oslo, and also in Tokyo)

- "Bad" (performed from Munich to Oslo, and also in Tokyo)
- "Black or White"
- "We Are the World" (video interlude)
- "Heal the World"
- "Man in the Mirror"

## Second Leg (1993)

The second leg of the *Dangerous* tour took Michael further afield, and included shows in Asia, Europe, and South America. Michael concluded the tour with five sold-out shows in Mexico City, attended by at least 500,000 people.

- August 24, 27: Suphachalasai Stadium, Bangkok, Thailand: Originally, Michael was scheduled to perform on August 25, but had to postpone the show due to severe dehydration. On August 27 he finally played the show, with a capacity audience of 70,000 in attendance.
- August 29, September 1: Singapore National Stadium, Singapore: During the show, the 47,000-capacity audience sang "Happy Birthday" to the singer on his thirty-fifth birthday.
- September 4, 6: Taipei Municipal Stadium, Taipei, Taiwan
- September 10–11: Fukuoka Dome, Fukuoka, Japan
- September 15: Luzhniki Stadium, Moscow, Russia: This ill-fated concert became one of the most controversial stops on the *Dangerous* Tour. Over 20,000 seats remained empty; the cool, rainy weather dampened the proceedings; and the show began over two hours late. Many soaked fans had already departed, and as the *Chicago Tribune*'s James P. Gallagher reported, those who stayed did not count themselves as ardent fans. Thus only a few songs received an enthusiastic reception (such as "Black or White"), as many tracks were unknown in Russia. An ill-tempered air swept over the crowd, as evidenced by the moment when a fan somehow ran onto the stage. After hugging her, Jackson appeared to cry, causing some in the audience to chant "Fake! Fake!"
- Overall, ticket sales disappointed, with prices slashed days before the concert; according to the *Tribune* article, some attendees reported receiving free tickets through their jobs. A documentary about the troubled event, *Michael Jackson: Moscow Case 1993*, was released in 2013.
- September 19, 21: Yarkon Park, Tel Aviv, Israel
- September 23: İnönü Stadium, Istanbul, Turkey
- September 26: Port of Santa Cruz de Tenerife, Tenerife, Canary Islands
- October 8, 10, 12, 1993: Estadio River Plate, Buenos Aires, Argentina
- October 15, 17: Estádio do Morumbi, Sao Paulo, Brazil
- October 23: Estadio Nacional, Santiago, Chile
- October 29, 31, November 7, 9, 11: Estadio Azteca, Mexico City, Mexico

## Set List

Michael's set list for these shows included:

- "Jam"
- "Wanna Be Startin' Somethin'"
- "Human Nature"
- "Smooth Criminal"
- "I Just Can't Stop Loving You" (featuring Siedah Garrett)
- "She's Out of My Life"
- "Jackson 5 Medley"

- "Thriller"
- "Billie Jean"
- "Black or White" (panther video interlude)
- "Someone Put Your Hand Out" (instrumental)

- "Will You Be There"
- "Dangerous"
- "Black or White"
- "We Are the World" (interlude)
- "Heal the World"
- "Man in the Mirror"

## 1996–97: HIStory World Tour

Promoting his greatest-hits collection *HIStory*, Michael embarked on his final world tour in 1996. He played eighty-two concerts to a total of four and a half million fans, spanning fifty-eight cities, thirty-five countries, and five continents. Unlike previous tours, he played only two dates in the United States, both in Hawaii. While the venture grossed over $40 million, it also became Michael's most troubled tour since 1984's *Victory*. The shows were dogged by negative reviews mixed with his own health issues, which ultimately forced him to cancel the rest of the planned tour.

### First Leg (1996–97)

The first phase of the *HIStory* tour began in Eastern Europe and ended with Michael's first concerts on US soil in seven years.

- September 7: Letna Park, Prague, Czech Republic: In a largely negative review, *Entertainment Weekly* writer Nisid Najari reported that the lackluster sound system and poorly placed video screens resulted in an underwhelming experience for the 100,000-strong audience. Najari wrote that the crowd responded most enthusiastically to the Jackson 5 medley, "Billie Jean," "Thriller," and his cover of the Beatles' "Come Together."
- September 10: Népstadion, Budapest, Hungary
- September 14: Lia Manoliu Stadium, Bucharest, Romania
- September 17: Dynamo Stadium, Moscow, Russia
- September 20: Bemowo Airport, Warsaw, Poland
- September 24: Estadio La Romareda, Zaragoza, Spain
- September 28, 30, October 2: Amsterdam Arena, Amsterdam, Netherlands
- October 7: Stade El Menzah, Tunis, Tunisia
- October 11, 13: Olympic Stadium, Seoul, South Korea
- October 18: Chungshan Soccer Stadium, Taipei, Taiwan
- October 20: Chungcheng Stadium, Kaohsiung, Taiwan
- October 22: Chungshan Soccer Stadium, Taipei, Taiwan
- October 25: National Stadium, Singapore
- October 27, 29: Merdeka Stadium, Kuala Lumpur, Malaysia
- November 1: Andheri Sports Complex, Mumbai, India
- November 5: Muang Thong Thani City Center, Bangkok, Thailand
- November 9, 11: Ericsson Stadium, Auckland, New Zealand
- November 14, 16: Sydney Cricket Ground, Sydney, Australia
- November 19: ANZ Stadium, Brisbane, Australia
- November 22, 24: Melbourne Cricket Ground, Melbourne, Australia
- November 26: Adelaide Oval, Adelaide, Australia
- November 30, December 2, 4: Burswood Dome, Perth, Australia

- December 8, 10: Asia World City Concert Grounds, Manila, Philippines
- December 13, 15, 17, 20: Tokyo Dome, Tokyo, Japan
- December 26, 28: Fukuoka Dome, Fukuoka, Japan
- December 31: Jerudong Park, Bandar Seri Begawan, Brunei: The Sultan of Brunei organized this special performance. In attendance were 4,000 invited guests as well as the public.
- January 3–4, 1997: Aloha Stadium, Honolulu, Hawaii: In his first US concerts since 1989, Michael played two sold-out shows at this 35,000-seat stadium. According to Grant's *Michael Jackson: A Visual Documentary*, no other artist had sold out the stadium. Since few acts of Michael's stature visit the islands, the concerts became must-see spectacles. In the *Los Angeles Times* article "A Big Aloha for Michael," a fan discussed Michael's visit to the Big Island. "It's an honor for him to pick Hawaii as his US stop. He's an icon."

**Set List**

Michael played the following songs on the first leg of his *HIStory* tour:

- Medley: "Scream / They Don't Care About Us / In the Closet"
- "Wanna Be Startin' Somethin'"
- "Stranger in Moscow"
- "Smooth Criminal"
- "You Are Not Alone"
- "The Way You Make Me Feel"
- "Jackson 5 Medley"
- "Off the Wall Medley"
- "Billie Jean"
- "Thriller"
- "Beat It"
- "Come Together / D.S." (performed for the first three months only)
- "Dangerous"
- "Black or White"
- "Earth Song"
- "Heal the World"
- "HIStory"

**Second Leg (1997)**

The second leg of the tour comprised three months of shows in Europe followed by a handful of concerts in South Africa.

- May 31: Weserstadion, Bremen, Germany
- June 3: Mungersdorfer Stadion, Cologne, Germany
- June 6: Weserstadion, Bremen, Germany
- June 8, 10: Amsterdam Arena, Amsterdam, Netherlands
- June 13: Nordmarksportfield, Kiel, Germany
- June 15: Parkstadion, Gelsenkirchen, Germany
- June 18: San Siro, Milan, Italy
- June 20: Stade Olympique de la Pontaise, Lausanne, Switzerland
- June 22: Krakelshaff, Bettembourg, Luxemborg
- June 25: Stade de Gerland, Lyon, France
- June 27, 29: Parc des Princes, Paris, France
- July 2: Ernst-Happel-Stadion, Vienna, Austria
- July 4, 6: Olympic Stadium, Munich, Germany
- July 9: Don Valley Stadium, Sheffield, England: *Uncut* ran an unusual review of the show, mainly focusing on Michael's appearance and the military themes

of the concert. Critic Paul Lester commented that the 50,000-strong audience reacted most to the iconic choreography of "Smooth Criminal" and "Billie Jean," and reached the following conclusion: "He should be judged on his music and public image, which combine to make him the most fascinating entertainer this century." The *New Musical Express*'s Paul Moody disagreed, his July 19 review "King of Pap: Michael Jackson: Don Valley Stadium, Sheffield" accusing him of insincerity and getting too wrapped up in his "King of Pop" status.

- July 12, 15, 17: Wembley Stadium, London, England: *Melody Maker*'s Chris Roberts lamented the "astonishingly sour, curdled reviews" the *HIStory* Tour had been receiving. Expressing misgivings over the military themes and what he termed "Messiah complex" of the star, he called the show "gross indulgence, narcissism, bombast." Yet the Wembley show was also "net magic, fantasy, travel, displacement, dissimulation, derailment. He dances with grace notes, his knees have Elvis dust. Ridiculous, religiose, it adds to the sum of unusual and radiant things that have been attempted."
- July 19: RDS Arena, Dublin, Ireland
- July 25: St. Jakob Stadium, Basel, Switzerland
- July 27: Stade Charles-Ehrmann, Nice, France
- August 1: Olympic Stadium, Berlin, Germany
- August 3: Festwiese, Leipzig, Germany
- August 10: Hockenheimring, Hockenheim, Germany
- August 14: Parken Stadium, Copenhagen, Denmark
- August 16: Ullevi, Gothenburg, Sweden
- August 19: Valle Hovin, Oslo, Norway
- August 22: Tallinn Song Festival Grounds, Tallinn, Estonia
- August 24, 26: Helsinki Olympic Stadium, Helsinki, Finland
- August 29: Parken Stadium, Copenhagen, Denmark
- September 3: Hippodrome Wellington, Ostend, Belgium
- September 6: Estadio José Zorrilla, Valladolid, Spain
- October 4, 6: Greenpoint Stadium, Cape Town, South Africa
- October 10, 12: Johannesburg Stadium, Johannesburg, South Africa
- October 15: Kings Park Stadium, Durban, South Africa

## Set List

Michael performed a slightly modified set for the second leg of the tour:

- Medley: "Scream / They Don't Care About Us / In the Closet"
- "Wanna Be Startin' Somethin'"
- "Stranger in Moscow"
- "Smooth Criminal"
- "You Are Not Alone"
- "Jackson 5 Medley"
- "Billie Jean"
- "Thriller"
- "Beat It"
- "Blood on the Dance Floor" (performed for the first three months only)
- "Dangerous"
- "Black or White"
- "Earth Song"
- "Heal the World"
- "HIStory"

## 1999: MJ & Friends

While not a full tour, MJ & Friends played in Korea and Germany. Intended as a fundraiser for children in Kosovo and Africa, Michael along with a full roster of other artists performed for crowds at Seoul's Olympic Stadium (June 25) and Munich's Germany's Olympic Stadium (June 27). At both shows, Michael performed a medley of his greatest hits ("Don't Stop 'Til You Get Enough," "The Way You Make Me Feel," "Scream," "Beat It," "Black or White," and "Billie Jean"), plus "Dangerous," "Earth Song," and "You Are Not Alone." Along with his band, longtime friend Slash joined him for both performances.

The MJ & Friends tour became notorious for an onstage equipment malfunction during Michael's Munich show. During "Earth Song," he stood on a prop bridge that spanned the stage. The stage collapsed with Michael still on the bridge, plunging him over fifty feet to the floor. He was able to continue the show, although did not change costumes for the remainder of the concert. After finishing the performance, he was rushed to the hospital to check for injuries.

Other artists who appeared during the MJ & Friends events include the following:

### Seoul

- Barenaked Ladies
- Boyz II Men
- Mariah Carey
- H.O.T.
- Patricia Kaas
- Philipp Kirkorov
- Andy Lau
- Coco Lee
- Vanessa Mae
- Scorpions
- S.E.S.
- Steven Seagal
- Slash
- Spirit of the Dance
- Status Quo
- Luther Vandross

### Munich

- A. R. Rahman
- Mario Adorf
- Roberto Alagna
- All Saints
- Barenaked Ladies
- Andrea Bocelli
- Boyzone
- Angela Gheorghiu
- Udo Jürgens
- Patricia Kaas
- Kelly Family
- Philipp Kirkorov
- Helmut Lotti
- Vanessa Mae
- Peter Maffay & Noa
- Alan Parsons
- André Rieu
- Sasha
- Scorpions
- Slash
- Spirit of the Dance
- Ringo Starr
- Status Quo
- Luther Vandross
- Zucchero

# 37

# We've Been Together for Such a Long Time Now

## Michael Jackson's Studio MVPs

**F**rom *Off the Wall* through *Invincible*, Michael Jackson surrounded himself with trusted friends and colleagues to help him craft his sound. Read the liner notes of his albums, and certain names appear again and again. This chapter pays tribute to Michael's MVPs—the names seen on album credits but deserving of greater attention.

### Quincy Jones

Perhaps Michael's best-known collaborator, the composer, producer, and arranger helmed *Off the Wall*, *Thriller*, and *Bad*. Beginning his career as a trumpet player and bandleader, he transitioned into an arranger and producer for artists as varied as Frank Sinatra, Paul Simon, and Lesley Gore ("It's My Party" was Jones's first foray into pop). As his career grew, he began releasing his own albums, beginning with 1969's *Walking in Space*. In the 1970s he worked with a variety of R&B acts, including the Brothers Johnson and Rufus and Chaka Khan.

After he added movie scoring to his resume, his role as music supervisor for the 1978 film *The Wiz* introduced him to Michael. At that point, Michael was an artist at a crossroads, wanting to establish a separate musical identity from his Jacksons material. Jones volunteered to helm *Off the Wall*, and the two began what would become a highly successful and influential partnership.

### Bruce Swedien

A highly respected and award-winning recording engineer, Swedien first met Jones in the 1960s when the producer was vice-president for Mercury Records in Chicago. Swedien had first received national attention for his work on Frankie Valli and the Four Seasons' 1962 hit "Big Girls Don't Cry," earning a Grammy nomination for his work. The two worked on recordings by jazz artists such as Sarah Vaughan and Dinah Washington before Swedien relocated to Los Angeles to work for Brunswick

Records. They reunited in 1977 to work on the soundtrack to *The Wiz*, and Swedien subsequently found himself engineering Michael's albums *Off the Wall*, *Thriller*, *Bad*, *Dangerous*, *HIStory*, and *Invincible*.

Among many reasons Swedien's talents remain in demand is his patented "Acusonic Recording Process," which he describes as using multiple multitrack tape machines to create a fuller, warmer effect that envelops the listener in crystal-clear, multilayered sound. On August 21, 2006, Swedien posted on GearSlutz.com that during the recording of the *Wiz* soundtrack he "came up with the basic system of organizing the tracks, the master tapes and the slave tapes that I still use. I call it 'Multi-Track Multiplexing.'" He used a combination of digital and analog multi-track machines to generate an unlimited number of recording tracks, creating what he called an "accurate" and "sonic" effect.

## Rod Temperton

The English songwriter, producer, and keyboardist got his start with the late 1970s funk/disco band Heatwave. He wrote some of the group's biggest hits, including "Boogie Nights," "Always and Forever," and "The Groove Line." Intrigued, Jones expressed interest in working with this young songwriter with a gift for memorable hooks. By the time Jones contacted him in 1979 for help on *Off the Wall*, Temperton

had already retired from performing in the band to focus on songwriting. Relocating to Los Angeles from Germany, Temperton began work on the tracks "Rock with You," "Off the Wall," and "Burn This Disco Out." To Temperton's surprise, Jones accepted all three of the songs for Michael's album.

After the huge success of "Rock with You," Temperton reunited with Jones and Michael to work on *Thriller*. His hit-making streak continued with "Thriller" along with "Baby Be Mine" and "The Lady in My Life." After the Michael Jackson projects, he continued working

Rod Temperton, a former member of Heatwave and one of Quincy Jones's favorite songwriters, penned the iconic title track to *Thriller*. Recorded in 1982, the track was released as a single in 1983 in 7-inch and 12-inch formats; the latter is pictured here.    *Author's collection* with Jones and other artists such as Donna Summer, Michael McDonald, George Benson, Manhattan Transfer, and Karen Carpenter.

## Greg Phillinganes

One of Michael's closest collaborators, keyboardist Phillinganes worked on all of Michael's Epic releases. Their association stretched back to 1978, when the top session musician arranged the Jacksons' *Destiny*. He subsequently played keyboards on *Triumph*, played on all of Michael's solo albums, and served as the musical director for the *Bad* and *Dangerous* tours, as well as Michael's thirtieth-anniversary concerts. In a touching tribute, he also served as music director for Cirque du Soleil's *Michael Jackson: The Immortal World Tour*.

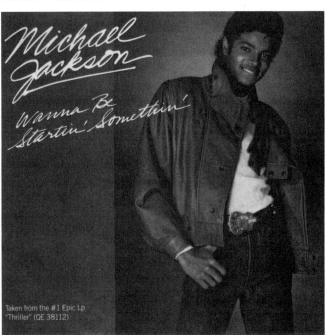

In a 2012 interview with *Atlanta*, Phillinganes credited his and Michael's mutual respect and kinship as the key to their collaborative relationship, mentioning "Thriller" as his favorite track from the album. "I did the synth bass part, those high-pitched synth parts, I did the Rhodes [keyboard] part and even did the pipe organ that Vincent Price does his rap over. It was crazy!" he said. "When I listen to it now, I just think about all the fun we had creating all those layers in the studio."

Keyboardist Greg Phillinganes performed on virtually all of Michael's Epic solo albums, including the *Thriller* track "Wanna Be Startin' Somethin.'"    *Author's collection*

## Jerry Hey

Considered one of the top session horn players, string and horn arrangers, and orchestrators, Hey has graced more albums (and earned more Grammy Awards) than can be listed here. He began as a member of Seawind, a Hawaii-based jazz-fusion group featuring Hey and horn players Larry Williams (another frequent Michael collaborator) and Kim Hutchcroft. This trio formed the Seawind Horns, an offshoot group that quickly became in-demand session horn players. Hey left Seawind as a touring member in 1979 but continued recording with the group through 1980.

Due to his reputation and fusion background, Hey became Jones's go-to musician for intricate horn arrangements integrating jazz, R&B, and pop. Their association began with Jones's 1976 album *I Heard That!!!* when Jones asked the Seawind Horns to play on some album tracks. That led to Hey's first full collaboration with Jones, playing on the Brothers Johnson's 1978 LP *Blam!*

It was when Hey played on *Off the Wall*, he told the website Hip-Bone Music, that he finally fully appreciated Jones's style. "He treats everyone with such respect that people working with Quincy want to do their absolute best for him. Of course, every session with Quincy is as good as it gets, but Michael Jackson's have to be at or near the top," said Hey. "As Quincy said, everyone playing on these sessions was at the height of his career, the songs were incredible, Bruce Swedien's engineering was groundbreaking, and Quincy's production was second to none."

## Paulinho da Costa

Brazilian master percussionist Paulinho da Costa has applied his considerable skills to thousands of albums as well as film soundtracks and TV music. A frequent Jones collaborator, Da Costa appears on all of Michael's albums as well as the Jacksons' *Triumph*. In *Moonwalk*, Michael singles out da Costa's percussion on "Don't Stop 'Til You Get Enough" as being a crucial ingredient to the song.

## Andraé Crouch Choir

One of Michael's secret weapons, Andraé Crouch and his choir were crucial contributors to some of Michael's most powerful and dramatic tracks, including "Man in the Mirror," "Keep the Faith," "Will You Be There," "Earth Song," and "Speechless." Crouch and his choir even joined Michael onstage during the 1988 Grammy Awards for a rendition of "Man in the Mirror." An arranger, producer, singer, and songwriter, Crouch melded traditional gospel with modern R&B, bringing spiritual music to a larger audience with songs like "The Blood Will Never Lose Its Power," "My Tribute (to God Be the Glory)," and "Soon and Very Soon." From the 1960s through the 2000s, Crouch served as an in-demand choir leader and arranger for artists such as Madonna and Paul Simon.

## Toto

- David Paich (keyboards, vocals)
- Steve Porcaro (keyboards)
- Steve Lukather (guitars, vocals)
- Jeff Porcaro (drums)

While Toto enjoyed a successful career as a band, releasing 1970s and 1980s classics such as "Hold the Line," "Rosanna," and "Africa," the band members were also songwriters and top session musicians. They wrote for and played with everyone from Steely Dan to Boz Scaggs, earning Jones's attention. They became crucial to *Thriller*, playing on several tracks. As Lukather told CNN in 2009, he contributed rhythm guitar and bass on "Beat It," while Jeff Porcaro played drums. In addition, Lukather played guitar and synthesizer on "Human Nature."

In fact, "Human Nature" was Toto's chief contribution to *Thriller*, as Steve co-wrote the track with lyricist John Bettis. He then submitted the original demo to Jones, and the producer loved the song so much that the instantly accepted it, with Temperton's composition "Carousel" bumped from the *Thriller* lineup to make room.

Toto members Steve Porcaro and David Paich also appear on *Bad*, and Paich appears on some *HIStory* tracks. Lukather continued collaborating with Michael, playing on *HIStory: Past, Present, and Future, Book 1* (1995) and *Blood on the Dance Floor* (1997). He looked back fondly on his years working with the singer, telling CNN on June 26, 2009, "He was very specific, he was very focused on the work. He knew what he wanted. And if he liked something, you could tell right away. If he was iffy about it, he would let you know. But he was very pleasant."

## Jeremy Lubbock

Beginning his career as a singer and pianist in England, Jeremy Lubbock received his first big break in 1953, when he recorded a version of "Catch a Falling Star," produced by George Martin (who would go on to greater fame producing the Beatles). Lubbock transitioned to arranging in the 1970s, working for the broadcasting companies BBC and ITV, before relocating to Los Angeles. After doing arrangements for Joni Mitchell and Minnie Riperton, Jones and keyboardist/producer David Foster recruited him for their projects. Lubbock's classical and jazz backgrounds made him a versatile musician, equally comfortable in various genres.

His first encounter with Michael was arranging 1982's *E.T. the Extra-Terrestrial* storybook album, a project Jones and Michael were working on alongside *Thriller*. After that, Lubbock would collaborate on several more tracks with Michael, conducting and arranging the *HIStory* songs "Smile" and "Childhood." In his memoir, *In the Studio with Michael Jackson*, Bruce Swedien describes how Michael wanted to meet the orchestra members who had performed on the two songs. Lubbock readily agreed, and when Michael entered the studio, he received a standing ovation from the musicians. "Jeremy stood up on the conductor's podium and also applauded as loud as he could! Michael was thrilled!"

Lubbock returned a few years later for the *Invincible* tracks "Speechless," "Whatever Happens," and "Heaven Can Wait." Michael clearly valued his work, as he tapped Lubbock to arrange 3T's 1996 single "Why."

## Slash

It's no secret that Michael enjoyed merging harder-edged rock with his music, as evidenced by Eddie Van Halen's solo on "Beat It" and Steve Stevens tearing up "Dirty Diana." His most frequent guest star from the rock world, however, was Guns N' Roses guitarist Slash, who appears on *Dangerous*, *HIStory*, *Blood on the Dance Floor*, and *Invincible*. The two would share an unlikely friendship for almost two decades.

Their collaborations began with *Dangerous*, when Slash guested on the rocker "Give In to Me." During his 1992 interview with Oprah Winfrey, Michael discussed their developing friendship and Slash's appearance in the accompanying video. "Slash, who's a dear friend of mine—we love animals and things like that—he wanted to play guitar and I wanted him to play guitar. We got together and we went to Germany and we shot this thing in just like two hours." In a lesser-known cameo, Slash plays the guitar riffs at the beginning of the "Black or White" video.

Slash made a return appearance on *HIStory*, playing on the funky and contro-versial "D.S." Two years later, he contributed to the *Blood on the Dance Floor* track "Morphine." His final collaboration with Michael would occur on *Invincible*, when he played lead on "Privacy." In addition, Slash would occasionally perform live with the singer, rocking the crowd during the 1995 MTV Video Music Awards per-formance of "Black or White"; his final public appearance with Michael occurred during the 2001 *30th Anniversary Special*, where they reprised "Black or White" as well as "Beat It."

## Dallas Austin

The Atlanta-based producer first gained fame when he helped to make Boyz II Men's debut album *Cooleyhighharmony*, but his biggest break came through his longtime creative partnership with TLC. He produced their huge albums *OOOOOOOOh . . . on the TLC Tip* (1992) and *CrazySexyCool* (1994), and co-produced their final effort, 1999's *FanMail*. These albums caught Michael's attention, and the star tapped him to produce three *HIStory* tracks: "They Don't Care About Us," "This Time Around," and "2 Bad." The first two became the most notorious tracks on the collection due to their controversial content, while "2 Bad" later appeared in the 1996 short film *Ghosts*.

## R. Kelly

R&B singer, songwriter, and producer R. Kelly enjoyed a longtime collaboration with Michael, penning and producing songs for *HIStory*, *Invincible*, and the *Number Ones* collection. Known for his combination of smooth R&B and hip hop, the Chicago-born Kelly shook up the music scene with his 1993 solo debut *12 Play*. Featuring raunchy lyrics and heavy beats grounded by his Marvin Gaye–like voice, he scored hits with "Bump N' Grind," "Your Body's Callin'," and "Sex Me." He continued to develop as an artist, producing Aaliyah's debut album and releasing singles that dealt with sexual themes ("Ignition" and "Feelin' on Yo Booty") and uplifting, spiritual messages ("I Believe I Can Fly" and "I'm Your Angel").

R. Kelly first worked with Michael in 1995, when he forwarded a demo of "You Are Not Alone" to the singer. Liking the track, Michael not only recorded the song but invited Kelly to produce it. That collaboration became Michael's last massive hit, becoming the first song in the history of the *Billboard* Hot 100 to debut at #1. Hoping to repeat their success, the two teamed again on *Invincible*, with Kelly pen-ning the song "Cry"; due to a lack of publicity and Michael's refusal to appear in the video, however, the song experienced only modest success. It served as a departure for Kelly, however, as it addressed environmental themes and other world issues.

Their final teaming would occur on the 2003 greatest hits collection *Number Ones*, for which Kelly wrote and produced the mid-tempo love song "One More Chance." While receiving positive reviews, the song peaked at #83 on the *Billboard* Hot 100, but reached the Top 10 in several other countries. Michael remained a fan of Kelly's, as evidenced by an amusing scene in the 2003 TV special *Michael Jackson's Private Home Movies*. As friend and director Brett Ratner sits in the front seat of a car, Michael is seen grooving in the back seat to "Ignition."

## Teddy Riley

Credited with pioneering the new jack swing genre, Riley quickly gained stature as a singer/songwriter, keyboardist, and producer in the late 1980s and 1990s. He got his start in hip-hop, first working on Doug E. Fresh and the Get Fresh Crew's classic single "The Show" before forming a creatively and commercially successful partnership Kool Moe Dee. Still a teenager, Riley produced the rapper's major hits, including "Go See the Doctor" (1986), "How Ya Like Me Now" (1987), and "I Go to Work" (1989). His hard-hitting beats and signature keyboard riffs led to work with R&B artists such as Bobby Brown, with whom he co-wrote the massively successful hit "My Prerogative."

Riley balanced his production with his own group Guy, a trio who proved influential in crafting the new jack swing sound, later defined by the *Chicago Tribune*'s Kelley L. Carter as "a hybrid of rhythms and drum machine wizardry . . . that is used as the backbeat of much of what is now modern day R&B music. It combines elements of jazz, pop, hip-hop, funk and R&B." While the group was not a massive crossover success, singles like "Groove Me," "Teddy's Jam," and "I Like" proved major R&B hits.

As Guy was winding down, Riley formed a new act, the equally influential Blackstreet; their biggest hit, "No Diggity," stood among the most distinctive songs of the 1990s. He also became involved with the rap act Wreckx-N-Effect, co-writing, producing, and performing on their 1992 smash "Rump Shaker."

In the midst of Riley's run of hits, Michael began work on his follow-up to *Bad*. Looking for a newer sound, he elected not to work again with Jones, who in turn recommended Riley. In a 2007 interview with the Baller Status site, Riley admitted feeling trepidation at following a legend such as Jones. Still, Riley brought several songs for Michael's consideration, figuring he would select only one. Instead, he selected seven. "I expected not to have more than one song on the album, but then over the course we just developed this great relationship and chemistry. It's a magnificent feeling," Riley said. As well as producing over half of *Dangerous*, he also co-wrote tracks such as "Remember the Time," "Jam," "In the Closet," and the title song. To date, *Dangerous* remains the highest-selling album in the history of new jack swing, with over thirty million copies sold worldwide, according to Carter.

Their collaboration continued on 1997's *Blood on the Dance Floor*, with Riley co-writing and producing the title track and "Ghosts," the former originally intended for inclusion on *Dangerous*. During his interview with Baller Status's Lucy Diamonds, Riley mentioned that he and Michael wanted to work together again; while they never reteamed, they experienced a virtual reunion in 2010, when Riley was tapped to produce the tracks "Hollywood Tonight," "Monster," and "Breaking News." As discussed in chapter 40, the latter two songs became the most controversial elements of the album *Michael*, with challenges to the vocals' authenticity. On September 2, 2013, Riley issued an apology via Twitter for his involvement in the project. "I was giving a problem that involved my bestfriend [sic] and sign a contract to remix what I had. It was too late for me to turn back so I finished out the project. Now if you want me to apologize for that, yes I'm funkin sorry I did it."

## Rodney "Darkchild" Jerkins

One of the chief architects of *Invincible*, Jerkins has amassed an impressive resume, writing and producing for some of today's major artists. Among his clientele are Janet Jackson, Beyoncé, Mary J. Blige, Mariah Carey, Whitney Houston, Rihanna, Justin Bieber, Luther Vandross, Jennifer Lopez, Toni Braxton, Destiny's Child, Lady Gaga and Britney Spears. Melding hip hop, R&B, and pop, Jerkins has proven a consistent hit maker, his stamp present on most tracks via the artist whispering "Darkchild" at some point during a song.

Due to Jerkins's already remarkable success, he was tapped to write and produce tracks for what would become Michael's final album. At just 19, Jerkins was hired to update the singer's sound to place him firmly in the early 2000s pop landscape. In the 2009 *Vibe* article "Rodney Jerkins Talks MJ," he recalled how Michael used to repeat the phrase "Melody is king" and wanted *Invincible* to sound as futuristic as possible. "There's stuff we didn't put on the album that I wish was on the album. My first batch [of beats] is what I really wanted him to do," Jerkins said. "I was trying to really go vintage, old school Mike. And that's what a lot of my first stuff was, that I was presenting to him. He kept 'Rock My World.'" Of *Invincible*'s sixteen tracks, Jerkins produced six.

After Michael's death, Jerkins took part in the 2014 posthumous collection *Xscape*, co-producing the title track, an *Invincible* outtake. Jerkins said he and Jackson originally started work on the song "Xscape" in 1999. "Even when Michael was alive, we never stopped working on the song 'Xscape,'" he told the Huffington Post's Mesfin Fekadu. "It was one of those songs where he specifically said to me, 'It has to see the light of day one day.'"

## Brad Buxer

The keyboardist and composer enjoyed years of collaborating with Michael, even serving as his musical director for his tours. One of their strangest projects included writing music for the *Sonic the Hedgehog 3* video game; in a 2009 interview with the French magazine *Black & White*, Buxer confirmed that the two had worked on the music. "If he is not credited for composing the music, it's because he was not happy with the sound coming out of the console. At the time, game consoles did not allow an optimal sound reproduction, and Michael found it frustrating. He did not want to be associated with a product that devalued his music," Buxer said.

According to the *Black & White* interview, they co-wrote "Stranger in Moscow," while Buxer played virtually every instrument on "Morphine" and the *Ultimate*

*Collection* song "In the Back." Of "Moscow," Buxer stated, "More than any other song that I worked with Michael, 'Stranger in Moscow' is where I made my most artistic leg. I'm not credited as co-composer on this track, but I have worked closely with Michael on the composition and structure of this song . . . I also played virtually all instruments."

## Dr. Freeze

The singer, songwriter, and producer was heavily influenced by new jack swing, writing and producing the Color Me Badd hit "I Wanna Sex You Up" and well as the Bell Biv DeVoe classic "Poison." He teamed up with Michael in 2001, contributing the ballad "Break of Dawn." In a 2011 interview with MJ France.com (translated on the Michael Jackson on Beat blog), Dr. Freeze revealed that he, not Michael, sang the chorus because Michael enjoyed his voice and performance.

Their other *Invincible* outtakes finally surfaced on 2014's *Xscape*, including "Blue Gangsta" and "A Place with No Name." Dr. Freeze looked back on his work with Michael as a learning experience. "Michael was more nervous with me than I was with him. He was simply the most wonderful person with whom you could never dream of working with. . . . He knew all about the music industry, everything about everything, nothing was foreign to him, and he taught me a lot. Finally, he was very humble and creative."

## Honorable Mentions

The following list includes other notable figures Michael frequently collaborated with in the studio.

### Glen Ballard

The hit-making songwriter composed two tracks for Michael: "Keep the Faith" and "Man in the Mirror," the latter written with Siedah Garrett.

### Siedah Garrett

The singer/songwriter first came to prominence duetting with Dennis Edwards on the 1984 single "Don't Look Any Further." Her compositions with Glen Ballard drew the attention of Jones, particularly their song "Man in the Mirror." In addition to songwriting duties, she sang backup on *Bad* and duetted with Michael on "I Just Can't Stop Loving You"; Garrett would reprise her role during the 1992–93 *Dangerous* World Tour. One of her compositions with Ballard, "Keep the Faith," also appeared on the 1991 album. In addition to her solo career, she was featured prominently on Jones's 1989 album *Back on the Block*.

### John J. R. Robinson

The top session drummer features prominently on *Off the Wall*, his backbeat crucial to the success of "Rock with You." Jones discovered the percussionist after seeing him perform with Rufus & Chaka Khan in 1978. After *Off the Wall*, Robinson performed on *Bad*, the "We Are the World" single, and Jones's albums *Back on the Block* and *Q's Jook Joint*, among too many other discs to mention.

## Jimmy Jam and Terry Lewis

The Minneapolis-based production duo may be primarily known for their work with Janet Jackson, but they applied their talents to Michael's music as well. They teamed up with the singer for *HIStory*, co-writing and producing "Scream" as well as "2 Bad," "HIStory," "Is It Scary," and "Tabloid Junkie." In addition, they would lend their mixing skills to the *Blood on the Dance Floor* track "Scream Louder," a reworking of the Michael and Janet duet.

## David Foster

The renowned songwriter and producer worked with Michael in several capacities. He played keyboards on *Off the Wall* and *Thriller*, co-wrote the *Off the Wall* song "It's the Falling in Love" with Carole Bayer Sager, and produced the *HIStory* songs "Smile," "Childhood," and "Earth Song."

## René Moore

Fans of 1980s R&B recall René & Angela, the duo who released the tracks "I'll Be Good," "Your Smile," and "You Don't Have to Cry"—all songs that saw renewed interest during the neo-soul movement of the 1990s. After his partnership with Angela Winbush ended, Moore transitioned into songwriting and producing. His association with Michael began with *Dangerous*, with Moore co-writing and co-producing the track "Jam." Their association continued on *HIStory*, as Moore co-wrote and produced "This Time Around" and "2 Bad." While Michael and Moore did not collaborate on original tunes again, Moore did help remix "2 Bad" for *Blood on the Dance Floor*.

## Bill Bottrell

The songwriter, producer, and engineer worked extensively with Michael, first meeting him while engineering and producing the Jackson's album *Victory*. He became heavily involved in the making of *Bad*, recording demos for songs including "Streetwalker." They continued their association on *Dangerous*, with Bottrell co-writing and producing the smash "Black or White" as well as "Give in to Me" and "Who Is It." *HIStory* saw their final collaboration, with Bottrell co-producing "Earth Song."

## Matt Forger

A sound engineer who has worked with everyone from Bruce Springsteen and Jones to Paul McCartney, Forger began his association with Michael on *Thriller*. He continued working with him on *Bad*, *Dangerous*, *HIStory*, and *Blood on the Dance Floor* as well as the *E.T.* storybook. In addition, he mixed and engineered the sound for the "Thriller" video and the film *Caption EO.* After designing his own sound systems while mixing live sound for rock bands in the northeast, he relocated to Los Angeles and began work at Westlake Studios. He gathered experience working under the best producers and artists, including Giorgio Moroder, Harold Faltermeyer, and George Duke, before teaming up with Jones and Michael. Soon he became an indispensable member of what Jones called the "A Team," which included Temperton and Swedien.

## Louis Johnson

A founding member of the 1970s group the Brothers Johnson, Johnson's bass slapping technique (which earned him the nickname "Thunder Thumbs") became a favorite for many artists. He played on almost every track on *Off the Wall* and *Thriller.* Louis and the Brothers Johnson were Jones protégés, and he referred to the producer as "my musical mentor and teacher" in the 2011 *Slap Masters Supplement* of *Bass Player* magazine. His last collaboration with Michael occurred on 1995's *HIStory.*

Beginning with the *Triumph* track "This Place Hotel," Michael increasingly experimented with integrating harder rock sounds into his music. He called upon rock's greatest guitarists to lay down edgy riffs, including Steve Stevens. The Billy Idol guitarist performed the lines that dominate the hit single "Dirty Diana." *Author's collection*

## Seth Riggs

The renowned vocal coach worked with Michael extensively from *Off the Wall* through *Invincible.* The creator of the "Speech Level Singing" (SLS) method, he accompanied Michael on the *Bad* Tour and frequently led Michael in vocal exercises during the recording of different albums. In an interview with Singeruniverse. com, he defined SLS as "an easy and applicable singing function which mirrors the old (seventeenth-century Italian) Bel Canto method of producing vocal sound. It is immediately adaptable to any style of singing." A search on YouTube reveals numerous clips of Riggs's sessions with Michael, demonstrating how he encouraged the artist to utilize his full range.

# 38

# Take You to the Max

## Odds and Ends

**M**ichael Jackson was a perfectionist, constantly tinkering with songs until he believed they were ready to be heard. If he remained dissatisfied with certain recordings, he would stow them in his vault, occasionally revisiting the material for future albums. Some of these outtakes were later issued on collections such as *The Ultimate Collection* and *Hello World*; others are available on bootlegs. They may have never been released on his studio albums, but they should not be overlooked, as they reveal his meticulous creative process.

This chapter presents an overview of notable outtakes and demos, some of which have resurfaced on later compilations. Because of the sheer volume of material Michael recorded, the following types are excluded from this list:

- Songs that were registered with the US Copyright Office but never recorded
- Tracks Michael mentioned in court depositions, but either never recorded or no other information exists
- Songs that have been discussed in other chapters
- Songs included on the posthumous releases *This Is It*, *Michael*, and *Xscape*, as they are discussed in chapter 40.

### "I'm Glad It Rained" (1972)

Recorded in August 1972 for the *Music and Me* sessions, this track ultimately appeared on the *Soulsation!* boxed set.

### "LuLu" (1971)

Recorded during the 1971 *Got to Be There* sessions, this song was later included on the *Soulsation!* collection.

### "You've Really Got a Hold on Me" (1973)

Michael Jackson recorded the Smokey Robinson cover on June 13, 1973, but it remained buried until 1984, when a remixed and overdubbed version appeared on the *Farewell My Summer Love 1984* album. Another version surfaced on the 1998 compilation *Motown Sings Motown Treasures: The Ultimate Rarities Collection* (credited to the Jackson 5); the original mix was included on the 2009 collection *Hello World*.

## "Call On Me" (1973)

Intended for a Michael Jackson solo album, the original version of this song was recorded on September 4, 1973. It stayed in the vaults until the 1984 collection *Farewell My Summer Love 1984*; not only did a remixed version appear on that album, it was also the B-side to the "Farewell My Summer Love" single. The original recording finally surfaced on the 1995 collection *Anthology: The Best of Michael Jackson*.

## "Don't Let It Get You Down" (1973)

Michael recorded a version of the Keni Lewis composition for a future solo album. While the original rendition finally appeared on 1995's *Anthology: The Best of Michael Jackson*, a remixed and overdubbed version was issued on the *Farewell My Summer Love 1984* compilation.

## "Farewell My Summer Love" (1973)

Originally recorded on August 31, 1973, this Lewis composition was shelved until *Farewell My Summer Love 1984*. Now overdubbed and remixed, this updated rendition became a surprise Top 10 hit in the UK and a Top 40 seller in the United States. The unmixed edition did not appear until the 2009 *Hello World* compilation.

## "Girl You're So Together" (1973)

While this Lewis-penned track eventually appeared on *Farewell My Summer Love*, it dates from August 31, 1973. The remixed version was issued as a single worldwide; in the US, it was the B-side to "Touch the One You Love." The original finally appeared on the 2009 *Hello World* collection.

## "A Pretty Face Is" (1974)

This Stevie Wonder composition is a mystery, as it may date to 1974 and the aborted project with the Jackson 5. In an interview with *Jet*'s Aldore Collier dated May 30, 1988, Wonder stated that they thought about reviving the song as duet for the album *Characters*, but chose "Get It" instead. "Michael and I had been talking for some years about doing some songs together. There were two songs that I had written that we talked about doing. One was called 'A Pretty Face Is' . . . We've been talking about doing 'A Pretty Face Is' at a later time." It is undetermined if the two ever recorded the track.

## "Iowa" (1977)

According to Cadman and Halstead's *For the Record*, Janet Jackson told *Q* in 1993 that Michael had composed a piece of classical music just before he filmed *The Wiz*. "He put all the songs he had written onto tape in the studio in our parents' house. . . . These are the things that he's written for orchestras, that are classical music—like something by Bach or Beethoven." To date, these tapes have never been heard.

## "You Can't Win (Parts I and 2)" (1979)

Michael recorded this *The Wiz* number twice—once for the movie and original soundtrack, and one more time with Jones. The final version features a different arrangement, including a heavier beat tailor-made for the discos. Michael's first solo single for Epic, the song peaked at #81 on the *Billboard* Hot 100 and #42 on the Hot Soul Singles chart.

## *Off the Wall* Demos and Outtakes (1979)

Flexing his songwriting muscles, Michael wrote a number of tracks for his solo efforts. In addition, he recorded material submitted by other writers. Some of these songs were eventually released as part of 2001's *Off the Wall Special Edition* package; others remain in the vaults.

- "Startin' Somethin'" (early version of "Wanna Be Startin' Somethin')
- "Don't Stop 'Til You Get Enough" (demo featuring Randy Jackson; available on *Off the Wall Special Edition*)
- "Rock with You" (featuring more strings and Michael's finger snaps)
- "Off the Wall" (home demo)
- "Get on the Floor" (demo featuring prominent hand clapping, new keyboard riffs, and prominent bass)
- "Working Day and Night" (demo, available on *Off the Wall Special Edition*)

## "The Toy" (1981)

*For the Record* cites a 1984 court deposition in which Michael discusses writing and recording a demo of this song. It was intended to be the title song to the Richard Pryor comedy of the same name, but Michael eventually canceled the project due to conflicts with making *Thriller*.

## "Someone in the Dark" (1982)

Recorded around the same time as *Thriller*, "Someone in the Dark" derives from the *E.T. the Extra-Terrestrial* storybook. Narrated by Michael and produced by Jones and Steven Spielberg, it included one new Michael track. Written by Temperton and the legendary songwriting duo of Alan and Marilyn Bergman, the song summarizes the story of Elliott and E.T.'s friendship. The lovely song lets Michael use his entire range and tap into his acting skills. While never released as a single, "Someone in the Dark" was eventually made available on the *Thriller 25* album, as well as *The Ultimate Collection*.

## "Can't Get Outta the Rain" (1982, B-side to "The Girl Is Mine")

This unusual B-side derives from *The Wiz* and is a reworking of Michael's recording of "You Can't Win" with Quincy Jones. Essentially a section of the extended version, the song was retitled "Can't Get Outta the Rain" and recycled as the B-side to "The Girl Is Mine."

## *Thriller* Demos and Outtakes

As usual, Michael submitted his own compositions and cut demos of other writers' submissions. The following list provides an overview of some of those tracks.

- "Sunset Driver" (demo; appears on *The Ultimate Collection*)
- "The Girl Is Mine" (demo; no Paul McCartney vocal)
- "P.Y.T. (Pretty Young Thing)" (demo; completely rewritten for the final version; available on *The Ultimate Collection*)
- "Starlight" (early version of "Thriller"; lyrics completely rewritten)
- "Carousel" (Michael Sembello outtake; appears on *Thriller 25*)
- "Hot Street" (Temperton outtake; originally called "Slapstick")
- "Nite Line"
- "She's Trouble"
- "Got the Hots" (co-written with Jones)
- "Billie Jean" (1981 home demo with different lyrics; available on *Thriller 25*)
- "Billie Jean" (two studio demos that sound closer to the final version)

## "Don't Be Messin' 'Round" (1986)

A demo recorded during the initial *Bad* sessions, this catchy, R&B/pop-fusion features a particularly strong Michael lead vocal, even on the demo. The track finally surfaced on *Bad 25* and provides an interesting glimpse into Michael's composing process. "Bridge!" he calls out at one point, scatting through that section as well as in the coda. He sings in lower ranges than usual, and according to engineer Bruce Swedien, played keyboards on this early version.

## "We Are the World" (1985)

The demo makes for a fascinating listen, as the lyrics are almost completely different except for the chorus. Lines such as "we're taking our own lives" were eventually rewritten with Lionel Richie. The melody remains the same, although Michael apparently tried to incorporate an African chant in the ending chorus. Along with tracks such as the early version of "P.Y.T.," this provides insight into Michael's composing process.

## "We Are Here to Change the World" (1986)

Co-written by Michael and John Barnes, this song appears in the Disney film *Captain EO* and was finally released on *The Ultimate Collection* in 2004.

## "Another Part of Me" (1986)

An earlier version of the *Bad* track, "Another Part of Me" is the final song in the *Captain EO* movie. While it differs little from the 1987 rendition, it does feature a different key.

## "Free" (circa 1986)

Also recorded during the *Bad* sessions, this lovely slice of breezy pop appears on *Bad 25*. Joyful lines like "The feel of letting my hair blow" accent the jazz-tinged chord changes, Michael's snapping fingers and clapping hands providing even better percussion than the drum machine. The song ends with Michael's contagious laughter as he exclaims, "Ronnie, you are so silly!" Why this gem failed to make the final album lineup remains a mystery.

During the height of Thriller-mania, K-Tel Records released *14 Original Hits with the Jackson 5*. Issued in 1984, the collection features cuts from Michael's group and solo years with Motown.     *Author's collection*

In an interview with Vogel for the *Atlantic*, Michael's friend and engineer Matt Forger discussed hearing this track while working on the *Bad 25* project. "When you listen to this song you hear Michael's spirit and joy. It's raw, it's loose, it's him in his element, doing what he loved to do. The first time I listened to it I broke down. This is what it was like every day."

## "I'm So Blue" (circa 1986)

A track that demonstrates how much Stevie Wonder influenced Michael, "I'm So Blue" tells of heartbreak, the sorrow balanced by a harmonica-powered melody. The song was included as part of the *Bad 25* set.

## "Song Groove / Abortion Papers" (circa 1986)

A long-discussed outtake, "Song Groove / Abortion Papers" failed to make the *Bad* album due to its controversial lyrical content. Michael penned this track about a teenaged girl trying to decide whether to terminate her pregnancy. His lyrics try to present both sides of the story, but ultimately his pro-life stance emerges. Vogel's "Abortion, Fame, and 'Bad': Listening to Michael Jackson's Unreleased Demos" explores the song, with Forger further explaining the track's origin. Forger states that Michael recognized the sensitivity of the topic, "but when you listen to the song there's a story being told. Michael really reflected on what the approach should be. He wasn't sure how to narrate it. There were different variations with vocals—he didn't want it to be judgmental. He was very clear about that. But he wanted to present a real, complicated situation."

## Other *Bad* Demos and Outtakes

The following list includes other notable songs recorded during the *Bad* sessions.

- "Pyramid Girl" (early version of "Liberian Girl")
- "Streetwalker" (available on *Bad 25*)
- "The Price of Fame" (was supposed to be used for a Pepsi campaign, but was replaced by a new version of "Bad"; available on *Bad 25*)
- "Who's Bad" (early demo version of "Bad"; originally titled "Pee")
- "Fly Away"
- "Groove of Midnight" (later given to Siedah Garrett)
- "Hot Fever" (early version of "The Way You Make Me Feel")
- "Scared of the Moon" (available on *Ultimate Collection*)
- "What You Do to Me"

## "Monkey Business" (1989)

Written with Bill Bottrell, this *Dangerous* outtake sees Michael occasionally using his lower range to match the song's funky give. "Lord have mercy," he sighs. "Don't you start no stuff with me!" It remained unreleased until the *Ultimate Collection* boxed set.

"Scream" was not Michael's first collaboration with sister Janet Jackson. He sang backup on "Don't Stand Another Chance," a track from her 1984 album *Dream Street*. Produced by Marlon Jackson, the single represented a mini family reunion.

*Author's collection*

## "Work That Body" (1989)

One of many compositions written with Bryan Loren (another being "Stay") for *Dangerous*, "Work That Body" features a typical new jack swing beat and synthesizer riffs. In a fascinating move, Michael references his Jackson 5 years by singing the "Sit down girl, I think I love you!" from "ABC." The bridge exudes a slightly jazzy air with Michael providing lush, multi-tracked backing vocals. Why this fun track failed to make the *Dangerous* lineup is unclear.

## "In the Closet" (1990)

As with many of Michael's demos, "In the Closet" sounds almost identical to the final version. On the demo, Michael's handclaps and snaps can be heard, and he speaks the lines that Princess Stephanie of Monaco recites on the *Dangerous* version. The beat and bass sound much stronger on this rough draft, and Michael's spoken lines add a new dimension to the track.

## "Give In to Me" (1990)

Intended to be part of a two-disc special edition of *Dangerous*, this demo version of "Give In to Me" can be easily found online. This version was apparently sent to Slash for him to improvise his guitar solo along to; the demo was subsequently re-recorded. Michael can be heard scatting and clapping his hands to the beat, ad-libbing the humorous line, "Love is a doughnut."

## "Gone Too Soon" (1990)

The demo version differs little from the final version, although Michael tempers his vocals more and does not break down in tears at the end.

## "She Got It" (1990)

Co-written with Teddy Riley, "She Got It" exudes the new jack swing style with its hard hip-hop beat and synthesizer riffs. In addition, it contains sexually explicit lyrics (at least for Michael), with lines like "netted stockings, purple panties that show" and "She's got the funky finger but she's giving him sex." The strong rock guitar sounds similar to "Black or White's" rock feel, but otherwise this is quite a departure from Michael's signature sound. Ultimately, he and Riley left it off *Dangerous*.

## "Jam" (1990)

This early version features an extended opening and a smoother, less raspy vocal. Michael seems to be working through the phrasing and rhythm, and not all the lyrics are complete. His scatting and finger snapping are prominent on the rough draft. Heavy D.'s rap is present, although his voice sounds slightly lower. Unlike some other demos, "Jam" provides insight into Michael's singing process and how he works through a rhythm and composes to fit the beat, not just the theme.

## "Keep the Faith" (1990)

While Michael does not use full vocal strength on this early version, and all backing vocals are not in place, it sounds very similar to the *Dangerous* track. Interestingly, Bruce Swedien admitted to *Rolling Stone* in 1992 that the recording session almost collapsed. "The day had come for Michael to put the lead on 'Keep the Faith'," he told Michael Goldberg. "He sang the first and second verses, and then he disappeared. It was very unlike Michael. I found him standing in the corner of his office crying his eyes out. He was absolutely heartbroken, to cut to the quick." Alarmed, Swedien told him to pull himself together; that Swedien would simply record "Keep the Faith" in another key.

"I told him, 'Michael we've got to face this right now.' I called the sync player and programmer. I felt we had to get the right key and get Michael to face it before it turned into something ugly." Swedien told Michael that they would not leave the studio until he had completed a take. "That was scary. But he did it. He pulled himself together. We went into the studio, cut a whole new demo and recorded a scratch vocal all the way through. A situation like that could have been a real block. We didn't leave the studio till dawn."

## "What About Us?" ("Earth Song" demo, 1990)

Michael began tinkering with "Earth Song" in 1990, hoping to include it on *Dangerous*. Originally called "What About Us," the song at this point had virtually identical lyrics, a slightly different vocal, and not all backing vocals. This early version does feature the André Crouch choir, although the back-and-forth exchange toward the end sees Michael singing in falsetto rather than yelling, as he does on the *HIStory* rendition. In the end he shelved the track, before reviving it five years later.

## "Serious Effect" (1990)

This hip-hop duet features LL Cool J performing the rap break; it failed to make the *Dangerous* lineup.

## Other *Dangerous* Demos and Outtakes

The following list includes additional material recorded during the *Dangerous* sessions.

- "Black or White" (demo)
- "Color of My Soul"
- "Dangerous" (early version, appears on *The Ultimate Collection*)
- "For All Time" (appears on *Thriller 25*)
- "Heal the World" (demo)
- "If You Don't Love Me"
- "Someone Put Your Hand Out" (originally recorded for *Bad*, reworked for *Dangerous*, and released in 1992 as a Pepsi promotional single; available on *The Ultimate Collection*)

## "In the Back" (1994–2004)

Michael worked on this track for a decade, eventually releasing it on *The Ultimate Collection*. He originally recorded a demo for *HIStory*, returned to it during *Blood on the Dance Floor* (ultimately selecting "Superfly Sister" instead), and finally for *Invincible*. The lyrics definitely fit *HIStory*'s angry tone, as they ask, "Why you wanna hit me? Why you stab me in the back?"

## *HIStory* Demos and Outtakes

During the *HIStory* sessions, Michael wrote and recorded a number of songs that ended up on other projects.

- "Fear"
- "Bass(z)ouille" (written with Bruce Swedien)
- "Ghosts" (early version, later reworked for *Blood on the Dance Floor*)

## "Mind Is the Magic" (1995)

A longtime fan of the Las Vegas illusionists Siegfried & Roy, Michael co-wrote what would become the theme song for their 1990s show. Songwriter Bryan Loren and Michael first wrote the track in 1989, then reworked it for the act's "Beyond Belief" show. Michael originally worked with the duo during his *Bad* World Tour but kept in touch with them. The song was not officially released until 1995, when Siegfried and Roy included it on their album *Dreams and Illusions* (released in Germany only).

## "On the Line"

In 1996, Spike Lee asked his friend Michael to record a song for his upcoming film *Get on the Bus*. Michael thus sang the Babyface composition "On the Line," which features in the movie's opening credits. The track was not included on the soundtrack, but was included on the 2004 boxed set *The Ultimate Collection*.

## "Angel" / "Do You Love Me" (1998–1999)

In conjunction with *HIStory*, Epic released a 12-inch single featuring remixes of "Scream" as well as older hits such as "Rock with You" and "Wanna Be Startin' Somethin'."

*Author's collection*

According to Cadman and Halstead's *For the Record*, Babyface mentioned in a 1999 interview that he and Michael had finished writing and recording some new songs. "Angel" was supposed to be part of a planned greatest hits package, but the project was shelved.

## *Invincible* Outtakes (1999–2001)

Michael wrote and recorded a vast amount of material for *Invincible*. The following list includes just a sampling of the still-unreleased songs.

- "Kick It"
- "I Don't Live Here Anymore"
- "Beautiful Girl" (demo, available on *The Ultimate Collection*)
- "Seeing Voices"
- "She Was Loving Me"
- "The Gloved One" (written by Sisqó)
- "This Is Our Time"
- "Pressure"
- "Fall Again" (co-written by Robin Thicke; available on *The Ultimate Collection*)
- "Stop the War"
- "Ekam Satyam (The One Truth)"
- "Cheater" (reworked from *Bad* sessions; original version on *The Ultimate Collection*)
- "Get Around"
- "Vibrationist"
- "Do You Want Me"
- "Maybe We Can Do It"
- "Seduction"
- "Tubeway"
- "Soldier's Entrance"
- "Belong 2"
- "The Pain"
- "We've Had Enough" (available on *The Ultimate Collection*)

## "Shout" (2001)

Co-written with Teddy Riley, this tribal beat–driven dance track was originally intended for *Invincible* but was replaced with "You Are My Life." It was eventually released in Europe on the "Cry" CD single.

## "Satisfy"—Mariah Carey (2002)

Written by Jimmy Jam and Terry Lewis, "Satisfy" features Carey on lead and Michael on backing vocals. Originally indeed for her album *Charmbracelet*, it was ultimately dropped and remains unreleased.

## "One More Chance" (2003)

The R. Kelly–penned ballad was originally intended for *Invincible*, but two years later was included on the greatest hits collection *Number Ones*. Michael began filming a music video for it in Las Vegas on November 17, 2003, but the shoot came to a halt when the Santa Barbara County Sheriff's Office raided Neverland that same night. A video featuring clips from throughout Michael's career was hastily compiled to promote the song; subsequently "One More Chance" reached the Top 10 in the UK, Italy, and Spain. In 2010, the DVD boxed set *Michael Jackson's Vision* included the original—yet still incomplete—video clip.

## "From the Bottom of My Heart" (2005)

After the devastation of Hurricane Katrina, Michael announced plans to record a benefit single. According to a 2005 *MTV News* report, "Michael Jackson Working on Katrina Song—But with Whom?," he had reached out to various stars, including R. Kelly, Jay Z, Ciara, Wyclef Jean, Mariah Carey, Lauryn Hill, Lenny Kravitz, James Brown, Yolanda Adams, and the O'Jays. In a 2009 interview with *Black & White*, engineer Brad Buxer confirmed that he worked on the song with Michael, but it remains unreleased.

## "He Who Makes the Sky Grey" (2005)

In 2005, Michael and his children briefly lived in Bahrain as the guest of Sheik Abdullah bin Khalifa, the prince of the country. The Sheik had started his own label, Two Seas Records, and began writing with Michael. As *Billboard* and other news outlets reported in spring 2006, Michael signed a two-year contract with the label. "I am incredibly excited about my new venture and I am enjoying being back in the studio making music," he said, in the article "Michael Jackson Sails with Two Seas," adding that he would release a new album in 2007. Just a few months later, Michael and the label canceled their agreement.

Michael did record some material while in Bahrain, however, including "He Who Makes the Sky Grey," co-written with the Sheik and Jermaine Jackson. Kim

Chandler, a session singer, lists on her website that she sang as part of a backing choir on an unreleased track, widely thought to be "He Who Makes the Sky Grey." The track has never surfaced.

## Will.i.am Collaborations (2006–2009)

When Michael and his children lived in Ireland, the Black Eyed Peas' will.i.am flew there to work on songs with him. In a November 2006 *Access Hollywood* interview, the duo discussed their ongoing collaboration. They entered the studio together to work on a series of tracks. As of this writing, these songs have never been released, but in a 2012 *Access Hollywood* interview, will.i.am stated he would only release them if Michael's mother Katherine approved the project.

- "I'm Dreamin'"
- "If You Don't Get It"
- "The Future"
- "If We Still Love"
- "Can You"
- "I Will Miss You"
- "I'm Still the King"

## "River Ripple" (2009)

Michael reportedly wrote this song with his children, intending to incorporate it into his *This Is It* concerts. According to Cadman and Halstead's *Michael Jackson: For the Record*, he planned to perform the ballad with an African choir.

# 39

# Let the Rhythm Get to You

## The Essential Michael Jackson Playlist

I magine creating a compilation for someone who has never heard Michael Jackson's music. Which songs best encapsulate his singing and performing style? Are there particular tracks that encompass the various genres comprising his sound? It is a challenge, and remains largely subjective. In compiling the hypothetical collection below, the following several factors were considered:

- song popularity
- vocal performance
- timeless quality
- distinctive instrumentation
- lyrical quality.

In creating a playlist, only officially released tracks were considered. Remixes, extended versions, live renditions, and unofficially released material require separate lists. This proposed collection provides an overview of Michael's solo years, including ballads and up-tempo tracks.

### Got to Be There (1972)

- "Got to Be There"
- "I Wanna Be Where You Are"
- "Rockin' Robin"
- "Ain't No Sunshine"

### Ben (1972)

- "Ben"
- "People Make the World Go Round"

### Music & Me (1973)

- "Music & Me"
- "With a Child's Heart"
- "Too Young"

### Forever, Michael (1975)

- "One Day in Your Life"
- "Just a Little Bit of You"
- "You Are There"

## Off the Wall (1979)

- "Don't Stop 'Til You Get Enough"
- "Rock with You"
- "Working Day and Night"
- "Off the Wall"
- "She's Out of My Life"
- "I Can't Help It"
- "Get on the Floor"

## Thriller (1982)

- "Wanna Be Startin' Somethin'"
- "Thriller"
- "Beat It"
- "Billie Jean"
- "Human Nature"
- "The Lady in My Life"
- "P.Y.T. (Pretty Young Thing)"

## Farewell My Summer Love 1984

- "Farewell My Summer Love"
- "You Really Got a Hold on Me"
- "Melodie"

## Bad (1987)

- "Bad"
- "Speed Demon"
- "The Way You Make Me Feel"
- "Liberian Girl"
- "Another Part of Me"
- "Man in the Mirror"
- "Smooth Criminal"
- "Leave Me Alone"
- "Dirty Diana"

After Michael Jackson left Motown, his former label released a 1975 greatest-hits collection featuring selections from his four solo albums. It sold moderately well in the US, peaking at #44 on the R&B charts and #156 on the *Billboard* 200. *Author's collection*

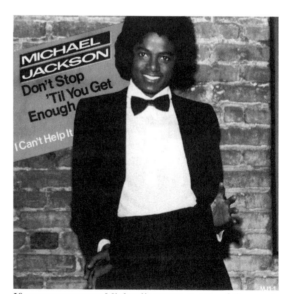

If any song proves Michael's status as one of the greatest "percussive singers," it is "Don't Stop 'Til You Get Enough," the first single from 1979's *Off the Wall*. *Author's collection*

## Dangerous (1991)

- "Jam"
- "Can't Let Her Get Away"
- "Remember the Time"
- "In the Closet"
- "Black or White"

- "Who Is It"
- "Give In to Me"
- "Will You Be There"
- "Keep the Faith"
- "Gone Too Soon"

## HIStory (1995)

- "Scream"
- "They Don't Care About Us"
- "Stranger in Moscow"
- "Earth Song"

- "You Are Not Alone"
- "Smile"
- "Money"
- "Childhood"

## Blood on the Dance Floor: HIStory in the Mix (1997)

- "Blood on the Dance Floor"
- "Superfly Sister"

- "Is It Scary"
- "Ghosts"

"Beat It" stands as one of Michael's most popular tracks of all time. *Rolling Stone* agreed, ranking it at #81 on its "100 Greatest Guitar Songs of All Time" list in 2008.

*Author's collection*

## Invincible (2001)

- "Unbreakable"
- "Heartbreaker"
- "Invincible"
- "Break of Dawn"
- "Heaven Can Wait"
- "Butterflies"
- "Whatever Happens"

## Number Ones (2003)

- "One More Chance"

## Michael (2010)

- "Hollywood Tonight"
- "Best of Joy"
- "(I Can't Make It) Another Day" (featuring Lenny Kravitz)
- "Behind the Mask"
- "Much Too Soon"

## *Xscape* (2014)

- "Love Never Felt So Good" (solo version)
- "Love Never Felt So Good" (Justin Timberlake duet)
- "A Place with No Name" (new version)
- "Xscape" (original version)

# 40

# I Am Forever

## The Posthumous Releases and Projects

After Michael Jackson's death in 2009, his estate announced a number of projects designed to pay tribute to the legendary entertainer. Films, albums containing material from his vaults, and collaborations with Cirque du Soleil have since appeared, not to mention reissues such as *Bad 25*. This chapter provides an overview of these releases up to 2015; more albums and films will surely surface in years to come.

### *Michael Jackson's This Is It* (Film and Soundtrack, 2009)

At the time of his death, Michael was deep in rehearsals for his planned fifty-concert series at London's O2 Arena. Titled *This Is It*, the shows were meant to mark his retirement from the stage; on a personal level, he wanted his children to see him perform live, something they had never witnessed. Along with choreographer Kenny Ortega, Michael planned an extravaganza celebrating his long career, treating audiences to live renditions of his biggest hits. No expense was spared, as he incorporated video, Cirque du Soleil–style acrobats, and state-of-the-art set design to showcase his music and dance. As with his other tours, his personal videographer filmed all the rehearsals; Michael and his staff would often watch the footage to make any necessary adjustments, then file the films in his archives.

When Michael unexpectedly passed, his estate, Ortega, and concert promoter AEG Live decided to edit over one hundred hours of footage into a film entitled *Michael Jackson's This Is It*. Released on October 28, 2009, just a few months after his death, *This Is It* was originally scheduled to run for a limited two-week engagement, and was subsequently issued on DVD and Blu-ray. Advance ticket sales broke records; a month before the documentary reached theaters, hundreds of showings across the US had already sold out. Abroad, the film performed even better: in Japan, over $1 million in tickets were sold in just one day, while in London fans bought over 30,000 tickets the day they went on sale. As MTV reported on September 29, 2009, a Los Angeles preview screening sold out within two hours.

During its first weekend, *This Is It* grossed over $23 million in the US alone; according to *Entertainment Weekly*'s box-office report from November 1, 2009, the documentary brought in $101 million worldwide that first weekend. Due to the high demand, the two-week engagement was extended up to Thanksgiving.

Overall, *This Is It* garnered positive reviews, assuring fans that the film portrays Michael as an in-control, relatively healthy entertainer driving himself as hard as his band and dancers. Rating the film a "B," *Entertainment Weekly* critic Owen Gleiberman praised it as "raw and entering sketch of a genius at work" but lamented that it does not showcase his "ferocity" as a singer and dancer. In its brief assessment, *Rolling Stone* gave *This Is It* three and a half stars, praising Michael's still powerful singing and dancing skills. "He's unguarded, assertive, far from childlike," Barry Walters wrote.

Other critics complained that the film kept Michael at a distance, both literally and figuratively. The *New York Post*'s Monohla Dargis disputed Ortega's contention that *This Is It* contains a portrayal that is "honest, raw, unguarded, right up until the day he died." "Truthfully, it is hard to imagine a supernova like Mr. Jackson, in particular one who grew up so publicly and at times pathetically, sharing anything honest, much less raw, on camera, either because he won't or he can't," Dargis wrote. "In the end, all you can expect from such manufactured lives—and perhaps all that we're really due—are glimmers of the figure left amid the fractured and distorting funhouse mirrors."

One of the film's most ecstatic reactions came from the late film critic Roger Ebert, who granted *This Is It* four stars and called it "one of the most revealing music documentaries I've seen." He marveled at Michael's physical condition and drive, noting that the cast and crew appeared to genuinely love him. In particular, Ebert seemed taken with Michael's still-impressive dancing abilities. "His movements are so well synchronized with the other dancers on stage, who are much younger and highly-trained, that he seems one with them," he wrote. "This is a man in such command of his physical instrument that he makes spinning in place seem as natural as blinking his eye."

Initially, *This Is It* generated controversy among family, critics, and fans. Had he lived, would Michael have wanted the rehearsal footage to be made public? Did it accurately portray Michael in terms of his physical and emotional condition, or was the film carefully edited to present an idealized version? Was a body double used for some of the sequences, even if Ortega insisted Michael appeared in every shot? Despite the concerns, *Michael Jackson's This Is It* transformed into an essential piece of Michael Jackson history—the only record of what those London concerts might have been.

The accompanying soundtrack was released in conjunction with the film, a collection of hits and demos in addition to a "new" track: "This Is It," one of several songs Michael wrote years earlier with composer Paul Anka (another track, "Love Never Felt So Good," resurfaced on 2014's *Xscape*). In 1983, the two musicians had met at Anka's California studio to write and record both tracks. Originally titled "I Never Heard," the renamed "This Is It" was slated to appear on Anka's duets album *Walk a Fine Line*. For unknown reasons, this version failed to make the album lineup; Anka subsequently gave the track to singer Sa-Fire, who recorded it in 1991.

As Michael's estate began compiling material for the *This Is It* soundtrack, they found the "I Never Heard" demo in his archives. Longtime collaborator Greg Phillinganes recorded new instrumentation and background vocals for the track along with several other musicians and the Jacksons. Lifting a line from the lyrics, the newly retitled "This Is It" appeared on the soundtrack album as two versions: a radio edit and an "orchestra version" featuring overdubbed strings. When Anka

MICHAEL JACKSON
BEHIND THE MASK

European vinyl collectors were undoubtedly excited by the limited edition "Behind the Mask" 7-inch single. The accompanying music video, titled the "Behind the Mask Project," compiled clips of fans from around the world lip-synching and dancing to the track.

*Author's collection*

discovered that the song had been issued without his knowledge, he threatened to sue; subsequently, the estate announced that they would give Anka 50 percent of the publishing rights.

"This Is It" was released for radio airplay only, and was available for purchase only as an album track. Despite not being downloadable as a single, it appeared on many charts due to massive radio airplay. In the US, it performed best on the R&B and Adult Contemporary charts, peaking at #18. Internationally, "This Is It" scored highest in Japan, reading #5 on the Hot 100 chart. The accompanying video, directed by Spike Lee, mixes vintage footage from Michael's career with shots of fans paying tribute to his memory.

Both the single and greatest hits package received some acclaim from reviewers. *Entertainment Weekly*'s Simon Vozick-Levinson enjoyed the demos of "She's Out of My Life," "Wanna Be Startin' Somethin'," and "Beat It," calling them "rare glimpses into Jackson's creative process." However, he dubbed "This Is It" a "decent if slight addition to Jackson's songbook."

All Music's Stephen Thomas Erlewine repeated that *This Is It* resembled a typical greatest-hits collection. He remained unimpressed with the "new" song, though he admitted "there's no denying the thrill of hearing an unheard vocal track of Michael at his prime, no matter how mediocre the song may be." In 2011, "This Is It" earned Michael his last Grammy nomination, for Best Male Pop Vocal Performance.

## *Michael* (2010)

The most controversial of all the posthumous releases, *Michael* consists of songs culled from the singer's archives, which were remastered to fit current trends.

Receiving lukewarm reviews, *Michael* suffered from an even bigger problem: authenticity.

Michael's longtime manager Frank DiLeo and the singer's estate cooperated with Sony to compile unfinished songs for a new collection. Deciding to focus on the most recent material, Sony singled out recordings from 2007–09. However, two tracks, "Much Too Soon" and "Behind the Mask," date from the *Thriller* era, while an earlier version of "(I Like) the Way You Love Me" first appeared on 2004's *The Ultimate Collection. Dangerous* producer Teddy Riley was named the producer for the project, and artists like Akon and Lenny Kravitz (who had recently collaborated with Michael) helped prepare the material for release. On the assumption that all tracks were authentic—indeed, most of the vocals sound typical of the singer's style—*Michael* was released on December 14, 2010. Immediately, family and friends emerged to dispute several tracks, the so-called "Cascio" recordings: "Breaking News," "Monster" (featuring 50 Cent), and "Keep Your Head Up."

As kids, brothers Frank and Eddie Cascio befriended Michael in the 1980s; their family subsequently became close friends and supporters of the singer. Michael would occasionally stay at the Cascios' house, and in 2007 he supposedly recorded several tracks with budding producer Eddie. Accusations that an impersonator had actually performed the vocals immediately surfaced upon *Michael*'s debut, with nephew T. J. Jackson tweeting that the vocals were fake. As reported by the *New York Daily News*' Joyce Chen, Michael's daughter Paris Jackson joined the chorus of naysayers; in a 2010 video chat, she even named the actual singer: impersonator Jason Malachi. The Black Eyed Peas' will.i.am, who had previously worked with Michael, expressed disgust with the entire project, claiming that the perfectionist singer would not want any of the material released.

To refute these accusations, Sony hired a forensic musicologist and recruited six producers and engineers who had previously worked with Michael to verify the vocals' authenticity. As Steve Knopper writes in "Inside Michael Jackson's Return," engineer Bruce Swedien believed the vocals were accurate, although the estate's own lawyer, Howard

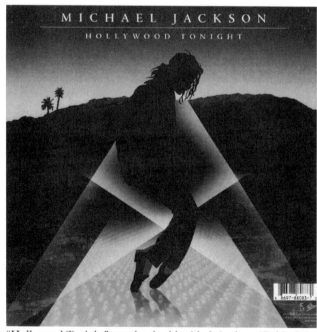

"Hollywood Tonight" was the double-sided single to "Behind the Mask," a limited-edition 7-inch single available only in Europe.

*Author's collection*

Weitzman, issued a vague statement. "Ultimately, Michael's fans will be the judges . . . as they always are." Fans continue to judge: according to a *New Musical Express* article from June 13, 2014, a woman sued the estate in 2014, accusing them of misrepresenting *Michael* as containing verified vocals. She plans to file a class-action lawsuit with the intention that everyone who bought *Michael* should receive financial compensation.

Expectations were high for *Michael*, as it was the first posthumous release other than the *This Is It* movie and soundtrack. Initial reactions were decidedly mixed, with *Rolling Stone*'s Jody Rosen assigning the disc three stars. While the critic praised "Behind the Mask," "(I Can't Make It) Another day," and "Much Too Soon," he argued that *Michael* does not represent a true Michael Jackson album. "Jackson was one of pop's biggest fussbudgets: Even when his songs were half-baked, the production was pristine. He would not have released anything like this compilation, a grab bag of outtakes and outlines," Rosen wrote.

Other reviewers expressed discomfort over listening to songs that Michael may have never wanted released. "But like some ghoulish postmodern joke on

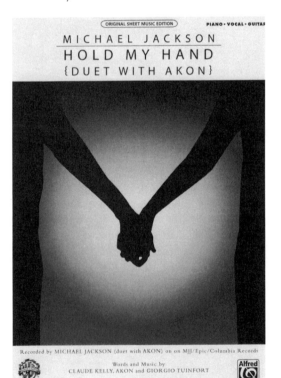

The first posthumous Michael Jackson compilation, 2010's *Michael* contains what his label claimed were previously unreleased demos. Controversy as to the authenticity of the songs dogged its release, resulting in disappointing sales. A duet with Akon, "Hold My Hand," was released as the first single. *Author's collection*

*Thriller*, *Michael* can't help but feel like the work of zombie hands—albeit tasteful zombie hands with ears finely attuned to the current whims and fancies of pop radio," wrote *Pop & Hiss*'s Margaret Wappler. "*Michael* often feels like a capitulation to those teeming masses who want one more shred of their beloved at any cost." All Music's Erlewine critiqued Riley's production, accusing him of making too many tracks sound like *Dangerous* outtakes, "heavy on rhythms but not melody, so desperate for relevance that every overdub is overworked." Rating the album two and a half stars, he ended his piece with a half-hearted compliment: "*Michael* is often tacky but considering how garish Jackson's taste could be, it winds up seeming almost respectful."

Internationally, *Michael* sold quite well, debuting at #1 in Germany, Austria, Italy, the Netherlands, and Sweden. It achieved platinum status in eighteen countries, and has sold 540,000 copies in the US. The highest chart positions reached in America include #1 on the R&B Albums chart and #3 on the *Billboard* 200. Only

"Hold My Hand," Michael's duet with Akon, was released as a single in the US as well as other countries; "Hollywood Tonight" and "Behind the Mask" were available internationally.

To promote Michael, three videos were made. Mark Wellington directed "Hold My Hand," a compilation of classic Michael footage and new scenes featuring Akon. The second, Wayne Isham–directed clip, "Hollywood Tonight," stars dancer Sofia Boutella as a young woman moving to Hollywood to realize her dream of becoming a dancer. The camera follows her as she takes dance classes, waitresses, and works in a strip joint in between auditions. Images of Michael are projected onto buildings, with Boutella executing Michael's signature moves as if he is inspiring her to continue.

Two videos were filmed for "Behind the Mask," but only one was ultimately shown. The officially issued clip resulted from the "Behind the Mask Project," where fans could submit videos of themselves lip-synching to the single in creative ways. The best footage was patched together to serve as a showcase for his biggest fans. However, this was not the original concept for "Behind the Mask": another version featuring elaborately masked dancers (directed by Alex Topaller and Daniel Shapiro) was eventually shelved in favor of the fan-made effort, but the first video finally appeared on YouTube in 2013.

Highlights of *Michael* include "Hollywood Tonight," where much of the rhythm track is based on Michael's beatboxing; the breezy, mid-tempo "(I Like) the Way You Love Me"; and the Babyface-esque "Best of Joy," featuring the now melancholy lines "I am forever / We are forever." Lenny Kravitz's crunching guitar riffs and sharp backing vocals let Michael indulge in his love of rock on the biting "(I Can't Make It) Another Day"; it would have been fascinating to hear these two collaborate on an album. "Behind the Mask" is a fun dance track, while "Much Too Soon" is a lovely, lilting ballad demonstrating his broad vocal range and gift for phrasing.

## *Bad 25* (Boxed Set and Documentary, 2012)

Celebrating the twenty-fifth anniversary of the *Bad* album, the Michael Jackson estate and Sony prepared a package containing the remastered album as well as related demos. A deluxe version also included the live CD and DVD *Live at Wembley July 16, 1988*, a performance previously unreleased but bootlegged. Recorded during the peak of his worldwide popularity, *Live at Wembley* displays Michael executing signature dance moves, performing his hits in front of an adoring, sold-out audience. Watching him playfully interact with then-unknown backup singer Sheryl Crow is a treat, and the entire show illustrates how Michael had finally surpassed his previous fame in the Jackson 5 to become a fully independent artist.

The CD containing outtakes and demos provides a rare glimpse into Michael's writing and recording process, finally issuing tracks such as the fierce "Streetwalker" and an early version of "Smooth Criminal," then titled "Al Capone." The controversial song "Abortion Papers" (listed as "Song Groove" on the cover) revealed Michael's opinion on abortion, although his lyrics try to present the pregnant teen's side as well as his own perspective. "Fly Away" and "Free" typify his love

songs, both revisiting themes of escapism in different sense ("Fly Away" addressing leaving a relationship, "Free" about love itself as a liberating force). "Don't Be
Messin' 'Round" resembles "Get on the Floor" in theme, but this time adds a Latin
flavor. Similar to "Leave Me Alone," "Price of Fame" reveals Michael's increasing
discomfort with being a superstar, a theme he would revisit many times after *Bad*.
Finally, the mid-tempo "I'm So Blue" sounds like Michael's take on a Stevie Wonder
track, complete with a harmonica-driven melody. Remixes of "Speed Demon" and
"Bad" as well as French and Spanish versions of "I Just Can't Stop Loving You"
round out the package.

Critical response to *Bad 25* was mixed. The *Los Angeles Times*' Randall Roberts
labeled the original album "one of the touchstone pop records of the era," but he
thoroughly disliked the two remixes, dubbing them "terrible commercial house
tracks" that diminish his legacy and "signal a future in which Jackson's music is officially deconstructed to unfortunate ends with full sanction of the singer's estate."

*Rolling Stone*'s Jody Rosen disagrees, rating *Bad 25* four and a half stars and
arguing that the album has grown in stature over the years. "Twenty-five years on,
*Bad* sounds less like *Thriller*'s underachieving follow-up than a masterpiece of pure
pop," Rosen writes. *Entertainment Weekly* awarded *Bad 25* an "A," citing the previously unreleased tracks as standouts. Ray Rahman concludes his review by calling
the package "a potent reminder of just how much *Bad*'s pulsing pop holds up."

In conjunction with the *Bad 25* boxed set, Spike Lee directed a documentary
about the making of the album, as well as its lasting impact. Premiering at the
69th Venice International Film Festival in August 2012, *Bad 25* contained archival
footage from the studio sessions, new interviews with *Bad* musicians and collaborators, and reflections from current artists. In her *Rolling Stone* article about the film,
Karen Bliss criticizes the movie for feeling "clinical at times" as it chronicles the
album track by track. However, she enjoyed the interesting facts it revealed, such
as the origins of the expression "shamon" and the anti-gravity lean in the "Smooth
Criminal" video.

Audiences responded positively at *Bad 25*'s Venice debut, with the *Hollywood
Reporter*'s David Rooney praising Lee's presentation of "a sensational snapshot
of the peak of the music video as art form, as well as the intricately layered process by which superior pop is crafted." After showing at Venice and the Toronto
International Film Festival, *Bad 25* received limited screenings in New York and Los
Angeles on October 19, 2012. ABC broadcast an edited version of the documentary
on November 22, and it was also broadcast in the UK and Germany. The entire film
was finally released on DVD, Blu-ray, and streaming video on July 3, 2013.

## Cirque du Soleil: *Immortal World Tour* and *One* (2011 and 2013)

Cirque du Soleil, the Canadian theatrical troupe that has dazzled audiences with
its elaborately staged shows, sophisticated themes, and spectacular acrobatics,
partnered with the Michael Jackson estate in 2011 to produce two shows. *Michael
Jackson: The Immortal World Tour* bowed in Montreal on October 2, 2011; the permanent Las Vegas production *Michael Jackson ONE* opened at the Mandalay Bay

Resort & Casino on May 23, 2013. Both shows feature remixed and mashed-up versions of Michael's best-known songs, with Cirque du Soleil's cast interpreting those songs through dance and dazzling costumes. While both productions seek to portray Michael's life through his music, they each incorporate different songs and storylines. As Cirque's director of creation Welby Altidor told *USA Today* in 2013, *ONE* aimed to be more intimate and interactive than *Immortal*. "It's another story about Michael's genius," he said. "There will be experiences above [the audience], on the side and in the front."

During its three-year run, *Immortal* toured 141 cities and 27 countries, playing to over 3.5 million people. According to *Billboard*'s Bob Allen, the show ranks at #8 on its Highest Grossing Tours list, earning $360 million. The Cirque production outsold events such as Bruce Springsteen's *Wrecking Ball* tour and the Rolling Stones' *Voodoo Lounge* outing.

The *Immortal* soundtrack album helped boost sales, debuting on November 21, 2011. Peaking at #24 on the *Billboard* 200, the disc reached #5 on the Top R&B/Hip Hop Albums chart. Sales were greatest in Japan, where it reached #9.

Reviews for the set were mixed. NPR's Ann Powers pronounced the soundtrack "a fun new way to take on Jackson's music—not offering a ton of new insights, but helping us hear more clearly what we thought we knew so well," However, critics like the *Los Angeles Times*' Randall Roberts claimed the music was a victim of the show's pacing. "The soundtrack is beholden to the Cirque/*Immortal* storyline and therefore sequenced not for the dance floor but for a Las Vegas–style production," he wrote. "As a result, a wildly inventive remix, such as what [Kevin] Antunes does for 'Dancing Machine,' barely gets going before grinding to a halt a few minutes in."

*Michael Jackson ONE* continues to perform well. When tickets first went on sale before its official world premiere on June 29, 2013, sales were so brisk that Cirque du Soleil instantly sold out all performances through August 31. According to the *Las Vegas Sun*'s extremely positive article "Strip Scribbles: 'Michael Jackson One' Ticket Sales Exceed Expectations at Mandalay Bay," its two-shows-a-night schedule still could not accommodate the demand for seating.

## Xscape (2014)

Having learned from their experience with 2010's *Michael*, Jackson's estate and Sony planned their next compilation of demos and unfinished songs very carefully. They enlisted L. A. Reid to oversee the project, and he in turn tapped Timbaland to executive produce. Reid then enlisted an impressive list of today's hit makers, including Rodney "Darkchild" Jerkins, Dr. Freeze, Jerome "J-Roc" Harmon, and Stargate to enhance the recordings. The idea was to construct an album as Michael would have recorded it in the present day. Ensuring the veracity of the demos, the *Xscape Deluxe Edition* includes all the untouched songs in addition to the updated, rearranged versions.

*Xscape* draws from material Michael wrote and recorded between the early 1980s and 2001. Estate executor John Branca and assistant Karen Langford sorted through the music vault, selecting twenty-four tracks that best fit Reid's

The second posthumous release, *Xscape* (2014), received critical acclaim for Timbaland's production. The first single, "Love Never Felt So Good," features a virtual duet with faithful student Justin Timberlake.

*Author's collection*

specifications. Once Reid narrowed down the selections, he instructed the producers to create new tracks from Michael's a cappella vocals. According to the 2014 *Billboard* cover story on *Xscape*, Michael would record in multiple studios, sing chords or arrangements, and bring producers demos with voice orchestrations and his unsurpassed beatboxing. He would then work on the tracks over a period of years, occasionally revisiting them for consideration on future albums.

When the producers isolated the vocal tracks, they also kept any ambient noise. "You can hear his foot in the booth when he's singing, and his fingers snapping," Jerkins told *Billboard*'s Joe Levy in 2014. "It was all raw, it was real. It wasn't like, 'Take the snaps out, take the stomps out.' No — it's real. It's him in the booth, and he's feeling what he's doing."

The eight tracks on *Xscape* represents various stages of Michael's career. "Love Never Felt So Good" dates from the 1983 Anka collaborations; for the radio version, Justin Timberlake overdubbed his vocals, while Timbaland added the percussion track from 1979's "Working Day and Night." Originally based on a sample from America's "A Horse with No Name," the retitled "A Place with No Name" sports a pounding techno beat. A snaking bass line throbs through "Chicago," while the charming "Loving You" features a younger Michael easily navigating the airy melody. "Slave to the Rhythm," a track Michael had worked on since 1990, sounds modern with an EDM arrangement. The mid-tempo "Blue

Gangsta" contains a particular emotive lead vocal, as if Michael was acting out the story just with his voice. Recorded during the *Invincible* sessions, the title track revisits the theme of fame as prison; while the remixed version features blasting horns, the original demo's heavy, minimal percussion surpasses the remake. The most controversial song, "Do You Know Where Your Children Are?" addresses sexual abuse and teenage runaways. While the song invited derision from many critics, the *New York Daily News*' Jim Farber highlighted it in his review, saying that it "suggests what Jackson might have sounded like had he made an EDM record. The stripped electronics have real bite, equaling the energy of Jackson's whoops."

Upon its release, *Xscape* received mixed reviews. *Classic Pop*'s Kate Allen cites the untouched "Love Never Felt So Good" as superior, calling it "goose bump– if not tear-inducing. "This purity and integrity should be the aim for any future Michael Jackson release." While Pitchfork's Douglas Wolk agrees with this assessment, he dislikes the rest of the album, summing up the tracks as "outtakes and misfires."

In contrast, *Billboard*'s Levy thoroughly enjoyed the album, awarding it four and a half stars out of five. He praises the producers for working with Michael's a cappella vocals, thus placing "Jackson's vocal abilities—his smooth ecstasy and pained grit; his swoops, pops, shouts and grunts; those moments when he's overcome by emotion, or breaking free of all restraint and gravity—front and center." He singles out "A Place with No Name" as a standout, comparing its keyboards to a Stevie Wonder cut and describing the melody as reminiscent of "Remember the Time." The *New Musical Express*'s review was largely positive, with Mark Beaumont calling tracks like "Chicago" and "Slave to the Rhythm" "ultra-modern" and describing "Love Never Felt So Good" as placing Michael "right back in his disco heyday."

Unlike *Michael*, *Xscape* received heavy promotion on several fronts. "Love Never Felt So Good" and "A Place with No Name" both appeared in Jeep's summer campaign, and the latter song became the first to be premiered exclusively on Twitter. The video for "Love Never Felt So Good" mixes vintage Michael footage with shots of Timberlake dancing and singing his sections. Fans sporting *Xscape* T-shirts also lip-synch to the song while dancers reenact scenes from his most famous videos. The most unusual marketing occurred at the 2014 *Billboard Music Awards*, when a "hologram" of Michael appeared on stage to perform "Slave to the Rhythm" with real backup dancers.

Overall, *Xscape* performed well on the charts, topping the *Billboard* R&B Album chart and reaching #2 on the pop 200. The lead single "Love Never Felt So Good" hit the Top 10 on the Adult Contemporary chart and the Hot 100. In the UK, *Xscape* became Michael's tenth #1 album, debuting in the position. As of January 2015, *Xscape* has sold over 459,000 copies in the US, and has been certified platinum in Brazil and Poland and gold in over thirteen other countries.

These CDs, films, and theatrical productions will assuredly be the first of many planned Michael Jackson projects. His huge amount of unreleased material, along with his continuing popularity, ensures that his legacy will endure for years to come.

# 41

# Every Path You Take You're Leaving Your Legacy

## Michael Jackson's Lasting Impact on Music, Dance, and Pop Culture

*"To give in the best way I can through song and through dance and through music. I believe that all art has as its ultimate goal the union between the material and the spiritual, the spiritual and the divine. I believe that that's the reason for the very existence of art, and I feel I was chosen as an instrument to give music and love and harmony to the world."*

—Michael Jackson's response to Oprah Winfrey's question concerning his life's purpose, *Michael Talks to . . . Oprah Live*, ABC-TV, February 10, 1993

FADE IN.
INT. COFFEE SHOP—DAY

A fortysomething woman sits at a table, sipping hot chocolate while working on her laptop. She surfs the Internet, looking for new music. Browsing YouTube, she soon learns that the adage "everything old is new again" still largely rings true.

*Click.* Usher's 2014 "Good Kisser" video appears, during which he breaks out dance moves such as the "walking against the wind" step and standing on his toes.

*Click.* Justin Timberlake's 2013 hit "Take Back the Night" flashes on the computer screen. As he stands on his toes and glide his feet across the stage, he croons lines such as "taking over!" over strings and horns right out of *Off the Wall*. A brief search reveals his ongoing devotion to Michael, which includes often singing in falsetto and performing dance tunes such as "Rock Your Body" (a track originally written for Michael) and "Like I Love You" (where Timberlake dons a fedora and red shirt for the video, executing Michael-esque dance routines).

*Click.* Beyoncé has posted clips of interviews promoting her self-titled 2013 visual album. What inspired her to create videos for every song on her new collection? The singer explains in her electronic press kit for her self-titled album that she fondly remembered seeing the "Thriller" video premiere, adding, "I miss that immersive experience. Now people only listen to a few seconds of song on the iPods and they don't really invest in the whole experience."

*Click.* Lady Gaga's 2014 video for "G.U.Y." features a cameo from a Michael lookalike, and past videos such as "Born This Way" and "Telephone" display Michael's influence in their dance routines and mini-movie quality featuring special effects.

*Click.* A brief visit to Spotify and a listen through Mary J. Blige's 2014 album *The London Sessions* reveals a subtle Michael tribute. During the track "Pick Me Up," Blige begins chanting "shamon," a reference to one of Michael's favorite ad-libs.

FADE OUT.

Since Michael Jackson's tragic 2009 death, interest in his music has steadily increased. In 2014, Michael's estate earned more than $140 million; his second posthumous collection, *Xscape*, debuted at #2 on the *Billboard* 200, and his virtual duet with Timberlake, "Love Never Felt So Good," reached #9 on the Hot 100 in May. Cirque du Soleil's tribute *ONE* will play in Las Vegas for the foreseeable future,

and more collections of previously unreleased material will continue being released.

Even more important than sales figures, however, is how he forever changed music, videos, and pop culture. He broke through racial and musical barriers, creating a genre-spanning sound. His military jackets, fedora, white socks, loafers, and single glove served as his trademarks, his dance steps and stage presence establishing him as a well-rounded entertainer. In addition, his heavily percussive singing style influenced generations of artists, as did his tenor and falsetto. Those techniques communicated a wide range of emotions, making songs dramatic readings as much as enjoyable pop tunes. His music videos set the standard all future clips tried to emulate, bringing movie-making techniques to what was considered a throwaway medium.

Today's pop charts are dominated by R&B and hip hop, a trend Michael began with *Thriller* and subsequent albums. Before the blockbuster's release, music tended to be heavily segregated. Pop tracks were played on Top 40 radio, and R&B songs were

*Michael Jackson's This Is It*, a documentary detailing the rehearsals for Michael's 2009 London concerts, gave fans a glimpse into preparations for what would have been his final stage performances. Despite showing for only two weeks in theaters, the film became the highest-grossing concert movie and documentary of all time, earning more than $260 million worldwide.

*Author's collection*

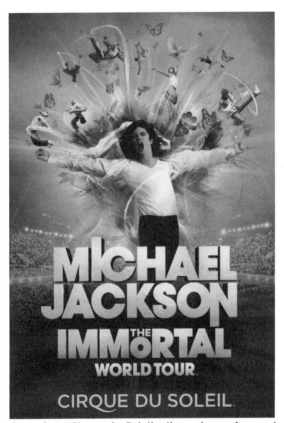

One of two Cirque du Soleil tribute shows, *Immortal* toured the world in 2014, delighting audiences with remixed versions of Michael Jackson favorites as well as dazzling staging and choreography. A permanent Cirque du Soleil show, *One*, is currently playing at Mandalay Bay in Las Vegas.                      *Author's collection*

aired on urban stations. When tracks such as "Billie Jean," "Beat It," "Thriller," and "Wanna Be Startin' Somethin'" were released, their across-the-board popularity demanded that they be played on both kinds of stations. At that time, few artists enjoyed such massive crossover success—a phenomenon that has since become common. For that reason alone, Michael's title of "King of Pop" is well deserved, as he changed the sound and style of contemporary pop music.

In addition to expanding pop's musical boundaries, he also elevated disco and dance music to a more respected level. The last years of disco saw oversaturation, with producers often receiving top billing over the artist. Thus the artists became somewhat interchangeable and faceless, the tracks cranked out to satisfy the public's insatiable taste for disco regardless of quality. Michael and Quincy Jones changed the trend with *Off the Wall*, a masterpiece melding jazz, R&B, and pop to create a sophisticated, adult kind of dance music. Instead of simply drawing people to the dance floor, tracks such as "Don't Stop 'Til You Get Enough" and "Working Day and Night" intrigued with their intricate percussion as well as Michael's innovative singing style. His use of gasps, breaths, hiccups, and beatboxing enhanced the percussion, a technique emulated by Timberlake, Usher, and British techno artist Jamie Lidell.

Unlike other artists, Michael wanted to master several talents: singing, songwriting, dancing, acting, and filmmaking. Future artists would try to emulate these skills, but no one has approached his level as a full entertainer. A bridge between old Hollywood and contemporary flash, Michael's art was an homage to legends such as Judy Garland, Gene Kelly, Fred Astaire, and Sammy Davis Jr., but he updated their music and dance to fit the disco era, the 1980s glam years, and the hip hop– and rock-dominated 1990s.

Michael's final album, *Invincible*, saw itself competing against a musical climate the singer greatly shaped. In 2001, pop artists such as the Backstreet Boys, *NSYNC, 98

Degrees, Christina Aguilera, and Britney Spears ruled the charts, and all of them owed a great debt to the King of Pop. Blending pop, R&B, and hip hop; filming expensive videos with complicated, heavily synchronized dance routines; staging elaborate live performances virtually recreating their videos: years earlier, Michael had pioneered these techniques, and by the 2000s they had become the norm. The Backstreet Boys even paid tribute to the "Thriller" video in their clip for "Everybody (Backstreet's Back)," transforming into monsters and executing a distinctly familiar dance routine.

Finally, Michael helped make message songs "cool." While he did not invent the charity concert and single, he helped elevate them to greater heights beginning with "We Are the World." A slew of songs followed, such as "Sun City" by Artists United Against Apartheid (1985); "That's What Friends Are For" by Dionne Warwick, Stevie Wonder, Gladys Knight, and Elton John (1985); "Let It Be" by Ferry Aid (1987); and 2010's "We Are the World 25" benefiting victims of the Haitian earthquake. Throughout his solo years, he continually wrote and recorded songs spotlighting poverty, war, child abuse, the environment, and AIDS, eventually establishing his Heal the World Foundation to raise money for various causes. Through these actions, Michael demonstrated that R&B and pop could be used for the greater good.

When he was a child performer, Michael set new expectations for young talent by convincingly singing intelligent pop songs. As a teenager, he elevated disco to new heights by writing sophisticated songs that also lured listeners to the dance floor. As he entered his adult years and embarked on a full-time solo career, he demonstrated that pop songs could encompass seemingly disparate genres and address complex issues. He also revealed the visual aspects of his music, with

Released in 2008, *Thriller 25* marked the twenty-fifth anniversary of the landmark album. In addition to remastered versions of the original tracks, the package contains remixes overseen by will.i.am as well as bonus tracks such as Vincent Price's complete rap from "Thriller" and the previously unreleased "For All Time."                    *Author's collection*

The *Xscape Deluxe Edition* includes this poster by Mr. Brainwash, an artist
Michael admired and befriended.                    *Author's collection*

cinematic videos becoming inextricably tied to the original recordings. Instead of
viewing music videos as throwaway promotional tools, he saw them as an art form
in themselves. His innovative dance moves, the special effects, and story lines
transformed the music video into a must-see event, both bolstering his career and
essentially molding MTV. Finally, he proved that musicians could also make fine
actors, his turn in *The Wiz* and *Ghosts* as well as his short videos daring artists to
stretch their skills beyond singing.

To paraphrase his 1991 *Dangerous* track, he was indeed gone too soon. But
Michael's legacy as an all-around entertainer will remain through his videos and
music. As younger artists such as Justin Bieber, Rihanna, and Pharrell prove,
future generations continue to rediscover Michael's timeless art and choose to
follow his lead.

During his final major interview, Michael told *Ebony* in 2007, "I always want to
do music that inspires or influences another generation. You want what you create
to live, be it sculpture or painting or music. Like Michelangelo, he said, 'I know
the creator will go, but his work survives.'" Michael Jackson may no longer be with
us, but his body of work lives on and will inspire future artists to shatter boundaries
of popular music, video, dance, and film.

# Bibliography

"40 Years Ago Today: The Jim Nabors Hour." J5 Collector. September 17, 2010, http://j5collector.blogspot.com/2010/09/jim-nabors.html.

"50 Best Michael Jackson Songs." *Rolling Stone*, June 23, 2014. Accessed February 7, 2015. www.rollingstone.com/music/pictures/50-best-michael -jackson-songs-20140623.

"500 Greatest Albums of All Time." *Rolling Stone*, May 31, 2012. Accessed January 11, 2015. www.rollingstone.com/music/lists/500-greatest-albums -of-all-time-20120531.

Abbey, John. "The Jacksons: *Triumph* (Epic)." *Blues & Soul*, October 21, 1980. Accessed January 15, 2015. www.rocksbackpages.com/Library/Article/ the-jacksons-itriumphi-epic.

———. "Michael Jackson: Michael's Peacock Music." *Blues & Soul*, August 1970. Accessed January 20, 2015. www.rocksbackpages.com/Library/Article/michael -jackson-michael-jacksons-peacock-music.

"Action Jackson." *Vibe*, June/July 1995: 52–57.

Adams, Michael. "The Cold Case: Director Mick Garris on Michael Jackson's Forgotten *Ghosts*." *Movieline*, July 14, 2009. Accessed February 19, 2015. http:// movieline.com/2009/07/14/the-cold-case-director-mick-garris-on-michael -jacksons-forgotten-ghosts/.

Allen, Bob. "Michael Jackson *Immortal* Tour Wraps with Eighth-Best Gross of All Time." *Billboard*, September 11, 2014. Accessed January 22, 2015. www .billboard.com/articles/columns/chart-beat/6251218/michael-jackson -immortal-tour-eighth-best.

Allen, Kate. "Michael Jackson: *Xscape* (Epic)." *Classic Pop*, August 2014. Accessed January 22, 2015. www.rocksbackpages.com/Library/Article/ michael-jackson-ixscapei-epic-.

———. "When Michael Was Bad: Michael Jackson: *Bad 25*." *Rock's Backpages*, September 24, 2012. Accessed June 5, 2015. www.rocksbackpages.com/ Library/Article/when-michael-was-bad-michael-jackson-ibad-25i.

Alletti, Vince. "Album Reviews: Michael Jackson—*Ben*." *Rolling Stone*, December 7, 1972. Accessed February 7, 2015, http://web.archive.org/web/20080618104812/ www.rollingstone.com/artists/michaeljackson/albums/album/187701/ review/5946973/ben.

Anderson, Kyle. "Why Is 'Man in the Mirror' Jackson's Top-Selling Song on iTunes?" *MTV*, June 30, 2009. Accessed February 23, 2015. www.mtv.com/ news/1615049/why-is-man-in-the-mirror-jacksons-top-selling-song-on-itunes/.

"An Interview with Dr. Freeze" (translated). *Michael Jackson on Beat*, January 28, 2011. Accessed February 4, 2015. http://michaeljacksonbeat.blogspot .com/2011/02/dr-freeze-on-michael-jackson.html.

Ankeny, Jason. "Foster Sylvers." All Music, accessed December 18, 2014. www .allmusic.com/album/foster-sylvers-pride-mgm-mw0000858451.

*Bad 25.* Directed by Spike Lee. 2012. New York, NY: Epic Legacy, 2013. DVD.

Baker, Danny. "The Jacksons: The Great Greenland Mystery." *New Musical Express*, April 4, 1981. Accessed January 15, 2015. www.rocksbackpages.com/Library/ Article/the-jacksons-the-great-greenland-mystery.

Beaumont, Mark. "Michael Jackson: *Invincible*." *New Musical Express*, September 12, 2005. Accessed January 12, 2005. www.nme.com/reviews/5780.

———. "Michael Jackson—*Xscape*." *New Musical Express*, May 23, 2014. Accessed January 22, 2015. www.nme.com/reviews/michael-jackson/15336.

Beaumont-Thomas, Ben. "*Dangerous* Was Michael Jackson's True Career High." *The Guardian*, July 6, 2009. Accessed June 10, 2015. www.theguardian.com/ music/musicblog/2009/jul/06/michael-jackson-dangerous.

"Bee Gees' Barry Gibb Reveals Michael Jackson Collaboration—Video." *New Musical Express*, May 26, 2011. Accessed January 28, 2015. www.nme.com/news/ michael-jackson/56886.

Bernhard, Lisa. "The Once and Future King." *TV Guide*, December 4, 1999. Reprinted in *Michael Jackson: The King of Pop, The Big Picture! The Music! The Man! The Legend! The Interviews!* Ed. Jel D. Lewis (Jones). Phoenix, AZ: Amber Books, 2005. Kindle edition.

Betts, Graham. *Motown Encyclopedia.* AC Publishing, 2009.

Bezner, Kevin. "Concert Rewind: Jacksons' Victory Tour Show Offers Lights, Lasers . . . Perfection." *Florida Times–Union*, July 22, 1984. Accessed January 31, 2015. http://jacksonville.com/news/metro/2009-06-25/story/concert_rewind_ jacksons%E2%80%99_victory_tour_show_offers_lights_lasers_perfecti.

"Biography." *Joe King Carrasco.* 2011. Accessed February 2, 2015. www.joeking.com/ joe-king-carrasco-media-pages/joe-king-carrasco-biography.

"Biography." *Mick Jackson*, accessed January 14, 2015, www.mickjacksonmusic. com/page1/page1.html.

Bliss, Karen. "Spike Lee Revisits Michael Jackson's Career for 'Bad 25' Documentary." *Rolling Stone*, September 17, 2012. Accessed January 22, 2015. www.rollingstone.com/music/news/spike-lee-revisits-michael-jacksons-career -for-bad25-documentary-20120917.

Boddicker, Michael. "Michael Jackson Keyboard Sounds of His Signature Songs Then and Now." *Keyboard Magazine*, September 1, 2009. Accessed June 3, 2015. www.keyboardmag.com/artists/1236/michael-jackson-keyboard-sounds -of-his-signature-songs-then-and-now/27406.

Bottrell, Bill. "Post Here If You Worked on Michael Jackson's DANGEROUS Album." *Gearslutz*, September 16, 2009. Accessed January 27, 2015. https:// www.gearslutz.com/board/so-much-gear-so-little-time/403276-post-here-if-you -worked-michael-jacksons-dangerous-album-24.html#post4582524.

Bowen, John. "Gothic Motifs." *Discovering Literature: Romantics and Victorians.* Accessed February 12, 2015. www.bl.uk/romantics-and-victorians/articles/gothic-motifs.

Brackett, Nathan, and Christina David Hoard, eds. "The Jackson 5." *The New Rolling Stone Album Guide.* New York: Simon and Schuster, 2004: 410.

"Brad Buxer Interview," *Black & White* (translation). November/December 2009. Accessed February 4, 2015. http://info.sonicretro.org/Brad_Buxer_Interview_%28Black_%26_White,_November/December_2009%29.

Bream, Jon. "Review of Jackson's 1988 Met Center Concert." *Minneapolis Star Tribune,* May 5, 1988. Accessed January 25, 2015. www.startribune.com/entertainment/49123542.html.

Brown, Geoff. *Michael Jackson: A Life in Music.* London: Omnibus, 2009.

Browne, David. "*HIStory.*" *Entertainment Weekly,* June 23, 1995. Accessed February 15, 2015. www.ew.com/article/1995/06/23/history-past-present-and-future-book-i.

———. "*Invincible* (2001)—Michael Jackson." *Entertainment Weekly,* November 9, 2001. Accessed January 12, 2015. www.ew.com/ew/article/0,,20396305_253595,00.html.

———. "Michael Jackson's 20 Greatest Videos: The Stories Behind the Vision." *Rolling Stone,* June 24, 2014. Accessed February 19, 2015. www.rollingstone.com/music/pictures/michael-jacksons-20-greatest-videos-the-stories-behind-the-vision-20140624.

Buzwell, Greg. "Dracula: Vampires, Perversity, and Victorian Anxieties." *Discovering Literature: Romantics and Victorians.* Accessed February 12, 2015. www.bl.uk/romantics-and-victorians/articles/dracula.

Cadman, Chris, and Craig Halstead. *Michael Jackson: For the Record.* London: New Generation Publishing, 2009.

———. *Michael Jackson: The Early Years.* Hertford, England: Authors OnLine, 2002.

Calabrese, Peter. *How Michael Jackson and the Moonwalk Saved NBC.* Calabrese Books, 2012. Kindle edition.

Callahan, Joe. "Ocala Sound Engineer Saw Jackson at His Best." *The Gainesville Sun,* June 27, 2009. Accessed January 28, 2015. www.gainesville.com/article/20090627/articles/906271005.

Campbell, Lisa. *Michael: The Complete Story of the King of Pop.* Apogee, 2012. Kindle edition.

Canby, Vincent. "'Big Screen' Takes on New Meaning." *The New York Times,* April 19, 1987: A18.

Carter, Kelley L. "5 Things You Can Learn about New Jack Swing." *Chicago Tribune,* August 10, 2008. Accessed February 4, 2015. http://articles.chicago-tribune.com/2008-08-10/news/0808080318_1_new-edition-new-jack-city-swing.

Chen, Joyce. "Michael Jackson's Daughter Paris Claims Singer's Last Album Used Impostor Jason Malachi's Voice." *New York Daily News,* February 29, 2012. Accessed January 21, 2015. www.nydailynews.com/entertainment/music-arts/michael-jackson-daughter-paris-claims-legendary-singer-album-impostor-voice-article-1.1030559.

Christgau, Robert. "The Christgau Consumer Guide." *Creem*, October 1973. Accessed February 7, 2015. www.robertchristgau.com/xg/cg/crm7310.php.

———. "Christgau's Consumer Guide." *Village Voice*, March 17, 1975. Accessed February 5, 2015. www.robertchristgau.com/xg/cg/cgv3-75.php.

———. "Christgau's Consumer Guide: *Bad* (Epic, 1987)." Accessed June 4, 2015. www.robertchristgau.com/get_artist.php?id=932.

———. "Consumer Guide Reviews: *Invincible* (Epic, 2001)." Accessed February 25, 2015. www.robertchristgau.com/get_artist.php?id=932&name=Michael +Jackson.

Clerk, Carol. "Michael Jackson: The Bowl, Milton Keynes." *Melody Maker*, September 17, 1988. Accessed January 25, 2015. www.rocksbackpages.com/Library/Article/michael-jackson-the-bowl-milton-keynes.

Cocks, Jay. "The Badder They Come: Michael Jackson Busts out with His First Album Since *Thriller*." *Time*, September 14, 1987: 85-86.

Colacello, Bob, and Andy Warhol. "Michael Jackson." *Interview*, October 1982. Accessed January 29, 2015. www.interviewmagazine.com/music/michael-jackson-1982/#_.

Collier, Aldore. "Stevie Wonder Says His Message Music May Shock but His Songs Talk about Social Wrongs." *Jet*, May 30, 1988: 58–60.

Committee on Commerce, Science, and Transportation. *Record Labeling: Hearing before the Committee on Commerce, Science, and Transportation*. 99th Cong., 1st session, September 19, 1985.

Concepcion, "Michael Jackson Cameo Shocks Akon Songwriter." *Billboard*, July 3, 2008. Accessed January 29, 2015. www.billboard.com/articles/news/1044909/michael-jackson-cameo-shocks-akon-songwriter.

Connelly, Christopher. "Michael Jackson Gets Serious." *Rolling Stone*, January 20, 1983: 46–47.

Cook, Richard. "Welcome to the Bad Boy's Island: Michael Jackson: *Bad*." *Sounds*, September 12, 1987. Accessed June 2, 2015. www.rocksbackpages.com/Library/Article/welcome-to-the-bad-boys-island-michael-jackson-ibadi-epic-.

Cooper, Mark. "The Jacksons: Off the Cuff." *Record Mirror*, March 2, 1981. Accessed January 20, 2015. www.rocksbackpages.com/Library/Article/the-jacksons-off-the-cuff.

Corliss, Richard. "Let's Go to the Feelies: Michael Jackson and George Lucas Give Disney A 3-D Dream." *Time*, September 22, 1986: 80–81.

Cromelin, Richard. "Michael Jackson Has a Good Thing in 'Bad.'" Los Angeles Times, August 31, 1987. Accessed June 5, 2015. www.latimes.com/la-archive-bad-review-aug31-story.html.

Currell, Christopher. "The Event Horizon: Synclavier, Music and Michael Jackson." *Headphone.Guru*, March 31, 2015. Accessed June 3, 2015. http://headphone.guru/the-event-horizon-synclavier-music-and-michael-jackson/.

Curtis, Jim. *Rock Eras: Interpretations of Music and Society 1954-1984*. Bowling Green, OH: Bowling Green State University Press, 1987.

"*Dangerous* Deposition." *MJ Translate*, accessed December 15, 2015. www.mjtranslate.com/en/interviews/1228/.

Dargis, Manohla. "Michael Jackson's This Is It: The Pop Spectacular That Almost Was." *The New York Times*, October 28, 2009. Accessed January 21, 2015. www .nytimes.com/2009/10/29/movies/29this.html.

Dasun, Allah. "When 'Heaven Can Wait': Teddy Riley Remembers Michael Jackson." *Hip Hop Wired*, July 8, 2009. Accessed January 13, 2015. http:// hiphopwired.com/2009/07/08/when-heaven-can-wait-teddy-riley-remembers -michael-jackson/.

Davis, Johnny. "Quincy Jones: 'I Knew How to Handle Michael." *The Guardian*, September 8, 2010. Accessed January 26, 2015. www.theguardian.com/music/ 2010/sep/08/quincy-jones.

Diamonds, Lucy. "The Teddy Riley Interview." *Baller Status*, August 30, 2007. Accessed February 4, 2015. www.ballerstatus.com/2007/08/30/the-teddy -riley-interview-by-lucy-diamonds/.

Dolan, Jon. "On the Edge." *Michael*. Ed. Jann S. Wenner. New York: Harper Studio, 2009. 138-143.

Ebert, Roger. "*The Wiz.*" *Chicago Sun-Times*, October 24, 1978. Accessed February 17, 2015. www.rogerebert.com/reviews/the-wiz-1978.

———. "*This Is It.*" *Roger Ebert*, October 27, 2009. Accessed January 21, 2015. www .rogerebert.com/reviews/this-is-it-2009.

*Ebony/Jet Showcase*. Episode no. 75, first broadcast 13 November 1987. Syndicated.

Echols, Alice. *Hot Stuff: Disco and the Remaking of American Culture*. New York: W. W. Norton, 2010. Kindle edition.

Eddy, Chuck. "Sound of Breaking Glass: Michael Jackson's *Dangerous.*" *Village Voice*, December 17, 1991. Accessed February 24, 2015. www.rocksbackpages. com/Library/Article/sound-of-breaking-glass-michael-jacksons-dangerous.

Eldredge, Richard L. "Q&A with Greg Phillinganes." *Atlanta*, June 1, 2012. Accessed February 2, 2015. www.atlantamagazine.com/culture/qa-with-greg -phillinganes1/.

Elias, Jason. "The Jacksons." All Music, accessed December 19, 2014, www.allmusic .com/album/the-jacksons-mw0000194277.

Erlewine, Stephen Thomas. "*Dangerous*—Michael Jackson." All Music. Accessed June 11, 2015. www.allmusic.com/album/dangerous-mw0000674875.

———. "Michael Jackson—Michael." All Music. Accessed January 21, 2015. www .allmusic.com/album/michael-mw0002079107.

———. "Michael Jackson: *Off the Wall.*" All Music. Accessed January 11, 2015. www .allmusic.com/album/off-the-wall-mw0000190332.

———. "'Michael Jackson's This Is It.'" All Music. Accessed January 21, 2015. www .allmusic.com/album/michael-jacksons-this-is-it-mw0001379083.

Essoyan, Susan. "A Big Aloha for Michael." *Los Angeles Times*, January 6, 1997. Accessed January 25, 2015. http://articles.latimes.com/1997-01-06/ entertainment/ca-15947_1_michael-jackson.

"Exclusive Interview: Michael Jackson." *TV Guide*, November 10–16, 2001. *Michael Jackson the King of Pop: The Big Picture, the Music! The Man! The Legend! The Interviews! An Anthology*, ed. Jel Jones. INgrooves, 2005.

"Fan Files Lawsuit and Alleges That Michael Jackson Doesn't Sing on 2010 Posthumous Album." *New Musical Express*, June 13, 2014. Accessed January 21, 2015. www.nme.com/news/michael-jackson/77888.

Farber, Jim. "'Xscape,' Michael Jackson's Second Posthumous Album." *New York Daily News*, May 9, 2014. Accessed January 22, 2015. www.nydailynews.com/entertainment/music-arts/stars-new-michael-jackson-album-article-1.1786008.

Fast, Susan. *Michael Jackson's Dangerous (33 1/3)*. New York: Bloomsbury Publishing. 2014. Kindle Edition.

Fekadu, Mesfin. "Rodney 'Darkchild' Jerkins Dishes on Michael Jackson's Posthumous Album 'Xscape.'" *Huffington Post*, May 3, 2014. Accessed February 4, 2015. www.huffingtonpost.com/2014/05/03/rodney-darkchild-jerkins-posthumous-michael-jackson-xscape_n_5258854.html.

Fisher, Mark. "And When the Groove Is Dead and Gone: The End of Jacksonism." *The Resistible Demise of Michael Jackson*, ed. Mark Fisher. New Alresford, Hampshire: Zero Books, 2009.

Flick, Larry. "Jackson's 'Story'—Track by Track." *Billboard*, May 20, 1995. 14.

Fong-Torres, Ben. *The Motown Album*. New York: St. Martin's, 1990: 9–17.

———. "The Jackson 5: The Men Don't Know but the Little Girls Understand." *Rolling Stone*, April 29, 1971: 24.

———. "The Jackson 5." *Rock and Roll Hall of Fame*, 1997, www.rocksbackpages.com/Library/Article/the-jackson-5.

Fricke, David. "The Jacksons: U.S. Tour July-December 1981." *Rolling Stone*, June 4, 1987: 109–110.

Friedlander, Paul. *Rock and Roll: A Social History*. Cambridge, MA: Westview, 2006.

*Future Music*. "Michael Jackson: Recording Dangerous with Teddy Riley." *MusicRadar.com*, July 3, 2009. Accessed June 9, 2015. www.musicradar.com/news/guitars/michael-jackson-recording-dangerous-with-teddy-riley-211776.

Gallagher, James P. "Jackson No Thriller in Rainy Moscow Concert." *Chicago Tribune*, September 16, 1993. Accessed January 25, 2015. http://articles.chicagotribune.com/1993-09-16/news/9309160283_1_free-tickets-michael-jackson-concert-wednesday-night.

George, Nelson. *Thriller: The Musical Life of Michael Jackson*. Cambridge, MA: Da Capo, 2010.

———. *City Kid: A Writer's Memoir of Ghetto Life and Post-Soul Success*. New York: Penguin, 2009.

———. "The Rhythm & the Blues: Prince Agrees to Talk—A Little." *Billboard*, December 18, 1982: 52; 54.

———. *Where Did Our Love Go? The Rise and Fall of the Motown Sound*. Chicago: University of Illinois Press, 2007.

Giles, Jeff. "35 Years Ago: Kenny Loggins Keeps the Fire Burning Bright." *Ultimate Classic Rock*, October 29, 2014. Accessed February 2, 2015. http://ultimateclassicrock.com/kenny-loggins-keep-the-fire/.

———. "Rumor Debunked: Michael Jackson Never Sang on a Doobie Brothers Record." *Ultimate Classic Rock*, April 18, 2014. Retrieved February 1, 2015. http://ultimateclassicrock.com/doobie-brothers-michael-jackson-debunked/.

Gleiberman, Owen. "Michael Jackson's This Is It (2009)," *Entertainment Weekly*, October 28, 2009. Accessed January 21, 2015. www.ew.com/ew/article/ 0,,20396305_20315850,00.html.

Goldberg, Michael. "Michael Jackson: The Making of the King of Pop." *Rolling Stone*, January 9, 1992. Accessed February 5, 2015. www.rocksbackpages.com/ Library/Article/michael-jackson-the-making-of-the-king-of-pop.

——, and Christopher Connelly. "Trouble in Paradise?" *Rolling Stone*, March 15, 1984. Accessed January 30, 2015. www.rollingstone.com/music/news/ trouble-in-paradise-19840315.

Goldman, Albert. "A Black Teen Breakthrough." *Life*, November 27, 1970, 12.

Goodman, Dean. "'New' Michael Jackson Single Written in 1983." *Billboard*, October 13, 2009. Accessed January 30, 2015. www.billboard.com/articles/ news/267087/new-michael-jackson-single-written-in-1983.

Gordy, Berry. *To Be Loved*. New York: Warner, 1994.

Graham, Renée. "The Thriller Is Back with 'Ultimate' Set." *Boston Globe*, November 16, 2004. Accessed January 28, 2015. www.boston.com/news/globe/ living/articles/2004/11/16/the_thriller_is_back_with_ultimate_set/.

Grant, Adrian. *Making HIStory*. New York: Omnibus, 1998.

——. *Michael Jackson: A Visual Documentary 1958-2009, Tribute Edition*. London: Omnibus, 2009. Kindle edition.

Graves, Tom. "Michael Jackson: *Bad*." *Rock and Roll Disc*, November 1987. Accessed March 2, 2015. www.rocksbackpages.com/Library/Article/michael -jacksoni-badi.

Greenburg, Zach O'Malley. *Michael Jackson, Inc.: The Rise, Fall, and Rebirth of a Billion-Dollar Empire*. New York: Atria Books, 2014.

Gundersen, Edna. "Archive: Man in the Mirror." *USA Today*, December 14, 2001. Accessed January 27, 2015. http://usatoday30.usatoday.com/life/music/ news/2009-06-26-mj-archive_N.htm.

Hajari, Nisid. "The King of Pap." *Entertainment Weekly*, September 20, 1996. Accessed January 15, 2015. www.ew.com/ew/article/0,,20396305_294175,00. html.

Hampp, Andrew, and Jason Lipshutz. "Beyoncé Unexpectedly Releases New Self-Titled 'Visual Album' on iTunes." *Billboard*, December 13, 2013. Accessed February 25, 2015. www.billboard.com/articles/columns/the-juice/5827398/ beyonce-unexpectedly-releases-new-self-titled-visual-album-on.

Hanford, Searl. "Talent in Action: Jacksons, Staci Lattisaw, Memorial Auditorium, Buffalo, N.Y." *Billboard*, September 5, 1981: 44.

Harmetz, Aljean. "Disney Gets Top Names for 3-D Film." *New York Times*, July 24, 1985: C13.

Harrington, Richard. "'Moonwalker': It's Baad: Michael Jackson's Extravagant New Arrival." *Washington Post*, January 10, 1989: b01.

Heckel, Aimee. "Chris Modell, Quirky Boulder Lyricist, Wrote Lyrics for Newly Released Michael Jackson Song." *Daily Camera*, January 15, 2011. Accessed January 20, 2015. www.dailycamera.com/entertainment/ci_17086830.

Herrera, Monica. "Akon on Michael Jackson: 'He Was Completely Healthy.'"
    *Billboard*, June 26, 2009. Accessed January 29, 2015. www.billboard.com/
    articles/news/268266/akon-on-michael-jackson-he-was-completely-healthy.
Hiatt, Brian. "Michael Jackson Nearing Completion of New LP." *MTV News*,
    December 21, 2000. Accessed January 13, 2015. www.mtv.com/news/1435389/
    michael-jackson-nearing-completion-of-new-lp/.
Hilburn, Robert. "Behind the Scenes of A Pop Miracle." *Los Angeles Times*, March
    24, 1985: 70.
———. "Michael Jackson's 'Invincible.'" *Los Angeles Times*, October 28, 2001.
    Accessed January 27, 2015. www.latimes.com/la-archive-invincible-review
    -oct28-story.html.
Himes, Geoffrey. "Prince/Michael Jackson/Luther Vandross: Live at the Capital
    Centre." *Columbia Flier*, October 20, 1988. Accessed January 25, 2015.
    www.rocksbackpages.com/Library/Article/princemichael-jacksonluther
    -vandross-live-at-the-capital-centre.
Hobbs, Linda. "V Exclusive: Rodney Jerkins Talks MJ's Last Studio Album,
    *Invincible*." *Vibe*, September 5, 2009. Accessed January 15, 2015. www.vibe
    .com/article/v-exclusive-rodney-jerkins-talks-mjs-last-studio-album-invincible.
Hoff, David J. "A Blueprint for Change." *Education Week*, April 21, 1999, www
    .edweek.org/ew/articles/1999/04/21/32gary.h18.html.
Hoffman, Rob. "In Studio with Michael Jackson." *True Michael Jackson*. Accessed
    January 18, 2015. www.truemichaeljackson.com/true-stories/in-studio/.
Holden, Stephen. "The Jacksons' Family Entertainment." *Rolling Stone*, January
    24, 1980: 76.
———. "Kenny Rodgers [sic] in A Fresh Vein." *The New York Times*, August 9, 1981.
    Accessed February 2, 2015. www.nytimes.com/1981/08/09/arts/kenny-rodgers-
    in-a-fresh-vein.html.
———. "*Off the Wall*—Michael Jackson." *Rolling Stone*, November 1, 1979: 64.
Hoskyns, Barney. "The Jacksons: *Victory*." *New Musical Express*, August 4, 1985.
    Accessed January 29, 2015. www.rocksbackpages.com/Library/Article/
    the-jacksons-ivictoryi-epic.
———. "The Jacksons: Meadowlands Stadium, New Jersey." *New Musical Express*,
    August 1984. Accessed January 31, 2015. www.rocksbackpages.com/Library/
    Article/the-jacksons-meadowlands-stadium-new-jersey.
Huey, Steve. "Artists: Michael Jackson." *Billboard*. Accessed February 24, 2015.
    www.billboard.com/artist/310778/michael-jackson/biography.
Hunt, Dennis. "Jackson Shows Up to Gather Awards, Despite Ankle Injury."
    *Los Angeles Times*, March 11, 1993. Accessed January 24, 2015. http://articles
    .latimes.com/1993-03-11/entertainment/ca-1327_1_michael-jackson.
———. "Music Video Makes Bet on 'Moonwalker.'" *Los Angeles Times*, January 6,
    1989: 22.
Hunter, James. "Being Like Mike." *Rolling Stone*, December 6, 2001. 149.
———. "*Invincible*—Michael Jackson." *Rolling Stone*, December 6, 2001.
    Accessed February 25, 2015. www.rollingstone.com/music/albumreviews/
    invincible-20011206.

———. "King of Pain: *HIStory: Past, Present and Future, Book 1*, Michael Jackson." *Rolling Stone*, August 10, 1995: 55; 57–58.

"In New York It's Jackson Power: Jackson 5: Madison Square Garden, New York." *New Musical Express*, August 14, 1971, www.rocksbackpages.com/Library/Article/in-new-york-its-jackson-power-jackson-5-madison-square-garden-new-york.

"In Profile: Thomas W. (Tom) Sneddon, Jr." *National District Attorneys Association*, 2007. Accessed February 17, 2015. http://web.archive.org/web/20080102103101/www.ndaa.org/ndaa/profile/tom_sneddon_jan_feb_2003.html.

"Interview: Jay Gruska." *Jermaine Jackson Music*, April 2012. Accessed January 29, 2015, http://jermainejacksonmusic.com/Site/Interviews.html.

"Interview: Jerry Hey." *Hip-Bone Music*. Accessed February 2, 2015. www.hip-bonemusic.com/b2p_hey1.html.

"Interviews: The Floacist." *Yazmar.com*, December 10, 2010. Accessed January 13, 2015. www.yazmar.com/2010/12/02/exclusive-interviewnatalie-the-floacist-stewart/.

Ivory, Steven. *"Thriller." Electronic Urban Report*, December 4, 2007. Accessed October 31, 2013. www.eurweb.com/story/eur39005.cfm.

*J5 Collector Blog*. http://j5collector.blogspot.com/search/label/1974.

"Album Reviews: *Jackson 5 Christmas Album*." *Billboard*, December 5, 1970: 63.

Jackson, Jermaine. *You Are Not Alone: Michael Through a Brother's Eyes*. New York: Simon and Schuster, 2012.

Jackson, Michael. *Moonwalk*. New York: Harmony Books, 1988.

"Jackson Plans Record for Attack Victims." BBC News, September 17, 2001. Accessed February 25, 2015. http://news.bbc.co.uk/2/hi/entertainment/1548056.stm.

"Jackson Pens, Produces New Tune for Holiday." *Jet*, June 10, 1985: 58.

Jefferson, Margo. *On Michael Jackson*. New York: Vintage Books, 2007.

Johnson, Billy Jr. "Songwriter Gets the Butterflies." Yahoo Music, November 15, 2001. Accessed February 1, 2015. http://new.music.yahoo.com/michael-jackson/news/artist-name-michael-jackson-id-1013025-songwriter-gets-the-butterflies--12063973.

Johnson, Robert E. "Michael Jackson: Breaking Eight-Year Silence, Superstar Talks Freely to JPC." *Ebony*, November 1992: 126-128.

———. "The Jackson Family Talk about Michael." *Jet*, March 26, 2009: 39–40.

Jones, Lucy. "The Incredible Way Michael Jackson Wrote Music." *New Musical Express*, April 2, 2014. Accessed January 18, 2015. www.nme.com/blogs/nme-blogs/the-incredible-way-michael-jackson-wrote-music.

Jones, Quincy. *Q: The Autobiography of Quincy Jones*. New York: Broadway Books, 2002.

Jones, Regina. "MJ: Unbreakable." *Vibe*, March 2002: 108-116.

Kaufman, Gil. "Michael Jackson's Posthumous Sales Surge." MTV, June 29, 2009. Accessed February 23, 2015. www.mtv.com/news/1614952/michael-jacksons-posthumous-sales-surge/.

———. "'Michael Jackson's This Is It' Ticket Sales Break International Records." MTV, September 29, 2009. Accessed January 21, 2015. www.mtv.com/

news/1622528/michael-jacksons-this-is-it-ticket-sales-break-international
-records/.

———. "Michael Jackson Working on Katrina Song—But with Whom?" MTV News,
September 19, 2005. Accessed February 4, 2015. www.mtv.com/news/1509834/
michael-jackson-working-on-katrina-song-but-with-whom/.

Kaufman, Sara. "Sara Kaufman Analyzes the Magic Behind Jackson's Dancing."
*Washington Post*, June 27, 2009. Accessed January 18, 2015. www.washington-
post.com/wp-dyn/content/article/2009/06/26/AR2009062604257.html.

Kiersh, Ed. "Run-D.M.C. Is Beating the Rap." *Rolling Stone*, December 4, 1986.
Accessed January 26, 2015. www.rollingstone.com/music/news/beating
-the-rap-19861204.

Knopper, Steve. "Inside Michael Jackson's Return." *Rolling Stone*, December 9,
2010: 13; 16.

Kot, Greg. "Justin Timberlake, 'The 20/20 Experience 2 of 2' Review." *Chicago
Tribune*, September 30, 2013. Accessed January 12, 2015. http://articles
.chicagotribune.com/2013-09-30/entertainment/chi-justin-timberlake
-review-20130929_1_20-20-experience-wallrdquo-producer-timbaland.

Leach, Robin. "Strip Scribbles: 'Michael Jackson One' Ticket Sales Exceed
Expectations at Mandalay Bay." *Las Vegas Sun*, June 5, 2013. Accessed January
22, 2015. www.lasvegassun.com/vegasdeluxe/2013/jun/05/strip-scribbles
-michael-jackson-one-ticket-sales-/.

Lester, Paul. "Michael Jackson's Twenty Greatest Hits." *The Resistible Demise of
Michael Jackson*, ed. Mark Fisher. Washington: Zero, 2009: 18–36.

———. "The Starman who Fell to Earth: Michael Jackson: Don Valley
Stadium, Sheffield." *Uncut*, September 1997. Accessed January 25, 2015.
www.rocksbackpages.com/Library/Article/the-starman-who-fell-to-earth
-michael-jackson-don-valley-stadium-sheffield-.

Levy, Joe. "Bringing Michael Jackson Back: The Inside Story of 'Xscape.'"
*Billboard*, May 5, 2014. Accessed January 22, 2015. www.billboard.com/
articles/news/6077455/michael-jackson-billboard-cover-story-xscape-full
-album-details?page=0%2C1.

———. "Michael Jackson's 'Xscape': Track-by-Track Review." *Billboard*, May 13,
2014. Accessed January 22, 2015. www.billboard.com/articles/review/6084867/
michael-jackson-xscape-album-review-track-billboard.

Lewis, Randy. "A Time for '86 Turkeys—And A Time for Thanks." *Los Angeles
Times*, November 27, 1986: 1.

Light, Alan. "*Dangerous*—Michael Jackson." *Rolling Stone*, January 1, 1992.
Accessed February 24, 2015. www.rollingstone.com/music/albumreviews/
dangerous-19920101.

Lipp, Chaz. "An Interview with Jimmy Jam of the Original 7even, Part Two."
*The Morton Report*, April 19, 2012. Accessed February 16, 2015. www
.themortonreport.com/entertainment/music/an-interview-with-jimmy-jam
-of-the-original-7ven-part-two//.

"Louis Johnson: 'Stomp!'" *Bass Player: Slap Masters Supplement*, Summer 2011.
Accessed February 4, 2015. www.nxtbook.com/nxtbooks/newbay/bp_
slapmasters/index.php?startid=24.

Lyle, Peter. "Michael Jackson's Monster Smash." *The Guardian*, November 25, 2007. Accessed January 8, 2015. www.telegraph.co.uk/culture/3669538/Michael -Jacksons-monster-smash.html.

Mansfield, Brian. "'We Are the World' at 30: 12 Tales You Might Not Know." *USA Today*, January 28, 2015. Accessed February 23, 2015. www.usatoday.com/story/ life/music/2015/01/27/we-are-the-world-30th-anniversary/22395455/.

Markovitz, Adam. "Box Office Report: 'Michael Jackson's This Is It' Makes $101 Million Worldwide." *Entertainment Weekly*, November 1, 2009. Accessed January 21, 2015. http://insidemovies.ew.com/2009/11/01/this-is-it-box-office/.

Maslin, Janet. "At the Movies." *The New York Times*, December 6, 1985: C8.

Martin, Gavin. "Michael Jackson: *Thriller*." *New Musical Express*, December 4, 1982. Accessed January 11, 2015. www.rocksbackpages.com/Library/Article/ michael-jackson-ithrilleri-epic.

McBride, James. "Tito and Randy: Facing Life After the Victory Tour." *People*, December 30, 1984. Accessed January 30, 2015. www.people.com/people/ archive/article/0,,20196977,00.html.

McCormick, Neil. "Michael Jackson, Bruce Springsteen & Bono: Great Singing Is About More Than the Notes." *The Telegraph*, June 30, 2009. Accessed January 18, 2015. http://blogs.telegraph.co.uk/culture/neilmccormick/100000966/ michael-jackson-bruce-springsteen-bono-great-singing-is-about-more-than -the-notes/.

McCready, John. "Michael Jackson: *Bad*." *New Musical Express*, September 12, 1987. Accessed January 29, 2015. www.rocksbackpages.com/Library/Article/ michael-jackson-bad.

McGee, David. "Chestnuts Roasting on an Electric Guitar." *Rolling Stone*, December 30, 1976: 63.

McMillian, Stephen. "Classic *Soul Train* Album Spotlight: The Jackson 5's *ABC*." *Soul Train*, June 3, 2013. http://soultrain.com/2013/06/03/classic-soul -train-album-spotlight-the-jackson-5s-abc/.

McNair, James. "Michael Jackson: Dead Man, Moonwalking: Michael Jackson: *Invincible*." *MOJO*, December 2001. Accessed January 12, 2015. www .rocksbackpages.com/Library/Article/dead-man-moonwalking-michael -jackson-iinviniblei-epic.

Meyers, Kate. "Jackson 5's Final Tour Was 12 Years Ago." *Entertainment Weekly*, July 12, 1996. Accessed January 30, 2015. www.ew.com/article/1996/07/12/ jackson-5s-final-tour-was-12-years-ago.

"Michael and the Jacksons Get Ready for Tour." *Jet*, May 21, 1984: 60–64.

"Michael Jackson's and Lionel Richie's Song Earns Millions for Africa's Famine Victims." *Jet*, April 8, 1985: 60–64.

"Michael Jackson Fans Shouldn't Question New Single 'Hold My Hand' (Should They?)" Pop & Hiss: The *L.A. Times* Music Blog, November 15, 2010. Accessed January 29, 2015. http://latimesblogs.latimes.com/music_blog/2010/11/ michael-jackson-fans-shouldnt-question-new-single-hold-my-hand.html.

"Michael Jackson: *Invincible*." *New Musical Express*, September 12, 2005. Accessed January 12, 2015. www.nme.com/reviews/5744.

"Michael Jackson, Live, on HBO in October." *New York Times*, August 13, 1992. Accessed January 24, 2015. www.nytimes.com/1992/08/13/arts/michael -jackson-live-on-hbo-in-october.html.

"Michael Jackson: My Pain." *The Daily Mirror*, April 12, 1999. Reprinted in *Michael Jackson: The King of Pop, The Big Picture! The Music! The Man! The Legend! The Interviews!* Ed. Jel D. Lewis (Jones). Phoenix, AZ: Amber Books, 2005. Kindle edition.

"Michael Jackson Plays Weird Role in 'Ghosts.'" *Manila Standard*, July 26, 1997: 39.

"Michael Jackson Remembered: The Tributes." *Rolling Stone*, June 25, 2014. Accessed January 27, 2015. www.rollingstone.com/music/pictures/michael-jackson -remembered-the-tributes-20140625/stevie-wonder-0704616.

"Michael Jackson Sails with Two Seas." *Billboard*, April 18, 2006. Accessed February 4, 2015. www.billboard.com/articles/news/58713/michael-jackson -sails-with-two-seas.

*Michael Jackson Talks to . . . Oprah Live*. Directed by Roger Goodman. 1993.

"Michael Jackson: The Peter Pan of Pop." *Newsweek*, January 9, 1983. Accessed January 28, 2015. www.newsweek.com/michael-jackson-peter-pan-pop-207034.

"Michael Jackson: The Star Studded TV Special, the New Album (at Last), the Famous Friends, the 'Wacko Jacko' Image—Does it Add Up to Comeback?" *TV Guide*, November 10, 2001. Reprinted in *Michael Jackson: The King of Pop, The Big Picture! The Music! The Man! The Legend! The Interviews!* Ed. Jel D. Lewis (Jones). Phoenix, AZ: Amber Books, 2005. Kindle edition.

"Michael Jackson Turns on the Crowd and Helps the Doobie Brothers Celebrate Their 10th Anniversary." *Rock & Soul*, March 1980. Accessed February 1, 2015. www.the-michael-jackson-archives.com/rcksoul80.html.

Michaels, Sean. "Bee Gees Singer Reveals Footage of Michael Jackson Collaboration." *Guardian*, May 26, 2011. Accessed January 28, 2015. www.the guardian.com/music/2011/may/26/bee-gees-michael-jackson-collaboration.

Miller, Carl. "'We Are Here to Change the World': *Captain EO* and the Future of Utopia." *Michael Jackson: Grasping the Spectacle*, ed. Christopher Smit. Burlington, VT: Ashgate, 2012: 117–129.

Monroe, Bryan. "Michael Jackson in His Own Words." *Ebony*, December 2007: 94–109.

Montgomery, James. "Did Michael Jackson Compose 'Sonic the Hedgehog 3' Soundtrack?" *MTV News*, December 4, 2009. Accessed February 4, 2015. www .mtv.com/news/1627664/did-michael-jackson-compose-sonic-the-hedgehog -3-soundtrack/.

Moore, Jayne. "Renowned Vocal Coach Seth Riggs Talks about His Special Technique, Workshops, and Camp." *Singeruniverse.com*. Accessed February 26, 2015. www.singeruniverse.com/riggs.htm.

Murph, John. "Michael Jackson's 'Bad' Just Wasn't That Good." *The Atlantic*, September 18, 2012. Accessed June 5, 2015. www.theatlantic.com/entertainment/ archive/2012/09/michael-jacksons-bad-just-wasnt-that-good/262551/.

Murphy, Austin. "It's Halftime!" *Sports Illustrated*. Accessed February 1, 2015. www .si.com/longform/halftime/.

Murphy, Keith. "'Happy Birthday MJ: How 'Remember the Time' Reminds Us of Michael Jackson's Greatness." *Vibe*, August 29, 2014. Accessed June 11, 2015. www.vibe.com/2014/08/happy-birthday-mj-how-remember-time-reminds-us -michael-jacksons-greatness/.

"Music in Slave Life: Recreational Songs—"Shortenin' Bread." *Slavery and the Making of America*, 2004. www.pbs.org/wnet/slavery/experience/education/ feature11.html.

Nathan, David. "The Jackson 5, Junior Walker, the Sisters Love: Empire Pool, Wembley." *Blues & Soul*, December 1, 1972. www.rocksbackpages.com/Library/ Article/the-jackson-5-junior-walker-the-sisters-love-empire-pool-wembley.

———. "The Jacksons." *Blues & Soul*, February 1977. www.rocksbackpages.com/ Library/Article/the-jacksons.

Neal, Mark Anthony. "The Return of the Scarecrow: Michael Jackson's 'Invincible.'" *SeeingBlack.com*, December 21, 2001. Accessed January 13, 2015. www.seeingblack.com/x122101/michaeljackson.shtml.

Newton, Steve. "Jacksons." *Georgia Straight*, November 23, 1984: 16.

Nobleman, Marc Tyler. "The Girl in the Video: 'Smooth Criminal' (1988)." *Noblemania*, July 29, 2013. Accessed February 19, 2015. http://noblemania .blogspot.com/2013/07/the-girl-in-video-smooth-criminal-1988.html.

Palmer, Robert. "Jagger Finishes First Solo Album, 'She's the Boss.'" *New York Times*, January 28, 1985. Accessed January 28, 2015. www.nytimes .com/1985/01/28/arts/jagger-finishes-first-solo-album-she-s-the-boss.html.

———. "Pop: 'Victory' Album Echoes Jacksons' Tour." *New York Times*, July 7, 1984. Accessed January 30, 2015. www.nytimes.com/1984/07/07/arts/pop-victory -album-echoes-jacksons-tour.html.

Pareles, Jon. "Music: To Regain Glory, the New Michael Imitates the Old." *New York Times*, October 28, 2001. Accessed February 25, 2015. www.nytimes .com/2001/10/28/arts/music-to-regain-glory-the-new-michael-imitates-the-old .html?sec=&spon=&pagewanted=2.

———. "Pop View: Michael Jackson Is Angry, Understand?" *New York Times*, June 18, 1995. Accessed February 24, 2015. www.nytimes.com/1995/06/18/arts/ pop-view-michael-jackson-is-angry-understand.html.

Patoski, Joe Nick. "When Michael Jackson Sang with Joe 'King' Carrasco." *Notes and Musings*, June 25, 2009. Accessed February 1, 2015. http://joenickp .blogspot.com/2009/06/when-michael-jackson-sang-with-joe-king.html.

Peel, John. "Review: Michael Jackson." *The Observer*, July 17, 1988. Accessed January 25, 2015. www.theguardian.com/music/2009/jun/28/michaeljackson -popandrock.

Phelan, Kevin. "Dave Mason Brings A Traffic Jam to Tarrytown." *Journal News*, January 6, 2015. Accessed February 2, 2015. www.lohud.com/story/ entertainment/2015/01/06/dave-mason-traffic-jam/21338569/.

"Picks and Pans Review: *Farewell My Summer Love 1984*," *People*, June 25, 1984. Accessed February 5, 2015. www.people.com/people/archive/article/ 0,,20088131,00.html.

Pidgeon, John. "Ever-So-Slightly-Wacko: The Day I Interviewed Michael Jackson (Via Little Sister Janet)." *Rock's Backpages*, June 15, 2009. Accessed January 20,

2015. www.rocksbackpages.com/Library/Article/ever-so-slightly-wacko-the
-day-i-interviewed-michael-jackson-via-little-sister-janet.

"Pipes of Peace." *The Beatles Bible*. Accessed January 28, 2015. www.beatlesbible
.com/people/paul-mccartney/albums/pipes-of-peace/.

"Post Here If You Worked on Michael Jackson's Dangerous Album." *Gearslutz*,
November 14, 2010. Accessed February 16, 2015. https://www.gearslutz.com/
board/so-much-gear-so-little-time/403276-post-here-if-you-worked-michael
-jacksons-dangerous-album-31.html#post6002031.

Powers, Ann. "Ann Powers and Other Pop Critics Remember Michael Jackson's
'Thriller.'" Pop & Hiss: The *L.A. Times* Music Blog, June 25, 2009. Accessed
January 9, 2015, http://latimesblogs.latimes.com/music_blog/2009/06/ann
-powers-and-other-pop-critics-remember-michael-jacksons-thriller-.html.

———. "First Listen: Michael Jackson 'Immortal.'" *NPR Music*, November 18, 2011.
Accessed January 22, 2015. www.npr.org/2011/11/16/142418013/first-listen
-michael-jackson-immortal.

"Quincy Jones on Michael Jackson: 'We Made History Together.'" Pop & Hiss:
The *L.A. Times* Music Blog, June 29, 2009. Accessed January 28, 2015. http://
latimesblogs.latimes.com/music_blog/2009/06/quincy-jones-on-michael
-jackson-we-owned-the-80s-and-our-souls-would-be-connected-forever.html.

Rabin, Nathan. "Joel Schumacher." *A.V. Club*, April 2, 2003. Accessed February
18, 2015. www.avclub.com/article/joel-schumacher-13804.

———. "Spooktastic Case File #174: 'Michael Jackson's Ghosts.'" A.V. Club,
October 27, 2010. Accessed February 20, 2015. www.avclub.com/article/
spooktastic-case-file-174-michael-jacksons-ghosts-46847.

Rahman, Ray. "*Bad 25* (2012)." *Entertainment Weekly*, September 7, 2012. Accessed
January 22, 2015. www.ew.com/ew/article/0,,20396305_20627104,00.html.

*Recording Industry of America (RIAA)*, August 21, 2009. Accessed January 11,
2015. https://www.riaa.com/goldandplatinumdata.php?content_selector=
gold-platinum-searchable-database.

"Remembering Michael: Sheryl Crow." *Time*, 2009. Accessed January 25, 2015.
http://content.time.com/time/specials/packages/article/0,28804,1907409_
1907413_1907489,00.html.

Ressner, Jeffrey. "Stevie Wonder Releases 'Characters.'" *Rolling Stone*, November
19, 1987: 15.

Reynolds, Simon. "The Top Ten Most Underrated Albums of All Time." *Spin*,
February 1991: 17.

Rice, Lynette. "Michael Jackson in 'Captain EO': A Fellow Dancer Remembers."
*Entertainment Weekly*, June 29, 2009. Accessed February 18, 2015. www.ew.com/
article/2009/06/29/michael-jackson-captain-eo.

Richards, Chris. "B-sides: Mavis Staples Talks Prince, Michael Jackson, Bob
Dylan and President Obama." *Click Track*, September 3, 2010. Accessed June
5, 2015. www.washingtonpost.com/blogs/click-track/post/b-sides-mavis-staples
-talks-prince-michael-jackson-bob-dylan-and-president-obama/2010/12/20/
ABAMq5F_blog.html.

Riley, Teddy. Twitter post, September 2, 2013. www.twitlonger.com/show/mjiirb.

Roberts, Chris. "Michael Jackson: *Invincible.*" *Uncut*, January 2002. Accessed January 12, 2015. www.rocksbackpages.com/Library/Article/michael -jackson-iinvinciblei-epic.

——. "Michael Jackson: Wembley Stadium, London." *Melody Maker*, July 26, 1997. Accessed January 25, 2015. www.rocksbackpages.com/Library/Article/ michael-jackson-wembley-stadium-london.

Robert, Randall. "First Listen: Michael Jackson, 'Immortal.'" NPR Music, November 18, 2011. Accessed January 22, 2015. http://latimesblogs.latimes. com/music_blog/2011/11/album-review-michael-jacksons-immortal.html.

——. "Michael Jackson's 'Bad 25' Box: Is It Worth Your Time and Money?" *Los Angeles Times*, September 18, 2012. Accessed January 22, 2015. http://articles .latimes.com/2012/sep/18/entertainment/la-et-ms-michael-jacksons-bad-25-is -it-worth-your-money-20120918.

Rockwell, John. "Michael Jackson's *Thriller*: Superb Job." *New York Times*, December 19, 1982. Accessed January 11, 2015. www.nytimes.com/1982/12/19/arts/ michael-jackson-s-thriller-superb-job.html.

Rooney, David. "*Bad 25*: Venice Review." *Hollywood Reporter*, August 31, 2012. Accessed January 22, 2015. www.hollywoodreporter.com/review/bad-25 -venice-review-367157.

Rosen, Jody. "Jackson's Patchwork Jams." *Rolling Stone*, December 23, 2010: 113.

——. "Michael Jackson—*Bad: 25 Anniversary Deluxe Edition.*" *Rolling Stone*, October 25, 2012: 77.

Rothman, Lily. "An Oral History of Michael Jackson's *Bad.*" *Time*, August 22, 2012. Accessed June 4, 2015. http://entertainment.time.com/2012/08/29/ michael-jackson-bad/slide/the-making-of-bad/.

Ruhlmann, William. "The Jacksons: *Victory.*" *All Music.* Accessed January 29, 2015. www.allmusic.com/album/victory-mw0000650297.

Sandomir, Richard. "How Jackson Redefined the Super Bowl." *New York Times*, June 29, 2009. Accessed January 24, 2015. www.nytimes.com/2009/06/30/ sports/football/30sandomir.html?_r=1&.

Sclafani, Tony. "Jackson Changed Course of Music, Society." *Today*, June 26, 2009. www.today.com/id/31567490/ns/today-today_entertainment/t/jackson -changed-course-music-society/#.VIDyFqTF8YK.

Sexton, Paul. "The Jacksons: No Sign of Slackening." *Record Mirror*, October 7, 1978, www.rocksbackpages.com/Library/Article/the-jacksons-no-signs -of-any-slackening.

Sheffield, Rob. "The 25 Essential Moments." *Michael.* Ed. Jann S. Wenner. New York: Harper Studio, 2009. 202-211.

Shrum, Margi. "Sauce: In the '80s, MJ Was Raisin Awareness." *Pittsburgh Post-Gazette*, July 2, 2009. Accessed February 19, 2015. www.post-gazette.com/ life/food/2009/07/02/Sauce-In-the-80s-MJ-was-raisin-awareness/stories/ 200907020278.

Siegerson, Davitt. "Michael Grows Up." *Rolling Stone*, October 22, 1987: 87–88.

——. "Olivia Newton-John: *Soul Kiss*/Diana Ross: *Eaten Alive.*" *Rolling Stone*, February 13, 1986: 78.

Site Administrator. "Re: Michael Jackson Sang Backup???" Michael McDonald, August 21, 2009. Accessed February 1, 2015. www.bvcdesign.com/forum/viewtopic.php?f=2&t=803&p=8249&hilit=michael+jackson#p8249.

Skow, John. "Nowhere Over the Rainbow." *Time*, October 30, 1978: 118.

Smith, Alan. "Jackson 5: Jacksons Give Teenyblacks Hope." *New Musical Express*, May 29, 1971. www.rocksbackpages.com/Library/Article/jackson-5-jacksons-give-teenyblacks-hope.

Smith, Christopher. "Michael Jackson's 'Motown 25' Performance." *Los Angeles Times*, June 27, 2009. Accessed March 3, 2015. http://articles.latimes.com/2009/jun/27/entertainment/et-jackson-motown27.

Smith, Dinitia. "Jackson Plans New Lyrics for Album." *New York Times*, June 23, 1995. Accessed February 16, 2015. www.nytimes.com/1995/06/23/arts/jackson-plans-new-lyrics-for-album.html.

Smith, Mike. "Michael Jackson: Bad Word Tour, Cardiff Arms Park, July 26, 1988." *Western Mail*. Accessed January 15, 2015. www.walesonline.co.uk/news/wales-news/looking-back-michael-jackson-brought-1824418.

Smyers, Darryl. "Joe King Carrasco Talks Dogs, Michael Jackson and *Tlaquepaque*." *Dallas Observer*, August 29, 2013. Accessed February 1, 2015. www.dallas observer.com/2013-08-29/music/joe-king-carrasco-talks-dogs-michael-jackson-and-tlaquepaque/2/.

Snow, Mat. "Michael Jackson: *Dangerous*." *Q*, January 1992. Accessed February 24, 2015. www.rocksbackpages.com/Library/Article/michael-jackson-idangerousi.

———. "Michael Jackson: Wembley Stadium, London." *Sounds*, July 23, 1988. Accessed January 25, 2015. www.rocksbackpages.com/Library/Article/michael-jackson2-wembley-stadium-london.

Solomon, Charles. "Movie Review: A Cosmic Journey in 'Born of Stars.'" *Los Angeles Times*, October 9, 1986: 7.

"Sounding Off: The Best in Recorded Music." *Ebony*, December 1987.

Spooner, Catherine. "Spine-Chillers and Suspense: A Timeline of Gothic Fiction." BBC. Accessed February 11, 2015. www.bbc.co.uk/timelines/zyp72hv.

Staff. "Review: *Moonwalker*." *Variety*, December 31, 1988. Accessed February 19, 2015. http://variety.com/1987/film/reviews/moonwalker-1200427521/.

St. Pierre, Roger. "Michael Jackson: Schmaltz or Genius?" *New Musical Express*, March 18, 1972. Accessed February 5, 2015. www.rocksbackpages.com/Library/Article/michael-jackson-schmaltz-or-genius.

"Steve Lukather Remembers Michael Jackson." CNN, June 26, 2009. Accessed February 3, 2015. www.stevelukather.com/news-articles/2009/06/steve-lukather-remembering-michael-jackson.aspx.

Stillwater, Willa. *M Poetica: Michael Jackson's Art of Connection and Defiance*. Amazon Digital Services, 2013. Kindle Edition.

Stubbs, David. "Michael Jackson: *Off the Wall*, *Thriller*, and *Bad*." *Uncut*, December 2001. Accessed June 5, 2015. www.rocksbackpages.com/Library/Article/michael-jackson-off-the-wall-thriller-and-bad-epic.

Sullivan, Randall. *Untouchable: The Strange Life and Tragic Death of Michael Jackson*. New York: Grove Press, 2012.

Swedien, Bruce. *In the Studio with Michael Jackson*. New York: Hal Leonard, 2009.

Swenson, John. "Michael Jackson." *Rolling Stone Illustrated History of Rock & Roll*, eds. Anthony DeCurtis, James Henke, and Holy George-Warren. New York: Random House, 1992: 649–655.

Symes, Phil. "Michael Jackson: The One Who Got Away." *Disc and Music Echo*, March 18, 1972. Accessed February 5, 2015. www.rocksbackpages.com/ Library/Article/michael-jackson-the-one-who-got-away.

Taete, Jamie Lee Curtis. "Meet the Mystery Man Who Rapped on Michael Jackson's 'Black or White.'" *Vice*, May 5, 2015. Accessed June 10, 2015. www.vice.com/ read/meet-the-guy-who-did-the-rap-on-michael-jacksons-black-or-white-213.

Taraborrelli, J. Randy. *Michael Jackson: The Magic, the Madness, the Whole Story, 1958–2009*. New York: Grand Central, 2009. Kindle edition.

"The Making of Michael Jackson's *Thriller*." *Future Music*, October 1, 2009. Accessed February 21, 2015. www.musicradar.com/news/guitars/the-making-of-michael -jacksons-thriller-222109.

*Thriller 25: The Book*. Orlando, FL: ML Publishing Group, 2008.

"Top Album Picks: Michael Jackson—*Thriller*." *Billboard*, December 11, 1982: 61.

Troupe, Quincy. "Michael Jackson: The Pressure to Beat It." *Spin*, June 1987: 44-49.

Trust, Gary. "'Say Say Say' Ranks as Michael Jackson's Biggest *Billboard* Hit." *Billboard*, June 17, 2010. Accessed January 28, 2015. www.billboard.com/articles/ news/957728/say-say-say-ranks-as-michael-jacksons-biggest-billboard-hit.

Tucker, Ken. "The Jacksons." *Rolling Stone*, January 27, 1977: 70.

Tweedle, Sam. "Raw, Rare, Well Done: The Rock and Roll Journey of Reed Kailing." *Confessions of a Pop Culture Addict*, June 13, 2009. http://popculture addict.com/interviews/reedkailing-htm/.

Van Metre, Lynn. "Will 'Victory' Be A Winner?" *Chicago Tribune*, July 5, 1984: c4.

———."The Jacksons Polish *Victory* Tour into A Slick Special-Effects Show." *Chicago Tribune*, October 14, 1984: b4.

Vigo, Julian. "Michael Jackson and the Myth of Race and Gender." *Michael Jackson: Grasping the Spectacle*, ed. Christopher R. Smit. Burlington, VT: Ashgate, 2012: 27–37.

Vineyard, Jennifer. "Michael Jackson Special to Re-Air, with Britney This Time." *MTV*, December 27, 2001. www.mtv.com/news/1451617/michael-jackson -special-to-re-air-with-britney-this-time/.

Vogel, Joseph. "Abortion, Fame, and 'Bad': Listening to Michael Jackson's Unreleased Demos." *The Atlantic*, September 11, 2012. Accessed February 2, 2015. www.theatlantic.com/entertainment/archive/2012/09/abortion-fame -and-bad-listening-to-michael-jacksons-unreleased-demos/262242/.

———. "How Michael Jackson Made 'Bad.'" *The Atlantic*, September 10, 2012. Accessed June 2, 2015. www.theatlantic.com/entertainment/archive/2012/09/ how-michael-jackson-made-bad/262162/.

———. "Michael Jackson, *Dangerous*, and the Reinvention of Pop." *Pop Matters*, September 27, 2011. Accessed June 11, 2015. www.popmatters.com/feature/ 148850-michael-jackson-dangerous-and-the-reinvention-of-pop/.

———. *Earth Song: Inside Michael Jackson's Magnum Opus*. New York: BlakeVision Books, 2011. Kindle edition.

———. *Man in the Music: The Creative Life and Work of Michael Jackson.* New York: Sterling, 2011.

Vozick-Levinson, Simon. "The Music Mix: Michael Jackson's 'This Is It' Soundtrack: EW's Review." *Entertainment Weekly,* October 26, 2009. Accessed January 21, 2015. http://music-mix.ew.com/2009/10/26/michael-jackson-this-is-it-review/.

Walters, Barry. "DVDs: Michael Jackson's This Is It." *Rolling Stone,* February 4, 2010: 64.

Wappler, Margaret . "Album Review: Michael Jackson's 'Michael.'" Pop & Hiss: The *L.A. Times* Music Blog, December 14, 2010. Accessed January 21, 2015. http://latimesblogs.latimes.com/music_blog/2010/12/album-review-michael-jacksons-michael.html.

Warwick, Jacqueline. "'You Can't Win, Child, But You Can't Get Out of the Game': Michael Jackson's Transition from Child Star to Superstar." *Popular Music and Society,* 35.2 (May 2012): 241–259.

Webb, Robert. "Story of the Song: 'Man in the Mirror,' Michael Jackson, 1987." *The Independent,* December 10, 2010. Accessed February 24, 2015. www.independent.co.uk/arts-entertainment/music/features/story-of-the-song-man-in-the-mirror-michael-jackson-1987-2156491.html.

Weintraub, Bernard. "In New Lyrics, Jackson Uses Slurs." *The New York Times,* June 15, 1995. Accessed February 16, 2015. www.nytimes.com/1995/06/15/arts/in-new-lyrics-jackson-uses-slurs.html.

White, Cliff. "The Jacksons, Wild Cherry: Convention Arena, Fort Worth, Texas." *New Musical Express,* May 7, 1977. Accessed January 19, 2015. www.rocksbackpages.com/Library/Article/the-jacksons-wild-cherry-convention-arena-fort-worth-texas.

"will.i.am Will Only Release Michael Jackson Songs at Request of Jackson's Mother." *Access Hollywood,* January 5, 2012. Accessed February 2, 2015. www.accesshollywood.com/william-will-only-release-michael-jackson-songs-at-request-of-jacksons-mother_article_58649.

Willman, Chris. "Hits and Missives." *Los Angeles Times,* June 18, 1995. Accessed February 16, 2015. www.latimes.com/la-archive-history-review-story-story.html.

Wolk, Douglas. "Michael Jackson: *Xscape.*" *Pitchfork,* May 15, 2014. Accessed January 22, 2015. http://pitchfork.com/reviews/albums/19333-michael-jackson-xscape/.

"Woman Recalls 1984 Meeting with Michael Jackson." *Dallas Morning News,* June 29, 2009. Accessed January 30, 2015. www.dallasnews.com/sharedcontent/dws/dn/latestnews/stories/062909dnmetladonna_video.1b2fa297.html.

Wynn, Ron. "The Jackson 5." *All Music Guide to Soul: The Definitive Guide to R&B and Soul.* Ann Arbor, MI: Hal Leonard, 2003.

Yancey, Kitty. "Cirque Tells More about New Michael Jackson Show." *USA Today,* February 21, 2013. Accessed January 22, 2015. www.usatoday.com/story/dispatches/2013/02/21/new-michael-jackson-show-called-one-to-open-at-mandalay-bay/1935905/.

Yeo Kah Sin, Dennis. "'Did I Scare You?': The Curious Case of Michael Jackson as Gothic Narrative." *Studies in Gothic Fiction* 1.1 (2010): 13–30.

Zambrano, Mark. "Jacksons Stage A Thriller." *Chicago Tribune,* October 13, 1984: 5.

# Index

# THE FAQ SERIES

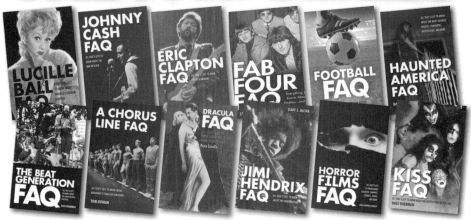

**AC/DC FAQ**
*by Susan Masino*
Backbeat Books
978-1-4803-9450-6.......... $24.99

**Armageddon Films FAQ**
*by Dale Sherman*
Applause Books
978-1-61713-119-6.................. $24.99

**Lucille Ball FAQ**
*by James Sheridan
and Barry Monush*
Applause Books
978-1-61774-082-4............$19.99

**The Beach Boys FAQ**
*by Jon Stebbins*
Backbeat Books
978-0-87930-987-9...........$22.99

**The Beat Generation FAQ**
*by Rich Weidman*
Backbeat Books
978-1-61713-601-6 ...............$19.99

**Black Sabbath FAQ**
*by Martin Popoff*
Backbeat Books
978-0-87930-957-2............$19.99

**Johnny Cash FAQ**
*by C. Eric Banister*
Backbeat Books
978-1-4803-8540-5.......... $24.99

**A Chorus Line FAQ**
*by Tom Rowan*
Applause Books
978-1-4803-6754-8 ...........$19.99

**Eric Clapton FAQ**
*by David Bowling*
Backbeat Books
978-1-61713-454-8................$22.99

**Doctor Who FAQ**
*by Dave Thompson*
Applause Books
978-1-55783-854-4.............$22.99

**The Doors FAQ**
*by Rich Weidman*
Backbeat Books
978-1-61713-017-5................ $24.99

**Dracula FAQ**
*by Bruce Scivally*
Backbeat Books
978-1-61713-600-9 ..............$19.99

**The Eagles FAQ**
*by Andrew Vaughan*
Backbeat Books
978-1-4803-8541-2 ............. $24.99

**Fab Four FAQ**
*by Stuart Shea and
Robert Rodriguez*
Hal Leonard Books
978-1-4234-2138-2.................$19.99

**Fab Four FAQ 2.0**
*by Robert Rodriguez*
Backbeat Books
978-0-87930-968-8...........$19.99

**Film Noir FAQ**
*by David J. Hogan*
Applause Books
978-1-55783-855-1...............$22.99

**Football FAQ**
*by Dave Thompson*
Backbeat Books
978-1-4950-0748-4 .......... $24.99

**The Grateful Dead FAQ**
*by Tony Sclafani*
Backbeat Books
978-1-61713-086-1............. $24.99

**Haunted America FAQ**
*by Dave Thompson*
Backbeat Books
978-1-4803-9262-5............$19.99

**Jimi Hendrix FAQ**
*by Gary J. Jucha*
Backbeat Books
978-1-61713-095-3...............$22.99

**Horror Films FAQ**
*by John Kenneth Muir*
Applause Books
978-1-55783-950-3.............$22.99

**James Bond FAQ**
*by Tom DeMichael*
Applause Books
978-1-55783-856-8.............$22.99

**Stephen King Films FAQ**
*by Scott Von Doviak*
Applause Books
978-1-4803-5551-4 ............ $24.99

**KISS FAQ**
*by Dale Sherman*
Backbeat Books
978-1-61713-091-5................$22.99

**Led Zeppelin FAQ**
*by George Case*
Backbeat Books
978-1-61713-025-0 ..............$19.99

**Modern Sci-Fi Films FAQ**
*by Tom DeMichael*
Applause Books
978-1-4803-5061-8............ $24.99

Prices, contents, and availability
subject to change without notice.

**Morrissey FAQ**
*by D. McKinney*
Backbeat Books
978-1-4803-9448-3............ $24.99

**Nirvana FAQ**
*by John D. Luerssen*
Backbeat Books
978-1-61713-450-0............. $24.99

**Pink Floyd FAQ**
*by Stuart Shea*
Backbeat Books
978-0-87930-950-3............$19.99

**Elvis Films FAQ**
*by Paul Simpson*
Applause Books
978-1-55783-858-2............. $24.99

**Elvis Music FAQ**
*by Mike Eder*
Backbeat Books
978-1-61713-049-6............. $24.99

**Prog Rock FAQ**
*by Will Romano*
Backbeat Books
978-1-61713-587-3............... $24.99

**Pro Wrestling FAQ**
*by Brian Solomon*
Backbeat Books
978-1-61713-599-6............... $29.99

**Rush FAQ**
*by Max Mobley*
Backbeat Books
978-1-61713-451-7................. $24.99

**Saturday Night Live FAQ**
*by Stephen Tropiano*
Applause Books
978-1-55783-951-0............. $24.99

Prices, contents, and availability
subject to change without notice.

**Seinfeld FAQ**
*by Nicholas Nigro*
Applause Books
978-1-55783-857-5............. $24.99

**Sherlock Holmes FAQ**
*by Dave Thompson*
Applause Books
978-1-4803-3149-5............. $24.99

**The Smiths FAQ**
*by John D. Luerssen*
Backbeat Books
978-1-4803-9449-0........... $24.99

**Soccer FAQ**
*by Dave Thompson*
Backbeat Books
978-1-61713-598-9............... $24.99

**The Sound of Music FAQ**
*by Barry Monush*
Applause Books
978-1-4803-6043-3............ $27.99

**South Park FAQ**
*by Dave Thompson*
Applause Books
978-1-4803-5064-9........... $24.99

**Bruce Springsteen FAQ**
*by John D. Luerssen*
Backbeat Books
978-1-61713-093-9................$22.99

**Star Trek FAQ**
**(Unofficial and Unauthorized)**
*by Mark Clark*
Applause Books
978-1-55783-792-9................$19.99

**Star Trek FAQ 2.0**
**(Unofficial and Unauthorized)**
*by Mark Clark*
Applause Books
978-1-55783-793-6.................$22.99

**Star Wars FAQ**
*by Mark Clark*
Applause Books
978-1-4803-6018-1.............. $24.99

**Quentin Tarantino FAQ**
*by Dale Sherman*
Applause Books
978-1-4803-5588-0 ........... $24.99

**Three Stooges FAQ**
*by David J. Hogan*
Applause Books
978-1-55783-788-2................$22.99

**The Who FAQ**
*by Mike Segretto*
Backbeat Books
978-1-4803-6103-4 ........... $24.99

**The Wizard of Oz FAQ**
*by David J. Hogan*
Applause Books
978-1-4803-5062-5............ $24.99

**The X-Files FAQ**
*by John Kenneth Muir*
Applause Books
978-1-4803-6974-0............ $24.99

**Neil Young FAQ**
*by Glen Boyd*
Backbeat Books
978-1-61713-037-3.................$19.99

HAL•LEONARD®
PERFORMING ARTS
PUBLISHING GROUP

**FAQ.halleonardbooks.com**

0815